Lecture Notes of the Institute for Computer Sciences, Social Informatics and Telecommunications Engineering   424

More information about this series at https://link.springer.com/bookseries/8197

Dingde Jiang · Houbing Song (Eds.)

Simulation Tools and Techniques

13th EAI International Conference, SIMUtools 2021
Virtual Event, November 5–6, 2021
Proceedings

Editors
Dingde Jiang (iD)
University of Electronic Science
and Technology of China
Chengdu, China

Houbing Song (iD)
Embry-Riddle Aeronautical University
Daytona Beach, FL, USA

ISSN 1867-8211 ISSN 1867-822X (electronic)
Lecture Notes of the Institute for Computer Sciences, Social Informatics
and Telecommunications Engineering
ISBN 978-3-030-97123-6 ISBN 978-3-030-97124-3 (eBook)
https://doi.org/10.1007/978-3-030-97124-3

This Springer imprint is published by the registered company Springer Nature Switzerland AG
The registered company address is: Gewerbestrasse 11, 6330 Cham, Switzerland

Preface

We are pleased to introduce the proceedings of the 13th European Alliance for Innovation (EAI) International Conference on Simulation Tools and Techniques (SIMUtools 2021). This conference brought together researchers, developers, and practitioners around the world who are leveraging and developing system modeling and simulation, software simulation, communication network modeling and analysis, AI system simulation and performance analysis, and big data simulation analysis to address current and future trends in simulation techniques, systems, networks, methods, platforms, models, practices, and software, as well as emulation software, simulation tools, and emulation tools. The conference is dedicated to fostering interdisciplinary collaborative research in these areas and across a wide spectrum of application domains.

The technical program of SIMUtools 2021 consisted of 63 full papers, including 49 papers in oral presentation sessions at the main conference track. The conference track covered the topics of Big Data, Deep Learning, Wireless Communication, Target Detection and Machine Learning, Mathematic Modeling, and Networking and Intelligent Algorithms. Aside from the high-quality technical paper presentations, the technical program also featured five keynote speeches. The six keynote speeches were given by Dingde Jiang from the University of Electronic Science and Technology of China, China, Houbing Song from Embry-Riddle Aeronautical University, Daytona Beach, USA, Lei Shi from the Institute of Technology Carlow Ireland, Lei Chen from the Xuzhou University of Technology, China, Junyuan Wang from Tongji University, China, and Shanshan Zhang from the Nanjing University of Science and Technology, China.

Coordination with the steering chair, Imrich Chlamtac, was essential for the success of the conference. We sincerely appreciate his constant support and guidance. It was also a great pleasure to work with such an excellent organizing committee team for their hard work in organizing and supporting the conference. In particular, we are grateful to the Technical Program Committee, who completed the peer-review process for the technical papers and helped to put together a high-quality technical program. We are also grateful to all the authors who submitted their papers to the SIMUtools 2021 conference and workshops.

We strongly believe that SIMUtools conference provides a good forum for all researchers, developers and practitioners to discuss all science and technology aspects that are relevant to simulation. We also expect that the future SIMUtools conference will be as successful and stimulating, as indicated by the contributions presented in this volume.

December 2021

Dingde Jiang
Houbing Song
Lei Chen
Liuwe Huo
Lei Shi
Feng Wang

Organization

Steering Committee

Imrich Chlamtac — University of Trento, Italy

Organizing Committee

General Chairs

Dingde Jiang — University of Electronic Science and Technology of China, China

Houbing Song — Embry-Riddle Aeronautical University, Daytona Beach, USA

Technical Program Committee Chairs

Lei Chen — Xuzhou University of Technology, China

Liuwe Huo — University of Electronic Science and Technology of China, China

Lei Shi — Institute of Technology Carlow, Ireland

Feng Wang — University of Electronic Science and Technology of China, China

Sponsorship and Exhibit Chairs

Changsheng Zhang — Northeastern University, China

Dan Li — Xuzhou University of Technology, China

Local Chair

Lei Chen — Xuzhou University of Technology, China

Workshops Chairs

Zhi Zhu — National University of Defense Technology, China

Jianguang Chen — University of Electronic Science and Technology of China, China

Publicity and Social Media Chairs

Litao Zhang   Zhengzhou Institute of Aeronautics, China
Zhihao Wang   University of Electronic Science and Technology
                               of China, China

Publications Chairs

Qingshan Wang   Hefei University of Technology, China
Lu Zhang   Xuzhou University of Technology, China

Web Chairs

Xiongzi Ge   NetApp, USA
Wei Yang   University of Electronic Science and Technology
                               of China, China

Posters and PhD Track Chairs

Lulu Bei   Xuzhou University of Technology, China
Zhihao Wang   University of Electronic Science and Technology
                               of China, China

Panels Chairs

Lei Miao   Middle Tennessee State University, USA
Yuan An   Xuzhou University of Technology, China

Demos Chairs

Minhong Sun   Hangzhou Dianzi University, China
Kailiang Zhang   Xuzhou University of Technology, China

Tutorials Chairs

Peiying Zhang   China University of Petroleum, China
Ping Cui   Xuzhou University of Technology, China

Technical Program Committee

Lei Chen   Xuzhou University of Technology, China
Wang Feng   University of Electronic Science and Technology
                               of China, China
Jianguang Chen   University of Electronic Science and Technology
                               of China, China
Zhihao Wang   University of Electronic Science and Technology
                               of China, China
Liuwei Huo   University of Electronic Science and Technology
                               of China, China

Contents

Big Data

Modeling and Simulation

Deep Learning

Network Simulations

Target Detection and Machine Learning

Life and Medical Sciences

Wireless Communication

Emulation of Multipath Solutions in Heterogeneous Wireless Networks Over Ns-3 Platform

Vadym S. Hapanchak[1]($\boxtimes$) and António D. Costa[2]

[1] Algoritmi Center, University of Minho, Braga, Portugal
b7768@algoritmi.uminho.pt
[2] Algoritmi Center, Department of Informatics, University of Minho, Braga, Portugal
costa@di.uminho.pt

Abstract. The increased availability of devices equipped with multiple wireless interfaces leads to consider multihoming as one of the key features of the next generation 5G networks. This paper discusses the emulation technique that integrates Linux Container and ns-3 network simulator to evaluate emerging multipath applications and protocols. The presented solution was utilized as an experimental platform to analyze the performance of Multipath TCP (MPTCP) protocol in heterogeneous network environments, particularly wireless ones, such as WLAN and cellular networks. We tested the MPTCP in fixed and mobility scenarios, exploiting the ns-3 to provide multipath wireless connectivity. The obtained results show the protocol behaviour that might have been expected from the system under investigation. Thus, one could use the presented scheme to get emulation results with reasonable accuracy, as long as ns-3 follows up with external real-time events. We further discuss the main limitations of the described method, observed in large-scale scenarios.

Keywords: Simulation · Ns-3 · Multipath · MPTCP · Network emulation · LXC · Heterogeneous · Wireless networks

1 Introduction

Nowadays, mobile devices support different types of wireless interfaces, such as WiFi and LTE, to connect to the Internet. The commonly used TCP/IP standard supports only one interface per connection since it cannot handle multiple data streams. It has been shown that multipath transmission can improve network resilience and increase data throughput by using multiple links simultaneously [3,11]. The use of multipath approach has been recently adopted for the fifth generation (5G) cellular networks for use in services that aim at supporting the requirements of high data rate, high reliability and low latency [1].

Multipath TCP (MPTCP) [4] is the well known multipath transmission protocol that has attracted significant attention in both academia and industry.

© ICST Institute for Computer Sciences, Social Informatics and Telecommunications Engineering 2022
Published by Springer Nature Switzerland AG 2022. All Rights Reserved
D. Jiang and H. Song (Eds.): SIMUtools 2021, LNICST 424, pp. 3–18, 2022.
https://doi.org/10.1007/978-3-030-97124-3_1

MPTCP is an extension to the regular TCP that allows single end-to-end connection data traffic to be split across different interfaces (also paths). In the context of wireless communication with mobility, MPTCP aims to provide reliable connectivity by seamlessly switching between different interfaces during data transmission.

Many researchers tend to evaluate the performance of multipath solutions by using a discrete-event network simulators or via a controlled environment. Simulation tools offer a possibility of testing new applications and protocol stacks for arbitrary complex scenarios. Generally, network simulators do not allow running "real" code and require dedicated implementations of newly designed algorithms for communication systems. However, it takes time for new protocols to be implemented and integrated into the simulator. For example, MPTCP is still not included as a module in any stable version of ns-3 simulator, and the available 3rd-party simulation modules are not fully compliant with the actual MPTCP specifications.

Therefore, we believe testing new multipath solutions using their real implementation is more realistic than developing a new module within the simulation tool. Controlled environment tests require real testbed deployment, which can be expensive and hard to manage. For instance, studying the performance of multipath solutions in the controlled heterogeneous wireless environment requires real testbed deployment of WiFi, 4G/5G systems, which brings upon high costs. Furthermore, real hardware equipment is challenging to modify, upgrade and scale.

On the other hand, the emulation technique can combine real application with the controlled and reproducible network scenario to obtain more accurate and credible results. The unmodified application code can be used in controlled networking environments. Thus, the emulation model can provide more realistic results than simulation but have a higher maintenance complexity.

Motivated by all these factors, in this work, we conduct container-based emulation to analyze how multipath protocols can be further tested by the advantages of using their real implementation. To demonstrate the abilities of the emulation method, we carried out a simple study of MPTCP using the ns-3 in emulation mode. In particular, we focus on wireless networks with differing characteristics, such as Wi-Fi and 4G.

However, the main contribution of this paper is the integration of Linux Container (LXC) with the ns-3 simulator that allows conducting complex real-time experiments, with realistic link-layer emulation (i.e., signal propagation, modulation techniques, antenna design, etc.) and mobility models. Detailed description of the implementation and configuration of the emulation framework is provided in this paper. In addition, the main limitations of the presented approach are discussed as well.

This paper is organized as follows. Section 2 presents the related works that have used the same emulation strategy. Section 3 presents the concepts and tools used to create an emulation environment and provide a detailed description of the emulator setup. Section 4 shows some scenarios used to study the behaviour of

MPTCP over heterogeneous wireless networks and analyzes the achieved results. Section 5 discusses the limitations of the proposed emulation method. Finally, Sect. 6 presents our conclusions and future work.

2   Related Works

There are various tools for simulation or emulation available for the scientific and research community. Network simulation tools, such as NS-3[1] and OMNET++[2], among others, offer a greater degree of flexibility and sufficient accuracy to analyze large network topologies. In contrast to simulation, where the entire experiment is modelled in software, emulation interacts with the real systems, such as end hosts and physical networks, to run the experiments. This provides the means to generate more accurate results from the experiment, close to the real environment.

CORE[3] and Mininet[4] are two well known lightweight emulators, which use Linux namespaces to provide isolation between emulated hosts. However, at the moment, these emulators have limited realism in modelling the physical layer effects of wired and wireless connections, such as signal interference and propagation.

Some works have successfully exploited the combination between Docker and ns-3 simulator [7–9,12]. The Docker framework is used to create LXCs, while ns-3 is used for network scenario generation. Nevertheless, the authors of these works do not discuss whether the presented emulators have any limitations.

Authors in [10] successfully simulated large LTE topologies by integrating the ns-3 simulator with the CORE emulator. Different scenarios and topologies were tested, and the real-time traffic was successfully exchanged between LTE devices in simulation and external equipment. Zhang et al. [13] proposed a high-fidelity experiment platform for mobile networks (FEP). A presented testbed interconnect ns-3, VirtualBox, Android and Docker, and the platform was tested with customized MPTCP-enabled Android.

The integration of ns-3 and Mininet was evaluated by Pakzad et al. [6] regarding experiment result accuracy, performance fidelity and scalability limits. The authors consider the great potential of the emulation platform, which shows a high degree of accuracy and fidelity of the achieved results as long as the scheduler of ns-3 can keep up with external real-time events. Arroyo et al. [2] study the limitations of the interaction of networks simulated in ns-3 with real nodes to analyze video streaming applications. The evaluation was presented considering several LXCs and a simulated WiFi network. The authors conclude that the number of devices deployed within the scenario substantially impacts the fidelity of achieved results than the traffic load.

---

[1] https://www.nsnam.org/.
[2] https://omnetpp.org/.
[3] http://coreemu.github.io/core/.
[4] http://mininet.org/.

However, none of the above works has focused on multipath emulation, including the detailed description of the employed testbed and the scalability limits. In this paper, we aim to address this critical gap.

3   Emulation of Multipath Connectivity

Our emulator integrates a Linux Container (LXC) into an ns-3 network simulation tool to provide realistic behaviour of emerging multipath solutions Fig. 1. Although this paper focuses on MPTCP protocol, one can also use this approach to integrate arbitrary software into the emulation. Firstly, this section gives a brief overview of the LXC technology, ns-3 platform and MPTCP protocol. Then, the emulation scheme is explained in detail.

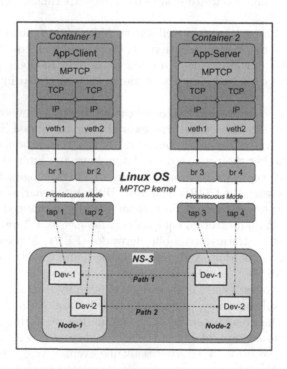

Fig. 1. Integration between LXC and ns-3 to emulate multipath connectivity

3.1   Background

Multipath connectivity is particularly useful in wireless networks and allows the concurrent use of different Radio Access Technologies (RAT). For example, if a mobile device has several interfaces (e.g., WiFi and 4G), it can simultaneously use both networks to provide reliable connectivity. This work focuses on standardized Multipath TCP (MPTCP) [4], one of the most prominent candidate multipath protocols in the future 5G networks. MPTCP extends the standard TCP enabling transmission of a single connection (session) through several *subflows* Fig. 2.

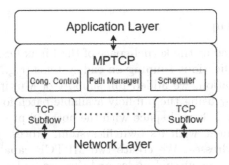

Fig. 2. Multipath TCP extension

MPTCP exploits multiple interfaces to aggregate the available bandwidth and enhance communication reliability. The advantage of the MTCP is that additional *subflows* may be created as soon as the mobile node has network coverage. Once a *subflow* is established, the application can send and receive data over multiple interfaces without disrupting the ongoing connection.

Linux Container (LXC) is a set of processes isolated from the rest of the operating system leveraging the *namespaces* and *cgroups* Linux kernel features. LXC is executed as simple processes with an independent view of system resources, a separate process tree and networking interfaces. Therefore, we select LXC as the primary node virtualization method since it has the flexibility of having several small virtual hosts implemented on a single physical system. Unlike full virtualization provided by Virtual Machines (VM), LXC is a lightweight virtualization technique that has reduced resource demands and shares the kernel with the host operating system (OS).

Network Simulator 3 (ns-3) is one of the most widely used open-source network simulators. It implements realistic modeling of different communication technologies, supports a wide variety of routing protocols and configuration of network parameters. It is a modular simulator based on the C++ language. Ns-3 enables the design, evaluation, and validation of various communication technologies with near real-life performance measurements.

NS-3 can work in so-called *real-time mode*, which allows network emulation, i.e., the integration of a simulation environment with real devices. When ns-3 runs in emulation mode, external devices can exchange packets with the simulated network in real-time using the *FdNetDevice* or *TapBridge* ns-3 modules. For instance, the link between Linux OS and ns-3 can be implemented using *tap* virtual network devices, allowing Layer-2 packet reception and transmission. Here, the *tap* device interacts with the *TapBridge* and is represented as a common *NetDevice* in the ns-3 environment.

3.2   Emulation Setup

MPTCP is implemented at the kernel-space of the Linux OS, working transparently for the user applications running on end-systems (e.g., client and server). To perform our evaluation, we added full support of Multipath TCP v0.94 to the Linux 5.4 kernel by using the publicly available patch for it.

LXC shares the same kernel space with the host OS providing a lightweight and isolated environment with its own filesystem, process hierarchy, network interfaces, and IP addresses. We create two MPTCP capable containers that represent client and server virtual nodes and can use multiple interfaces simultaneously. As shown in Fig. 1, our emulation framework incorporates the Linux bridges (*br*), tap devices (*tap*) and virtual interfaces (*veth*) in order to interconnect the corresponding container with the associated ns-3 *Node* in the simulator. It can be seen as a simple wired connection between two virtual interfaces that allow interaction with the deployed LXCs.

After LXC is binding with the *Node* inside ns-3, the ns-3 *Node* sends all the incoming network traffic to the LXC through a virtual *tap* interface connected to the *veth* of the container through a Linux *bridge*. Similarly, the LXC sends the outgoing traffic over the ns-3 network. All the required components (*bridge*, *tap*, *veth*) should be created and configured before the emulation session starts for the experiment to work correctly.

Ns-3 support gives the ability to generate network scenarios and simulate several types of wired/wireless communication technologies such as Ethernet, Wi-Fi, LTE, 5G, among others, with realistic physical layer signal propagation models in addition to different types of mobility models. In order to synchronise ns-3 simulation clock with the real-time (*wall*) clock an *real-time scheduler* should be used during experiments.

3.3   Implementation Details

This study focuses on multipath connectivity in heterogeneous wireless networks, such as WLAN and LTE. As for the LTE technology simulations, we have utilized the LENA open-source module provided by the ns-3 platform. It includes the radio protocol stack and LTE access mechanism defined by the *3GPP* standard that controls the connection between User Equipment (*UE*) and the eNodeB(*eNB*). In addition, *eNB* is connected via a point-to-point link to the Evolved Packet Core(*EPC*) network with a single Serving Gateway (*SGW*) and Packet Data Network Gateway(*PGW*).

In order to conduct our multipath experiments, we create two MPTCP-capable containers with two virtual interfaces (*veth*) each, linked to the ns-3 over Linux *bridge* interfaces Fig. 3. The combination of the *left* container and UE Node on ns-3, can be seen as one whole representing a client node. Accordingly, the *right* container and *Remote* node can be seen as one single host running application server logic.

The UE node has two wireless interfaces to perform multipath connectivity. One interface is connected to the LTE network via the *eNb*, and the other is connected to a WiFi network via Access Point (*AP*). The *Remote* node is connected to the EPC as well as to the AP via two dedicated wired links with the same characteristics.

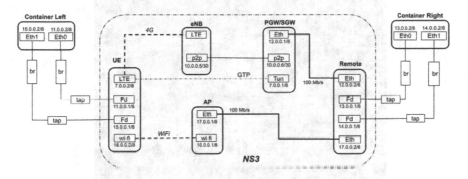

Fig. 3. Detailed scheme of emulated multipath environment

Many emulation based studies use the ns-3 *TapBridge* module since it allows the interface of the ns-3 node to be mapped directly into a tap device in the host OS. In that case, external devices can exchange Layer-2 network traffic with the simulator. However, not all ns-3 *NetDevices* support this type of connection, e.g., LTE devices do not support bridging of *tap* devices. Instead, *FdNetDevice* (*FD*) was used to connect Linux containers with the simulated environment. *FD* can read and write traffic using a file descriptor associated with a tap device, a socket, or a user-space process. Also, we found *FD* to be more stable during the simulation experiments, providing accurate and reproducible results.

UE and Remote nodes relay traffic from LXC to the ns-3 network and vice versa through the *tap* device bound to the *FD*. This approach results in the additional hop and requires more careful configuration, but on the other hand, it allows the simulation of all network models currently available in ns-3. It is essential to mention that the upper bound limit for TCP throughput that can be achieved for this configuration with *FD* is around 70 Mbps and the delay induced by the additional hop is less than 0.5 ms. As mentioned by the ns-3 documentation[5], this limit is most likely due to the hardware's processing power involved in the tests.

---

[5] https://www.nsnam.org/docs/models/html/fd-net-device.html.

As shown in Fig. 3, there are two available ways by which UE can reach the Remote host: via LTE network (*path1*) and WiFi network (*path2*). To create a multipath communication environment, routing tables of LXC containers were configured such that all traffic from the first interface (*veth0*) are sent over *path1*, and all traffic from the second interface (*veth1*) are routed through *path2*. Furthermore, routing paths have to be defined for each ns-3 node to access the external networks Fig. 4.

```
routing table of PGW
Node: 4, Time: +0s, Local time: +0s, Ipv4StaticRouting table
Destination     Gateway         Genmask             Flags Metric Ref     Use Iface
127.0.0.0       0.0.0.0         255.0.0.0           U     0      -       -   0
7.0.0.0         0.0.0.0         255.0.0.0           U     0      -       -   1
14.0.0.4        0.0.0.0         255.255.255.252     U     0      -       -   2
12.0.0.0        0.0.0.0         255.0.0.0           U     0      -       -   3
11.0.0.0        7.0.0.2         255.0.0.0           UGS   0      -       -   1
13.0.0.0        12.0.0.2        255.0.0.0           UGS   0      -       -   3

routing table of AP (wifi)
Node: 2, Time: +0s, Local time: +0s, Ipv4StaticRouting table
Destination     Gateway         Genmask             Flags Metric Ref     Use Iface
127.0.0.0       0.0.0.0         255.0.0.0           U     0      -       -   0
16.0.0.0        0.0.0.0         255.0.0.0           U     0      -       -   1
17.0.0.0        0.0.0.0         255.0.0.0           U     0      -       -   2
15.0.0.0        16.0.0.2        255.0.0.0           UGS   0      -       -   1
14.0.0.0        17.0.0.2        255.0.0.0           UGS   0      -       -   2

routing table of UE
Node: 0, Time: +0s, Local time: +0s, Ipv4StaticRouting table
Destination     Gateway         Genmask             Flags Metric Ref     Use Iface
127.0.0.0       0.0.0.0         255.0.0.0           U     0      -       -   0
16.0.0.0        0.0.0.0         255.0.0.0           U     0      -       -   1
7.0.0.0         0.0.0.0         255.0.0.0           U     0      -       -   2
15.0.0.0        0.0.0.0         255.0.0.0           U     0      -       -   3
11.0.0.0        0.0.0.0         255.0.0.0           U     0      -       -   4
0.0.0.0         7.0.0.1         0.0.0.0             UGS   0      -       -   2
14.0.0.0        16.0.0.1        255.0.0.0           UGS   0      -       -   1

routing table of Remote
Node: 1, Time: +0s, Local time: +0s, Ipv4StaticRouting table
Destination     Gateway         Genmask             Flags Metric Ref     Use Iface
127.0.0.0       0.0.0.0         255.0.0.0           U     0      -       -   0
17.0.0.0        0.0.0.0         255.0.0.0           U     0      -       -   1
12.0.0.0        0.0.0.0         255.0.0.0           U     0      -       -   2
14.0.0.0        0.0.0.0         255.0.0.0           U     0      -       -   3
13.0.0.0        0.0.0.0         255.0.0.0           U     0      -       -   4
0.0.0.0         12.0.0.1        0.0.0.0             UGS   0      -       -   2
15.0.0.0        17.0.0.1        255.0.0.0           UGS   0      -       -   1
16.0.0.0        17.0.0.1        255.0.0.0           UGS   0      -       -   1
```

Fig. 4. Routing tables of principal nodes in simulation

In LTE networks, the end-to-end IP connectivity is provided within the EPC through the PGW. The PGW uses the destination IP address to identify a single UE and the eNB to which it is attached. Therefore, the 3GPP specification does not allow transmission of the packets with destination IP addresses different from registered UE. The PGW silently drops those packets because it would not know through which eNB it should be routed.

We first define a static routing at the PGW to access the external network outside the LTE to overcome this problem. Next, we replace the IP address bonded to UE on the PGW application with the IP address of the left container. Thus, all traffic in the LTE path destined to the container is routed to UE by the PGW, then UE reroutes it to the container via the FD interface.

4   Experimental Validation

This section presents the evaluation scenario, parameters setting, metrics used, validity tests, and corresponding results. The emulation environment was configured as realistic as possible to get reliable results. We have created different network topologies under various conditions to evaluate the proposed multipath emulation method. However, in this paper, we present only a short part of the obtained results since a detailed evaluation of MPTCP is out of the scope of this paper. All other scenarios we make publicly available[6] for research and use.

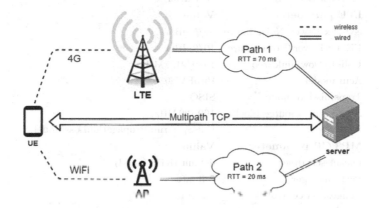

Fig. 5. The topology used for the emulation

4.1   Framework Configuration

Most protocols and channel configurations in our experiments use their default settings unless otherwise specified. The emulation parameters used for analysis are configured as listed in Table 1.

The *default* EPS bearer was used in the LTE network with the channel error models disabled. In addition, the number of resource blocks for uplink and downlink is set to 100 to achieve a bandwidth of 20 MHz. The eNb uses the FDD mode with a downlink frequency of 2120 MHz and an uplink frequency of 1930 MHz. In the simulation, the transmission power of 10 and 30 dBm was used by UE and eNB, respectively. Also, The *FriisSpectrumPropagationLossModel* is used to model signal fading.

---

[6] https://github.com/vandit86/ns3-scratch.

Table 1. Network configuration parameters

WiFi parameter	Value
Standard	802.11a
Phys. channel model	YansWifiChannel
Channel number	36
Channel width	20 MHz
Frequency	5180 MHz
Data mode	OfdmRate6Mbps
TX-power level	23 dBm
Rx-sensitivity	-101 dBm
LTE parameter	**Value**
eNb Tx Power/Noise figure	30/5 dBm
UE Tx Power/Noise figure	10/9 dBm
Uplink/Downlink freq	1930/2120 MHz
Acm model	PiroEW2010
Transmission mode	SISO
Number of resource blocks	100 (20 MHz)
Loss model	FriisSpectrumPropagationLossModel
MPTCP parameter	**Value**
Packet scheduler	default (RTT-based)
Path manager	full mesh
Congestion control	OLIA

Linux kernel implementation of MPTCP provides flexibility to select the path manager, congestion control algorithm, and packet scheduler to be used. In our experiments, we use the *"default"* RTT-based packet scheduler with the *"full mesh"* path manager, which ensures the creation of multiple sub-flows per connection. The original TCP configuration parameters were left unchanged. We employ the *OLIA* congestion control as it is less aggressive toward other TCP sessions over congested paths, which satisfies the design goals of MPTCP. The experiments were carried out on an AMD EPYC 7302 machine running a VM Linux Mint 20 (Kernel v.5.4.0) with MPTCP v0.95 configured with eight cores and 20 GB of RAM.

Once the experiment is deployed, we can "attach" to any container and perform metric tests with the common tools. During the emulation, data traffic is generated using the *Iperf3*, which allows the adjustment of TCP-related parameters like congestion control algorithm and receiver buffer size (*TCP RWND*). Furthermore, *Iperf3* works in client-server mode, measuring goodput at each end of the network path. *Tcpdump* and *Wireshark* tools are used to capture packets and analyze communication details, such as packet loss or round-trip time (RTT). In addition, the Linux Traffic Control may be used to change delay, jitter, bandwidth shaping, among others, of the LXC interface.

4.2   Simple Scenario

The network topology of the evaluation scenario is the one shown in Fig. 5. We simulate a scenario where a multihomed UE is connected to the server with two network interfaces, i.e. WiFi and 4G, each with unique IP addresses. Two transmission paths are used to evaluate the performance with heterogeneous links. The average RTT configured for *path 1* is 70 ms and for *path 2* is 20 ms. The WiFi AP and LTE-PGW are connected to the server with 100 Mbps wired links. All nodes remain stationary during the simulation.

To perform our experiments, we use the *Iperf3* tool to run MPTCP sessions between the UE and server with an unlimited load that guarantees link saturation. As can be seen on Fig. 6, MPTCP splits the generated traffic amongst two *subflows*. It aggregates the bandwidth of available links, and we get increased overall throughput as expected. The average RTT on *path 2* grows rapidly due to the saturation of the wireless AP capacity Fig. 7.

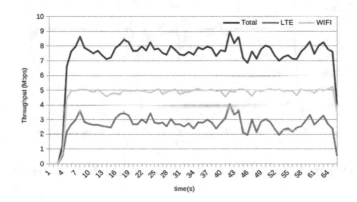

Fig. 6. Registered throughput with enabled MPTCP

4.3   Mobility Scenario

Multipath TCP supports seamless handovers by design, i.e., traffic flow switches from one network without disrupting application-layer data flow. Therefore, MPTCP is considered to be a promising approach in mobility scenarios, as it can migrate connections between different wireless interfaces.

One of the main features of the ns-3 based emulation is the ability to create mobility scenarios depending on the need of the experiment. We create a simple mobility scenario where the UE moves away from WiFi AP, with a constant velocity of 2 m/s, to trigger the handover procedure. Figure 8 shows the average downlink throughput for UE with rate-limited traffic, i.e., the *Iperf3* data rate was limited to 1 Mbps.

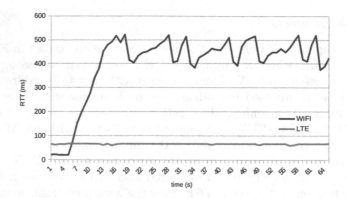

Fig. 7. Measured delay on each path

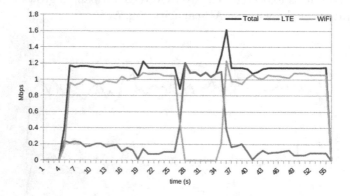

Fig. 8. Throughput on each interface during the handover

A UE is initially connected to both cellular and WiFi networks while receiving data simultaneously. The default MPTCP scheduler selects a path that guarantees the lowest delay for each segment. Although MPTCP transmits data via all available paths, almost all the traffic is sent via WiFi network (*path 2*). It can be seen that when the UE goes out of the coverage of the WiFi network, MPTCP can detect the connection loss and switch traffic flow to the *path 1* (LTE network), thus guarantee throughput required by the application. Notice that the application layer is unaware that the WiFi link goes down since data transmission proceeds on an alternate path.

Next, UE moves back to AP, and after some time, as the WiFi connectivity is restored, the MPTCP scheduler selects the path with the lowest RTT as the primary network path to send data. With this example, we evaluate the performance of MPTCP during the handover and show that our emulation technique responds as expected to the mobility aspect.

5   Limitations

As mentioned previously, during the tests with the FdNetDevice we have found a maximum achieved TCP throughput of approximately 70 Mbps. This result confirms the limits declared in ns-3 documentation. In this section, we evaluate the scalability of the described emulation method by increasing the complexity of the network topology. Afterwards, we discuss the limitations exhibited by the simulator and point out the possible solutions to overcome these constraints.

5.1   Scalability Evaluation

Low scalability is a common problem for all emulation-based experiments. Due to the limited hardware resources, emulators cannot reproduce the correct behaviours of a real network with a large topology and high traffic load. The fidelity of the emulator's results relies on physical resources of the host system, such as memory and CPU.

Ns-3 itself is an event-driven single-threaded[7] simulator that uses one CPU core to execute all the simulated events that are enqueued according to the simulation time they take place. Ns-3 applies a *real-time scheduler* in emulation mode that synchronizes the simulation clock with the hardware clock (*wall clock*). Thus, the events in the simulation are processed according to the system time.

However, in large scale scenarios, numerous events can occur within a short period. The simulation becomes time-consuming, so the execution of the enqueued event may be delayed. This delay, or *"jitter"*, is defined as a difference between the time an event should be handled and when it actually does. Ns-3 can control the fidelity of emulation if the real-time scheduler is configured to run in *"HardLimit"* mode. Thus, the simulator continually monitors *jitter* value. When the *HardLimit* mode is enabled, the experiment will abruptly stop if the *jitter* becomes too large (100 ms by default).

To investigate the scalability of our experiments, we studied the impact of the number of LTE devices in simulation by measuring the *jitter* of the simulator and RTT between two LXC. The same static scenario was employed, as described in the previous section Fig. 5. Several additional LTE devices created within the simulation are connected to the same eNb, downloading a 512 Kbps UDP data stream from a separate server connected to the same PGW.

Similar to our first experiment, we created the MPTCP session by performing an *iperf3* test with an unlimited load between two LXCs for 30 s. Figure 9 shows the evolution of the *jitter* during one simulation for a different number of connected LTE devices. The results indicate that the ns-3 can maintain a low *jitter* value when the number of LTE devices within the scenario is below twenty. However, with the 25 LTE devices, the processing of simulation events cannot keep up with the wall clock. Thus the emulation cannot guarantee a reasonable accuracy of the experimental results.

---

[7] *FdNetDevice* and *TapBridge* use auxiliary threads.

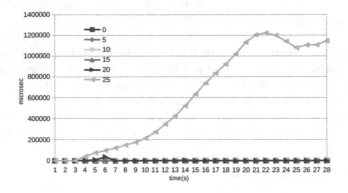

Fig. 9. The impact of LTE devices on simulation delay (*jitter*)

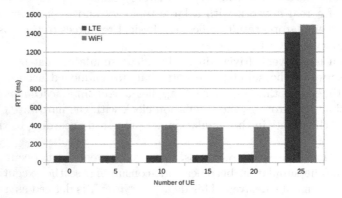

Fig. 10. RTT between LXCs with different number of LTE devices

Figure 10 confirms this conclusion by evaluating the RTT between two LXC's on both paths (LTE and WiFi). It shows that the number of network devices within the ns-3 simulator can limit the fidelity of the produced results by raising the *jitter*. This happens since the CPU cannot keep up with the increasing computational load; thus, the difference between the simulator and system clocks is growing. Therefore, it is important to find a limit that guarantees acceptable *jitter* for a particular emulation scenario.

One can use a faster host system for the network emulation (i.e., more CPU, larger RAM) in order to improve the scalability of the container-based experiments. The time dilation technique [5] is another promising approach to deal with the system's scalability issues. It's consists of a notion of *virtual time* that allows scaling system time for some selected processes. Thus, the real-time clock value is replaced by the virtual time clock tied to each process. For instance, when LXC is attached to a virtual clock scaling by a factor of N, it is considered to run N times more slowly than on the actual execution platform. Thus, by simply slowing the advancement of virtualized time, LXC will not exceed the rate at which ns-3 can advance. However, some modification to the Linux kernel is needed to use this approach.

6 Conclusions and Future Work

This work presents an emulation technique to analyze multipath data delivery over heterogeneous wireless links. It exploits the realistic network behaviour offered by the ns-3 platform and the functioning of real nodes provided by the Linux containers.

In particular, we have carried out an illustrative study on the behaviour of MPTCP protocol when used over wireless networks with differing characteristics., such as Wi-Fi and LTE. First, we have described in detail the emulation scheme, which allows the interaction of ns-3 with real systems. The proposed emulation method was validated for various scenarios in terms of accuracy and fidelity of achieved results. The expected MPTCP behaviour and experiment outcomes were registered through the experiments, validating the presented method as a flexible way to test emerging multipath protocols and applications.

Finally, we have discussed the limitations exhibited by the presented emulation technique. It is shown that the processing load of the ns-3 based emulation has a significant impact on the capacity of the simulator to perform a real-time execution. The emulator can produce sufficiently accurate results if the number of physical devices is low. The simulation delay (*jitter*) was used as a primary fidelity indicator.

Our current work explores the proposed emulation technique for a wide range of wireless networks (e.g., 5G). As future work, we plan to extend the presented scheme with realistic mobility models by using a traffic simulator. Furthermore, future work should improve the capacity of the emulator to perform a real-time execution to provide support for large-scale experiments.

References

1. 3GPP: Ts 23.501, system architecture for the 5g system, v16.4 (2020)
2. Arroyo, J., Diez, L., Agüero, R.: On the use of emulation techniques over the ns-3 platform to analyze multimedia service QoS. In: Agüero, R., Zinner, T., García-Lozano, M., Wenning, B.-L., Timm-Giel, A. (eds.) MONAMI 2015. LNICST, vol. 158, pp. 196–208. Springer, Cham (2015). https://doi.org/10.1007/978-3-319-26925-2_15
3. Elattar, M., Wendt, V., Neumann, A., Jasperneite, J.: Potential of multipath communications to improve communications reliability for internet-based cyberphysical systems. In: IEEE International Conference on Emerging Technologies and Factory Automation, ETFA 2016-November (2016). https://doi.org/10.1109/ETFA.2016.7733536
4. Ford, A., Raiciu, C., Handley, M.J., Bonaventure, O.: TCP Extensions for Multipath Operation with Multiple Addresses. RFC 6824 (2013). https://doi.org/10.17487/RFC6824, https://rfc-editor.org/rfc/rfc6824.txt

5. Lamps, J., Nicol, D., Caesar, M.: Timekeeper: a lightweight virtual time system for Linux (2014). https://doi.org/10.1145/2601381.2601395
6. Pakzad, F., Layeghy, S., Portmann, M.: Evaluation of Mininet-WiFi integration via ns-3. In: 26th International Telecommunication Networks and Applications Conference, ITNAC 2016, pp. 243–248 (2017). https://doi.org/10.1109/ATNAC. 2016.7878816
7. Petersen, E., Antonio To, M.: DockSDN: a hybrid container-based software-defined networking emulation tool. Int. J. Network Manage. (2021). https://doi.org/10. 1002/nem.2166
8. Petersen, E., Cotto, G., To, M.A.: Dockemu 2.0: evolution of a network emulation tool. In: 2019 IEEE 39th Central America and Panama Convention, CONCAPAN 2019 2019-November (2019). https://doi.org/10.1109/CONCAPANXXXIX47272. 2019.8977002
9. Portabales, A.R., Nores, M.L.: Dockemu: extension of a scalable network simulation framework based on docker and ns3 to cover IoT scenarios. In: SIMULTECH 2018 - Proceedings of 8th International Conference on Simulation and Modeling Methodologies, Technologies and Applications (Simultech), pp. 175–182 (2018). https://doi.org/10.5220/0006913601750182
10. Sabbah, A., Jarwan, A., Issa, O., Ibnkahla, M.: Enabling LTE emulation by integrating CORE emulator and LTE-EPC Network (LENA) simulator. In: IEEE International Symposium on Personal, Indoor and Mobile Radio Communications, PIMRC, 1–6 October 2017 (2018). https://doi.org/10.1109/PIMRC.2017.8292642
11. Suer, M.T., Thein, C., Tchouankem, H., Wolf, L.: Multi-connectivity as an enabler for reliable low latency communications - an overview. IEEE Commun. Surv. Tutor. **22**(1), 156–169 (2020). https://doi.org/10.1109/COMST.2019.2949750
12. To, M.A., Cano, M., Biba, P.: DOCKEMU - a network emulation tool. In: Proceedings - IEEE 29th International Conference on Advanced Information Networking and Applications Workshops, WAINA 2015, pp. 593–598 (2015). https://doi.org/ 10.1109/WAINA.2015.107
13. Zhang, T., Zhao, S., Cheng, B., Ren, B., Chen, J.: FEP: High fidelity experiment platform for mobile networks. IEEE Access **6**, 3858–3871 (2018). https://doi.org/ 10.1109/ACCESS.2018.2793943

A Dynamic Migration Strategy of SDN Controllers in LEO Networks

Liuwei Huo, Dingde Jiang^(✉), Wei Yang, and Jianguang Chen

School of Information and Communication Engineering, University of Electronic Science and Technology of China, Chengdu 611731, China

Abstract. Multiple low earth orbit (LEO) satellites form a constellation that can construct the network to achieve full coverage of the ground. However, the topology of the LEO satellite network is highly dynamic, and end-to-end transmission is a huge challenge for the LEO satellite network. As an important technology to solve the network dynamic management, the software defined network (SDN) has been introduced into the LEO satellite network. To manage the LEO network efficiently, the controllers of the SDN-based LEO satellite network can be deployed on some satellites and directly controlled by the ground base stations (GBSs). Since GBSs are static, so the controller should be migrated from one LEO satellite to another LEO satellite. Controller migration as an elastic control method plays an important role in the SDN-based LEO satellite network. Aiming at the problems of low migration efficiency and high migration cost in existing migration schemes, we propose a dynamic migration strategy of the controller. First, we analyze the load composition of the controller, and construct a load function, set the trigger factor to determine the load imbalance. Then, we determine the migration target and establish a migration efficiency model, and consider the load balancing rate and migration cost to determine the migration switch and the migration controller. Finally, by setting migration triplets to complete the migration mapping, to achieve efficient controller migration in the LEO satellite network. Simulation results show that this strategy can effectively reduce the controller response time, reduce the migration cost, and improve the controller throughput.

Keywords: Low earth orbit satellite · Dynamic migration · Controller · Software-defined network

1 Introduction

With the rapid development of communication technology, the Internet has penetrated all areas of human daily activities and has become an infrastructure for human daily and industrial production. The rapid deployment and application of 5G have brought tremendous changes to the human lifestyle, at the same time, it has a huge impact on economic, political, and military activities [1]. Due to the influence of geographical, population density, natural environment, and other factors, the basic network with wired as the backbone network has achieved full coverage in densely populated areas, however,

© ICST Institute for Computer Sciences, Social Informatics and Telecommunications Engineering 2022
Published by Springer Nature Switzerland AG 2022. All Rights Reserved
D. Jiang and H. Song (Eds.): SIMUtools 2021, LNICST 424, pp. 19–28, 2022.
https://doi.org/10.1007/978-3-030-97124-3_2

it is impossible to establish base stations or access points in many areas restricted by geographical conditions, such as in the air, oceans, deserts, deep mountains [2]. In many remote areas or areas with sparse populations, it is difficult and expensive to establish base stations. Besides, in the face of natural disasters (such as typhoons, mountain torrents) or emergencies (such as terrorist attacks, riots), the networks are extremely susceptible to damage, which will cause the network connection to be interrupted. The satellite communication network is not affected by geography and is a supplement to the ground communication system, so it is widely used in areas where the ground communication system is not easy to cover or where the network construction cost is high [3]. In recent years, satellite communications have aroused great attention from academia and industry.

Satellite networks have significant advantages, such as wide-area coverage, full-time and -space interconnection, and multi-satellite coordination, which have received great attention in terms of the global network. According to the satellite orbit height, satellites can be divided into geostationary earth orbit satellites (GEO), medium earth orbit satellites (MEO), and low earth orbit satellites (LEO) [4]. The orbital altitude of GEO is about 35786 km, and the orbital altitude of the LEO satellite is ranging from 500 km to 1200 km. The round-trip transmission delay of GEO and LEO are in the range [239, 278] ms and [8, 11] ms, respectively [5]. As we all know, the quality of service (QoS) of the communication system is very sensitive to transmission delay, so LEO has a stronger advantage in communication. However, LEO satellites move at high speeds in space, so ground equipment must frequently hand over the access satellites, but frequent satellite handover is a very serious challenge for network communications. To solve this problem, routing algorithms of LEO and software-defined satellites network are widely studied. In [6], Xiao et al. proposed the LEO satellite network capacity model which to value the influence of topology and routing strategy on throughput capacity. In [7], Chen et al. studied the distributed congestion avoidance routing algorithm in the large-scale constellation networks and proposed the Longer Side Priority (LSP) strategy to maximize the path searching space.

Although the routing algorithm research can help the LEO satellite network enhance the QoS of communications, the problem of the frequent handover of LEO satellites still cannot be solved. Therefore, the concept of software defined network (SDN) was introduced into the LEO satellite networks. SDN decouples the control plane and forwarding plane in switches and centralizes the control plane into the controller as the logical control center. So the network management of SDN is flexible, and the routing rules of the flow are optimal and programmable. In [8], Ling et al. designed an OpenSatNet architecture based on the SDN scheme in the satellite network and proposed an optimized forward scheduling algorithm (OFSA) to solve the multi-objective optimization problem of tasks. In [9], Zhu et al. proposed a software defined routing algorithm in the SDN-based LEO satellite network to obtain the optimal routing path by a centralized routing strategy. In SDN, the controller is the core of network control and management, so the number and deployment location of controllers have a great impact on the performance of the SDN network. In [10], Papa et al. studied the dynamic SDN controller placement in the LEO constellation satellite network and formulated the dynamic controller placement as an Integer Linear Programming (ILP). The number of satellite communications requests is proportional to users, while the distribution of ground users is uneven. Therefore, to improve the ability of the controller for managing the network, we hope that the controller will always locate at the position of the control center, which requires controllers to be able to dynamically deploy or migrate between different LEO satellites. The development of virtualization, Docker, and network function virtualization (NFV), provides solutions for the dynamic deployment and migration of controllers in the LEO satellite network.

The rest of this paper is organized as follows. Section 2 is a problem statement. Section 3 is to derive our prediction approach, and perform some simulaitons and i analyze the simulation resutls. Finally, we concluded our works in Sect. 4.

2 Problem Statement

The space-ground integrated network (SGIN) consists of satellites and ground base stations(BSs), as Fig. 1 shows. In the SGIN, the satellites move around the earth at high speed along their orbits, so satellites cannot continuously cover a certain ground area, the satellite-ground links are dynamic. The LEO satellite constellations are highly concerned and can provide continuous service to terrestrial users by switching the access LEO satellites.

The SGIN is formed by connecting satellites to the ground and satellites to satellites. The space-based network is mainly composed of satellites in the air; the air-based network is mainly composed of helicopters; the ground-based network is mainly composed of fixed, mobile nodes, ships on the ground, and so on.

SDN is a new type of network architecture system, which supports control and data plane resolution, and has the characteristics of centralized control, making the bottom layer equipment transparent to the upper layer applications. In response to the problems in the SGIN, we apply SDN technology to it, which brings the following advantages to the entire SGIN: (1) Reduce the cost of network equipment maintenance. In the existing network, the control and data forwarding functions of the network equipment are closely coupled, and the design and development of the software and hardware of the equipment depend on different manufacturers, making the maintenance cost of the equipment higher. SDN solves the problem of control and data plane, and provides a unified and open programming interface, which reduces the cost of network equipment maintenance and brings great convenience to on-board equipment; (2) Improve the centralized control capability of the network. In the traditional network, the different hardware and software of the devices, make the equipment in the network is independent. In the traditional equipment, because of different hardware and proprietary software of manufacturers, makes the equipment in the network independent, and the equipment is heterogeneous, and the management compatibility is poor. Under the open architecture of SDN. (3) The SGIN can better adapt to new business needs. SDN has a unified and open programming interface, which enables the design of the controller to adapt to the underlying business requirements, without having to operate each device independently, making the network more convenient to adapt to new business requirements. (4) Enhance the safety and reliability of data transmission in the network. SDN can configure different control strategies for different flows to achieve multi-granularity network control capabilities, enhancing network security and reliability.

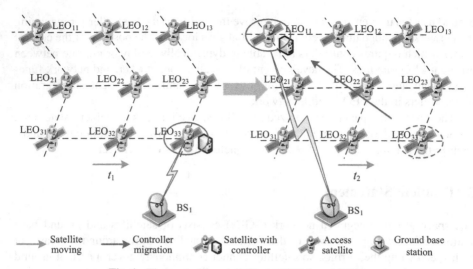

Fig. 1. The controller migration in SDN-based SGIN.

The SDN controller can obtain all the information from the data plane and construct a global view of the network, and the open northbound interface can realize rapid and automatic configuration according to different dynamic needs in the network, which meets the flexible and changeable characteristics of the world network [10]. The SGIN is composed of a space-based network and ground network, that is, a large-scale hierarchical network. According to the distance between the satellite and the ground, the space-based network consists of satellites. SDN architecture is also layered architecture. Corresponding to the SDN layered architecture in a multi-layer world network is an issue we need to study. The complex heterogeneity of the SGIN and the single controller's single point of failure and failure to meet cross-domain deployment requirements, so the multi-controller distributed deployment solution needs to be studied. Because of the frequent and highly dynamic characteristics of link switching in the SGINs, studying the reliability of the network requires studying the load balancing problem between controllers.

In the SDN-based SGIN, the controllers are deployed on some LEO satellites. Users on the ground are stationary relative to LEO satellites. When the controller on the LEO is far away from the users, the QoS (quality of service) for ground users will be greatly reduced. To solve this problem, we propose that moving the controller in the LEO, so that the controller will not be far away from the controller, as Fig. 1 shows.

In the LEO satellite network, the overload of the controller in LEO can be represented as

$$LS(j) = \sum_{i=1}^{n} r_i LR(i) \tag{1}$$

where $LS(j)$ is the total overload of the LEO satellite j, n represents the number of LEO satellites r_i represents the coefficient of the weight, $LR(i)$ represents the utilized state of the controller overload factor i. Assuming that the load of the controller close value of the threshold is $MAX(j)$, there are two situations about the controller migration:

In the SDN-based LEO satellite network, the flexibility of a dynamic SDN control plane concerning the number of controllers taking migration time constraints into account. There are two reasons for triggering the controller migration:

(1) $LS(j) \geq MAX(j)$ indicates that the controller has been overloaded or disconnect from the ground, so it should be migrated to the other satellite.
(2) $P(j) \leq P\min$ indicates that the signal strength between the LEO satellite with a controller and the GBS cannot meet the needs of measurement and control communication.
(3) $LS(j) < MAX(j)$, $P(j) \leq P\min$ which means that the controller does not need to migrate from the current LEO satellite to other LEO satellites.

In the process of controller migration, we set the signal strength from GBS to the LEO satellite with a controller as one of the triggering conditions, the signal strength from the GBS to the satellite with a controller can be written as

$$LR(i) = \sum_{f=1}^{F_i} B_f C \Big/ B_{\max} \tag{2}$$

where B_f is the bandwidth that the satellite forwarding the data; f represents the index of the flow processed by the LEO satellite i; F_i is the total number processed on the LEO satellite i; B_f is the bandwidth of flow f; $B_{\max}$ is the maximum bandwidth that can be processed by the LEO satellite i, it is limited by the memory and backplane bandwidth on the LEO satellite i; C is the utilization rate of CPU on LEO satellite, which can be obtained by reading the status information of LEO satellite.

The controller migration cost contains the network status information that needs to be migrated from the current LEO satellite to the candidate LEO satellite, the network status information is not only the dynamic information of the LEO satellite network but also the static information of the LEO satellite network. When calculating the controller migration cost value and selecting the candidate LEO satellite, the weight factors $a_i(t)$ are mainly considered.

The *controller migration Delay* (η): we use migration delay as the metric that the overhead considered in the controller migration process. The controller migration overhead in time can be quantified as:

$$\eta = \sum_{i=1}^{N} a\lambda_i \tag{3}$$

where a is the weight factor; λ_i is the migration delay that transmits the static information of the LEO satellite network, and they can be calculated as

$$a = \begin{cases} 1/h_{ij}, & h_{ij} < n \\ 0, & LS(j) \geq MAX(j) \end{cases} \tag{4}$$

$$\lambda_i = I_i / B_{ij} \tag{5}$$

where h_{ij} means the hops from the current LEO satellite i to the candidate satellite j; I_i is the static information of the LEO satellite; B_{ij} is the minimum bandwidth between the current LEO satellite i to the candidate satellite j.

The *switch access cost* (ξ) is the delay that the LEO satellite as switch on the data plane accesses to the controller to reconstruct the control link. The switch reconstruct overhead can be rewritten like that

$$\xi = \sum_{i=1}^{N_j} t_i \tag{6}$$

where t_i is the duration that the LEO satellite i as switch on the data plane accesses to the controller to reconstruct the control link; N_j is the number of switches access into the controller in SDN-based LEO satellite network.

The migration cost of the controller is the issue that we should pay attention to at present. When the controller is migrated from the current LEO satellite into another satellite, the switch satellite on the transmission path needs to be re-connected to the new controller periodically to adjust the control plane of the network. The goal of the controller migration in the LEO satellite network is to minimize the response time and handover time of the controller while keeping control flow overhead low. Therefore, we apply the weighting factor to the response time in the objective function.

$$
\begin{aligned}
& \min \max(\eta + \xi) \\
& s.t. \\
& \quad C1 : a \geq 0 \\
& \quad C2 : t_i \geq 0 \\
& \quad C3 : C < MAX(j)
\end{aligned}
\tag{7}
$$

where conditions $C1$ and $C2$ ensure that the weight factor of the candidate LEO satellite and the duration of the re-access controller is not negative. Condition $C3$ means that the candidate LEO satellite can deploy the controller. The objective function (7) is an optimization problem, we use the optimization algorithm to solve it.

Then, the controller migration step can be written as:

Step 1: Measure the signal strength between the LEO satellite with a controller and obtain the load of the LEO satellite with the controller.

Step 2: If the signal strength of the control satellite and the ground station is weakened $P(j) \leq P$ min or the load of the current LEO satellite is high $LS(j) \geq MAX(j)$, the controller triggers the process of controller migration.

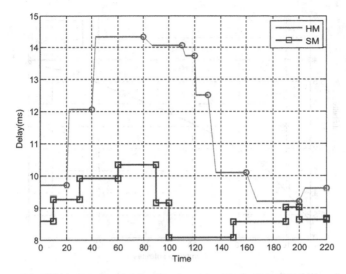

Fig. 2. The delay between the controller and the GBS.

Step 3: The controller obtains the global view of the LEO satellite network, including the current network topology, satellite memory, backplane bandwidth, etc.;

Step 4: Take all the satellites that connect to GBS directly as a set of candidate satellites, and calculate the migration cost of each candidate LEO satellite in the set, then select the LEO satellite with the least migration cost as the candidate LEO satellite with the objective function (7).

Step 5: The controller sends the network status to the candidate LEO satellite, and sends notifications to all LEO satellites as the switch in the data plane to access the candidate LEO satellite with the controller.

Step 6: Each LEO satellite as the switch access the LEO satellite that deploys the new controller.

Step 7: Return to step 2.

3   Simulation Result and Analysis

3.1   Simulation Environment

In this section, we use Matlab to simulate the proposed method, and AGI STK(Systems Tool Kit) issued to export satellite orbit data. In the simulation, all the location of the satellites are known based on data set from AGI STK. The number of satellites is 66 and we deploy satellite constellations according to the Iridium satellite system. There are two controller migration schemes, we named our method as soft migration (SM) and comparing it with the hard migration method (HM) that the controller will migrate when the GBS cannot directly communicate with the LEO satellite with a controller.

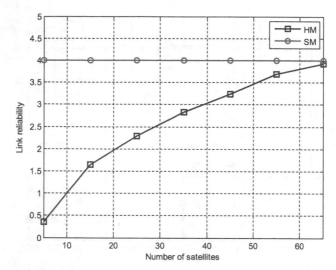

Fig. 3. The link reliability between the satellite deployed controller and the GBS

3.2 Simulation Results Analysis

Figure 2 shows the delay between the satellite deployed controller and the GBS. The red line represents the delay of HM and the blue line represents the delay with the proposed method SM. The red dotted line indicates that the link between the satellite deployed controller and the GBS is broken. In Fig. 2, we find that most of the transmit delay of HM is bigger than that of our method. The average number of handovers increases significantly. For the HM, when the signal strength of the satellite received by the GBS does not meet the communication conditions, the satellite will start the migration of the controller. Since the migration of the controller consumes time, the communication will be temporarily disconnected. For the SM, when the satellite has not reached the hard handover condition, the controller on the LEO satellite has been migrated, and the principle of SDN redirection is used to connect other switches to the controller. The satellites are connected, so the delay of the controller switching for SM is very short. This is the phenomenon shown in Fig. 2.

Figure 3 shows the link reliability between the satellite deployed controller and the GBS. The relationship between the number of satellites and the link reliability in this paper. As can be seen from Fig. 3, as the number of satellites increases, the link reliability of the network increase for the HM method, but the line is stable for the SM method. With the increasing number of satellites, then there are a large number of alternative satellites as the controller, so the deployment position of the controller migration between satellites will be frequent. The link reliability increasing with the number of satellites. For the SM, we always choose the appropriate satellite as an alternative satellite, so the links between satellite and GBS are reliable.

Figure 4 shows the mean delay between the satellite deployed controller and the GBS. The average delay is reduced to the lowest value. Continuing to deploy controllers, latency began to show an upward trend. This is mainly because the end-to-end delay of the network is mainly the delay between the controller and the switch. When there are a little number of controllers and switches, the shortest connection path between the switch and the controller in the network is always long, resulting in network control delay with the number of controllers increases, the distance between the controller and the switch begins to decrease, and the average control delay decreases continuously until the controller is migration.

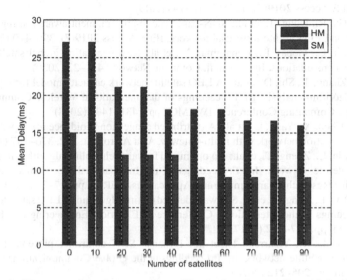

Fig. 4. **The** mean delay between the satellite deployed controller and the GBS

4 Conclusions

The architecture of the SDN enhances the flexibility of the satellite network and provides compatibility of multiple networks. The LEO satellite SDN-based network, which combines the SDN and the satellite network, is an important part of the future 5G network. However, the current LEO satellite SDN control strategy has the problem that a large amount of control information brought about by frequent handovers affects the network communication quality. Considering the problem of link stability between switches and controllers in LEO satellite SDN-based networks, we studied the migration strategy of controllers migrated between the satellites based on the soft-ware-defined network in the LEO satellite network.

Acknowledgments. This work was supported in part by the National Natural Science Foundation of China (No. 61571104), the Sichuan Science and Technology Program (No. 2018JY0539), the Key projects of the Sichuan Provincial Education Department (No. 18ZA0219), the Fundamental Research Funds for the Central Universities (No. ZYGX2017KYQD170), the CERNET Innovation Project (No. NGII20190111), the Fund Projects (Nos. 2020-JCJQ-ZD-016–11, 61403110405, 315075802, JZX6Y202001010161), and the Innovation Funding (No. 2018510007000134). The authors wish to thank the reviewers for their helpful comments.

References

1. Long, Q., Chen, Y., Zhang, H., et al.: Software defined 5G and 6G networks: a survey. Mob. Netw. Appl. **2019**, 1–21 (2019). https://doi.org/10.1007/s11036-019-01397-2
2. Papa, A., Cola, T., Vizarreta, P., et al.: Design and evaluation of reconfigurable SDN LEO constellations. IEEE Trans. Netw. Serv. Manage. **2020**, 1–14 (2020)
3. Nie, Y., Fang, Z., Gao, S.: Survivability analysis of LEO satellite networks based on network utility. IEEE Access **2019**(7), 123182–123194 (2019)
4. Guo, Q., Gu, R., Dong, T., et al.: SDN-based end-to-end fragment-aware routing for elastic data flows in LEO satellite-terrestrial network. IEEE Access **2019**(7), 396–410 (2019)
5. Ravishankar, C., Gopal, R., Benammar, N., et al.: Next-generation global satellite system with mega-constellations. Int. J. Satell. Commun. Network. **4**, 1–23 (2020)
6. Xiao, Y., Zhang, T., Shi, D., et al.: A LEO satellite network capacity model for topology and routing algorithm analysis. In: Proceedings of the International Wireless Communications and Mobile Computing Conference (IWCMC), pp. 1431–1436 (2018)
7. Chen, Q., Chen, X., Yang, L., et al.: A distributed congestion avoidance routing algorithm in mega-constellation network with multi-gateway. Acta Astronaut. **162**, 376–387 (2019)
8. Ling, T., Liu, L., Zheng, C., et al.: An optimized forward scheduling algorithm in a software-defined satellite network. In: Proceedings of the International Conference on Software Engineering Research, Management and Applications (SERA), pp. 27–32 (2019)
9. Zhu, Y., Qian, L., Ding, L., et al:. Software defined routing algorithm in LEO satellite networks. In: Proceedings of the International Conference on Electrical Engineering and Informatics (ICELTICS), pp. 257–262 (2017)
10. Papa, A., Cola, T., Vizarreta, P., et al.: Dynamic SDN controller placement in a LEO constellation satellite network. In: Proceedings of the Global Communications Conference (Globecom), pp. 206–212 (2018)
11. Jiang, D., Xu, Z., Liu, J., Zhao, W.: An optimization-based robust routing algorithm to energy-efficient networks for cloud computing. Telecommun. Syst. **63**(1), 89–98 (2015). https://doi.org/10.1007/s11235-015-9975-y
12. Jiang, D., Nie, L., Lv, Z., et al.: Spatio-temporal Kronecker compressive sensing for traffic matrix recovery. IEEE Access (2016)
13. Jiang, D., Wang, F., Lv, Z., et al.: QoE-aware efficient content distribution scheme for satellite-terrestrial networks. IEEE Trans. Mob. Comput. (2021)
14. Jiang, D., Zhao, Z., Xu, Z., et al.: How to reconstruct end-to-end traffic based on time-frequency analysis and artificial neural network. AEU-Int. J. Electron. Commun. **68**(10), 915–925 (2014)
15. Wang, Y., Jiang, D., Huo, L., et al.: A new traffic prediction algorithm to software defined networking. Mob. Netw. Appl. **26**(2), 716–725 (2021)

A Network Traffic Measurement Approach for Edge Computing Networks

Xi Song[1], Wansheng Cai[2], Chuan Liu[3]($\boxtimes$), Dingde Jiang[4], and Liuwei Huo[4]

[1] State Grid Gansu Electric Power CORP., Lanzhou 730000, China
[2] State Grid Electric Power Research Institute, Nanjing 210003, China
[3] Global Energy Interconnection Research Institute Co., Ltd., Nanjing 210003, China
liuchuan@geiri.sgcc.com.cn
[4] School of Astronautics and Aeronautic, University of Electronic Science and Technology of China, Chengdu 611731, China

Abstract. Edge computing is one of the key technologies in 5G networks, it can collect and process data on the access network and decrease the transmission load of the network. The data exchange in the Edge computing network Software Defined Networking (SDN) decouples the control plane and forwarding plane in traditional switches and plans to route in the global view, making network management more flexible and efficient. The accurate and comprehensive network traffic measurement is the key to traffic management of edge computing networks. Then, we propose a novel edge computing network traffic measurement approach to SDN. The proposed measurement methods use the In SDN by collecting statistics in OpenFlow-based switch and utilize the LSTM model and GNN method to infer the fine-grained measurement. Then, we construct an objective function to optimize the estimation results. Finally, we conduct a series of simulations to evaluate the performance of the proposed scheme. Simulation results show that our approach is feasible and has low measurement cost.

Keywords: Edge computing · Internet of things · Software defined networking

1 Introduction

Smart cities use billions or even trillions of devices to collect various information in urban areas, such as transportation, power plants, water supply networks, schools, and hospitals [1, 2]. The data of the smart city is generated by a large number of distributed devices and transmitted to the cloud computing server through the network. This information is used to improve the management and utilization efficiency of urban resources and improve the quality of life of residents [3]. In the traditional Internet of Things architecture, smart city data is integrated and processed in cloud computing. The cloud computing center consists of hundreds of thousands of servers, allowing users to use various terminals to access application services at any location. The storage location of the requested resource in the cloud is not fixed. Cloud computing is a general computing platform that

D. Jiang and H. Song (Eds.): SIMUtools 2021, LNICST 424, pp. 29–37, 2022.
https://doi.org/10.1007/978-3-030-97124-3_3

has powerful computing and storage capabilities and supports simultaneous operation of different applications [2]. The scale of the cloud can be dynamically expanded to meet the growing needs of applications and users, and cloud resources can be sold according to customer needs. In the IoT architecture of smart cities, cloud computing collects and centrally processes a large amount of monitoring data from distributed devices. Therefore, citizens can obtain more comprehensive and effective information from the cloud. Although the data volume of each device is small, a large number of devices simultaneously transmit data to cloud computing, which will cause congestion and delay, and pose a major challenge to the fast transmission capability of cloud computing servers, data processing.

Chen et al. [4] Designed a scalable, accurate, and fast measurement scheme in SDN using packet-level statistical data, and proposed a low-latency load-aware two-layer measurement platform that can estimate link utilization. Aslan et al. [5] studied the influence of active and passive network state collection methods in SDN. Liu et al. [6] shows a flow measurement and reasoning framework that performs adaptive measurement through online learning. Shu et al. [7] proposed a reference framework for traffic engineering in SDN, and proposed a framework for traffic measurement. These programs try to use estimation methods to measure network traffic, however, measurement errors are not unpredictable. Jiang et al. [8, 9] studied the characteristics of network traffic in wireless access networks.

Based on the above analysis, we have considered pull-based and flow-based network traffic measurement in the edge computing architecture. In this article, we propose a low-overhead measurement scheme and build a new edge computing network measurement architecture. We directly measure some data of network traffic and predict fine-grained network traffic. Then, we propose an objective optimization model to reduce the fine-grained measurement error of reasoning, and propose a heuristic algorithm to find the optimal solution of the model. Our main contributions in this article are as follows:

(1) The measurement overhead and accuracy of flows as the core factor in the edge computing network. To obtain the measurement results with low overhead and high accuracy, we propose to measure the coarse-grained traffic of flows and fine-grained traffic of links.
(2) Multiple decision factors, including bandwidth, link load and flow conservation principle, are jointly considered in networking, an objective function is proposed to decrease the estimate errors.
(3) We present a LSTM and GNN algorithm to obtain the optimal solution of the fine-grained measurement, and conduct some simulations to verify the validate the proposed measurement scheme.

The rest of this paper is organized as follows. Section 2 presents a novel lightweight measurement architecture of edge computing and analyzes the traffic matrix. We propose a coarse-grained measurement and optimization to measure the fine-grained traffic of the edge computing network. Section 3, we use a simulation to verify the novel measurement architecture and the performance of the proposed method and then analyze simulation results. Finally, Sect. 4 is the conclusion of our work.

2   Problem Statement

Edge computing frequently requests the resource from cloud computing to decrease the network. Network measurements such as load balancing, path planning, and anomaly detection are required, and SDN is based on traffic measurement is easier and more flexible than traditional networks.

2.1   Traffic Matrix Construction

OD (Origin-Destination) traffic refers to the amount of data transmitted from any node to another node in the network, and it describes the dynamic changes of data transmitted between the source and the destination. In the edge-computing network, flow traffic is dynamically changing and can be expressed as

$$\mathbf{x} = \{x_1, x_2, ..., x_t, ...\} \tag{1}$$

The flow traffic in the network is very important for the network management, but it is difficult to measure the traffic of each flow in the edge computing network. However, the link load in the network can be directly measured through SNMP(simple network management protocol). Therefore, we use the network traffic matrix to invert the network traffic in the edge-computing network. The relationship between flow traffic and link load can be expressed as a linear equation that

$$[y_1, y_2, ..., y_n]^T = [a_{ij}]_{n \times k} [x_1, x_2, ...x_k]^T \tag{2}$$

where $[y_1, y_2, ..., y_n]^T$ is a column vector representing link traffic, $[x_1, x_2, ...x_k]^T$ is also a column vector representing the traffic matrix and $[a_{ij}]_{n \times k}$ is the routing matrix, $i \in \{1, 2, ..., n\}$ $i \in \{1, 2, ..., n\}$, and $a_{ij} \in \{0, 1\}$.

The network traffic flow forecasting problem can be regarded as describing the non-linear mapping function f that maps historical traffic data to future traffic data.

The flows in the edge computing network have periodic changes in both time and space dimensions. To obtain complex spatial and time dependence is an important issue for network traffic inversion. In a non-dynamic network topology, the device nodes in the network constitute a point set, and the connections between nodes constitute a combination of edges. Therefore, the network topology can be expressed as a graph composed of points and edges $G = (N_p, E_p)$, where $N_p = \{n_1, n_2, ..., n_{NP}\}$, $E_p = \{e_1, e_2, ..., e_{EP}\}$. Using traditional convolutional neural networks (CNN) can obtain local spatial features, but CNN is limited to processing European data (such as images, speech, etc.). However, the network topology exhibits a non-Euclidean topology, which indicates that the CNN model cannot directly represent the complex topology of the network, that is, it cannot correctly capture the spatial correlation of traffic in the network topology. GCN (Graph convolutional network) is widely used to extract the spatial correlation of graph-based data.

Many researchers only use the first few time intervals (usually a few minutes or hours) to predict the network traffic. These methods ignore long-term correlations (such as periodicity), and periodicity is regarded as an important feature of spatiotemporal forecasting problems. Edge computing network data exhibits periodic changes in temporal and spatial correlation, considering not only short-term information, but also long-term periodic information. After extracting the spatial characteristics of the data, LSTM is usually used to obtain the time series dependency. Edge computing network traffic data is constantly changing with time and space, showing strong uncertainty and complexity. Therefore, in the measurement and prediction of edge computing network traffic, it is necessary to consider the impact of these complexity and uncertainty on the prediction results.

$$h_{i,t} = LSTM\left([x_{i,t}; e_{i,t}], h_{i,t-1}\right) \qquad (3)$$

where $h_{i,t}$ is the network traffic i at time t. $e_{i,t}$ is the external influence variable. The $h_{i,t}$ contains spatial and short-term time information. This method only uses historical time series fragments adjacent to the forecast period, because the traffic data of a node at the previous moment will inevitably have a greater impact on the traffic at the next moment. This kind of network only uses the most recent time interval. To make better long-term predictions, we need consider the periodic information. Since people's lives and work are usually regular, usually everyone's living habits and work content are relatively fixed, and have a certain degree of repetition, which makes network business traffic also have time characteristics. In addition, different types of business flows occur during working hours or during breaks, and they are located in different spatial locations during working hours and off hours. That is, the network traffic data also has an obvious weekly cycle pattern. We can find that the network traffic pattern of the previous Monday is usually similar to the network traffic pattern of the previous Monday, but is slightly different from the network traffic pattern of the weekend.

Training LSTM to handle long-term information is a difficult task. As the length of the time series increases, the periodic effects reduce significantly. To solve this problem, the relative time period of the forecast target should be modeled. However, it is not enough to consider only the relative time period, because it ignores the traceability of time changes, that is, the data of network traffic is periodic. During daily working hours, the traffic on the network will suddenly increase, and during the rest period, the network traffic will decrease, which shows that network traffic sequence changes periodically.

Therefore, we designed a periodic attention mechanism to constrain the predicted value of network traffic. For daily time changes, these times can solve potential time changes. Using LSTM to process daily sequence information, the formula as shown

$$h_{i,t}^{p,q} = LSTM\left([x_{i,t}^{p,q}; e_{i,t}^{p,q}], h_{i,t}^{p,q-1}\right) \qquad (4)$$

where $h_{i,t}^{p,q}$ is the network traffic i at time t at precious p days at time period q. $e_{i,t}^{p,q}$ is the external influence variable. The $h_{i,t}$ contains spatial and short-term time information. We use LLAMM as our proposed network traffic measurement methods.

Not every previous network traffic measurement has the same contribution to the target prediction. Then, we introduce the attention mechanism to capture the changes in time and obtain a weighted representation of each period in the previous measurement. The representation of each period of the previous measurement is the weighted sum of each selected period, and its definition as shown

$$h_{i,t}^{p} = \sum_{q \in Q} \alpha_{i,t}^{p,q} h_{i,t}^{p,q} \qquad (5)$$

where $\alpha_{i,t}^{p,q}$ is the weighted factor which used to represent the importance of p days at time period q. $\alpha_{i,t}^{p,q}$ is obtained by comparing the space-time representation obtained from LSTM with the previous hidden state $h_{i,t}^{p,q}$, and its calculation uses the attention mechanism, and its calculation as shown that

$$\alpha_{i,t}^{p,q} = \frac{\exp(score(h_{i,t}^{p,q}, h_{i,t}))}{\sum\limits_{q \in Q} \exp(score(h_{i,t}^{p,q}, h_{i,t}))} \tag{6}$$

The definition of attention score can be viewed as a content-based function that

$$score(h_{i,t}^{p,q}, h_{i,t}) = v^T \tanh(W_H h_{i,t}^{p,q} + W_X h_{i,t} + b_X) \tag{7}$$

where W_H, W_X, b_X, v are parameters and v^T is the transpose of v. For each previous periodic p, we get a period representing $h_{i,t}^p$. Then, we use another LSTM to use these period representations as the input and save the time sequence, as shown that

$$h_{i,t}^p = \text{LSTM}(h_{i,t}^p, h_{i,t}^{p-1}) \tag{8}$$

The output $h_{i,t}^p$ of the last period as a representation of time dynamic similarity.

We will concatenate short-term dependence $h_{i,t}$ and long-term dependence, $h_{i,t}^p$ to obtain $h_{i,t}^c$, as shown in the formula that

$$h_{i,t}^c = [h_{i,t} : h_{i,t}^p] \tag{9}$$

where the symbol: means splicing. For the predicted link and time, both short-term and long-term dependence are retained. We input $h_{i,t}^c$ to the fully connected layer. To obtain the final predicted value of traffic flow for each link, and represent it as $y_{i,t+1}$, so the final prediction function is defined as follows:

$$\hat{y}_{i,t+1} = \tanh(W_{fa} h_{i,t}^c + b_{fa}) \tag{10}$$

where W_{fa} and b_{fa} are parameters. Due to the normalization operation, the output range of the model is (1,1). Then, the predicted value is normalized and reversed to bring it back to the actual range.

In the training phase, the goal is to minimize the error between the actual traffic flow on links and the predicted value. The loss function of the model can be written as

$$L = \sum_{i=1}^{n} \|\hat{y}_{i,t+1} - y_{i,t+1}\| + \lambda L_{reg} \tag{11}$$

where $\hat{y}_{i,t+1}$ and $y_{i,t+1}$ are the predicted result and actual network traffic, respectively. λ is a hyperparameter. The first term of formula (11) is used to minimize the error between the actual traffic flow and the predicted flow. The second term L_{reg} is the L2 regularization term, which can effectively prevent over-fitting.

3 Simulation Result and Analysis

3.1 Simulation Environment

In order to evaluate the performance of the measurement scheme proposed, we built an SDN test platform and wrote the measurement module in python. We import the measurement module programmed import into the controller and call the Periodic Sampling module to send a Read-state message to switches via OpenFlow protocol. To verify the performance of the measurement scheme proposed, we introduce some common error evaluation metrics, such as the Relative Error (RE). The AE of the flow traffic reflects the deviations between the actual traffic and the measurement results. The RE is the ratio of measured absolute error to the actual value, reflecting the credibility of the measurement.

3.2 Simulation Evaluation

Figure 1 shows that the transmission rate of LLAMM is generally relatively stable, and is higher than the transmission rate of R60 and U60, and is closest to the transmission rate of the real network stream, indicating that the measurement performance of LLAMM is more stable.

It can be seen from Fig. 2 that the relative error produced by U60 at the beginning of the measurement is relatively large, and the relative error is relatively stable over time, and the average relative error of most network traffic measurement is about 0.2. The relative error of R60 is relatively small in the early stage, while the relative error of the later measurement is always high. Although the measurement relative error of LLAMM will suddenly increase at some moments. LLAMM still maintains a relatively stable relative error, and the measurement result of LLAMM is relatively stable and similar

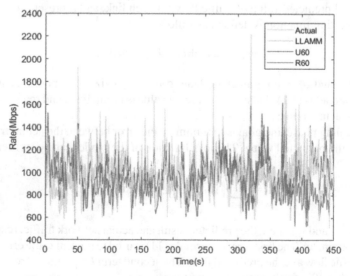

Fig. 1. The network traffic measurement of different methods.

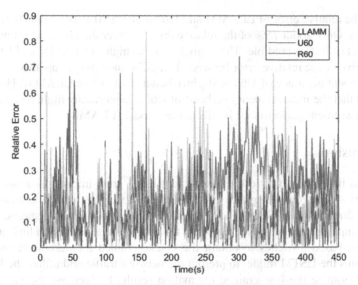

Fig. 2. The RE of network traffic measurement.

with the U60. This shows that our proposed method can continuously and steadily measure network traffic.

We introduce the cumulative distribution function (CDF) to describe the relative error more intuitively. Figure 3 shows the CDF of the relative error produced by different sampling schemes. The relative error is the ratio of the absolute error of the measurement to the actual value, which reflects the credibility of the measurement. It can be seen from

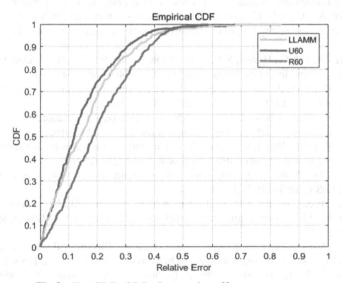

Fig.3. The CDF of RE of network traffic measurement.

Fig. 3 that the relative error of LLAMM and U60 is about 90% lower than 0.3, and R60 is even lower. Only about 75% of the relative error is lower than 0.3, indicating that the measurement of R60 is credible. The degree is not as high as LLAMM and U60. From the CDF curve of the relative error between LLAMM and U60, it can also be seen that the measurement accuracy of U60 is slightly better than that of LLAMM. However, it can be seen that the measurement overhead of U60 is abnormally high, resulting in the overall measurement performance is still not as good as LLAMM.

4   Conclusions

Fine-grained flow-based network measurement has a great impact on network traffic management of edge computing networks. In this paper, we propose a novel measurement method for flow traffic of SDN. The proposed scheme has two main stages. The first stage, the sampling method is used to collect the statistics information of links and flows in OpenFlow-based switches to obtain the coarse-grained measurement; the second stage performs the LSTM model to predict the network traffic and utilize the LLAMM method to optimize the fine-grained estimation results to decrease the measurement errors. Finally, the simulation results show that the proposed measurement method is feasible and effective.

References

1. Memos, V.A., Psannis, K.E., Ishibashi, Y., et al.: An efficient algorithm for media-based surveillance system (EAMSuS) in IoT smart city framework. Futur. Gener. Comput. Syst. **83**(4), 619–628 (2018)
2. Hossain, M.S., Muhammad, G., Abdul, W., et al.: Cloud-assisted secure video transmission and sharing framework for smart cities. Futur. Gener. Comput. Syst. **83**, 596–606 (2018)
3. Ali, I., Gani, A., Ahmedy, I., et al.: Data collection in smart communities using sensor cloud: recent advances, taxonomy, and future research directions. IEEE Commun. Mag. **56**(7), 192–197 (2018)
4. Chen, M.H., Tien, Y.C., Huang, Y.T., et al.: A low-latency two-tier measurement and control platform for commodity SDN. IEEE Commun. Mag. **54**(9), 98–104 (2016)
5. Aslan, M., Matrawy, A.: On the impact of network state collection on the performance of SDN applications. IEEE Commun. Lett. **20**(1), 5–8 (2016)
6. Liu, C., Malboubi, A., Chuah, C.N.: OpenMeasure: adaptive flow measurement and inference with online learning in SDN. In: Proceedings of the INFOCOM 2016, pp. 47–52 (2016)
7. Shu, Z.G., Wan, J.F., Wang, S.Y., et al.: Traffic engineering in software-defined networking: measurement and management. IEEE Access **4**, 3246–3256 (2016)
8. Jiang, D.D., Huo, L.W., Li, Y.: Fine-granularity inference and estimations to network traffic for SDN. PLoS ONE **13**(5), 1–23 (2018)
9. Jiang, D.D., Huo, L.W., Lv, Z.H., et al.: A joint multi-criteria utility-based network selection approach for vehicle-to-infrastructure networking. IEEE Trans. Intell. Transp. Syst. **19**(10), 3305–3319 (2018)
10. Pappas, S.S., Ekonomou, L., Karamousantas, D.C., et al.: Electricity demand loads modeling using AutoRegressive Moving Average (ARMA) models. Energy **33**(9), 1353–1360 (2008)
11. Xu, C., Li, Z., Wang, W.: Short-term traffic flow prediction using a methodology based on autoregressive integrated moving average and genetic programming. Transport **31**(3), 343–358 (2016)

12. Li, X.L., Qian, J.X.: Studies on artificial fish swarm optimization algorithm based on decomposition and coordination techniques. J. Circ. Syst. (2003)
13. Roughan, M., Zhang, Y., Willinger, W., et al.: Spatio-temporal compressive sensing and internet traffic matrices. IEEE/ACM Trans. Netw. (ToN) **20**(3), 662–676 (2012)

End User Experience Evaluation of Map Navigation and Location Service

Kai Chen, Lei Chen(✉), Zichen Tang, Qimeng Zhang, Yulong Jiang, Jun Yin, Jian Tao, and Ping Cui

Jiangsu Province Key Laboratory of Intelligent Industry Control Technology, Xuzhou University of Technology, Xuzhou 221018, China
chenlei@xzit.edu.cn

Abstract. The Map Navigation and Location Service is one of the most popular service types. To analyze the quality of the end-user experience, we identify the key indicators of quality of experience (QoE) for these services, and estimate the weights of these indicators. Based on the SERVPERF model, we collect the feedback data of college students and workers to build an index system of map navigation and location service. Using this index system, we can help users choose high-quality map navigation and location service, and to improve the end user experience for these services.

Keywords: Navigation service · Quality of experience · Location service

1 Introduction

Right now, drivers significantly depend on the online navigation service. Because the urban road conditions are more and more complex, drivers need map navigation service to route [1]. Many navigation service platforms focus on user experience, however, in the current market, we lack unified evaluation of navigation service quality [2–5]. The evaluation index system proposed by our experiment provides methods to evaluate and select high-quality map navigation and location services and provides a reference basis for improving the quality of map navigation and location service. This study also provides an improvement suggestion to current navigation software.

The common methods of user experience evaluation mainly include subjective evaluation methods, behavior data method, interview method, literature method, questionnaire method and physiological methods [6, 7]. By using the above methods, we can understand all the users feel when using the map software. In the process of establishing an index system, it is necessary to design an index system first, and then through rating and analysis by the expert. This study used questionnaire method, literature method, statistical analysis method and AHP hierarchical analysis method, with college students and social people as the sample group [8, 9]. Through literature, interviews, and analysis, 6 primary indicators and 18 secondary-level indicators were finally established to make the index system more objective and reasonable. The reliability analysis makes the

D. Jiang and H. Song (Eds.): SIMUtools 2021, LNICST 424, pp. 38–50, 2022.
https://doi.org/10.1007/978-3-030-97124-3_4

research results stable and reliable, the effectiveness analysis reflects the effectiveness of the research results, the consistency analysis and the determination of index weight make the results more real and accurate [10–13]. Analytic Hierarchy Process (AHP) provides a powerful tool for the research results [14]. Through the above methods, relatively accurate research results are obtained.

From the results of the survey, college students and social people pay more attention to the security and functionality and empathy of the map services. Map software can improve these three aspects to improve the user service experience and user stickiness [15]. This survey provides a future improvement direction for all map software, provides a reference to promoting the development of map software for multi-level personalized users, and promotes the positive circular development of the software ecosystem.

2 Investigation Method

The evaluation index of map navigation and location service is different from SERVPERF model. According to the particularity of map navigation and location service and user needs, the physical ability of the primary index in the SERVPERF model is removed, and the top-level index such as security and functionality is added. Then the main indicators of more comprehensive addition are obtained through literature and interview methods. Based on the characteristics of the map navigation user group and their requirements, we modify the indicators and questionnaires. For the preliminary construction of map navigation and location service evaluation index platform, design questionnaire, and let users according to their own understanding of the importance of map navigation and positioning service evaluation indicators, rate and evaluation system of relevance to fill out the questionnaire. The smaller the arithmetic mean, the lower the perception to the end users. The indicators with low score of Eq. (1) can be deleted.

$$M_y = \frac{1}{m_y} \sum_{x-1}^{m_x} C_{xy} \tag{1}$$

M_y is the arithmetic average of y index score. m and C_{xy} represent the number of users and the index score respectively. The larger the M_y value, the greater the user thinks that the more important the index is in the evaluation of map navigation and location service. And the smaller the M_y value, the smaller the user thinks the index on the evaluation map navigation and location service.

The degree of coordination is inversely proportional to the coefficient of variation, the greater the coefficient, the greater the user divergence. For the coordination of user opinions V_y, the following calculation methods are adopted in the pre-research:

First, the sample standard deviation for the evaluation results of the y index is calculated, as shown in formula 2:

$$\beta_y = \sqrt{\frac{1}{m_y - 1} \sum_{x-1}^{m_i} (C_{xy} - M_y)^2} \qquad y = 1, 2, 3 \ldots \ldots, n \tag{2}$$

Then, the coefficient of variation of y index score was calculated, as shown in Formula 3:

$$V_y = \frac{\beta_y}{M_y} \quad y = 1, 2, 3 \ldots \ldots, n \tag{3}$$

Furthermore, index weighting shows the importance of each index in the whole evaluation system. Reasonable weight distribution can ensure that the evaluation results are more realistic and effective.

First, the judgment matrix of the evaluation index of map navigation and location service is constructed, and the 1–9 scale method is proposed by T.L. Saaty in reference [16].

Factor i versus j comparison of the judgment is a_{ij}, so factor j versus i comparison of the judgment is a_{ji} or $1/a_{ij}$.

The construction matrix is listed below, as shown in Table 1:

Table 1. Scales of judgment matrix 1–9 and their implications

Scale	Meaning
1	Compared with the two indicators, they are equally important
3	Compared with the two indexes, index A is slightly more important than index B
5	Compared with the two indexes, index A is obviously more important than index B
7	Compared with the two indicators, indicator A is more important than indicator B
9	Compared with the two indexes, index A is more important than index B
2, 4, 6, 8	Compared with the two indexes, it is between the two judgment scales
1/3	Compared with the two indexes, index B is slightly more important than index A
1/5	Compared with the two indexes, index B is obviously more important than index A
1/7	Compared with the two indexes, index B is more important than index A
1/9	Compared with the two indexes, index B is more important than index A
1/2, 1/4, 1/6, 1/8	Compared with the two indexes, it is between the two judgment scales

To facilitate the calculation of the weight of map navigation and location service, according to the hierarchical order ranking and the consistency inspection and its consistency inspection, there are the following formulas as follow:

We test *CI* whether A is a consistent matrix, and when λ_{max} larger than n, the more consistent the degree is, so we can test the consistency through this method.

$$CI = \frac{\lambda_{max} - n}{n - 1} \qquad (4)$$

λ_{max} is the maximum eigenvalue of the matrix A, and the n represents the order of the matrix.

$$CR = \frac{CI}{RI} \qquad (5)$$

RI is the average random consistency index, and the value of the *RI* is a set of standard metrics generated by random methods.

$$CR = \frac{\sum_{j=1}^{m} CI(j)a_j}{\sum_{j=1}^{m} CR(j)a_j} \qquad (6)$$

Generally, when the consistency ratio *CR* <0.1, it demonstrates that the inconsistency of A is within the admissible range and can use the normalized eigenvectors as the weight vector, otherwise it needs to be reconstructed into a pair comparison matrix to adjust the A.

Indicator specified processing process is shown in the following Fig. 1:

Step1	Based on the SERVPERF model [17], combined with the particularity of map navigation and location services and user needs, six top-level indicators are selected.
Step2	Several users who have long used map software are selected for interviews to understand their feelings about using map software and discuss the most important performance of map software.
Step3	Summarize the main opinions of the interview, obtain secondary-level indicators.

Fig. 1. Indicators selection flow

Step1	The questionnaire was designed according to Likert scale and the scores were set to 1-5, indicating ' very insignificant, not important, average, important and very important '.
Step2	Several college students who use map navigation and location services are selected to score map software indicators.
Step3	According to the collected scoring data, the formula (1), (2) and (3) is used to calculate the user opinion consistency and user opinion coordination index and compared with the standard value to analyze whether it is reasonable.
Step4	According to the reasonable results, the index system is adjusted. After adjustment, the quality survey is carried out until all indicators are reasonable, and the evaluation index system of map navigation and location service is obtained.
Step5	22 preliminary questionnaires have been released and restored. SPSS22.0 is used to analyze the reliability and effectiveness of the evaluation index system, and to check whether the index system standard.
Step6	The 1-9 scale method proposed by T.L. Saaty was used to compare and analyze various indicators. The questionnaire was designed, and the weight of indicators at all levels was calculated.
Step7	Through (4), (5) and (6) consistency test, check the coordination between the indicators.

Fig. 2. Questionnaire design flow

Table 2. Evaluation indicators of map navigation and location services

Top-level indicators	The secondary-level indicators
Security A	Identity information A1
	Authorized security A2
	Location information security A3
Reliability B	System stability B1
	Navigation accuracy B2
	Sustainability B3
Responsibility C	Route planning delay C1
	Route update delay C2
	Customer service response delay C3
Assurance D	Service quality D1
	Version update D2
	Product brand and strength D3
Functionality E	Search function E1
	Location function E2
	Features E3
Empathy F	Value-added services F1
	Humanized experience F2
	Use costs F3

3 Results Analysis

3.1 Indicator Analysis

The questionnaires created by this experiment will be distributed to full-time students through electronic questionnaires and other ways. This time 22 questionnaires were collected, all valid. The results of the questionnaire were imported into the SPSS22.0 for reliability and effectiveness analysis. Reliability analysis is to calculate the data results obtained and the output data results to determine the stability of the questionnaire. The results of the same survey on the same index reflect the strength of the consistency trend. The safety coefficient of Krenbach α coefficient of level I index is 0.961, reliability coefficient is 0.778, use experience coefficient is 0.858, value-added service coefficient is 0.918, function coefficient is 0.762, and guarantee coefficient is 0.740. The Cronbach's Alpha value of each level index is greater than 0.7, and the overall calculated questionnaire is greater than 0.9, which can verify that the index system is of very high reliability.

Secondly, the evaluation matrix of the evaluation index of the map navigation and positioning system is constructed and the 1–9 scale method proposed by T.L. Saaty is used to compare and obtain the weight: first-level index: safety A, reliability B, use experience C, value-added service D, function E, guarantee F. Secondary-level indicators: identity information A1, authorized security A2, personal security A3. System stability B1, navigation accuracy B2, continuity B3. Route planning delay C1, route update delay C2, problem feedback response delay C3. Quality of Service D1, version update D2, product brand and strength D3. Search function E1, location E2, feature E9. Personalized service F1, priority customer interest F2, use cost F3. Through the calculation of the research data, the first-level index weight table, the secondary-level indicator weight table and the AHP level analysis results table are obtained. The exact values are shown in the Table 3, 4, 5, 6, 7, 8, 9 and 10 below.

Finally, the weight distribution of the secondary-level indicators in the primary evaluation index and the primary weight in the overall objective evaluation index are the combined weight of the secondary-level evaluation indicators, as shown in Table 11. And we get a Weight graph as the Fig. 3 shown.

Table 3. Questionnaire reliabilities test a value

Dimension	Cronbach a coefficient	N of items
Security	0.961	3
Reliability	0.778	3
Use experience	0.858	3
Value-added services	0.918	3
Functionality	0.762	3
Guarantee	0.740	3
Overall questionnaire	0.960	18

Table 4. A-F weights of grade I indicators

Evaluation index	Security A	Reliability B	Responsiveness C	Guarantee D	Functionality E	Empathy F
Security A	1	3	1	1	3	5
Reliability B	1/3	1	1/3	1/3	1	3
Responsiveness C	1	3	1	1	3	5
Guarantee D	1	3	1	1	3	5
Functionality E	1/3	1	1/3	1/3	1	3
Empathy F	1/5	1/3	1/5	1/5	1/3	1

Table 5. Weights of secondary-level indicators A1–A3

	A1	A2	A3	Wi
A1	1.0	8	8	33.654%
A2	0.8	1.0	9	33.654%
A3	0.8	0.9	1.0	32.692%
Summary of consistency check results				
Maximum characteristic root	CI value	RI value	CR value	Consistency test results
3.000	0.000	0.520	0.000	Pass

Table 6. Weights of secondary-level indicators B1–B3

	B1	B2	B3	Wi
B1	1.0	3	2	31.884%
B2	0.33	1.0	9	33.816%
B3	0.23	0.9	1.0	34.300%
Summary of consistency check results				
Maximum characteristic root	CI value	RI value	CR value	Consistency test results
3.000	0.000	0.520	0.000	Pass

Table 7. Weights of secondary-level indicators C1–C3

	C1	C2	C3	Wi
C1	1.0	5	7	35.577%
C2	0.5	1.0	7	32.692%
C3	0.7	0.7	1.0	31.731%
Summary of consistency check results				
Maximum characteristic root	CI value	RI value	CR value	Consistency test results
3.000	0.000	0.520	0.000	Pass

Table 8. Weights of secondary-level indicators D1–D3

	D1	D2	D3	Wi
D1	1.0	6	7	32.701%
D2	0.6	1.0	9	33.175%
D3	0.7	0.9	1.0	34.123%
Summary of consistency check results				
Maximum characteristic root	CI value	RI value	CR value	Consistency test results
3.000	0.000	0.520	0.000	Pass

Table 9. Weights of secondary-level indicators E1–E3

	E1	E2	E3	Wi
E1	1.0	3	7	34.762%
E2	0.3	1.0	3	33.810%
E3	0.7	0.3	1.0	31.429%

Summary of consistency check results

Maximum characteristic root	CI value	RI value	CR value	Consistency test results
3.000	0.000	0.520	0.000	Pass

Table 10. Weights of secondary-level indicators F1–F3

	F1	F2	F3	Wi
F1	1.0	8	2	32.353%
F2	0.8	1.0	2	31.863%
F3	0.2	0.2	1.0	35.764%

Summary of consistency check results

Maximum characteristic root	CI value	RI value	CR value	Consistency test results
3.000	0.000	0.520	0.000	Pass

3.2 QoE Analysis

In this paper, we adopt several representative AMap, Baidu Maps, Map Bar, Tiger Maps, Search Dog, Navigation Dog Map and so on. This paper analyzes the service platforms of AMap, Tencent Maps, Baidu Maps, and Apple Maps.

In this section, the quality evaluation index system of map navigation and location service is analyzed, and the data collected by the questionnaire survey are used for analysis and calculation to determine samples with judgment scores for each Secondary-level index. The volunteers of this questionnaire are mainly frequent users of map navigation software, almost college students and social people.

In the qualitative index, each Secondary-level index scored in 5 points, indicating very insignificant, not important, average, important and very important, we rank according to our own understanding, according to the importance of the evaluation index and each index, then multiplied by the weight, the overall score, each index is weighted by 10 volunteers, and then multiplied by the weight of the corresponding index for each index. Finally, the comprehensive score is summarized.

In the questionnaire survey, 10 volunteers have both chosen the AMap, and we can find that college students and civil servants are more concerned about C1, E1, F3, that is, Route Planning Delay, Search Feature and Use Cost when using these services. But also, can see that the AMap product service and quality is very good, so we mainly go to the AMap analysis and research.

Table 11. AHP results

Items	Eigenvector	Weight value	Maximum eigenvalue	CI value
A1	1.010	5.609%	18.000	0.000
A2	1.010	5.609%		
A3	0.981	5.449%		
B1	0.952	5.288%		
B2	1.010	5.609%		
B3	1.024	5.689%		
C1	1.067	5.929%		
C2	0.981	5.449%		
C3	0.952	5.288%		
D1	0.995	5.529%		
D2	1.010	5.609%		
D3	1.038	5.769%		
E1	1.053	5.849%		
E2	1.024	5.689%		
E3	0.952	5.288%		
F1	0.952	5.288%		
F2	0.938	5.208%		
F3	1.053	5.849%		

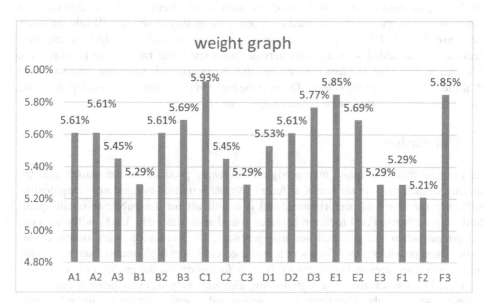

Fig. 3. Weight graph

Table 12. A M_y and V_y analysis was performed for the retrieved questionnaire samples

Selected Map	AMap	AMap	AMap	AMap	AMap	AMap	AMap	AMap	AMap	AMap	M_y	β_y	V_y
A1	4	5	5	5	5	5	4	5	4	5	4.7	0.483	0.103
A2	4	5	5	5	5	5	3	5	4	5	4.6	0.699	0.152
A3	3	5	5	5	5	5	3	5	4	5	4.5	0.699	0.155
B1	3	5	5	4	5	4	3	5	4	5	4.3	0.823	0.191
B2	3	5	5	4	5	5	4	5	4	5	4.5	0.707	0.157
B3	4	5	5	4	5	5	4	5	4	5	4.6	0.516	0.112
C1	5	5	5	4	5	5	5	5	5	5	4.9	0.316	0.065
C2	4	5	5	1	5	5	5	5	5	5	4.5	1.269	0.282
C3	4	5	5	3	5	5	3	5	5	5	4.4	0.843	0.192
D1	4	5	5	5	5	5	4	5	4	4	4.6	0.516	0.112
D2	5	5	5	3	5	5	4	5	5	5	4.6	0.699	0.152
D3	5	5	5	4	5	5	4	5	5	5	4.7	0.483	0.103
E1	5	5	5	3	5	5	4	5	5	5	4.7	0.675	0.144
E2	4	5	5	5	5	4	4	5	5	5	4.7	0.483	0.103
E3	4	5	5	2	5	5	2	5	4	4	4.4	1.197	0.292
F1	4	5	5	3	5	5	4	5	4	4	4.4	0.699	0.159
F2	4	5	5	1	5	5	4	5	4	4	4.2	1.229	0.293
F3	4	5	5	4	5	5	3	5	5	5	4.5	0.707	0.157

From the Table 12, as can be seen, the higher ones are C1, A1, D3, E1, and E2, it also shows the route planning delay, identity information, product brand and strength of AMap, location function in the map products in the forefront. At the same time for other map software can also be used to improve the quality of services. While the lower ones are B1, C3, E3, F1, F2. Customer service response delay, navigation accuracy, features, value-added services, and personalized experience have yet to be improved. For example, AMap is often pointed out that the interface is too large, and so on, so that the user's experience is poor. Despite the high overall rating of the AMap, there are some shortcomings that merit further improvement.

4   Conclusion

At present, there are many map navigation software products in the market, and the quality of each product service is different. We lack a unified evaluation of map quality, software function and performance, and it is difficult for the public to obtain quali-fied map navigation and location services issued authoritatively. Users will have poor experience when using unqualified map software. The evaluation index system of this experiment provides a tool for users to evaluate and select high quality map navigation and location services and provides a reference for improving the quality of map naviga-tion and location services. Through investigation and analysis, in the primary indicators, people care more about security, functionality and empathy services. Through further analysis, Secondary-level indicators, people pay more attention to the route planning delay, search feature and use cost. Through the establishment of the index system, some problems existing in the map navigation and location service can be found. In view of these problems, the corresponding improvement suggestions are put forward to improve the service quality of the map navigation and location service products. Therefore, it is expected that the map navigation and location service products can provide better information services and improve the user experience.

According to the results of the user experience survey, customer service response delay, navigation accuracy, features, value-added services, personalized experience has yet to be improved. We can take the following measures to improve the quality of product service. Some professionals can be trained to provide a better service, and some intelligent robot services can be used to improve customer service response delay. When optimizing an upgrade to the software, Map Software Company can add recommended algorithms based on the current location or route duration, and when the current location is identified as Home or Company, the home page will recommend a work route or an off-duty route, prioritizing the recommended time for the user's commute or recording the user's commute time to improve navigation accuracy and experience. For users travelling in different modes of transport, according to the user's history of off-duty navigation time, time-consuming, through the APP push personalized timing to remind users of departure time, push road conditions, etc., to do intelligent commute butler, to solve the problem of users late due to road conditions. At the same time, can cooperate with the audio class APP, the navigation process recommends the audio class content direct entry, for the audio products to draw, meet the user's expectations at the same time to realize the flow of cash. Other map software companies can also adopt the above recommendations to further improve the quality of product service to enhance the user's experience.

Acknowledgements. This work was supported in part by Xu Zhou Science and Technology Plan Project (Grant No. KC21309).

References

1. Liu, M., Zhao, F., Yin, J., Niu, J., Liu, Y.: Reinforcement-tracking: an effective trajectory tracking and navigation method for autonomous urban driving. IEEE Trans. Intell. Transp. Syst. (2021) https://doi.org/10.1109/TITS.2021.3066366
2. Abdelhamid, S., Elsayed, S.A., AbuAli, N., Hassanein, H.S.: Driver-centric route guidance. IEEE Glob. Commun. Conf. (GLOBECOM) **2016**, 1–6 (2016). https://doi.org/10.1109/GLOCOM.2016.7841755
3. Maheshwari, S., Zhang, W., Seskar, I., Zhang, Y., Raychaudhuri, D.: EdgeDrive: supporting advanced driver assistance systems using mobile edge clouds networks. In: IEEE INFOCOM 2019 - IEEE Conference on Computer Communications Workshops (INFOCOM WKSHPS), pp. 1–6 (2019). https://doi.org/10.1109/INFCOMW.2019.8845256
4. Ebenezer, R.P., Priya, M.V., Nivetha, B.: GPS navigation with voice assistance and live tracking for visually impaired Travelers. In: 2019 International Conference on Smart Structures and Systems (ICSSS), pp. 1–4 (2019). https://doi.org/10.1109/ICSSS.2019.8882833

5. Klafft, M.: Including weather forecasts in routing decisions of navigation systems for road vehicles: The users' view. In: 2017 36th International Conference of the Chilean Computer Science Society (SCCC), pp. 1–5 (2017). https://doi.org/10.1109/SCCC.2017.8405124
6. Yuling, F., Shengli, D., Lina, Y.: Research on comprehensive evaluation method of user experience in information interaction. J. Inf. Resour. Manage. **1**, 38–43 (2015)
7. Zhang, C.: The Why, What, and How of Immersive Experience, IEEE. Access **8**(1), 90878–90888 (2020)
8. Haiyan, Y.: Research and implementation of evaluation index system optimization. Sci. Technol. Manage. Res. **12**, 128–205 (2009)
9. Tjong, Y., Sugandi, L., Nurshafita, A., Magdalena, Y., Evelyn, C., Yosieto, N.S.: User satisfaction factors on learning management systems usage. Int. Conf. Inf. Manage. Technol. (ICIMTech) **2018**, 11–14 (2018)
10. Wuyi, Z., Bingyi, H.: Analysis of reliability and validity of questionnaire. Stat. Inf. Forum **6**, 11–15 (2005). (In Chinese)
11. Li, Y., Han, Z., He, Q.: Multi-criteria sorting method based on AHP and variable precision rough set. Int. Conf. Mach. Learn. Cybern. **2012**, 261–266 (2012)
12. Boral, S., Chaturvedi, S.K., Howard, I.M., McKee, K., Naikan, V.A.: An integrated approach for fuzzy failure mode and effect analysis using fuzzy AHP and fuzzy MARCOS. In: 2020 IEEE International Conference on Industrial Engineering and Engineering Management, pp. 395–400 (2020)
13. Li, M., Li, Q., Wang, X.: Determination of index weight of minimum price method for technical scoring based on AHP-BP model. In: Conference Proceedings of the 7th International Symposium on Project Management (ISPM2019). Ed. Aussino Academic Publishing House, pp.448–454 (2019)
14. Jinyu, G., Zhongbin, Z., Qingyuan, S.: Research and application of analytic hierarchy process. China Saf. Sci. J. **5**, 148–153 (2008)
15. Wang, Y., Qiu, W.: Optimization of distribution path for community group buying considering customer satisfaction. Tongji University. In: Proceedings of IAECST-International Conference on Traffic and Transportation Engineering and Management. International Conference on Humanities and Social Science Research, Shanghai, China (2019)
16. Saaty, T.L.: Deriving the AHP 1–9 scale from first principles. In: ISAHP 2001 Proceedings (2001)
17. Fragoso, J.T., Espinoza, I.L.: Assessment of banking service quality perception using the SERVPERF model. Contaduría y Administración, 1294–1316 (2017)

Native Versus Overlay-Based NDN over Wi-Fi 6 for the Internet of Vehicles

Ygor Amaral B. L. de Sena[1,2]($\boxtimes$) and Kelvin Lopes Dias[1]

[1] Centro de Informática, Universidade Federal de Pernambuco, Recife, Brazil
ygor.amaral@ufrpe.br, kld@cin.ufpe.br
[2] Unidade Acadêmica de Serra Talhada, Universidade Federal Rural de Pernambuco,
Serra Talhada, Brazil

Abstract. Internet of Vehicles (IoV) is a cornerstone building block
of smart cities to provide better traffic safety and mobile infotainment. Recently, improved efficiency in WLAN-based dense scenarios has
become widespread through Wi-Fi 6, a license-free spectrum technology that can complement the cellular-based infrastructure for IoV. In
addition, Named Data Networking (NDN) is a promising Internet architecture to accomplish content distribution in dynamic IoV scenarios.
However, NDN deployments, i.e., native (clean-slate) and overlay (running on top of IP stack), require further investigation of their performance over wireless networks, particularly regarding the IoV scenario.
This paper performs a comparative simulation-based study of these NDN
deployments over Wi-Fi 6 for IoV using real vehicular traces. To the best
of our knowledge, this is the first effort that extends ndnSIM 2 with an
overlay-based NDN implementation and that compares it with the native
approach. Results show that the overlay-based NDN consistently outperforms the native one, reaching around 99% of requests satisfied, against
only 42.35% in the best case of native deployment.

Keywords: Named Data Networking · Wi-Fi 6 · Internet of Vehicles ·
NDN deployments

1 Introduction

Vehicular Networks have attracted much attention from the industry and
research community since an increasing number of vehicles will be connected
to the wireless infrastructure of smart cities. Besides traditional traffic safety
applications, bandwidth-hungry infotainment services will require efficient distribution of content to vehicles. Despite the wide-area coverage of cellular communications and 5G advancements for vehicular networking, access via Wireless
Local Area Network (WLAN) has also evolved as an outdoor alternative for free
of charge/public access and complementary technology to cellular connectivity.
Nowadays, the IEEE 802.11ax standard, also known as Wi-Fi 6, promotes highly
efficient communication in dense scenarios [9]. This way, WLAN connectivity has

© ICST Institute for Computer Sciences, Social Informatics and Telecommunications Engineering 2022
Published by Springer Nature Switzerland AG 2022. All Rights Reserved
D. Jiang and H. Song (Eds.): SIMUtools 2021, LNICST 424, pp. 51–63, 2022.
https://doi.org/10.1007/978-3-030-97124-3_5

gained momentum in smart cities. Similar to cellular networks, the IEEE 802.11 family has evolved and can benefit the efficient content distribution within limited coverage for mobile users and vehicles.

Recently, Named Data Networking (NDN) [21], a promising Internet architecture for content distribution, has also embraced the realm of vehicular networks through the so-called Vehicular NDN (VNDN) [8]. Instead of using the traditional end-to-end IP-based communication, NDN adopts a hop-by-hop approach to distributing and retrieving content on the Internet. Thus, NDN does not need network layer addressing but relies on names to request the desired content. This solution has several advantages, especially in mobility contexts. When it comes to vehicles as end-users, this architecture has been promoted to overcome the intrinsic dynamic and challenging scenarios of wireless networks and, in particular, is well-suited to the Internet of Vehicles (IoV) through different solutions based on VNDN.

However, NDN is a clean-slate network architecture, breaking the compatibility with applications devised to provide services over IP networks. We refer to this approach as native NDN, because it performs a full replacement of IP protocol and a direct NDN deployment over the link layer [14]. In order to tackle this issue, the NDN can also be deployed as an overlay network, that is, NDN over IP [1, 21], thus, enabling coexistence with the traditional Internet architecture and benefiting from existing IP-based applications. We call this deployment overlay NDN. In general, NDN networks in testbed experiments commonly use only the overlay NDN deployment, while proposals evaluated through simulated environments commonly use only native NDN.

Despite existing works on the synergy between NDN and IoV [2,4,6,8,19], they analyzed their proposal either considering native or overlay deployment, but there are no insights on the comparative performance of both approaches. This is due to the lack of an out-of-the-box tool to evaluate both deployments. Furthermore, when modeling vehicle traffic, the works do not consider real traces from transportation authority and use low-throughput wireless networks, which limits the comparison between different approaches. Besides that, contention-based wireless technologies such as Wi-Fi 6 may suffer from broadcast storms or degradation of transmission rates due to the switching to basic service [16].

Hence, we conducted a performance evaluation of native and overlay deployments in an IoV context considering a Wi-Fi 6 hotspot. The vehicular traffic has been modeled based on real traces. To the best of our knowledge, this is the first effort to implement the overlay NDN in ndnSIM 2 [13] and perform a comparative evaluation with native deployment. Our simulation results show that the overlay deployment outperforms native in our scenarios, always reaching around 99% of requests satisfied, against only 42.35% in the best case of native deployment.

The remainder of this paper is organized as follows. Section 2 describes the general architecture of NDN to support different deployments flavors. In Sect. 3 we describe related work. We address all the implementation details of the simulation-based experiments in Sect. 4. We then discuss the performance evaluation results in Sect. 5. Finally, we conclude our paper in Sect. 6.

2   NDN Deployment Flavors

NDN networks have an architecture that works differently than IP networks, focusing mainly on content rather than device addressing, as shown in the narrow waist in Fig. 1. The problem with addressing IP networks is that they rely on end-to-end application communications and depend on the device's location. With the emergence of IoV, IP addressing has become a limitation due to the high mobility of these nodes.

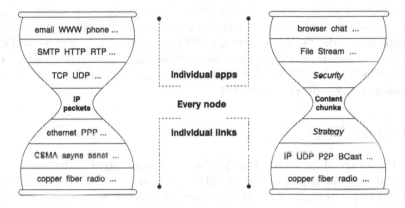

Fig. 1. Architectural differences between IP and NDN networks [21].

Applications on NDN networks request data by using the name of desired content, without informing the destination address, through hop-by-hop communication. This modus operandi brings several advantages. One of them is that the NDN architecture remains simple, and despite being clean-slate, NDN is also a universal overlay; it can run as an overlay network over anything that can forward packets, including IP networks [21], as also shown in Fig. 1.

Even when the NDN is deployed as an overlay network over IP, hop-by-hop communication is employed if there are intermediate NDN nodes between consumer and producer and thus the change of IP address due to mobility should not have the same negative impact when compared to a purely IP-based network. In this way, the overlay NDN provides its primary feature of distributing named-based content, while taking advantage of the existing and mature infrastructure of IP networks. However, this deployment increases the network management complexity due to the extra layer of tunnel handling that encapsulates NDN packets [14].

Although native deployment is the goal preconized by NDN researchers, IP networks are ubiquitous. Therefore, NDN needs incremental penetration on the

Internet, either on top of IP networks or linked via translators, to be feasible in current real-world scenarios. As described earlier, NDN is a universal overlay and runs over IP. In addition, approaches that interconnect native NDN and IP networks through translator gateways have been proposed [7,14], where IP nodes can communicate with NDN nodes and the other way around, without the need for overlapping. In this way, these network architectures must coexist, and after reaching a sufficient number of NDN nodes, the IP protocol could be gradually replaced by native NDN. Thus, the native deployment must perform satisfactorily during a transition period.

The NDN project provides its tools with an open-source license, including NDN Forwarding Daemon (NFD) [1]. This official forwarder has been designed to support the NDN in various deployment types, providing several lower-level transport mechanisms to run NDN over UDP, TCP, Ethernet, WebSocket, and others. In addition, NFD can be easily extended to provide new transport mechanisms compatible with other underlying technologies. Despite this, the official NDN simulator, ndnSIM 2 [13], provides NFD only with transport to NetDevice (abstraction of link technology), thus, supporting only native NDN deployments. To support NDN over IP in ndnSIM 2, we have implemented a new transport mechanism and described it in Sect. 4.

3   Related Work

We are not aware of any study that performs a comparative evaluation between native and overlay deployments of NDN networks. Hence, this study is of paramount importance for further investigation of NDN performance over wireless networks. Furthermore, simulation-based studies commonly work with native NDN, while studies based on testbed experiments usually work with overlay NDN. Thus, we believe that this work is the first effort to compare these NDN deployments.

The standard NDN architecture has no layer-2 address resolution. Thus, the native NDN only transmits through broadcast communication, which requires several precautions to avoid storms in wireless networks, since a broadcast transmission uses only the basic service [16] provided by most 802.11 variants, where throughput is much lower and retransmissions are disabled, providing less reliability. Conversely, the overlay NDN, when running over the IP, can use the existing layer-2 address resolution mechanism. Thus, overlay NDN has name-based routing, with hop-by-hop communication, but without the need for all transmissions to occur through broadcast.

Some works have proposed mechanisms to make broadcast transmissions more responsive on the wireless channel. Those researches [10,11,17,20] neither consider IoV scenarios nor comparisons between native and overlay deployments of NDN. An approach called NLB [10] has been proposed for efficient live video broadcasting over overlay NDN in wireless networks. NLB is a leader-based mechanism to suppress duplicate requests, where a single consumer requests (via UDP unicast) and everyone receives the same data (via UDP broadcast).

A multicast rate adaptation scheme in wireless networks has been proposed in [20]. With this approach, interests are always sent via layer-2 broadcast. However, a mapping mechanism between the Pending Interest Table (PIT) entry and the layer-2 address has been developed that allows the sending of data via layer-2 unicast. In this way, the proposed scheme can decide when it is better to send data packets via unicast or broadcast.

A broadcast-based adaptive forwarding strategy called self-learning has been proposed [17] and improved [11] to learn paths without needing routing algorithms. This is useful in wireless networks where nodes can be mobile and routes can change dynamically. To learn routes, the strategy broadcasts the first interest and upon receiving the data, it learns which paths have the content with the respective prefix. This way, the next interests can be sent via unicast to the learned paths. However, this approach does not perform layer-2 address mapping, and it is not possible to perform unicast with native NDN. The experiment in [11] were performed with overlay NDN, using UDP unicast and UDP broadcast.

In the specific context of VNDN, [8] performed a study in which all packets are sent via layer-2 broadcast. However, to reduce the disadvantages of exhaustive broadcast, the authors created a mechanism that uses Global Positioning System (GPS) information to perform forwarding based on distance, avoiding two nearby cars from sending packets simultaneously to use the wireless channel more efficiently. Moreover, to restrict the spread of interest packets, a hop limitation has been applied.

The dynamic unicast [2] is a routing protocol devised to perform an implicit content discovery through broadcast transmissions and dynamic content retrieval with efficient unicast links, without the need for location information. When a unicast path is broken, it can be reestablished when new interests are sent via broadcast by neighboring nodes.

Another protocol, called LOCOS [4], has been proposed for content discovery and retrieval in VNDN. LOCOS performs a directed search for content based on the location. Once the producer changes their location, requests cannot be satisfied until the new location is discovered. The protocol will periodically conduct a controlled search in the vicinity area to find the new location through transmissions of interests via broadcast. In this way, LOCOS reduces the storm problem while forwarding is directed to the nearest source.

MobiVNDN [6] is a variant of the NDN for VNDN and has been proposed to mitigate the performance problems of VNDN in wireless networks. In this proposal, the interest and data packets have some differences from the standard NDN. Moreover, a new packet called advertisement has been proposed to propagate content availability. In MobiVNDN, vehicles exchange location and speed information with each other to assist in forwarding and calculating the probability of communication interruptions. In this approach, the geographical location provided by the GPS also performs a key role in preventing unnecessary use of the wireless channel and thus minimizing the problems of broadcast storms. Still, even though MobiVNDN makes better use of the wireless channel, communication is also done through broadcast at layer 2.

An approach has been proposed [19] to improve data delivery on VNDN with a scheme in which the vehicular backbone has a unicast data delivery process. Despite a small scenario with few vehicular nodes, the simulation results show an increase in efficiency and the authors conclude that unicast is one of the responsible for reducing communication costs in wireless networks.

In summary, while some works focus on improving VNDN by suppressing redundant transmissions of interest packets based on the location to minimize the broadcast storm problem, other address the problem by creating strategies where communication changes from broadcast to unicast. In this work, we take another approach by not modifying any standard NDN behavior. We evaluate and compare the vanilla NDN in two different deployments, the native and the overlay.

4   Experimental Setup

We performed our experiments with ndnSIM 2.8 [13], adding the NDN stack to a modified ns-3 [15]. However, the version used is still 3.30.1, so we migrated to ns-3.33 due to the new features of the 802.11ax module. Our experiments used two NDN deployments (see Fig. 2) over Wi-Fi 6 networks in the vehicular context.

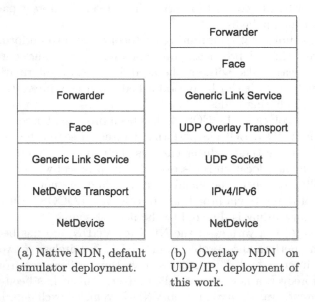

(a) Native NDN, default simulator deployment.

(b) Overlay NDN on UDP/IP, deployment of this work.

Fig. 2. Overview of the NDN deployments in the network simulator.

Figure 2a shows the overview of native NDN, which is the default deployment in ndnSIM 2. On the top is the forwarder that creates and manages faces (interface generalization). In the end nodes, the forwarder intermediates the communication between application and face. Each face is composed of link service and transport mechanism, the former translates the packets to lower layers, while the latter deals with the underlying communication [1]. Finally, NetDevice is an abstraction in the ns-3 of the network interface, which can be Ethernet, Wi-Fi, point-to-point, among other link technologies.

The forwarder included in ndnSIM 2, known as NFD [1], does not implement any overlay NDN approach into the simulator. Thus, we developed our implementation. Figure 2b shows the overview of our deployment of the overlay NDN on top of IP network. The main change is that the transport layer of each face creates an unicast tunnel to a remote face through UDP socket over IPv4 or IPv6. These tunnels are created hop-by-hop between each NDN node. Therefore, in this deployment, a UDP socket is the underlying communication mechanism for the NDN network. Finally, for this deployment to work properly in ndnSIM 2, we need to modify the stack helper and global routing helper to configure the communication via UDP sockets automatically.

4.1 Vehicular Traffic Modeling

To model vehicular traffic realistically in Simulation of Urban Mobility (SUMO) [12], we collected open data [5] from the transportation authority of Recife, Brazil, and we chose the data of 2019, as this year vehicular traffic was not influenced by the Covid-19 pandemic. The transport authority provides data such as the date/time and speed of each car traveling the streets for all city traffic sensors. The traffic sensor identified by FS037REC was chosen to have its data analyzed. As shown in Fig. 3, it monitors one of the main avenues in the city.

Fig. 3. Avenue with four lanes modeled on SUMO.

We calculate the average traffic on business days and based on this, we model the scenario with 172 m of avenue, 3 bus stops and 125 vehicles over 300 s, with an average and a maximum speed of 31 km/h and 60 km/h, respectively. Finally, we performed 31 simulations of this modeling to import the flow generated in each of the instances of the network simulations (see Table 1) and calculate the statistical tests.

4.2   Scenarios

Our simulation scenarios consist of 125 vehicular nodes that, along the 172 m of the avenue, will be connected to an NDN router through a Wi-Fi 6 network, 802.11ax standard with Modulation and Coding Set (MCS) 11 and 800ns of Guard Interval (GI). As shown in Fig. 4, the NDN router has been placed halfway. In addition, it is connected to the remote server (the producer) with a 1 Gbps point-to-point link and 30 ms delay. The Content Store (CS) size of the NDN router is 10,000 packets and for all other nodes it is 0. The payload of the data packets is 1024 bytes. Finally, when using the overlay NDN deployment, we configure the networks with IPv4 addressing.

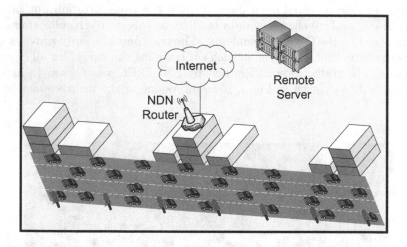

Fig. 4. Vehicular NDN network topology.

In our scenarios, the vehicular nodes send interest packets at a constant rate, defined uniformly between 50 and 100 packets per second for each vehicle. We created two scenarios identified by a suffix 1 or 2 at the end of the name for each instance of deployment (please, see Table 1). In the first, all vehicular nodes use the *ConsumerCbr* application, available by default in the ndnSIM 2. We define that each vehicle requests content with a different prefix, so we force all vehicles to request distinct data between them. Because of this peculiarity, there should be no advantage to broadcast traffic. In the second scenario, we randomly choose 50% of the vehicles to use the *ConsumerCbr* application in the same way as in the first scenario, and the rest to use the *ModifiedConsumerCbr*, a new application modified by us that sends interest packets with the sequence number based on the simulation time, therefore, vehicles request contents with the same name at the same time. Consequently, many vehicles request the same content and there may be an advantage in broadcast traffic. In these proposed scenarios, we performed 31 simulations for each instance present in Table 1.

Table 1. List of evaluated instances

NDN deployment	Scenarios	Instance
Native	1	Native-1
	2	Native-2
Overlay	1	Overlay-1
	2	Overlay-2

5 Performance Evaluation

In this section, we inform the statistical methods used, as well as present and discuss the results obtained with the simulations performed.

5.1 Statistical Tests

Arcuri and Briand [3] discuss the usage of statistical testing to analyze randomized algorithms in software engineering. Based on that, we chose Shapiro-Wilk to test the normality of the results. Although the data follow a normal distribution, homoscedasticity is not satisfied, that is, the variances between the distributions are not equivalent. Thus, we chose to use the following statistical tests: Mann-Whitney U-test, a non-parametric significance test; Vargha and Delaney's $\hat{A}_{12}$, a non-parametric effect size test, for assessing whether there are statistical differences among the obtained results. We used a confidence level of 95% in all cases. All statistical analyses and tests were run using SciPy [18], an open-source scientific tool.

5.2 Results

We started the discussion with the Mann-Whitney U-test, that deals with their stochastic ranking [3] to observe the probability that one population will have its values higher than the other and thus verify the statistical significance between these populations. Our null hypothesis (H_0) is not rejected when the p-value is greater than 0.05, suggesting that the evaluated instances achieved the same performance, otherwise, our alternative hypothesis (H_a) suggests that the instances achieved statistically different performances.

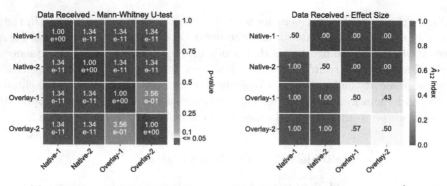

(a) The Mann-Whitney U-test.   (b) The Vargha and Delaney's $\hat{A}_{12}$ index.

Fig. 5. Statistical tests of significance and effect size.

Figure 5a shows U-test p-values for the metric of data received in vehicles in each instance evaluated (see Table 1). The only time that the H_0 was not rejected was when we compared the overlay NDN network in the two scenarios. It occurred because the transmissions for this NDN deployment are face-to-face unicast, and due to the layer-2 address resolution traditionally provided by the IP stack was possible to have full access to wireless network services. Thus, there was no performance difference of overlay deployment in the two evaluated scenarios. It is also important to note that the H_a was accepted when comparing the native NDN deployment in the two evaluated scenarios. Since this deployment performs only broadcast transmissions, it is expected to have a performance difference in the scenarios evaluated, even having access only to basic service [16] of wireless network, due to the exhaustive broadcast.

We use the $\hat{A}_{12}$ effect size test to analyze also the magnitude of the difference. This test presents an intuitive result, measuring the probability that one approach is better than another. Figure 5b shows $\hat{A}_{12}$ index for the metric of data received. The native deployment presented the worst $\hat{A}_{12}$ index, mainly in the first scenario. According to the result of this test, it is unlikely that the native deployment will perform better than the overlay deployment. When looking at Native-1 versus Native-2 instances, it is clear that if consumers request the same content for this deployment, it will make a significant difference, improving performance. When observing the Overlay-1 and Overlay-2 instances, the $\hat{A}_{12}$ index for the second presented a slight superiority despite the U-test showing no statistical difference. The slight difference could be explained because much of the data requested is already in the NDN router's CS. Thus, other vehicles have already requested data, something that does not occur in the first scenario.

Figure 6a shows the total number of interest packets sent and the data received in each evaluated instance. The number of interest packets sent is the same, regardless of the instance. Therefore, only one bar has been placed on the chart with this information. It is possible to observe that there is a considerable superiority of Native-2 over Native-1, around 70% of more data received, with Native-1 reaching only 18.25% of requests satisfied, against 31.1% reached by

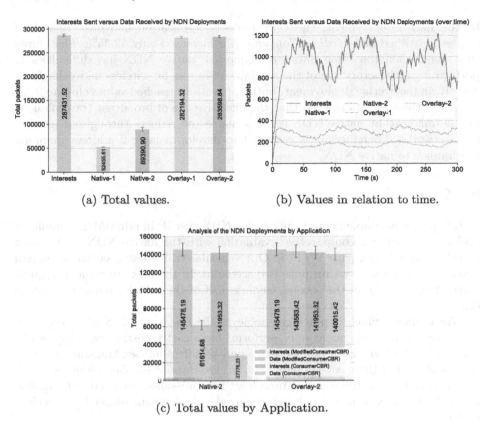

(a) Total values.

(b) Values in relation to time.

(c) Total values by Application.

Fig. 6. Relation between interest sent and data received by evaluated instances.

Native-2. Thus, it confirms the importance of vehicles requesting the same content in the native deployment. However, when comparing Native-2 with the two instances of the overlay deployment, the performance difference is significant, receiving more than 200% of data received than Native-2, reaching values close to 99% of requests satisfied in overlay deployments.

This difference is explained by the fact that the wireless network standard offers a basic service of communication for broadcast transmissions [16], as a consequence, the performance of this traffic is reduced. The Fig. 6b shows the same information, but from a new perspective to show the packets in relation to the simulation time. The lines of data received in the overlay instances always follow the interests sent, taking advantage of wireless network resources, unlike the instances of native deployment that always use the basic service of the wireless network, falling away from optimal performance.

Figure 6c also shows this analysis of the relationship between interests and data, but by application, which is why it contains instances only from the second scenario. In our experiments the vehicles running *ConsumerCbr* requests distinct data, while the vehicles running *ModifiedConsumerCbr* requests same data. Hence, we compared NDN deployments with these two types of traffic.

In the native deployment, the *ConsumerCbr* application had only 19.57% of requests satisfied and *ModifiedConsumerCbr* increased only 42.35%. This shows that even when the same data are requested, native NDN has difficulties in performing satisfactory use of the available resources on wireless networks. Conversely, in the overlay deployment, both applications reached values close to 99%.

All of these results showed that the excessive use of broadcast transmissions in the link layer by native NDN is not scalable and reduces throughput in wireless networks. Therefore, it is essential to develop a layer-2 address mapping mechanism to native NDN.

6 Conclusions

In this paper, we implemented the overlay NDN over IP in ndnSIM 2.8 simulator and we conducted a comparative evaluation with the native NDN deployment in vehicular network with Wi-Fi 6. Our vehicular traffic has been based on real traces, and from this, we propose two scenarios. In the first, all vehicles request distinct data, while in the second scenario half of the vehicles request the same data.

We evaluate which deployment achieves the best rate of satisfied requests, since the native deployment only performs broadcast transmission. Oppositely, the overlay deployment in our scenarios only performs unicast transmission. Our results show that the native deployment has low rates of satisfied requests in Wi-Fi 6 due to the extensive use of broadcast transmissions, achieved only 42.35% in the best case. On the other hand, the overlay deployment reached values close to 99%.

NDN is a clean-slate network architecture. It is unlikely to be initially deployed in the native form. A transition period will be necessary for this migration to take place smoothly. Thus, comprehensively understanding the performance of the overlay NDN deployment is a necessary step for its adoption in vehicular networks. As future work, a layer-2 address mapping mechanism should be devised to improve the performance of native NDN deployment in wireless networks and compared with existing solutions. In addition, more scenarios should be investigated considering heterogeneous nodes with native NDN, overlay NDN, and nodes that have only IP stack, all communicating with each other.

Acknowledgments. This work was partially supported by the National Council for Scientific and Technological Development (CNPq) (Grant No. 312831/2020-0).

References

1. Afanasyev, A., et al.: NFD Developer's Guide. Technical Report NDN-0021 (2018)
2. Anastasiades, C., Weber, J., Braun, T.: Dynamic unicast: information-centric multi-hop routing for mobile ad-hoc networks. Comput. Netw. **107**, 208–219 (2016). Mobile Wireless Networks
3. Arcuri, A., Briand, L.: A practical guide for using statistical tests to assess randomized algorithms in software engineering. In: 2011 33rd International Conference on Software Engineering (ICSE), pp. 1–10 (2011)

4. Coutinho, R.W.L., Boukerche, A., Yu, X.: A novel location-based content distribution protocol for vehicular named-data networks. In: 2018 IEEE Symposium on Computers and Communications (ISCC), pp. 01007–01012, June 2018
5. CTTU: Open data of vehicle traffic from Recife-Brazil (2019). http://dados.recife.pe.gov.br/dataset/velocidade-das-vias-quantitativo-por-velocidade-media-2019
6. Duarte, J.M., Braun, T., Villas, L.A.: MobiVNDN: a distributed framework to support mobility in vehicular named-data networking. Ad Hoc Netw. **82**, 77–90 (2019)
7. Fahrianto, F., Kamiyama, N.: A low-cost IP-to-NDN translation gateway. In: 2021 IEEE 22nd International Conference on High Performance Switching and Routing (HPSR), pp. 1–5, June 2021
8. Grassi, G., Pesavento, D., Pau, G., Vuyyuru, R., Wakikawa, R., Zhang, L.: VANET via named data networking. In: 2014 IEEE Conference on Computer Communications Workshops (INFOCOM WKSHPS), pp. 410–415, April 2014
9. Khorov, E., Kiryanov, A., Lyakhov, A., Bianchi, G.: A tutorial on IEEE 802.11ax high efficiency WLANs. IEEE Commun. Surv. Tutor. **21**(1), 197–216 (2019)
10. Li, M., Pei, D., Zhang, X., Zhang, B., Xu, K.: NDN live video broadcasting over wireless LAN. In: 2015 24th International Conference on Computer Communication and Networks (ICCCN), pp. 1–7, August 2015
11. Liang, T., et al.: Enabling named data networking forwarder to work out-of-the-box at edge networks. In: 2020 IEEE International Conference on Communications Workshops (ICC Workshops), pp. 1–6 (2020)
12. Lopez, P.A., et al.: Microscopic traffic simulation using SUMO. In: 2018 21st International Conference on Intelligent Transportation Systems (ITSC), pp. 2575–2582 (2018)
13. Mastorakis, S., Afanasyev, A., Zhang, L.: On the evolution of ndnSIM: an open-source simulator for NDN experimentation. SIGCOMM Comput. Commun. Rev. **47**(3), 19–33 (2017)
14. Nour, B., Li, F., Khelifi, H., Moungla, H., Ksentini, A.: Coexistence of ICN and IP networks: an NFV as a service approach. In: 2019 IEEE Global Communications Conference (GLOBECOM), pp. 1–6, December 2019
15. ns-3: ns-3 Network Simulator Website (2021). https://www.nsnam.org/
16. SA, I.: IEEE standard for information technology - telecommunications and information exchange between systems - local and metropolitan area networks-specific requirements - Part 11: wireless LAN Medium Access Control (MAC) and Physical Layer (PHY) Specifications. In: IEEE Std 802.11-2020 (Revision of IEEE Std 802.11-2016), pp. 1–4379, February 2021
17. Shi, J., Newberry, E., Zhang, B.: On broadcast-based self-learning in named data networking. In: 2017 IFIP Networking Conference (IFIP Networking) and Workshops, pp. 1–9, June 2017
18. Virtanen, P., et al.: SciPy 1.0: fundamental algorithms for scientific computing in python. Nat. Methods **17**, 261–272 (2020)
19. Wang, X., Wang, Z., Cai, S.: Data delivery in vehicular named data networking. IEEE Netw. Lett. **2**(3), 120–123 (2020)
20. Wu, F., Yang, W., Fan, Z., Tian, K.: Multicast rate adaptation in WLAN via NDN. In: 2018 27th International Conference on Computer Communication and Networks (ICCCN), pp. 1–8, July 2018
21. Zhang, L., et al.: Named data networking. SIGCOMM Comput. Commun. Rev. **44**(3), 66–73 (2014)

An Adaptive and Efficient Network Traffic Measurement Method Based on SDN in IoT

Wansheng Cai[1], Xi Song[2], Chuan Liu[3], Dingde Jiang[4(✉)], and Liuwei Huo[4]

[1] State Grid Electric Power Research Institute, Nanjing 210003, China
[2] State Grid Gansu Electric Power CORP., Lanzhou 730000, China
[3] Global Energy Interconnection Research Institute Co., Ltd., Nanjing 210003, China
liuchuan@geiri.sgcc.com.cn
[4] School of Astronautics and Aeronautics, University of Electronic Science and Technology of China, Chengdu 611731, China

Abstract. The Internet of Things (IoT) is a worldwide information network that connects thousands of technological gadgets. We incorporate the SDN network architecture into IoT networks and investigate the characteristics of SDN-based IoT networks in order to make the IoT more flexible and extendable. SDN (Software Defined Networking) is a logical control center with a centralized control plane that makes network management more flexible and efficient. For IoT network management, fine-grained and reliable traffic information is critical. Then, in SDN-based IoT networks, we construct a network traffic model by analyzing the self-similarity of network traffic in IoT network. Then, we collect some traffic statistics in OpenFlow-based switches as the source data and use it to train the proposed network traffic estimation model. Using the measured network traffic in the IoT network, we use the Kalman Filtering to measure and estimate each flow, this scheme just increases a little overhead. Then, we propose to an algorithm to search the more accuracy of traffic. Finally, we run additional simulations to ensure that the suggested measuring system is accurate. Simulation findings suggest that using intelligent optimization approaches, we can improve the granularity and accuracy of traffic data.

Keywords: Internet of Things · Software Defined Network · Optimization algorithm · Network measurement

1 Introduction

The Internet of Things (IoT) is a widely used communication technology that has changed people's lifestyles. It has been widely used in smart homes, intelligent transportation, intelligent logistics, smart medical, smart factories, intelligent agriculture, and other areas to create a more convenient life for citizens [1]. Cloud computing is at the heart of the IoT, processing and storing data. Hundreds of thousands of computers make up the cloud computing center, which allows customers to access application services from any location via a variety of terminals. Cloud computing is a general-purpose computing

D. Jiang and H. Song (Eds.): SIMUtools 2021, LNICST 424, pp. 64–74, 2022.
https://doi.org/10.1007/978-3-030-97124-3_6

platform with significant computing and storage capabilities that allows multiple programs to run concurrently [2]. Cloud resources can be sold based on consumer demand, and their scale can be dynamically adjusted to meet the needs of rising applications and users. In cloud computing, there is a lot of data to process and exchange, therefore accurate network traffic statistics is critical for network management.

The network architecture of the legacy IoT network is not scalable and does not meet the requirements of the increasing devices. The goal of Software Defined Networking (SDN) is to make network management easier and the IoT more flexible. To simplify network management policies and dynamically configure network rules, SDN isolates the control plane from the underlying forwarding device and incorporates it into the logically centralized controller [3–5]. Because the controller in SDN has a global view of the networks, it may build global traffic dispatching optimization rules. However, the applications process associated to cloud computing for requesting specific services, such as long-term data storage, applications requests, and resource requests, is susceptible to latency and bandwidth constraints. As a result, most cloud computing services are primarily concerned about latency and bandwidth. In a cloud computing network, fine-grained network traffic information acquisition is critical for traffic control. The importance of traffic engineering for cloud computing architecture cannot be overstated. Hardware support and remote monitoring agent software are required for each of them. SDN offers a revolutionary flow-based statistical measuring method that is both versatile and convenient for collecting traffic statistics from switches.

Through the OpenFlow protocol, SDN provides two techniques for collecting flow statistics: pull-based and push-based [6]. A pull-based technique is an active method of gathering statistical data that does not require any additional hardware or software. All that is required is for the controller to deliver commands to the OpenFlow-based switch. Programs for controlling devices to collect flow statistics or port statistics information, read-state messages and deliver them to OpenFlow-based switches [7]. Jiang et al. [8, 9] investigated network traffic aspects in a communications access network.

We discuss pull-based and flow-based network traffic measurement in cloud computing architecture based on the aforesaid analysis. In this research, we present a low-overhead traffic information acquisition scheme and build a unique cloud computing network measurement architecture. We directly measure some network traffic metrics and forecast fine-grained network traffic. Then, to reduce the fine-grained measurement error inferred, we propose an intelligent optimization model and a heuristic approach to find the model's optimal solution. We offer a model to forecast network traffic and use an optimization approach to achieve fine-grained network traffic in this system. The following are the primary contributions we make in this paper:

- We present a framework for measuring network traffic in IoT networks. We collect statistics of flow traffic to construct a traffic matrix and clean them as the training set of the proposed model.
- We proposed the NEKF algorithm to measure and estimate the network traffic in the IoT network.
- Finally, we run additional simulations to test the suggested measuring scheme's performance.

The following is how the rest of the paper is structured: The key security challenges of SDN are discussed in Sect. 2, after which we present a fine-grained measurement method and describe fine-grained measurement prediction and optimization in the IoT paradigm. The performance of fine-grained measurement with the scheme is simulated in Sect. 3. Finally, Sect. 4 brings our works to a conclusion.

2 Problem Statement

In the IoT network, there are huge amount of devices that connect into the network, and network architecture is dynamic, to measure and manage the network effectively, we think about the IoT network architecture based on SDN, and proposed the active network traffic measurement scheme in the SDN-based IoT network.

2.1 The Self-similarity of IoT Network Traffic

In the Internet, the network traffic obeys the Poisson distribution, then we can construct a mathematic model of Internet with Poisson distribution function. However, the traffic in SDN-based IoT network is different from the traffic in Internet, although the packet of devices in IoT network is relatively small, and the data volume is relatively large, so we need to analyze the flow traffic characteristic in IoT network.

The discovery of the self-similarity of flow traffic has led people to find the theoretical reasons for the actual network performance and the theoretical performance using the traditional Poisson model. First, analyze the causes of self-similarity. Aiming at the propagation characteristics of self-similar business between sensor nodes in the Internet of Things, the self-similarity analysis of the business after the network researches self-similar traffic entering the Internet of Things network through the access point, etc. Through these analyses, to comprehensively describe the business characteristics of the Internet of Things. Finally, analyze and study the impact of business self-similarity on the derived performance of network nodes and on the quality of network service.

The scale of networks has grown as the telecommunications business has grown, and user data needs have emerged; different sorts of services, such as voice data, video, and formal streaming media, have distinct features. IP addresses are used in a variety of business streams on the Internet. The expected result is quite different from the real situation when the Poisson service model of the data service flow in the network is utilized in the data transmission network. The enormity of the network and the intricacy of the service in this situation can no longer be evaluated through the lens of a single call. The establishment cannot be determined by making multiple calls; rather, it must be determined from a broad perspective, depending on the data flow method and rate. Data on Internet communication, video, and VBR traffic was thoroughly examined, and the following key results were reached:

(1) Business flow can be self-similar at any moment and in any network environment.
(2) Self-similarity is common in the IP network environment, whether at the network layer, transport layer, or application layer, and it is linked to certain applications and protocol networks.

(3) Network performance is influenced by self-similarity. The notion of business self-similarity, as well as an examination of the sources of similarity, as well as an examination of network performance based on self-similarity, estimation, optimization, necessity, and possibility.

The local features of the curve seem to have the same similar performance on different space or time scales. Self-similarity refers to network traffic that has the same burstiness and similarity in different time scales and different locations. When the business flow in the network is increasing rapidly, the suddenness of the flow growth is easy to be noticed. The larger the number of samples, the more it can reflect the characteristics of the network traffic, and there are many similarities.

The flow traffic in IoT network is a generalized stationary random process $\mathbf{X} = \{X_n, n = 1, 2, 3, ...\}$, where X_n represents the k-th network traffic entities (such as data packets, bytes, bits). $N[t]$ is the number of the network traffic arrived between the time period $[0, t]$, and can be written as

$$N(t) = \int_0^t dN\tau \tag{1}$$

where $dN\tau$ is the process of each packets arrived.

The mathematical expectation and variance of a stationary time series X_n are

$$\mu = E[(X_n)] \tag{2}$$

$$\sigma^2 = E[(X_n - \mu)^2] \tag{3}$$

The autocorrelation function is

$$r(k) = \frac{E[(X_n - \mu)(X_{n+k} - \mu)]}{\sigma^2} \tag{4}$$

The random process obtained after time aggregation with a block size of m has the same autocorrelation function as the original random process. When the condition $k \to \infty$, so

$$\lim_{k \to \infty} r(k) = H(2H - 1)k^{2H-2} \tag{5}$$

where $H \in (0.5, 1)$ is the Hurst parameter [10]. The actual network traffic is positively correlated, so the value range of H is in the range $(0.5, 1)$. The larger the H value, the higher the degree of self-similarity of the process, the slower the variance reduction rate of the random process after time averaging, and the stronger the correlation of the business flow. When $H = 0.5$, the self-similar process degenerates into a Poisson process. The transmission of the flow in the IoT network has short correlation, that is, the data volume of the packet in the arrival time interval is self-similar.

As we all know that the network traffic is the rate of packets/bytes/bites arrived, so it has the rate change and can be regarded as the acceleration of the flow. So, we use the Nosie Estimation Kalman Filtering (NEKF) to predict the network traffic. NEKF overcomes the limitation that the state transition matrix in the classic Kalman filter model needs to be reversible, and expands the application range of the Kalman filter. Using the statistical characteristics of noise estimation, open source to achieve higher prediction accuracy. The core function of Kalman filter is that

$$\mathbf{X}_k = \mathbf{K}_k \cdot \mathbf{Z}_k + (1 - \mathbf{K}_k) \cdot \mathbf{X}_{k-1} \tag{6}$$

where $\mathbf{K}_k$ is the k-th Kalman Gain. $\mathbf{Z}_k$ is the measurement results and $\mathbf{X}_{k-1}$ is the (k − 1)-th estimation results. The state equation and observation equation of Kalman filter can be written as follows

$$\mathbf{X}_k = \mathbf{F}_k \cdot \mathbf{X}_{k-1} + \mathbf{w}_{k-1} \tag{7}$$

$$\mathbf{Y}_k = \mathbf{H}\mathbf{X}_k + \mathbf{v}_k \tag{8}$$

where Eq. (7) represents the state equation, $\mathbf{X}_k$ is the $M \times 1$ dimensional state vector, which is unobservable; $\mathbf{F}_k$ is the $M \times M$ dimensional state transition matrix, which is used Describe the transition of the system from the state at time $k-1$ to the state at time k; $\mathbf{w}_{k-1}$ is the $M \times 1$ dimensional process error vector. Equation (8) represents the observation equation, $\mathbf{Y}_k$ is an $N \times 1$ dimensional observation vector; $\mathbf{H}$ is an $N \times M$ dimensional observation matrix, and the unobservable state vector $\mathbf{X}_k$ undergoes the action of $\mathbf{H}$, It becomes the observation vector $\mathbf{Y}_k$; $\mathbf{v}_k$ is the $N \times 1$ dimensional observation error vector.

Assuming that the observation time interval is T, the problem of concern is to predict the traffic arrival volume in the next T based on the current and previous observations. Let x_k denote the amount of traffic arriving at time n, and use x'_{k-1} to denote the first-order differential of x_k. When the observation time interval T is not too large, the relationship can be obtained using the first-order difference equation:

$$x_k = x_{k-1} + Tx'_{k-1} \tag{9}$$

where x'_k is the rate of flow change, namely the flow rate. In the same way, we can get that

$$x'_k = x'_{k-1} + Tx''_{k-1} \tag{10}$$

where x'_{k-1} is the rate of flow change.

There are many reasons can lead to changes in the rate of flow traffic at the node, such as the randomness of channel status, the uncertainty of terminal access, the distribution of service duration, the role of protocols, and various interferences. Consider these factors as "noise" with unknown statistical characteristics that cause the flow velocity change, and set it as w_k, so we can get that

$$x''_k = w_k \tag{11}$$

Then, we combine Eqs. (8)–(10) into a vector, then

$$\mathbf{X}_k = \begin{bmatrix} x_k \\ x'_k \\ x''_k \end{bmatrix} \tag{12}$$

The Eq. (6) can be written as

$$\mathbf{X}_k = \mathbf{F}_k\mathbf{X}_{k-1} + \mathbf{w}_k \tag{13}$$

where $\mathbf{F}_k$ is the state transition matrix (as $\mathbf{F}$), namely

$$\mathbf{F}_k = \mathbf{F} = \begin{bmatrix} 1 & T & 0 \\ 0 & 1 & T \\ 0 & 0 & 0 \end{bmatrix} \tag{14}$$

w_k is the state noise vector, and it can be expressed as

$$\mathbf{w}_k = \begin{bmatrix} 0 \\ 0 \\ w_k \end{bmatrix} \tag{15}$$

The observation equation can be expressed as

$$y_k = \mathbf{H}\mathbf{X}_k + v_k \tag{16}$$

where $\mathbf{H}$ is the observation matrix, $\mathbf{H} = [1\,0\,0]$; v_k represents the observation noise. Note that $\mathbf{H}$ is 1×3-dimensional, and $\mathbf{X}_k$ is 3×1-dimensional, so the matrix form $\mathbf{Y}_k$ in Eq. (7) becomes the scalar form y_k.

2.2 Estimation Model

The traffic noise in IoT network obeys Gaussian distribution with zero mean, namely $G(0, \sigma)$. In multi-dimensional network traffic forecasting, to comprehensively consider the degree of deviation of each dimension from its mean, it is necessary to introduce a covariance matrix. $\mathbf{w}_k$ and $\mathbf{v}_k$ are the noise variables. The means of $\mathbf{w}_k$ and $\mathbf{v}_k$ are both 0, and the covariance matrix of $\mathbf{w}_k$ and $\mathbf{v}_k$ are $\mathbf{Q}_k$ and $\mathbf{R}_k$, respectivley. The covariance matrix estimation $\mathbf{P}_{k,k-1}$ at k-th can be expressed at that

$$\mathbf{P}_{k,k-1} = \mathbf{F}_k\mathbf{P}_{k-1,k-1}\mathbf{F}_k^T + \mathbf{Q}_k \tag{17}$$

Then, the Kalman Gain can be written as that

$$\mathbf{K}_k = \frac{\mathbf{P}_{k,k-1}\mathbf{H}_k^T}{\mathbf{R}_k + \mathbf{H}_k\mathbf{P}_{k,k-1}\mathbf{H}_k^T} \tag{18}$$

The estimation results can be written as that

$$\mathbf{X}_k = \mathbf{F}_k \cdot \mathbf{X}_{k-1} + \mathbf{K}_k[\mathbf{Y}_k - \mathbf{H}_k\mathbf{X}_{k-1}] \tag{19}$$

The updated minimum mean square error matrix is that

$$\mathbf{P}_{k,k} = [1 - \mathbf{K}_k\mathbf{H}_k]\mathbf{P}_{k,k-1}\beta \tag{20}$$

Base on the above analysis, we proposed an algorithm (NEKF) to measure and estimate network traffic in IoT network, the process of the algorithm as follows:

Step 1: Measuring the network traffic in the IoT network, and construct the traffic matrix X; Initialing the noise error w_k, v_k and β; construct the transfer matrix F_k and observation matrix H.

Step 2: Calculate the covariance matrix Q_k and R_k; Then, with the Eq. (16) to calculate the covariance matrix estimation $P_{k,k-1}$;

Step 3: Based on the Eq. (17), calculating the Kalman Gain K_k;

Step 4: With the Eqs. (17) and (18) to calculate the estimation results X_k and update the minimum mean square error matrix $P_{k,k}$;

Step 5: Go back to step 2 until the maximum repeat times.

3 Simulation Result and Analysis

3.1 Simulation and the Simulation Metrics

In order to verify the algorithm proposed in this article, we built an SDN test platform based on the Ryu controller and Mininet network simulation tool, and wrote the network traffic measurement and prediction module in the Ryu controller with python language. Absolute error (AE) and relative error (RE) are two commonly used indicators to measure network traffic estimation errors. The AE of the flow rate reflects the deviation between the actual flow rate and the measurement result. RE is the ratio of AE to the actual traffic value, which reflects the reliability of the measurement. AE and RE can be expressed as

$$AE_i = \left| x_i - \hat{x}_i \right| \tag{21}$$

$$RE_i = \left| x_i - \hat{x}_i \right| / x_i \tag{22}$$

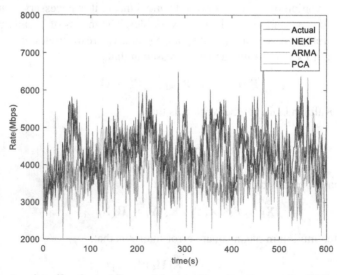

Fig. 1. The network traffic of actual flow and three traffic estimation results. (Color figure online)

3.2 Simulation Evaluation

We use Iperf to simulate network traffic in the network and randomly select a business flow for analysis. Traffic in the network. In this article, we use the traffic model (NEKF) mentioned in this article to estimate and optimize network traffic, and compare and analyze it with real network traffic, ARMA and PCA and other network traffic estimation methods.

Figure 1 shows the results of network traffic measurement and estimation with a sampling interval of 1 s in 10 min. The red line uses the real traffic value generated by the simulation tool, while the blue line, pink line and green line represent the results of network traffic measurement and estimation by NEKF, ARMA, and PCA, respectively. From the figure, we can see that the three network traffic measurement and estimation methods can basically reflect the trend of traffic changes in the network as a whole. It can be seen from the whole that our proposed algorithm can still more accurately reflect the changes in network traffic compared with the other two methods.

To reflect the accuracy of network traffic estimation more accurately, we use absolute error and relative error to further analyze the network traffic. Figure 2 shows the absolute error of the network flow estimation error of several different network flow estimation methods. We also find that the error of our proposed method is relatively small compared with the other two network traffic estimation methods, and the average is less than 500 Mbps.

Figure 3 shows the CDF distribution diagram of the absolute error of network traffic. From the figure, it can be seen that 80% of the network traffic error of our proposed algorithm is less than 720 Mbps, while the other two algorithms are less than 1080 Mbps and 1470 Mbps, respectively, which fully demonstrates the stability and the accuracy of network traffic estimation of our proposed methods. In Fig. 3, we also find that the

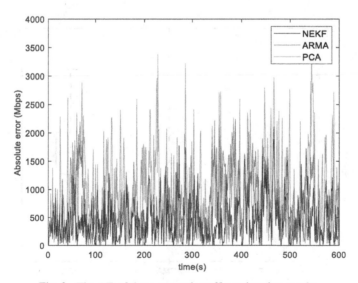

Fig. 2. The AE of three network traffic estimation results.

slope of NEKF is the largest, that is, the probability distribution of absolute error of NEKF is very concentrated, which shows that the performance of our proposed method is relatively stable.

Figure 4 shows the distribution of the relative error of network traffic with the boxplot. T The red line in the box represents the median value of RE ranking, while the upper and lower edge distributions of the blue box represent the distribution points of RE at 75% and 25%. Then, compare with the other two methods, the median value of RE of

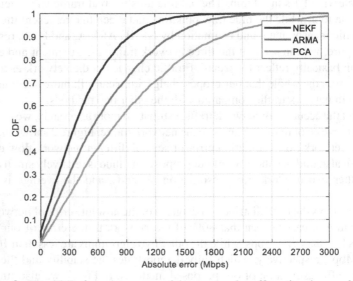

Fig. 3. The CDF of absolute errors of three network traffic estimation results.

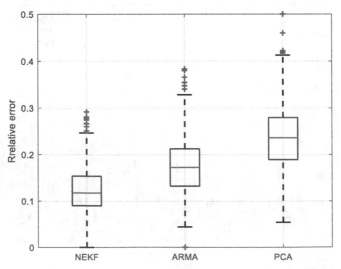

Fig. 4. The mean and variance of relative errors. (Color figure online)

our proposed method is the smallest, and the value is 0.118, namely the RE of traffic estimation results is about 11.8%, and the RE of the traffic estimation results is about 17.3% and 23.6%, respectively. The black line represents the distribution area of most of the measured values. It can be seen from the figure that the black interval of our proposed algorithm is smaller than that of the other two methods, which fully illustrates the stability of our proposed algorithm. It can be seen that our proposed algorithm is not only stable, but also has high network traffic estimation accuracy. The RE of traffic results is about 11%, which has strong usability.

4 Conclusions

As the basic network for information collection, the Internet of Things allows millions of electronic devices to be connected to the network. The traditional architecture of the SDN-based Internet of Things network has strong flexibility and strong scalability, and can allocate resources to users in a personalized manner and perform network management and scheduling according to user needs. In order to better manage the network, the measurement and estimation of network traffic is the basis to ensure the efficient prototype of the network. In order to overcome the high cost of traditional measurement methods and poor deployment flexibility, we propose a novel network traffic measurement and measurement method in this article.

By measuring the network traffic, the network traffic is estimated, so as to obtain the dynamic change trend of the network traffic, and provide data support for the efficient management of the network. Finally, we built a network simulation verification platform to analyze the performance of the algorithm proposed in this paper. The simulation results show that our proposed measurement approach is feasible and effective.

References

1. Memos, V., Psannis, K., Ishibashi, Y., et al.: An efficient algorithm for media-based surveillance system (EAMSuS) in IoT smart city framework. Futur. Gener. Comput. Syst. **83**(4), 619–628 (2018)
2. Hossain, M., Muhammad, G., Abdul, W., et al.: Cloud-assisted secure video transmission and sharing framework for smart cities. Futur. Gener. Comput. Syst. **83**, 596–606 (2018)
3. Ali, I., Gani, A., Ahmedy, I., et al.: Data collection in smart communities using sensor cloud: recent advances, taxonomy, and future research directions. IEEE Commun. Mag. **56**(7), 192–197 (2018)
4. Suarez-Varela, J., Barlet-Ros, P.: Towards a NetFlow implementation for OpenFlow software-defined networks. In: Proceedings ITC 2017, vol. 1, pp. 187–195 (2017)
5. Huang, L., Zhi, X., Gao, Q., et al. Design and implementation of multicast routing system over SDN and sFlow. In: Proceedings ICCSN 2016, pp. 524–529 (2016)
6. Yu, C., Lumezanu, C., Zhang, Y., Singh, V., Jiang, G., Madhyastha, H.V.: FlowSense: monitoring network utilization with zero measurement cost. In: Roughan, M., Chang, R. (eds.) PAM 2013. LNCS, vol. 7799, pp. 31–41. Springer, Heidelberg (2013). https://doi.org/10.1007/978-3-642-36516-4_4
7. Xu, H., Zong, X., Su, J., et al.: Formalization of SNMP messages using composite-elements based on extenics for software-defined networking. In: Proceedings the 9th International Conference on Communication Software and Networks, May 2017, pp. 989–992 (2017)

8. Jiang, D.D., Huo, L.W., Li, Y.: Fine-granularity inference and estimations to network traffic for SDN. PLoS ONE **13**(5), 1–23 (2018)
9. Jiang, D.D., Huo, L.W., Lv, Z.H., et al.: A joint multi-criteria utility-based network selection approach for vehicle-to-infrastructure networking. IEEE Trans. Intell. Transp. Syst. **19**(10), 3305–3319 (2018)
10. Kermarrec, G.: On estimating the Hurst parameter from least-squares residuals. Case study: correlated terrestrial laser scanner range noise. Mathematics **8**(5), 1–23 (2020)
11. Wang, J., Wen, R., Li, J., et al.: Detecting and mitigating target link-flooding attacks using SDN. IEEE Trans. Dependable Secur. Comput. **1**, 1–10 (2018)

Mobility-Aware Resource Allocation Based on Matching Theory in MEC

Bin Niu[1](✉), Wei Liu[1], Yinghong Ma[1], and Yue Han[2]

[1] State Key Labs of ISN, Xidian University, Xi'an 710071, China
niubin@stu.xidian.edu.cn, liuweixd@mail.xidian.edu.cn, yhma@xidian.edu.cn
[2] College of Information and Communication,
National University of Defense Technology, Xi'an 710106, China

Abstract. Mobile Edge Computing (MEC) is a technology that provides communication, computing, and storage resources at the edge of a mobile network to improve the Quality of service (Qos) for mobile users. However, the conflict between the mobility of the user and the limited coverage of the edge server may interrupt the ongoing service and cause a decrease in the quality of the service. In this context, we jointly formulate service migration and resource allocation in MEC by considering user mobility, service migration, communication and computing resources in the edge server to minimize the total service delay. Then we propose a matching algorithm that takes into account the selection preferences of users and Edge servers, and effectively solves the integer nonlinear programming problem we formulated. Finally, the simulation results prove the effectiveness of the proposed algorithm.

Keywords: MEC · Mobility · Resource allocation · Matching theory

1 Introduction

With the rapid development of 5G and the Internet of Things (IoT), many new applications have emerged in mobile terminals, which put forward high requirements for delay and bandwidth. However, the limited computing resources on mobile devices are not enough to support these applications. Although traditional cloud computing provides a lot of computing resources, due to the centralized architecture of cloud computing, a lot of time is wasted in the process of data transmission. Mobile Edge Computing (MEC) has become an effective method to provide users with communication, computing and storage resources closer to users [1]. Therefore, users can offload tasks to Edge servers to improve the Qos of user.

The financial support of the National Natural Science Foundation of China (61871452), and the Fundamental Research Funds for the Central Universities under Grant JB210106.

D. Jiang and H. Song (Eds.): SIMUtools 2021, LNICST 424, pp. 75–88, 2022.
https://doi.org/10.1007/978-3-030-97124-3_7

Resource allocation and task offloading in MEC network has been widely considered. In [2], jointly optimizing local computing frequency, task splitting and transmission power, while ensuring strict delay requirements and remaining energy constraints, an algorithm for dynamic resource allocation based on user tasks is proposed. The work in [3] takes into account the service delay of users, channel quality, Edge server resources and service provider revenue, and proposes a SPA matching algorithm, which effectively reduces the service delay of users and increases the revenue of service provider.

However, none of the above works consider the mobility of users, which is fundamental for mobile users in MEC. Due to the conflicts between the mobility of users and limited coverage of Edge servers, providing continuous service to users becomes challenging. Considering the mobility of users, the work in [4,5] formulated the mobility of users as a 1-D and 2-D Markov decision process respectively and proposed an algorithm for service migration. Different from the previous study, the authors of [6–10] exploited user mobility can be predicted accurately based on the movement trajectory of user [11]. In [6], considering the user mobility, distributed resources, task properties and energy constraint of the user equipment, jointly formulate task assignment and power allocation to minimize the service delay of user.

Although the mobility of users is considered in the above work, the proposed resource allocation algorithms are all based on providing services for a single user. In fact, in the real mobile edge computing scenario, the edge server provides services for multiple users at the same time, and there is task conflict between users, which is not considered in the above work. The work in [7] jointly considered the limited battery of mobile devices and the service delay requirement of task, two algorithms are proposed for single user and multi-user to minimize the service delay. In [8], a joint service migration and mobility optimization method for vehicle edge computing is developed. In addition, a multi-agent deep reinforcement learning algorithm is proposed. The proposed method can effectively reduce system cost and vehicle service delay. The work in [9] focus on the provisioning of virtualized network function services for mobile users in MEC that takes into account user mobility and service delay requirements. The above work is based on the resource allocation on the user side without considering the perspective of the edge server. The work in [10] proposed a matching algorithm in Vehicular MEC to minimize the service delay and power consumption. However, the work in [10] did not consider the migration of some user tasks, only considered the case where calculations are performed on the same server and the calculation results are returned through the connection between Edge servers.

Although the prior works have studied mobility-aware computation offloading and resource allocation, it is still a challenging problem. Our contributions can be summarized as follows.

1) We study the service migration and resource allocation in mobile edge computing. Considering both the mobility of users and the limited resources of Edge Servers, we formulate the resource allocation problem as a integer nonlinear problem to minimize the service delay.

2) We propose an effective matching algorithm, taking into account the selection preferences of users and Edge servers, and effectively solve the proposed inte-

ger nonlinear problem. Compared with other algorithms, the proposed matching algorithm achieves lower service delay.

The rest of the paper is organized as follows. Section 2 presents the system model and discuses the mobility of user, communication model, computation model and migration model in detail. Section 3 discusses the service delay minimization problem formulation, while Sect. 4 describes our proposed Matching algorithm to obtain effective resource allocation. Section 5 presents the results and performance analysis. Section 6 finally concludes this work and highlights future direction.

2   System Model

2.1   System Configuration

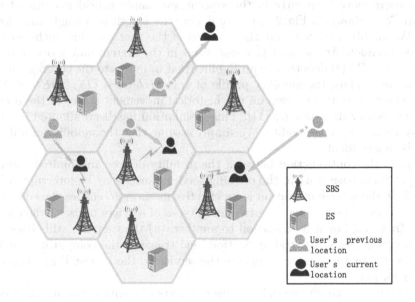

Fig. 1. Mobile edge computing network

As shown in Fig. 1, we consider a mobile edge computing system that includes K Small base stations ($SBS = \{SBS_1, SBS_2, \ldots, SBS_K\}$) with co-located Edge servers ($ES = \{ES_1, ES_2, \ldots, ES_K\}$) and N users ($U = \{u_1, u_2, \ldots, u_N\}$). In the paper, we consider the mobility of users and the delay-sensitive requirement of task. The task of user u_i can be described by a tuple $\{D_i, DC_i, T_i^{req}, Mob_i(t)\}$ [9], where D_i is the data size (bits) of u_i, DC_i is the required computing resources (CPU cycles) of u_i, T_i^{req} is the delay requirement of u_i and $Mob_i(t)$ is the mobility profile of u_i that will be introduced later [9]. Due to the limited computing resources of user, the user has to offload its task to the Edge server.

The k-th Edge server ES_k can be described by a tuple $\{C_k, \gamma_k\}$, where C_k is the computing capacity (CPU cycles per second) of Edge Server ES_k, and γ_k is the maximum numbers of users that the k-th Edge server ES_k can simultaneously serve [12]. Furthermore, B_k is the bandwidth that Small base station SBS_k provides to a single user [3]. It should be noted that the coverage of Small base station is relatively small, so users will not stay in a certain area for a long time because of the mobility [13]. It's noted that Small base stations are connected by backhaul links [8].

Fig. 2. Time-slotted system

As users move frequently in the system, we simply consider a time-slotted system [5] as shown in Fig. 2. And we denote the length of a single timeslot as t_{slot}. We simply assumed that the position of the user remains unchanged for a single timeslot. At the next timeslot, users in the system may move to a new position. Let $P_{i,k}(t)$ denotes the probability that u_i moves to the coverage of ES_k at timeslot t. Thus, the mobility profile of u_i is $Mob_i(t) = \{P_{i,k}(t)|ES_k \in ES\}$, which can be estimated based on the historical movement traces of the user by using trajectory data mining [11]. This assumption has been adopted in [9,14] too. Without loss of generality, We simply assume that the mobility of different users is independent.

Due to the contradiction between the mobility of user and limited coverage of single Small base station, the ongoing service of user may be interrupted [15]. Therefore, the service migration is an effective measure to ensure the continuity of the service of user. There are two main types of services of user, when a user moves from one Small base station to another, (a) the user can still choose the previous Edge server for task execution, and transmit the computing result to the user, (b) or the user can migrate the service to the closest Edge server for task execution.

In summary, the service delay of user consists of communication delay, computation delay and migration delay.

2.2 Communication Model

When user in the system has a computation task, it offloads task to ES through the closest SBS. As we mentioned earlier, we consider the delay-sensitive requirement of the task, and the transmission delay is an important part of the service delay of the user. Moreover, we assume the radio resources used between users are orthogonal to avoid the interference [3]. Thus, the transmission rate $R_{i,k}$ between user u_i and Small base station SBS_k is given by

$$R_{i,k} = B_k log_2(1 + \mathrm{SNR}_{i,k}) \tag{1}$$

where B_k is the bandwidth provided to u_i, and $\text{SNR}_{i,k}$ is the received signal-to-noise ratio given by

$$\text{SNR}_{i,k} = \frac{P_i h d_{i,k}^{-\theta}}{\delta^2} \qquad (2)$$

where P_i is the transmit power of u_i, h is the channel power gain, and $d_{i,k}$ is the distance from u_i to SBS_k, θ is the path loss, and δ^2 is the Noise power. Thus, the transmission delay $T_{i,k}^{comm}$ from the u_i to SBS_k is [3]:

$$T_{i,k}^{comm} = \frac{D_i}{R_{i,k}} \qquad (3)$$

2.3 Computation Model

Due to the delay-sensitive requirement of user, computation delay by the Edge server significantly affects the Qos of the user. For Edge server, it allocates its computing resources reasonably to serve multiple users simultaneously. We assume that users share the computing resources of the Edge server equally. Therefore, we define a matching matrix $M(t) \in \mathbb{R}^{N \times K}$ to represent the relationships between users and Edge servers in timeslot t. The matching matrix $M(t)$ of timeslot t is a correspondence between users and Edge servers.

$$M_{i,k}(t) = \begin{cases} 1, & \text{if } u_i \text{ chooses } ES_k \text{ to execute in timeslot t} \\ 0, & \text{otherwise} \end{cases} \qquad (4)$$

We also assume that the task of user u_i can only be computed in single Edge server in any timeslot [8]. As we mentioned earlier, the users of any Edge server ES_k can served simultaneously is γ_k. Therefore, the two constraints are as follows.

$$\sum_{ES_k \in ES} M_{i,k}(t) \le 1, \forall u_i \in U \qquad (5)$$

$$\sum_{u_i \in U} M_{i,k}(t) \le \gamma_k, \forall ES_k \in ES \qquad (6)$$

Since the task of user u_i may have been partially calculated in the previous timeslot, let denote the requirement of computation resources by u_i in timeslot t as $DC_i(t)$, which is given by:

$$DC_i(t) = \mu(t)DC_i \qquad (7)$$

where the $\mu(t)(\mu(t) \in (0,1))$ is the percentage of task that has not been calculated at the beginning of timeslot t.

As we mentioned earlier, the users share the computation resources of Edge server equally. Due to the limited computing capacity of Edge server, not all tasks can be completed in the current timeslot and the unfinished tasks need to be calculated in the next timeslot. Thus, we denote the computation delay of u_i who use the ES_k to execute the task in timeslot t as $T_{i,k}^{comp}(t)$, which is given by:

$$T_{i,k}^{comp}(t) = \begin{cases} \frac{DC_i(t)}{C_k / \sum\limits_{u_i \in U} M_{i,k}(t)} & u_i \text{ can be completed in timeslot t} \\ t_{slot} & \text{otherwise} \end{cases} \quad (8)$$

2.4 Migration Model

As we mentioned earlier, providing continuous service to users becomes challenging due to mobility of users and limited coverage of Edge servers. In order to ensure that users continue to receive services, service migration is an important measure. Since the user move in the coverage of multiple Small base stations, the user should make a decision to choose whether to migrate. Therefore, there are two main types of service of user, when a user moves from one Small base station to another, (a) the user can still choose the previous Edge server for task execution, and transmit the computing result to the user, (b) or the user can migrate the service to another Edge server for task execution [15]. Furthermore, it is also essential to decide where to migrate. As we mentioned earlier, the migration strategy of migrating computing tasks to the closest server for task processing is considered to be an effective migration strategy [4]. When the migration is completed, the Edge server restores the previous computing service of user.

As we noted earlier, Small base stations are connected by backhaul links. Thus, the migration delay is composed of transmission, propagation, processing and queuing [8]. The transmission delay between Small base station SBS_p and Small base station SBS_k in timeslot t is denoted as: $\eta(t)D_i/\omega_{p,k}$, where $\eta(t)$ ($\eta(t) \in (0,1)$) is the percentage of task which has not been computed in timeslot t, and $\omega_{p,k}$ is the transmit rate (bps) through the Small base station SBS_p and Small base station SBS_k. Due to the data of computing result is relative small, we ignore the transmission time of computing result. In addition, the propagation, processing and queuing delays are determined by the hop count between the previous Edge server ES_p and the current Edge server ES_k [8]. Therefore, we denote the migration delay of u_i between Edge server ES_p and Edge server ES_k in timeslot t as $T_{i,p,k}^{mig}(t)$, which is described as:

$$T_{i,p,k}^{mig}(t) = \begin{cases} 0 & ES_k = ES_p \\ \eta(t)D_i/\omega_{p,k} + \lambda h(ES_p, ES_k) & ES_k \neq ES_p \end{cases} \quad (9)$$

where $M_{i,p}(t-1) = 1$, $M_{i,k}(t) = 1$, the λ is a positive coefficient, and $h(ES_p, ES_k)$ represents the hop count between the ES_p and ES_k. And we also denote the binary $\alpha_i^{p,k}(t)$ to represent the migration between Edge server ES_p and Edge server ES_k of user u_i in timeslot t.

$$\alpha_i^{p,k}(t) = \begin{cases} 1 & \text{migrate } u_i \text{ service from } ES_p \text{ to } ES_k \text{ in timeslot t} \\ 0 & \text{otherwise} \end{cases} \quad (10)$$

We assume that the task of user u_i can only be computed in single Edge server in any timeslot. Thus, the migration of any user task can not occur on different Edge servers. The constraint is as follows.

$$\sum_{ES_p \in ES} \sum_{ES_k \in ES} \alpha_i^{p,k}(t) \leq 1, \forall u_i \in U \tag{11}$$

3   Problem Formulation

In the previous section, we discuss the communication delay, computation delay and migration delay of user, all of which are very essential for the total service delay of user. When user u_i has a new task, it offloads the task to the closest Edge server ES_{close}, and the transmission delay is $T_{i,close}^{comm}$. Since the user u_i may experience multiple timeslots in the process of receiving service, we denote that the start timeslot for user u_i to receive service from Edge server as ts_i, and the last time for user u_i to receive service from Edge server as tl_i. Thus, the total computation delay of user u_i can be denoted as T_i^{comp}, which can be described as:

$$T_i^{comp} = \sum_{t=ts_i}^{tl_i} \sum_{ES_k \in ES} M_{i,k}(t) T_{i,k}^{comp}(t) \tag{12}$$

Furthermore, user u_i may move in the coverage of multiple base stations during the service period. Therefore, the service of user may be migrated many times, and the total migration delay of user u_i can be denoted as T_i^{mig}, which can be described as:

$$T_i^{mig} = \sum_{t=ts_i}^{tl_i} \sum_{ES_p \in ES} \sum_{ES_k \in ES} \alpha_i^{p,k}(t) T_{i,p,k}^{mig}(t) \tag{13}$$

To sum up, the total service delay of user u_i is composed of the transmission delay, total computation delay and total migration delay. As a result, the service delay of u_i is denoted as T_i, which can be described as follows:

$$T_i = T_{i,close}^{comm} + T_i^{comp} + T_i^{mig} \tag{14}$$

It is obvious that the service delay of user u_i must satisfy request latency T_i^{req} of user u_i, which is shown as follows.

$$T_i \leq T_i^{req}, \forall u_i \in U \tag{15}$$

Thus, we are ready to formulate the optimization problem, which is shown below.

$$\min_{M(t)} \quad \frac{\sum_{u_i \in U} T_i}{N} \tag{16}$$

s.t   Service delay constraint: (15)

Edge server constraint: (6)

Computation constraints: (4), (5)

Migration constraints: (10), (11)

where (16) is the optimal target of the system, representing the average service delay of all users. The formulated problem falls in the form of a Integer nonlinear program, which is an NP-hard problem. Therefore, we adopt the matching theory to find the suboptimal solution.

4   Matching Based Computation Resource Allocation and Task Migration Scheme

As we mentioned earlier, the service of user may last for multiple timeslots. Therefore, we consider the resource allocation scheme in each timeslot, that is, the user chooses the best resource in each timeslot. Thus the final resource allocation scheme for users is also a suboptimal solution.

This resource allocation problem can be seen as a matching problem between users and Edge servers [16]. In our model, the Edge servers provide computing resources for users to select, and the matching is between the set of users ($U = \{u_1, u_2, \ldots, u_N\}$) and the set of Edge servers ($ES = \{ES_1, ES_2, \ldots, ES_K\}$). Therefore, we design a matching algorithm to get a competitive resource allocation scheme.

Since the matching is between the users and Edge servers, each user gives a preference list over the Edge servers that it can find acceptable, and each Edge server gives a preference list over the users that it can provide service before matching process. Since our goal is to minimize the service delay of user, the preference list of each user is determined by the service delay of the Edge servers available, while the preference list for each Edge server is determined by the computation delay of user. Let PL^{User} denotes preference list of users, and PL^{ES} denotes the preference list of Edge servers.

As we mentioned earlier, a single Edge server can provide computation service for multiple users simultaneously, and the users who choose the same Edge server share the computation resources equally. Although any Edge server ES_k has quota γ_k to limit the maximum number of users, the number of users that a Edge server serves in timeslot t is unknown for both users and Edge servers before matching. Therefore, we assume that user who choose any Edge server ES_k shares $1/\gamma_k$ of Edge server ES_k computation resources when build the preference list of users and Edge servers [3]. Denote the maximal computation delay of user u_i who use Edge server ES_k in timeslot t as $T_{i,k}^{maxcomp}(t)$.

$$T_{i,k}^{maxcomp}(t) = \frac{DC_i(t)}{C_k/\gamma_k} \tag{17}$$

Furthermore, when the user selects which Edge server to compute task, the user consider the service delay of user. Denote the preference of user u_i over Edge server ES_k in timeslot t as $PL_i^{User}(k,t)$, which is based on the transmission delay, maximal computation delay and migration delay.

$$PL_i^{User}(k,t) = T_{i,k}^{comm} + T_{i,k}^{maxcomp}(t) + T_{i,p,k}^{mig}(t); \tag{18}$$

where p satisfied the $M_{i,p}(t-1) = 1$.

When Edge server selects which the users to serve, the Edge server only consider the maximal computation delay of user. Denote the preference of Edge server ES_k over user u_i in the current timeslot t as $PL_k^{ES}(i,t)$, which is based on the maximal computation delay.

$$PL_k^{ES}(i,t) = T_{i,k}^{maxcomp}(t) \tag{19}$$

Then, we design the matching algorithm to decide whether to migrate and where to compute the task [17].

Step 1: Establishment of user preference list

As we mentioned earlier, there are at most two Edge servers for any user u_i to select: one is the Edge server ES_{pre} which the user selected in the previous timeslot $t-1$, and the other is the Edge server ES_{close} in timeslot t which is the closest to the user. If the previous Edge server ES_{pre} is different from the closest Edge server ES_{close}, the user can select one of them. If the user select the previous Edge server, it means the Edge server continues to serve user. If the user select the closest Edge server, it means the service needs to be migrated. Furthermore, if the previous Edge server is also the closest Edge server in current timeslot t, the user has only one Edge server to select.

When the previous Edge server is different from the closest Edge server in timeslot t, the user has two Edge servers to select: the closest Edge server and the previous Edge server. And the preference list of user is determined by the service delay which is calculated by (18). The smaller the service latency, the higher the priority. For example, if the $PL_i^{User}(close,t) \leq PL_i^{User}(pre,t)$, the preference list of user u_i in timeslot t is $PL_i^{User}(t) = [ES_{close}, ES_{pre}]$. When the user has only one Edge server to select. Thus, the preference list of user in timeslot t is $PL_i^{User}(t) = [ES_{close}]$.

Step 2: Establishment of Edge server preference list

For any Edge server ES_k, the user it can provide service consists of two kinds of users: one is the user who selected ES_k in the previous timeslot $t-1$, the other is the closest Edge server of user who did not select ES_k in the previous timeslot $t-1$. Define the number of the above two kinds of users as N_1 and N_2 respectively. Therefore, we assume the number of users which can potentially be

---

Algorithm 1: Matching Algorithm

Input: $ES, U, PL^{User}, PL^{ES}$

Output: Matching matrix $M(t)$

1　**while** *some user u_i has task to process and u_i has not matched with Edge server* **do**

2　　**for** $u_i \in U$ **do**

3　　　　u_i proposes the first Edge server ES_{first} in current preference list $PL_i^{user}(t)$ of u_i;

4　　　　remove the first Edge server ES_{first} from current preference list $PL_i^{user}(t)$;

5　　　　$M(t) \leftarrow M(t) \cup (u_i, ES_{first})$;

6　　**end**

7　　**for** $ES_k \in ES$ **do**

8　　　　**while** ES_k *is over-subscribed* **do**

9　　　　　　Find the worst users u_{wst} from the users who have selected ES_k according to the current preference list $PL_k^{ES}(t)$ of ES_k;

10　　　　　$M(t) \leftarrow M(t)/(u_{wst}, ES_{wst})$;

11　　　　**end**

12　　**end**

13　**end**

14　Return matching results $M(t)$.

---

served by the Edge server ES_k is $N_1 + N_2$. It is noted that $N_1 + N_2$ may be more than γ_k and the user who selected the Edge server in previous timeslot has higher priority than other users. Therefore, the preference list of Edge server ES_k consists of two parts, the two kinds of users are sorted by the maximal computation delay respectively, which is described by (19).

For example, we simply assume that the maximal computation delay of users which selected the Edge server ES_k in previous timeslot $t - 1$ is $PL_k^{ES}(1, t) \leq PL_k^{ES}(2, t) \leq \cdots \leq PL_k^{ES}(N_1, t)$ and the maximal computation delay of other users which Edge server ES_k can potentially serve is $PL_k^{ES}(N_1 + 1, t) \leq PL_k^{ES}(N_1 + 2, t) \leq \cdots \leq PL_k^{ES}(N_1 + N_2, t)$. Therefore, the preference list of Edge server ES_k in timeslot t is $PL_k^{ES}(t) = [user_1, user_2, \ldots, user_{N_1}, user_{N_1+1}, \ldots, user_{N_1+N_2}]$.

Step 3: Match selection of user

For any user u_i, if the Edge server ES_k is the first Edge server in its preference list, the matching matrix is $M(t)_{i,k} = 1$. Then, the user removes the first Edge Server from its preference list. For example, if the preference list of user u_i before Step 3 is $PL_i^{User}(t) = [ES_{pre}, ES_{close}]$, then the preference list after the matching selection of user is $PL_i^{User}(t) = [ES_{close}]$, and the matching matrix is $M(t)_{i,pre} = 1$.

Step 4: Match selection of Edge server

According to the current matching matrix $M(t)$, for any Edge server ES_k in the system, it judges whether it has reached the limit on the number of service users γ_k. If it has not reached the limit, go straight to the next step. Otherwise, if the number of user who selects the ES_k is $\gamma_k + k_1$, the Edge server ES_k will select the k_1 worst users among the current users based on the preference list and set the element corresponding to the matching matrix to 0. For example, if user u_i is one of the k_1 worst users, the matching matrix is $M(t)_{i,k} = 0$.

Step 5: Estimate of Matching result

If there still some users who does not match with the Edge servers, the process will go back to Step 3. Otherwise, if all the users match with the Edge servers, the process of matching in current timeslot t is finished. Furthermore, the details of matching algorithm is shown as Algorithm 1.

According to the matching result we get, we recalculate the service delay of users in the current timeslot, which is given by (14). At the next timeslot, due to the mobility of the user, the user may move to a location which is in the coverage of another Small base station. If the task of user has not completed, the process of this timeslot will be repeated. Meanwhile, the preference list will be recalculated, and the matching algorithm will be used until all users in the network have finished the services.

5 Performance Evaluation

In this section, we evaluate the performance of the proposed algorithm through experimental simulations.

We consider a mobile edge computing system that includes 20 Small base stations with co-located Edge servers and the number of users is from 50 to 140. The computing capacity of Edge Server varies from 1 GHz to 10 GHz, and the maximum numbers of users that Edge server can simultaneously serve is 7. Furthermore, the data size of user task varies from 10 MB to 20 MB, and the required CPU cycle of user varies from 5 GHz to 10 GHz. The other parameters used in the simulation are shown in Table 1.

Table 1. Parameters description

Parameter	Value
The delay requirement of user, T_i^{req}	5–6 s
The length of timeslot, t_{slot}	2 s
The bandwidth, B_k	200 kHz
The transmit rate through Base station $\omega_{p,k}$	100 Mbps
hop	0.05 s
The transmit power of user, P	200 mW
Noise spectral density	−174 dBm/Hz
Pass loss exponent, α	3

We evaluate the performance of Algorithm 1 against the Algorithm MobMig which is proposed by [12] and the Algorithm AMA which means always migrating

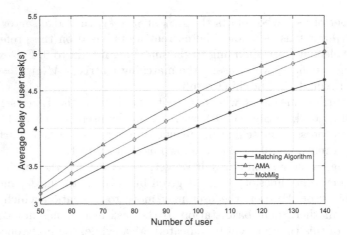

Fig. 3. The average service delay of user task

the service with the movement of user. In Fig. 3, the service delay of user versus the number of user is plotted for the above three algorithms. As seen from Fig. 3, the service delay of user increases with the increasing of number of user, as the computation resources provided to single user decreases with the increasing of the number of user task, resulting the increasing of user service delay. As our proposed matching algorithm makes the task offload decision and allocates the computing resources of the edge servers reasonably, the performance of Matching Algorithm we proposed is obviously better than the other two algorithms.

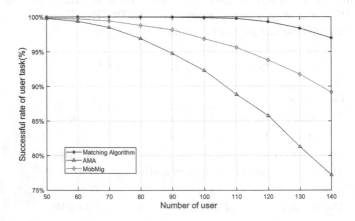

Fig. 4. The successful rate of user task

In Fig. 4, the successful rate of user task versus the number of user is plotted for the above three algorithms. As seen from Fig. 4, the successful rate of user task decreases with the increasing of number of user. When user service delay exceeds the delay requirements of tasks, the task fails. As the number of server service users increases, service delay for users increase, resulting the decrease of successful rate of user task. Furthermore, Fig. 4 shows that the Matching Algorithm also has the best performance among the three algorithms.

6 Conclusion

In this paper, we study the service migration and resource allocation in mobile edge computing. We use the timeslot system to represent the continuous movement process of the user discretely. We formulate the resource allocation problem as a integer nonlinear problem to minimize the service delay by taking account of the mobility of user. Then we propose the Matching Algorithm taking into account of the preferences of users and Edge servers to solve the formulated problem. Finally, the simulation results show the effectiveness of the proposed algorithm.

References

1. Mach, P., Becvar, Z.: Mobile edge computing: a survey on architecture and computation offloading. IEEE Commun. Surv. Tutor. **19**(3), 1628–1656 (2017)
2. Qin, M., et al.: Service-oriented energy-latency tradeoff for IoT task partial offloading in MEC-enhanced multi-RAT networks. IEEE Internet Things J. **8**(3), 1896–1907 (2021)
3. Gu, Y., Chang, Z., Pan, M., Song, L., Han, Z.: Joint radio and computational resource allocation in IoT fog computing. IEEE Trans. Veh. Technol. **67**(8), 7475–7484 (2018)
4. Wang, S., Urgaonkar, R., He, T., Zafer, M., Chan, K., Leung, K.K.: Mobility-induced service migration in mobile micro-clouds. In: 2014 IEEE Military Communications Conference, pp. 835–840 (2014)
5. Wang, S., Urgaonkar, R., Zafer, M., He, T., Chan, K., Leung, K.K.: Dynamic service migration in mobile edge computing based on Markov decision process. IEEE/ACM Trans. Netw. **27**(3), 1272–1288 (2019)
6. Saleem, U., Liu, Y., Jangsher, S., Li, Y., Jiang, T.: Mobility-aware joint task scheduling and resource allocation for cooperative mobile edge computing. IEEE Trans. Wirel. Commun. **20**(1), 360–374 (2021)
7. Zhu, T., Shi, T., Li, J., Cai, Z., Zhou, X.: Task scheduling in deadline-aware mobile edge computing systems. IEEE Internet Things J. **6**(3), 4854–4866 (2019)
8. Yuan, Q., Li, J., Zhou, H., Lin, T., Luo, G., Shen, X.: A joint service migration and mobility optimization approach for vehicular edge computing. IEEE Trans. Veh. Technol. **69**(8), 9041–9052 (2020)
9. Ma, Y., Liang, W., Li, J., Jia, X., Guo, S.: Mobility-aware and delay-sensitive service provisioning in mobile edge-cloud networks. IEEE Trans. Mob. Comput. 1 (2020)
10. Gu, B., Zhou, Z.: Task offloading in vehicular mobile edge computing: a matching-theoretic framework. IEEE Veh. Technol. Mag. **14**(3), 100–106 (2019)
11. Feng, Z., Zhu, Y.: A survey on trajectory data mining: techniques and applications. IEEE Access **4**, 2056–2067 (2016)

12. Peng, Q., et al.: Mobility-aware and migration-enabled online edge user allocation in mobile edge computing. In: 2019 IEEE International Conference on Web Services (ICWS), pp. 91–98 (2019)
13. Liu, Z., Wang, X., Wang, D., Lan, Y., Hou, J.: Mobility-aware task offloading and migration schemes in SCNs with mobile edge computing. In: 2019 IEEE Wireless Communications and Networking Conference (WCNC), pp. 1–6 (2019)
14. Taleb, T., Ksentini, A., Frangoudis, P.A.: Follow-me cloud: when cloud services follow mobile users. IEEE Trans. Cloud Comput. **7**(2), 369–382 (2019)
15. Wang, S., Xu, J., Zhang, N., Liu, Y.: A survey on service migration in mobile edge computing. IEEE Access **6**, 23511–23528 (2018)
16. Zhang, Y., Qin, X., Song, X.: Mobility-aware cooperative task offloading and resource allocation in vehicular edge computing. In: 2020 IEEE Wireless Communications and Networking Conference Workshops (WCNCW), pp. 1–6 (2020)
17. El-Atta, A.H.A., Moussa, M.I.: Student project allocation with preference lists over (student, project) pairs. In: 2009 Second International Conference on Computer and Electrical Engineering, vol. 1, pp. 375–379 (2009)

On Jamming Game in Multi-user MIMO Downlink AF Relay System

Bai Shi[1], Kai Cui[1], Jihong Jiang[1], and Huaizong Shao[1,2](✉)

[1] University of Electronic Science and Technology of China, Chengdu 611731,
Sichuan, People's Republic of China
hzshao@uestc.edu.cn

[2] Peng Cheng Laboratory, Shenzhen 519012, Guangdong, People's Republic of China

Abstract. Wireless devices may threaten urban security if they are maliciously used. Some Internet-of-things (IoT) devices have already troubled the city management even hurt citizens. Jamming technique is one of the effective approaches to prevent these malicious activities. In addition, some IoT devices may locate far from base station and the power of received signals may be low. In this paper, we discuss a jamming power allocation problem in a multi-user multiple-input multiple-output (MU-MIMO) downlink relay system when the communication and jamming signals are relatively low due to the long distance between them, in which jammer tries to minimize the sum rate of IoT devices while these devices try to communicate at the fastest rate. Besides, jammer transmits jamming signals after detecting the communication request of devices so base station should decide how to transmit first, which is modeled by a two-person zero-sum Stackelberg game. However, the sum rate in such a scenario is non-convex. Finding the equilibrium strategy is general N-P hard. To address this complex problem, we decompose it into several easy-solved sub-problems and adopt an alternating optimization over them. Further, we simulate the proposed method numerically and results suggest the superiority.

Keywords: Urban security · Relay · MIMO · Jamming · Sum rate ·
Zero-sum game · Stackelberg game

1 Introduction

The widely used wireless devices facilitate daily life but it threatens urban security. For example, terrorists may use wireless Internet of Things (IoT) devices to destroy public facilities even endanger life safety. The characteristic of exposure to the open-access environment of wireless communication systems makes it susceptible to deliberate jamming attacks. In this way, jammer limits the communication among opponents to protect itself. Traditional adversarial jamming

Supported by National Natural Science Foundation of China: NSFC61871092.

D. Jiang and H. Song (Eds.): SIMUtools 2021, LNICST 424, pp. 89–100, 2022.
https://doi.org/10.1007/978-3-030-97124-3_8

methods against wireless communication systems include tone jamming, barrage jamming and narrow-band jamming. These methods are widely applied but they are inefficient. On the other hand, jamming techniques are facing the challenges of anti-jamming techniques. For example, cognitive radio (CR) [8] techniques have the inherent merit of evading the jamming signal intelligently. Jamming techniques need to be upgraded.

One of the effective theories referred to by much intelligent jamming research about countering the CR system is game theory. Most related research can be divided into two types: correlated and uncorrelated jamming. Correlated jamming [1,2,7,13,14] means jamming signal correlates to communication signal, while uncorrelated jamming [3–6,9,15–17,19] means they are independent. Obviously, uncorrelated jamming is easier to be implemented. In [4], a Bayesian game between transceiver and jammer was formulated, where jammer did not know the user type (smart or regular one) clearly. In [17], the best strategy (Nash equilibrium) for both authorized users and jammer is to uniformly allocate all power to all the subchannels in AWGN channel in Orthogonal Frequency Division Multiplexing (OFDM) system. Some researchers concentrated on the multi-user system. In the uplink of multi-tone interference single-input-single-output (SISO) channel, the jamming-transmitting capacity game has a Nash equilibrium and it can be achieved by the generalized iterative water-filling algorithm [6]. In [18], a Stackelberg game of a base station and a jammer in nonorthogonal multiple access (NOMA) downlink system was investigated and a Q-learning-based power allocation algorithm was proposed. Furthermore, some researchers were interested in the relay system. In a single-transmitter, single-user and multi-relay communication system, in which some relays are non-cooperative to others and behave maliciously to transceiver like a jammer, it proved that the Nash equilibrium is transmitting Gaussian white noise [3], and [15] extended this research in a two-way relay channel.

Previous research gives much insight into the jamming strategy, however, little research investigates the optimal jamming strategy in the time-invariant multi-user multiple-input multiple-output (MU-MIMO) downlink relay scenario which is common in reality. Besides, the distances between base station and IoT devices may sometimes be long and jammer may be far away from them so signal-to-noise ratio (SNR) and jamming-to-noise ratio (JNR) are relatively low. To jam these devices in such a scenario, we formulate a new static zero-sum Stackelberg game of intelligently jamming MIMO downlink relay system, in which base station tries to maximize the sum rate of the whole communication system while jammer tries to minimize it. However, it is hard to find this equilibrium since the sum rate is non-convex [10]. We propose a feasible algorithm to address this complex problem. We first approximate the sum rate by an inequality. Subsequently, we decompose it into several easy-solved sub-problems and adopt an alternating optimization over them. Finally, we solve every sub-problem by the Lagrange method or majorization-minimization (MM) algorithm.

The rest of this paper is organized as follows. The system model and the jamming-transmitting zero-sum game model are formulated in Sect. 2. In Sect. 3,

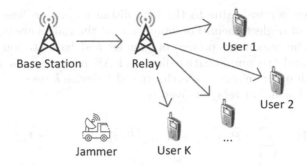

Fig. 1. Downlink model with relay.

we show how to find an approximate equilibrium strategy of the transmitting-jamming zero-sum game in time-invariant channel. Then we simulate those algorithms by numerical method in Sect. 4 and conclude this paper in Sect. 5 (Table 1).

Table 1. Notation table

Notation	Discription
$\mathbf{H}_{(*)(\cdot)}$	channel matrix of $(*)$ to $(\cdot)$
μ	power amplification coefficient of relay
P_S, P_J	power of base station and jammer
k	k-user, $k = 0, 1, ..., K$, 0 means relay
n_k	white Gaussian noise at k-user
$\mathbf{x}_k$	transmitting symbols of base station to k-user
$\mathbf{j}$	jamming symbols
$\mathbf{K}_{Xk}, \mathbf{K}_J$	covariance matrices of $\sqrt{\alpha_k P s}\mathbf{x}_k, \sqrt{\beta P s}\mathbf{j}$
$\mathbf{y}_R, \mathbf{y}_k$	receiving symbols at relay and k-user
$\mathbf{H}_{SRk}$	$\mu\mathbf{H}_{Rk}\mathbf{H}_{SR}$
$\mathbf{H}_{JRk}$	$\mu\mathbf{H}_{Rk}\mathbf{H}_{JR}$
$\tilde{\mathbf{N}}_k$	$\mathbf{H}_{RK}N_0\mathbf{H}_{RK}^H + N_k\mathbf{I}$

2   System Model

2.1   Wireless Communication and Jamming Model

As shown in Fig. 1, we consider the downlink model of a MIMO communication system with one amplify-and-forward (AF) relay and K devices. A jammer tries to disrupt this system by transmitting jamming signals to relay and devices. The power of jammer is limited. We assume that the wireless signals from base station attenuate seriously due to the long distance between base station and devices so we can neglect them. For simplicity, all the radios are equipped with M antennas. The maximum powers of jammer and base station are P_J and P_S separately and the amplification factor of AF relay is μ. In addition, for consistency with other related research, we call k-device k-user.

The received signal at relay is given by

$$\mathbf{y}_R = \mathbf{H}_{SR} \sum_{k=1}^{K} \sqrt{P_S \alpha_k} \mathbf{x}_k + \mathbf{H}_{JR} \sqrt{P_J \beta} \mathbf{j} + \mathbf{n}_0, \quad k = 1, 2, ..., K \qquad (1)$$

and the received signal at k-th user is given by

$$\begin{aligned} \mathbf{y}_k &= \mu \mathbf{H}_{Rk} \mathbf{y}_R + \mathbf{H}_{Jk} \sqrt{P_J \beta} \mathbf{j} + \mathbf{n}_k \\ &= \mathbf{H}_{Rk} \mathbf{H}_{SR} \sum_{l=1}^{K} \sqrt{\mu P_S \alpha_l} \mathbf{x}_l + \mathbf{H}_{Rk} \sqrt{\mu} \mathbf{n}_0 + \mathbf{n}_k \qquad (2) \\ &\quad + \mathbf{H}_{Rk} \mathbf{H}_{JR} \sqrt{\mu P_J \beta} \mathbf{j} + \mathbf{H}_{Jk} \sqrt{P_J \beta} \mathbf{j}, \qquad k = 1, 2, ..., K \end{aligned}$$

where $\mathbf{H}_{(\cdot)(*)}$ denotes the $M \times M$ channel matrix from $(\cdot)$ to $(*)$ and the subscript "S", "R", "J", "k" means base station, relay, jammer and k-user respectively. Each element of $\mathbf{H}_{(\cdot)(*)}$ is supposed to be identically independently distributed (i.i.d.), i.e., $\mathbf{H}_{(\cdot)(*)} = [g_{ij(\cdot)(*)}]_{1 \leq i,j \leq M}$ and $g_{ij(\cdot)(*)} \sim \mathcal{CN}(0, \sigma_{(\cdot)(*)}^2)$ where $\mathcal{CN}$ is circular symmetric complex Gaussian distribution. $\mathbf{y}_{(\cdot)}$ is the received signal at $(\cdot)$. $\mathbf{x}_{(\cdot)}$ and $\mathbf{j}_{(\cdot)}$ are the transmitting and jamming symbol to $(\cdot)$ and the subscript "0" means "to relay". Every symbol of $\mathbf{x}_{(\cdot)}$ and $\mathbf{j}_{(\cdot)}$ is normalized and i.i.d. so $\mathbb{E}(x_{(\cdot)i}) = 0$, $\mathbb{E}(j_{(\cdot)i}) = 0$ and $\mathbb{E}(x_{(\cdot)i} x_{(\cdot)l}^H) = 0$, $\mathbb{E}(j_{(\cdot)i} j_{(\cdot)l}^H) = 0$, $l \neq i$. $\alpha_{(\cdot)}$ and $\beta_{(\cdot)}$ are the power proportion allocated to $(\cdot)$ by base station and jammer. $\mathbf{n}_o$ and $\mathbf{n}_k$ are white Gaussian noise and $\mathbf{n}_{(\cdot)} \sim \mathcal{CN}(0, N_{(\cdot)}\mathbf{I})$. SNR is defined by the power of base station P_S divided by the power of noise, P_S/N, and JNR is P_J/N. The covariance matrix of transmitting signal to user k denotes as $\mathbf{K}_{Xk}$ and that of jamming signal is $\mathbf{K}_J$.

2.2   Stackelberg Game Formulation

In this section, we introduce the jamming game model with respect to sum rate. A standard strategic game consists of a finite set of players $\mathcal{N}$ for each play $i \in \mathcal{N}$, a non-empty action set $\mathcal{A}_i$ and for each player a preference relation on $\mathcal{A} = \times_{i \in \mathcal{N}} \mathcal{A}_i$ [11]. We define $\mathcal{N} = \{\text{base station, jammer}\}$. The action spaces of them are $\mathcal{A}_1 = \{\mathbf{K}_{Xk} \in \mathbb{C}^{M \times M} | \mathbf{K}_{Xk} \succeq 0, \sum_{k=1}^{K} \text{Tr}(\mathbf{K}_{Xk}) \leq P_S, k = 1, 2, ..., K\}$ and $\mathcal{A}_2 = \{\mathbf{K}_{Jk} \in \mathbb{C}^{M \times M} | \mathbf{K}_{Jk} \succeq 0, \sum_{k=0}^{K} \text{Tr}(\mathbf{K}_{Jk}) \leq P_J, k = 0, 1, ..., K\}$ respectively. The preference relations are defined by positive associated utility functions: $u_1(\mathbf{K}_{Xk}; \mathbf{K}_{Jk}) = R(\mathbf{K}_{Xk}, \mathbf{K}_{Jk}) = \sum_{k=1}^{K} R_k(\mathbf{K}_{Xk}, \mathbf{K}_{Jk})$ for base station and $u_2(\mathbf{K}_{Jk}; \mathbf{K}_{Xk}) = -R(\mathbf{K}_{Xk}, \mathbf{K}_{Jk}) = -\sum_{k=1}^{K} R_k(\mathbf{K}_{Jk}; \mathbf{K}_{Xk})$ for jammer, where $R_k(*, \cdot)$ is the data rate of k-th user

$$R_k = \log \det(\mathbf{I} + \mu\mathbf{H}_{Rk}\mathbf{H}_{SR}\mathbf{K}_{Xk}\mathbf{H}_{SR}^H\mathbf{H}_{Rk}^H(\tilde{\mathbf{N}}_k + \sum_{l=1,l\neq k}^{K} \mu\mathbf{H}_{Rk}\mathbf{H}_{SR}\mathbf{K}_{Xl}\mathbf{H}_{SR}^H\mathbf{H}_{Rk}^H$$

$$+ \mu\mathbf{H}_{Rk}\mathbf{H}_{JR}\mathbf{K}_J\mathbf{H}_{JR}^H\mathbf{H}_{Rk}^H + \mathbf{H}_{Jk}\mathbf{K}_J\mathbf{H}_{Jk}^H)^{-1}) \tag{3}$$

and $\tilde{\mathbf{N}}_k = \mu\mathbf{H}_{Rk}N_0\mathbf{H}_{Rk}^H + N_k\mathbf{I}$. We define $u(*) = u_1(*) = -u_2(*)$. In such case, the jamming game is denoted by $G_1 = <\mathcal{N}, (\mathcal{A}_1, \mathcal{A}_2), (u_1, u_2)>$ in brief.

Moreover, in a practical reactive jamming regime, jammer usually sends jamming signals after detecting communication signals, and base station is aware of this, which means that base station and jammer must decide in order. On the other hand, base station and jammer are both intelligent enough to choose an optimal transmitting strategy (covariance matrices). Thus, we model game G_1 as a Stackelberg game, which is given by

$$\max_{\mathbf{K}_{X1},...,\mathbf{K}_{XK}} \cdot \min_{\mathbf{K}_J} \cdot R(\mathbf{K}_{X1},...,\mathbf{K}_{XK},\mathbf{K}_J)$$

$$s.t. \begin{cases} \sum_{k=1}^{K} \text{Tr}(\mathbf{K}_{Xk}) \leq P_S \\ \text{Tr}(\mathbf{K}_J) \leq P_J \\ \mathbf{K}_{Xk} \succeq 0, \qquad k = 1, 2, ..., K \\ \mathbf{K}_J \succeq 0 \end{cases} \tag{4}$$

3 Stackelberg Equilibrium of Jamming Game in Time-Invariant Channel

In this section, we will address the optimal jamming power allocation problem in the MU-MIMO downlink system in the time-invariant channel. However, problem (4) is quite complex. We first simplify the sum rate function in the regime of low SNR and JNR. Then, we decouple it into two simple sub-problems to find the jamming strategy.

Due to the low SNR and JNR, the covariance matrices of communication and jamming signals are smaller than those of noise. For relatively smaller matrix $\mathbf{X}, \mathbf{Y}$,

$$\log \det(\mathbf{I} + \mathbf{X}(\mathbf{N} + \mathbf{Y})^{-1}) \approx \text{Tr}(\mathbf{X}\mathbf{N}^{-1}(\mathbf{I} - \mathbf{Y}\mathbf{N}^{-1})) \tag{5}$$

It is easy to prove it.

$$\log \det(\mathbf{I} + \mathbf{X}(\mathbf{N} + \mathbf{Y})^{-1})$$
$$\approx \text{Tr}(\mathbf{X}(\mathbf{N} + \mathbf{Y})^{-1}) \tag{6}$$
$$= \text{Tr}(\mathbf{X}\mathbf{N}^{-1}(\mathbf{I} + \mathbf{Y}\mathbf{N}^{-1})^{-1}(\mathbf{I} - \mathbf{Y}\mathbf{N}^{-1})^{-1}(\mathbf{I} - \mathbf{Y}\mathbf{N}^{-1}))$$
$$\approx \text{Tr}(\mathbf{X}\mathbf{N}^{-1}(\mathbf{I} - \mathbf{Y}\mathbf{N}^{-1}))$$

Substituting formula (5) into (3), R_k can be approximated by

$$R_k \approx \mathrm{Tr}(\mathbf{H}_{SRk}\mathbf{K}_{Xk}\mathbf{H}_{SRk}^H\tilde{\mathbf{N}}_k^{-1} - \mathbf{H}_{SRk}\mathbf{K}_{Xk}\mathbf{H}_{SRk}^H\tilde{\mathbf{N}}_k^{-1}\mathbf{H}_{Jk}\mathbf{K}_J\mathbf{H}_J^H\tilde{\mathbf{N}}_k^{-1}$$
$$- \mathbf{H}_{SRk}\mathbf{K}_{Xk}\mathbf{H}_{SRk}^H\tilde{\mathbf{N}}_k^{-1}\mathbf{H}_{JRk}\mathbf{K}_J\mathbf{H}_{JRk}^H\tilde{\mathbf{N}}_k^{-1}$$
$$- \mathbf{H}_{SRk}\mathbf{K}_{Xk}\mathbf{H}_{SRk}^H\tilde{\mathbf{N}}_k^{-1}\sum_{l=1,l\neq k}^{K}\mathbf{H}_{SRk}\mathbf{K}_{Xl}\mathbf{H}_{SRk}^H\tilde{\mathbf{N}}_k^{-1})$$

Suppose that

$$\mathbf{A} = \sum_{k=0}^{K} -\mathbf{H}_J^H\tilde{\mathbf{N}}_k^{-1}\mathbf{H}_{SRk}\mathbf{K}_{Xk}\mathbf{H}_{SRk}^H\tilde{\mathbf{N}}_k^{-1}\mathbf{H}_{Jk} - \mathbf{H}_{JRk}^H\tilde{\mathbf{N}}_k^{-1}\mathbf{H}_{SRk}\mathbf{K}_{Xk}\mathbf{H}_{SRk}^H\tilde{\mathbf{N}}_k^{-1}\mathbf{H}_{JRk}$$

$$(7)$$

and

$$\mathbf{B}_{1k} = \mathbf{H}_{SRk}^H\tilde{\mathbf{N}}_k^{-1}\mathbf{H}_{SRk} - \mathbf{H}_{SRk}^H\tilde{\mathbf{N}}_k^{-1}\mathbf{H}_{Jk}\mathbf{K}_J\mathbf{H}_J^H\tilde{\mathbf{N}}_k^{-1}\mathbf{H}_{SRk}$$
$$- \mathbf{H}_{SRk}^H\tilde{\mathbf{N}}_k^{-1}\mathbf{H}_{JRk}\mathbf{K}_J\mathbf{H}_{JRk}^H\tilde{\mathbf{N}}_k^{-1}\mathbf{H}_{SRk}$$

$$(8)$$

$$\mathbf{B}_{2k} = \mathbf{H}_{SRk}^H\tilde{\mathbf{N}}_k^{-1}\mathbf{H}_{SRk} \tag{9}$$

Given $\mathbf{K}_{Xk}$, $k = 1, 2, ..., K$, $R(\mathbf{K}_J; \mathbf{K}_{X1}, ..., \mathbf{K}_{XK}) = \mathrm{Tr}(\mathbf{A}\mathbf{K}_J)$, and given $\mathbf{K}_J$ $R(\mathbf{K}_{X1}, ..., \mathbf{K}_{XK}; \mathbf{K}_J) = \sum_{k=0}^{K}\mathrm{Tr}(\mathbf{B}_{1k}\mathbf{K}_{Xk} - \mathbf{K}_{Xk}\mathbf{B}_{2k}\sum_{l\neq k}\mathbf{K}_{Xl}\mathbf{B}_{2k})$. The original problem (4) is decoupled into two sub-problems:

$$\min_{\mathbf{K}_J}. \quad \mathrm{Tr}(\mathbf{A}\mathbf{K}_J)$$
$$s.t. \quad \begin{cases} \mathrm{Tr}(\mathbf{K}_J) \leq P_J \\ \mathbf{K}_J \succeq 0 \end{cases} \tag{10}$$

and

$$\max_{\mathbf{K}_{X1},...,\mathbf{K}_{XK}}. \quad \sum_{k=0}^{K}\mathrm{Tr}(\mathbf{B}_{1k}\mathbf{K}_{Xk} - \mathbf{K}_{Xk}\mathbf{B}_{2k}\sum_{l\neq k}\mathbf{K}_{Xl}\mathbf{B}_{2k})$$
$$s.t. \quad \begin{cases} \sum_{k=1}^{K}\mathrm{Tr}(\mathbf{K}_{Xk}) \leq P_S \\ \mathbf{K}_{Xk} \succeq 0, \quad k = 1, 2, ..., K \end{cases} \tag{11}$$

3.1   Jamming Power Allocation Strategy Design

Jamming power allocation strategy is acquired by solving problem (10). It is a convex problem. The Lagrangian of it reads

$$L(\mathbf{K}_J, \lambda, \mathbf{Q}) = \mathrm{Tr}(\mathbf{A}\mathbf{K}_J) + \lambda(\mathrm{Tr}(\mathbf{K}_J) - P_j) - \mathrm{Tr}(\mathbf{Q}\mathbf{K}_J) \tag{12}$$

and the Karush-Kuhn-Tucker (KKT) Conditions of it are given by

$$\mathbf{Q} = \mathbf{A} + \lambda\mathbf{I}$$
$$\mathrm{Tr}(\mathbf{K}_J) \leq P_J, \quad \mathbf{K}_J \succeq 0 \tag{13}$$
$$\lambda \geq 0, \quad \mathbf{Q} \succeq 0$$
$$\lambda(\mathrm{Tr}(\mathbf{K}_J) - P_J) = 0, \quad \mathbf{Q}\mathbf{K}_J = 0$$

The solution is discussed as follows: (a) When $\lambda = 0$, $\mathbf{Q} = \mathbf{A}$, leading to $\mathbf{A} \succeq 0$. The optimal jamming covariance matrix $\mathbf{K}_J^*$ satisfies $\mathrm{Tr}(\mathbf{K}_J) \leq P_J, \mathbf{K}_J \succeq 0, \mathbf{A}\mathbf{K}_J = 0$. Obviously, $\mathbf{K}_J = 0$ is one of the solutions. (b) When $\lambda > 0$, $\mathbf{Q} = \mathbf{\Lambda} + \lambda\mathbf{I}$. If $\mathbf{Q} \succ 0$, $\mathbf{K}_J = 0$ since $\mathbf{Q}\mathbf{K}_J = 0$. It contradicts with $\mathrm{Tr}(\mathbf{K}_J) = P_J$. Moreover, $\mathbf{A} \succeq 0$ is impossible since $\mathbf{Q}$ can not be strictly positive definite. Let $\mathbf{Q} = \mathbf{A} + \lambda_{Amin}\mathbf{I}$ where λ_{Amin} is the minimum eigenvalue of matrix $\mathbf{A}$. $\mathbf{K}_J^*$ should satisfy $\mathbf{Q}\mathbf{K}_J^* = 0$, $\mathrm{Tr}(\mathbf{K}_J^*) = P_J$ and $\mathbf{K}_J^* \succeq 0$. If $\mathbf{u}$ is one of the bases of the null space of $\mathbf{Q}$, then $\mathbf{Q}\mathbf{u}\mathbf{u}^H = 0$. Consequently, $P_J\mathbf{u}\mathbf{u}^H$ is one of the solutions of $\mathbf{K}_J$.

3.2 Optimizing Base Station Transmitting Strategy

The transmitting power allocation strategy of base station is acquired by solving problem (11). However, it is non-convex. It can be rewritten as

$$\min_{\mathbf{K}_{X1},\ldots,\mathbf{K}_{XK}} \cdot \mathrm{Tr}(\mathbf{K}_X\mathbf{B}_2\mathbf{I}_M\mathbf{K}_X\mathbf{I}_v\mathbf{I}_v^H\mathbf{B}_2 - \mathbf{B}_1\mathbf{K}_X) \triangleq f(\mathbf{K}_X)$$

$$s.t. \quad \begin{cases} \mathrm{Tr}(\mathbf{K}_X) \leq P_S \\ \mathbf{K}_X = \mathrm{blkdiag}(\mathbf{K}_{X1}, \mathbf{K}_{X2}, \ldots, \mathbf{K}_{XK}) \\ \mathbf{K}_{Xk} \succeq 0, \quad k = 1, 2, \ldots, K \end{cases} \tag{14}$$

where $\mathbf{B}_1, \mathbf{B}_2$ are the block diagonal concatenation of $\mathbf{B}_{1k}$ and $\mathbf{B}_{2k}$ respectively. $\mathbf{I}_v = (\mathbf{I}, \mathbf{I}, \ldots, \mathbf{I})^T$.

$$\mathbf{I}_m = \begin{bmatrix} \mathbf{0} & \mathbf{I} & \ldots & \mathbf{I} \\ \mathbf{I} & \mathbf{0} & \ldots & \mathbf{I} \\ \ldots & \ldots & \ldots & \ldots \\ \mathbf{I} & \mathbf{I} & \ldots & \mathbf{0} \end{bmatrix} \tag{15}$$

$\mathbf{I}$ is the $M \times M$ identity matrix. $\mathbf{B}_2\mathbf{I}_M$ may not be positive semidefinite.

To solve problem (14), we use the majorization-minimization (MM) method. MM method consists of two steps: (a) find a surrogate function which is the tight upper bound of original objective. (b) minimize surrogate function. The first critical thing is to find the tight upper bound $\check{f}(\mathbf{K}_X)$ of the objective $f(\mathbf{K}_X)$.

Definition 1 (Lipschitz Continuous [12]). *Given two metric spaces (X, d_X) and (Y, d_Y) where d_* denotes the metric on set $(*)$. A function $f : X \mapsto Y$ is called Lipschitz continuous if there exists a real constant $L \geq 0$ such that for all $x_1, x_2 \in X$, $d_Y(f(x_1), f(x_2)) \leq Ld_X(x_1, x_2)$.*

The second-order Taylor expansion of the quadratic matrix function $g(\mathbf{X}) = \mathrm{Tr}(\mathbf{X}\breve{\mathbf{A}}\mathbf{X}\breve{\mathbf{B}})$ is convex. Thus, if the gradient of $g(\mathbf{X})$ is Lipschitz continuous, it can be bounded by a convex quadratic function

$$\breve{g}(\mathbf{X}) = g(\mathbf{X}_0) + \nabla g(\mathbf{X}_0)(\mathbf{X} - \mathbf{X}_0) + \frac{L}{2}||\mathbf{X} - \mathbf{X}_0||^2 \tag{16}$$

where $||\nabla g(\mathbf{X}) - \nabla g(\mathbf{X}_0)|| \leq L||\mathbf{X} - \mathbf{X}_0||$ and $\nabla g(\mathbf{X}) = (\breve{\mathbf{A}}\mathbf{X}\breve{\mathbf{B}} + \breve{\mathbf{B}}\mathbf{X}\breve{\mathbf{A}})^T$. Define

$$\mathbf{V} \triangleq \breve{\mathbf{A}}^T \otimes \breve{\mathbf{B}} + \breve{\mathbf{B}}^T \otimes \breve{\mathbf{A}} \tag{17}$$

so

$$
\begin{aligned}
L &\triangleq \sup_{\mathbf{X}} \frac{||\nabla g(\mathbf{X}) - \nabla g(\mathbf{X}_0)||_F}{||\mathbf{X} - \mathbf{X}_0||_F} \\
&= \sup_{\mathbf{X}} \frac{||(\breve{\mathbf{A}}(\mathbf{X} - \mathbf{X}_0)\breve{\mathbf{B}} + \breve{\mathbf{B}}(\mathbf{X} - \mathbf{X}_0)\breve{\mathbf{A}})^T||_F}{||(\mathbf{X} - \mathbf{X}_0)||_F} \\
&\overset{\mathbf{Y} \triangleq \mathbf{X} - \mathbf{X}_0}{=} \sup_{\mathbf{Y}} \frac{||\mathrm{vec}(\breve{\mathbf{A}}\mathbf{Y}\breve{\mathbf{B}} + \breve{\mathbf{B}}\mathbf{Y}\breve{\mathbf{A}})||}{||\mathrm{vec}(\mathbf{Y})||} \\
&= \sup_{\mathbf{Y}} \frac{||(\breve{\mathbf{A}}^T \otimes \breve{\mathbf{B}} + \breve{\mathbf{B}}^T \otimes \breve{\mathbf{A}})\mathrm{vec}(\mathbf{Y})||}{||\mathrm{vec}(\mathbf{Y})||} \\
&= \sup_{\mathbf{Y}} \frac{||\mathbf{V}\mathrm{vec}(\mathbf{Y})||}{||\mathrm{vec}(\mathbf{Y})||}
\end{aligned}
$$

There is a natural bound of L: the spectral norm of $\mathbf{V}$. Let $\breve{\mathbf{A}} = \mathbf{B}_2\mathbf{I}_M$, $\breve{\mathbf{B}} = \mathbf{I}_v\mathbf{I}_v^H\mathbf{B}_2$, so the upper bound is expressed as

$$\breve{f}(\mathbf{K}_X) = \breve{g}(\mathbf{K}_X) - \mathrm{Tr}(\mathbf{B}_1\mathbf{K}_X) \tag{18}$$

$$\min_{\mathbf{K}_{X1},\dots,\mathbf{K}_{XK}} \cdot \quad \breve{f}(\mathbf{K}_X; \mathbf{K}_{X0})$$

$$s.t. \quad \begin{cases} \mathrm{Tr}(\mathbf{K}_X) \leq P_S \\ \mathbf{K}_X = \mathrm{blkdiag}(\mathbf{K}_{Xk}), \quad k = 1, 2, \dots, K \\ \mathbf{K}_{Xk} \succeq 0, \quad k = 1, 2, \dots, K \end{cases} \tag{19}$$

Thus, the problem (11) can be solved by successively solving convex problem (19).

In summary, the original optimal jamming power allocation Stackelberg game (4) of the MU-MIMO downlink system in the time-invariant channel can be solved by alternatively optimizing problem (10) and problem (11). Furthermore, problem (11) can be converted into sub-problem (19). The procedures to find the jamming strategy are in Algorithm 1.

Algorithm 1. Jamming Power Allocation Strategy of Stackelberg game

---

Input: Action Spaces $\mathcal{A}_1$ and $\mathcal{A}_2$, CSI of all channel
Output: $\mathbf{K}_J$
1: **repeat**
2:     calculate $\mathbf{A}$ in (7) and its minimum eigenvalue λ_{Amin}
3:     **if** $\mathbf{A} \succeq 0$ **then**
4:         $\mathbf{K}_J = 0$
5:     **else**
6:         find a base vector $\mathbf{u}$ of null space of $\mathbf{K}$
7:         $\mathbf{K}_J = P_J \mathbf{u} \mathbf{u}^H$
8:     **end if**
9:     init $\mathbf{K}_X^0$ and $t := 0$
10:    **repeat**
11:        $t \leftarrow t + 1$
12:        $\mathbf{K}_X^t$: solve problem (19) at $\mathbf{K}_{X0} = \mathbf{K}_X^{t-1}$ by some convex solvers
13:    **until** convergence
14: **until** convergence
15: Return $\mathbf{K}_J$.

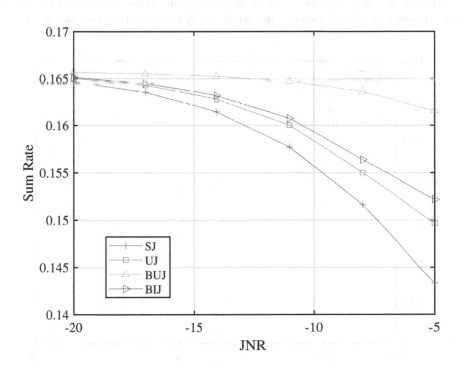

Fig. 2. Sum rate in time-invariant channel against JNR when $M = 2$, $K = 5$, SNR $= -10$ dB, $\mu = 2$.

4   Numerical Results

In this section, we will verify the performance of the proposed jamming power allocation algorithm. We compare the proposed method with several widely-used jamming methods numerically. Results indicate that the proposed jamming method is superior to other methods. We present the performance of four methods: Stackelberg jamming (SJ) strategy, the uniformly jamming (UJ) strategy, the strategy of matching the jamming channel to base station but uniformly allocating power ($\mathbf{K}_J = \frac{P_J}{n}\mathbf{V}\mathbf{V}^H$, marked as 'BUJ'), the strategy of inverting the channel between jammer and base station (marked as 'BJI'). Without loss of generality, the channel matrices $\mathbf{H}_{(\cdot)(*)} = [g_{ij(\cdot)(*)}]_{1 \le i,j \le M}$ and $g_{ij(\cdot)(*)} \sim \mathcal{CN}(0,1)$ and $N_k = 10$ for all $k = 0, 1, ..., K$.

We first focus on Fig. 2. Obviously, all the sum rates under different jamming and transmitting strategies decrease with SNR. The sum rate of the proposed method (marked as 'SJ') is the lowest compared to other methods. Then we turn to reveal the performances with different SNR in Fig. 3. With SNR increases, the sum rate of all users increases with no doubt for all methods. So proposed equilibrium jamming strategy is still the lowest one. These two results manifest that jammer can jam adversaries more effectively by using the proposed method.

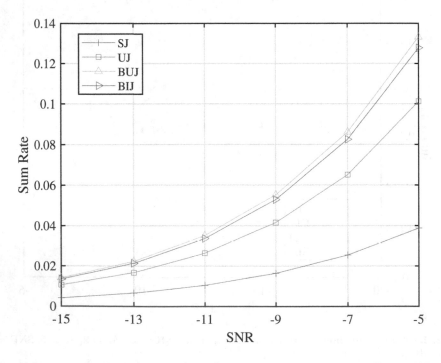

Fig. 3. Sum rate in time-invariant channel against SNR when $M = 2$, $K = 5$, JNR = -10 dB, $\mu = 2$.

5   Conclusion

In this paper, we formulate a two-person zero-sum Stackelberg game about jamming power allocation problem in MU-MIMO downlink system with smart jammers in low SNR and JNR regime. We derive the approximated form of the original problem and solve the approximated equilibrium strategy by an iterative method. Numerical results show that the proposed jamming power allocation method can successfully jam such a system. In the future, we plan to extend this work in a non-orthogonal multiple-access (NOMA) regime.

References

1. Akyol, E.: On optimal jamming in strategic communication. In: 2019 IEEE Information Theory Workshop (ITW), pp. 1–5 (2019). https://doi.org/10.1109/ITW44776.2019.8989298
2. Basar, T.: The Gaussian test channel with an intelligent jammer. IEEE Trans. Inf. Theory **29**(1), 152–157 (1983). https://doi.org/10.1109/TIT.1983.1056602
3. Chen, M., Lin, S., Hong, Y.P., Zhou, X.: On cooperative and malicious behaviors in multirelay fading channels. IEEE Trans. Inf. Forensics Secur. **8**(7), 1126–1139 (2013). https://doi.org/10.1109/TIFS.2013.2262941
4. Garnaev, A., Petropulu, A.P., Trappe, W., Vincent Poor, H.: A jamming game with rival-type uncertainty. IEEE Trans. Wirel. Commun. **19**(8), 5359–5372 (2020). https://doi.org/10.1109/TWC.2020.2992665
5. Garnaev, A., Trappe, W.: A prospect theoretical extension of a communication game under jamming. In: 2019 53rd Annual Conference on Information Sciences and Systems (CISS), pp. 1–6 (2019). https://doi.org/10.1109/CISS.2019.8692847
6. Gohary, R.H., Huang, Y., Luo, Z., Pang, J.: A generalized iterative water-filling algorithm for distributed power control in the presence of a jammer. IEEE Trans. Signal Process. **57**(7), 2660–2674 (2009). https://doi.org/10.1109/TSP.2009.2014275
7. Kashyap, A., Basar, T., Srikant, R.: Correlated jamming on MIMO Gaussian fading channels. IEEE Trans. Inf. Theory **50**(9), 2119–2123 (2004). https://doi.org/10.1109/TIT.2004.833358
8. Liang, Y., Chen, K., Li, G.Y., Mahonen, P.: Cognitive radio networking and communications: an overview. IEEE Trans. Veh. Technol. **60**(7), 3386–3407 (2011). https://doi.org/10.1109/TVT.2011.2158673
9. Liu, Q., Li, M., Kong, X., Zhao, N.: Disrupting MIMO communications with optimal jamming signal design. IEEE Trans. Wirel. Commun. **14**(10), 5313–5325 (2015). https://doi.org/10.1109/TWC.2015.2436385
10. Luo, Z., Zhang, S.: Dynamic spectrum management: complexity and duality. IEEE J. Sel. Top. Signal Process. **2**(1), 57–73 (2008). https://doi.org/10.1109/JSTSP.2007.914876
11. Osborne, M.J., Rubinstein, A.: A Course in Game Theory. The MIT Press, Cambridge (1994)
12. O'Searcoid, M.: Metric Spaces. Springer Undergraduate Mathematics Series. Springer, London (2006)
13. Shafiee, S., Ulukus, S.: Capacity of multiple access channels with correlated jamming. In: MILCOM 2005–2005 IEEE Military Communications Conference, vol. 1, pp. 218–224 (2005). https://doi.org/10.1109/MILCOM.2005.1605689

14. Shafiee, S., Ulukus, S.: Mutual information games in multiuser channels with correlated jamming. IEEE Trans. Inf. Theory **55**(10), 4598–4607 (2009). https://doi.org/10.1109/TIT.2009.2027577
15. Shao, Y., Chen, M., Lin, S., Lin, W.S.: On two-way relay channel with an active malicious relay. In: 2015 International Conference on Wireless Communications Signal Processing (WCSP), pp. 1–6 (2015). https://doi.org/10.1109/WCSP.2015.7341118
16. Signori, A., Chiariotti, F., Campagnaro, F., Zorzi, M.: A game-theoretic and experimental analysis of energy-depleting underwater jamming attacks. IEEE Internet Things J. **7**(10), 9793–9804 (2020). https://doi.org/10.1109/JIOT.2020.2982613
17. Song, T., Stark, W.E., Li, T., Tugnait, J.K.: Optimal multiband transmission under hostile jamming. IEEE Trans. Commun. **64**(9), 4013–4027 (2016). https://doi.org/10.1109/TCOMM.2016.2597148
18. Xiao, L., Li, Y., Dai, C., Dai, H., Poor, H.V.: Reinforcement learning-based NOMA power allocation in the presence of smart jamming. IEEE Trans. Veh. Technol. **67**(4), 3377–3389 (2018). https://doi.org/10.1109/TVT.2017.2782726
19. Zhou, X., Qiu, M., Lin, S.C., Hong, Y.W.P.: On the jamming power allocation and signal design in DF relay networks. In: 2013 Asilomar Conference on Signals, Systems and Computers, pp. 1268–1272 (2013). https://doi.org/10.1109/ACSSC.2013.6810497

An Energy-Efficient Dynamic Spectrum Access Approach for Internet of Things Applications

Jianguang Chen[1], Dingde Jiang[1($\boxtimes$)], Wei Yang[1], and Xiaoqian Fan[2]

[1] School of Information and Communication Engineering, University of Electronic Science and Technology of China, Chengdu 611731, China
jiangdd@uestc.edu.cn
[2] School of Computer Science and Engineering, Northeastern University, Shenyang 110819, China

Abstract. Energy efficiency has become the main problem of the communication network for sustainable development. The highly energy-efficient communication has become research focus and hotspot. Traditional network designs only consider network efficiency or network minimum energy consumption, but rarely consider maximum energy efficiency of networks. This paper presents an energy-efficient dynamic spectrum access approach for internet of things applications. We consider that communications between secondary users does not affect normal communications of primary users. The minimum interference problem between secondary users and primary users is discussed. By taking maximal energy efficiency as the optimal goal, we propose the energy efficient channel allocation strategy and sleeping mechanism. Then by minimizing the interference between secondary users and primary users, we can improve system throughput. The sleeping mechanism is utilized to minimize network energy consumption and establish the end-to-end cognitive multi-hop routing. Simulation results show that our algorithm is effective and feasible.

Keywords: Energy efficiency · Channel allocation · Sleeping mechanism · Spectrum access · Cognitive networks

1 Introduction

With communication technologies advancing, network energy efficiency receives many attentions from academic and industry communities. At the same time, the dynamic spectrum access requirements for Internet of Thing applications become current research hotspots [1, 2]. However, it is a huge challenge how to attain highly efficient-energy dynamic spectrum access for Internet of Things applications [3, 4]. This has brought forth extensive research interests and attentions in current network communications.

R. Prajapat et al. proposed a highly energy-efficient k-Hop clustering method to solve the energy consumption problem in the cognitive radio sensor network [1]. Y. Yilmaz utilized jointly sequential spectrum sensing and channel estimation to obtain highly

© ICST Institute for Computer Sciences, Social Informatics and Telecommunications Engineering 2022
Published by Springer Nature Switzerland AG 2022. All Rights Reserved
D. Jiang and H. Song (Eds.): SIMUtools 2021, LNICST 424, pp. 101–110, 2022.
https://doi.org/10.1007/978-3-030-97124-3_9

efficient dynamic spectrum access performance [2]. X. Liu et al. exploited reinforcement learning to improve dynamic spectrum access performance for cognitive Internet of Vehicles applications [3]. Y. Pei et al. used blockchain theory to realize dynamic spectrum access which took into account with the cooperation of sensing, access and mining [4]. J.A. Ansere et al. studied the energy efficiency problem in cognitive radio Internet of Things networks, and proposed a reliable and highly energy-efficient dynamic spectrum access approach [5]. S. Debroy et al. presented an energy-efficient routing method with spectrum aware ability to improve device-to-device communication performance in Internet of Things [1]. X. Liu et al. designed an highly energy-efficient network resource allocation method to raise the performance of the cognitive industrial Internet of Things [6]. V.K. Shah et al. proposed an efficient dynamic spectrum access approach with band-aware abilities to improve delay-tolerant smart city applications [7]. Energy-efficient networking, efficient content distribution scheme, and network performance measurements can be found in our previous work [8–10].

Different from these work, we propose an energy-efficient dynamic spectrum access approach for internet of things applications in this paper. Firstly, we consider that communications between secondary users does not affect normal communications of primary users. The minimum interference problem between secondary users and primary users is discussed. Secondly, by taking maximal energy efficiency as the optimal goal, the energy efficient channel allocation strategy and sleeping mechanism are proposed. Thirdly, by minimizing the interference between secondary users and primary users, the system throughput is raised and improved. The sleeping mechanism is utilized to minimize network energy consumption and establish the end-to-end cognitive multi-hop routing. Finally, simulation results show that our algorithm is effective and feasible.

2 Problem Statements

In the wireless cognitive network, communications between nodes consume huge energy. To overcome this problem, we define the path energy as:

$$E = \sum_{i=1}^{l} P_i \cdot T_i \tag{1}$$

where P_i denotes the power of node i which processing information, T is the time of each node which processing information, l represents the total number of the path nodes.

In this paper, the power of each node is divided into three parts power. They include the sending power, receiving power, and sleeping power, which are respectively denoted as P_{send}, $P_{receive}$ and P_{sleep}. The time of each node processing information is divided into three parts. They include the sending time, receiving time, and sleeping time, which are expressed as T_{send}, $T_{receive}$, and T_{sleep}. Thereby, we define the path energy efficiency as:

$$EE = \sum_{i=1}^{l} C/E_i \tag{2}$$

where c is the transferred information in the process of communication, E denotes the energy consumption that each node consumes, l is the total number of the path nodes.

The energy consumption of each node is divided into three parts. They include sending energy consumption, receiving energy consumption, and sleeping energy consumption, which are respectively denotes as E_{send}, $E_{recieve}$, E_{sleep}. In this paper we assume that the transmitted information C between communication nodes is constant. Then we solve the energy efficiency value according to Eqs. (1) and (2).

There are a lot of channel allocation methods in the modern wireless communication field. Because we here consider the energy efficiency of the cognitive multi-hop spectrum access, the channel allocation scheme is accomplished in the process of establishing link. Then we can guarantee the connectivity of the path.

Then we establish the path based on energy efficiency. The sleeping mechanism for the path node is considered, which increases energy efficiency of the communication path further. We assumed that the location of secondary users is randomly distributed, and each node can send data, receive data and come into sleeping. The awakening mechanism of each node is intelligent, that is, the node wakes up automatically when the link transmits information.

When the primary user communicates with each other, the secondary user processes the multi-hop communication with the primary user's channel. The network model is shown as Fig. 1. In this model, the primary user uses the base station for communications. We assume that primary user is $M_m = \{m_1, m_2, m_3..., m_m, m_d\}$, where m_d is base station, secondary user is $C_n = \{c_1, c_{2,...}, c_n\}$, there are M_m available channels, $H = \{h_1, h_2, \ldots, h_M\}$ are used for different primary users. There are interferences for the corresponding primary user when the secondary users communicates with each other. There also exist interferences between the primary users. Thereby in this network model, we consider that the communication between the secondary users does not affect the primary user communications. And we need to eliminate the interference between the secondary users in the process of communications.

For the secondary user and primary user, the transmitting terminals and the receiving terminals both use the omni-directional antenna to send and receive signal. Within the limits of sending nodes, the network node is connected. Then we simply introduce the omni-directional antenna transmit model. We assume that the received signal power is $p_c d^{-\beta}$ in this paper, where p_c is the sending power of sending node c, d is the distance between the sending node and the receiving node, the value of β depends on the channel characteristics, and β is 2–4. We assume that the position of the network node is the same, and the power between nodes i and j is $p_{ij} = d_{ij}^{\beta}$, where d_{ij} is the distance between nodes i and j. In this paper the value of β is 2.

Now we discuss energy consumption and energy efficiency model. According to Eq. (1), the path energy consumption is the sum of the product of each node power and the processing information time. We assume that the node has three states, namely sending state, receiving state, sleeping state. The process of energy consumption also includes similar three states. Therefore, based on Eq. (1), the path energy can also be denoted as follows:

$$E = \sum_{i=1}^{l} \left(E_{send} + E_{receive} + E_{sleep} \right)_i \qquad (3)$$

Energy consumption of each state is:

$$E_{send} = P_{send} * T_{send} \tag{4}$$

$$E_{receive} = P_{receive} * T_{receive} \tag{5}$$

$$E_{sleep} = P_{sleep} * T_{sleep} \tag{6}$$

Then energy efficiency can be denoted as follows:

$$EE = \sum_{i=1}^{l} (EE_{send} + EE_{reveive} + EE_{sleepi} \tag{7}$$

Energy efficiency of each state is:

$$EE_{send} = C/E_{send} \tag{8}$$

$$EE_{receive} = C/E_{receive} \tag{9}$$

$$EE_{sleep} = C/E_{sleep} \tag{10}$$

Next, we deduce the maximum energy efficiency multi-hop spectrum access app-roach. To establish a maximum energy efficiency path between source node and destination node, we need to consider the distribution of link channels in the process of building the path. Then we ensured the connectivity of the path. When we construct this path, we put in the sleeping mechanism for the path. And the sleeping method can improve the energy efficiency further. Now we discuss the details about energy efficiency path, the channel allocation strategy of energy efficiency priority, and the sleeping mechanism module.

The secondary user can communicate with each other in the maximum emission radius when the primary user stays in the idle state. The emission radius under the condition that the communications between secondary users do not affect the communication of primary users is called as the limited radius. When there are more than two secondary users in the network, it is difficult to calculate the variable value of secondary users. To improve the calculation efficiency, we propose a novel algorithm to reduce the computational complexity.

According to the energy consumption and energy efficiency models, the calculation process of this algorithm is denoted as follows:

Step1: Considering the influence from the primary user to the secondary user, we calculate the emission radius of the secondary user on the premise that secondary users do not affect the normal communications between primary users;
Step2: As shown in Fig. 1, we determine the coverage Φ centered at the source node, with a radius of the distance between the source node and the destination node;

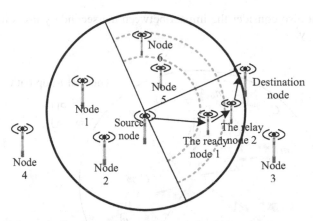

Fig. 1. The schematic diagram of the multi-hop path with maximum energy efficiency.

Step3: We remove the secondary user outside the circle Φ, which reduced the calculation overhead of the algorithm. As shown in Fig. 1, nodes 3 and 4 are outside the round Φ. Then we delete them;

Step4: Determine the circle centering in the source node and with a radius of the distance between the source node and the destination node. We need the semicircle that on the direction of the source node to the destination node and delete the secondary user on the other semicircle. As shown in Fig. 1, based on a radius of the distance between the source node and the destination node, we delete the semicircle on the opposite direction of the destination node, that is, node 1 and 2.

Step5: To begin with the source node and ending with the destination node, we determine the node of the biggest energy efficiency of single relay route according to Eq. (2). As shown in Fig. 2, we put the node 1 into the route.

Step6: We delete the node in the semicircle with the radius of the distance between the source node and the relay node that in the Step5 joined in the route. Then we reduce the computation between the secondary users further. As shown in Fig. 2, we delete node 5.

Step7: According to the above principles, we put many relay nodes into the path.

Step8: We determine the path of the maximum energy efficiency eventually. And we decrease the calculation greatly between the secondary user s in the process.

As shown in Fig. 2, we get the maximum energy efficiency of the path with the above algorithm. In the legend of 3, there are 50 secondary user. We get the route, which start with node 6 and end with node 1. The number of hops is 4.

Now we discuss the energy efficiency priority of the channel allocation strategy. In the wireless cognitive network, not only the primary user has the impact on the secondary user but also the other secondary user has the impact on the primary user. Thereby it is necessary to carry on the channel allocation.

Each channel in the spectrum is orthogonal completely in the wireless cognitive network, and the secondary user can use multiple channels. However, when several secondary users use the same channel in a certain range, there will be conflicts and interference between the secondary users. So we not only consider the impact of the primary user but also consider the impact between the secondary users in the channel allocation strategy.

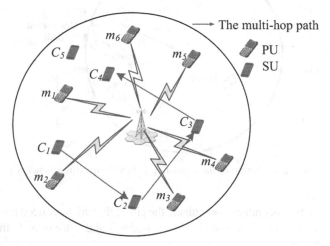

Fig. 2. The multi-hop cognitive network model for IoT applications.

The distribution of channel allocation strategy and the process of setting up the maximum energy efficiency path are interdependent. We supposes that the topological structure of the secondary users is not changed in a network perception period. We define the network topology of the secondary users is $C_n = \{c_1, c_{2,...,}c_n\}$, and the number of secondary users n. And we use matrix $M_m = \{m_1, m_2, m_3..., m_m\}$ to represent the network topology of the primary users, and the number of primary users is m. We use matrix $Ch\_use = \{h_{rr}|h_{rr} \in (0, 1)\}_{m \times n}$ to denote the condition of the secondary users' channel when eliminating the interference of the primary user. Each column of the matrix represents the available channel condition under the influence of the primary user, where 0 stands for the available channel and 1 denotes the unavailable channel. We use matrix $Ch\_use\_CU = \{u_{ii}|u_{ii} \in (0, 1)\}_{n \times n}$ to stand for the condition of the secondary users' channel. We have thought about the influence between the secondary users, where 0 stands for the available channel and 1 denotes the unavailable channel. When accomplished the single relay energy efficiency maximum link, we judge the channel if can be used or not in this link according to the obtained situation *RTS* of the channel. If available, we assign the channel to the link; if not, we establish the second largest energy efficiency link based on Eq. (2). And we detect the link if there is an available channel, until the link has the available channel. When we have allocated the channel for the first link, we assign the second relay node based on the Eq. (1). We allocate the channel for this link. We determine whether the primary user and secondary user have affected the node respectively, based on $Ch\_use = \{h_{rr}|h_{rr} \in (0, 1)\}_{m \times n}$ and $Ch\_use\_CU = \{u_{ii}|u_{ii} \in (0, 1)\}_{n \times n}$. Then we judge if the link has the available channel or not. And we also determine if the link has the available channel or not according to the above principles in the subsequent links. If there was no available channel between the source node and the destination node, the path can not be established, that is we can not establish the maximum energy efficiency path.

Next, we use the schematic to illustrate the principle of this strategy. As shown in Fig. 2, if the emission radius of the first secondary user is RS, the second link can't use the channel of the first link because of the influence from the RS to the second link. If the emission radius of the first link is the rest radius that as shown in Fig. 2, there is no effect on the second channel of the link because of its emission radius is small, so that the channel of the second link doesn't conflict with the channel of the first link. If the emitting radius of the first node is RS and the emitting radius of the third relay node is $R3$, there is a conflict for the link between the third node and the first node. So the third link can't use the channel of the first. The rest of the link channel allocations is similar. In short, when considering the influence between the secondary users, we should take the interference between the secondary users into account successively. Only in this way can we eliminate the interference between the links and achieve the channel assignment effectively.

3   Simulation Results and Analysis

In order to validate the proposed algorithm in this paper, we present the simulations of different network system algorithm scenes. For simulation, we suppose that the primary user and secondary user obey random distribution, the channel number of primary user is $M - 15$ and the number of the secondary user is changed according to the need of the simulation environment. We also assume that there are two packets in the channel and their size are random. *EECM* represents the scene where the path does not use the sleeping mechanism, while $EECM_{sleep}$ stands for our proposed approach using the sleeping mechanism.

Now we analyze the impacts of hop counts on the energy consumption of the network path. In the simulation, we test how the path energy efficiency changes with the path hop counts. We assume that the number of secondary users is stochastic. Then we set the number of the secondary users as $N = 50$, and set the link number being increased from 1 to 5. From Fig. 3, we find that the path energy consumption value increases with the increase of the number of hop count. We can also see that the path energy consumption value of $EECM_{sleep}$ is smaller than that of *EECM*. Therefore, this shows that our approach can reduce the power consumption greatly.

Next, we discuss the impacts of hop counts on the path energy efficiency. We get the value of energy efficiency at the same simulation environment with Fig. 3. From Fig. 4, we find that the value of the path energy efficiency is on the decline with the increase of the hop count. Figure 4 show that the energy efficiency of our approach $EECM_{sleep}$ is bigger than that of *EECM*. This further indicates that our method holds better performance.

We analyze the impact of the number of secondary users on the path energy consumption. We obtain the energy consumption with the number of secondary users in the same simulation scene. In the our simulation, the distribution of the primary and secondary users' positions is random. We set the number of secondary users being increased from 10 to 18. Then we obtain the energy consumption and energy efficiency of the path

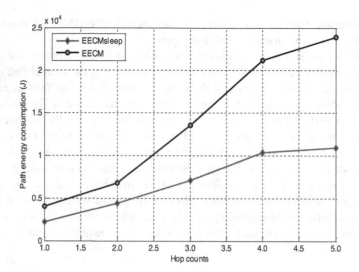

Fig. 3. The impact of hop counts on energy consumption.

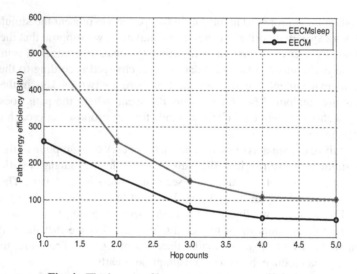

Fig. 4. The impact of hop counts on energy efficiency.

with the sleeping mechanism and without the sleeping mechanism. From Fig. 5, we can see that the energy consumption increases with the increase of the number of secondary users. Figure 6 also show that the path energy consumption of our method $EECM_{sleep}$ is smaller than that of $EECM$. Therefore, this also shows our method has much better energy efficiency performance.

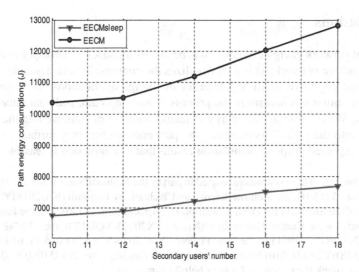

Fig. 5. The impact of secondary users' number on energy consumption.

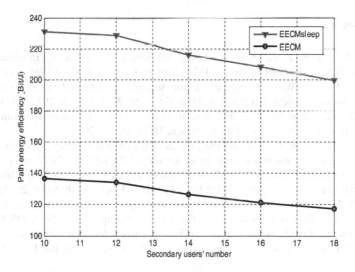

Fig. 6. The impact of secondary users' number on energy efficiency.

Next we further discuss the impact of the number of the secondary users on the path energy efficiency. We get the path energy efficiency in the same simulation environment with Fig. 5. From Fig. 6, we can find that the value of the path energy efficiency becomes more small with the increase of the number of secondary users. And we can see that the path energy efficiency of our method $EECM_{sleep}$ is bigger than that of $EECM$. This also indicate our approach indeed hold better performance.

4 Conclusions

The study of network energy efficiency has been the emphases and hotspot issues in the wireless cognitive network. This paper realizes the energy-efficient dynamic spectrum access for the cognitive multi-hop Internet of Things applications. We consider the channel distribution mechanism in the process of building path, and guarantee the path is connected. When building the energy efficiency maximum path, we join the sleeping mechanism into the path. This increases the path energy efficiency further. Finally, we achieve the expected purpose. Simulation results that our approach is feasible.

Acknowledgments. This work was supported in part by the National Natural Science Foundation of China (No. 61571104), the Sichuan Science and Technology Program (No. 2018JY0539), the Key projects of the Sichuan Provincial Education Department (No. 18ZA0219), the Fundamental Research Funds for the Central Universities (No. ZYGX2017KYQD170), the CERNET Innovation Project (No. NGII20190111), the Fund Projects (Nos. 2020-JCJQ-ZD-016-11, 61403110405, 315075802, JZX6Y202001010161), and the Innovation Funding (No. 2018510007000134). The authors wish to thank the reviewers for their helpful comments.

References

1. Prajapat, R., Yadav, R.N., Misra, R.: Energy-efficient k-Hop clustering in cognitive radio sensor network for Internet of Things. IEEE Internet Things J. **8**(17), 13593–13607 (2021)
2. Yilmaz, Y., Guo, Z., Wang, X.: Sequential joint spectrum sensing and channel estimation for dynamic spectrum access. IEEE J. Sel. Areas Commun. **32**(11), 2000–2012 (2014)
3. Liu, X., Sun, C., Zhou, M., et al.: Reinforcement learning based dynamic spectrum access in cognitive Internet of Vehicles. China Commun. **18**(7), 58–68 (2021)
4. Pei, Y., Hu, S., Zhong, F., et al.: Blockchain-enabled dynamic spectrum access: cooperative spectrum sensing, access and mining. In: Proceedings GLOBECOM 2019, pp. 1–6 (2019)
5. Ansere, J.A., Han, G., Wang, H., et al.: A reliable energy efficient dynamic spectrum sensing for cognitive radio IoT networks. IEEE Internet Things J. **6**(4), 6748–6759 (2019)
6. Debroy, S., Samanta, P., Bashir, A., et al.: SpEED-IoT: spectrum aware energy efficient routing for device-to-device IoT communication. Futur. Gener. Comput. Syst. **93**(1), 833–848 (2019)
7. Liu, X., Hu, S., Li, M., et al.: Energy-efficient resource allocation for cognitive industrial Internet of Things with wireless energy harvesting. IEEE Trans. Ind. Inf. **17**(8), 5668–5677 (2021)
8. Shah, V.K., Luciano, B., Silvestri, S., et al.: A diverse band-aware dynamic spectrum access network architecture for delay-tolerant smart city applications. IEEE Trans. Netw. Serv. Manage. **17**(2), 1125–1139 (2020)
9. Jiang, D., Wang, Z., Wang, W., et al.: AI-assisted energy-efficient and intelligent routing for reconfigurable wireless networks. IEEE Trans. Netw. Sci. Eng. (2021). https://doi.org/10.1109/TNSE.2021.3075428
10. Jiang, D., Wang, F., Lv, Z., et al.: QoE-aware efficient content distribution scheme for satellite-terrestrial networks. IEEE Trans. Mob. Comput. (2021). https://doi.org/10.1109/TMC.2021.3074917
11. Jiang, D., Wang, Z., Huo, L., et al.: A performance measurement and analysis method for software-defined networking of IoV. IEEE Trans. Intell. Transp. Syst. (2020). https://doi.org/10.1109/TITS.2020.3029076

A New End-To-End Network Traffic Reconstruction Approach Based on Different Time Granularities

Wei Yang[1], Dingde Jiang[1]([✉]), Jianguang Chen[1], Zhihao Wang[1], Liuwei Huo[1], and Wenhui Zhao[2]

[1] University of Electronic Science and Technology of China, Chengdu 611731, China
[2] College of Information Science and Engineering, Northeastern University, Shenyang 110819, China

Abstract. End-to-end network traffic is an important input parameter for network planning and network monitoring, which plays an important role in network management and design. This paper proposes a new end-to-end network traffic reconstruction algorithm based on different time granularity. This algorithm reconstructs the end-to-end network traffic with fine time granularity by taking advantage of the characteristics of the link traffic which is easy to be measured directly in the network with coarse time granularity. According to the fractal and self-similar characteristics of network traffic found in existing studies, we first carry out fractal interpolation for link traffic measurement under coarse time granularity to obtain link traffic under fine time granularity. Then, by using the compressive sensing theory, an appropriate sparse transformation matrix and measurement matrix are constructed to reconstruct the end-to-end network traffic with fine time granularity. Simulation results show that the proposed algorithm is effective and feasible.

Keywords: End-to-end network traffic reconstruction · Fractal interpolation · Compression sense · Dictionary Learning Algorithm

1 Introduction

The end-to-end network Traffic Matrix (TM) is an overview of the entire network Traffic. The elements in the matrix represent the traffic in the network that starts at one node (source node) and ends at another node (destination node) [1]. The traffic can be in packets or bytes. Source and Destination Pairs are called OD Pairs. Traffic matrix is not only the key input of network management and traffic engineering tasks, but also can be applied to network management, network security and other fields.

In recent years, with the continuous expansion of network functions and the diversification of users' requirements for network performance [2–4], the end-to-end network traffic is very important for the network management [5], and it has become a hot topic for the network traffic measurement. There are many network traffic measurement scheme, such as SNMP (Simple Network Management Protocol), sending probing packet [6],

D. Jiang and H. Song (Eds.): SIMUtools 2021, LNICST 424, pp. 111–122, 2022.
https://doi.org/10.1007/978-3-030-97124-3_10

and so on. The end-to-end network traffic reconstruction in the traffic matrix has become an important research field that recover the end-to-end network traffic with measured coarse-granularity network traffic of link load.

For the end-to-end network traffic, it has become a hot research field that how to reconstruct the traffic matrix to meet the requirement of certain accuracy through limited measurement information [7]. At present, there are many reconstruction methods of the traffic matrix. Fan et al. sparsely represent the normal and anomalous traffic in wavelet and time domain, and use the convex program to estimate both the normal and anomalous components of the traffic matrix [8]. Pachuau et al. use the traffic to represent all traffic flows and use the Genetic algorithm (GA) based optimization method to further the solutions of the Gravity model [9], and authors use the Gravity model to obtain an initial solution and use GA model to solve link load-TM. Amoroso et al. [10] propose a super resolution technique for traffic matrix inference that does not require any knowledge on the structural properties of the matrix elements to infer, nor a large data collection. Jiang et al. [11] study the measurement and analysis technology for software-defined networking of IoV and propose a performance measurement and analysis method to measure and characterize its performance.

This paper studies the reconfiguration of end-to-end network traffic under the granularity of fine time measurement by using the information that is easy to be directly measured in the existing network: link load and routing matrix under the granularity of coarse time measurement. Whether the end-to-end network traffic can be reconstructed at different time granularity depends to a great extent on how to obtain the link load required by the traffic matrix at fine time granularity from the link load at coarse time granularity. The traditional mathematical interpolation of link load, such as Lagrange interpolation, linear interpolation, etc. cannot well reflect the characteristics of network traffic in time scale because these interpolation methods are only numerical interpolation, so the traditional interpolation cannot well meet the characteristics of traffic data. Given that network traffic has self-similarity characteristics in a larger time scale and fractal characteristics in a smaller time scale link load, as a linear weight of end-to-end network traffic, should also have fractal characteristics. In this paper, the application of fractal interpolation to link load is first proposed, that is, the link load under coarse time measurement granularity is fractal interpolation and the link load under fine time measurement granularity is obtained.

In the following, the paper is organized that Sect. 2 makes a problem elaboration in. Then, the end-to-end traffic is reconstructed and proposed the RLS-DLA algorithm in Sect. 3. Finally, we perform some simulations to verify our proposed methods in Sect. 4 and make a conclusion for our works in Sect. 5.

2 Problem Elaboration

The end-to-end network traffic matrix represents the traffic transmission between all OD pairs in the network. If there are n nodes in a network, then there are n^2 OD flows. The end-to-end network traffic matrix at time t can be expressed as $x(t) = [x_1(t), x_2(t), \ldots, x_k(t), \ldots, x_{n^2}(t)]^T$, where $x_k(t)$ represents the traffic of OD flow in article k at time t. Then, there are $k = (i-1) * n + j$ OD flows that $x_k(t)$ starts from the source node i and ends at the node j.

Link load matrix represents the change in traffic rate over each link at time t. The link traffic matrix can be expressed as $y(t) = [y_1(t), y_2(t), \ldots, y_r(t), \ldots, y_l(t)]^T$, where l represents the total number of links in the entire network. y_r represents the traffic rate change of time t on link r. The size of the routing matrix A is $l \times c(c = n^2)$. When OD flow j passes link i, route matrix element $a_{ij} = 1$, otherwise $a_{ij} = 0$. Each list in matrix A shows all the links that OD flows through as it traffic through the entire network. The routing matrix contains the actual routing information of the network. In this paper, it is considered that the routing matrix is stable and does not change in the period of traffic matrix reconstruction. The relationship between link load, routing matrix, and end-to-end network traffic matrix can be expressed as

$$y(t) = Ax(t) \tag{1}$$

The link load matrix can be directly measured through SNMP. There are many ways to obtain route matrix $y(t)$, usually by collecting the configuration information of IGP (Interior Gateway Protocol) or collecting the link state information of the interaction between routers and calculating the number of shortest paths. Therefore, the end-to-end network traffic reconfiguration problem is transformed into the problem of knowing $y(t)$ and A and solving $x(t)$. If A is a full rank square matrix, then the solution of Eq. (1) exists and is unique. However, in the actual network, the number of OD flow is often much greater than the number of links, that is $c \gg l$. The matrix A is not a full rank matrix. According to $x(t) = A^{-1}y(t)$, it is difficult to obtain the exact solution of end-to-end network traffic, so it is a great challenge to reconstruct the end-to-end network traffic.

More importantly, existing IP network devices do not always support direct measurements of end-to-end network traffic for a variety of reasons. And some devices support this kind of measurement. However, due to the rapid increase of network services, the equipment will need to collect a lot of measurement data. This will add additional burden to network equipment, which will affect network performance and affect the normal operation of the network.

In view of the above problems, this paper proposes to reconstruct the end-to-end traffic of the entire network under the fine time measurement granularity by directly measuring the link traffic under the coarse time granularity. The goal is to obtain end-to-end network traffic with as few measurements as possible to minimize the impact on network equipment and network performance. Fractal interpolation of link load $y_c(t)$ under coarse time measurement granularity is performed to obtain link load $y_f(t)$ under fine time granularity. Then, given $y_f(t)$ and A, the end-to-end solve the network traffic matrix $x(t)$.

Through the first time for coarse granularity fractal interpolation to get the link traffic $y_c(t)$ under the link traffic $y_f(t)$ under fine granularity of time, and then using the theory of compressed perception by reconstructing the corresponding time $y_f(t)$ under the granularity of end-to-end network traffic $x_f(t)$, and the $x_f(t)$ satisfy the following conditions:

$$y_f(t) = Ax_f(t) \tag{2}$$

Here, according to the above elaboration, we propose an end-to-end network traffic reconstruction model based on different time granularity.

The end-to-end network traffic $x_1(t), x_2(t), \ldots, x_k(t), \ldots, x_c(t)$ has significant self-similarity and fractal characteristics $y_1(t), y_2(t), \ldots, y_r(t), \ldots, y_l(t)$ also have obvious self-similarity and fractal characteristics. We propose to use fractal interpolation to solve the link traffic reconstruction problem under fine time granularity.

A. Fractal Interpolation of Link Flow Signal

Network traffic reflects the activities of network devices and users accessing the network. It has obvious long correlation, short correlation, self-similarity and heavy tail distribution. Reflect the local and the whole have obvious similarity. For objects with this fractal feature, we can use a fractal interpolation algorithm. The link traffic with fine time granularity can be obtained by interpolating the measured link traffic with coarse time granularity.

Suppose the known coarse time granularity is N times the fine time granularity (where $N \geq 2$ is an integer). For the link traffic $y_c(t)$ under coarse time granularity, we can get the following equation:

$$
\begin{cases}
\{(t, y_{1c}(t))|y_{1c}(t) \in R; t = 1, 1+N, \ldots, 1+(T-1)N\} \\
\{(t, y_{2c}(t))|y_{2c}(t) \in R; t = 1, 1+N, \ldots, 1+(T-1)N\} \\
\ldots \\
\{(t, y_{lc}(t))|y_{lc}(t) \in R; t = 1, 1+N, \ldots 1+(T-1)N\}
\end{cases}
\tag{3}
$$

where T represents the number of moments under coarse granularity of link traffic.

For each link traffic, we hope to construct the following function to obtain the link traffic data at $[t, t+N]$ time points within the measurement interval T:

$$
f_i : \begin{cases} y_{ic}(t) \to y_{ic}(\hat{t}) \\ t \to \hat{t} \end{cases}
\tag{4}
$$

where $i = 1, 2, \ldots, l, t = 1, 1+N, \ldots, 1+(T-1)N$.

According to Eq. (4), we use the fractal theory to construct the function f_i through iteration, that is:

$$
w_{ij}\begin{pmatrix} \hat{t} \\ y_{ic}(\hat{t}) \end{pmatrix} = \begin{pmatrix} a_{ij} & 0 \\ c_{ij} & s_{ij} \end{pmatrix}\begin{pmatrix} t \\ y_{ic}(t) \end{pmatrix} + \begin{pmatrix} d_{ij} \\ e_{ij} \end{pmatrix}
\tag{5}
$$

where $\hat{t}$ represents the corresponding moment calculated through the transformation of equation t (5). Similarly, $y_{ic}(\hat{t})$ represents the link traffic value at the corresponding $\hat{t}$ moment calculated by $y_{ic}(t)$ transformation. $i = 1, 2, \ldots, l$ and $j = 2, 3, \ldots, T$, w_{ij} represents the functional relationship within the measurement interval $[t, t+N]$, and $f_i = (w_{i2}, w_{i3}, \ldots, w_{iT})$. Therefore, f_i represents the iterative function system composed of $(T-1)$ functions.

For $t = 1, 1+N, \ldots, 1+(T-1)N$, at $\hat{t} = 1, 1+(T-1)N$, Eq. (5) must satisfy:

$$
\begin{cases}
w_{ij}\begin{pmatrix} 1 \\ y_{ic}(1) \end{pmatrix} = \begin{pmatrix} t_{j-1} \\ y_{ic}(t_{j-1}) \end{pmatrix} \\
w_{ij}\begin{pmatrix} 1+(T-1)N \\ y_{ic}(1+(T-1)N) \end{pmatrix} = \begin{pmatrix} t_j \\ y_{ic}(t_j) \end{pmatrix}
\end{cases}
\tag{6}
$$

where t_{j-1} and t_j represent the $j-1$ and j values in t respectively.
According to Eqs. (5) and (6):

$$
\begin{cases}
a_{ij} + d_{ij} = t_{j-1} \\
a_{ij}(1 + (T-1)N) + d_{ij} = t_j \\
c_{ij} + s_{ij}y_{ic}(1) + e_{ij} = y_{ic}(t_{j-1}) \\
c_{ij}(1 + (T-1)N) + s_{ij}y_{ic}(1 + (T-1)N) + e_{ij} = y_{ic}(t_j)
\end{cases}
\tag{7}
$$

where $i = 1, 2, \ldots, l$ and $j = 2, 3, \ldots, T$. In general, s_{ij} is chosen as a constant, and $0 \le s_{ij} < 1$. Then, we can calculate a_{ij}, d_{ij}, c_{ij} and e_{ij} according to Eq. (7), and uniquely determine the iterative function system f_i represented by Eqs. (5)–(6). In general, in order to ensure that the function w_{ij} (where $j = 2, 3, \ldots, T$) can well describe the fractal characteristics of link traffic, a_{ij}, c_{ij} and s_{ij} meet the following constraints:

$$
\max\left(\sqrt{a_{ij}^2 + (1+\varepsilon)c_{ij}^2}, \sqrt{\frac{1}{\varepsilon} + 1}|s_{ij}|\right) < 1
\tag{8}
$$

where ε is an constant that $\varepsilon = 0$.

According to coarse time, the link load $y_{ic}(t)$ under granularity was measured, and the iteration coefficient $a_{ij}, c_{ij}, d_{ij}, e_{ij}$ was first obtained through formula (7). When $j = 2, \ldots, T$, in formula (5), $t = 1, 1+N, 1+2N, \ldots, 1+(T-1)N$, the corresponding w_{ij} is obtained in turn, and the interpolation process of fractal interpolation is completed. The attractor $G' = \cup_{j=2}^{T} w_j(G)$ of IFS is a graph of continuous function $f[1, 1 + (T-1)N] \to R$ through all interpolation points $(t, y(t))$, $t = 1, 1+2N, \ldots, 1+(T-1)N$. The continuous Function is called Fractal Interpolation Function (FIF).

B. Link Flow Interpolation Reconstruction
In this paper, fractal interpolation is applied successively to link load under coarse time measurement granularity of l bar to obtain link load under fine time measurement granularity of l bar. According to the principle of fractal interpolation, it can be seen that, if the coarse time measurement granularity is known, the link load t has T moments, then $\hat{t}$ in the obtained fractal interpolation function G' has $T(T-1)$ moments. Obviously, the number of moments obtained is far more than the required moment $1 + (T-1)N$.

There are only two moments that are closest to the required $\tilde{t}$ moment are selected from the obtained $\hat{t}$ moment, and the corresponding two link traffic values are averaged as the link traffic values at the required moments.

In summary, it is known that the link load of t at T moments under coarse time measurement granularity is known, and the interval is N. Through fractal interpolation and selection of required moments, the link load of $1 + (T-1)N$ at $\tilde{t}$ moments under fine time measurement granularity is finally obtained. As Eq. (9) shows:

$$
\begin{cases}
\{(\tilde{t}, y_{1f}(\tilde{t}))|y_{1f}(\tilde{t}) \in R; \tilde{t} = 1, 2, 3, \ldots, 1 + (T-1)N\} \\
\{(\tilde{t}, y_{2f}(\tilde{t}))|y_{2f}(\tilde{t}) \in R; \tilde{t} = 1, 2, 3, \ldots, 1 + (T-1)N\} \\
\cdots \\
\{(\tilde{t}, y_{lf}(\tilde{t}))|y_{lf}(\tilde{t}) \in R; \tilde{t} = 1, 2, 3, \ldots, 1 + (T-1)N\}
\end{cases}
\tag{9}
$$

3   End-To-End Network Traffic Reconfiguration

In the third part of this paper, fractal interpolation is used to obtain the link load with fine time measurement granularity corresponding to the traffic matrix. Then, we use the compressive sensing framework to reconstruct end-to-end network traffic $x_f(\tilde{t})$.

A. Sparse Transformation Matrix Construction

According to the compressive sensing theory, when the original traffic signal is not k-sparse signal, the original signal $x_f(\tilde{t})$ in Eq. (2) needs to be sparse represented by the transformation matrix Ψ, that is:

$$x_f(\tilde{t}) = \Psi * s(\tilde{t}) \tag{10}$$

where $s(\tilde{t})$ after transformation is sparse signal or compressible signal, $\tilde{t} = 1, 2, 3, \ldots, 1 + (T - 1)N$.

Signal sparse representation is widely used in various fields of signal processing and image processing. It is also the basis of compressed sensing theory. Only by selecting an appropriate transformation matrix, can the sparse representation coefficient $s(\tilde{t})$ be ensured to have sufficient sparsity or attenuation and the reconstruction accuracy of compressed sensing. The most prominent advantage of this algorithm is that in the algorithm, the forgetting factor λ and $0 \leq \lambda < 1$ are introduced to gradually get rid of the dependence on the initial dictionary in the training process and enhance the sparse representation ability of the RLS learning dictionary.

In this paper, under the fine-time measurement granularity, the real end-to-end traffic data at the first T' moments is taken as the training data $x\_train(t), t = 1, 2, ..., T'$, where $T' < 1 + (T - 1)N$, and RLS-DLA is adopted for sparse representation or sparse approximation, then according to Eq. (10):

$$x\_train(t) = D * s\_train(t) \tag{11}$$

where, $c \times 1$ is the size of $x\_train(t)$, $c = n^2$ is the total number of OD flow in the network with n nodes, D is the over-complete dictionary, and its size is $c \times c$. $s\_train(t)$ is the sparse representation coefficient of D under the dictionary of the training data $x\_train(t)$, and its size is $c \times 1$. The pseudo code for RLS-DLA as Table 1 shows.

B. Obtain End-To-End Traffic

In this paper, the dictionary D obtained by training with some real traffic data is taken as the sparse transformation matrix Ψ in the reconstruction of all end-to-end network traffic. Then, combining Eqs. (2) and (10) can be written as follows:

$$y_f(\tilde{t}) = A * x_f(\tilde{t}) = A * D * s(\tilde{t}) \tag{12}$$

where $\tilde{t} = 1, 2, 3, \ldots, 1 + (T - 1)N$.

The problem is transformed into: given the link load $y_f(\tilde{t})$, routing matrix A and sparse transformation matrix D under the granularity of fine time measurement, how to solve $s(\tilde{t})$ through the compressed sensing reconstruction algorithm. In the compressive sensing theory, a sufficient condition for the reconstruction algorithm to accurately reconstruct the original signal is that $\Theta = \Phi * \Psi$ meets the RIP criterion, which is equivalent to that the measurement matrix Φ is irrelevant to the transformation matrix Ψ.

In Eq. (12), A is the fixed routing matrix, and the matrix element is 0 or 1; D is a fixed sparse transformation matrix, and obviously $A * D$ cannot meet the RIP criterion. We generate a random Gaussian matrix $R \sim N(0, \frac{1}{n^2})$ of size $m \times l$, l is the total number of links under link load, and $m < l \ll n^2$. For formula (12), multiply left and right sides by the matrix R at the same time:

Table 1. The pseudocode for RLS-DLA

Algorithm: Recursive Least Squares Dictionary Learning Algorithm

---

Input: training data: $x\_train(t)$

Output: overcomplete dictionary: D

Initialization:

$D = x\_train(:, 1 : n^2)$ {use first n^2 training vectors as initial dictionary and then normalize D}

$S = \phi$ {initial coefficient matrix}

$m - 1$ {the number of iterations}

$K = 10$ {sparsity of OMP}

repeat

　　get the forgetting factor: $0 \le \lambda_m < 1$

　　$x = X\_train(:, m)$ {every training vector}

　　$s = OMP(x, D, K)$ {coefficient vector}

　　$r = x - D * s$ {signal residual}

　　$S = S \cup s$

　　$C = S * S^T$

　　$C_\lambda = \lambda^{-1} * C$ {apply forgetting factor}

　　$u = C_\lambda * s$

　　$\alpha = 1 / (1 + w^T * u)$

　　$D = D + \alpha * r * u^T$ {update the dictionary}

　　　　$C = C_\lambda - \alpha * u * u^T$ {update C from m = 2}

　　　　$m = m + 1$

until $m > T'$ 　　{T' training vectors}

Output: D

$$R * y_f(\tilde{t}) = R * A * D * s(\tilde{t}) = \Phi' * D * s(\tilde{t}) \tag{13}$$

Therefore, the new measurement matrix $\Phi' = R * A$ constructed in this way is still an independent co-distributed Gaussian random matrix, which is highly irrelevant to the fixed sparse transformation matrix D, so $\Theta' = \Phi' * D$ can meet the RIP criterion. The new observation vector $z(\tilde{t}) = R * y_f(\tilde{t})$ has a size of $m \times 1$. Finally, for the observation vector $z(\tilde{t})$ of each time, the OMP (Orthogonal Matching Pursuit) algorithm is called to reconstruct the sparse representation coefficient $s(\tilde{t})$ of the corresponding time. Note: the desired end-to-end network traffic $x_f(\tilde{t}) = D * s(\tilde{t})$. The measurement matrix Φ' constructed in this way not only meets the RIP criterion but also reduces the dimension of the observation vector $z(\tilde{t})$ while ensuring the reconstruction accuracy. IPFP constraint optimization is carried out on the obtained initial traffic matrix $x_f(\tilde{t})$ to obtain the network end-to-end traffic $x(\tilde{t})$ under the fine time measurement granularity.

4 The Simulation Analysis

In this paper, the simulation experiment used the real traffic data from the Abilene backbone network for one week to verify. Under different time measurement granularity, the link load with coarse time measurement granularity was used to reconstruct the network end-to-end traffic with fine time granularity, that is, the traffic matrix. Abilene network has a total of $n = 12$ nodes, that is, there is $c = n^2 = 144$ OD flow. The Abiline network has 30 links, plus the two outgoing and incoming links of each node, a total of 54 links, so $l = 54$. In the actual construction of the measurement matrix, a random Gaussian matrix R of size 20×54 is generated, that is $m = 20 < l = 54 < c = 144$. TomoG, SRSVD, and PCA methods are considered to be more accurate methods for end-to-end network traffic reconstruction. This paper will compare the new method of reconstructing end-to-end traffic of finer-grained network from coarse-grained time measurement link load with the above three methods, and analyze and compare the effect of OD flow reconfiguration, Spatial relative errors (SREs) and Temporal relative errors (TREs) of the four methods.

A. Reconstruction Effect of Traffic

In this paper, the OD20 stream was randomly selected from 144 OD streams. The reconstruction effect of OD20 under different coarse time measurement granularity is compared with TomoG, SRSVD and PCA respectively. The reconstruction effect with coarse time measurement granularity of 10 min is demonstrated. When the time measurement granularity of link load is 10 min, the OD20 reconstructed and the OD20 reconstructed through SRSVD, TomoG and PCA are compared with the true value of OD20, as shown in Fig. 1. Real20 represents the true values of OD20 under 5 min measurement granularity; In Fig. 1, NEW 10 min represents the OD20 reconstructed when the measurement granularity is 10 min. It can be seen from the reconstruction results of OD20 that OD flow has the best reconstruction effect when the coarse-time measurement granularity is 10 min, which is better than the other three reconstruction methods and other coarse-time measurement granularity. As the granularity of time measurement increases, it can be seen that the accuracy of reconstruction decreases gradually, which is related to the decrease of known link load time.

B. Error Assessment

The SREs of traffic matrix estimation represent the spatial relationship of the estimation error with OD flow, which reflects the estimation accuracy of the estimation method in space. The TREs represent the variation of the estimation error with time, reflecting the estimation accuracy of the estimation method in time. SREs and TREs of traffic matrix are important indicators to measure the quality of estimation methods. They are respectively defined as follows:

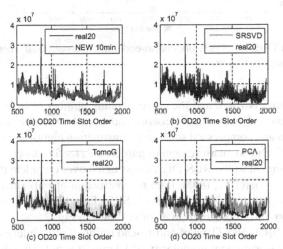

Fig. 1. The reconstruction effect of OD20 at particle size was measured in 10 min

$$\begin{cases} err_s(i) = \frac{||\hat{x}_M(i) - x_M(i)||_2}{||x_M(i)||_2}, & t = 1, 2, \ldots, M \\ err_t(t) = \frac{||\hat{x}_c(t) - x_c(t)||_2}{||x_c(t)||_2}, & i = 1, 2, \ldots, c \end{cases} \tag{14}$$

where $c = n^2$ represent the total number of OD streams in IP backbone network, and M represents the number of moments of network traffic reconstructed under fine time measurement granularity; $err_{sp}(i)$ represents the SREs of OD flow $err_{sp}(i)$ in article i relative to all measuring moments; $x_M(i)$ and $\hat{x}_M(i)$ respectively represent the true value and estimated value of OD flow in article i relative to all measuring moments. $err_{tm}(t)$ represents the TREs of all OD flow at time t. $x_c(t)$ and $\hat{x}_c(t)$ represent the true and estimated values of all OD flow at time t, respectively.

Given the real traffic data of the Abilene network for one week, the time measurement granularity is 5 min, the data of 2016 real end-to-end network traffic moments. In this paper, link loads with coarse time measurement granularity of 10 min are used to reconstruct the network end-to-end traffic with fine time measurement granularity of 5 min. For coarse time measurement, the known number of time T corresponding

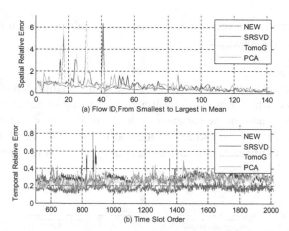

Fig. 2. SREs (a) and TREs (b) of network end-to-end traffic reconstructed when the coarse-time measurement granularity is 10 min.

to particle size 10 min is 1008, and the corresponding number of time interval N is 2. Therefore, the number of moments of network end-to-end traffic measured at 5 min by fractal interpolation and compressed sensing reconstruction algorithm: $1 + (T-1) * N$ corresponds to 2015. Due to measurement of particle size for 5 min before the real traffic data $T' = 500$ a moment as the RLS-DLA constructed over complete dictionary when training data x_train, therefore, in the final reconstruction of traffic data to remove its 500 times before, then the results with TomoG, SRSVD and PCA method carries on the analysis comparison, the reconstruction error is shown in Fig. 2.

Figure 2 shows SREs and TREs of end-to-end traffic of the Abilene network reconstructed from time measurement granularity of 10 min. It is not difficult to find that for different coarse time granularity, SREs of the new method proposed in this paper are all smaller than TomoG, SRSVD and PCA. However, with the increase of time granularity, the TREs of the new method increases obviously, and the performance of end-to-end traffic reconstruction becomes worse. The reason is that, with the increase of time measurement granularity, the number of moments of known link load becomes less and less, the network traffic error obtained by reconstruction will inevitably increase, and the reconstruction effect will also become worse and worse.

To evaluate the reconstruction accuracy of the four methods more accurately, the CDFs (Cumulative Distribution Function) of SREs and TREs are analyzed below. That is, CSRE (Cumulative distribution function of Spatial Relative Errors) and STRE (Cumulative distribution function of Temporal Relative Errors). Figure 3 is the CSRE and CTRE of end-to-end traffic of Abilene network reconstructed by time measurement granularity of 10 min.

In Fig. 3, coarse time measurement granularity is 10 min, that is, when the number of moments to be obtained is about twice the number of known moments. When SREs is 0.71, the new method proposed in this paper-reconstructing fine-grained traffic matrix from coarse-grained link load can accurately reconstruct 90.3% OD flow. When TREs is 0.21, the new method can accurately reconstruct 90.0% OD flow.

It is not difficult to find that the CDF curve of spatial relative error changes little with the increase of time measurement granularity. The performance of the new method proposed in this paper is superior to the other three existing methods. But time relative error of the CDF curves in rough time measuring particle size for 10 min while performance gradually decline, but are better than the other three kinds of existing methods. This also reflects that, as the number of known moments decreases, the known information decreases, so the effect of reconstructing the entire network end-to-end traffic gradually becomes worse.

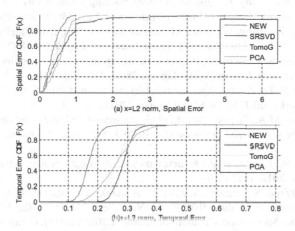

Fig. 3. CSRE (a) and CTRE (b) of network end-to-end traffic reconstructed when the coarse-time measurement granularity is 10 min.

5   Conclusions

Network end-to-end traffic reconstruction is a highly ill-posed linear inverse problem. How to obtain more accurate estimation of network end-to-end traffic through appropriate methods is a hot and difficult issue in current research. In this paper, the link load under coarse time measurement granularity, which is easy to be directly measured in the network, is used to reconstruct the network end-to-end traffic under fine time measurement granularity under the precondition that the routing matrix is known. Then, a new sparse transformation matrix and measurement matrix are constructed, and the compressive sensing framework is used. The network end-to-end traffic under fine time measurement granularity is obtained from the link load reconstruction under fine time measurement granularity. Simulation results show that with the increase of the time measurement granularity, the reconstruction performance of the new method becomes worse gradually.

Acknowledgments. This work was supported in part by the National Natural Science Foundation of China (No. 61571104), the Sichuan Science and Technology Program (No. 2018JY0539), the Key projects of the Sichuan Provincial Education Department (No. 18ZA0219), the Fundamental

Research Funds for the Central Universities (No. ZYGX2017KYQD170), the CERNET Innovation Project (No. NGII20190111), the Fund Projects (Nos. 2020-JCJQ-ZD-016–11, 61403110405, 315075802, JZX6Y202001010161), and the Innovation Funding (No. 2018510007000134). The authors wish to thank the reviewers for their helpful comments.

References

1. Hashemi, H., Abdelghany, K.: End-to-end deep learning methodology for real-time traffic network management. Comput.-Aided Civ. Infrastruct. Eng. **33**(10), 849–863 (2018)
2. Jiang, D., Wang, Z., Wang, W., et al.: AI-assisted energy-efficient and intelligent routing for reconfigurable wireless networks. IEEE Trans. Netw. Sci. Eng. **9**, 78–88 (2021)
3. Clemm, A., Zhani, M.F., Boutaba, R.: Network management 2030: operations and control of network 2030 services. J. Netw. Syst. Manage. **28**(4), 721–750 (2020)
4. Jiang, D., Wang, F., Lv, Z., et al.: QoE-aware efficient content distribution scheme for satellite-terrestrial networks. IEEE Trans. Mob. Comput. (2021)
5. Petrov, V., Lema, M.A., Gapeyenko, M., et al.: Achieving end-to-end reliability of mission-critical traffic in softwarized 5G networks. IEEE J. Sel. Areas Commun. **36**(3), 485–501 (2018)
6. Zhang, H., Cai, Z., Liu, Q., et al.: A survey on security-aware measurement in SDN. Secur. Commun. Netw. **2018**, 1–15 (2018)
7. Kumar, A., Vidyapu, S., Saradhi, V.V., et al.: A multi-view subspace learning approach to internet traffic matrix estimation. IEEE Trans. Netw. Serv. Manage. **17**(2), 1282–1293 (2020)
8. Fan, X.B., Xu, X.: Sparse representation for network traffic recovery. Comput. Commun. **160**, 547–553 (2020)
9. Pachuau, J.L., Roy, A., Krishna, G., et al.: Estimation of traffic matrix from links load using genetic algorithm. Scalable Comput.: Pract. Exp. **22**(1), 29–38 (2021)
10. Amoroso, R., Esposito, F., Merani, M.: Estimation of traffic matrices via super-resolution and federated learning. In: Proceedings of the 16th International Conference on emerging Networking EXperiments and Technologies, pp. 560–561 (2020)
11. Jiang, D., Wang, Z., Huo, L., et al.: A performance measurement and analysis method for software-defined networking of IoV. IEEE Trans. Intell. Transp. Syst. **22**, 3707–3719 (2020)

A Botnet Detection Method Based on SCBRNN

Yafeng Xu, Kailiang Zhang[(⊠)], Qi Zhou, and Ping Cui

Jiangsu Province Key Laboratory of Intelligent Industry Control Technology,
Xuzhou University of Technology, Xuzhou 221018, China
zhangkailiang@xzit.edu.cn

Abstract. With the rapid development of the social network and Internet of things, the complex network environment has led to more serious network security issues. Botnets have always been one of the most important issues in network security. The continuous update of botnet technology has severely influence the network operation of Internet service providers, posing a huge threat to security. Effective detection of botnets is the focus of related security solutions. In the new environment, traditional solutions have become inefficient. In recent years, botnet detection results based on machine learning technology continue to emerge. From the perspective of small batch gradient sample collection, this article optimizes the two-way neural network model and adopts approximate entropy to determine the abnormality of the data, thereby effectively detecting botnets. Research data shows that the model has good performance and can accurately identify botnets. Compared with the traditional model method, when the small batch sampling range is reduced, the accuracy is significantly improved, which provides effective help for Internet service providers to accurately detect botnets, improves service security mechanisms, and improves core competition force.

Keywords: Botnet · SCBRNN · Small batch · ApEn

1 Introduction

With the development of emerging technologies such as artificial intelligence, big data and 5G, some emerging network technologies and communication methods have been proposed [1, 2], and network quality and experience quality have been continuously improved [3, 4]. The energy efficiency methods improve the performance of internet of things [5–8]. However, the large number of devices accessing to the network pose challenges in security. The security threats facing the network are increasing, and security problems and attacks related to global networks often occur [9]. In the global risk factor rankings of the World Economic Forum, cyber attacks ranked the top five, becoming the third largest risk factor, causing great damage to production and life [10]. As a common method of network attacks, botnets have caused huge damage to the normal operation of the network and the security of information [11]. Network operators provide the most important basic services including network data transmission services and DNS resolution services. However, botnets can take advantage of their characteristics to

D. Jiang and H. Song (Eds.): SIMUtools 2021, LNICST 424, pp. 123–131, 2022.
https://doi.org/10.1007/978-3-030-97124-3_11

easily launch targeted Various attacks and damages to basic network operations, including DDoS attacks and DNS attacks, which have caused huge damage to basic network operations and services, severely undermined network information security [12, 13]. Therefore, effective response to botnets is the core security task of each operator, and accurate detection is the key. In recent years, artificial intelligence and machine learning have greatly changed the network security industry. The traffic analysis methods [14, 15] and complex web data analysis on cloud platform can help recognition [16–21]. Because behavior characteristic statistical analysis and behavior simulation monitoring are difficult to extract and detect target data, this paper proposes an efficient optimization method SCBRNN (bidirectional recurrent neural network for small batch data acquisition), which optimizes based on the characteristics of network traffic data Improve the two-way recurrent neural network to improve learning efficiency, and finally judge whether the target network host is invaded by a botnet based on the characteristics of entropy.

2 Related Work

Among the existing botnet detection methods, emerging methods based on machine learning are constantly being proposed. Most of these methods are based on the characteristics of traffic for qualitative analysis. The literature [22] conducted a study on the network behaviors with potential hidden dangers, fully analyzed the characteristics of these network behaviors (ActBehavior, FailBehavior, ScanBehavior), found the difference signs from the network level, and then used the mean algorithm to compare the hosts in the botnet Members confirm. [23] From the perspective of communication characteristics and traffic classification, some scholars proposed a cluster correlation verification method. Through the clustering and judgment of malicious traffic, the host in the network was identified by the botnet. Literature [24] proposed a detection method based on P2P traffic feature extraction, which extracts the traffic of P2P-related applications, such as artificial intelligence, application software, entertainment terminals, and basic services, and then uses the Bayes method for detection. This method has Higher detection accuracy. Literature [25] proposed a detection algorithm based on the concept of random walk statistics. The feature of the algorithm is to target unstructured P2P botnets and use graph data in real-world scenarios for detection. The evaluation results show that better detection accuracy can be obtained. However, for the network robot targets below 5%, the detection effect needs to be studied. GetoarGallopeni et al. [26] proposed a traffic analysis method based on DNS attacks and Mirai. Its main feature is to capture characteristic traffic for analysis while performing simulated attacks. Although this method has better proactive defensive detection, it has better performance in experiments. Indoor hardware testing environment requirements are high, and social applicability needs to be further confirmed. S. Chen et al. [27] used feedforward artificial neural networks to extract effective traffic convolution from the target network, which can effectively identify botnets. Although this method has a certain accuracy, the confidence level needs to be further improved. In the literature [28], scholars analyzed the transmission path of botnets through TCP/HTTP protocol, confirmed the connection characteristics based on TCP, and proposed a technology based on traffic behavior to detect botnets, because robots in the target network The nature of the difference is not suitable for feature-based detection. There are also scholars [29] using statistical learning methods, using a lightweight logistic regression model to identify the characteristics of the botnet traffic, and then confirm it through the Bro network monitoring framework, and classify malicious and benign traffic. In the literature [27, 30], a test method and system based on convolutional network are proposed, which is characterized by collecting, merging, and measuring data flow in a flow counter, which has good accuracy. In actual production and life, network operators, in order to be able to respond well to the threats and destruction brought by botnets, have deployed targeted solutions [31]. Existing solutions based on intrusion detection mainly use active detection methods to trigger targeted defense actions. Based on intrusion detection technology, it relies on various technologies to detect botnets, including request recognition [33], statistical recognition and entropy detection. The characteristics of these methods are all based on collecting botnet traffic characteristics to define them the behavior of. Due to their different development environments, the existing test technology has a challenging task, which is the reliability of operation in actual scenarios. Therefore, designing an intrusion detection method model for Internet service providers will provide adequate protection for end users and the underlying network, and can adapt to frequent changes. More accurate and effective botnet detection methods and mechanisms are of great significance for Internet service providers to reduce the harm of botnets to basic networks, improve service efficiency, protect the interests of end users, and enhance corporate competitiveness.

3 Model

Based on the characteristics of mini-batch gradient descent, this paper proposes an efficient optimization method SCBRNN, which uses a part of the sample to update the parameters in each iteration. Its advantage is that optimizing the neural network parameters of a part of the sample each time is not much slower than that of a single data, and using a part of the sample for each training can greatly reduce the number of iterations required for convergence, reduce the probability of gradient explosion, and perform effective convergence at the same time. To make the results more real and reliable, the relevant algorithms are shown in Table 1.

In Table 1, m represents the sample size, P is the sample collection amount, l and r are the sample collection boundaries, and g() and f() are the activation functions, thus showing the process of the bidirectional recurrent neural network based on small batch sample collection. The structure is shown in Fig. 1.

Table 1. SCBRNN Algorithm.

Heading level
1. Input layer X
2. Initialize the input layer data
3. While time node t has not ended
4. Computed hiding layer A and A′ with f()
5. If t < m * P
6. Take samples 1 to r(t + m * P)
7. Else if t > m − m * P
8. Take samples l(t − m * P) to m
9. Else
10. Take samples l(t − m * P) to r(t + m * P)
11. Calculate the target value Y with g()
12. Output layer Y
13. End

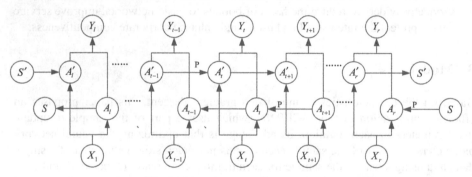

Fig. 1. Model structure of SCBRNN.

In Fig. 1, not every node has a connection between the hidden layers. For the node information at time t, part of the data before and after it will be collected instead of all of it. This is essentially different from the W in the model itself. Combining the recursive formula of the unidirectional cyclic neural network and the bidirectional cyclic neural network, adding the acquisition rate P, the information of the hidden layer is obtained as follows:

$$A_t = f(WPA_{t+1} + Ux_t) \tag{1}$$

$$A'_t = f(W'PA'_{t-1} + U'x_t) \tag{2}$$

Among them (1) is the A_t calculated by the forward input layer, and (2) is the A_t' calculated by the forward input layer. P and WA are the vector product, and the total data amount before and after the t node is collected is the data amount of P. In this way, the recurrence formula can be used to perform calculations based on part of the data, thereby increasing the fault tolerance rate and reducing the probability of gradient problems. The output formula (3) obtained by combining formulas (1) and (2) is:

$$Y_t = g(Vf(WPA_{t+1} + Ux_t) + V'f(W'PA'_{t-1} + U'x_t)) \tag{3}$$

Incorporating formulas (1) and (2) into (3) for continuous iteration, the sample collection formula (4) for the previous sequence of the t node is:

$$LA' = V'f(W'P(\ldots f(W'PA_{t-1+1}\ldots Ux_{t-1})) + U'x_t) \tag{4}$$

The sample collection formula (5) for the subsequent sequence of the t node is:

$$RA = Vf(WP(\ldots f(WPA_{t+r-1}\ldots Ux_{t+1})) + Ux_t) \tag{5}$$

4 Model Training

Select the network traffic data set for training. The data set spans three months and involves 10 local workstation IPs. According to the improved model, we will combine the data set and use RNN, BNRR and SCBRNN according to the changes in the data collection rate to determine whether the 10 local workstation IPs have been invaded and become members of the botnet. Existing research has collected data characteristics in the tuple of network information flow for identification, which is composed of interface index, source IP address, destination IP address, source port number, destination port number, and protocol number. The device performs network information flow statistics on past data packets according to the tuple information. However, in order to make better use of the time dynamic information of network traffic, this article does not care about the internal load information of network traffic, nor does it involve the privacy of network traffic. In this way, on the basis of improving security, the data characteristics are collected on the remote ASN (integer that identifies the remote ISP) and traffic (the number of connections in a day). The data set collected this time is based on network data traffic using ten different IP addresses in the past three months. The compiled data information statistics are shown in Table 2.

Table 2. Network data traffic statistics under different IP.

IP	Count	IP	Count
0	3980	5	1249
1	2159	6	1305
2	2416	7	2233
3	1186	8	2230
4	1308	9	2737

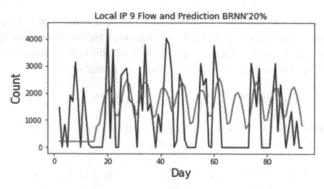

Fig. 2. Network traffic value of IP 9 predicted by SCBRNN.

It can be seen from Table 2 that in order to make more objective predictions and training, a total of 20,802 pieces of data have been prepared, and each piece of data contains Date information, that is, the time of data collection, which ensures the objectivity of the data. It also contains the IP number. For better data analysis, the IP address has been converted into a number. The ISP in the data bar is used to remotely identify the number of remote ASNs, and Stream is used to mark the IP at a specific time. How many network traffic connections have been made, these two data information we will use as the data characteristics of the information. Use Python's pandas library to perform statistics on the data and fill in the default values in the data information. The results of SCBRNN are shown in Fig. 2.

In Fig. 2, the sampling rate of SCBRNN is 20%. It can be seen that this method inherits the advantages of the two-way cyclic neural network, fully expresses the fluctuation trend of the data, and combines the characteristics of some data before and after each time. But not all. The data can better represent the data near the peak and more accurately predict the exact value of the network data flow.

5 Result Analysis

In order to test the accuracy of the model method, ApEn (Approximate Entropy) is introduced to evaluate the performance of the model. Approximate entropy is a nonlinear dynamic parameter used to quantify the regularity and unpredictability of time series fluctuations. The more complex the time series, the greater the approximate entropy. Approximate entropy has strong anti-interference ability. If the data contains abnormal values, ApEn can be compared with the abnormal level to determine the degree of expression of the true information in the original data. Taking IP6 as an example, the approximate entropy calculation process of setting the N-dimensional time series according to the statistical data is u(1), u(2) . . . u(N).

Define algorithm related parameters m, r, where m is an integer, which represents the length of the comparison vector, m in this article is the interval of days, which is 2, and r is a real number, which represents the measure of "similarity", in general, r = 0.2* std, where std is the standard deviation of the sample, r = 150 in this article.

Then, the approximate entropy can be expressed as shown in the following formula (6).

$$\text{ApEn} = \Phi^m(r) - \Phi^{m+1}(r) \tag{6}$$

Combined with the keras and numpy libraries in Python, the approximate entropy time changes of IP6 in cyclic neural algorithms are shown in Fig. 3.

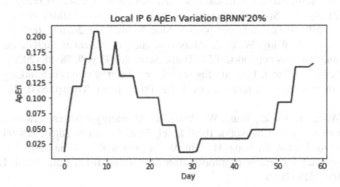

Fig. 3. Time trend of ApEn with IP 6 based on the predicted values of three algorithms.

It can be seen from Fig. 3 that in the approximate entropy calculation process, the vector that meets the condition will be extracted when the vector is reconstructed. Therefore, only 60 vectors are extracted in the ApEn timing diagram. On the whole, it can be found that the ApEn of the LocalIP6 host is relatively large, exceeding the level of 0.1, indicating that the statistical data has a large abnormal fluctuation during the model training process, indicating that it has been hacked. And become a member of the botnet.

6 Conclusion

This paper proposes a botnet detection method based on deep learning. From the perspective of small batch gradient sample collection, the two-way neural network model is optimized, and the approximate entropy method is used to judge data anomalies, thereby effectively detecting botnets. Research data shows that the model has good performance and can identify botnets more accurately. Compared with traditional model methods, this model method can learn the characteristics of botnet traffic more comprehensively and efficiently. When the small batch sampling range is reduced, the accuracy of botnet detection is significantly improved. The ability to detect unknown botnets can effectively solve the problem of accurate identification of botnets by Internet service providers, improve the quality of service security, and enhance the core competitiveness of enterprises.

Acknowledgment. This work is partly supported by Jiangsu technology project of Housing and Urban-Rural Development (No. 2019ZD041).

References

1. Zhang, K., Chen, L., An, Y., et al.: A QoE test system for vehicular voice cloud services. Mob. Netw. Appl. **26**, 700–715 (2019)
2. Chen, L., Jiang, D., Bao, R., Xiong, J., Liu, F., Bei, L.: MIMO scheduling effectiveness analysis for bursty data service from view of QoE. Chin. J. Electron. **26**(5), 1079–1085 (2017)
3. Chen, L., et al.: A lightweight end-side user experience data collection system for quality evaluation of multimedia communications. IEEE Access **6**(1), 15408–15419 (2018)
4. Chen, L., Zhang, L.: Spectral efficiency analysis for massive MIMO system under QoS constraint: an effective capacity perspective. Mob. Netw. Appl. **26**, 691–699 (2020)
5. Jiang, D., Wang, Z., Wang, W., et al.: AI-assisted energy-efficient and intelligent routing for reconfigurable wireless networks. IEEE Trans. Netw. Sci. Eng. **9**, 78–88 (2020)
6. Jiang, D., Huo, L., Zhang, P., et al.: Energy-efficient heterogeneous networking for electric vehicles networks in smart future cities. IEEE Trans. Intell. Transp. Syst. **22**, 1868–1880 (2020)
7. Jiang, D., Wang, Y., Lv, Z., Wang, W., Wang, H.: An energy-efficient networking approach in cloud services for IIoT networks. IEEE J. Sel. Areas Commun. **38**(5), 928–941 (2020)
8. Jiang, D., Huo, L., Lv, Z., Song, H., Qin, W.: A joint multi-criteria utility-based network selection approach for vehicle-to-infrastructure networking. IEEE Trans. Intell. Transp. Syst. **19**(10), 3305–3319 (2018)
9. Mohammadian, M.: Network security risk assessment using intelligent agents. In: 2018 International Symposium on Agent, Multi-Agent Systems and Robotics (ISAMSR), Putrajaya, pp. 1–6 (2018)
10. Huang, K., Yang, L., Fu, R., Zhou, S., Hong, Z.: HASN: a hierarchical attack surface network for system security analysis. China Commun. **16**(5), 137–157 (2019)
11. Vormayr, G., Zseby, T., Fabini, J.: Botnet communication patterns. IEEE Commun. Surv. Tutor. **19**(4), 2768–2796 (2017)
12. Shafi, Q., Basit, A.: DDoS botnet prevention using blockchain in software defined internet of things. In: 2019 16th International Bhurban Conference on Applied Sciences and Technology (IBCAST), Islamabad, Pakistan, pp. 624–628 (2019)
13. Li, W., Jin, J., Lee, J.: Analysis of Botnet domain names for IoT cybersecurity. IEEE Access **7**, 94658–94665 (2019)
14. Jiang, D., Wang, Z., Huo, L., et al.: A performance measurement and analysis method for software-defined networking of IoV. IEEE Trans. Intell. Transp. Syst. **22**, 3707–3719 (2020)
15. Jiang, D., Wang, W., Shi, L., Song, H.: A compressive sensing-based approach to end-to-end network traffic reconstruction. IEEE Trans. Netw. Sci. Eng. **7**(1), 507–519 (2020)
16. Yang, B., Bao, W., Huang, D.-S.: Inference of large-scale time-delayed gene regulatory network with parallel MapReduce cloud platform. Sci. Rep. **8**(1), 1–11 (2018). https://doi.org/10.1038/s41598-018-36180-y
17. Yang, B., Bao, W.: Complex-valued ordinary differential equation modeling for time series identification. IEEE Access **7**(1), 41033–41042 (2019)
18. Jiang, D., Huo, L., Song, H.: Rethinking behaviors and activities of base stations in mobile cellular networks based on big data analysis. IEEE Trans. Netw. Sci. Eng. **7**(1), 80–90 (2020)
19. Jiang, D., Wang, Y., Lv, Z., Qi, S., Singh, S.: Big data analysis based network behavior insight of cellular networks for industry 4.0 applications. IEEE Trans. Ind. Inform. **16**(2), 1310–1320 (2020)
20. Yang, B., Wang, G., Bao, W.: CSE: complex-valued system with evolutionary algorithm. IEEE Access **7**(1), 90268–90276 (2019)
21. Ghafir, I., et al.: BotDet: a system for real time botnet command and control traffic detection. IEEE Access **6**, 38947–38958 (2018)

22. Qiu, Z., Miller, D.J., Kesidis, G.: Flow based botnet detection through semi-supervised active learning. In: 2017 IEEE International Conference on Acoustics, Speech and Signal Processing (ICASSP), New Orleans, LA, pp. 2387–2391 (2017)
23. Mai, L., Park, M.: A comparison of clustering algorithms for botnet detection based on network flow. In: 2016 Eighth International Conference on Ubiquitous and Future Networks (ICUFN), Vienna, pp. 667–669 (2016)
24. Dhayal, H., Kumar, J.: Botnet and P2P botnet detection strategies: a review. In: 2018 International Conference on Communication and Signal Processing (ICCSP), Chennai, pp. 1077–1082 (2018)
25. Muhs, D., Haas, S., Strufe, T., Fischer, M.: On the robustness of random walk algorithms for the detection of unstructured P2P botnets. In: 2018 11th International Conference on IT Security Incident Management & IT Forensics (IMF), Hamburg, pp. 3–14 (2018)
26. Gallopeni, G., Rodrigues, B., Franco, M., Stiller, B.: A practical analysis on Mirai Botnet traffic. In: 2020 IFIP Networking Conference (Networking), Paris, France, pp. 667–668 (2020)
27. Chen, S., Chen, Y., Tzeng, W.: Effective botnet detection through neural networks on convolutional features. In: IEEE International Conference on Trust, Security and Privacy in Computing and Communications/12th IEEE International Conference on Big Data Science and Engineering (TrustCom/BigDataSE), pp. 372–378 (2018)
28. Kapre, A., Padmavathi, B.: Behaviour based botnet detection with traffic analysis and flow interavals using PSO and SVM. In: International Conference on Intelligent Computing and Control Systems (ICICCS), pp. 718–722 (2017)
29. Bapat, R., et al.: Identifying malicious botnet traffic using logistic regression. In: Systems and Information Engineering Design Symposium (SIEDS), pp. 266–271 (2018)
30. Kant, V., Singh, E.M., Ojha, N.: An efficient flow based botnet classification using convolution neural network. In: International Conference on Intelligent Computing and Control Systems (ICICCS), pp. 941–946 (2017)
31. Garg, S., Sharma, R.M.: Anatomy of botnet on application layer: mechanism and mitigation. In: International Conference for Convergence in Technology (I2CT), pp. 1024–1029 (2017)

Big Data

3 Big Data

A Video Parallel Retrieval Method Based on Deep Hash

Jiayi Li[1], Lulu Bei[2(✉)], Dan Li[2], Ping Cui[2], and Kai Huang[3]

[1] Transportation, Shenyang Aerospace University, Shenyang 110136, China
[2] School of Information and Electrical Engineering, Xuzhou Institute of Technology, Xuzhou, China
[3] JiangSu XCMG Information Technology Co., LTD., Xuzhou 221008, China

Abstract. This paper designs a parallel video retrieval based on Spark and deep hash. The method comprises deep feature extraction using a convolution neural network based on partial semantic weighted aggregation; filtering features of image information in deep networks; the extraction and distributed storage of video summary keys; the establishment of distributed product quantitative hash coding model of image, realizing the distributed coding compression of high-dimensional features. The video parallel retrieval method proposed in this design has the advantages of high retrieval accuracy and good retrieval efficiency.

Keywords: Deep hash · Convolution neural network · High precision

1 Introduction

In terms of video image feature extraction, content-based video retrieval initially mainly manually extracted features through subjective judgment for specific scenes, such as texture, edge, shape, and color features, which is easy to lead to incomplete image feature extraction [1–5]. The emergence of convolution neural networks (Convolution Neural Networks,CNN) provides an implicit automatic image feature extraction scheme for learning. The CNN-based depth feature can not only retain more image detail information, but also perform traditional features in terms of image feature representation. In recent CNN-based video retrieval studies [6–9]. The VGG model has deep network layers and good versatility, but the number of training features is very large, and more noise features are independent of the image information. Therefore, it is necessary to suppress the background noise in the deep feature extraction part and highlight the effective discrimination part, so as to extract the more effective depth feature information [10–14].

To improve the accuracy of video retrieval, the extracted video key-frame image features need to retain more image information. Thus its features tend to include higher dimensions such as the CNN model extracted by VGG-16 based deep features of 4096 dimensions and large feature dimensions also reduce the efficiency of feature storage and retrieval [15–19]. Therefore, the coding compression of the high-dimensional characteristic vector is achieved by using the hash coding method, thus saving the storage

D. Jiang and H. Song (Eds.): SIMUtools 2021, LNICST 424, pp. 135–141, 2022.
https://doi.org/10.1007/978-3-030-97124-3_12

space and improving the computational efficiency [20–24]. However, these studies are generally in a single-machine environment, and for distributed storage scenarios, we still need to first concentrate all the data on a single node for coding model training, bringing higher data calculation and storage pressure. Therefore, it is urgently necessary to adapt to the video image distributed storage environment for distributed hash coding model training, so as to optimize the process of hash model training and computational storage [25–29].

In order to solve the above existing technical problems and improve the accuracy and efficiency of video retrieval. A deep hash-based parallel video retrieval method is proposed, combined with the characteristics of large-scale video retrieval.

2 System Design

The method of video parallel retrieval based on deep hash, the overall architecture schematic diagram is shown in Fig. 1, mainly includes 2 parts:

(1) Video depth feature extraction of frame image based on CNN: extract the original video data set to obtain video summary data set; conduct weighted aggregation based on VGG network and PWA model, screen and form deep feature extraction model; and generate image depth feature set based on the trained model.
(2) Video key-image feature quantification based on distributed hash: the training set is divided according to the video summary image depth feature set, and the distributed hash coding model is trained; the image is generated according to the coding model; the coding search according to the coding model to improve the efficiency of searching.

3 Specific Implementation Plan

3.1 Deep Feature Extraction of Video Key-Images

First, the video summary image is extracted by the key-frame, and then the deep convolution feature set through the convolution neural network VGG16 network model, and then select the partial semantic based weighted aggregation method PWA to obtain the final feature vector. The feature screening process utilizes an unsupervised strategy to select a partial convolution layer filter to generate a probabilistic weight scheme, and obtains the final feature representation by aggregating the weighted region representation corresponding to each semantic content.

As shown in Fig. 2, the video key-image depth feature extraction process is as follows:

(1) For the input query image I, first pass to the restrained deep network VGG-16 model to extract deep convolution layer features f (consisting of C channel feature maps, each with height H and width W). The image is represented by N a filtered partial detector weighted aggregate, which is a vector representation in $N * C$ dimensions.

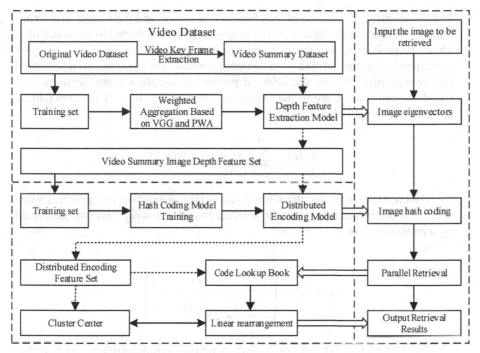

Fig. 1. Schematic drawing of the overall architecture

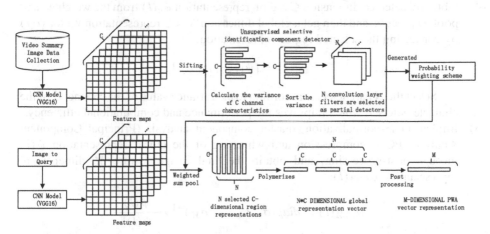

Fig. 2. Diagrammatic of depth feature extraction process of video frame image

(2) The selection of partial discriminant detectors is trained based on the video key-image feature data-set, and the feature graph channels with larger differences are selected. Therefore, screened by calculating the variance of each channel feature, the C channel variance of the C dimension vector $V = \{v_1, v_2, ..., v_c, ..., v_C\}$:

$$V = \frac{1}{D} \sum_{i=1}^{D} (g_i - \overline{g})^2$$

(3) The variance $\{v_1, v_2, ..., v_C\}$ of the channel C is sorted, and the former N discriminant convolution layer filter with the largest variance is selected as some detector. Then, the probability weight scheme is generated via unsupervised policies, each corresponding to the implied fixed semantic content. The construction represented by the weighted PWA of the selected probability weight scheme begins with a weighted sum set of dimensional depth convolution $C \times W \times H$ features f of an image I with height H and width W:

$$\psi_n(I) = \sum_{x=1}^{W} \sum_{y=1}^{H} w_n(x, y) f(x, y)$$

The coefficients w_n are the normalized weight, depending on the active value $v_n(x, y)$ in the position (x, y) of the selected probability weight scheme generated by a partial detector n:

$$w_n(x, y) = \left(\frac{v_n(x, y)}{(\sum_{x=1}^{W} \sum_{y=1}^{H} v_n(x, y)^\alpha)^{1/\alpha}} \right)^{1/\beta}$$

The sum of and are the parameters of power normalization α and β power scaling, respectively.

(4) Obtain N selected dimension C region representation $\psi_n(I)$ from the weighted and pooling process, and then get a global dimension $N \times C$ representation vector $\psi(I)$ by connecting the selected region representation:

$$\psi(I) = [\psi_1, \psi_2, ..., \psi_N]$$

Select the N part detector according to the variance value of the channel C of the characteristic set, which improves the performance and computational efficiency.

(5) Implement l_2-normalization, master component analysis (Principal Component Analysis, PCA) compression and whitening of the global representation $\psi(I)$ through post-processing, and obtain the final image feature M dimensional representation $\psi_{PWA}(I)$:

$$\psi_{PWA}(I) = diag(\sigma_1, \sigma_2, \ldots, \sigma_M)^{-1} V \frac{\psi(I)}{\|\psi(I)\|_2}$$

Where V is the PCA matrix of size $M \times N$, M is the number of reserved dimensions, $\sigma_1, \sigma_2, \ldots, \sigma_M$ is the associated singular value.

3.2 Distributed Hash Encoding Model

Distributed feature encoding model training is a hash product quantization coding for the image feature set output by a convolution neural network and achieves fast retrieval of an arbitrary image query via distributed coding storage. First, hash coding learning on

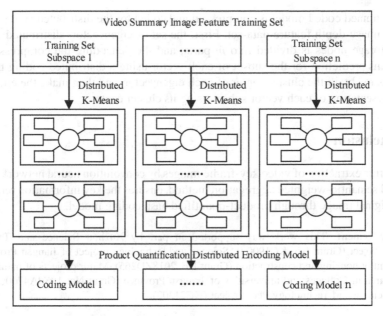

Fig. 3. Schematic of distributed hash coding model

the training data-set to obtain the feature coding model; then the trained coding model is applied to the original video key-image feature data-set to realize its compression coding representation and data distributed storage.

As shown in Fig. 3, the video key-image feature quantification process based on distributed hash is as follows:

(1) The distributed computing process in the Spark platform distributed stores the summary image feature data-set in the data store RDD, divided into multiple partitions on different nodes in the cluster.

(2) For a summary image feature data-set X of one dimension p. Data distributed stored on m computing nodes and thus divided into m subsets $X = [X_1, \ldots, X_m]$.

(3) K-Means clustering for each subset. Each subset contains n cluster centers. Total $m \times n$ distributed matrix is required for storage. The encoding matrix is represented by the $B = [B_1, B_2, \ldots, B_S]$. According to the characteristics of distributed data, the target function of distributed product quantification is:

$$\ell_{PQ} = \min \sum_{t=1}^{S} \left\| X_t - \begin{bmatrix} C^1 B_t^1 \\ \ldots \\ C^m B_t^m \end{bmatrix} \right\|_F^2$$

$$= \min \sum_{t=1}^{S} \left\| \begin{matrix} X_t^1 - C^1 B_i^1 \\ \ldots \\ X_t^m - C^m B_i^m \end{matrix} \right\|_F^2$$

(4) The trained coded model is compressed and coded for the distributed stored video key-image depth feature data-set. First, the set of eigenvectors distributed on the m storage nodes is divided into m parts, and then encoding the compressed K-Means prediction for the subset of each vector using a distributed coding model, so as to obtain the cluster center of each eigenvector, and then make the encoding representation of each vector subset using its cluster center.

4   Conclusion

Deep feature extraction of video key-frame images by convolution neural network based on partial semantic-weighted aggregation method, ensures the key information retention of the original image through product-quantified hash coding model.

Acknowledgement. This work was supported in part by Xuzhou Science and Technology Plan Project (Grant No. KC19003). Science and technology project of Jiangsu Provincial Department of housing and construction (Grant No. 2018ZD265). Major projects of natural science research in Colleges and universities of Jiangsu Province (Grant No. 19KJA470002) and Xuzhou Science and Technology Plan Project (KC21303).

References

1. Xiong, S., Lei, M., Liu, C.: Batch Images parallel retrieval based on deep hashing. J. Chongqing Univ. Technol. (Nat. Sci.) (2018)
2. Jiang, Y., Zhuo, J., Zhang, J., et al.: The optimization of parallel convolutional RBM based on spark. Int. J. Wavelets Multiresolut. Inf. Process. (2018)
3. Mou, F.U., Yang, H., Tangmei, W.U., et al.: Fast video transcoding method based on spark streaming. J. Comput. Appl. **38**, 3500 (2018)
4. Qin, J., Chen, J., Xiang, X., et al.: A privacy-preserving image retrieval method based on deep learning and adaptive weighted fusion. J. Real-Time Image Process. **17**(1), 161–173 (2020)
5. Dong, Y., Li, J.: Video retrieval based on deep convolutional neural network (2017)
6. Wan, L., Zhang, G., Li, H., et al.: A novel bearing fault diagnosis method using spark-based parallel ACO-K-means clustering algorithm. IEEE Access **PP**(99), 1 (2021)
7. Shi, L., Liu, S., Shi, Y., et al.: Sea ice concentration products over polar regions with Chinese FY3C/MWRI Data (2021)
8. Liu, P., Ye, S., Wang, C., et al.: Spark-based parallel genetic algorithm for simulating a solution of optimal deployment of an underwater sensor network. Sensors **19**(12), 2717–2727 (2019)
9. Langer, M., Hall, A., He, Z., et al.: MPCA SGD—a method for distributed training of deep learning models on spark. IEEE Trans. Parallel Distrib. Syst. **29**, 2540–2556 (2018)
10. Hou, J., Sheng, W.U., Yingna, L.I.: Research on parallel K-means clustering model based on spark. Comput. Digit. Eng. (2018)
11. Qin, J., Li, H., Xiang, X., et al.: An encrypted image retrieval method based on Harris corner optimization and LSH in cloud computing. IEEE Access **7**, 24626–24633 (2019)
12. Cao, Y., Wang, N., Xu, Z., et al.: Network big data classification processing method based on Spark and distributed KNN classifier. Appl. Res. Comput. (2019)
13. Deng, Q., Yang, N.: Research of improved parallel K-means algorithm based on spark framework. Intell. Comput. Appl. **8**, 76–78 (2018)

14. Jing, W., Zhang, D., Song, H.: An application of ternary hash retrieval method for remote sensing images in panoramic video. IEEE Access **8**, 140822–140830 (2020)
15. Wang, Y., Nie, X., Shi, Y., et al.: Attention-based video hashing for large-scale video retrieval. IEEE Trans. Cogn. Dev. Syst. **PP**(99), 1 (2019)
16. Hajkacem, M., N'Cir, C., Essoussi, N.: A parallel text clustering method using Spark and hashing. Computing (6) (2021)
17. Gupta, A., Thakur, H., Shrivastava, R., et al.: A big data analysis framework using apache spark and deep learning. In: IEEE International Conference on Data Mining Workshops (2017)
18. Lunga, D., Gerrand, J., Yang, L., et al.: Apache spark accelerated deep learning inference for large scale satellite image analytics. IEEE J. Sel. Top. Appl. Earth Observ. Remote Sens. **13**, 271–283 (2020)
19. Khan, S., Liu, X., Alam, M.: A spark ML driven preprocessing approach for deep learning based scholarly data applications (2019)
20. Uddin, M.A., Joolee, J.B., Sohn, K.A.: Dynamic facial expression understanding using deep spatiotemporal LDSP on spark. IEEE Access **PP**(99), 1 (2021)
21. Yang, F., Wang, H., Fu, J.: Improvement of recommendation algorithm based on collaborative deep learning and its parallelization on spark. J. Parallel Distrib. Comput. **148**(2), 58–68 (2021)
22. Zaouk, K., Song, F., Lyu, C., et al.: Neural-based modeling for performance tuning of spark data analytics (2021)
23. Takam, C.A., Samba, O., Kouanou, A.T., et al.: Spark architecture for deep learning-based dose optimization in medical imaging. Inform. Med. Unlocked **19**, 100335 (2020)
24. Sundareswaran, A., Lavanya, K.: Real-time vehicle traffic prediction in apache spark using ensemble learning for deep neural networks. Int. J. Intell. Inf. Technol. (IJIIT) **16**, 19–36 (2020)
25. Khan, S., Khan, M., Iqbal, N., et al.: Spark based parallel deep neural network model for classification of large scale RNAs into piRNAs and non-piRNAs. IEEE Access **PP**(99), 1 (2020)
26. Singh, P., Singh, S., Mishra, P.K., et al.: A data structure perspective to the RDD-based Apriori algorithm on spark. SSRN Electron. J. (2019)
27. Wang, L., Chen, C., Yun, S.U.: Design and implementation of massive ship density distribution calculation system based on spark. Ship Electron. Eng. (2019)
28. Lunga, D., Gerrand, J., Yang, H.L., et al.: Apache spark accelerated deep learning inference for large scale satellite image analytics (2019)
29. Shmeis, Z., Jaber, M.: A rewrite-based optimizer for spark. Future Gener. Comput. Syst. **98**, 586–599 (2019)

Cosmetics Sales Data Classification Method of Japanese Cross-Border E-Commerce Platform Based on Big Data

Jingxian Huang$^{(\boxtimes)}$

Guizhou Minzu University, Guiyang 550025, Guizhou, China

Abstract. Data analysis is playing an increasingly important role in the cross-border e-commerce platform in the cosmetics industry. Therefore, this paper proposes a cosmetics sales data classification method for the Japanese cross-border e-commerce platform based on big data. Taking the cosmetics sales data on the Japanese cross-border e-commerce platform as the research object, the development model of Japanese cross-border e-commerce and the connotation of cosmetics are expounded. Take targeted methods and measures; extract consumer purchase behavior characteristics on Japanese cross-border e-commerce platform, conduct in-depth analysis of customer relationship from three aspects: customer analysis, sales analysis and e-commerce platform analysis, and guide the behavior of maintaining customer relationship; Big data technology is used to predict the sales potential of cosmetics, determine the output according to the actual sales volume, and design the sales data classification model according to the characteristics of the data samples. Experimental results have classify the sales data, it is of great significance to the cosmetics sales of the e-commerce platform.

Keywords: Big data · Japanese cross-border e-commerce platform · Cosmetics sales · Data classification · Consumer · Sales potential

1 Introduction

The essence of cross-border e-commerce is an international business activity [1, 2]. The buyers and sellers of the transaction subjects come from different customs territories and complete the online communication, payment and other links of normal e-commerce activities through a common e-commerce platform. The difference is that the logistics links are carried out cross-border by international logistics companies. This is a very popular e-commerce model in modern society [3, 4]. Cross border e-commerce includes four elements: commodity logistics, enterprise talents, trading platform and commodity warehousing [5]. These four elements determine the advantages and disadvantages of the development of cross-border e-commerce enterprises. In Japan, cross-border e-commerce really began in the second half of the 1990s, and Lotte market began to operate in 1997. Three years later, Yahoo shopping was born. In 2000, Amazon began selling books in Japan and opened a cross-border E-commerce mall the next year. Due to the rise

© ICST Institute for Computer Sciences, Social Informatics and Telecommunications Engineering 2022
Published by Springer Nature Switzerland AG 2022. All Rights Reserved
D. Jiang and H. Song (Eds.): SIMUtools 2021, LNICST 424, pp. 142–153, 2022.
https://doi.org/10.1007/978-3-030-97124-3_13

of cloud services that can build the company's cross-border e-commerce website at a low price, and the cross-border e-commerce market exceeded 5 trillion yen in 2005. During the first growth period (2001–2005), with the increase of cross-border e-commerce website users year by year, there were many consumer problems, such as operational errors. In order to solve this dispute, the electronic consumer contract was implemented in 2001. Amazon Japan began to sell in the form of "Amazon market plays". In the second growth period (2007–2009), in 2008, Amazon, a cross-border e-commerce enterprise exhibited on Amazon market plays, began to provide services from commodity custody to distribution function entrustment. In addition, in 2009 the next year, Amazon began to provide the same day delivery service, and Lotte market also began to provide the next day delivery service "easy tomorrow'. Because of the cooperation between the two large companies, cross-border e-commerce has entered the era of service competition, that is, "you can shop easily and deliver goods quickly". In the third growth period (2010 - present), in 2010, the so-called flash marketing coupon websites that can discount in joint purchase appeared one after another. First, in Japan's cross-border e-commerce enterprises, although there are constraints such as language but also a growth field, which may become the driving force of Japan's economic activation. The proportion of Japan (6%) is lower than that of the United States and China. On the other hand, compared with imported goods, Japan has a low sense of presence in purchasing cross-border e-commerce. The proportion of cross-border e-commerce buyers among online buyers in Japan is 5%. Compared with other major countries, all levels are low, and there is no progress in the use of cross-border e-commerce at the time of import. Second, the reason why Japanese users do not conduct cross-border e-commerce is that "it is enough on their own cross-border e-commerce websites", and half of the netizens are very satisfied on Japan's domestic websites. The second reason is the language barrier of "foreign language is very hard", the third reason is the worry of "return is very troublesome or return freight is relatively expensive", and the fourth reason is the speed of arrival of goods "because of the need for delivery date table" and "because of distrust of overseas cross-border e-commerce websites" This sense of distrust leads to a distance. At present, the academic research data on classifying big data technology and cosmetics sales data of Japan's cross-border e-commerce platform are not very rich.

Some scholars on e-commerce platform cosmetics sales data analysis method, document [6] in order to obtain micro consumer characteristics, based on marketing data, put forward a more micro sales data analysis, using K-means store classification and feature extraction, verify the relationship between the sales characteristics and actual sales, and on this basis, carried out the precise distribution recommended for retail stores.

Based on the above research literature, this paper proposes a cosmetics sales data classification method for the Japanese cross-border e-commerce platform based on big data.

2 Overview of Cross Border E-Commerce and Cosmetics in Japan

2.1 Development Mode of Cross-Border E-Commerce in Japan

In Japan, cross-border e-commerce is a commercial transaction between enterprises, families, individuals, the government and other public or private institutions. Its main forms are roughly divided into six types [7]. This form has the longest history and the largest transaction volume is inter enterprise transaction (B2B). B2B is widely used with the development of EDI and Internet. In addition to using EDI for orders, there are also enterprises that create shopping corners in their own company's websites and use B2B dedicated cross-border e-commerce websites. After B2B, the largest transaction volume is the computer of Japanese cosmetics enterprises and consumers (B2C). The transaction volume of B2C has also increased year by year. Consumers purchase goods and services on cross-border e-commerce websites, and the official website purchase of enterprises is also included in B2C. As other forms, consumers and governments also become suppliers. There are two forms of cross-border e-commerce in which consumers become suppliers: inter consumer transaction (C2C) and consumer to enterprise transaction (C2B). C2C refers to transactions between individuals, and C2B refers to transactions between individuals and enterprises, including transactions in which individuals accept translation work as freelancers. The forms in which the Japanese government becomes the supplier are also divided into government to enterprise transaction (G2B) and government to consumer transaction (G2C). Both refer to the government's services on the Internet and the electronic application of various applications. There are many advantages for Japanese cosmetics enterprises to engage in cross-border e-commerce, but the biggest advantage is that it is easier and cheaper to sell to a wide range of customers than ever before. If there is information about goods and services on the e-commerce platform and the environment for accepting orders is good, cross-border e-commerce will be established. In order to sell to overseas customers, sales can be carried out under different mechanisms from the past, such as local distribution of salespeople, establishment of sales bases and cooperation with agency stores, so as to greatly reduce the cost of developing new markets. Market Research and advertising can be carried out efficiently and at low cost. Based on the purchase records on cross-border e-commerce, the reading history of web pages, the flexible use of consumer action modes and other information, advertising is more efficient. The transaction volume of B2B in the world is more than 7 times that of B2C. However, 80% of enterprises with B2C growth rate exceeding b2bo replied that the development of B2C had an impact on the application of B2B cross-border e-commerce. Especially in the aspects of sales mode and consumers' way, B2C has a great impact on B2B.

2.2 Cosmetic Connotation

In today's era, cosmetics have become a necessity of people's daily life [8]. Cosmetics refer to daily chemical industrial products that are spread on any part of the human body surface (skin, hair, nails, lips, etc.) and decoration. According to the product classification standard. Cosmetics can be divided into skin care products, hair products, beauty products, cleaning products and other cosmetics [9, 10]. Product attribute refers to the collection of various characteristics of a product. It includes natural attributes and social attributes. Natural attributes mainly refer to the inherent properties and characteristics of products, such as product appearance, performance, etc. Social attributes refer to various characteristics formed after the product is integrated into the social category, such as brand characteristics. Brand identity is an important index to measure the online sales attraction of products. As far as cosmetics are concerned, their natural attributes include packaging and beautifying functions. Social attributes include the social recognition of its functions and the brand awareness of some cosmetics. From the natural attributes of products, the characteristics of small packaging volume and convenient storage and transportation of finished cosmetics are suitable for online sales. From the perspective of product social attributes, the use value of cosmetics is beauty, which can meet consumers' emotional needs. Selling cosmetics is not only a tangible product, but also an intangible service and the added value of a product. From the perspective of online sales, the sensory attraction of cosmetic functional effects and appearance characteristics to consumers is an important factor leading consumers to buy online. Generally speaking, products with visual impact are more conducive to online sales mode.

3   Cosmetics Sales Data Classification Method of Japanese Cross-Border E-Commerce Platform Based on Big Data

3.1   Extracting the Characteristics of Consumers' Purchase Behavior on Japanese Cross-Border E-Commerce Platforms

Due to the emergence of Japan's cross-border e-commerce platform, important changes are taking place in the consumption concept, consumption mode and consumer status of cosmetics audience, which makes contemporary consumer psychology present new characteristics and trends compared with the past. Only when enterprises and e-commerce platform vendors understand the demand characteristics of e-commerce platform consumers can they make better sales decisions [11–13]. In the past quite a long historical period, industry and Commerce served consumers as individual individuals. Only in modern times, the industrialization and standardized mode of production submerged the personality of consumers in the flood of a large number of low cost and unitary products. However, no consumer's psychology is exactly the same. Psychological identity has become a prerequisite for consumers to make purchase decisions, and personalized consumption is and will become the mainstream of consumption [14, 15]. It is not only the personalized consumption of consumers that makes the consumption needs of e-commerce platforms different. Different e-commerce platform consumers have different needs due to different times and environments, and different e-commerce platform consumers have different needs at the same demand level. Therefore, in order to succeed in e-commerce platform sales, we must seriously consider this difference and take targeted methods and measures according to the characteristics of different consumers. Product is anything that can be used to meet some human needs or desires. Modern marketing concept believes that enterprises should provide products centered on customer needs. Cosmetics enterprises should understand their expectations for e-commerce platform sales in order to meet the needs of consumers by using platform sales. Knowing which attributes of e-commerce platform sales can affect consumers' acceptance of this model requires understanding the types of e-commerce platform consumers, their e-commerce platform purchase motivation and demand characteristics. Consumer research shows that different historical and cultural environments, especially different media environments, breed consumer groups in different times. The rise of the Internet has created a third new media. The popularization of platform media has spawned a new third generation of consumers, also known as consumers in the era of e-commerce platform. The research on the purchase behavior of consumers on e-commerce platform is the basis for e-commerce platform sales enterprises to improve customer service. To understand the main categories of e-commerce platform consumers, we must first understand the main types of online population. The types of online population can be divided into: simple type, surfing type, access type, bargaining type, regular type and sports type. What simple customers need is convenient and direct online shopping. We must provide real convenience for this type of consumers and make them feel that selling through e-commerce platform can save more time. Surfers are interested in websites that are constantly updated and have innovative design features. Access Internet users are novices who have just come into contact with e-commerce platforms. They rarely shop. Companies with famous traditional brands should pay enough attention to this group of potential consumers, because novices on e-commerce platforms are more willing to trust the brands they are familiar with in life. Negotiators have an instinct to buy cheap goods, so the low price feature of e-commerce platform sales can attract such people. Regular and sports e-commerce platform users are usually attracted by the content of the website. At present, the challenge faced by e-commerce platform enterprises is how to attract more Internet users and strive to turn website visitors into consumers. Through the analysis and Research on the consumer categories of e-commerce platform, it can be found that shoppers' purchase motivation and purchase behavior are of great value to e-commerce platform enterprises to improve services [16, 17]. In fact, it is obvious that the three most attractive factors for consumers of e-commerce platforms are convenience, wide range of options and low price. The purchase motivation of e-commerce platform consumers refers to some internal driving forces that can make e-commerce platform consumers produce purchase behavior in the purchase activities of e-commerce platform. Motivation is an internal psychological state, which is not easy to be observed or measured directly, but it can be understood and summarized according to people's long-term behavior or self statement. For enterprises, by understanding consumers' motivation, they can explain and predict consumers' behavior and take corresponding promotion measures. For e-commerce platform sales, motivation research is more important. Because e-commerce platform sales is an invisible sales, the complex, multi-level, intertwined and changeable purchase behavior of e-commerce platform consumers can not be observed directly, but can only be imagined and experienced through text or language communication. The former refers to people's purchase motivation caused by various needs, including low-level and high-level needs, while the latter is caused by people's psychological processes such as cognition, emotion and will. From the perspective of consumers, price is not the only factor that determines consumers' purchase, but it is a very important factor that consumers must consider when buying goods. For general commodities, there is often an inverse relationship between price and demand. For the same commodities, the lower the price, the greater the sales volume. Because e-commerce platform sales can reduce the intermediate costs and some additional information costs required by traditional retail, and reduce product costs and sales costs, the commodity prices sold by e-commerce platforms are generally low. Based on this, the steps to extract the characteristics of consumers' purchase behavior on Japan's cross-border e-commerce platform.

3.2 Big Data Technology Predicts Cosmetics Sales Potential

Big data refers to data sets whose size exceeds the acquisition, storage, management and analysis capabilities of conventional database tools [18]. But it also emphasizes that it does not mean that data sets that exceed a specific TB value must be considered big data. At present, most cosmetic stores in the market regularly make sales reports and sales analysis, which are generally divided into classified sales data summary reports by week, month, quarter and year. Sales forecasting is one of the important functions of data mining. Sales forecast refers to the estimated sales amount and sales quantity of all or some products in the future. It is the core part of sales plan. Sales forecast affects all aspects of sales management, including plan, budget and sales, which is not directly related to the scale of the enterprise and the number of salespeople. Sales forecast is a sales target put forward through relatively reliable analysis method on the basis of fully considering various factors that may affect the actual situation of the enterprise. Through forecasting, enterprises can determine the output according to the sales volume, so as to arrange production and avoid inventory backlog.

For sales personnel, they can mobilize their enthusiasm to achieve sales goals as soon as possible, and actively manage customer relationship according to customer churn prediction. For cosmetics sales enterprises, it is necessary to timely adjust the corresponding product inventory guarantee under different situations or events and the number of on-site workers at the sales point through the prediction method to market demand. These

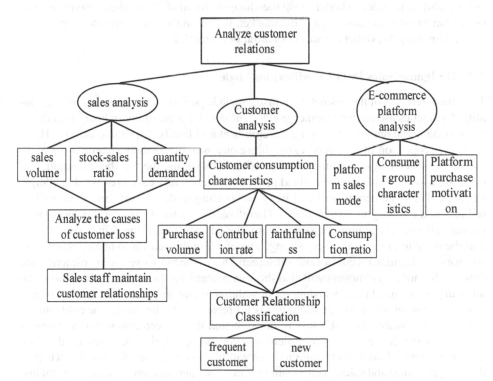

Fig. 1. The customer relationship data model.

information or knowledge may be hidden in a large number of original data and need to be extracted and analyzed by technology [19, 20]. The customer relationship data model. Are shown in Fig. 1:

As can be seen from Fig. 1, according to the cosmetics sales data, due to the relatively stable customer relationship, the purchase volume of old customers is far greater than that of new customers, reaching a contribution of more than 82%. After the background investigation of cosmetics, we found that the loyalty of old customers of high-end skin care series is higher. Their cultural level is relatively high, and they will not choose to buy skin care products aimlessly. Especially for the company's skin care projects, the proportion of re consumption of old customers is getting higher and higher. However, with the fierce competition and insufficient grasp of the market situation, the old customers of the cosmetics company also have a certain loss. According to the results, compare the completion of the scheduled plan and analyze the reasons for non completion. Predicting future sales, demand and so on through time series. Through sales analysis, you can understand the sales volume, sales inventory ratio, old customer contribution rate and other information. After subdividing the data, you can analyze the performance completion of salespeople. With the advent of the era of big data, the concept of cosmetics sales also needs to keep pace with the times. How to attract customers in the era of big data, accurately predict, predict inventory through big data marketing and maintain good customer relations have become the problems that some representative enterprises need to solve at present, and use big data to predict sales related situations to improve their coping ability, In order to better grasp the changing trend of the market, enterprises will better have customers and occupy the market. Based on this, complete the steps of big data technology to predict the sales potential of cosmetics.

3.3 Designing Sales Data Classification Mode

The characteristics of the cosmetics industry include periodicity, seasonality and regionality. Cosmetics are daily consumer goods. The development of the industry is in direct proportion to the national economic development and family disposable income. However, the proportion of residents' expenditure on cosmetics in their income is not high, so the periodicity of the industry is not obvious. In spring, the weather is humid, and there are a lot of dust and pollen mixed in the air, which is very easy to cause skin allergy. In particular, some people will feel itchy and peeling in this season, and there will be redness and swelling in serious cases. Therefore, the focus of skin care in spring is to prevent allergy. The summer weather is hot, the oil secretion of the skin is very strong, and the ultraviolet ray is also very strong. Therefore, in this season, skin care should pay attention to cleaning, oil control and sunscreen. Due to the extensive use of cosmetics, the demand for makeup removers will also show an upward trend this season. In autumn, the air is dry, so we need to replenishment. In addition to choosing some skin care products to replenishment, there will be more needs for replenishing the mask. The cold climate in winter accelerates the water loss of the skin, and the oil secretion is not as strong as that in summer. It is necessary to replenish water and appropriate nutrition for the skin. Seasonal commodities refer to commodities with obvious seasonal characteristics in production, purchase and sales, such as summer mats, winter supplements, agricultural and sideline products, etc. In order to ensure the normal supply of seasonal commodities in the market, enterprises generally purchase and reserve seasonal commodities in advance according to the characteristics of production and sales, and supply them to the market at an appropriate time. Although the seasonal sales characteristics of cosmetics are not as obvious as seasonal products, the sales volume of functional cosmetics will fluctuate with the seasons in different seasons. For example, lip balm and hand cream will be significantly higher in summer than in summer. Cosmetics sales are related to residents' income and consumption level. The market consumption in economically developed areas is relatively high, and that in eastern and coastal areas is higher than that in inland areas. The sales volume in the first tier and second tier areas is larger than that in other third tier and county-level areas. Women's demand potential for cosmetics is unlimited. Mastering customers' psychology and timely launching member services can not only promote secondary shopping, but also enhance customers' loyalty to products.

For consumers, buying directly from overseas manufacturers can ensure the quality of goods and can be bought cheaply. However, there are risks in the popularity of cross-border e-commerce. In cross-border e-commerce, because intermediary companies such as online stores are often used to circulate goods, goods may circulate in large quantities when manufacturers do not expect. As a result, there is also a price collapse in China. In addition, the system has not been improved. There may be urgent changes and restrictions in the future. In the case of cross-border goods trading, the way of "general trade" is usually adopted according to the inter enterprise transaction called B2B. As far as China's imports are concerned, trading companies and retail companies will enter the market before overseas sellers deliver goods to Chinese consumers. In contrast, "cross-border e-commerce" basically connects overseas sellers with domestic consumers in China. However, even for cross-border e-commerce with direct transactions, the cross-border movement of goods is the same as that of general trade. The difference between the two lies in the tax methods and procedures. When using cross-border e-commerce to import goods from overseas, there are two modes: "bonded zone mode" and "direct delivery mode". From the perspective of consumers, "direct delivery mode" is an international mail. The cycle from ordering to receiving goods is very long. The use of air transportation not only requires logistics costs, but also has problems such as difficult to accept after-sales service when there are problems with imitation products, defective products and other goods. In contrast, the "bonded area model" shortens the cycle from ordering to receiving goods, which can not only maintain the quality of goods, but also reduce the cost due to large-scale procurement and maritime use, which may be cheaper than the direct delivery model. For the original data to be analyzed, in order to determine whether the original variables are suitable for data analysis, we need to do the correlation analysis of variables. In the significance detection, the methods include double tail detection and single tail detection. The result of double tail detection is to compare whether there is significant difference between the two variables. Single tail detection is based on the size difference of variables when the directivity is known. In statistical analysis, the result of using double tail detection is more strict. Exponential smoothing method is a common method of time series analysis. It can be used to predict the medium and long-term development trend of a phenomenon. It is also one of the most frequently used prediction methods. The traditional full period average method makes equal use of all data and data from the past to the present, while the weighted moving average method gives greater weight to the recent data and data. The exponential smoothing method needs to weight the current actual observation value and the predicted smoothing value of the phenomenon, which is compatible with the advantages of the above two methods. The basic formula of exponential smoothing method is:

$$D = Qr + (1 - \varphi)_{r-1} \tag{1}$$

In formula (1), Q represents the time prediction value, r represents the actual measurement value, and φ represents the smoothing constant. According to the principle of exponential smoothing method, when the initial value of time is 1, formula (1) becomes the following form:

$$W = \alpha h + (1 - \varphi)_{\eta} \tag{2}$$

In formula (2), α represents predicted sales, h represents actual sales, φ represents smoothing constant, and η represents the number of multi class data samples. Multi classification problem is the most important branch in the field of data classification. It studies the data samples to be classified and extracts feature information to represent the data. In multi classification problems, category decision-making is a very important problem. It is the ultimate goal of classification problems. The quality of decision-making principles will directly affect the final classification efficiency. Decision function is a mathematical model that classifies the samples according to some characteristics of the data set through the analysis and research of the classified data. Then the data classification problem description is defined as:

$$L = \frac{1}{2}\left(l^{ij} \cdot k^{ij}\right) + \sum g_{ij} \tag{3}$$

In formula (3), l represents the numerical quantization result, k represents the minimum threshold, g represents the maximum threshold, and i, j represent the predicted and actual number of training samples of the objective function respectively. The most intuitive and commonly used method to solve the problem of unbalanced classification is to reduce the imbalance of data samples to be classified. Resampling methods include over sampling (up sampling) method and under sampling (down sampling) method. Oversampling method refers to increasing the number of minority training samples through certain principles. The initial oversampling method is simply to copy the minority training samples. This learning process sometimes leads to over learning, which is not significantly helpful to improve the classification accuracy of minority samples. Some improved methods choose to add some heuristic ideas to the sampling scheme and selectively expand some small class data samples. These methods have achieved satisfactory results in practical application. Under sampling method is to reduce the sample imbalance by reducing the number of multi class samples in unbalanced data samples. The commonly used methods to reduce multi class data samples include unilateral detection, large sample pruning, maximum (small) closed value processing, sample noise reduction, etc. Resampling method reduces the imbalance of training samples and improves the classification accuracy of small class data samples to a certain extent, but there are also some fatal problems, such as whether the new small class samples can fully characterize the characteristics of small class data without causing over learning, and whether the effective information can be retained in the process of multi class sample reduction. Based on this, complete the steps of designing sales data classification mode.

4   Comparative Experiments and Analysis

In order to verify whether the cosmetics sales data classification method of Japanese cross-border e-commerce platform can be actually applied, the test data selects 390M data in a Japanese cosmetics sales database of Japanese cross-border e-commerce platform and classifies it through the present method and document [6] method respectively.

The experiment doped the sales data and non-sales data, divided the overall data into 40 categories, 20 copies of the sales data and non-sales data, using two methods, and observed the classification results in Fig. 2:

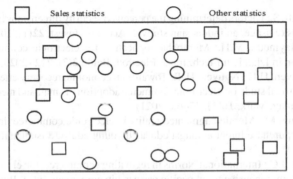

A.document [6] classification results

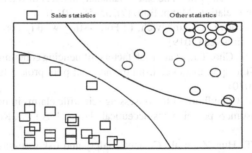

B.Classification results of the method presented in this paper

Fig. 2. Classification results for both methods

As can be seen in Fig. 2, this method divides the sales data to the left of Fig. 2(b), and the other data to the right of Fig. 2(b). However, literature [6] cannot distinguish the categories of data, reflecting that this method can distinguish sales data from sales data, and there is no unclear classification or misclassification, because this method can accurately excavate data attributes and links between projects, so as to achieve accurate classification.

5 Conclusion

The sales data used in this paper comes from the sales of new brand cosmetics in Japan on the e-commerce platform. Although this part of data can not represent the sales of all cosmetics enterprises, and the amount of data is not very huge, it can represent the sales of high-end health and skin care products. In order to study the sales characteristics in the big data environment, we combined the sales data of the store and external data sources such as weather, air quality and date type to extract and convert the data, and established the corresponding data classification model. Limited by the research conditions, the article has not studied the complex relationship of sample data thoroughly enough, and will continue to improve in the future.

References

1. Marianus, S., Ali, S.: Factors determining the perceived security dimensions in B2C electronic commerce website usage: an indonesian study. J. Account. Invest. **22**(1), 104–132 (2021)
2. Hamid, O., Allaymoun, M.H.: Murabaha application for electronic commerce internet of things utilisation in Islamic fin-tech. Int. J. Electron. Bank. **2**(3), 212 (2020)
3. Hoang, T., Nguyen, H.K., Nguyen, H.T.: Towards an economic recovery after the COVID-19 pandemic: empirical study on electronic commerce adoption of small and medium enterprises in Vietnam. Manag. Mark. **16**(1), 47–68 (2021)
4. Haile, T.T., Kang, M.: Mobile augmented reality in electronic commerce: investigating user perception and purchase intent amongst educated young adults. Sustainability **12**(21), 9185 (2020)
5. Azmi, I., Phuoc, J.C.: International Norms in regulating ecommerce: the electronic commerce chapter of the comprehensive trans-pacific partnership agreement. Int. J. Bus. Soc. **21** (2020)
6. Wang, L.Y., Gao, S., Li, J., et al.: The sales character analysis of retails based on K-means method and spatial correlation. Mapp. Bull. (9), 55–58 (2019)
7. Kirichenko, L., Radivilova, T., Zinkevich, I.: Forecasting weakly correlated time series in tasks of electronic commerce (2019)
8. Kim, H.W., Seok, Y.S., Cho, T.J., et al.: Risk factors influencing contamination of customized cosmetics made on-the-spot: evidence from the national pilot project for public health. Sci. Rep. **10**(1), 1561 (2020)
9. Jie, G.F., Carlson, L., Chaudhuri, H.R.: Assessing scientific claims in print ads that promote cosmetics: how consumers perceive cosmeceutical claims. J. Advert. Res. **59**(4), JAR-2018-048 (2019)
10. Zhaolun, Z., Ying, T., Hua, Z., et al.: Cosmetic safety and risk assessment under the "new" regulations. China Deterg. Cosmet. **5**(04), 24–32 (2020)
11. Yano, Y., Kato, E., Ohe, Y., et al.: Examining the opinions of potential consumers about plant-derived cosmetics: an approach combining word association, co-occurrence network, and multivariate probit analysis. J. Sens. Stud. **34**, e12484 (2019)
12. Yao, Y.: Changes of Chinese cosmetics consumers markets by scale. China Deterg. Cosmet. **4**(04), 22–23 (2019)
13. Zbib, I., Ghaddar, R., Samarji, A., et al.: Examining country of origin effect among Lebanese consumers: a study in the cosmetics industry. J. Int. Consum. Mark. **33**(2), 1–15 (2020)
14. Huang, S.: Identity construction of female consumers in Chinese and American cosmetics advertisements: a critical pragmatic study. Int. Linguist. Res. **3**(4), 131 (2020)

15. Long, V.T.: Research on the influence of transportation services quality on purchasing intention of customer in E-commerce - evidence from purchasing intention of Vietnamese consumer in cosmetic industry. Int. J. Soc. Sci. Educ. Res. **3**(5), 45–53 (2020)
16. Sohn, H.J., You, S.H., Park, C.H.: Relationship between consumers' exploring cosmetics information behavior and satisfaction and recommendation intention. Asian J. Beauty Cosmetol. **17**(4), 499–509 (2019)
17. Sama, R., Trivedi, J.: Factors affecting consumers loyalty towards halal cosmetics: an emerging market perspective. Int. J. Bus. Emerg. Mark. **11**(1), 1 (2019)
18. Du, G., Liu, Z., Lu, H.: Application of innovative risk early warning mode under big data technology in internet credit financial risk assessment. J. Comput. Appl. Math. **386**(12), 113260 (2021)
19. García-Gil, D., Holmberg, J., García, S., et al.: Smart data based ensemble for imbalanced big data classification (2020)
20. Yue, G., Liu, J., Liu, F.: Medical big data filling and classification simulation based on decision tree algorithm. Comput. Simul. **38**(1), 451–454, 459 (2021)

Modeling and Simulation

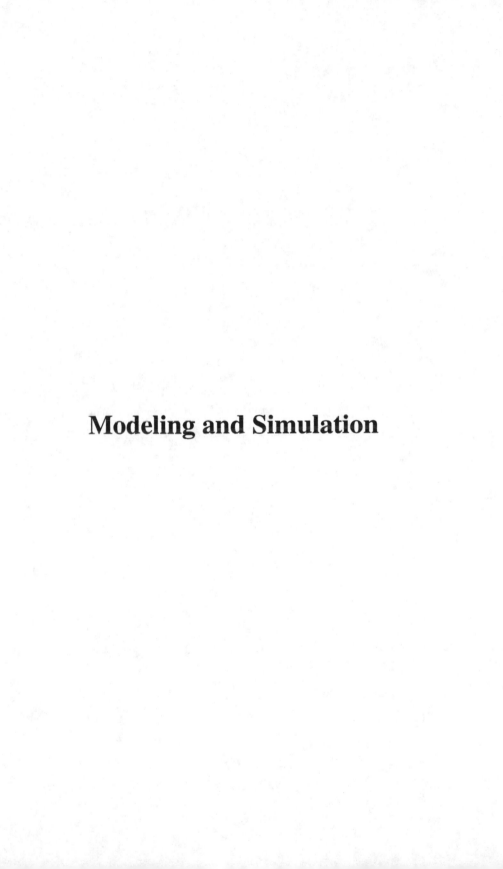

Feature Filtering Spectral Clustering Method Based on High Dimensional Online Clustering Method

Zizhou Feng[1], Yujian Gu[1], Bin Yang[2], Baitong Chen[3], and Wenzheng Bao[1(✉)]

[1] School of Information Engineering, Xuzhou University of Technology, Xuzhou 221000, China
[2] School of Information Science and Engineering,
Zaozhuang University, Zaozhuang 277160, China
[3] Xuzhou No. 1 People's Hospital, Xuzhou 221000, China

Abstract. Golgi is an important eukaryotic organelle. Golgi plays a key role in protein synthesis in eukaryotic cells, and its dysfunction will lead to various genetic and neurodegenerative diseases. In order to better develop drugs to treat diseases, one of the key problems is to identify the protein category of Golgi apparatus. In the past, the physical and chemical properties of Golgi proteins have often been used as feature extraction methods, but more accurate sub-Golgi protein identification is still challenged by existing methods. In this paper, we use the tape-bert model to extract the features of Golgi body. To create a balanced dataset from an unbalanced Golgi dataset, we used the SMOTE oversampling method. In addition, we screened out the important eigenvalues of 300 dimensions to identify the types of Golgi proteins. In 10-fold cross validation and independent test set test, the accuracy rate reached 90.6% and 95.31%.

Keywords: Golgi appratus · Malonylation · SMOTE · Protein

1 Introduction

In recent years, spectral clustering has become one of the most popular clustering algorithms [1]. It is easy to implement, can be solved effectively by standard linear algebra software, and is often better than traditional clustering algorithms, such as k-means algorithm [2].

Common spectral clustering algorithms usually include loading data, calculating Euclidean distance to obtain distance matrix, calculating adjacency matrix W and degree matrix D through distance matrix, so as to obtain Laplacian matrix $L = D - W$, then decomposing Laplacian matrix L to obtain characteristic matrix, and then clustering with k-means algorithm to obtain clustering results [3–6]. This spectral clustering algorithm is easy to understand and implement, but it has the disadvantages of slow running speed and low precision, and there is still a lot of optimization space [7–9].

There is a spectral clustering method for high-dimensional online clustering [10–12]. By further optimizing the Laplacian matrix (i.e. feature matrix), the feature matrix is

D. Jiang and H. Song (Eds.): SIMUtools 2021, LNICST 424, pp. 157–164, 2022.
https://doi.org/10.1007/978-3-030-97124-3_14

processed by using cropdiagonal, Gaussian blur, rowwise threshold, symmetry, diffusion and rowwise normalize, The feature matrix similar to Laplacian matrix is obtained, which can provide real-time and effective clustering for data [13–15].

The purpose of this paper is to improve the speed and accuracy of clustering by feature processing on the basis of the high-dimensional online clustering and removing the features with low correlation coefficient through the correlation coefficient matrix.

2 Methods and Materials

2.1 Optimization Idea of Spectral Clustering Model

Spectral clustering is a clustering algorithm based on graph theory. Therefore, the standard spectral clustering algorithm first regards the data as a graph. If the data is two-dimensional, it can be intuitively represented by image. If the data is multi-dimensional or even high-dimensional, it can only be represented by abstract formula.

If the intra cluster similarity is high and the inter cluster similarity is low, the clustering performance is better. Therefore, the standard of optimizing the clustering model is to improve the cluster similarity and reduce the inter cluster similarity.

The optimization idea of spectral clustering model is also based on this standard.

The optimization method of spectral clustering model is to minimize the objective function.

2.2 The Definition of Graph and Adjacency Matrix and Degree Matrix

Graph G is composed of the set of points V (vertex) and the set of edges e (edge), that is, g = (V, e), where V is the data set V = {V1, V2, ... VN}, e is the weight of the sample point VI and the sample point VJ, represented by Wij, Wij equal to 0 means that the sample point VI is not connected with the sample point VJ. Therefore, the directed adjacency matrix w of the graph for the data set with capacity n is expressed as: $W = (w_{ij})_{i,j=1,...,n}$ Weight of undirected graph $w_{ij} = w_{ji}$.

The undirected weight W in the figure above is expressed as:

$$\begin{pmatrix} w_{11} & w_{12} & 0 & w_{14} & 0 \\ w_{21} & w_{22} & w_{23} & 0 & 0 \\ 0 & w_{32} & w_{33} & 0 & w_{35} \\ w_{41} & 0 & 0 & w_{44} & w_{45} \\ 0 & 0 & w_{53} & w_{54} & w_{55} \end{pmatrix} \tag{1}$$

definition d_i It is the sample point v_i Degree of freedom:

$$d_i = \sum_{j=1}^{n} w_{ij} \tag{2}$$

The meaning of sample point degree is the sum of all weights connected with the sample point.

The degree of all sample points in the dataset is defined as the degree matrix D:

$$D = \begin{pmatrix} d_1 & & & \\ & d_2 & & \\ & & \ddots & \\ & & & d_n \end{pmatrix} \tag{3}$$

The matrix D is a diagonal matrix and the off diagonal elements are all zero.

2.3 Representation of Adjacency Matrix

The weight of adjacency matrix is the similarity between sampleseIn this paper, Euclidean distance is used to express the similarity between sample points

$$d(x, y) := \sqrt{(x_1 - y_1)^2 + (x_2 - y_2)^2 + \cdots + (x_n - y_n)^2} = \sqrt{\sum_{i=1}^{n} (x_i - y_i)^2} \tag{4}$$

2.4 Laplacian Matrix and Its Properties

Laplacian matrix L is the basis of spectral clustering algorithm. There are two kinds of Laplacian matrices and their attributes, namely non standardized Laplacian matrix and standardized Laplacian matrix.

1 Nonstandardized Laplacian matrix.

The non Laplacian matrix is defined as the difference between the degree matrix D and the adjacency matrix W. the expression is as follows:

$$L = D - W \tag{5}$$

We have two methods to define the standardized Laplacian matrix L_{sym} and L_{rw}, defined as:

$$L_{sym} = D^{-1/2}LD^{-1/2} = I - D^{-1/2}WD^{-1/2}$$
$$L_{rw} = D^{-1}L = I - D^{-1}W \tag{6}$$

2.5 The Meaning of Cut Graph of Undirected Graph

An undirected graph is composed of sample points and edges. The clustering of data set can be regarded as the segmentation of undirected graph. Suppose that graph G contains two connected subsets A and B after segmentation, then the weight of tangent graph between AB is as follows:

$$cut(A, B) = \sum_{i \in A, j \in B} w_{ij} \tag{7}$$

among Denotes the adjacency matrix of graph G.

If G is cut into k connected subsets AI(I = 1, 2, ..., K), the simplest method is to minimize the following formula:

$$\text{cut}(A_1, \ldots, A_k) := \sum_{i=1}^{k} \text{cut}(A_i, \overline{A_i}) \tag{8}$$

among $\overline{A_i}$ express A_i The complement of.

This segmentation method only considers minimizing the similarity between clusters, and does not consider the similarity within clusters, so this segmentation standard is not accurate, so we need to optimize the segmentation method, and there are two kinds of optimal segmentation methods: ratiocut segmentation and ncutt segmentation. Ncutt cut graph is also called standardized spectral clustering algorithm, and ratiocut cut graph is called non standardized spectral clustering algorithm.

$$RatioCut(A_1, A_2, \ldots, A_k) = \sum_{i=1}^{k} \frac{cut(A_i, \overline{A_i})}{|A_i|} \tag{9}$$

$$Ncut(A_1, \ldots, A_k) = \sum_{i=1}^{k} \frac{cut(A_i, \overline{A_i})}{vol(A_i)} \tag{10}$$

2.6 The Choice of Laplacian Matrix

There are two kinds of algorithms for Laplacian matrix. Which algorithm to choose is a basic problem of spectral clustering. If the graph is regular and the degrees of most sample points are approximately equal, it is feasible to choose any kind of Laplacian matrix. If the degree difference of most sample points is large, it is recommended to use the standardized Laplacian matrix. Because the nonstandardized Laplacian matrix corresponds to the ratiocut cut graph, the similarity within the cluster described by the ratiocut cut graph is the number of samples contained in the cluster |a|, the standardized Laplacian matrix corresponds to the ncutt cut graph, and the ncutt cut graph describes the similarity within the cluster as Vol (a). Because Vol (a) is better than |a| in reflecting the similarity within clusters, this paper chooses the standardized Laplacian matrix.

2.7 Selection of the Number of Cluster Classes

The first problem of spectral clustering algorithm is the selection of the number of clusters. The common way is to use the heuristic eigenvalue difference search (eigengap heuristic), meaning: if the first k eigenvalues are very small, and the K + 1 eigenvalue is quite different from the previous eigenvalue, then the number of clusters is K. Let G be partitioned into k connected subsets without intersection, then K eigenvalues are equal to 0 and K + 1 eigenvalues are greater than 0. Therefore, we can assume that the smaller the eigenvalue is, the better the clustering performance is, and select the number of clusters with very small eigenvalue as the number of clusters. In this paper, the high-dimensional online clustering algorithm based on links selects cluster K automatically according to the samples.

2.8 Feature Filtering

For a specific learning algorithm, which feature is effective is unknown. Therefore, it is necessary to select the useful features from all the features. And in practical application, the problem of dimension disaster often appears. If only some of the features are selected to build the model, the running time of the learning algorithm can be greatly reduced, and the interpretability of the model can be increased.

The principle of feature selection is to obtain as small a feature subset as possible, not to significantly reduce the classification accuracy, not to affect the classification distribution, and the feature subset should be stable and adaptable.

There are many methods of feature selection, such as chi square test, information gain, correlation coefficient and so on. This paper adopts the correlation coefficient method to judge the correlation coefficient and a certain threshold between each column of data (each column of data is a different sample value represented by the same feature) and the label, It can be considered that the column features have little correlation with the results, which will affect the classification effect, and the column is removed, that is to complete a feature filtering.

Feature filtering has the following advantages: first, reduce the number of features, dimension reduction; second, reduce the difficulty of learning tasks, improve the efficiency of the model; third, make the model more pan Chinese ability, reduce over fitting; fourth, enhance the understanding between features and eigenvalues.

3 Algorithm

3.1 Standard Spectral Clustering Algorithm

Spectral clustering is a clustering algorithm based on graph theory. Therefore, the standard spectral clustering algorithm first regards the data as a graph. If the data is two-dimensional, it can be intuitively represented by image. If the data is multi-dimensional or even high-dimensional, it can only be represented by abstract formula.

After the data is regarded as undirected weight graph, the specific process of spectral clustering is as follows:

1. By Euclidean distance or ε-Neighborhood method, k-nearest neighbor method and other methods are used to calculate the distance between each node and get the distance matrix.
2. The adjacency matrix A and degree matrix D are calculated by the distance matrix.
3. The nonstandardized Laplacian matrix $L = D - A$ is obtained.
4. Normalized Laplacian matrix: $l \rightarrow D - 1 / 2ld - 1 / 2$.
5. The eigenvector HN is obtained by eigendecomposition of the normalized Laplacian matrix.
6. The feature vector HN is sent to kmeans clustering as a sample.
7. The clustering result $c = (C1, C2, \ldots, CN)$ is obtained.

Spectral clustering is a kind of clustering method based on data similarity matrix. It defines the optimization objective function of subgraph partition, introduces indicator variables, and transforms the partition problem into solving the optimal indicator variable matrix HH.Then, by using the properties of Rayleigh entropy, the problem is further transformed into solving the K minimum eigenvalues of Laplacian matrix. Finally, as some expression of samples, the traditional clustering method is used for clustering.

3.2   High Dimensional Online Clustering Method

The spectral clustering method in this paper is based on this method. This spectral clustering method is called links, which aims to cluster the unit vectors of high-dimensional Euclidean space online. This algorithm is suitable for the situation that the data need to be effectively clustered when the data stream enters. What this paper focuses on is the excellent running speed and accuracy of this method when processing high-dimensional data.

This method uses six default optimization methods: cropdiagonal, Gaussian blur, rowwise threshold, symmetry, diffuse and rowwise normalize to refine the feature matrix, so as to get more accurate results.The specific steps are as follows:

1. The similarity matrix affinity is calculated by sample data
2. Six default optimization methods are used to optimize the similarity matrix affinity
3. The similarity matrix affinity is decomposed into feature matrix and feature vector
4. Through the characteristic matrix, the characteristic vector, the maximum number of clusters and the minimum number of clusters, the number of clusters K is obtained.
5. The first k minimum eigenvalues of feature vector are taken and sent to kmeans clustering
6. The result $c = (C1, C2, \ldots, CN)$.

3.3   High Dimensional Spectral Clustering Algorithm Based on Feature Filtering

In this paper, based on the links spectral clustering algorithm, the feature selection function is added. Many processed data are high-dimensional data, some data samples may have more than ten, dozens or hundreds of thousands of dimensional data features, some of which have little correlation with the clustering results, that is to say, it will play a role of interference, resulting in the accuracy of clustering results. The innovation of this paper lies in the feature selection of data, filtering out the data with low correlation of clustering results, so as to improve the accuracy of clustering results.

The algorithm is as follows

1. Extract and separate the data information and tags contained in the data
2. Obtain the correlation coefficient (COR) between each column of data (each column of data is a different sample value represented by the same feature) and the tag
3. The average exp of all correlation coefficients is calculated as the threshold to judge the correlation
4. Traverse the correlation coefficient of each column of data, when corn < exp, delete the column, otherwise keep the column
5. Get the filtered new data
6. The new data is sent to the links spectral clustering method for clustering
7. The result $c = (C1, C2, \ldots, CN)$.

4   Conclusion

In this paper, three spectral clustering methods, standard spectral clustering, high-dimensional online clustering (links) and feature filtered high-dimensional spectral clustering, are compared in terms of algorithm accuracy and operation time, It can be seen from the above figures and that the precision of the feature filtered high-dimensional spectral clustering is higher than the high-dimensional online clustering (links) and table quasi spectral clustering, and the clustering speed is much faster than the standard spectral clustering algorithm. It can be seen that this model not only retains the high speed of high-dimensional online clustering (links), but also improves the accuracy of clustering results (Table 1).

Table 1. The comparison of three method

Method	Standard spectral clustering	High dimensional online clustering	High dimensional spectral clustering based on feature filtering
Run time	2503.372078180313 s	769.8853192329407 s	775.8828499317169 s

Acknowledgement. This work is supported by the fundamental Research Fundo for the Central Universities, 2020QN89, Xuzhou science and technology plan project (KC19142), the talent project of 'Qingtan scholar' of Zaozhuang University, Jiangsu Provincial Natural Science Foundation, China (SBK2019040953), Youth Innovation Teamof Scientific Research Foundation of the Higher Education Institutions of Shandong Province, China (2019KJM006), the Key Research Program of the Science Foundation of Shandong Province (ZR2020KE001), the PhD research startup foundation of Zaozhuang University (2014BS13) and Zaozhuang University Foundation (2015YY02), the Natural Science Foundation of China (61902337), Natural Science Fund for Colleges and Universities in Jiangsu Province (19KJB520016), Xuzhou Natural Science Foundation KC21047 and Young talents of science and technology in Jiangsu.

References

1. Molinie, B., Giallourakis, C.C.: Genome-wide location analyses of N6-Methyladenosine modifications (m(6)A-Seq). Methods Mol. Biol. **1562**, 45–53 (2017)
2. Nye, T.M., van Gijtenbeek, L.A., Stevens, A.G., et al.: Methyltransferase DnmA is responsible for genome-wide N6-methyladenosine modifications at non-palindromic recognition sites in Bacillus subtilis. Nucleic Acids Res. **48**, 5332–5348 (2020)
3. O'Brown, Z.K., Greer, E.L.: N6-methyladenine: a conserved and dynamic DNA mark. In: Jeltsch, A., Jurkowska, R. (eds.) DNA Methyltransferases-Role and Function, vol. 945, pp. 213–246. Springer, Cham (2016). https://doi.org/10.1007/978-3-319-43624-1_10
4. Zhang, G., et al.: N6-methyladenine dna modification in drosophila. Cell **161**(4), 893–906 (2015)
5. Janulaitis, A., et al.: Cytosine modification in DNA by BCNI methylase yields N4-methylcytosine. FEBS Lett. **161**, 131–134 (1983)

6. Unger, G., Venner, H.: Remarks on minor bases in spermatic desoxyribonucleic acid. Hoppe-Seylers Z. Physiol. Chem. **344**, 280–283 (1966)
7. Fu, Y., et al.: N6-methyldeoxyadenosine marks active transcription start sites in Chlamy-domonas. Cell **161**, 879–892 (2015)
8. Greer, E.L., et al.: DNA methylation on N6-adenine in C. elegans. Cell **161**, 868–878 (2015)
9. Zhang, G., et al.: N6-methyladenine DNA modification in Drosophila. Cell **161**, 893–906 (2015)
10. Wu, T.P., et al.: DNA methylation on N6-adenine in mammalian embryonic stem cells. Nature **532**, 329–333 (2016)
11. Xiao, C.L., et al.: N-methyladenine DNA modification in the human genome. Mol. Cell **71**, 306–318 (2018)
12. Zhou, C., et al.: Identification and analysis of adenine N6-methylation sites in the rice genome. Nat. Plants **4**, 554–563 (2018)
13. Chen, W., et al.: i6mA-Pred: identifying DNA N6-methyladenine sites in the rice genome. Bioinformatics **35**, 2796–2800 (2019)
14. Almagor, H.A.: A Markov analysis of DNA sequences. J. Theor. Biol. **104**, 633–645 (1983)
15. Borodovsky, M., et al.: Detection of new genes in a bacterial genome using Markov models for three gene classes. Nucleic Acids Res. **17**, 3554–3562 (1995)

Research on CRM Boost PFC Converter Based on GaN Device

Yao Ding[1,2] and En Fang[1,2(✉)]

[1] School of Electrical and Control Engineering, Xuzhou University
of Technology, Xuzhou 221018, Jiangsu, China
fangen@cumt.edu.cn
[2] Jiangsu Key Construction Laboratory of Large Engineering Equipment Testing and Control
Technology, Xuzhou 221018, Jiangsu, China

Abstract. There is a need for Power Factor Correction (PFC) converters to improve performance and reduce device size while maintaining a high power factor in the consumer electronics arena. Increasing the switching frequency is the essential way to increase the power density of the PFC converter. When the switching frequency of the converter is close to the MHz level, the switching loss of the conventional Si MOSFET increases sharply, resulting in a decrease in the overall efficiency of the converter. The dual-pulse test platform based on the cascode GaN transistor TPH3206PD and the experimental platform of 200 W single-phase CRM boost PFC converter is introduced. Then, the stability of the high frequency driving circuit of the GaN device is verified by the dual-pulse test platform, which effectively avoids the false turn-off phenomenon in the turn-on process. The switching loss of TPH3206PD is measured experimentally, and the accuracy of theoretical calculation is verified. The experimental results show that when the operating frequency of the CRM boost PFC converter is close to 1 MHz. GaN devices can effectively reduce switching loss and improve overall efficiency.

Keywords: Boost PFC converter · Critical current mode · GaN devices

1 Introduction

The performance of switch-mode power supply (SMPS) is the key to the reliable operation of power equipment. Among the performance parameters of SWPs, the power factor (PF) is the most crucial parameter for energy saving and environmental protection. PF is the ratio of active power to total power. The reduction of PF means an increase in power consumption and harmonic pollution, which leads to circuit failure, equipment damage, and electromagnetic interference. Power Factor Correction (PFC) improves the harmonic generation equipment in rectification, which is the primary method to solve the problem of low PF. PFC converter improves pf value, makes input current and input voltage in phase, corrects the input current waveform, and reduces distortion and harmonics. It is more and more necessary for power conversion equipment to improve

D. Jiang and H. Song (Eds.): SIMUtools 2021, LNICST 424, pp. 165–177, 2022.
https://doi.org/10.1007/978-3-030-97124-3_15

efficiency and minimize module size while maintaining or improving electrical and thermal performance in consumer electronics. At the same time, following the development concept of socialism with Chinese characteristics in the new era, power products have the development goals of high efficiency and miniaturization. The volume of the PFC converter usually accounts for a large percentage of power supply equipment, which directly affects the power density of the power adapter. In response to the advocacy of gradually building energy consumption mode of saving, efficient, clean, and low-carbon society, improving the efficiency and power density of PFC converter is an effective way to realize efficient and clean power products.

2 Analysis of Theory of CRM Boost PFC Converter Based on GaN Device

The cascode GaN transistors are more suitable for Critical Current Mode (CRM) boost PFC Converters. Analyzing and comparing the static characteristics of the cascode GaN transistors and Si devices can help to analyze the conducting losses of both. The principle analysis of GaN devices and CRM boost PFC converters is the basis of applying GaN devices to high-frequency CRM boost PFC converters. Therefore, the static characteristics of the cascode GaN transistors and Si devices are analyzed and compared in this paper. The power factor correction principles with switching mode and steady-state for the CRM boost PFC converters are discussed.

2.1 Static Characteristics of Cascode GaN Transistors

The cascode GaN transistor TPH3206PD (600 V/17 A/150 mΩ) of Transphorm company is selected as the research object. TPH3206PD is composed of Si MOSFET IRF8707 and depletion GaN HEMT via the cascode packaging technology. Their parameters are shown in Table 1. The drain-source voltage $V_{\text{ds-Si}}$ of Si MOSFET is used as the driving voltage of GaN HEMT. In order to cut off the drain current of GaN HEMT, it is necessary to select Si MOSFET with enough breakdown voltage to meet condition $V_{\text{dsmax\_Si}} > |V_{\text{th\_GaN}}|$ for turning off the GaN HEMT. GaN HEMT has an insulator between the gate electrode and the AlGaN barrier layer, selecting Si MOSFET with high breakdown voltage. It shows that the cascode structure can drive the GaN HEMT with a large dv/dt. As shown in Table 1, the rated voltage V_{dss} of IRF8707 is 30 V, and the absolute value of threshold voltage of GaN HEMT $|V_{\text{th\_GaN}}|$ is 20 V, which meets the academic requirements.

Table 1. Parameters table of Cascode GaN transistor and its components.

Parameters	TPH3206PD	Depletion GaN HEMT	IRF8707
Rated voltage V_{dss}	600 V	600 V	30 V
Rated current $I_d(T_c = 25\ °C)$	17 A	17 A	17 A
Conducting resistance R_{ds_on}	150 mΩ	140 mΩ	11.9 mΩ
Threshold voltage V_{th}	2.1 V	−20 V	2.1 V
Gate source voltage V_{gs}	−18 V–18 V	−40 V–2 V	−20 V–20 V

Output Characteristics of Si MOSFET IRF8707

Si MOSFET IRF8707 is a bidirectional conducting device with a parasitic diode, so its output characteristic curve includes the first and third quadrant. Figure 1 shows the output characteristic curves of Si MOSFET IRF8707. The first quadrant curve shows the relationship between voltage and current when the device is in forwarding conduction. The third quadrant curve shows the relationship between voltage and current when the device is under reverse voltage.

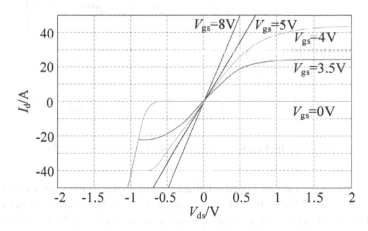

Fig. 1. Output characteristic curve of Si MOSFET IRF8707.

When the Si MOSFET is under forwarding voltage, the driving voltage V_{gs_Si}, larger than the threshold voltage, is applied to the gate-source and the device is on. Under the same voltage, the higher the driving voltage is, the smaller the on-resistance and the smaller the conducting state loss is. When the driving voltage applied to the gate-source is 8 V, the output characteristic is approximately linear.

When Si MOSFET withstands reverse voltage, if V_{gs_Si} is less than V_{th_Si}, the conduction channel of Si MOSFET is blocked, and the current flows through the body diode of the device. The device shows diode characteristics, and the reverse voltage drop of the device is the body diode voltage drop V_F. Suppose the gate-source driving voltage is large enough, the reverse conduction resistance of the device decreases. When the reverse current flows through the channel, the voltage drop of the source and drain is V_{sd_Si}. The output characteristic curve of Si MOSFET is almost symmetrical with the first quadrant. V_{gs_Si} is greater than its threshold voltage V_{th_Si}. At this time, current flows through both the channel and the bulk diode, and the device works in the reverse saturation region. The reverse conduction voltage is clamped as the voltage drop of the bulk diode V_F.

Output Characteristics of Depletion GaN HEMT

There is no parasitic diode in the lateral structure of depletion GaN HEMT, which determines the symmetry of its conduction characteristics, i.e., gate-source voltage V_{gs_GaN} and gate-drain voltage V_{gd_GaN} can drive the device on and off.

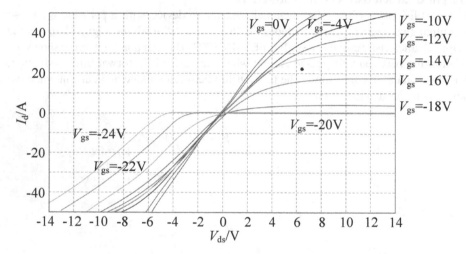

Fig. 2. Output characteristic curve of depletion GaN HEMT.

Figure 2 shows the first and third quadrant output characteristic curves of depletion GaN HEMT in TPH3206PD. It can be seen that the output characteristic curve of depletion GaN HEMT in the third quadrant is different from that of Si MOSFET due to the absence of parasitic diode and its symmetrical conduction characteristics. Because there is no bulk diode in GaN HEMT, the reverse conduction characteristics are obviously different from that of Si MOSFET, which leads to the difference between the cascode GaN transistor and Si MOSFET.

Figure 3 shows the output characteristic curve of TPH3206PD. It can be seen that the output characteristics of the cascode GaN transistor are similar to that of power Si MOSFET in the first quadrant. Still, it does not show diode characteristics in the case of reverse conduction in the third quadrant. It is mainly because the cascode GaN transistor has a cascode structure. Its reverse conduction voltage is the sum of reverse conduction voltage of power Si MOSFET and depletion GaN HEMT. Therefore, the reverse conduction voltage of the cascode Gan transistor is slightly higher than that of Si MOSFET of the same voltage level.

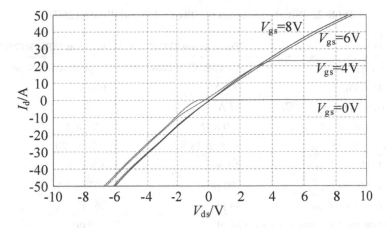

Fig. 3. Output characteristic curve of TPH3206PD.

2.2 Comparison of Static Characteristics Between the Cascode GaN Transistor and Si Device

According to the difference of static characteristics between the cascode GaN transistor and Si devices, the super junction Si MOSFET of Infineon CoolMOS IPP65R125C7 (650 V/13 A/125 mΩ) as representatives of current high-performance Si devices are selected. The rated voltage and current are similar to TPH3206PD, which is suitable for comparative analysis. Some parameters of TPH3206PD and IPP65R125C7 are shown in Table 2.

The conduction characteristics of the cascode GaN transistor TPH3206PD at different working junction temperatures of $T_J = 25\,°C$ and $175\,°C$ are shown in Figs. 2, 3 and 4. It can be seen that in the actual operating range of 0–17 A, the conduction characteristics can be approximately linear. The R_{ds_on} value at any temperature can be calculated from Fig. 4 by the ratio of V_{ds} to I_d in the linear region.

The R_{ds_on} performance of Si device IPP65R125C7 is 0.057–0.150 Ω, 38%–100% better than that of the cascode GaN transistor in the same condition.

3 Analysis of Basic Principles of CRM Boost PFC Converter

The basic principle of a single-phase CRM boost PFC converter consists of two parts. The first part is the working mode of main switch S in a switching cycle, and the second part is the principle of power factor correction. The central circuit topology of the single-phase boost PFC converter is shown in Fig. 5. The primary circuit includes AC power supply v_{in}, EMI filter, rectifier bridge, boost filter inductor L, switch S, diode D, input capacitor C_{in}, output regulator capacitor C_o and load, etc.

3.1 Analysis of CRM Boost PFC Converter

Figure 6 shows the equivalent circuit of the converter when the switch is on and off. Figure 7 shows the changes in switch voltage, inductance current, and voltage. At $t = t_0$,

Table 2. Partial parameters of TPH3206PD and IPP65R125C7.

Parameters	Transphorm TPH3206PD	Infineon IPP65R125C7
Technology type	Cascade GaN transistor	Superjunction Si MOSFET
Rated voltage V_{ds}	600 V	650 V
Rated current I_d ($T_c = 25\ ^{\circ}C$)	17 A	13 A
Conducting resistance R_{ds_on}	150 mΩ	125 mΩ
Gate-source voltage V_{gs}	-18 V–18 V	-20 V–20 V
Threshold voltage V_{TH}	2.1 V	3.5 V
Input capacitance C_{iss}	760 pF	1670 pF
Output capacitance C_{oss}	44 pF	26 pF
Reverse transmission capacitor C_{rss}	34 pF	579 pF
Total charge of gate-source Q_{gs}	2.1 nC	8 nC
Total gate-drain charge Q_{gd}	2.2 nC	11 nC
Total gate-charge Q_g	6.2 nC	35 nC
Total reverse recovery charge Q_{rr}	54 nC	7 μC
Reverse recovery time t_{rr}	17 ns	800 ns

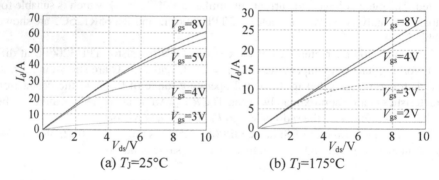

(a) $T_J=25^{\circ}C$ (b) $T_J=175^{\circ}C$

Fig. 4. Conduction characteristic of TPH3206PD at 25 $^{\circ}$C and 175 $^{\circ}$C.

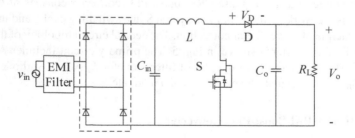

Fig. 5. Main circuit of single-phase Boost PFC.

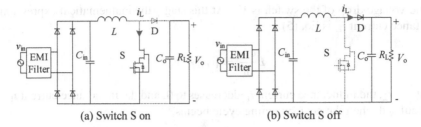

(a) Switch S on   (b) Switch S off

Fig. 6. Equivalent circuit of CRM Boost PFC working mode.

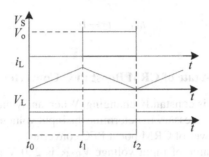

Fig. 7. Equivalent waveforms of CRM Boost PFC key parameters.

the switch S turns on, and the diode D turns off. The AC power v_{in} charges the inductor L, and C_o discharges the load R_L. The inductance current i_L rises from zero and can be calculated by Eqs. (1) and (2) between $[t_0, t_1]$.

$$L\frac{di_L}{dt} = |v_{in}| \tag{1}$$

$$v_{in} = V_{in}\sin\omega t = \sqrt{2}V_{RMS}\sin\omega t \tag{2}$$

Where, V_{in} is the peak value of AC power supply voltage, and V_{RMS} is the effective value of AC power supply voltage. ω is the angular frequency of the AC supply voltage.

In this stage, v_{in} can be considered as the instantaneous value of the AC power supply. Because the power frequency of the AC power supply is far less than the switching frequency, v_{in} is almost unchanged in a switching cycle. When $t = t_1$, the inductance current i_L rises to the peak i_{LP}. The growth of i_L is expressed as follows.

$$i_{LP} = \frac{|v_{in}|}{L}t_{on} \tag{3}$$

$$t_{on} = t_1 - t_0 \tag{4}$$

At $t = t_1$, switch S turns off, and diode D turns on. v_{in} and L charge C_o through D and discharge R_L at the same time. Inductance current i_L drops to 0 due to the discharge, and the voltage drop of the switch is V_0. At this stage, the mathematical expression of inductance current i_L is Eq. (5).

$$L\frac{di_L}{dt} = |v_{in}| - V_o \tag{5}$$

At $t = t_2$, the inductance current i_L decreases to 0, and the inductance current i_L can be calculated when the next switching cycle begins.

$$i_{LP} = \frac{V_o - |v_{in}|}{L}t_{off} \tag{6}$$

$$t_{off} = t_2 - t_1 \tag{7}$$

3.2 Analysis of Steady-State of CRM Boost PFC Converter

The switching frequency is constantly changing. When analyzing the specific range of switching frequency, it is necessary to determine the input voltage, output voltage, boost inductance and output power of CRM boost PFC converter.

When the practical value of input voltage V_{RMS} is 220 V and the output voltage V_{out} is 390 V, if the input voltage reaches the peak value, the minimum switching frequency f_{s_min} is 1. Mathcad can be used to show the change curve of the switching frequency of AC power supply in one cycle, as shown in Fig. 8. It can be seen that the maximum frequency is about 4.5 times the minimum frequency. If the minimum switching frequency of the designed PFC converter is 200 kHz, the switching frequency range is about 200 kHz–900 kHz.

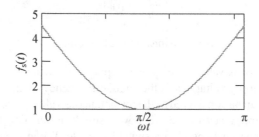

Fig. 8. Diagram of switching frequency variation.

4   Experimental Research

4.1 Dual-Pulse Test Platform

In order to verify the theoretical analysis results, a dual-pulse test apparatus based on the cascode GaN transistor TPH3206PD is built. And a 200 W single-phase CRM boost

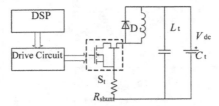

Fig. 9. Structure diagram of the dual-pulse test platform.

PFC converter experimental platform is made to verify the dynamic performance and loss of TPH3206PD. The control performance is proved, and power loss of CRM boost PFC converter based on GaN is calculated to prove the efficiency improvement. The input current zero-crossing distortion is suppressed.

Figure 9 is the structure diagram of the dual-pulse test platform, which includes driving circuit and DC power supply V_{dc}, filter capacitor C_t, inductance L_t, freewheeling diode D_t and switch S_t to be tested. Other parameters of the dual pulse test platform are shown in Table 3.

Table 3. Parameters table of double pulse test platform.

Parameter	Values
Input Voltage V_{dc}	390 V
Driving voltage V_{GS}	12 V
Driving resistor R_G	5 Ω, 20 Ω
Switching frequency f_{sw}	550 kHz

4.2 Cascode Gan Transistor Switching Loss Verification

In the dual-pulse test of the cascode GaN transistor, the current before turning on is zero, and the conducting current is 3.84 A, 2.04 A, 1.48 A, and 1.23 A, respectively. Four groups of switching waveforms are obtained by changing the switching current by changing the time of the first pulse, as shown in Figs. 10, 11, 12 and 13.

According to the switching waveforms, the switching losses of four groups of different switching currents are calculated and compared with the theoretical calculation. The theoretical and actual switching losses of TPH3206PD shown in Table 4 are obtained. The theoretical value of turn-on loss is quite different from the actual value because the turn-on process of TPH3206PD has a specific oscillation. In the experiment, the parasitic parameters caused by PCB layout are challenging to be quantified. So the oscillation waveform in the investigation is slightly different from that in the simulation, which causes the accuracy of the theoretical value of turn-on loss to be lower than that of turn-off loss. According to the parameters in Table 4, the maximum difference between the theoretical and actual values is 4.99%, and the minimum difference is 1.73%. The

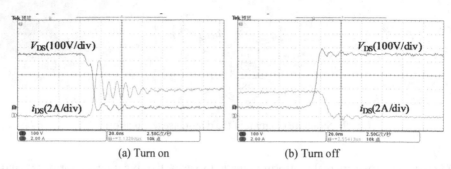

(a) Turn on   (b) Turn off

Fig. 10. Switching waveforms when the switching current is 3.84 A.

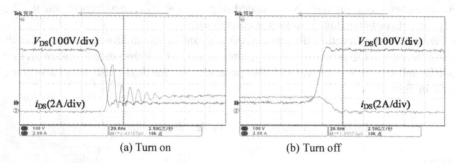

(a) Turn on   (b) Turn off

Fig. 11. Switching waveforms when the switching current is 2.04 A.

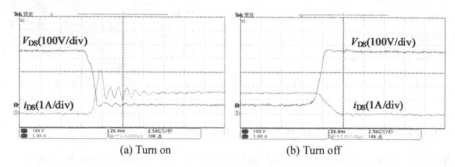

(a) Turn on   (b) Turn off

Fig. 12. Switching waveforms when the switching current is 1.48 A.

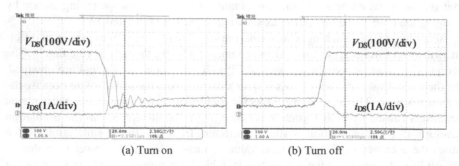

(a) Turn on   (b) Turn off

Fig. 13. Switching waveforms when the switching current is 1.23 A.

leading difference between the theoretical and actual values is 3.71%, and the minimum difference is 0.08%. The accuracy of switching loss is within the allowable error range, which shows that the theoretical and simulation analyses are in line with reality.

Table 4. Comparison of theoretical and actual values of TPH3206PD switching.

	Theoretical turn-on loss/μJ	Actual turn-on loss/μJ	Theoretical turn-off loss/μJ	Actual turn-off loss/μJ
$i_{rms} = 3.84$ A	26.232	25.677	4.410	4.543
$i_{rms} = 2.04$ A	14.340	14.657	3.658	3.799
$i_{rms} = 1.48$ A	11.158	11.745	3.206	3.231
$i_{rms} = 1.23$ A	8.625	8.924	3.003	3.079

4.3 Experimental Analysis of Converter Performance

The converter reaches steady-state quickly. In order to test whether the CRM boost PFC converter based on GaN device can achieve the goals of high power factor and more than 90% efficiency in the entire input range, the VRMs of 85 V, 160 V, 220 V, and 265 V are selected for the experiment, and the results are shown in Fig. 14.

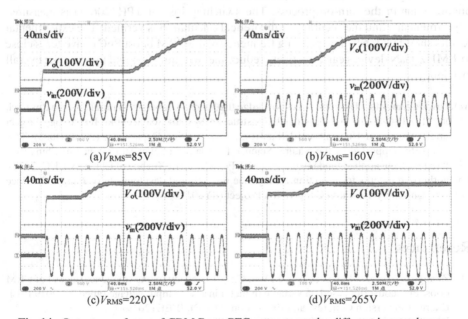

(a)V_{RMS}=85V

(b)V_{RMS}=160V

(c)V_{RMS}=220V

(d)V_{RMS}=265V

Fig. 14. Output waveforms of CRM Boost PFC converter under different input voltages.

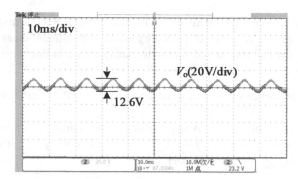

Fig. 15. Steady-state waveforms of output voltage.

When the CRM boost PFC converter reaches the steady-state, the output voltage waveform is shown in Fig. 15. The measured output voltage ripple is 12.6 V, less than 5%, which conform to the theoretical and simulation analyses.

5   Conclusions

The dual-pulse test platform based on the cascode GaN transistor TPH3206PD is built, and the experimental platform of a 200 W single-phase CRM boost PFC converter is described. Then, the stability of the high-frequency driving circuit of the GaN device is verified by the dual-pulse test platform, which effectively avoids the false turn-off phenomenon in the turn-on process. The switching loss of TPH3206PD is measured experimentally, and the accuracy of theoretical calculation is verified. The experimental results show that when the operating frequency of the CRM boost PFC converter is close to 1 MHz, GaN devices can effectively reduce the switching loss and improve the overall efficiency.

Acknowledgements. The authors acknowledge the Jiangsu University Natural Science Research Project (18KJB470024) and Provincial Construction System Science and Technology Project of Jiangsu Provincial Housing and Urban-Rural Construction Department (2018ZD088). This work is partly supported by the Natural Science Foundation of Jiangsu Province of China (No. BK20161165), the applied fundamental research Foundation of Xuzhou of China (No. KC17072). The authorized patents for invention are also the research and development of Jiangsu Province Industry-University-Research Cooperation Project (BY2019056).

References

1. Zhang, Z., Yao, K., Ma, C., Chen, J., Wu, C.: All-fixed switching frequency control of CRM boost PFC converter based on variable inductor in a wide input voltage range. In: 2019 IEEE Energy Conversion Congress and Exposition (ECCE). IEEE (2019)
2. Wu, Y., Ren, X., Zhou, Y., Chen, Q., Zhang, Z.: Dynamic AC line frequency response method for LUT-based variable on-time control in 360 Hz–800 Hz CRM boost PFC converter. IEEE Trans. Power Electron. **PP**(99), 1 (2020)

3. Chen, Y.L., Chen, Y.M., Chen, H.J.: On-time compensation method for CRM/DCM Boost PFC converter. In: 2013 Twenty-Eighth Annual IEEE Applied Power Electronics Conference and Exposition (APEC). IEEE (2013)
4. Yao, K., Zhang, Z., Yang, J., Liu, J., Shao, F.: Quasi-fixed switching frequency control of CRM boost PFC converter based on variable inductor in wide input voltage range. IEEE Trans. Power Electron. **PP**(99), 1 (2020)
5. Wei, X.F., Chen, S.Y., Zhu, H.K., Yang, X., Guo, X.: Research on high power density LLC resonant converter based on GaN device. Adv. Technol. Electr. Eng. Energy (2019)
6. Fang, Y., et al.: Research on novel bridgeless dcm pseudo-boost PFC converter. J. Electr. Eng.
7. Jang, P., Kang, S., Cho, B., et al.: Totem-pole bridgeless boost PFC converter based on GaN FETs. In: Power Electronics Annual Conference, pp. 185–186 (2014)
8. Yang, F.: Interleaved critical conduction mode boost PFC converter with coupled inductor. IEEE Trans. Power Electron. PE (2011)
9. Ren, X., Wu, Y., Guo, Z., Zhang, Z., Chen, Q.: An online monitoring method of circuit parameters for variable on-time control in CRM boost PFC converters. IEEE Trans. Power Electron. **32**, 1786–1797 (2019)
10. Gao, J.: Analysis of a boost PFC pre-regulator operated in both CRM and DCM (2015)
11. Yao, K., Liu, J., Zhu, D., Jin, Z.: High power factor CRM boost PFC converter with optimum switching frequency variation range control based on variable inductor. IEEE Trans. Power Electron. **PP**(99), 1 (2021)
12. Ren, X., Wu, Y., Chen, Q., Zhang, Z.: Accurate operation analysis based variable on-time control for 360 Hz–800 Hz CRM boost PFC converters. IEEE Trans. Ind. Electron. **PP**(99), 1 (2019)
13. Wu, Y., Ren, X., Li, K., Zhang, Z., Chen, Q.: An accurate variable on-time control for 400 Hz CRM boost PFC converters *. In: 2019 IEEE Applied Power Electronics Conference and Exposition (APEC). IEEE (2019)
14. Sun, J., Huang, X., Strain, N.N., Costinett, D.J., Tolbert, L.M.: Inductor design and ZVS control for a GaN-based high efficiency CRM totem-pole PFC converter. In: 2019 IEEE Applied Power Electronics Conference and Exposition (APEC). IEEE (2019)
15. Ren, X., Yu, W., Guo, Z., Zhang, Z., Chen, Q.: An online monitoring method of circuit parameters for variable on-time control in CRM boost PFC converters. IEEE Trans. Power Electron. **34**(99), 1786–1797 (2018)
16. Chen, Y.L., Chen, Y.M.: Line current distortion compensation for DCM/CRM boost PFC converters. IEEE Trans. Power Electron. **31**(3), 2026–2038 (2015)

Application of Cascode GaN HEMT in LLC Soft Switching Converter

Kaiyuan Qin[1], En Fang[1,2(✉)], and Yuan-ming Zhang[3]

[1] School of Electrical and Control Engineering, Xuzhou
University of Technology, Xuzhou 221018, Jiangsu, China
fangen@cumt.edu.cn
[2] Jiangsu Key Construction Laboratory of Large Engineering Equipment Testing and Control
Technology, Xuzhou 221018, Jiangsu, China
[3] State Grid Suqian Power Supply Company, Suqian 223800, Jiangsu, China

Abstract. After decades of development, the performance of Si-based power switching devices is approaching its material limits. The power electronic converter is limited to further growth in the direction of high frequency, high efficiency, and high power density. As an outstanding representative of the third generation of wide bandgap semiconductor devices, the cascode GaN HEMT utilizes a cascode structure to achieve the normally-off nature of GaN devices, with unmatched steady-state and dynamic performance of Si-based devices. In order to promote its replacement of Si devices and give full play to the performance advantages, the cascode GaN HEMT is applied to the soft-switching topology of the LLC resonant converter in this paper. The relationship between the output capacitance and the dead-time of the switching device is analyzed. The effects with root mean square values of the first and second side currents are also considered. Taking advantage of the small output capacitance of the cascode GaN HEMT, the circulating current of the converter is reduced, which leads to further reduction of the conduction and transformer loss. Thus, the efficiency of the converter is improved. An LLC converter with 97% maximum efficiency and 96.2% total load efficiency was built to prove the correctness and effectiveness of the analysis.

Keywords: Cascode GaN device · Hard switch · Soft switch · Application research

1 Introduction

High frequency, high efficiency, and high power density are the inevitable trend of the development of power electronic converters. High frequency is an effective way to reduce the volume of passive components and improve the converter's power density. However, with the increase of switching frequency, the switching loss and driving loss of the converter rise rapidly, which leads to the converter's efficiency reduction. With the development of power electronics in recent years, a few high-performance Si MOS-FETs can reach a switching frequency of more than 1 MHz. But the switching speed

D. Jiang and H. Song (Eds.): SIMUtools 2021, LNICST 424, pp. 178–193, 2022.
https://doi.org/10.1007/978-3-030-97124-3_16

is still limited due to the significant parasitic parameters determined by their materials and packages, resulting in high switching and driving losses. So the devices can not be applied on a large scale. Therefore, in recent years, the development of power electronic converters mainly improves the power density and efficiency of the converter by researching the converter topologies and the performance of magnetic components.

Due to the material advantages of GaN devices and the reduction of parasitic parameters, the switching speed of GaN devices is much faster than that of Si MOSFETs. So it is possible to increase the switching frequency of the converters with GaN devices. The research on the static and dynamic characteristics and application of GaN devices is of great significance to improve the power density and efficiency of the converter.

The static and dynamic characteristics of the cascode GaN devices are different from those of traditional Si MOSFETs because of the unique structure and material aspects of the composite of Si MOSFET and GaN HEMT. Moreover, the change rate of voltage and current in the switching process of GaN devices is very high, and the influence of parasitic parameters at a low switching operation speed of GaN devices can not be ignored. The resulting voltage and current spikes and oscillations bring about the reliability reduction of the switching process, the switching loss increase, and the switching frequency limit of GaN devices. The advantages of GaN devices can not be fully utilized. Therefore, the parasitic parameters in the application of GaN devices are studied for optimization to reduce the switching loss and control the voltage and current spikes. The switching oscillation is critical to the application of GaN devices and also the inevitable choice to improve the power density, efficiency, and stability of GaN-based converters. At the same time, in soft-switching topology, it is an effective way to improve the efficiency of the soft-switching converter by using the smaller parasitic parameters of GaN devices to improve the conditions of soft switching and further reduce the converter loss.

In 2016, the industry market of gallium nitride power devices was about $12 million. In 2018, it accounted for 0.67% of the world semiconductor power market. The demand for gallium nitride power devices is expected to increase with explosive growth from 2018 to 2022, and the value will reach $450 million by 2022.

As the essential component of modern industry, China also attaches importance to the development of wide bandgap power devices. In the China-made 2025 plan, five major projects are proposed. In this plan, about the industrial foundation project, it is put forward that by 2020, 40% of the essential core parts and critical basic materials will be independently supported, including aerospace equipment, communication equipment, power generation, transmission equipment, rail transportation equipment and other equipment. The advanced manufacturing process of essential core components (components) and critical basic materials urgently needed by household appliances and other industries has been popularized and applied. By 2025, 70% of essential core parts and critical basic materials will be guaranteed independently. Therefore, accelerating the research and application of GaN power devices is also the need of the times and the nation, which is of great significance to enhance China's comprehensive competitiveness and support the world power status.

The factors that limit the frequency rise and stability of the cascode GaN HEMT in high-speed hard-switching applications are studied in this paper. And the devices are applied to a hard-switching buck converter. Under the given optimization measures, the advantages of high-frequency and high-speed are brought into play, and the stability of the converter is guaranteed. Switching loss becomes the main part of system loss.

ZVS (zero voltage switch) is realized in LLC resonant soft-switching converter on the primary side and ZCS (zero current switch) on the secondary side. High energy conversion efficiency is achieved. In recent years, it has been widely used in switching power supply, LED-drive power supply, intermediate bus converter, power electronic transformer, and other occasions. In this chapter, the cascode GaN HEMT is applied to LLC resonant converter with a soft-switching topology. Using the characteristics of GaN device with small output junction capacitance, the converter's cycle current and dead time are reduced. The loss of the converter decreases and the efficiency of the converter is improved.

2 LLC Resonant Converter Principle

2.1 Circuit Topology

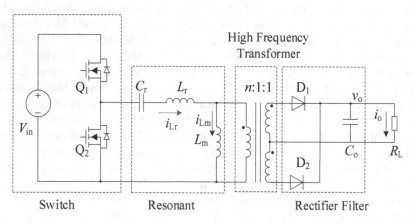

Fig. 1. Half-bridge LLC resonant converter topology.

Figure 1 shows the topology of the half-bridge LLC resonant converter, which mainly includes four parts. The switching network generates the square waves. The resonant network consists of resonant capacitor C_r, resonant inductor L_R, and excitation inductor L_m. The rectifier and filter network is composed of a high-frequency transformer with a middle tap, rectifier diode, and filter capacitor. The switching network consisting of main switches Q_1 and Q_2 generates a square wave voltage with a 50% duty cycle and adjustable frequency through complementary conduction. The dead time is inserted between the complementary conduction of Q_1 and Q_2 to prevent the bridge arm from passing through. Thus, ZVS on the primary side is realized. The impedance of the resonant network changes with the change of switching frequency, and the output voltage is adjusted with the switching frequency. The rectifier diodes D_1 and D_2 are full-wave rectified, and the output voltage is filtered by filter capacitor C_o.

2.2 Working Principle

The resonant network composed of resonant capacitor C_r, resonant inductor L_r and excitation inductor L_m has two resonant frequencies. The resonant frequency f_s of resonant capacitor C_r and resonant inductor L_r can be obtained by Eq. (1).

$$f_s = \frac{1}{2\pi\sqrt{L_r C_r}} \tag{1}$$

Resonant frequency f_m of resonant capacitor C_r and resonant inductor L_r can be driven from Eq. (2).

$$f_m = \frac{1}{2\pi\sqrt{(L_r + L_m)C_r}} \tag{2}$$

When the converter switching frequency f works in different load ranges, the system operates in three states. Figure 2 shows the waveforms of the converter working in different switching frequency ranges. LLC resonant converter can realize ZVS on the primary side in the entire load range and ZCS on the secondary side when $f_m < f < f_s$. The resonant network voltage is zero when the converter works at f = fs, and the efficiency reaches the maximum. Taking the converter working in $f_m < f < f_s$ state as an example, the working process of the converter is divided into six stages. The operational circuit diagrams of different phases are shown in Fig. 3, and working principles are analyzed in detail

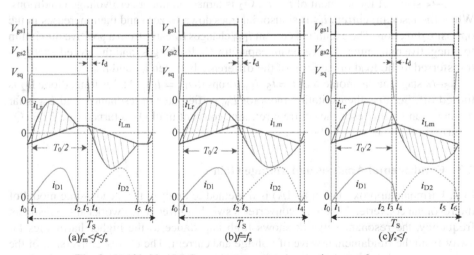

Fig. 2. Half-bridge LLC resonant converter operating waveforms.

$t_0 - t_1$ stage: at the moment of $t = t_0$, the lower transistor Q_2 is turned off. At the same time, the resonant current i_{Lr} discharges the junction capacitor of the upper transistor Q_1. The body diode of Q_1 turns on, and the drain-source voltage drops to the reverse conduction voltage drop. The voltage on the excitation inductor L_m is clamped by the voltage reflected from the secondary side, and only the resonant capacitor C_r and inductor L_r participate in the resonance.

t_1–t_2 stage: at the moment of $t = t_1$, the upper device Q_1 is conducting under zero voltage conditions. The input voltage V_{in} is added to the resonant network, and the current i_{Lr} changes sinusoidally. And the excitation current i_{Lm} increases linearly. The difference between i_{Lr} and i_{Lm} is shown in the shaded part of the figure. And the current is transmitted to the load through the high-frequency transformer after diode rectification. Since the switching period is greater than the resonant period, the resonant current i_{Lr} drops to the equivalent of the excitation current i_{Lm} before Q_1 is turned off. At the moment of $t = t_2$, the diode D_1 is turned off, and this stage ends. When the converter works with $f_s < f$, the resonance current i_{Lr} is more significant than the excitation current i_{Lm} until Q_1 is turned off.

t_2–t_3 stage: at the moment of $t = t_2$, Q_1 is still conducting, and D_1 is off. The resonant capacitor C_r, resonant inductor L_r, and excitation inductor L_m participate in the resonance. At the same time, because the resonant current i_{Lr} is equal to the excitation current i_{Lm}, the primary current of the high-frequency transformer is zero, and the primary and secondary sides are disconnected.

t_3–t_4 stage: at the moment of $t = t_3$, the upper tube Q_1 is turned off. The resonant current i_{Lr} discharges the capacitor of the lower tube Q_1 junction, and the body diode is turned on. The voltage on L_m is clamped by the voltage reflected from the secondary side, and the resonant capacitor C_r and resonant inductor L_r participate in the resonance. The resonance current i_{Lr} decreases sinusoidally, and the excitation current i_{Lm} decreases linearly.

t_4–t_5 stage: at the moment of $t = t_4$, Q_2 is turned on under zero voltage conditions. When the resonant current i_{Lr} is sinusoidal goes down to zero and then increases in the opposite direction. The excitation current i_{Lm} changes linearly from a positive maximum to a negative maximum. The resonant capacitor C_r discharges, and the stored energy is transferred to the load in the form of the difference between i_{Lr} and i_{Lm}.

t_5–t_6 stage: at the moment of $t = t_5$, i_{Lm} drops to $i_{Lr} = i_{Lm}$. At this time, diode D_2 is turned off. Because the excitation inductor L_m participates in resonance, and L_m is far greater than L_r, the resonance current remains constant until Q_2 is turned off. When Q_2 is turned off, the next cycle begins.

2.3 Fundamental Analysis and Voltage Gain

First harmonic approximation (FHA) is a method to analyze the steady-state model of the resonant converter. When the converter's switching frequency works at the resonant frequency, the resonant network shows high impedance to the higher harmonics far away from the fundamental wave of voltage and current. The energy conversion of the converter is mainly completed by the fundamental wave in the Fourier series of voltage and current. At this time, the steady-state analysis of the converter only considers the fundamental component, and the error is tiny when the converter works near f_s. The AC steady-state model of LLC Resonant Converter in fundamental analysis is shown in Fig. 4. Among them, v_{fund} is the fundamental neutral point voltage in the switching network. $R_L{}'$ is the AC equivalent resistance after the load resistance, and the secondary side of the high-frequency transformer is converted to the primary side.

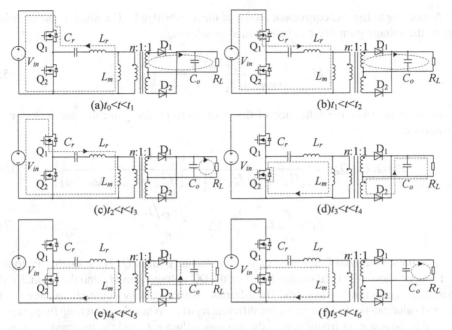

Fig. 3. Working mode analysis of half bridge LLC resonant converter.

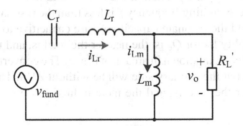

Fig. 4. AC steady-state model of a half-bridge LLC resonant converter.

The fundamental voltage is obtained by the Fourier decomposition of the neutral point voltage.

$$v_{\text{fund}} = \frac{2}{\pi} V_{\text{in}} \sin(2\pi f \cdot t) \tag{3}$$

Where, V_{in} is the DC input voltage, and f is the switching frequency of the converter. AC equivalent resistance R_L' can be rewritten as follows.

$$R_L' = \frac{8n^2}{\pi^2} \cdot R_L \tag{4}$$

Where, n is the transformation ratio of the high-frequency transformer and R_L is the value of load resistance.

According to the AC equivalent model of the half-bridge LLC resonant converter in Fig. 4, the voltage gain Mg can be obtained as follows.

$$M_g = \left| \frac{(j\omega L_m) \| R_L'}{(j\omega L_m) \| R_L' + j\omega L_r + \frac{1}{j\omega C_r}} \right| \tag{5}$$

In order to study the influence of the parameters on the gain, the parameters are normalized.

$$M_g(f_n, L_n, Q_e) = \left| \frac{L_n \cdot f_n^2}{\left[(L_n + 1) \cdot f_n^2 - 1\right] + j\left[(f_n^2 - 1) \cdot f_n \cdot Q_e \cdot L_n\right]} \right| \tag{6}$$

$$f_n = \frac{f}{f_s}; L_n = \frac{f_m}{f_r}; Q_e = \frac{\sqrt{L_m/L_r}}{R_L'} \tag{7}$$

f_n is the normalized frequency. L_n is the inductance ratio. Q_e is the quality factor.

Figure 5 shows the relationship between the DC voltage gain M_g and the normalized frequency f_n under different loads. The difference between the switching frequency f and the load value can be divided into three different regions. When the switching frequency f is equal to the resonant frequency f_s, the resonant inductor L_r and the resonant capacitor C_r resonate in series. They are short-circuited, and the voltage drop is zero. The input voltage is directly applied to the excitation inductance and load, so the voltage gain is constant at 1. When the switching frequency f is less than the resonant frequency f_s, the resonant inductor L_r and the resonant capacitor C_r are capacitive to the outside. At this time, the larger the quality factor Q_e is, the heavier the load is, and the more capacitive the total input impedance is, as shown in area ① of Fig. 5. The converter can achieve ZCS on the secondary side, but the primary side will be without ZVS. The lower the quality factor Q_e is, the lighter the load is, and the more inductive the total input impedance

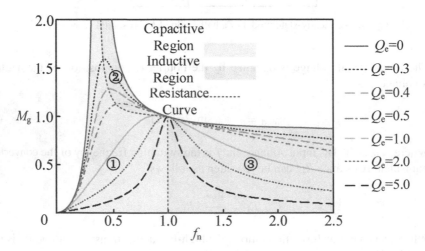

Fig. 5. Voltage gain vs. normalized frequency curves.

is. The voltage gain is greater than 1, which is shown in area ② of Fig. 5. At this time, the converter can realize ZVS on the primary side and ZCS on the secondary side. The intersection line between them is the total load curve, which is shown as a resistance. When the switching frequency f is greater than the resonant frequency f_s, the resonant inductor L_r and the resonant capacitor C_r are inductive. The excitation inductor L_m and the load capacitor parallel network are inductive, and the voltage gain is less than 1. The converter works in the inductive region, that is, region ③. The converter can achieve ZVS on the primary side but lose ZCS on the secondary side. In order to realize ZVS on the primary side, the converter should be designed to work in zone ② and zone ③.

2.4   Effect of Output Capacitance of Switch on LLC Resonant Converter

When the converter's switching frequency works at $f = f_s$ point, the resonant network voltage is zero as a whole, and the efficiency of transferring energy to the secondary side reaches the maximum value. Generally, this point is designed as the rated working state of the converter. Based on the analysis of the working condition of the converter at $f = f_s$, the dead time of the LLC resonant converter is much less than the switching cycle time. In the dead time, the primary and secondary sides are disconnected, and the excitation current i_{Lm} is equal to the resonant current i_{Lr}. The voltage on the excitation inductor is the value of the secondary side output voltage converted to the primary side, which is converted linearly in a quarter cycle and reaches the peak value in the dead time. The waveform is shown in Fig. 6, and the peak value of the primary excitation current is I_{Lm_p} can be calculated as follows.

$$I_{\text{Lm\_P}} = \frac{nV_o}{L_m} \cdot \frac{T_0}{4} \tag{8}$$

In order to realize ZVS at the primary side, the peak value of excitation current i_{Lm_p} in dead time should charge and discharge the output junction capacitance C_{oss} of Q_1 and Q_2, and the PCB distributed capacitance C_{stray} in the switching network to make the drain-source voltage drop to zero before the device is turned on.

$$I_{\text{Lm\_P}} \geq \frac{2V_{in}(2C_{oss} + C_{stray})}{t_d} \tag{9}$$

The distributed capacitance C_{stray} of PCB is mainly the capacitance between the gate and source lying in pads and the routing line of PCB, which should be optimized in PCB plate making. Generally, its value is far less than the output junction capacitance C_{oss} of the power devices. $2C_{oss} + C_{stray} = C_{eq}$ is proposed, and Eq. (8) is substituted into Eq. (9) to get the following formula.

$$L_m \leq \frac{T_0 t_d}{16 C_{eq}} \tag{10}$$

From the above analysis, it can be seen that in $T/2$, the resonance current i_{Lr} changes according to the sinusoidal quantity, and the excitation current i_{Lm} changes linearly.

$$i_{Lr}(t) = \sqrt{2} I_{\text{RMS\_P}} \sin(\omega t + \Phi) \tag{11}$$

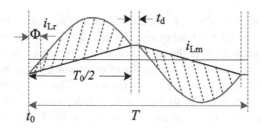

Fig. 6. Resonant current and excitation current at $f = f_s$.

Among them, I_{RMS_P} is the practical value of primary current, ω is the angular frequency of the resonant frequency, Φ is the phase difference between resonance current and excitation current. In the dead time, the excitation current i_{Lm} is equal to the resonance current i_{Lr}.

$$i_{Lr}(t_0) = \sqrt{2}I_{RMS\_P}\sin(\Phi) = -\frac{nV_0}{L_m} \cdot \frac{T}{4} \tag{12}$$

At the same time, the difference between the primary resonance current i_{Lr} and the excitation current i_{Lm} is the current transmitted to the secondary side in half a period.

$$\frac{\int_0^{\frac{T_0}{2}}\left[\sqrt{2}I_{RMS\_P}\sin(\omega_0 t + \Phi) + \frac{nV_0}{L_m}\frac{T_0}{4} - \frac{nV_0}{L_m}t\right]dt}{T/2} = \frac{V_0}{nR_L} \tag{13}$$

The excitation inductance L_m is taken as the maximum value under ZVS.

$$L_m = \frac{T_0 t_d}{16C_{eq}} \tag{14}$$

From Eq. (13) and Eq. (14), the relationship among the practical values of primary current I_{RMS_P}, C_{eq}, and dead time t_d can be obtained.

$$I_{RMS\_P} = \frac{1}{4\sqrt{2}}\frac{V_0}{nR_L}\sqrt{\frac{256C_{eq}^2 n^4 R_L^2}{t_d^2} + 4\pi^2 + \frac{16\pi^2(T_0 t_d + t_d^2)}{T_0^2}} \tag{15}$$

The RMS of the secondary side current is the current transferred to the secondary side by the difference between the resonance current i_{Lr} and the excitation current i_{Lm}.

$$I_{RMS\_S} = \sqrt{\frac{\int_0^{\frac{T_0}{2}}[i_{Lr}(t) - i_{Lm}(t)]^2 dt}{T_S/2}}$$

$$= \frac{\sqrt{3}}{24\pi}\frac{V_0}{R_L}\sqrt{\frac{256C_{eq}^2(5\pi^2 - 48)n^4 R_L^2 T_0}{t_d^2(T_0 + 2t_d)} + \frac{12\pi^4 T_0}{T_0 + 2t_d} + \frac{48\pi^4(T_0 t_d + t_d^2)}{T_0(T_0 + 2t_d)}} \tag{16}$$

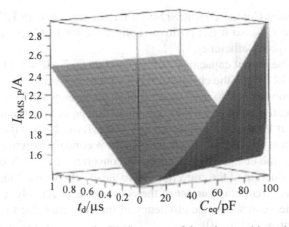

Fig. 7. Relationship between the RMS current of the primary side and C_{eq} and t_d.

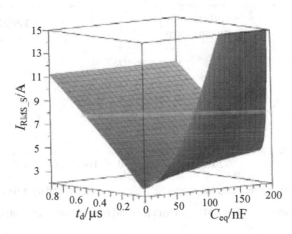

Fig. 8. Relationship between the RMS current of the secondary side and C_{eq} and t_d.

The current RMS determines the conduction loss of the primary side and secondary side switching devices and rectifier diodes. In the case of ZVS on the primary side and ZCS on the secondary side, the conduction loss accounts for an essential part of the total loss of the converter. Reducing the RMS current of the primary and secondary side is of great significance to improve the converter's efficiency. Figure 7 and Fig. 8 respectively draw the graphs of the primary and secondary side current practical value changing with the equivalent capacitance C_{eq} and dead time t_d by Maple mathematical software. It can be seen that under the condition of a specific dead time t_d, the primary and secondary side currents have a minimum value. And with the increase of C_{eq}, the primary and secondary side current also increases. Since C_{eq} is mainly composed of the output capacitance C_{oss} of switching devices, the smaller output capacitance of C_{oss} corresponds to the smaller RMS currents of the primary and secondary sides. It is of great significance to reduce the conduction loss and transformer loss of the converter and improve its efficiency. Compared with Si MOSFET, the cascade GaN HEMT has smaller output capacitance C_{oss}, so it has positive significance for LLC resonant converter to reduce loss and improve efficiency.

According to the output capacitance of the cascode GaN HEMT TPH3206PSB and Si MOSFET IPI60R199CP, the change of RMS current at primary and secondary sides of LLC resonant converter with dead time is obtained, as shown in Fig. 9. It can be seen that the optimal dead time of Si MOSFET is about 200ns, and the optimal dead time of GaN device is about 100ns. Compared with Si MOSFET, the RMS of the primary current for GaN device is less than 0.2A, and the RMS of the secondary current is less than 1.5A. It can be seen that the design of LLC resonant converter using GaN device results in the turn-off loss reduction of the converter due to the excellent switching characteristics of the devices. The circulating current of the converter is effectively reduced. The loss of the converter decreases, and the efficiency of the converter due to its small output capacitance is improved (Fig. 10).

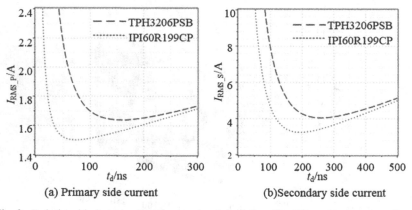

(a) Primary side current   (b)Secondary side current

Fig. 9. Relationship between RMS current and dead time for different output capacitors.

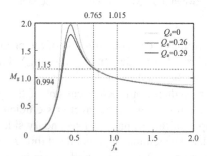

Fig. 10. Parameter design verification.

3   Experimental Verification and Loss Analysis

3.1   Experimental Verification

A half-bridge LLC resonant converter based on the cascode GaN HEMT TPH3206PSB is built. It is tested under different load conditions, and the working waveforms of the converter are shown in Fig. 11. The energy increases with the growth of the load, which is transferred from the converter to the load. The resonant current rises, and the primary side cycle energy increases. The converter can realize ZVS at the primary side in the full load range. Compared with hard-switching applications, the peak and oscillation problems in soft switching applications vanish, and the stability of the converter is greatly improved. At the same time, the efficiency of the converter under different loads is tested. As shown in Fig. 12, the maximum efficiency of the converter can reach 97%, and the full load efficiency of 96.2% is achieved.

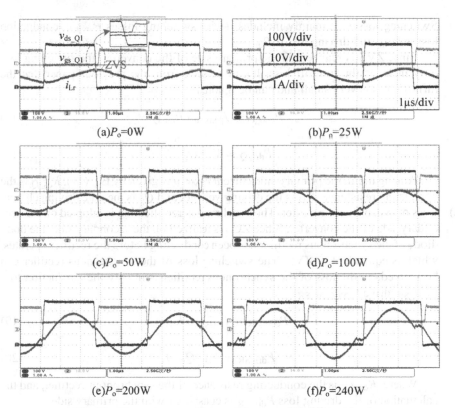

Fig. 11. Converter operating waveforms under different loads.

3.2   Loss Analysis

In order to make further efforts on the influence of the cascode GaN HEMT on LLC resonant conversion, the loss of the converter is analyzed.

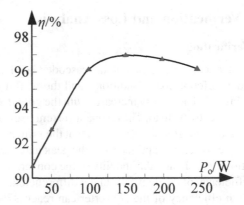

Fig. 12. Converter efficiency curve.

(1) Switching losses. It mainly includes device switching losses P_{switch}, conduction losses P_{con}, and driving losses P_{dri}.

Since ZVS is realized on the primary side of the converter, the switching loss only includes the turn-off loss. It can be seen from the previous paper that the turn-off loss is very small and can be ignored.

$$P_{\text{con\_Q}} = I_{\text{RMS\_P}}^2 \cdot R_{\text{ds\_Q}} \tag{17}$$

$$P_{\text{dri\_Q}} = V_{\text{D}} \cdot Q_{\text{g}} \cdot f_{\text{s}} \tag{18}$$

Among them, the primary side current $I_{\text{RMS\_P}}$ is given by Eq. (11). $R_{\text{ds\_Q}}$ is the conducting resistance. V_{D} is the driving voltage, and Q_{g} is the gate driving charge.

(2) Loss of synchronous rectifier. The synchronous rectification is adopted on the secondary side of the converter. Since ZCS is realized on the secondary side, the body diode of the synchronous rectifier has been conducting before the rectifier operates, which is equivalent to ZVS. The switching loss of the synchronous rectifier can be ignored, so the loss of the synchronous rectifier is mainly the conduction loss $P_{\text{con\_SR}}$, drive loss $P_{\text{dri\_SR}}$.

$$P_{\text{con\_SR}} = I_{\text{RMS\_S}}^2 \cdot R_{\text{ds\_SR}} \tag{19}$$

$$P_{\text{dri\_SR}} = V_{\text{D}} \cdot Q_{\text{g}} \cdot f_{\text{s}} \tag{20}$$

Where, $R_{\text{ds\_SR}}$ is the conducting resistance of the synchronous rectifier, and the calculation of the driving loss $P_{\text{dri\_SR}}$ is consistent with the primary side.

(3) Loss of magnetic devices. In this paper, the excitation inductance and resonant inductance are designed as leakage inductance and excitation inductance of the high-frequency transformer. The loss of magnetic devices is mainly copper loss P_{Cu} and iron loss P_{Fe} of the high-frequency transformer. The copper loss P_{Cu} is obtained as follows.

$$P_{\text{Cu}} = R_{\text{Cu\_P}} \cdot I_{\text{RMS\_P}}^2 + R_{\text{Cu\_S}} \cdot I_{\text{RMS\_S}}^2$$

$$= 2\sigma j N_P \sqrt{\pi A_e} I_{RMS\_P} + 2\sigma j N_S \sqrt{\pi A_e} I_{RMS\_S} \tag{21}$$

Among them, σ is the copper resistivity. N_P and N_S are the primary and secondary turns, respectively. j is the current density. A_e is the conductor cross-sectional area. The iron loss P_{Fe} is calculated in Eq. (22).

$$P_{Fe} = P_v \cdot V_e = k \cdot f^m \cdot B_p^n \cdot V_e \tag{22}$$

Where, P_v is the magnetism core specific loss. k, m, and n are constants. f is the equivalent frequency. B_p is the flux density. V_e is the effective volume of the core. The loss of each part of the converter is calculated as shown in Fig. 13.

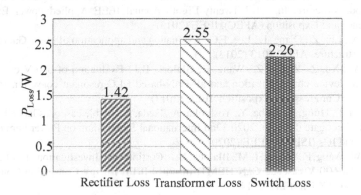

Fig. 13. LLC resonant converter loss analysis.

In LLC resonant converter based on the cascode GaN HEMT, the device loss does not account for most of the converter loss, and the high-frequency transformer loss becomes the most significant part of the system loss under full load. Therefore, to further improve the converter's efficiency, it is necessary to use a planar high-frequency transformer to reduce the transformer loss further.

4 Conclusions

The ccascode GaN HEMTs are applied to LLC resonant converter with the soft-switching topology. The relationship between dead time, primary and secondary current RMS, and output capacitance is analyzed. At the same time, relying on the advantage of cascode GaN HEMT with small output capacitance, the soft-switching condition of the LLC resonant converter is improved. The RMS current of the primary and secondary sides is reduced. The conduction loss and transformer loss are further reduced. The converter efficiency is improved. The hardware platform of 240W LLC resonant converter based on the cascode GaN HEMT is built. The maximum efficiency of the converter is 97%, and the total load efficiency can reach 96.2%. The loss of each part of the converter is analyzed, and the direction of further improving the efficiency of the converter is proposed.

Acknowledgements. The authors acknowledge the Jiangsu University Natural Science Research Project (18KJB470024) and Provincial Construction System Science and Technology Project of Jiangsu Provincial Housing and Urban-Rural Construction Department (2018ZD088). This work is partly supported by the Natural Science Foundation of Jiangsu Province of China (No. BK20161165), the applied fundamental research Foundation of Xuzhou of China (No. KC17072). The authorized patents for invention are also the research and development of Jiangsu Province Industry-University-Research Cooperation Project (BY2019056).

References

1. Huang, X., Liu, Z., Qiang, L., Lee, F.C.: Evaluation and application of 600V GaN HEMT in cascode structure. In: 2013 Twenty-Eighth Annual IEEE Applied Power Electronics Conference and Exposition (APEC). IEEE (2013)
2. Huang, X., Liu, Z., Qiang, L., Lee, F.C.: Evaluation and application of 600V GaN HEMT in cascode structure. APEC 2013 (2013)
3. Zhang, W., Xu, Z., Zhang, Z., Wang, F., Blalock, B.J.: Evaluation of 600 V cascode GaN HEMT in device characterization and all-GaN-based LLC resonant converter. In: Energy Conversion Congress and Exposition. IEEE (2013)
4. Sugiyama, T., Hung, H., Isobe, Y., Yoshioka, A., Ikeda, K.: Stable cascode GaN HEMT operation by direct gate drive. In: 2020 32nd International Symposium on Power Semiconductor Devices and ICs (ISPSD). IEEE (2020)
5. Zhang, W., Wang, F., Tolbert, L.M., Blalock, B.J., Costinett, D.: Investigation of soft-switching behavior of 600 V cascode GaN HEMT. In: 2014 IEEE Energy Conversion Congress and Exposition (ECCE). IEEE (2014)
6. Li, Q., Liu, B., Duan, S.: Simplified analytical model for estimation of switching loss of cascode gan hemts in totem-pole pfc converters. Chin. J. Electr. Eng. **5**(3), 1–9 (2019)
7. Liu, Z.: Characterization and failure mode analysis of cascode gan HEMT. Virginia Tech (2014)
8. Katzir, L., Shmilovitz, D.: A 1-MHZ 5-kV power supply applying SiC diodes and GaN HEMT cascode mosfets in soft switching. IEEE J. Emerg. Sel. Top. Power Electron. **4**(4), 1474–1482 (2016)
9. Huang, X., Li, Q., Liu, Z., Lee, F.C.: Analytical loss model of high voltage gan hemt in cascode configuration. IEEE Trans. Power Electron. **29**(5), 2208–2219 (2014)
10. Wang, N., Jia, H., Tian, M., Li, Z.W., Xu, Y.: Impact of transformer stray capacitance on the conduction loss in a GaN-based LLC resonant converter. In: 2017 IEEE 3rd International Future Energy Electronics Conference and ECCE Asia (IFEEC 2017 - ECCE Asia). IEEE (2017)
11. Liu, Z., Huang, X., Lee, F.C., Qiang, L.: Simulation model development and verification for high voltage GaN HEMT in cascode structure. In: Energy Conversion Congress and Exposition. IEEE (2013)
12. Park, H.P., Jung, J.H.: Design considerations of 1 MHz LLC resonant converter with GaN E-HEMT. In: European Conference on Power Electronics & Applications. IEEE (2015)
13. Xiang, J., Ren, X., Wang, Y., Yue, Z.: Investigation of cascode stucture GaN devices in ZCS region of LLC resonant converter. In: 2017 IEEE Energy Conversion Congress and Exposition (ECCE). IEEE (2017)
14. Cheng, S., Chou, P.C.: Power conditioning applications of 700V GaN-HEMTs cascode switch. In: Conference of the IEEE Industrial Electronics Society. IEEE (2016)

15. Huang, X., Qiang, L., Liu, Z., Lee, F.C.: Analytical loss model of high voltage GaN HEMT in cascode configuration. In: 2013 IEEE Energy Conversion Congress and Exposition. IEEE (2013)
16. Attia, Y., Youssef, M.: GaN on silicon E-HEMT and pure silicon MOSFET in high frequency switching of EV DC/DC converter: a comparative study in a nissan leaf. In: 2016 IEEE International Telecommunications Energy Conference (INTELEC). IEEE (2016)
17. Li, Q., Liu, B., Duan, S., Wang, L., Luo, C.: Analytical switching loss model of cascode GaN HEMTs based totem-pole PFC converters considering stray inductances. In: 2018 1st Workshop on Wide Bandgap Power Devices and Applications in Asia (WiPDA Asia). School of Electrical and Electronic Engineering, Huazhong University of Science and Technology, Wuhan (2018)
18. Galanos, N., Popovic, J., Ferreira, J.A., Gerber, M.: Influence of the magnetic's parasitic capacitance in the switching of high-voltage cascode GaN HEMT. In: Cips, International Conference on Integrated Power Electronics Systems. VDE (2016)
19. Chou, P.-C., Cheng, S.: Performance characterization of gallium nitride hemt cascode switch for power conditioning applications. Mater. Sci. Eng. B (2015)

Characteristics and Application of Cascode GaN HEMT

En Fang[1,2(✉)]

[1] School of Electrical and Control Engineering, Xuzhou
University of Technology, Xuzhou 221018, Jiangsu, China
fangen@cumt.edu.cn
[2] Jiangsu Key Construction Laboratory of Large Engineering Equipment
Testing and Control Technology, Xuzhou 221018, Jiangsu, China

Abstract. For the particular structure of cascode GaN HEMT, the parameters related to its output characteristics, transfer characteristics, driving characteristics, and switching characteristics are compared with Si MOSFETs under the same voltage and current level. And it is better than Si MOSFET. To obtain accurate switching loss and clarify the influence of various parameters on the switching process, a practical segmentation analysis model is established for the dynamic process of cascode GaN HEMT turn-on and turn-off, which is verified by the dual-pulse test hardware platform. The prediction of the process voltage and current waveform is accurate.

Keywords: Cascode · GaN device · Characteristics

1 Introduction

As the most important secondary energy in social production, electrical energy is widely used in the production and life of human society because of its clean, manageable control and easy transmission. Multiple transformations are needed in the process of power production, transmission, and consumption. As one of the critical technologies of power conversion, power electronic technology is more and more profoundly going into human life and affecting the progress of human civilization. After more than half a century of development, power electronics technology has been widely used in transportation, energy, national defense, and other fields of the national economy and people's livelihood. In today's world, energy shortage and environmental protection problems are becoming increasingly severe, and photovoltaic power generation, wind power generation and electric vehicle industry promote the continuous development of power electronic technology. At the same time, it also puts forward new requirements for power electronic devices and encourages them to develop in the direction of high frequency, high efficiency, and high power density.

After decades of development, the performance of Si-based power switching devices is approaching its material limits. The power electronic converter is limited to further

D. Jiang and H. Song (Eds.): SIMUtools 2021, LNICST 424, pp. 194–204, 2022.
https://doi.org/10.1007/978-3-030-97124-3_17

growth in the direction of high frequency, high efficiency, and high power density. As an outstanding representative of the third generation of wide bandgap semiconductor devices, Cascode GaN HEMT utilizes a cascode structure to achieve the normally-off nature of GaN devices, with unmatched steady-state and dynamic performance of Si-based devices. In order to promote its replacement of Si devices and give full play to the performance advantages of cascode GaN HEMTs, this thesis studies its characteristics and applications in hard switching and soft switching states.

2   Characteristics and Analysis of Cascode GaN HEMT

2.1 Performance Comparison

Table 1. List of device models.

Current/A	Transphorm	Infineon	Fairchild	Vishay
16	TPH3206PSB	IPD65R250E6	FCPF190N65 S3R0L	
20	TPH3208PS	IPP60R190C6	FCPF190N60	SiHA22N60AE
27	TPH3212PS			SiHP28N65E
35	TPH3205WSBQA	IPP65R099C6	FCP125N65S3	SiHG33N65EF
47	TP65H035WS	SPW47N65C3	FCH47N60	SiHW47N65E

The FOM (figure of merit) of the device is the product of gate charge Q_g and the conducting state resistance R_{ds_on} in normal operation. Generally, the FOM or the product of gate-drain charge Q_{gd} of the device and the conducting resistance R_{ds_on} is used for measuring device performance. The smaller the product is, the better the device performance is.

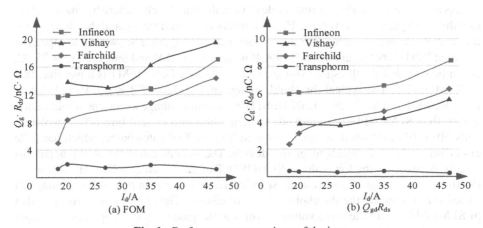

Fig. 1. Performance comparison of devices.

With the continuous improvement of caspode GaN HEMT devices of Transphorm company and the introduction of improved models, the products are becoming more and more mature. At present, commercial products mainly include 650 V and 900 v series devices. Table 1 shows the selection of 650 V series devices of Transphorm with different current levels and Si MOSFETs with corresponding voltage and current levels from Infineon, Fairchild, and Vishay companies. Figure 1 shows the FOM value, gate-drain charge Q_{gd}, and conducting resistance R_{ds_on} of the above devices. The product results are compared. It can be seen that the quality factor and $Q_{gd}R_{ds\_on}$ of GaN device are almost only 1/10 to 1/5 of that for Si MOSFET. And the performance gap becomes more and more evident with the increase of current. The results show that cascode GaN HEMT has better performance than Si MOSFET, and the higher the power level is, the more pronounced the advantage is.

2.2 Transfer Characteristics Analysis

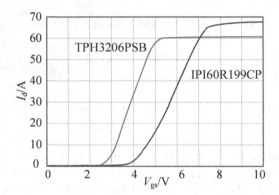

Fig. 2. Transfer characteristic curves comparison.

As a voltage-controlled current mode device, the transfer characteristic characterizes the ability of gate-source voltage V_{gs} to amplify drain current I_d, and the slope of the transfer characteristic curve is transconductance g_{fs}. Figure 2 shows the comparison between TPH3206PSB and IPI60R199CP when $V_{ds} = 10$ V and temperature is 25 °C. It can be seen that the threshold voltage V_{TH} of cascode GaN HEMT is lower than that of Si MOSFET. The typical threshold voltage of TPH3206PSB is 2.1 V, and that of IPI60R199CP is 3 V. Cascode GaN HEMTs have better voltage to current amplification ability than Si MOSFETs. In cascode structure, the turn-on and turn-off of depletion GaN HEMT is controlled by low voltage Si MOSFET of gate-source, which has little effect on the overall threshold of the device. The overall threshold of the apparatus mainly depends on the low voltage Si MOSFET of gate-source of GaN HEMT, while the threshold voltage of low voltage Si MOSFET is lower than that of high voltage Si MOSFET. Therefore, the threshold voltage of cascode GaN HEMT is lower than that of Si MOSFET with the same voltage level, and the gate-source voltage has a stronger amplification ability to drain current.

2.3 Driving Characteristic Analysis

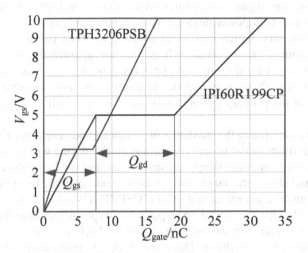

Fig. 3. Gate charge curves comparison.

The gate charge characteristic is the relation curve between the driving charge and the gate-source voltage of the device in the switching process. Because the switching time of the device in the circuit is related to the inter-electrode parasitic capacitance, and the inter-electrode parasitic capacitance is a function of the drain-source voltage VDS of the device, in order to facilitate the circuit design, in the actual application process, Generally, the switching speed is calculated. The driving circuit is designed by the gate charge characteristic curve of the device. Figure 3 shows the comparison of gate charge characteristic curves of TPH3206PSB and IPI60R199CP at $V_{ds} = 400$ V and $I_d = 10$ A. Taking the gate characteristic of IPI60R199CP as an example, Q_{gs} is the charge required to charge the gate-source parasitic capacitor C_{gs} to the threshold voltage, and Q_{gd} is the charge required to overcome the "Miller effect" in the switching process of the device, also known as "Miller charge". It can be seen that the gate charge of GaN device is much less than that of Si MOSFET, significantly the Miller platform charge Q_{gd} is only one-fifth of it. It ensures faster-driving speed, shorter switching time, and less loss of Gan devices under the same driving conditions.

Table 2. Contrast of driving characteristic related parameters.

Device model	Driving voltage range/V	Threshold voltage/V	Q_{gs}/nC	Q_{gd}/nC	Q_g/nC
TPH3206PSB	±18	2.1	2.1	2.2	6.2
IPI60R199CP	±20	3	8	11	32

Table 2 shows the parameters related to device driving. It can be seen that the driving voltage range of cascode GaN HEMT is similar to that of Si MOSFET. The Si MOSFET driver chip widely used at present can be directly used to drive cascode GaN HEMT, but the threshold voltage of the latter is lower than that of Si MOSFET, which is more likely to lead to misdirection of gate-source interference. Due to the high dv/dt and di/dt in the switching process of Gan power devices, the switching process is more easily affected by parasitic parameters, which makes the coupling between the drive circuit and the power circuit become serious, and the voltage and current oscillation of the drive circuit may be intensified or turned on by mistake. Therefore, it is necessary to optimize the switching speed of GaN by selecting the appropriate driving resistor and optimizing the PCB layout of the primary power circuit and driving circuit to reduce the parasitic parameters.

At the same time, due to the existence of common-mode capacitor C_{IO} in the drive isolator, the high dv/dt in the process of turning on the device will generate common-mode current in the front controller of the driver chip, and the larger the common mode capacitor C_{IO} and dv/dt, the larger the common-mode current. Because the dv/dt of GaN devices is much higher than that of Si MOSFET, it is essential to select a suitable low common-mode capacitor driver. In response to this problem, a digital isolator can be added between the driver chip and the front-end controller, but this undoubtedly increases the complexity and cost of the driver. Therefore, the development and production of driver isolation chips with low common-mode capacitance is a better choice for the application of GaN devices in the future.

2.4 Comparison of Switch Characteristic Parameters

The switching characteristics of power devices are mainly related to the inter-electrode parasitic capacitance. The smaller the inter-electrode parasitic capacitance is, the shorter the charging time is, and the closer the switching process is to the ideal state. The inter-electrode parasitic capacitance of power devices mainly consists of gate-source parasitic capacitance C_{gs}, gate-drain parasitic capacitance C_{gd}, drain-source parasitic capacitance C_{ds}. In practical application, input capacitance C_{iss}, feedback capacitance C_{rss} and output capacitance C_{oss}. Equation (1) is usually used to express the conversion relationship among them.

$$
\begin{cases}
C_{iss} = C_{gs} + C_{gd} \\
C_{rss} = C_{gd} \\
C_{oss} = C_{ds} + C_{gd}
\end{cases}
\tag{1}
$$

Table 3 shows the comparison of switching characteristic parameters between TPH3206PSB and IPI60R199CP. The test conditions of TPH3206PSB are: $V_{gs} = 0V$, $V_{ds} = 400V$, $f = 1$ MHz. The test conditions of IPI60R199CP parameters are: $V_{gs} = 0$ V, $V_{ds} = 100$ V, $f = 1$ MHz (Generally speaking, the parasitic capacitance between electrodes is constant when V_{ds} exceeds 100 v. therefore, the difference of V_{ds} test conditions does not affect the comparison. It can be seen that the parasitic capacitance of cascode GaN HEMT is much smaller than that of Si MOSFET, which makes the switching characteristics better. Compared with Si MOSFET, the turn-on delay $t_{d(on)}$, turn-on gate-source voltage-rise time t_r, turn off delay $t_{d(off)}$, and turn off gate-source voltage drop time t_f are greatly reduced so that the voltage and current intersection time in the switching process is reduced, and the switching loss is reduced, which provides the necessary conditions for greatly increasing the switching frequency of the converter.

Table 3. Switching characteristic related parameters comparison.

Device model	C_{iss}/pF	Crss/pF	C_{oss}/pF	t_d(on)/ns	t_r/ns	t_d(off)/ns	t_f/ns
TPH3206PSB	720	5.5	46	6	4.5	9.7	4
IPI60R199CP	1520		72	10	5	50	5

Table 4 shows the reverse recovery characteristic parameters of TPH3206PSB and IPI60R199CP: peak reverse recovery current I_{RP}, reverse recovery time t_{rr}, reverse recovery charge Q_{rr}. Because the depletion type high voltage GaN HEMT in cascode GaN HEMT structure adopts two-dimensional electron gas conduction channel, there is no PN junction in Si based device and parasitic body diode, so there is no reverse recovery problem. At the same time, the breakdown voltage of Si MOSFET in cascode structure is lower, the reverse recovery characteristic of the parasitic diode is better than that of high voltage Si MOSFET, and the reverse recovery charge Q_{rr} is much smaller. Therefore, the reverse recovery charge Q_{rr} of cascode GaN HEMT is much smaller than that of Si MOSFET with the same voltage and current. It can be seen from Table 4 that the reverse recovery charge Q_{rr} of TPH3206PSB is less than 1% of IPI60R199CP. In some bridge topologies, due to the sizeable reverse recovery charge of Si MOSFET, the current spike is often caused when the complementary transistor is turned on, so it is easy to damage the device. In order to solve this problem, the fast recovery diodes are paralleled in engineering applications. When Gan devices are used, the anti-parallel fast recovery diode can be omitted, and the stability of the converter can be improved.

Table 4. Comparison of parameters related to reverse recovery characteristics.

Device model	I_{RP}/A	t_{rr}/ns	Q_{rr}/nC
TPH3206PSB	10	17	52
IPI60R199CP	33	340	5500

2.5 Working Modal Analysis

According to the common-gate and common-source structure of cascode GaN HEMT, its different working modes are analyzed. In order to study its working principle under different working modes, the equivalent circuit model of cascode GaN HEMT is given in Fig. 4.

When the drain and source of the device are under forwarding voltage, the applied voltage is divided on different parasitic capacitors in the machine. When the gate-source

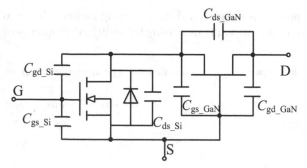

Fig. 4. Cascode GaN HEMT equivalent circuit.

driving voltage V_{gs} of cascode GaN HEMT is less than the threshold voltage V_{TH_Si} of Si MOSFET, the Si MOSFET and depletion GaN HEMT are both in the off state, and there is no current flowing through the device, so the device is in the forward blocking state. When the gate-source driving voltage V_{gs} is greater than the threshold voltage V_{TH_Si} of Si MOSFET, Si MOSFET starts to turn on, and its drain-source parasitic capacitance C_{ds_Si} begins to discharge due to the parallel with gate-source parasitic capacitance C_{gs_GaN} of depletion GaN HEMT and drain-source parasitic capacitance C_{ds_Si} of Si MOSFET. C_{gs_GaN} also starts to release the power, and the gate-source voltage V_{gs_GaN} of depletion GaN HEMT rises. The conduction channel is open, and the whole device is opened in the positive direction. The current flow in the device is shown in Fig. 5.

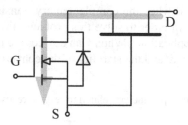

Fig. 5. Cascode GaN HEMT forward conduction mode.

When the drain and source of the device bear the reverse voltage, the device is in reverse conduction mode. Due to the existence of Si MOSFET parasitic diode, the current may flow through different conductive channels, resulting in an additional reverse conduction voltage drop of the device. The main problems are as follows:

(1) Si MOSFET body diode conduction: when the gate-source driving voltage V_{gs} is less than the threshold voltage V_{TH_Si} of Si MOSFET, the bulk diode is on, and the channel is off. The current flows through the bulk diode of Si MOSFET, i_{sd} is the reverse conduction current, R_{ds_GaN} is GaN HEMT conducting resistance, V_{F_Si} is the diode voltage drop of Si MOSFET, as shown in Fig. 6(a). At this time, the

reverse conduction voltage drop of cascode GaN HEMT is as follows.

$$V_{sd} = i_{sd} \cdot R_{ds\_GaN} + V_{F\_Si} \qquad (2)$$

(2) Si MOSFET channel conduction: when the device gate-source driving voltage is large, the channel on state resistance R_{ds_Si} of Si MOSFET is small, and its source-drain voltage drop is less than the reverse conduction voltage drop of Si MOSFET body diode. The current flows through the channel of Si MOSFET, as shown in Fig. 6(b). In this case, the reverse conduction voltage drop of cascode GaN HEMT is as follows.

$$V_{sd} = i_{sd} \cdot (R_{ds\_Si} + R_{ds\_GaN}) \qquad (3)$$

(3) Si MOSFET channel and body diode conduct simultaneously: when the device gate-source driving voltage is greater than the threshold voltage VTH_Si of Si MOSFET, the driving voltage is small, the channel conducting state resistance R_{ds_Si} of Si MOSFET would be significant. When the current flows through the track, the source and drain voltage drop may be greater than the reverse conduction voltage V_{F_Si} of Si MOSFET bulk diode. At this time, the parasitic diode of Si MOSFET is turned on, and its reverse conduction voltage is clamped at V_{F_Si}. The current flows through the channel of Si MOSFET and the body diode at the same time, as shown in Fig. 6(c). The reverse conduction voltage drop of cascode GaN HEMT is as follows.

$$V_{sd} = i_{sd} \cdot R_{ds\_GaN} + V_{F\_Si} \qquad (4)$$

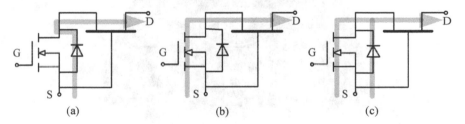

Fig. 6. Cascode GaN HEMT reverse conduction mode.

3 Experimental Verification

In order to verify the accuracy of the analytical model derived in this paper, the mathematical calculation software is used to solve the above analytical model of the switching process, and the voltage and current waveforms of the turn-on and turn-off process are made. The dual-pulse test platform is built and compared with the model results.

Table 5. Model verification experimental parameters.

Parameter	Values	Unit
Input voltage V_{in}	450	V
Drain parasitic inductance L_D	2	nH
Source parasitic inductance L_S	1.5	nH
Gate parasitic inductance L_G	2	nH
Driving resistor R_G	15	Ω

Both Q_L and D_H are cascode GaN HEMT TPH3206PSB made by Transphorm company. The upper D_H gate source is short-circuited and used as a freewheeling tube. The experimental parameters are shown in Table 5.

In the design of dual-pulse hardware platform, the value of parasitic inductance is not easy to control. Through the calculation of drive circuit and power circuit on PCB by Saturn PCB software, the parasitic inductance value of drive circuit $L_{Dri} = 3.2nH$, and the total parasitic inductance value of power circuit $L_{Pow} = 3.8nH$ are obtained. It is basically consistent with the model validation parameters. The double pulse test platform is shown in Fig. 7. Figure 8 shows the experimental waveforms and switching process waveforms when i_d is 10A.

Fig. 7. Gallium nitride device dual-pulse test experimental platform.

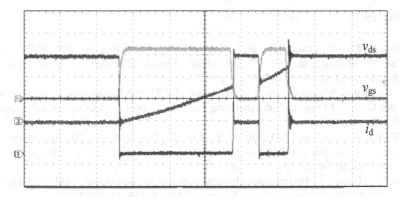

Fig. 8. Experimental waveforms of double pulse test.

4   Conclusions

In order to promote the substitution of cascode GaN HEMT for Si MOSFET, this chapter firstly compares the performance index of cascode GaN HEMT with Si MOSFET at the same voltage and current level. It makes clear that GaN device is superior to Si-based device. At the same time, the output characteristics, transfer characteristics, driving factors, and switching characteristics of cascode type GaN HEMT are compared with Si MOSFET at the same voltage and current level. The advantages of different attributes of cascode type GaN HEMT are explained. The reverse conduction voltage of cascode type GaN HEMT is slightly higher, and the size of common-mode capacitance should be paid attention to in driver selection. Finally, the different operation modes of cascode GaN HEMT are analyzed. In order to clarify the mechanism of the influence of various parameters on the switching process and obtain more accurate switching loss, an analytical model of cascode type GaN HEMT switching process is established in this chapter by reasonably segmenting and simplifying the switching process and considering the influence of reverse recovery of the complementary transistor. A double pulse test platform is built to verify the accuracy of the model. It is confirmed that the voltage and current waveforms in the switching process are more consistent with the measured waveforms, and the switching loss is more accurate.

Acknowledgements. The authors acknowledge the Jiangsu University Natural Science Research Project (18KJB470024) and Provincial Construction System Science and Technology Project of Jiangsu Provincial Housing and Urban-Rural Construction Department (2018ZD088). This work is partly supported by the Natural Science Foundation of Jiangsu Province of China (No. BK20161165), the applied fundamental research Foundation of Xuzhou of China (No. KC17072). The authorized patents for invention are also the research and development of Jiangsu Province Industry-University-Research Cooperation Project (BY2019056).

References

1. Huang, X., Liu, Z., Qiang, L., Lee, F.C.: Evaluation and application of 600V GaN HEMT in cascode structure. In: 2013 Twenty-Eighth Annual IEEE Applied Power Electronics Conference and Exposition (APEC). IEEE (2013)
2. She, S., Zhang, W., Huang, X., Du, W., Qiang, L.: Thermal analysis and improvement of cascode GaN HEMT in stack-die structure. In: Energy Conversion Congress and Exposition. IEEE (2014)
3. Li, Y., Zhang, Y., Zheng, T.Q., Huang, B., Guo, X.: Research on output volt-ampere characteristics of cascode gan hemt and its application in single-phase inverter. Trans. China Electrotechnical Soc. (2015)
4. Chou, P.C., Cheng, S.: Performance characterization of gallium nitride HEMT cascode switch for power conditioning applications. Mater. Sci. Eng. B **198**, 43–50 (2015)
5. Sriram, S., Alcorn, T., Radulescu, F., Sheppard, S.: Cascode structures for GaN HEMTs. US20140361341 (2014)
6. Elangovan, S., Lin, J., Heng, C.S.: Reliability characterization of Gallium Nitride (GaN) HEMT cascode switch for power electronics applications. In: Sixteenth International Conference on Flow Dynamics (2020)
7. Green, B.M., Chu, K.K.: Cascode connected algan/gan hemts on sic substrates. IEEE Microwave Guided Wave Lett. **10**(8), 316–318 (2000)
8. Chou, P.-C., Chen, S.-H., Hsieh, T.-E., et al.: Evaluation and reliability assessment of GaN-on-Si MIS-HEMT for power switching applications. Energies (2017)
9. Liu, Z.: Characterization and failure mode analysis of cascode GaN HEMT. Virginia Tech (2014)
10. Ma, H., Zhang, N., Lin, L.Y.: Switching model of GaN HEMT in cascode configuration. J. Zhejiang Univ. (2016)
11. Chou, P.-C., Cheng, S.: Performance characterization of gallium nitride HEMT cascode switch for power conditioning applications. Mater. Sci. Eng. B. Solid-State Mater. Adv. Technol. (2015)
12. Sriram, S.: Cascode structures for GaN HEMTs (2017)
13. Swain, R., Jena, K., Lenka, T.R.: Modelling of capacitance and threshold voltage for ultrathin normally-off algan/gan moshemt. Pramana - J. Phys. **88**, 3 (2017). https://doi.org/10.1007/s12043-016-1310-y
14. Liu, Z., Huang, X., Zhang, W., Lee, F.C., Li, Q.: Evaluation of high-voltage cascode GaN HEMT in different packages. In: IEEE Applied Power Electronics Conference and Exposition-APEC, pp.168–173. IEEE (2014)
15. Zhang, W., Xu, Z., Zhang, Z., Wang, F., Blalock, B.J.: Evaluation of 600 V cascode GaN HEMT in device characterization and all-GaN-based LLC resonant converter. In: Energy Conversion Congress and Exposition. IEEE (2013)
16. Huang, X., Liu, Z., Qiang, L., Lee, F.C.: Evaluation and application of 600V GaN HEMT in cascode structure. APEC (2013)
17. Cheng, S., Chou, P.C.: Power conditioning applications of 700V GaN-HEMTs cascode switch. in: Conference of the IEEE Industrial Electronics Society. IEEE (2016)

Simulation Research on Modular DC Grid-Connected PV System

Qi Zhou[1] and En Fang[1,2](✉)

[1] School of Electrical and Control Engineering, Xuzhou
University of Technology, Xuzhou 221018, Jiangsu, China
fangen@cumt.edu.cn
[2] Jiangsu Key Construction Laboratory of Large Engineering Equipment
Testing and Control Technology, Xuzhou 221018, Jiangsu, China

Abstract. An efficient three-port interleaved boost LLC resonant converter is used as the basic converter unit of the modular DC grid-connected photovoltaic system in this paper. The bi-directional port of the converters is connected through a low voltage DC bus to solve the problem of unbalanced output power and voltage oscillation of each module in the system. The simulation platform of modular DC grid-connected photovoltaic system based on three-port interleaved boost LLC resonant converters is built. The operational principles and characteristics of interleaved boost LLC resonant converter are verified by simulation. The rationality and effectiveness of the modular DC grid-connected photovoltaic system and its voltage sharing control strategy are also demonstrated.

Keywords: Three-port converter · Photovoltaic power generation system · Voltage sharing control

1 Introduction

Since the 21st century, with the economic development and population growth, the demand of human society for energy has been increasing. Oil, coal, and other traditional fossil energy consumption is rising and drying up, at the same time causing environmental pollution, ecological damage, greenhouse effect, and other problems. So it is imperative to develop new alternative energy. All countries worldwide are vigorously promoting the development of various new renewable energy sources, among which photovoltaic (PV) power generation with solar energy is considered one of the most promising renewable energy sources and has been widely studied and applied.

At present, the research on modular photovoltaic AC grid-connected system is mainly focused on the system structure. The inverter structure based on cascade H-bridge (CHB) [1–3] has been widely used. It can directly connect to a medium voltage AC grid without using a step-up transformer. At the same time, the system can realize independent MPPT control of all photovoltaic modules and improve power generation efficiency. However, the large CHB photovoltaic grid-connected system also faces many challenges, such as electrical isolation and leakage current suppression, the power imbalance between phases and phases, and low-frequency ripple disturbance.

D. Jiang and H. Song (Eds.): SIMUtools 2021, LNICST 424, pp. 205–219, 2022.
https://doi.org/10.1007/978-3-030-97124-3_18

2   Isolated Three-Port DC/DC Converter

In recent years, with the development of all kinds of independent power generation systems with energy storage devices, three-port DC/DC converters have been more developed and applied. According to the isolation between the three ports, these converters can be divided into non-isolation, semi-isolation, and full isolation types. The structure of the semi-isolation and fully isolation type three-port DC/DC converter is shown in Fig. 1.

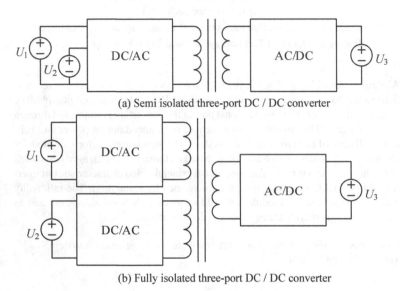

(a) Semi isolated three-port DC / DC converter

(b) Fully isolated three-port DC / DC converter

Fig. 1. Structures of isolated three-port DC/DC converters.

The fully isolated three-port DC/DC converter realizes complete electrical isolation between the three ports and can connect ports of different voltage levels simultaneously. It can also select appropriate DC/AC units according to the voltage and current characteristics of different ports, such as series resonant full-bridge [4, 5], voltage full-bridge [6, 7], voltage half-bridge [8] and current full bridge, etc.

In a stand-alone photovoltaic power generation system, three-port DC/DC converter can connect photovoltaic module, energy storage device and load simultaneously. This kind of system has a compact structure, low cost, high efficiency, and flexible power flow control. Through centralized control of three-port DC/DC converter, MPPT control of photovoltaic module, battery charge and discharge management, and voltage/power control of load can be realized at the same time.

In the distributed photovoltaic power generation system, the additional port of a three-port DC/DC converter can balance the mismatched photovoltaic input power [9, 10] between each module. Each module can achieve independent photovoltaic MPPT and output the same capacity at the same time. Therefore, the three-port DC/DC converter can be used to solve the problems of unbalanced output power and voltage oscillation in the modular photovoltaic DC grid-connected system.

3   Control Strategy of Modular DC Grid-Connected PV System Based on Three-Port IB-llC Resonant Converters

Integrated three-port DC/DC converter has been widely used in renewable energy systems because of its high power density, small size, and lightweight. Theoretically, any isolated three-port DC/DC converter can be used as the basic converter unit in the modular photovoltaic DC grid-connected system studied in this paper.

3.1   System Structure and Operation Modes

As the basic three-port DC/DC converter unit in the modular photovoltaic DC grid-connected system studied in this paper, the three-port IB-LLC resonant converter has the advantages of high gain range, soft switching, high power density, electrical isolation, and high conversion efficiency.

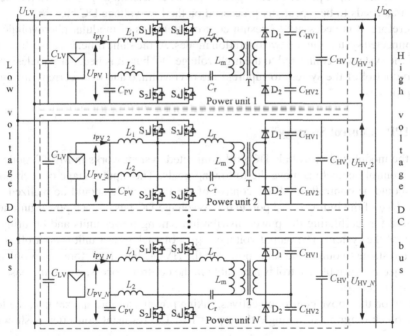

Fig. 2. Topology of modular DC grid-connected PV system based on three-port IB-LLC resonant converters.

The three-port IB-LLC resonant converter is used as the basic converter unit in the modular photovoltaic DC grid-connected system studied in this paper. Its structure is shown in Fig. 2. The input port of a single converter is connected with the photovoltaic module to form a basic power unit. The two-way ports of all converters are connected to the low-voltage DC bus in parallel, and the output ports are cascaded to the high-voltage DC bus. The number n of power units in the system can be determined according to the setting value UHV of the high voltage DC bus voltage UDC and single converter output voltage.

In general, in order to obtain as much energy as possible from the photovoltaic module, the modular photovoltaic DC grid-connected system needs to make each power unit work at the maximum power point of the photovoltaic module. However, sometimes for the safe operation of the power grid, it is necessary to make the whole system operate at a constant total output power to avoid generating too much power and causing the problem of grid overload [11]. Therefore, the system has two steady-state operation modes, namely MPPT operation mode and constant power operation mode.

When the modular photovoltaic DC grid-connected system works in MPPT operation mode, it is necessary to maximize the photovoltaic input power of each power unit in the system. All photovoltaic modules operate at the maximum power point. When the system works in the constant power operation mode, it is necessary to make the whole system obtain continuous photovoltaic input power. At the same time, in order to reduce the system loss and improve the conversion efficiency, it is necessary to make the photovoltaic input power of each power unit as consistent as possible to reduce the energy that needs to be repeatedly processed on the low-voltage DC bus.

Therefore, it is necessary to design control strategies of modular photovoltaic DC grid-connected systems under two operation modes. At the same time, because the output port of the system is connected to the high voltage DC bus, it is necessary to design the start-up control of the system to suppress the over-voltage and over-current during the start-up process.

3.2 MPPT Control Strategy

When the modular photovoltaic DC grid-connected system works in MPPT mode, the system control needs to achieve the following goals. The input voltage of each power U_{PV-i} should be controlled. MPPT control of the PV module should be realized. The voltage U_{LV} of the bidirectional port and low-voltage DC bus of each power unit needs to be held for facilitating the power distribution among power units and ensuring the stability of the system. The output voltage U_{HV_i} of each power unit is controlled precisely and stable to output the same power to the HVDC bus. Therefore, the problem of multi-objective variable control is inevitable in the control process, which increases the difficulty of control.

Based on the above control objectives, taking power unit i as an example, the local control block diagram of a single three-port IB-LLC resonant converter is shown in Fig. 3.

For the photovoltaic MPPT control of the three-port IB-LLC resonant converter input port, the actual output voltage U_{PV_i} and current i_{PV_i} of the photovoltaic module are sampled. And the maximum power point voltage $U_{PV\_i}^*$ obtained by the MPPT algorithm is used as the voltage reference value of the converter input port. Then, the duty cycle D_i^* is calculated by the PI controller and feedforward link.

For the voltage and power flow control of the bi-directional port and output port of the three-port IB-LLC resonant converter, the actual output voltage U_{HV_i} of the converter is obtained by sampling. And the voltage reference value of the bi-directional port is

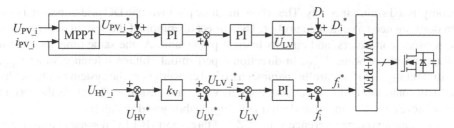

Fig. 3. MPPT control block of the converter in PV system.

adjusted by using the difference between its reference value U_{HV}^* and the actual output voltage U_{HV_i} as follows.

$$U_{LV\_i}^* = U_{LV}^* + k_V(U_{HV\_i} - U_{HV}^*) \tag{1}$$

Among them, U_{LV}^* is the set value of bidirectional port voltage and low voltage DC bus voltage of the converter. $U_{LV\_i}^*$ is the reference value of the bidirectional port voltage of converter in adjusted power unit i. And k_V is the coefficient greater than 0. Then the difference between the reference value $U_{LV\_i}^*$ and the actual U_{LV} obtained by sampling is calculated by the PI controller to get the switching frequency f_i^*.

Finally, according to the duty cycle D_i^* and switching frequency f_i^* obtained in the above process, PWM + PFM modulation method is used to generate the driving signals of four power MOSFETs in the three-port IB-LLC resonant converter to realize the control of the converter.

Assuming that no power is transmitted through the low-voltage DC bus during the operation of the modular photovoltaic DC grid-connected system, the system is equivalent to the cascade DC/DC converter structure. The output voltage U_{HV_i} of the three-port IB-LLC resonant converter with more considerable photovoltaic input power in the system is higher than the reference value U_{HV}^* set by the system. According to Eq. (1), the reference value $U_{LV\_i}^*$ of the bi-directional port voltage of the converter would be set higher. Part of the photovoltaic input power is transmitted to the low voltage DC bus through its bi-directional port, resulting in the decrease of the output power of the converter and the reduction of the output voltage U_{HV_i}.

Similarly, the output voltage U_{HV_i} of the three-port IB-LLC resonant converter with small PV input power in the modular PV DC grid-connected system should be lower than the reference value U_{HV}^*. The reference value $U_{LV\_i}^*$ of the bi-directional port voltage of the converter is reduced. The converter obtains power from the low voltage DC bus through the bi-directional port and transmits it to the output port, and the output voltage U_{HV_i} rises.

Finally, the unbalanced output voltage of every three-port IB-LLC resonant converter is eliminated, and the converters work at the same output voltage in steady-state operation.

According to the control block diagram in Fig. 3, the controller only needs to sample the power unit's internal voltage and current parameters to realize the photovoltaic MPPT control of the input port of the three-port IB-LLC resonant converter. The power control of the bidirectional port and the voltage sharing control of the output port are accomplished simultaneously. The whole modular photovoltaic DC grid-connected system does not need a central controller. The correct operation of the system only requires the sensors, controllers, and circuits in each power unit. At the same time, the output voltage reference value U_{HV}^*, bi-directional port initial voltage reference value U_{LV}^*, coefficient k_V, and PI controller parameters of all converters in the system can be set by the local controller in the power unit. And the values are the same. Therefore, the system can achieve an actual modular design with high stability and scalability.

The output voltage reference value U_{HV}^* of three-port IB-LLC resonant converter in modular photovoltaic DC grid-connected system can be set as follows:

$$U_{HV}^* = \frac{U_{DC}}{N} \tag{2}$$

Where, U_{DC} is the rated voltage of HVDC bus connected to the system output port, and N is the number of power units in the system. The voltage reference value U_{LV}^* of low voltage DC bus and bidirectional ports of all converters in the system can be set as follows.

$$U_{LV}^* = 0.5nU_{HV}^* = \frac{nU_{DC}}{2N} \tag{3}$$

Where, N is the transformation ratio of the converter isolation transformer.

3.3 Constant Power Control Strategy

When the modular photovoltaic DC grid-connected system works in the constant power operation mode, it is necessary to abandon the MPPT control of the photovoltaic module, and adjust the reference value P_{PV}^* of the photovoltaic input power of each power unit according to the difference between the monitoring value P_{DC} of the total output power of the system and the reference value P_{DC}^*. Therefore, it is necessary to add a central controller to the system to monitor the total output power P_{DC} of the system and calculate the reference value P_{PV}^* of photovoltaic input power.

$$P_{PV}^* = \frac{P_{DC}^*}{N} + \frac{P_{DC}^* - P_{DC}}{N} \tag{4}$$

Where, N is the number of power units in the system. According to Eq. (4), the control block diagram of the central controller is shown in Fig. 4.

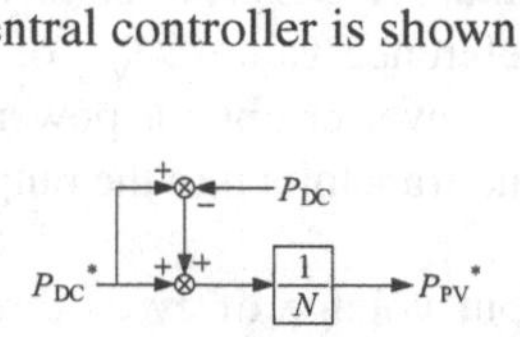

Fig. 4. Control block of central controller in PV system.

In addition, the control objectives of the modular PV DC grid-connected system under constant power operation mode are the same as those of MPPT operation mode for the bidirectional port and output port of each power unit. Combined with the control block diagram of the central system controller and the local controller of each power unit, the control block diagram of the whole system is shown in Fig. 4.

According to the control block diagram, during the constant power operation of the modular photovoltaic DC grid-connected system, if the photovoltaic input power of some power units can not reach the reference value P_{PV}^* due to working conditions or other reasons, the total output power P_{DC} of the system is lower than the reference value P_{DC}^*. According to Eq. (4), the reference value P_{PV}^* of output power sent by the central controller to the local controller of each power unit rises. The power unit with insufficient photovoltaic input power through the bidirectional port and low-voltage DC bus is supplemented so as to restore the total output power of the system to P_{DC}^*. Therefore, the control strategy is used to control the total output power of the system and make the photovoltaic input power of all power units as consistent as possible. The energy that needs to be repeatedly processed is reduced, and the conversion efficiency of the system is improved (Fig. 5).

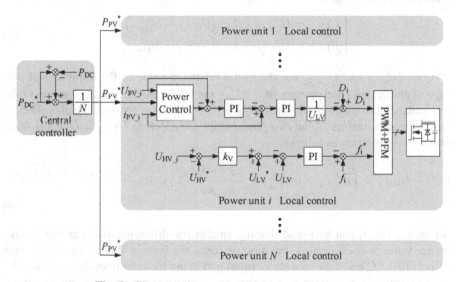

Fig. 5. Constant power control block in the PV system.

In the constant power operation mode, the central controller is required to monitor the operation status of the modular photovoltaic DC grid-connected system and send control commands to the local controller of each power unit to ensure the regular operation of the modular photovoltaic DC grid-connected system. All control commands and data are transmitted between the central controller of the system and the local controller of each power unit through the low-speed communication channel. It is important to note that in practical application, no matter in MPPT operation mode or constant power operation mode, all modular photovoltaic DC grid-connected systems of all structures need the central controller to monitor the whole system.

Since the reference value P_{PV}^* needs to be obtained in each power unit, the control in constant power operation mode is not strict for every modular. For the local controller of each power unit, since only the PV MPPT control of the input port in Fig. 3 is replaced with power control, the voltage equalization control of the output port and voltage stability of the bidirectional port can still be realized through the local controller, sensor and circuit inside each power unit.

3.4 Output Port Voltage Sharing Error Analysis

According to the above analysis, when the local controllers of all three-port IB-LLC resonant converters are set with the same voltage reference values as U_{HV}^* and U_{LV}^* and control coefficient k_V, the output ports of each converter in the modular photovoltaic DC grid-connected system can achieve complete voltage sharing. However, due to unavoidable errors in devices and circuits between converters in practical application, it is difficult for all power units to have precisely the same parameter characteristics. It is assumed that the converters of power unit i and power unit j have different voltage references and coefficients.

$$\begin{cases} U_{LV\_i} = U_{LV\_i0}^* + k_{V\_i}\left(U_{HV\_i} - U_{HV\_i}^*\right) \\ U_{LV\_j} = U_{LV\_j0}^* + k_{V\_j}\left(U_{HV\_j} - U_{HV\_j}^*\right) \end{cases} \tag{5}$$

Where, $U_{Lv\_i0}^*$ and $U_{LV\_j0}^*$ are the initial reference value of the bidirectional port voltage of power unit i and power unit j. $U_{HV\_i}^*$ and $U_{HV\_j}^*$ are the reference values of the output voltage of two power units, respectively. k_{V_i} and k_{V_j} are the control coefficient k_V of the local controller of the two power units. Considering $U_{LV\_i} = U_{LV\_j} = U_{LV}$, formula (5) is rewritten as follows.

$$U_{HV\_i} - U_{HV\_j} = \left(U_{HV\_i}^* - U_{HV\_j}^*\right) + \frac{k_{V\_j} - k_{V\_i}}{k_{V\_i}k_{V\_j}}U_{LV} + \frac{k_{V\_i}U_{LV\_j0}^* - k_{V\_j}U_{LV\_i0}^*}{k_{V\_i}k_{V\_j}} \tag{6}$$

From Eq. (6), it can be found that the smaller the difference between the voltage reference value or coefficient is, the more accurate the voltage sharing control of each three-port IB-LLC resonant converter output port in the modular photovoltaic DC grid-connected system is, and the more significant the equalizing error reduced by the control coefficient k_{V_i} and k_{V_j} is. However, according to Eq. (1), the increase of control coefficient k_V leads to the rise in the error between the reference value and the set value U_{LV}^* of the bidirectional port voltage of the converter. Thus the voltage regulation performance of the port is affected.

According to the above analysis, the voltage sharing control method used in this paper is similar to the droop control method [12, 13], which has been widely used in parallel DC/DC converter systems and DC/AC inverter systems. And the control coefficient k_V has a function similar to the droop coefficient. In the droop control, the reference value of output voltage is adjusted by detecting the output current of the module to realize the load current balance. Accordingly, with the control method used in this paper, the output voltage through the local controller in each power unit is sampled, and the reference value of the output voltage of the power unit is adjusted according to the sampling value so as to achieve the balance of the output voltage of each power unit. These two control methods do not need current sharing or voltage sharing buses and have good system modularity and high reliability, but also affect the voltage regulation ability of the system.

In addition, for the modular photovoltaic DC grid-connected system in this paper, the bidirectional ports of each power unit are connected to the low-voltage DC bus in parallel, and no load is connected, which is only used to deal with the mismatched input power between each power unit. Therefore, the voltage U_{LV} of bidirectional port and low-voltage DC bus does not need to be highly precisely controlled, and its error does not need to be eliminated entirely.

4 Simulation Results

The simulation model of the three-port IB-LLC resonant converter is built by using MATLAB/Simulink software to verify the working principle and characteristics of the converter. Then, based on the simulation model of the converter, the simulation model of the modular photovoltaic DC grid-connected system is built to verify the characteristics of the system and the effectiveness of the voltage sharing control method. The working principles and features of the three-port IB-LLC resonant converter and the modular photovoltaic DC grid-connected system based on the converter are simulated and verified.

4.1 Simulation of Three Port IB-LLC Resonant Converter

Simulation of three-port IB-LLC resonant converter was built according to the parameter as shown in Table 1. The capacitance C_r, inductance L_r and L_m are the resonant capacitance, resonant inductance and excitation inductance of the converter, respectively. Inductors L_1 and L_2 are interleaved boost inductors. The capacitors C_{PV}, C_{LV} and C_{HV} are the filter capacitors of PV input port, bi-directional port and output port, respectively. n is the transformation ratio of the converter isolation transformer. Capacitors C_{HV1} and C_{HV2} are voltage doubling rectifying capacitors of the output port of the converter. f_r is the resonant frequency of the converter.

Table 1. Simulation parameters of three port IB-LLC resonant converter

Parameters	Value	Parameters	Value
L_1/L_2	150 μH	n	1:1
C_{PV}	10 μF	C_{LV}	100 μF
C_r	1 μF	C_{HV}	30 μF
L_r	10 μH	C_{HV1}/C_{HV2}	10 μF
L_m	80 μH	f_r	50.3 kHz

Figure 6 shows the primary voltage and current waveforms of steady-state simulation of three-port IB-LLC resonant converter with switching frequency $f = 50$ kHz and duty cycle $D = 0.4$, 0.5 and 0.6, respectively. i_{L1}, i_{L2} and i_L are the current of two boost inductors L_1 and L_2 and the input current of the combined converter. i_{Lr} and i_{Lm} are the resonance current and excitation current, respectively. U_{PV}, U_{LV} and U_{HV} are the voltage of the input port, bidirectional port and output port, respectively. i_{D1} and i_{D2} are the current of rectifier diode D_1 and D_2, respectively. When the duty cycle D changes, the operating characteristics of the converter would change accordingly.

According to Fig. 6, when the duty cycle $D = 0.5$, the ripple of the input current i_L of the three-port IB-LLC resonant converter is the most negligible, almost zero, and the voltage relationship between the three ports of the converter meets $U_{HV} = 2U_{LV} = 4U_{PV}$. At the same time, the gain between the three ports of the converter changes with the duty cycle D. Specifically, the gain G_{PV_LV} from the input port to the bidirectional port of the converter increases with the decrease of duty cycle D. The gain G_{PV_HV} from the bidirectional port to the output port of converter is the largest when the duty cycle D = 0.5. And it decreases symmetrically with the distance of the duty cycle D away from 0.5. Total gain G_{PV_HV} from the input port to output port of converter increases with the decrease of duty cycle D. In addition, no matter what the duty cycle D is, the current i_{D1} and i_{D2} of the two rectifier diodes of the converter always naturally drop to 0 and rise from 0.

4.2   Simulation of Modular Photovoltaic DC Grid-Connected System

The parameters of the three-port IB-LLC resonant converter used in the simulation are the same as those in Table 1. The simulation parameters of the modular photovoltaic DC grid-connected system are shown in Table 2. U_{PV}, U_{LV} and U_{HV} are the rated voltages of the three ports of the converter, and U_{LV} is also the voltage of the low voltage DC bus in the system. SunPower SPR-305-WHT-U photovoltaic module in MATLAB/Simulink software is selected as the photovoltaic power supply. Each photovoltaic array contains five photovoltaic strings in parallel, and each photovoltaic string is composed of 10 photovoltaic units in series, with a total of 50 photovoltaic units. According to the photovoltaic power curve provided by MATLAB/Simulink software, under the standard working condition of light intensity $G = 1000$ W/m^2 and temperature $T_p = 25°C$, the maximum power point voltage of the photovoltaic power supply is about 550 V, and the maximum output power is about 15 kW. P_{PV} is the full power handled by a single converter. The system parameters N, P_{DC}, and U_{DC} are the number of power units in the system, the total capacity of the system, and the voltage of HVDC bus in the simulation model of the modular design, the control block diagram of each power unit is shown in Fig. 3. Only its voltage and current parameters are sampled and controlled to ensure the complete modularization of the system.

Figure 7 shows the simulation results of the modular photovoltaic DC grid-connected system when the photovoltaic input power of some power units changes due to the change of light intensity. Among them, Fig. 7(a) shows the photovoltaic input power of each power unit. All photovoltaic arrays work at the room temperature of $T_p = 25°C$. When $t = 0.02$ s, the photovoltaic arrays in power units 1–3 work at the standard condition of light intensity $G_{1-3} = 1000$ W/m^2. The maximum power point voltage is $U_{PV\_1-3} = 550$ V, and the power is $P_{PV\_1-3} = 15$ kW. The light intensity of the photovoltaic array in power unit 4 is $G_4 = 800$ W/m^2, and the maximum power point voltage is $U_{PV\_4} =$

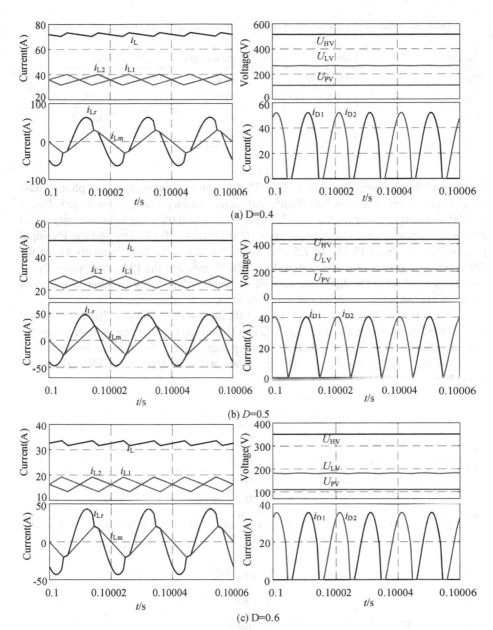

(a) D=0.4

(b) D=0.5

(c) D=0.6

Fig. 6. Steady-state operation simulation waveforms of converter.

Table 2. Simulation parameters of modular photovoltaic dc grid connected system.

Parameters	Value	Parameters	Value
U_{PV}	500–600 V	U_{LV}	1100 V
U_{HV}	2200 V	PPV	15 kW
N	5	P_{DC}	75 kW
U_{DC}	11 kV		

545 V, and the power is $P_{PV\_4} = 12$ kW. The illumination intensity of the photovoltaic array in power unit 5 is $G_5 = 500$ W/m^2, and the maximum power point voltage is $U_{PV\_5} = 540$ V, and the power is $P_{PV\_5} = 7.5$ kW. When $t = 0.05$ s, the light intensity G_1 of PV array in power unit 1 decreases from 1000 W/m^2 to 500 W/m^2, and the PV input power P_{PV_1} is from 15 kW to 7.5 kW. When $t = 0.1$ s, the light intensity G_1 of the PV module in power unit 1 is restored to 1000 W/m^2, and the PV input power P_{PV_1} increases to 15 kW. The light intensity of the photovoltaic array in other power units remains unchanged throughout the whole process.

In Fig. 7(b) and Fig. 7(d), the voltages of the high voltage DC bus U_{DC} at the output port of the system and the low voltage DC bus U_{LV} at the bidirectional port of the power unit are shown, respectively. When the input power of some power units in the system changes, the voltages on the two DC buses are stable as $U_{DC} = 11$ kV and $U_{LV} = 1100$ V.

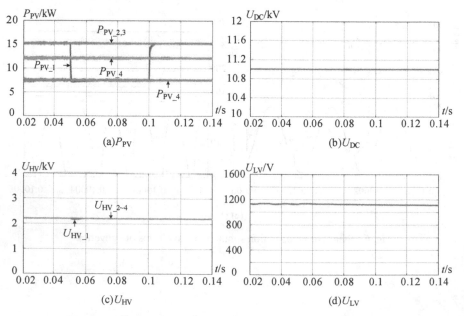

Fig. 7. System simulation waveforms of PV input power changing.

Figure 7(c) shows the output voltage U_{HV} of each power unit. During the whole simulation process, the output voltage U_{HV_1-5} of each power unit is the same, which is maintained at the rated value $U_{HV} = 2.2$ kV. When $t = 0.05$ s, there is only a slight fluctuation in the output voltage U_{HV_1} of power unit 1 when the photovoltaic input power P_{PV_1} drops sharply. The simulation verifies the effectiveness of voltage sharing control at the output port of the modular photovoltaic DC grid-connected system when the photovoltaic input power of each power unit is unbalanced, and the photovoltaic input power changes.

Figure 8 shows the simulation results of a modular photovoltaic DC grid-connected system based on the three-port IB-LLC resonant converter when the photovoltaic power supply of some power units is disconnected. Among them, Fig. 8(a) shows the photovoltaic input power of each power unit, and the working state of each power unit before $t = 0.05$ s is the same as that in Fig. 8. When $t = 0.05$ s, the PV array in power unit 1 is disconnected from the input port of the converter. The input port of the converter is open. There is no PV power input, and other power units have no change.

In Fig. 8(b) and Fig. 8 (d), the voltages of high voltage DC bus U_{DC} and the low voltage DC bus U_{LV} at bidirectional port of power unit are shown, respectively. During the simulation process, both of them are kept at $U_{DC} = 11$ kV and $U_{LV} = 1100$ V.

Figure 8(c) shows the voltage U_{HV} of the output port in each power unit. When $t = 0.05$ s, a slight fluctuation of the voltage U_{HV} in power unit 1 occurs and gradually recovers. And when $t - 0.1$ s, the output port of the system returns to the original steady-state voltage sharing operation state. The simulation results show that when the

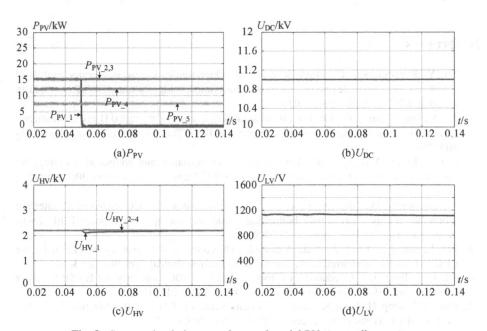

Fig. 8. System simulation waveforms of partial PV source disconnect.

photovoltaic power supply of some power units fails, the modular photovoltaic DC grid-connected system can still maintain regular and stable operation, and the system has good fault tolerance.

5 Conclusion

An efficient three-port interleaved boost LLC resonant converter is adopted as the basic converter unit of the modular DC grid-connected photovoltaic system in this paper. The bi-directional port of the converters is connected through a low voltage DC bus to solve the problem of unbalanced output power and voltage oscillation of each module in the system. The simulation platform of modular DC grid-connected photovoltaic system based on three-port interleaved boost LLC resonant converters is built. The operational principles and characteristics of interleaved boost LLC resonant converter are verified by simulation. The rationality and effectiveness of the modular DC grid-connected photovoltaic system and its voltage sharing control strategy are also demonstrated.

Acknowledgements. The authors acknowledge the Jiangsu University Natural Science Research Project (18KJB470024) and Provincial Construction System Science and Technology Project of Jiangsu Provincial Housing and Urban-Rural Construction Department (2018ZD088). This work is partly supported by the Natural Science Foundation of Jiangsu Province of China (No. BK20161165), the applied fundamental research Foundation of Xuzhou of China (No. KC17072). The authorized patents for invention are also the research and development of Jiangsu Province Industry-University-Research Cooperation Project (BY2019056).

References

1. Yu, Y., Konstantinou, G., Hredzak, B., et al.: Operation of cascaded h-bridge multilevel converters for large-scale photovoltaic power plants under bridge failures. IEEE Trans. Industr. Electron. **62**(11), 7228–7236 (2015)
2. Yu, Y., Konstantinou, G., Hredzak, B., et al.: Power balance of cascaded H-bridge multilevel converters for large-scale photovoltaic integration. IEEE Trans. Power Electron. **31**(1), 292–303 (2016)
3. Liu, L., Li, H., Xue, Y., et al.: Reactive power compensation and optimization strategy for grid-interactive cascaded photovoltaic systems. IEEE Trans. Power Electron. **30**(1), 188–202 (2015)
4. Krishnaswami, H., Mohan, N.: Three-port series-resonant DC-DC converter to interface renewable energy sources with bidirectional load and energy storage ports. IEEE Trans. Power Electron. **24**(10), 2289–2297 (2009)
5. Shi, J., Zhang, J., Long, J., et al.: A cascaded DC converter with primary series transformer LLC and output interleaved buck. Trans. China Electrotechnical Soc. **30**(24), 93–102 (2015)
6. Su, G.J., Tang, L.: A reduced-part, triple-voltage DC-DC converter for EV/HEV power management. IEEE Trans. Power Electron. **24**(10), 2406–2410 (2009)
7. Kim, S.Y., Song, H., Nam, K.: Idling port isolation control of three-port bidirectional converter for EVs. IEEE Trans. Power Electron. **27**(5), 2495–2506 (2012)
8. Wang, L., Wang, Z., Li, H.: Asymmetrical duty cycle control and decoupled power flow design of a three-port bidirectional DC-DC converter for fuel cell vehicle application. IEEE Trans. Power Electron. **27**(2), 891–904 (2012)

9. Lu, Y., Sun, K., Wu, H., et al.: A three-port converter based distributed dc grid connected pv system with autonomous output voltage sharing control. IEEE Trans. Power Electron. **34**(1), 325–339 (2019)
10. Wang, K., Wu, X., Liu, F., et al.: Cascaded H-bridge multilevel converter topology for large-scale photovoltaic system with balanced operation. In: IECON 2017 - 43rd Annual Conference of the IEEE Industrial Electronics Society. IEEE (2017)
11. Yang, Y., Wang, H., Blaabjerg, F., et al.: A hybrid power control concept for pv inverters with reduced thermal loading. IEEE Trans. Power Electron. **29**(12), 6271–6275 (2014)
12. Anand, S., Fernandes, B.G., Guerrero, J.: Distributed control to ensure proportional load sharing and improve voltage regulation in low-voltage DC microgrids. IEEE Trans. Power Electron. **28**(4), 1900–1913 (2013)
13. Lu, X., Sun, K., Guerrero, J.M., et al.: State-of-charge balance using adaptive droop control for distributed energy storage systems in dc microgrid applications. IEEE Trans. Industr. Electron. **61**(6), 2804–2815 (2014)

Key Quality Indicators of Social Networking Service

Jiachao Deng, Lei Chen[✉], Guiling Liu, Jing Guo, Yan Geng, Chenlu Wun, Jie Yan, and Ping Cui

Jiangsu Province Key Laboratory of Intelligent Industry Control Technology, Xuzhou University of Technology, Xuzhou 221018, China
chenlei@xzit.edu.cn

Abstract. Social Networking Service (SNS) is one of the most popular types of online services. To analyze the quality of the end-user experience, we study the key quality indicators (KQIs) of these services. Based on the servo model, we collect data from college students and obtain hierarchical KQIs. Using this KQIs system, we analyze three most popular SNSs as examples and give some improved suggestions.

Keywords: Key quality indicator · Social networking service · Quality of experience

1 Introduction

With the rapid development of the Internet in recent years, social networks have also developed rapidly [1–4]. And it has become an important channel for people to make friends and entertainment activities. Social software is characterized by a large number of user participation [5], large information scale, fast content update, diversified information communication methods, and the freedom of information editing. At present, there are many domestic social network operators, and fierce competition [6, 7]. In this case, the performance of social software platform services is very important and may affect user viscosity [8–10]. In the functions of social software, there are mainly five important performances: security, reliability, use experience, responsiveness and ease of use. It is found that these five important features can be improved again. Social software needs to pay attention to strengthening the response and security of its software and expanding its functions. Through these studies, we can promote each social software to enhance its value and development potential and enhance its competitiveness. On this basis, college students account for a large proportion of users, and their attention to performance is particularly important. Therefore, it is of great significance to study the service evaluation index system of socialized software.

The common methods of user experience evaluation [11] mainly include literature, interview, questionnaire survey, statistical analysis, hierarchical analysis, case analysis and statistical analysis [12–16]. By using the above methods, we can understand all the

D. Jiang and H. Song (Eds.): SIMUtools 2021, LNICST 424, pp. 220–229, 2022.
https://doi.org/10.1007/978-3-030-97124-3_19

users feel when using social software. In the process of establishing an index system, it is necessary to design an index system first, and then through rating and analysis by the expert. This study used the above seven methods to take college students as the sample groups. Through literature, interviews and analysis, four first-level indicators and 11 s-level indicators were finally established to make the index system more objective and reasonable. The reliability, effectiveness, consistency, and index weights [17–19]. Reliability analysis makes the research results stable and reliable, the effectiveness analysis reflects the effectiveness of the research results, the consistency complex analysis and the index weight determination make the results real and accurate. Case description by WeChat [20] makes the research more specific. Through the above methods, relatively accurate research results can be obtained.

According to the survey results, college students pay more attention to the security and reliability [21, 22] of social software when using social media platforms. Social software can improve both aspects to improve the user service experience and user stickiness. This survey provides a future improvement direction for all social software, provides a reference for promoting the development of social software for multi-level personalized users, and promotes the positive cycle development of the platform ecosystem.

2 Investigation Method

Using the interview method, this research evaluates social software from the perspective of users. Understanding the daily use of social software, the problems and expectations of social software provide the basis for determining the metrics in this paper. The evaluation index of social software is based on previous studies, combined with the current situation of personal social software, the user characteristics of social software and the needs of information service groups. In the process of index construction, the index is revised and improved through interviews and other methods. Using the questionnaire survey method, this survey refers to the previous research rules, constructs the sample and conducts the survey. By consulting and sorting out the literature published by predecessors, combined with model, information construction and user experience theory, the questionnaire is mainly distributed through network and face-to-face survey. Using statistical analysis methods, this research adopts more statistical analysis methods in daily life, makes a quantitative analysis of the data obtained from the questionnaire, and then makes a descriptive statistical analysis and the reliability and effectiveness of the questionnaire. Using analytic hierarchy process, the structure of social software evaluation index system is very complex. In the face of this complex decision-making process, the quantitative analysis method can be used in the index analysis at all levels to decompose the complex problems, so as to make the problems more hierarchical, so as to sort the advantages and disadvantages of the decision-making schemes according to the analysis classification. This paper uses this method to evaluate the indexes at all levels, compare the relative importance of the indexes at the same level, then analyze and calculate the index weight, and calculate the weight of each index, in order to make the setting of the index system more reasonable. Using the case analysis method, this paper takes China's largest social software QQ and WeChat as examples, determines the sample size and questionnaire according to the established evaluation index system, verifies the collected data, establishes SERVQUAL model and analyzes it. Finally, the feasibility and rationality of the model are proposed and demonstrated. Using the statistical analysis method, this survey determines the validity of the questionnaire data through SPSS reliability test and validity test, obtains the index system of social software service quality, makes descriptive statistics on the data, and obtains the overall situation of social software information service quality (Figs. 1 and 2).

Step 1	Based on the SERVPERF service model, combined with the particularity of social software and user needs, five first-level indicators were selected.
Step 2	By understanding how they feel about using social software and to discuss its most important performance.
Step 3	Summarize the main opinions of the interview and obtain 11 secondary indicators under literature classification as main indicators.
Step 4	Adjust to the established index system according to the reasonable results. After the adjustment, the quality investigation will be conducted until all the indicators are reasonable, and the social software service evaluation index system is obtained.
Step 5	After modification, four primary indicators and 11 secondary indicators were eventually formed

Fig. 1. Establishment table of the indicators

Primary indicators	The secondary indicators
Responsibility A	Response speed is fast A1
	Multiple-end login can be supported A2
	Update frequency is guaranteed A3
	File transfer is fast A4
Security B	Identity information security B1
	Authorized information security B2
	Transfer the file security B3
Ease of use C	Can be compatible with multiple browsing modes C1
Reliability D	Easy to use C2
	The stability is very good D1
	Can give timely help with difficulties D2

Fig. 2. Evaluation indicators of social software services

3   Results Analysis

3.1   Indicator Analysis

The questionnaire produced in this experiment will be distributed to full-time students by means of electronic questionnaire. A total of 15 questionnaires were collected this time, all of which were valid. The questionnaire results were imported into spss22.0 for reliability and effectiveness analysis.

The evaluation matrix of social software evaluation index is constructed. T. The 1–9 scale method proposed by L. ssty is used to compare and obtain weights: primary indicators: reactivity a, safety B, ease of use C and reliability D. Secondary indicator: response speed A1, support multi terminal login A2, ensure update frequency A3 and file transmission speed A4. Identity information security B1, authorization information security B2, storage file security B3. Compatible with multi browser mode C1, easy to use C2. Software stability D1, timely help in case of difficulties, Through the calculation of survey data, the weight tables of primary indicators and secondary indicators are obtained. The specific values are shown in the table below (Tables 1, 2, 3, 4 and 5).

Table 1. A-D weights of grade I indicators

	Responsibility A	Security B	Ease of use C	Reliability D	Wi
Responsibility A	1	5	3	3	41.714%
Security B	1/5	1	1/5	1/5	6.339%
Ease of use C	1/3	5	1	3	31.696%
Reliability D	1/3	5	1/3	1	20.251%

Table 2. Weights of secondary indicators A1–A4

	Response speed is fast A1	Multiple-end login can be supported A2	Update frequency is guaranteed A3	File transfer is fast A4	Wi
Response speed is fast A1	1	3	5	5	47.979%
Multiple-end login can be supported A2	1/3	1	3	1/3	18.847%
Update frequency is guaranteed A3	1/5	1/3	1	3	16.587%
File transfer is fast A4	1/5	3	1/3	1	16.587%

Table 3. Weights of secondary indicators B1–B3

	Identity information security B1	Authorized information security B2	Transfer the file security B3	Wi
Identity information security B1	1	5	3	63.698%
Authorized information security B2	1/5	1	5	25.828%
Transfer the file security B3	1/3	1/5	1	10.474%

Table 4. Weights of secondary indicators C1–C2

	Can be compatible with multiple browsing modes C1	Easy to use C2	Wi
Can be compatible with multiple browsing modes C1	1	3	75.000%
Easy to use C2	1/3	1	25.000%

Table 5. Weights of secondary indicators D1–D2

	The stability is very good D1	Can give timely help with difficulties D2	Wi
The stability is very good D1	1	5	83.333%
Can give timely help with difficulties D2	1/5	1	16.667%

3.2 QoE Analysis

In recent years, with the rapid development of the Internet, social networks have also developed rapidly. And it has become an important channel for people to make friends and entertainment activities. Social software is characterized by a large number of user participation, large information scale, fast content update, diversified information communication methods, and the freedom of information editing. At present, there are many domestic social network operators and the competition is fierce. Manufacturers for limited market customers have launched their own special services to stand out in a wave of social software. However, the functions of these social software tend to be very function-ally similar, making it difficult for consumers to choose between chaotic and complex markets.

This paper takes China QQ, WeChat and microblog as examples. The two social software platforms are studied and analyzed to determine the judgment score samples of each secondary index. The evaluators of this questionnaire are mainly regular users of social software, almost college students. Questionnaires will be issued on each sample to ensure effectiveness.

In qualitative indicators, each secondary indicator is scored 5 points, 1–5 points "very unimportant, unimportant, general, important, very important", We rank according to our own understanding. According to the evaluation indicators and the importance of each indicator, we multiply it by the weight and the total score. Each indicator is weighted by 15 volunteers, and then multiplied by the corresponding indicators to get the weight of each indicator. Finally, we summarize the comprehensive score.

Table 6. Design of social software service quality evaluation questions

Index	Questions corresponding to the questionnaire
Response speed is fast	Please evaluate the speed of the most frequent social software response combined with your own experience
Support-terminal login on	Please evaluate the supporting multi-terminal login of the most frequent social software combined with your own experience
Can ensure the update frequency	Please evaluate the guaranteed update frequency of the most frequent social software combined with your own experience
File transfer speed	Please evaluate the file transfer speed of the most frequent use of social software, combined with your own use experience
Identity information security	Please rate the identity information security indicators in the security
License information security	Please rate the authorized information security indicators in the security
Store the file security	Rate the storage file security metrics in the security

(*continued*)

Table 6. (*continued*)

Index	Questions corresponding to the questionnaire
Compatible with multiple browser modes	Please rate compatibility with multiple browser mode metrics in ease of use
Easy to use	Please rate the easy-of-use indicators in the ease of use
Stability of the software	Please score the stability indicators of the software in the reliability
When encountering difficulties in use, you can give and help in time	Please score the and help indicators when using difficulties in reliability

This is based on the above theory of social software service quality assessment questionnaire, as shown in Tables 6, 7, and 8.

Table 7. We Chat service quality evaluation data sheet

Index	Average
Response speed is fast	4.27
Support-terminal login on	4.6
Can ensure the update frequency	4.2
File transfer speed	3.73
Identity information security	3.73
License information security	3.87
Store the file security	3.6
Compatible with multiple browser modes	4.07
Easy to use	4.13
Stability of the software	4.2
When encountering difficulties in use, you can give and help in time	3.53

According to the above scoring rules, when conducting a questionnaire survey on WeChat service quality, we can find that college students are not satisfied with file transmission speed, identity security information, authorization information security, storage file security and help in case of difficulties. These indicators are lower than 4.0, indicating that we still need to improve our security and reliability.

According to the above scoring rules, when conducting a questionnaire survey on QQ service quality, we can find that college students are not satisfied with file transmission speed, identity security information, authorization information security and storage file security. These indicators are lower than 4.0, indicating that we still need to improve our security.

Table 8. QQ service quality evaluation data sheet

Index	Average
Response speed is fast	4
Support-terminal login on	4.65
Can ensure the update frequency	4.23
File transfer speed	3.8
Identity information security	3.71
License information security	3.9
Store the file security	3.6
Compatible with multiple browser modes	4
Easy to use	4.14
Stability of the software	4.2
When encountering difficulties in use, you can give and help in time	4

4   Conclusion

The above research shows that the secondary indicators related to the security and reliability of wechat and QQ are lower than 4.0. According to this phenomenon, we find that
college students are more concerned about the security and reliability of social software.
Social software generally meets the expectations of users, but there is still much room
for improvement in some indicators. Only by ensuring that it is in these areas can the
user experience be greatly improved. The survey results not only provide a reference for
users to choose social software, but also let social software companies understand the
advantages and disadvantages of their products and clarify the optimization direction. It
provides index system reference for social software service evaluation.

College students as the main force of social software, their social software service
evaluation has a great impact on the improvement of social software functions in the
future. Therefore, it is essential to discuss and study the social software service factors of
college students. It can provide a reference for the future development of social software
services.

Because sampling surveys are limited in scope and quantity, they do not fully represent the overall state of society. The results did not discuss the aspects of personalization,
and the applicability needs to be improved. Without considering various influential regulatory factors, choosing only two social software from many social software as empirical
research objects, so the conclusions have certain limitations. Further research is needed.

References

1. Chen, J., Kou, G., Wang, H., Zhao, Y.: Influence identification of opinion leaders in social networks: an agent-based simulation on competing advertisements. Inf. Fusion. **76**(532) (2021).
DOI:https://doi.org/10.1016/j.inffus.2021.06.004

2. Gozuacik, N., Sakar, C.O., Ozcan, S.: Social media-based opinion retrieval for product analysis using multi-task deep neural networks. Expert Syst. Appl. **183**(30) (2021). https://doi.org/10.1016/j.eswa.2021.115388

3. Cho, S.M.J., et al.: Association between social network structure and physical activity in middle-aged Korean adults. Soc. Sci. Med. (2021). https://doi.org/10.1016/j.socscimed.2021.114112

4. Molodetska, J.K.: Counteraction to strategic manipulations on actors' decision making in social networking services. In: 2020 IEEE 2nd International Conference on Advanced Trends in Information Theory (ATIT), pp. 266–269 (2020). https://doi.org/10.1109/ATIT50783.2020.9349347

5. Ye, Q.-W., Xu, J.-Q., Luo, Y.-M.: On adopted intention of short video apps based on perceived value and VAM Theory. Adv. Sci. Technol. Appl. Res. Cent. (2019). Proceedings of 2019

6. Kuo, T., Yeh, J., Lin, C., Lin, S.: Designing, analyzing and exploiting stake-based social networks. In: 2010 International Conference on Advances in Social Networks Analysis and Mining, pp. 402–403 (2010).https://doi.org/10.1109/ASONAM.2010.14

7. Delu, W.: Enterprise network marketing strategy based on SNS social network. In: 2019 12th International Conference on Intelligent Computation Technology and Automation (ICICTA), pp. 295–299 (2019). https://doi.org/10.1109/ICICTA49267.2019.00069

8. Liu, Z.-Y., Wang, J.-L., Liu, J., Liu, X.-Y., Liao, K.: Research on the influence of union-pay M-payment quality and brand personality on user viscosity. J. Korea Soc. Comput. Inf. **25**(4) (2020)

9. Yang, X., Yuan, H., Cheng, H., Liu, P.-S.A.: Case study on digital library's user viscosity in Chongqing University Library. Library Management, **33**(3) (2012)

10. Gao, W.C., Jiang, W.X., Gao, W.H., Liu, J.F., Chen, J.C.: Design and implementation of web instant communication system based on web 2.0. In: Advanced Materials Research, pp. 533–536 (2014)

11. Abdulhak, S.A., Hwang, G., Kang, D.: T-model for evaluation and identification of social network site: Usability drawbacks and user-experience enhancements. In: 2011 International Conference on User Science and Engineering (i-USEr), pp. 240–244 (2011). https://doi.org/10.1109/iUSEr.2011.6150573

12. Chou, Y.C., Yen, H.Y., Sun, C.C., Hon, J.S.: Comparison of AHP and fuzzy AHP methods for human resources in science technology (HRST) performance index selection. In: 2013 IEEE International Conference on Industrial Engineering and Engineering Management, pp. 792–796 (2013). https://doi.org/10.1109/IEEM.2013.6962520

13. Zhang, W.: The AHP-FM assement of audit risk in E-commerce enterprises. In: 2010 International Conference on E-Business and E-Government, pp. 592–595 (2010). https://doi.org/10.1109/ICEE.2010.157

14. Tsai, J., Cheng, H., Kao, Y.: Development of KM-based AHP method and auxiliary web questionnaire system for multi-criteria decision-making application. In: 2012 IEEE Symposium on Robotics and Applications (ISRA), pp. 485–489 (2012). https://doi.org/10.1109/ISRA.2012.6219230

15. Chen, S., Li, Y.: A research of fuzzy AHP approach in evaluating distance education system alternatives. In: 2009 First International Workshop on Education Technology and Computer Science, pp. 741–745 (2009).https://doi.org/10.1109/ETCS.2009.170

16. Wang, X.: Research on performance evaluation of architectural aesthetics with the AHP theory. In: 2013 Third International Conference on Intelligent System Design and Engineering Applications, pp. 1185–1190 (2013). https://doi.org/10.1109/ISDEA.2012.280

17. Bellenger, M.J., Herlihy, A.T.: Performance-based environmental index weights: are all metrics created equal? Ecol. Econ. **69**(5), 1043–1050 (2010)

18. Wu, Y., Ye, T., Wang, W., et al.: Index weight decision based on AHP for information retrieval on mobile device. In: Proceedings of 2010 2nd International Conference on Information and Multimedia Technology (ICIMT 2010). IACSIT Press, pp. 68–75 (2010)
19. Kang., M.S.: Efficient SAS programs for computing path coefficients and index weights for selection indices. J. Crop Improv. **29**(1), 6–22 (2015)
20. Dfz, A., et al.: WeChat use among family caregivers of people living with schizophrenia and its relationship to caregiving experiences. Comput. Hum. Behav. **123**(1) (2021). https://doi.org/10.1016/j.chb.2021.106877
21. Sahraoui, S., Henni, N.: SAMP-RPL: secure and adaptive multipath RPL for enhanced security and reliability in heterogeneous IoT-connected low power and lossy networks. J. Ambient Intell. Humanized Comput. 1–21 (2021).https://doi.org/10.1007/s12652-021-03303-9
22. Yuqing, L.: Research on personal information security on social network in big data Era. In: 2017 International Conference on Smart Grid and Electrical Automation (ICSGEA), pp. 676–678 (2017). https://doi.org/10.1109/ICSGEA.2017.91

Discussion on the Project Teaching Method of Investment Banking in Local Ethnic Colleges and Universities

Hongyan Zeng[✉]

Guizhou Minzu University, Guiyang 550025, China

Abstract. Beijing stock exchange setted up in 2021, direct financing is increasingly important for our country economy development high quality either the present or the future. Investment bank is the soul of the capital market, the investment banking course is a studying of the investment bank, is one of the important lessons of the financial discipline, so promoting its teaching effect is imperative keeping pace with The Times.Combined with the present "Investment Banking" teaching in colleges of ethnic areas and the needs of the development of the economic society in national regions,from understanding the theory and technology dimensions, improving practice ability and innovation ability, the characteristics of the project teaching method highly improve the teaching effect, raising favorable the nation's colleges and universities financial talent supply and demand in national regions matching degree,it is realized of the teaching aim of providing high quality human capital to boost the development of ethnic areas of local ethnic colleges and universities.

Keyword: Teaching reform · Project teaching method · Investment banking

1 Introduction

Investment Banking is a core course for finance majors in colleges and universities, and it is integrated with theory, technology and practice.The content involves the definition and theory of investment bank, asset securitization, corporate restructuring, the basic theory and basic knowledge of investment Banks's external supervision management, investment Banks's internal organization management, through teaching, and making students to form a relatively complete knowledge structure of investment Banks, grasping the basic rule of its development, and having a comprehensive understanding and profound understanding of the basic knowledge, concepts and theories of investment banking, and clearly knowing the innovation and practicability of this discipline, laying a solid foundation for future study and work.Teaching purpose is to cultivate students to be able to clear up the capital market operation and the economic theory, familiar with the basic process of each business investment and operation skills, understanding of capital operation skills, forming self cognition of economic phenomenon, and with the initiative of the source for ending problems, improving the learning ability, thinking

D. Jiang and H. Song (Eds.): SIMUtools 2021, LNICST 424, pp. 230–235, 2022.
https://doi.org/10.1007/978-3-030-97124-3_20

ability, practice and innovation ability.Therefore, the course characteristic determines the law that must be payed attention to the combination of theory, practice and innovation in the process of teaching, if still using traditional teaching as the main way of classroom teaching, it is unable to realize the course teaching effect, and the reality of capital market, investment Banks and other industries changing very fast, leading to the textbook content updating rhythm can't keep up with the reality.As well as the particularity of the financial industry, its openness to the outside world is limited, which also sets up the threshold to enter the reality and understand the development of the industry.Therefore, centering on the teaching effect objectives of improving theory, practice and innovation, this paper proposes to adopt the teaching method of "project" in the teaching of "Investment Banking" from the perspectives of improving students' initiative, updating teaching content and materials, and shaping talents in the industry.

2 The Theoretical Basis of Project-Based Teaching and Its Teaching Characteristics

2.1 The Basis of Learning Theory

Centering on the goal of improving learning effect, scholars have discussed and formed learning theories centering on the correct understanding and grasp of learning essence, which provides theoretical basis for educators to carry out teaching and can be used for reference.At present, learning theories mainly include behaviorism, humanism and cognitive theory, among which the object classification theory in Bloom's old cognitive theory is representative and is also one of the main theoretical bases of current teaching reform. Basing Bloom's old cognitive goal classification theory, cognitive goals are divided into six cognitive levels: Knowledge, Comprehension, Application, Analysis, Synthesis and Evaluation.Each cognitive goal contains two dimensions of "knowledge" and "cognitive process". The "knowledge" dimension refers to the relevant content involved in learning and clearly defines what to teach. Generally, there are four types:Factual knowledge, Conceptual knowledge, Procedural knowledge and Metacognitive knowledge;"Cognitive process" identifies the stages that facilitate students' acquisition and application of knowledge. It consists of six categories: memory, understanding, application, analysis, evaluation and creation, in order of cognitive complexity from lowest to highest.In a word, learning is an "input-process-output" process, and learning theory focuses on the learning process to find rules to further solve the problem of "what to learn" and the evolution of "how to learn".

2.2 Teaching Characteristics

Project-based teaching method aims at promoting students' enthusiasm and autonomy in knowledge construction. It adopts students' understanding or application of the central concepts and principles of a certain discipline and enables students to operate and jointly implement a complete "project" teaching activity.Project teaching method mainly has the following characteristics: (1) Project is as the carrier of teaching, each task is clear and specific; (2) Using real or simulated situations cultivate professional ability; (3) In order to complete the project tasks, it is necessary to consult multi-disciplinary materials or conduct field research, which improves students' learning autonomy, broadens their knowledge range and exercises their social ability; (4) The project is implemented by a group, which cultivates the students' spirit of organization, unity and cooperation; (5) Teachers change from "teaching" to "guiding" to improve the adequacy and feasibility of teachers' preparation materials, and teachers increase their own knowledge and practice performance to better guide students.

3   Design and Implementation of Investment Banking Course Project Method in Local Ethnic Colleges and Universities

3.1   Practical Design of Project Method

From mastering theory,enhancing the level of technology and innovation to improve, improve the teaching effect of the investment banking course, law of practice for the project teaching is designed by the practicality, autonomy, development, integrated, open ascending. The practicality is embodied by project topics is from the real world, promoting learning content pertinence and practicability;The autonomy is reflected in the students' choice freely of content and report form, learning autonomy and freedom are improved, effectively promoting the development of students' creative ability;The developmental performance is the combination of the curriculum project package and the sub-project content, and the design of the project package according to the law of the cognitive process of educational objectives.The comprehensiveness is reflected the characteristics of cross-disciplinary knowledge collection and learning as well as comprehensive application and disposal in the process of completing project contents;Openness is reflected in the diversity and free selectivity of methods, reports and presentations adopted by students around the theme. Meanwhile, project-based teaching focuses on students' performance in the process of ability development in project activities in the evaluation link.

In short, the project teaching method apply the teacher guidance behind the scenes, students act and implement in front of the scenes, centralized evaluation mode, the teaching content compiled into each subproject, and arranged by the order following the rules of cognitive goal theory.Each project is prepared by outside the classroom, discussions, speeches, reports during class. It changes the passive to active relying on the cognitive ability to connect scattered knowledge points and transform them into students' own memory and knowledge content. At last the initiative, practicality and innovation of students' independent learning can be fully mobilized and improved.

3.2   Implementation Process

3.2.1   Determine the Core Competencies of the Course

Combining with the economic development in national regions,the aim through the study of investment banking,which is the students can master the following six core competence: Resource packaging company for investment projects, Assessment and asset value, The design of asset securitization process, Operation stock issuance and listing, Analysis of investment project financial statements and The design of the risk management process.The ability requirements, knowledge content and project design arrangement in the course teaching objectives are shown in Fig. 1.

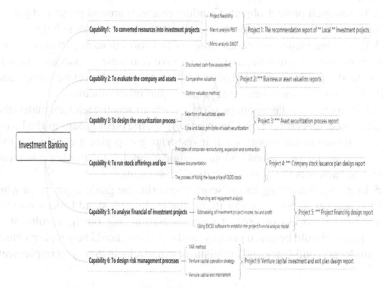

Fig. 1. The ability requirements, knowledge content and project DesignArrangement in the course teaching objectives of investment banking

3.2.2 Determine Knowledge Structure and Project Arrangement

According to the above 6 core competencies,are included 17 knowledge modules, Project feasibility, PEST for Macro analysis, SWOT for micro analysis and so on,and arranging 6 specific project tasks such as *** local *** investment promotion project recommendation report, *** enterprise or asset value evaluation report, *** asset securitization process report, *** Company stock issuance plan design report.

3.2.3 Examples of Project Teaching

During the first lesson new semeter, the undergraduates are divided into 6 groups, and are responsible for the project by random drawing. Eeach group start to study and prepare materials by themselves, and schedule tasks by discussing among members of group, and the teacher always gives help and solutions, and each group prepares reporting content of the project, especially before the team reporting content, teacher has lessen for related content that will be report by undergraduate, so that giving bedding on a theoretical foundation for the group report. Finally, the teacher and students graded the completion of the group project. Take "*** local *** investment promotion project recommendation report" as an example to explain the process of project teaching.

3.2.3.1 To sort and elaborate theory. First, the teacher sent the group articles and materials related to project feasibility, Macro analysis PEST, micro analysis SWOT, etc. After learning and absorbing, the group discuss and agreed with the teacher on the project completion plan. Then, the group introduce relevant knowledge in the first class, the teacher supplement it, and other students put forward suggestions or suggestions for improvement.

3.2.3.2 To research project object. Conduct research around project objects, adopt relevant materials, and teachers follow up and provide corresponding help.

3.2.3.3 To sort out project contents. Discuss and sort out each part according to the project recommendation template, and teacher give real-time guidances. The template content is divided into: Project background, Project content, Project advantage analysis, Project effect analysis, Project financing analysis and other modules.

3.2.3.4 To recommend classroom project. The group sent the relevant materials to the students in advance, this group as the financing group, the other groups as the investment group, after listening to the report, each investment group give a conclusion to invest or not to invest? And give reasons and suggestions. Finally, the teacher comments and summarizes, and answers the questions raised by students.

3.2.3.5 To grade. According to the scoring criteria, the grade is given, in which the weight of the teacher is 60%.Among them, the evaluation should focus on students' performance in the process of project implementation, not on the results of project completion. Praise should be given priority, and criticism should be supplemented, so as to enhance students' confidence and enthusiasm to participate in project implementation.

4 Suggestions on Improving the Effect of Project Teaching in the Implementation of Investment Banking

4.1 Project Teaching Methods to Be Coordinated with Traditional Teaching Methods

According to the cognitive goal theory, different knowledge needs different teaching methods, so in order to achieve a better teaching effect of each project, it is necessary to interweave various forms and methods. Because each project involves a lot of knowledge points, such as the theoretical basis and business development process involved in the project, the traditional teaching method is more effective, so it is necessary to flexibly adopt appropriate teaching methods into each project teaching process to ensure the quality of the project teaching.

4.2 Resource Endowment Plus Teaching Objectives to Determine Project Tasks

Each project task has a core ability training goal. Therefore, in order to effectively complete this teaching goal, the resource endowment of local colleges, teachers and other teaching objectives should be taken into account when determining the project task, so as to ensure the effective progress of the project and achieve the goal of training students' ability.

4.3 The Combination of Student Personality and Project Task Arrangement

Centering on the goal of improving learning initiative and enthusiasm, during the implementation of project teaching, the project tasks should be arranged by considering the personality of students and other factors, so as to fully mobilize each student and ensure that the comprehensive ability has a certain degree.

4.4 Teachers Playing a Leading Role Rehind the Scenes

In project teaching, teachers plan and guide behind the scenes to ensure the high-quality completion of the project teaching process, while students implement the project in front of the scene and report to the students in class. Therefore, teachers work more on pre-class preparation and resource provision, and fully tap the maximum potential of students through guidance.

4.5 Strengthening Evaluation and Reflection

After the completion of each project task, evaluation and reflection should be carried out to summarize the teaching process of the project and accumulate experience for the next project teaching. The focus is on the existing deficiencies and the need for improvement, so as to further clarify ideas for the project teaching method.

References

1. Xie, L.: Practical research on improving students' innovation consciousness by using project-based teaching method–a case study of money and banking. Educ. Teach. Forum **7**, 124–125 (2019)
2. Wang, W., Qiao, L.: Application and effect of project teaching method in investment banking teaching. J. Agric. Univ. Hebei (Agric. For. Educ.), **4**, 45–47 (2015)
3. Tingting, Y.: The systematic curriculum of work process from the perspective of modern cognitive theory. Educ. Modernization **9**, 103–104 (2019)
4. Li, M.: Practice and exploration of "curriculum ideology and politics" in financial management courses. Fireworks Market Technol. **3**, 91–92 (2020)

Engineering Ecosystem Models: Semantics and Pragmatics

Tristan Caulfield[1]([✉]), Marius-Constantin Ilau[1], and David Pym[1,2]

[1] University College London, London, UK
[2] Institute of Philosophy, University of London, London, UK
{t.caulfield,marius-constantin.ilau.18,d.pym}@ucl.ac.uk

Abstract. In a world of ever-increasing complexity, the smooth functioning of society is critically dependent on our ability to understand and manage both individual systems and complex ecosystems of systems. Models, combined with tools to reason about them, can provide a way to do this. In order for rigorous reasoning about models to be possible, they must have a robust mathematical foundation, which must also support tools for the engineering principles—compositionality, interfaces, and local reasoning—that are required to enable the practical construction of models of ecosystems. In this paper, we present a vision for a system of modelling, based on the concept of distributed systems as a metaphor for ecosystems of systems, that captures these requirements. We describe a mathematical foundation, identify the engineering principles needed, and show how they can be built in a rigorous way that preserves the ability to reason when dealing with complex, large-scale ecosystem models. We illustrate our ideas with examples and briefly explain how they apply in a practical modelling project.

Keywords: Distributed systems · Ecosystems · Modelling · Compositionality · Interfaces · Local reasoning

1 Introduction

The environment we inhabit is constantly increasing in complexity and with this comes a need for new ways of understanding and thinking about the world that can manage this complexity.

There is a famous quote from Grace Hopper:

'Life was simple before World War II. After that, we had systems.'

Now, systems are pervasive. They interact with and depend on each other and we, in turn, depend on them. It has become important to be able to think about

---

This work has been partially supported by the UK EPSRC research grant EP/R006865/1.

D. Jiang and H. Song (Eds.): SIMUtools 2021, LNICST 424, pp. 236–258, 2022.
https://doi.org/10.1007/978-3-030-97124-3_21

not just a single system, but also its interactions with other systems—it has become necessary to think of *ecosystems*.

Models are a way of understanding and reasoning about the world. There is a lot of existing modelling technology and practice that is good for capturing models of individual systems. The necessary shift to the ecosystem view means that we must consider not just the construction of models of individual systems but also how they are constructed in order to interact with one another.

Rigorous mathematical reasoning about models is important. In addition to the usual simulation techniques, it is necessary to be able to reason about models supports tools such as model checking, formal specification, and correctness and verification techniques. In order for a system of modelling to support this type of rigorous reasoning, it must itself have a rigorous mathematical foundation.

Ecosystems are systems of systems or, to put it another way, they are compositions of interacting subsystems. Examples include the global financial infrastructure of banks and exchanges, transportation networks, cyber-physical systems such as or workplace IoT networks and semi-automated manufacturing lines, and distributed databases. Other examples include electricity distribution networks, package delivery (or any supply chain using GPS and tags), and artificial organs (smart heart pumps, etc.).

What properties, built on the rigorous mathematical foundations, should a system of modelling have in order to make it a useful tool for capturing and reasoning about models of ecosystems?

Two of the first things that are required are systematic accounts of composition and interfaces. Composition is an important concept because it captures the structure of systems in the real world, but also because it is a useful tool for modelling—decomposing a large system or ecosystem into smaller subsystems allows us to manage the complexity of models. Interfaces are essential for understanding how systems are composed together. They specify what it is that interacting systems require of each other.

The notions of composition and interface support a range of useful modelling tools. For example, substitution—replacing one component model with another—which in turn supports refinement, abstraction, and extension of models.

Another requirement is local reasoning [26, 38, 39, 42, 51], which enables the specification of the conditions required for models to be composed with one another. The components used in forming compositions are the interfaces between the models. As such, the conceptual and technical complexity of reasoning about composite models is controlled. In the absence of local reasoning, actions such as the substitution of one (possibly small) component model for another might involve reasoning about the entire ecosystem. In general, such a situation would be conceptually and technically intractable.

In order to reason about systems, a rigorous mathematical foundation is required. In order to reason about ecosystems, these concepts of composition, interface, and local reasoning must build upon this rigorous foundation. With these three properties and the additional modelling tools they enable, a system of modelling can support practical and efficient modelling and reasoning about ecosystems. The question then is, of the ways of thinking about models, which ones are good ones that provide the substrate for thinking about ecosystems?

Other modelling approaches have tried to support, at least partially, the properties described above. For example, [13] describes an extension to the UML language [46] that facilitates composition using two different strategies—merging and overwriting, representing variations of the definition of the composition relationship—better to align object-oriented model structures with the structure of requirement specifications, [19] describes an event algebra for the synchronization and composition of labeled transition systems applied to timed automata, and Alloy [27], can be seen as an attempt at constructing a modelling framework based on rigorous mathematical concepts, but which does not focus on the composition of large-scale models. Furthermore, general techniques such as [31] focus on model decompositions that follow a modular approach.

When considering composition for more practical purposes, a particularly interesting class of modelling tools focused on transformation can be found in the model driven development literature. Focusing on the Model Transformation Chains abstraction, [1], practical tools such as MTCFlow or UniTI [50] support the composition of such chain abstractions and allow therefore the production of reusable modelling artefacts not only directly, but also through executable code generation [29].

This shows that composition—both at the level of the languages used to describe the components of the models and at the level of the construction and manipulation of the models themselves—is a useful tool in a variety of different modelling approaches. Here, we seek to present a *generic*, semantically-rigorous modelling approach that encompasses these concepts and can be implemented directly.

Computer science provides the concept of a *distributed system* (e.g., [16]) as a paradigm that encompasses not only single systems, but also ecosystems of systems. We propose that a theory of distributed systems models, based on a rigorous mathematical foundation, can meet these requirements. Thus our contribution is to capture the inherent semantic structure of ecosystems and derive appropriate tools for constructing and reasoning about systems—that is, accounts of interfaces, substitution, and local reasoning—from that structure.

In Sect. 2, we discuss how we use the distributed systems metaphor as a basis for modelling systems and their (de)composition. In Sect. 3, we sketch the process-algebraic foundation of models and logical tools for reasoning about them. In Sect. 4, we explain how we model locations and how this gives rise to an analysis interfaces, substitution, and local reasoning about components and (de)composition through reasoning about interfaces.

In Sect. 5, we discuss a practical example of the deployment of our modelling approach using tools—implemented in the Julia language [28], available at [8]—that capture our modelling framework (cf. [10,14]). Specifically, we consider a model of strategies for device recovery in the aftermath of security breaches that require the reinstallation of operating systems.

Finally, in Sect. 6, we discuss what is required to deliver fully our vision of a modelling framework.

2 Modelling Distributed Systems

The growth of interconnected networked systems led to the development of the concept and theory of distributed systems in computer science. This paradigm views systems as collections of components, in different locations, that work together to perform some task and communicate by sending information or messages over network connections.

This view is obviously very specific to its focus on computer systems, but its concepts can be taken more generally to provide a useful metaphor for understanding all types of systems and, finally, ecosystems. There are three key components upon which we draw.

- *Location*—Distributed systems naturally have a concept of different locations, which are connected to each other. In the CS view, components are present at different locations and connected by a network. In the more general view, locations can be physical (e.g., a room, a container), logical (e.g., an address in computer memory), or abstract (e.g., the location where a semaphore exists).
- *Resource*—Resources exist at locations and can move between them according to the locations' connections. In the general view, they can represent anything: physical objects, people, information.
- *Process*—Processes execute and manipulate resources as they do so.

These concepts can be used to build a representation of a system's structure and operation, but there is one more concept required: the environment in which the system operates.

- *Environment*—Environments capture the world outside of the system of interest and how the two interact.

This generalization provides concepts that can be used to model essentially any type of system, from physical to logical, or systems that incorporate both. We note also that these concepts are scale-free—they can be used at any level of abstraction or representation. However, we have not actually defined what it means to *build* a model using this distributed systems approach. This, too, is very flexible. Models can be largely conceptual, and use the ideas of location, resource, and process as a means to help think about the structure and behaviour of a system. Or distributed systems models can be mathematical, as we will show in the next section. Finally, this metaphor can be used to build executable models, in the spirit of Birtwistle's Demos [7], where a programmatic description of the system (in terms of locations, resources, and processes) is run to simulate the behaviour of the system [8–10,14]. An early implementation of these ideas, Gnosis [14], has been used in significant commercial applications [4–6] derived from an industry-based research project [22].

The ability to compose models is important for modelling larger systems and ecosystems. During the modelling process, these systems can be decomposed into smaller parts, which can be modelled separately and then recombined, and which helps manage complexity. What does composition look like in the distributed systems approach?

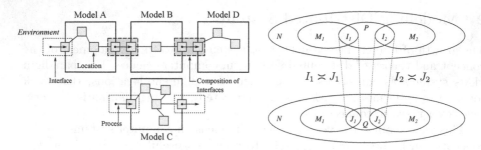

Fig. 1. Interfaces, composition, and substitution

Fig. 2. Interfaces and substitution

We start with interfaces. These define, for a model, the locations, resources, and processes involved in a composition. For a composition of two models to be valid, the interfaces in both models must match. Figure 1 depicts three models which compose together. When models with interfaces are not composed, the environment generates the events expected by the interface; when composed, the environment is replaced by a model. Also shown is an example of substitution: `Model C` can be substituted for `Model B` as the interfaces of the two models match; this allows a modeller to refine or increase detail in parts of a larger model. We give more detail about interfaces and composition in Sect. 4.

Interfaces and composition seem to support the concept of local naturally. Obtaining such an account of reasoning requires a mathematical conception of the distributed systems metaphor on top of which interfaces and composition can be defined. Milner [36, 37] considers the concept of interface from the point of view of a quite abstract graphical theory of processes. Our notion is more directly grounded in the concept of a distributed system, but we conjecture that the approaches can be understood comparatively. Our approach is more directly concerned with the logical concept of local reasoning.

3   A Sketch of the Mathematical Foundations

We begin by giving a formal framework for capturing the distributed systems metaphor that we are proposing as a basis for a semantically and logically well founded framework for modelling ecosystems of systems in the absence of locations. The basic theory of processes and their associated logics is technically essentially determined by the interaction between processes and resources, with locations playing a significant conceptual rôle only when the model-engineering concepts of interface, substitution, and local reasoning are considered, which we do in Sect. 4. The results presented in this section for states R, E extend to states L, R, E [14].

3.1   Processes and Resources

Our starting points are Milner's synchronous calculus of communicating systems, SCCS [33]—perhaps the most basic of process calculi, the collection of which includes also CCS [32], CSP [23], Meije [17], and their derivatives, as well as the π-calculus [35], bigraphs [36] and their derivatives—and the resource semantics of bunched logic [20,40,42,43]. The key components for our purposes are the following:

- A monoid of actions, Act, with a composition ab of elements a and b and unit 1;
- The following grammar of process terms, E, where $a \in$ Act and X denotes a process variable:

$$E ::= 0 \mid a \mid a : E \mid \sum_{i \in I} E_i \mid E \times E \mid \ldots$$

Most of the cases here, such as 0, action, action prefix, sum, concurrent product, and recursion, will seem quite familiar.

Mathematically, this notion of resource—which covers examples such as space, memory, and money—is based on (ordered, partial, commutative) monoids (e.g., the non-negative integers with zero, addition, and less-than-or-equals):

- each type of resource is based on a basic set of resource elements,
- resource elements can be combined, and
- resource elements can be compared.

Formally, we consider pre-ordered, partial commutative monoids of resources, $(\mathbf{R}, \circ, e, \sqsubseteq)$, where $\mathbf{R}$ is the carrier set of resource elements, $\circ$ is a partial monoid composition, with unit e, and $\sqsubseteq$ is a pre-order on $\mathbf{R}$. The basic idea is that resources, R, and processes, E, co-evolve,

$$R, E \xrightarrow{a} R', E',$$

according to the specification of a partial 'modification function', $\mu : (a, R) \mapsto R'$, that determines how an action a evolves E to E' and R to R'.

The base case of the operational semantics, presented in Plotkin's SOS style [41], is given by action prefix and concurrent composition, $\times$, exploits the monoid composition, $\circ$, on resources:

$$\frac{\mu(a, R) = R'}{R, a : E \xrightarrow{a} R', E'} \qquad \frac{R, E \xrightarrow{a} R', E' \quad S, F \xrightarrow{b} S', F'}{R \circ S, E \times F \xrightarrow{ab} R' \circ S', E' \times F'}.$$

This (rather general [17,33]) notion of composition at the level of process does not explain the engineering concept of the composition of models, with its requisite notions of interface and substitution, that we discuss in the sequel.

Sums, which represented choices, recursion, and other combinators are defined in similar ways.

A modification function is required to satisfy some basic coherence conditions (in certain circumstances, additional structure may be required [2]): for all actions a and b and all resources R and S, and where $\simeq$ is Kleene equality,

- $\mu(1, R) = R$, where 1 is the unit action, and
- if $\mu(a, R)$, $\mu(b, S)$, and $R \circ S$ are defined, then
  $\mu(ab, R \circ S) \simeq \mu(a, R) \circ \mu(b, S)$.

This function specifies the *signature* of the model.

3.2   Logic

Process calculi such as SCCS, CCS, and others come along with associated modal logics [21, 34, 47, 48]. Similarly, the calculus sketched here has associated modal logic, MBI [2, 14, 15]. The basic logical judgement is of the form

$$R, E \models \phi,$$

read as 'relative to the available resources R, the process E has property ϕ'.

Building on the ideas of the bunched logic BI (e.g., [20, 40, 42, 43]) and its application to Separation Logic [26, 44], MBI has, the usual *additive* connectives, $\top, \wedge, \rightarrow, \bot, \vee$.

These are all defined by semantic clauses of a satisfaction relation, where $\mathcal{V}$ is an interpretation of propositional letters in the usual way—see, for example, [49]—beginning as follows:

$$R, E \models p \text{ iff } (R, E) \in \mathcal{V}(p)$$

In addition, MBI also has a *multiplicative* conjunction, $*$,

$$R, E \models \phi * \psi \text{ iff there are } S, T \text{ and } F, G \text{ s.t. } S \circ T \sqsubseteq R, F \times G \sim E, \text{ and } S, F \models \phi \text{ and } T, E \models \psi \tag{1}$$

where $\sim$ is bisimulation (see, e.g., [33, 47, 48]) of processes, together with a multiplicative implication, $-\!*$. Note that the truth condition for $*$—sometimes called a 'separating conjunction', since its conjuncts use separate resources—combines the resources from the truth conditions for its component formulae.

The relationship between truth and action is captured by the clauses of the satisfaction relation for the (additive) modalities, given essentially as follows (recall that $R' = \mu(a, R)$):

$$R, E \models \langle a \rangle \phi \text{ iff there exists } E' \text{ s.t. } R, E \xrightarrow{a} R', E' \text{ and } R', E' \models \phi$$
$$R, E \models [a] \phi \text{ iff for all } E' \text{ s.t. } R, E \xrightarrow{a} R', E', R', E' \models \phi$$

Similarly, in addition to the usual additive quantifiers and modalities, MBI has multiplicative quantifiers and multiplicative modalities [14, 15] (we elide the details of MBI's predication).

The basic connection between the process calculus and the logic is given by a form of van Benthem-Hennessy-Milner theorem that relates process equivalence, as given by bisimulation, and logical equivalence (e.g., [2,14,15,21,34,47,48]), for MBI, defined by

$$R, E \equiv_{\text{MBI}} R, F \quad \text{iff} \quad \text{for all } \phi, R, E \models \phi \text{ iff } R, F \models \phi$$

For image-finite processes E and F and any R, [2,14,15],

$$R, E \sim R, F \quad \text{iff} \quad R, E \equiv_{\text{MBI}} R, F \qquad (2)$$

Under stronger assumptions about the nature of resources [2], or with restrictions to the logic [14], this equivalence can be extended to pairs R, E and S, F of states with distinct resources.

Logics based on the language of MBI have proved valuable in program analysis—see the Infer tool [18]—partly by virtue of their deployment of local reasoning, based on the connective $*$.

4 Ecosystem Modelling and Local Reasoning

As we have discussed, a key component of the distributed systems metaphor that we propose as a basis for a semantically and logically well-founded framework for modelling ecosystems of systems is location, logical or physical.

In general, we can identify a few requirements for a useful notion of location in systems modelling. Specifically,

- a collection of basic locations,
- directed connections between locations,
- a notion of substitution, which respects connections, and
- (optionally) a (monoidal) product of locations (a technical requirement).

In the presence of locations, the judgements for the transition relation for model states and the associated logical truth, respectively, take the forms

$$L, R, E \xrightarrow{a} L', R', E' \quad \text{and} \quad L, R, E \models \phi,$$

where the property ϕ of the process E holds relative to resources R at location L; that is, if a is an action guarding (the rest of) E, then $\mu(a, L, R)$ is defined, but are otherwise defined similarly as above [2,14].

4.1 Interfaces

The mathematical structure of models as described above provides the basis for the class of models that have been implemented in a systems modelling package [9,10] for the Julia language. Closely following [9,10], we describe interfaces more formally using well-motivated simplifications (that are, in fact, convenient to implement [10]) of the general semantic set-up [2,14,15].

Models in this methodology are designed to be composed with other models (Fig. 1). Composition allows two or more models to be combined and the resulting behaviour explored. When models are composed there are interactions at the location, process, and resource levels, and the role of their intended environments is critical. Processes evolve (transition) and resources are moved between models at locations shared between the models. To enable composition, models need interfaces, which define the locations at which models fit together and which actions, defined at appropriate locations within the interface, are party to the composition. Actions in the interface will nevertheless be able to execute only if the resources they require are available.

The locations and resources of a model are represented using a location graph, $\mathcal{G}(\mathcal{V}[\mathcal{R}], \mathcal{E})$, with a set of vertices, $\mathcal{V}$, representing the locations of the model, and a set of directed edges, $\mathcal{E}$, giving the connections between the locations. Vertices are labelled with resources $\mathcal{R}$. Rather than thinking of actions evolving processes, it is convenient to think of a process as a trace of actions—the history of actions that have evolved a process during the execution of the model. All of the actions in a model are contained in a set, $\mathcal{A}$, and process traces are comprised of these.

The environment a model sits inside causes actions within the model to be executed, at a particular location. A model contains a set of located actions, $\mathcal{L}$, and a located action, $l \in \mathcal{L}$, is given by an ordered pair $l = (a \in \mathcal{A}, v \in \mathcal{V})$. The environment associates these located actions with probability distributions: $Env : \mathcal{L} \rightarrow ProbDist$. During the execution of the model, the located actions are brought into existence by sampling from these distributions.

Writing I for the set of interfaces on a model, then an interface $I \in I$ on a model is a tuple (In, Out, L) of sets of input and output vertices, where $In \subseteq \mathcal{V}$ and $Out \subseteq \mathcal{V}$, and a set of located actions $L \subseteq \mathcal{L}$. The sets of input vertices and output vertices in interfaces must be disjoint; that is,

$$\bigcap_{i \in \mathcal{I}} In_i \in In = \emptyset \quad \text{and} \quad \bigcap_{i \in \mathcal{I}} Out_i \in Out = \emptyset.$$

Given this set-up, we can define a model as follows:

Definition 1. *A model $M = (\mathcal{G}(\mathcal{V}[\mathcal{R}], \mathcal{E}), \mathcal{A}, \mathcal{P}, \mathcal{L}, \mathcal{I})$ consists of a location graph $\mathcal{G}$, a set of actions $\mathcal{A}$, a set of processes $\mathcal{P}$, a set of located actions $\mathcal{L}$, and a set of interfaces $\mathcal{I}$. (Note that we can still consider the evolution of model states to be described as above.)* □

Our notion of interface is related to Lynch and Tuttle's input/output automata [30].

Two models, M_1 and M_2 are composed using specific interfaces $I_{1,1}, \ldots, I_{1,j}, \ldots, I_{1,n} \in \mathcal{I}_1$ and $I_{2,1}, \ldots, I_{2,k}, \ldots, I_{2,m} \in \mathcal{I}_2$ using the composition operator, to give $M_1 {}_{I_{1,j}}|_{I_{2,k}} M_2$, which is defined using an operation $\oplus$ on each of the elements of a model. First, we define the $\oplus$ operator for vertices and edges, $\mathcal{V}_1 \oplus \mathcal{V}_2 = \mathcal{V}_1 \cup \mathcal{V}_2$ and, for each $v \in \mathcal{V}_1 \oplus \mathcal{V}_2$, and then

$$v[\mathcal{R}_1 \oplus \mathcal{R}_2] = \begin{cases} v[\mathcal{R}_1] & \text{if } v \in \mathcal{V}_1 \wedge v \notin \mathcal{V}_2 \\ v[\mathcal{R}_2] & \text{if } v \in \mathcal{V}_2 \wedge v \notin \mathcal{V}_1 \\ v[\mathcal{R}_1 \cup \mathcal{R}_2] & \text{otherwise.} \end{cases}$$

Composition of edges, actions, and proceeses are straightforward: $\mathcal{E}_1 \oplus \mathcal{E}_2 = \mathcal{E}_1 \cup \mathcal{E}_2$, $\mathcal{A}_1 \oplus \mathcal{A}_2 = \mathcal{A}_1 \cup \mathcal{A}_2$, and $\mathcal{P}_1 \oplus \mathcal{P}_2 = \mathcal{P}_1 \cup \mathcal{P}_2$.

To define the $\oplus$ operator for locations and interfaces, we first need to introduce some notation. The interfaces on a model are a set of tuples; for example, the interfaces of M_1: $\mathcal{I}_1 = \{(In_1, Out_1, L_1)_i\}$. A particular interface from $\mathcal{I}_1$ is referred to as $I_{1,i}$, and the input locations from that interface are referred to as $In_{1,i}$, the outputs as $Out_{1,i}$, and the located actions as $L_{1,i}$.

When models are composed, the located actions in the interface that were executed by the environment in the uncomposed model are now executed as a consequence of the other model instead. As such, the composition of located actions is the union of both sets of located actions, minus those that are in interfaces used in the composition: $\mathcal{L}_1 \oplus \mathcal{L}_2 = \mathcal{L}_1 \cup \mathcal{L}_2 \setminus \{L_{1,j}, L_{2,k}\}$.

Interfaces can be used in just one composition, and the input and output locations of the interfaces from the two models must correspond, so their composition is $\mathcal{I}_1 \oplus \mathcal{I}_2 = (\mathcal{I}_1 \cup \mathcal{I}_2) \setminus \{I_{1,j}, I_{2,k}\}$, where we require $\bigcup_{j=1}^{n} In_{I_{1,j}} = \bigcup_{k=1}^{m} Out_{I_{2,k}}$ and $\bigcup_{j=1}^{n} Out_{I_{1,j}} = \bigcup_{k=1}^{m} In_{I_{2,k}}$. Models must be composed completely: any location that is in both of the models must belong to the interfaces used in the composition.

Definition 2. *With the data as established above, the composition of models M_1 and M_2 is given by*

$$M_1{}_{I_{1,j}}|_{I_{2,k}} M_2 = (\mathcal{G}((\mathcal{V}_1 \oplus \mathcal{V}_2)[\mathcal{R}_1 \oplus \mathcal{R}_2], \mathcal{E}_1 \oplus \mathcal{E}_2), \mathcal{A}_1 \oplus \mathcal{A}_2, \mathcal{P}_1 \oplus \mathcal{P}_2, \mathcal{L}_1 \oplus \mathcal{L}_2, (\mathcal{I}_1 \oplus \mathcal{I}_2))$$

with the constraint that $\mathcal{V}_1 \cap \mathcal{V}_2 = In_{1,j} \cup In_{2,k}$. (This constraint above represents a significant design choice in the definition of interfaces.)   □

Proposition 1 ([10]). $M_1{}_{I_{1,j}}|_{I_{2,k}} M_2$ *is a model.*   □

Proposition 2 ([10]). *For any models M_1 and M_2, let $I_{1,2}$ be the subset of interfaces in $\mathcal{I}_1$ that compose with M_2. Composition of models is commutative and associative:* $M_1{}_{I_{1,j}}|_{I_{2,k}} M_2 = M_2{}_{I_{2,k}}|_{I_{1,j}} M_1$ *and* $(M_1{}_{I_{1,1}}|_{I_{2,1}} M_2)_{I_{1,3} \cup I_{2,3}}|_{I_{3,1} \cup I_{3,2}} M_3 = M_1{}_{I_{1,2} \cup I_{1,3}}|_{I_{2,1} \cup I_{3,1}} (M_2{}_{I_{2,3}}|_{I_{3,2}} M_3)$ □

So far, this definition of interface says little about how a model becomes animated. How this actually works is that a model is animated when events occur at its boundaries. As we have seen, models exist within environments and, as we have remarked, environments are captured within our framework stochastically. In fact, our treatment of environment—that is, that part of a model that is not captured in detail, using the distributed systems structure of locations, resources, and processes—is rather simple.

These issues will be clear by a simple example: the conveyor belt, represented using the language of our distributed systems modelling metaphor, and explain how it can decomposed into two component subsystems using an appropriate choice of interface. Figure 3 depicts a conveyor belt in which resources r are moved along from right to left, with *in* and *out* locations at either end.

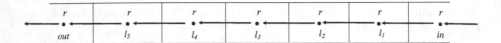

Fig. 3. A conveyor belt

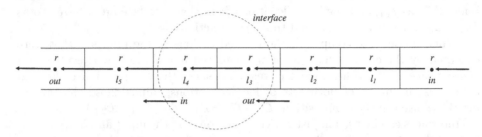

Fig. 4. A composite conveyor belt

The signature for this model, as described by its modification function, can be specified as follows:

$$\mu(move(r, in, l_1), in, r) = (l_1, r) \qquad \mu(move(r, l_5, out), l_5, r) = (out, r)$$
$$\mu(move(r, l_k, l_{k+1}), l_k, r) = (l_{k+1}, r) \qquad\qquad otherwise \quad \uparrow$$

where, as usual, $\uparrow$ denotes 'undefined'.

The process-component of the model is then defined, recursively, as follows:

$$ConBelt ::= (move(r, in, l_1) : ConBelt \times move(r, l_1, l_2) : ConBelt \times$$
$$\dots \times move(r, l_5, out) : ConBelt) + 0$$

Then the system Ls , Rs , $ConBelt$, where we right Ls and Rs for the evident lists of locations and resources, describes the basic operation of a conveyor belt, as depicted in Fig. 3. Either the belt moves with each section in lockstep or it stops (0 denotes termination).

Consider now a conveyor belt that consists of one belt passing on its items to another, perhaps because different machines are used to process the items on different belts. We can use our idea of interfaces to describe how to think of our $ConBelt$ as the composition of two, component, ConBelts.

The set-up is depicted in Fig. 4. Here we can see that the conveyor belt can be understood as the composition of two such belts, the right-hand one of which has l_3 as it's out location, which then leads to the in location, l_4, of the right-hand one. The interface consists of the two locations, l_3 and l_4, together with their associated data.

4.2   Substitution

As we have briefly discussed, the construction of models of complex systems may require the substitution of one component model for another; for example, perhaps, to either increase or reduce the level of detail; or, perhaps, to explore a quite different design for part of a model; or, perhaps, to replace part of the environment with a specific model. The typical situation is, more or less, as depicted in Fig. 2: a model N has components M_1 and M_2 connected by a model Q. We seek to replace Q with the model P.

For simplicity, denote the interfaces between M_1 and Q and Q and M_2—formally defined as composites, as above—by J_1 and J_2, respectively. Similarly, suppose that P, which replaces Q, has interfaces I_1 and I_2 to M_1 and M_2.

For substitution to behave as required, what must we require of P, I_1, and I_2? We identify the following requirements: (i) the pairs of substituting and substituted interfaces should be able to simulate one another; (ii) the distributions of the events that are incident upon the corresponding boundaries of the interfaces should be the same, up to choices of parameters. These two conditions together give us what we need: let $\mathcal{D}_M(L)$ denote a set of pairs of probability distributions and locations in a model M. We write $d_1 \asymp d_2$ if d_1 and d_2 are distributions that are the same up to choices of parameters and extend this notation to sets $\mathcal{D}_M(L)$. Then, we require:

- $\mathcal{D}_N(In_{I_1}) - \mathcal{D}_N(In_{J_1})$ and $\mathcal{D}_N(Out_{I_1}) - \mathcal{D}_N(Out_{J_1})$
- $\mathcal{D}_N(In_{I_2}) = \mathcal{D}_N(In_{J_2})$ and $\mathcal{D}_N(Out_{I_2}) = \mathcal{D}_N(Out_{J_2})$
- for $i = 1, 2$, abusing notation a little, $I_i \asymp J_i$.

Consider the example of a substitution depicted in Fig. 5, in which a small-scale road map of the roads in and out of a city is replaced by a larger scale map, which has more detail of the topography of the city. The relevant interfaces here are simply the points of contact between the roads within the city and their connections in the environment, together with their associated probability distributions.

The logic MBI allows us to assert some useful properties. For example, if $\mathcal{S}$ (i.e., some L, R, E) and $\mathcal{S}'$ (i.e., some L', R', E') denote states (we elide details) of the smaller and larger scale models, then we can write

$$\mathcal{S} \models \phi \quad \text{and} \quad \mathcal{S}' \models \phi'$$

where—writing c for a car, g_1, g_2, g_3 for the three city gates, and t and u for time periods, all as parameters for actions in the evident way—we can assert $\phi = [enter_{c,g_1}]\top \rightarrow (\langle exit_{c,g_2}\rangle\top \vee \langle exit_{c,g_3}\rangle\top)$ and

$$\phi' = [enter_{c,g_1}](\langle park_{c,t}\rangle\top \vee \langle gas_{c,u}\rangle\top) \rightarrow (\langle exit_{c,g_2}\top\rangle \vee \langle exit_{c,g_3}\rangle\top)$$

Here, just as in the transition from $\mathcal{S}$ to $\mathcal{S}'$, we give greater detail of the properties that may hold of a city location.

Note that the exit possibilities are not the only such possibilities (e.g., a car may remain in the town and never leave).

4.3   Local Reasoning

In this section, we introduce the concept of local reasoning, first introduced in the context of Separation Logic [26,45,51]. This conceptual design facilitates

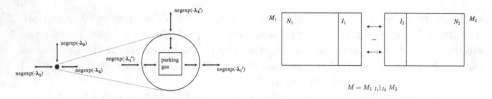

Fig. 5. Substitution   **Fig. 6.** Interfaces and local reasoning

the ability to reason locally about the underlying components of an system or ecosystem.

The primary advantage of this is that the properties of an specific component in a decomposition of a model can be reasoned about without the need to reason about other components other than in respect of the interfaces to the specific component. Consequently, modularity (and substitution) are supported, with the conceptual and computational complexity of reasoning constrained.

With respect to local reasoning, we argue that the combination of the mathematical foundations sketched in Sect. 3 and the conceptual separation of components, as described above, offers the ability to focus analyses on specific components and simply state the relevant aspects for intercommunication at the level of interfaces.

We can identify here a local reasoning principle, or *frame rule* [26,38,39,42, 51]. We begin by setting up some notation for the states of the various component models depicted in Fig. 6:

- let the model $M = M_1{}_{I_1}|_{I_2}M_2$ have state $\mathcal{S}$;
- let the component models (of the composition of interest) M_i have states $\mathcal{S}_i$, respectively;
- let the submodels N_i have states $\mathcal{U}_i$, respectively; and
- let the interfaces I_i have states $\mathcal{I}_i$, respectively.

Now, using $\circ$ for composition of states, we assume the following, for $i = 1, 2$:

- $\mathcal{S}_i \sim \mathcal{U}_i \circ \mathcal{I}_i$, $\mathcal{S} \xrightarrow{a} \mathcal{T}$, and $\mathcal{I}_i \xrightarrow{a} \mathcal{J}_i$
- $a\#N_i\backslash I_i$; that is, that the action a is 'separated from' that part of the model N_i that is not coincident with the interface I_i in that the execution of a does not affect N_i.

Now, suppose that $\mathcal{U}_i \models \phi_i$, for $i = 1, 2$. Then we have the following frame rule:

$$\frac{\mathcal{J}_1 \models \psi_1 \quad \mathcal{J}_2 \models \psi_2 \qquad \mathcal{S} \xrightarrow{a} \mathcal{T} \text{ and } \mathcal{I}_i \xrightarrow{a} \mathcal{J}_i}{\mathcal{T} \models (\phi_1 * \psi_1) * (\psi_2 * \phi_2) \qquad a\#N_i\backslash I_i}$$

This rule is sound with respect to bisimulation equivalence:

Proposition 3 (Soundness of the frame rule). *Suppose, for $i = 1, 2$, $\mathcal{J}_i \sim \mathcal{J}_i'$, $\mathcal{I}_1 \sim \mathcal{I}_i'$, and $\mathcal{S} \sim \mathcal{S}'$ and $\mathcal{T} \sim \mathcal{T}'$. Then $\mathcal{T}' \models (\phi_1 * \psi_1) * (\psi_2 * \phi_2)$.*

Proof Sketch. By (2), we have that that, for $i = 1, 2, \mathcal{U}_i \models \phi_i$ and $\mathcal{J}_i \models \psi_i$. Then, note that separation condition, $a \# N_i \backslash I_i$, and the definition (1) of satisfaction for $*$ are respected by bisimulation. Finally, further applications of (2) then give the required conclusion.

To understand how all this works, consider again Fig. 5 and suppose we have a model M for the part of the city that includes the parking and the gas station. That model is connected by interfaces—here again they are just point-to-point, respecting stochastic flows—to the rest of the more detailed model of the city. The facilities of the gas station and their operating capacities, which can be expressed logically, are properties of M that are independent of the model of the surrounding city. In this example, these properties correspond to the ϕ_is in the frame rule: separated by the multiplicative conjunction, $*$, they are invariant under changes to the surrounding model and the interfaces to it when the overall model evolves. The primary advantage of such a setting is that the modeller can confidently focus its analysis on a singular model component without the need to reason about its relationships with other components—the relevant aspects of intercommunication remain located at the interface level, acting as contracts that submodels have to fulfill in order for the composition to be possible.

Returning to our example of the conveyor belt, as depicted in Figs. 3 and 4, suppose the two component belts are there to support two different sequences of operations:

- The right-hand belt performs actions op_1 and op_2 on the resources at locations l_1 and l_2, respectively;
- At l_3, in the interface, the correct completion of the operations op_1 and op_2 is verified;
- At l_4, in the interface, the readiness of the resources for the operations of the left-hand belt is verified;
- The left-hand belt performs the operation op_5 on the resource at l_5.

What can a frame rule say about this situation? First, we give the conveyor belt a bit more to do. Suppose that at locations l_1, l_2, and l_5, the operations op_1, op_2, and op_5, respectively, may—provided the machines servicing the belts are functioning correctly—be performed. Then, using MBI's modalities, as defined in Sect. 3.2,

$$in, r, move(r, in, l_1) : ConBelt \models [move(r, in, l_1)]\langle op_1 \rangle \top$$

since $move(r, in, l_1)$ takes our focus to location l_1, at which point op_1 may be performed, and nothing else happens to the resource r until it moves to l_2. Similarly,

$$l_1, r, move(r, l_1, l_2) : ConBelt \models [move(r, l_1, l_2)]\langle op_2 \rangle \top$$

These properties hold of that part of the right-hand belt that lies outwith its interface to the left-hand belt.

A similar logical judgement holds for the left-hand belt:

$$in, r, move(r, l_4, l_5) : ConBelt \models [move(r, l_4, l_5)]\langle op_5 \rangle \top$$

Again, this property holds independently of properties of the right-hand belt.

Here we are assuming, for simplicity, that the belt(s) cannot stall or otherwise prevent the passing of resources from one location to the next—such a possibility would break our separation condition. This assumption, however, provides a clue to the use of the frame rule.

So far, our discussion of interfaces has been purely at the operational level: locations, actions, and so on. But the composition of models through interfaces might also be subject to some requirements that certain properties of the component models hold. That is, the composition

$$M_{1 I_{1,j}} |_{I_{2,k}} M_2$$

might be made subject to conditions, following the notational convention set out above, as follows: $\mathcal{I}_{1,j} \models \phi_{1,j}$, for each j and $\mathcal{I}_{2,k} \models \phi_{2,k}$, for each k, specifying the required properties of the output from one model and input to the other.

Within our conveyor belt(s) example, we can set up an example of such a situation. Let $Op_1(r)$ and $Op_2(r)$ be propositions that denote that the resource has received the operations op_1 and op_2, respectively. Then we may impose the conditions

- On the output of right-hand belt:

$$l_3, r, move(r, l_3, l_4) : ConBelt \models Op_1(r) \wedge Op_2(r)$$

- On the input to the left-hand belt:

$$l_4, r, move(r, l_4, l_5) : ConBelt \models Op_1(r) \wedge Op_2(r)$$

In order to check that the two conveyor belts can be composed, we need only check that the resources arriving at l_3 have received the operations op_1 and op_2. Of course, the left-hand belt may require that the resources it receives also carry a certification that these operations have been performed. Such a certification might be delivered as part of a check at l_3 and a verification at l_4:

- Check: $l_3, r, move(r, l_3, l_4) : ConBelt \models Check(op_1, op_2)$
- Validate: $l_4, r, move(r, l_4, l_5) : ConBelt \models Validate(op_1, op_2)$

Again, checking these properties would be independent of those parts of the belts outwith their interfaces.

5   Applying the Framework

Modelling tools based on the framework we have described above have been deployed in a range of applications that aim to support information security decision-making such as [9–12,24] or [25].

Recently—using tools, implemented in the Julia language [28] and available at [8], that capture the framework we have described—we have considered the problem of organizational recovery under ransomware attacks and constructed

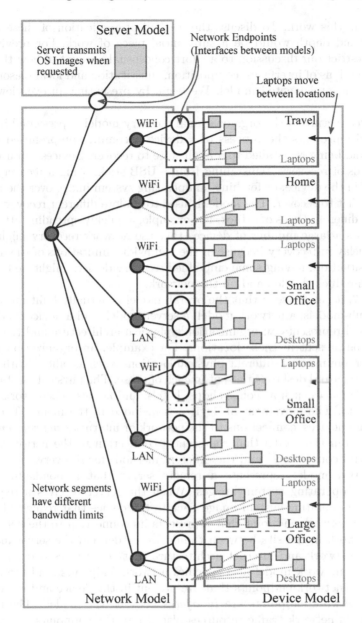

Fig. 7. The architecture of the recovery model

a model for exploring different attack scenarios for the purpose of increasing organizational resilience. This work, has been carried out in collaboration with industry colleagues, is reported in [3].

Here, we use this problem of organizational recovery to discuss how our analysis of compositionality and local reasoning can be applied to the models generated in this work. To discuss the method of application of these ideas in generality and depth would be a substantial piece of work. For brevity, here we must restrict our discussion to a short conceptual account of how the above described notions of interfaces, composition, substitution and local reasoning are utilized in an implemented model. We begin by presenting an overview of the model.

The architecture of the organizational recovery model is presented in Fig. 7. The model represents the process of a device becoming compromised by ransomware and being reinstalled to a fresh state to recover. Devices can use different methods of recovery: reinstalling from a USB stick, using a recovery image embedded in the device, or fetching an operating system image over the network and using that to recover. The model is used to explore different recovery strategies under different types of attack. For example, a quickly-spreading attack that compromises a large number of devices that use network recovery might cause a serious delay in recovery because of the bandwidth limitations of the network; in such a situation, having some embedded recovery devices might be beneficial as this can reduce the demand on the network.

In Fig. 7, it can be seen that the overall model is actually built out of three separate sub-models: a network model, a server model, and a device model. The device model represents an organization's physical architecture and the devices that may be present in those locations. For example, an organization may be spread over a number of different physical locations, such as offices, with devices such as laptops and desktops present in each of those. The physical locations also may include places such as coffee shops, hotels, and homes, where work devices may travel to. The movement of devices is included in the model. The model also includes devices' connections to the network or internet—*network endpoints* are locations in the model that represent a connection to the network, over a LAN or WiFi connection—and the different methods for recovery.

The server model represents a remote server that responds to devices' requests for operating system images. When the server receives a request, it transmits an operating system image back to the device that requested it. The server has a network endpoint that represents its connection to the network.

The network model sits between the device model and the server model. It defines the network and internet architecture that the devices and server connect to. The network model also specifies network endpoints, and these correspond to the network endpoints that are present in the device and server models. These network endpoints are *interfaces* between the models. The network model accepts network traffic resources placed into the endpoints by transmitting devices, and delivers them, after a delay, to the receiving network endpoint. The delay is based on the size of the data, the bandwidth of the different network segments, and how much other traffic is also being transmitted at the same time.

These three sub-models compose together at the interfaces—the network endpoints—to become a larger, complete model. In the complete model, when a device is compromised and initiates recovery over the network, it 'transmits' a request for an operating system image to the server over the network. It does this by moving a resource representing the request into the network endpoint. The network model waits for such resources to arrive in the endpoints; when one arrives, it begins the transmission process by calculating the transmission time (which can vary and is updated based on network utilization by other devices). When the transmission time has elapsed, the network model delivers the request resource to the server's endpoint. The server waits for these requests to arrive from the network and responds to them by transmitting an operating system image resource back to the device that requested it over the network using the same process. When the device receives the image, it completes the recovery process by installing it.

When considering substitution, two options are possible: substituting a model with another model or substituting an environment component with a model. For example, one might consider a single network storage point as too simplistic and wish to employ a more complex storage model that includes different servers, load balancing or back-up procedures. In such a case, the modeller can focus on developing the desired architecture as long as the output network packets have the same signature as the ones produced by the model to be substituted. Furthermore, perhaps the modeller considers that additional focus has to be placed on different types of malware that might affect the organization. In that case, the environmental process that stochastically triggered malware events can be developed into a fully structured model and then substitute that part of the environment.

Furthermore, we describe a plausible scenario for the application of local reasoning. Although the original model goal was to illustrate the different recovery times of different mechanisms and strategies, one might imagine that our model setting can be used for simulating the impact of different data loss policies. In that case, the modeller need not worry about having to fully re-implement the models to target data loss or perform a complete re-validation procedure. Different modelling approaches can tend to either take this consistency for granted or perform time consuming re-validation steps, whereas in our case, the frame rule described above ensures that the previously considered invariant components remain invariant as long as they don't interact with any of the new development additions.

To see how our approach to compositionality and local reasoning can be applied to such a setting, let's consider a stripped down, somewhat abstracted, version of the composite model. Here, for simplicity, we assume that composed models—Server–Network and Network–Device—have interfaces that are identical; that is, in terms of our definition in Sect. 4.1, this amounts to the interfaces from each of the models that are used in a composition being identical in each model. The simplified composite model is depicted in Fig. 8 .

By way of an example, consider the composition of the device model and the network model. A device may request an image from the server by sending a request from the endpoint interface for transmission over the network to the server. The server's response, including the image, is transmitted over the network and received at the Endpoint interface, which now holds the image for receipt by the device:

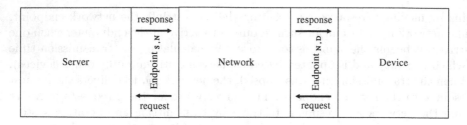

Fig. 8. A simplified recovery model

$$\text{Endpoint}_{N,D} \overset{response}{\longrightarrow} \text{Endpoint}'_{N,D}$$

The availability of the image that is appropriate for the device can be expressed by a logical assertion such as

$$\text{Endpoint}'_{N,D} \models \text{Image}_X \wedge \text{Device}_X$$

where X denotes the required OS, so that Image_X denotes a proposition asserting that an X image is available and Device_X denotes that the device requires the X image.

Note that the separation condition, as defined above,

$$response \,\#\, \text{Device} \backslash \text{Endpoint}_{N,D}$$

holds. Consequently, applying the frame rule, we can substitute a different device model, Device$'$, provided

$$\text{Endpoint}'_{N,D'} \models \text{Image}_X \wedge \text{Device}'_X$$

can be verified.

As the examples above and in Sect. 3 illustrate, the way in which composition, substitution, and local reasoning have been defined and supported by our modelling approach brings a certain set of advantages. Composition ensures model consistency. Substitution and the use of interfaces offers great flexibility while at the same time conserving model consistency. Lastly, local reasoning offers the confidence to focus model analysis on singular components and ability to better manage complexity in a timely manner when considering practical implementation.

6   Discussion and Future Work

We have explained the need for a compositional engineering methodology—using the ideas of interfaces and substitution—for constructing models of complex ecosystems. Our methodology is mathematically rigorous, itself building on a rigorous approach to modelling distributed systems, which are seen as a metaphor for the structure of complex ecosystems.

Models based on the distributed systems metaphor have found significant application in commercial contexts. As we have described in Sect. 2, an early implementation of these ideas, Gnosis [14], formed the basis of the application of an industry-based modelling project [22] to major clients [5,6]. However, Gnosis lacks the compositional engineering and reasoning tools that we have proposed in this paper, with only a very limited model-checker implemented. A compositional approach for executable models was subsequently developed in [8,10] and used in recent, as yet unpublished, work by some of us that has involved the application of our ideas to resource-allocation problems in hospitals, with a focus on emergency care and its follow-up. Here, the location-based, modular approach appears to be particularly valuable, as it allows different clinical departments, which must interact with one another, to be modelled and reasoned about independently.

While our current tools support the distributed systems modelling framework that we have described in Sect. 2, including the notion of interface, for a systematic approach to the construction of executable models much work remains to be done to deliver our vision of a fully developed practical methodology:

   tools to support the design and specification of models that support our theory of interfaces and substitution;
 – tools to support logical reasoning—in particular, tools based on model checking—about models; and
 – tools to support local reasoning about the compositional structure of models.

These additions will enable the construction of large-scale models of ecosystems that can be executed and reasoned about. This will allow us to better represent, understand, and make decisions about the complex systems in the modern world.

References

1. Alvarez, C., Casallas, R.: MTC flow: a tool to design, develop and deploy model transformation chains. In: Proceedings of the Workshop on ACadeMics Tooling with Eclipse, ACME '13, New York, NY, USA. Association for Computing Machinery (2013)
2. Anderson, G., Pym, D.: A calculus and logic of bunched resources and processes. Theoret. Comput. Sci. **614**, 63–96 (2016)
3. Anonymous authors. Modelling Organizational Recovery (2021, Submitted)
4. Baldwin, A., Beres, Y., Duggan, G.B., Mont, M.C., Johnson, H., Middup, C., Shiu, S.: Economic methods and decision making by security professionals. In: Schneier, B. (ed.) Economics of Information Security and Privacy III, pp. 213–238. Springer, New York (2013). https://doi.org/10.1007/978-1-4614-1981-5_10

5. Beres, Y., Griffin, J., Shiu, S., Heitman, M., Markle, D., Ventura, P.: Analysing the performance of security solutions to reduce vulnerability exposure window. In: 2008 Annual Computer Security Applications Conference (ACSAC), pp. 33–42 (2008)
6. Beresnevichiene, Y., Pym, D., Shiu, S.: Decision support for systems security investment. In: 2010 IEEE/IFIP Network Operations and Management Symposium Workshops, pp. 118–125 (2010)
7. Birtwistle, G.: Demos - Discrete Event Modelling on Simula. Macmillan, Basingstoke (1979)
8. Caulfield, T.: SysModels Julia Package. https://github.com/tristanc/SysModels. Accessed 10 May 2021
9. Caulfield, T., Pym, D.: Improving security policy decisions with models. IEEE Secur. Priv. **13**(5), 34–41 (2015)
10. Caulfield, T., Pym, D.: Modelling and simulating systems security policy. In: Proceedings of SimuTools (2015)
11. Caulfield, T., Fielder, A.: Optimizing time allocation for network defence. J. Cybersecur. **1**(1), 37–51 (2015)
12. Caulfield, T., Parkin, S.: Case study: predicting the impact of a physical access control intervention. In: Proceedings of the 6th Workshop on Socio-Technical Aspects in Security and Trust, pp. 37–46 (2016)
13. Clarke, S.: Extending standard UML with model composition semantics. Sci. Comput. Program. **44**(1), 71–100 (2002). Special Issue on Unified Modeling Language (UML 2000)
14. Collinson, M., Monahan, B., Pym, D.: A Discipline of Math. Systems Modelling. College Publns., Rickmansworth (2012)
15. Collinson, M., Pym, D.: Algebra and logic for resource-based systems modelling. Math. Struct. Comput. Sci. **19**, 959–1027 (2009)
16. Coulouris, G., Dollimore, J., Kindberg, T.: Distributed Systems: Concepts and Design, 3rd edn. Addison Wesley, Boston (2000)
17. de Simone, R.: Higher-level synchronising devices in Meije-SCCS. Theor. Comput. Sci. **37**, 245–267 (1985)
18. Facebook. Open-sourcing Facebook Infer. https://engineering.fb.com/2015/06/11/developer-tools/open-sourcing-facebook-infer-identify-bugs-before-you-ship/. Accessed 10 May 2021
19. Fares, E., Bodeveix, J.-P., Filali, M.: Event algebra for transition systems composition application to timed automata. Acta Informatica **55**(5), 363–400 (2017). https://doi.org/10.1007/s00236-017-0302-9
20. Galmiche, D., Méry, D., Pym, D.: The semantics of BI and resource Tableaux. Math. Struct. Comput. Sci. **15**, 1033–1088 (2005)
21. Hennessy, M., Milner, R.: On observing nondeterminism and concurrency. In: de Bakker, J., van Leeuwen, J. (eds.) ICALP 1980. LNCS, vol. 85, pp. 299–309. Springer, Heidelberg (1980). https://doi.org/10.1007/3-540-10003-2_79
22. Hewlett-Packard Laboratories. Security Analytics. https://www.hpl.hp.com/news/2011/oct-dec/security_analytics.html. Accessed 10 May 2021
23. Hoare, C.A.R.: Communicating Sequential Processes. Prentice-Hall International, London (1985)
24. Ioannidis, C., Pym, D., Williams, J.: Information security trade-offs and optimal patching policies. Eur. J. Oper. Res. **216**(2), 434–444 (2011). https://doi.org/10.1016/j.ejor.2011.05.050

25. Ioannidis, C., Pym, D., Williams, J.: Fixed costs, investment rigidities, and risk aversion in information security: a utility-theoretic approach. In: Schneier, B. (ed.) Economics of Information Security and Privacy III, pp. 171–191. Springer, New York (2013). https://doi.org/10.1007/978-1-4614-1981-5_8

26. Ishtiaq, S.S., O'Hearn, P.: BI as an assertion language for mutable data structures. In: Proceedings of POPL (2001)

27. Jackson, D.: Alloy: a lightweight object modelling notation. ACM Trans. Softw. Eng. Methodol. 11(2), 256–290 (2002)

28. julia. http://julialang.org

29. Kleppe, A.: MCC: a model transformation environment. In: Rensink, A., Warmer, J. (eds.) ECMDA-FA 2006. LNCS, vol. 4066, pp. 173–187. Springer, Heidelberg (2006). https://doi.org/10.1007/11787044_14

30. Lynch, N.A., Tuttle, M.R.: An introduction to input/output automata. CWI Q. 2, 219–246 (1989)

31. Ma, Q., Kelsen, P., Glodt, C.: A generic model decomposition technique and its application to the eclipse modeling framework. Softw. Syst. Model. 14(2), 921–952 (2015). https://doi.org/10.1007/s10270-013-0348-2

32. Milner, R.: A Calculus of Communicating Systems, vol. 92. Springer, Heidelberg (1980). https://doi.org/10.1007/3-540-10235-3

33. Milner, R.: Calculi for synchrony and asynchrony. Theor. Comput. Sci. 25(3), 267–310 (1983)

34. Milner, R.: Communication and Concurrency. Prentice Hall, New York (1989)

35. Milner, R.: Communicating and Mobile Systems: The π-Calculus. Cambridge University Press, Cambridge (1999)

36. Milner, R.: Bigraphs as a model for mobile interaction. In: Corradini, A., Ehrig, H., Kreowski, H.-J., Rozenberg, G. (eds.) ICGT 2002. LNCS, vol. 2505, pp. 8–13. Springer, Heidelberg (2002). https://doi.org/10.1007/3-540-45832-8_3

37. Milner, R.: The Space and Motion of Communicating Agents. Cambridge University Press, Cambridge (2009)

38. O'Hearn, P.: Resources, concurrency, and local reasoning. Theor. Comput. Sci. 375(1–3), 271–307 (2007)

39. O'Hearn, P., Reynolds, J., Yang, H.: Local reasoning about programs that alter data structures. In: Fribourg, L. (ed.) CSL 2001. LNCS, vol. 2142, pp. 1–19. Springer, Heidelberg (2001). https://doi.org/10.1007/3-540-44802-0_1

40. O'Hearn, P.W., Pym, D.J.: The logic of bunched implications. Bull. Symb. Logic 5(2), 215–244 (1999)

41. Plotkin, G.D.: A structural approach to operational semantics. Technical Report DAIMI FN-19, Computer Science Dept., Aarhus University, Aarhus, Denmark (1981)

42. Pym, D.: Resource semantics: logic as a modelling technology. ACM SIGLOG News 6(2), 5–41 (2019)

43. Pym, D.J., O'Hearn, P.W., Yang, H.: Possible worlds and resources: the semantics of BI. Theor. Comput. Sci. 315(1), 257–305 (2004)

44. Reynolds, J.: Separation logic: a logic for shared mutable data structures. In: Proceedings of LICS (2002)

45. Reynolds, J.C.: Separation logic: a logic for shared mutable data structures. In: Proceedings of the 17th Annual IEEE Symposium on Logic in Computer Science, LICS '02, Washington, DC, USA, pp. 55–74. IEEE Computer Society (2002)

46. Rumbaugh, J., Jacobson, I., Booch, G.: Unified Modeling Language Reference Manual, 2nd edn. Pearson Higher Education, Hoboken (2004)

47. Stirling, C.: Modal and Temporal Properties of Processes. Springer, Heidelberg (2001). https://doi.org/10.1007/978-1-4757-3550-5
48. van Benthem, J.: Logical Dynamics of Information and Interaction. Cambridge University Press, Cambridge (2011)
49. van Dalen, D.: Logic and Structure, 3rd edn. Springer, Heidelberg (1997)
50. Vanhooff, B., Ayed, D., Van Baelen, S., Joosen, W., Berbers, Y.: UniTI: a unified transformation infrastructure. In: Engels, G., Opdyke, B., Schmidt, D.C., Weil, F. (eds.) MODELS 2007. LNCS, vol. 4735, pp. 31–45. Springer, Heidelberg (2007). https://doi.org/10.1007/978-3-540-75209-7_3
51. Yang, H., O'Hearn, P.: A semantic basis for local reasoning. In: Nielsen, M., Engberg, U. (eds.) FoSSaCS 2002. LNCS, vol. 2303, pp. 402–416. Springer, Heidelberg (2002). https://doi.org/10.1007/3-540-45931-6_28

Meta-modelling for Ecosystems Security

Tristan Caulfield[1]([✉]), Marius-Constantin Ilau[1], and David Pym[1,2]

[1] University College London, London, UK
{t.caulfield,marius-constantin.ilau.18,d.pym}@ucl.ac.uk
[2] Institute of Philosophy, University of London, London, UK

Abstract. As the world has evolved to become ever more dependent on complex ecosystems of large, interacting systems, it has become ever more important to be able to reason rigorously about the design, construction, and behaviour not only of individual systems—which may include aspects related to all of people, process, and technology—but also of their assembly into ecosystems. In such situations, it is inevitable that no one type of model—such as mathematical models of dynamical systems, logical models of languages, or discrete event simulation models—will be sufficient to describe all of the aspects of ecosystems about which rigorous reasoning is required. We propose here a meta-theoretical framework, the 'triangle framework', within which different types of models may be categorized and their interactions, especially during the construction of models, can be understood. Its explicit goals are to facilitate a better understanding of the nature of models and to provide a more inclusive language for the description of heterogeneous models. Specifically, we identify three qualities of models, each derived from modelling goals—conceptuality, mathematicality, and executability—and explain how models will, typically, have all of these qualities to varying extents. We also show how the framework supports an analysis of how models can be co-designed by their various stakeholders within an identified translation zone within the process of model construction. We explore our ideas in the concrete setting of models encountered in a range of surveyed security papers, drawn from a diverse collection of security conferences. Although descriptive in nature, we envision this framework as a necessary first step in the development of a methodology for heterogeneous model design and construction, diverse enough to characterize the myriad of model types used in the field of information security while at the same time addressing validation concerns that can reduce their usability in the area of security decision-making.

Keywords: Systems · Ecosystems · Models · Qualities ·
Methodology · Co-design · Translation zone · Security · Modelling

This work has been partially supported by the UK EPSRC research grant EP/R006865/1.

D. Jiang and H. Song (Eds.): SIMUtools 2021, LNICST 424, pp. 259–283, 2022.
https://doi.org/10.1007/978-3-030-97124-3_22

1   Introduction

There is a famous quote from Grace Hopper:

'Life was simple before World War II. After that, we had systems.'

Now, systems are pervasive. They interact with and depend on each other and we, in turn, depend on them. It has become important to be able to think about not just a single system, but also its interactions with other systems—it has become necessary to think of *ecosystems*.

From the perspective of security, it is particularly significant that our ecosystems of concern are *socio-technical*, encompassing not only technical components, but also economic, human, and policy or regulatory aspects.

It is of increasing importance to be able to reason rigorously about the design and behaviour of systems and ecosystems. In particular, is of increasing importance to be able to reason rigorously about the security of systems and ecosystems. A key approach to reasoning about systems is based on the idea of modelling.

Systems models can take many forms. Here we discuss what, we shall argue, are the key categories of models.

- Models may, of course, be expressed in the language of mathematics—perhaps using tools such as differential and integral equations, stochastic processes, or even the methods of abstract algebra—in order to understand the structure of a system.
- Models may also be essentially computational, expressed in a programming language for the purpose of being executed—perhaps as simulations, such as in the *Monte Carlo*-style—in order observe the behaviours of the system.
- Models may be essentially conceptual, perhaps expressed using rigorous natural language or pictorial representation.

Different types of models are appropriate for capturing different types of questions about different types of models. However, it is often the case that combinations of different types of models are not only useful, but essential. For example, within security economics, it may be necessary to combine an executable model of a system, together with a mathematical/economic model of the value of different policy régimes, all based on a conceptual model of the choice of applicable policies and their implementation. See, for example, [11,13,14]. Similarly, Beautement et al.'s 'compliance budget' [8] combines a conceptual model of employees' behaviours within an organization and an economic model of the consequences of their behavioural choices for productivity.

In this paper, we present a meta-theoretical framework within which we can categorize the different types of ecosystem models that are available and understand their relationships to one another in general and the interactions of types of models of particular ecosystems. We argue that this framework represents an important first step in the development of a methodology for heterogeneous model design and construction because it offers a common language for the description of basic properties of models from different research traditions. Furthermore, the application of such a methodology on information security models requires an important, yet often omitted debate about validation. To even be able to define what validation is in the context of heterogeneous models requires at least a way of describing model properties in relation to model goals and types of knowledge employed. This is exactly what our framework focuses on. In the future, we hope to produce more practical results such as correlations between a model's goals, the types of knowledge it employs, the means of design in its translation zone, its triangle configuration, and its success of implementation and deployment in the real world. However, the domain exploration carried out using this approach in Sect. 5 shows that it manages to encompass the domain's diversity, making it a reasonable alternative for the description of information security models.

We begin, in Sect. 2, by considering the classical characterization of perspectives on modelling in terms Logical Empiricism and Relativism. We explain some of the philosophical background of the two paradigms and describe the methodological and practical issues that lead to a need for combining them in the context of modelling ecosystems.

In Sect. 3, by introducing the 'triangle' framework, we construct a conceptualization of the nature of models that characterizes the key categories of models according to three anchor points of properties:

- **Conceptuality**: describing the components of an ecosystem, their inter-relationships, and their evolution in informal, yet rigorous, terms. For example, a careful description of a river system, including its sources, its estuaries, and its flood plains, together with an explanation of the circumstance in which they might be overwhelmed.
- **Mathematicality**: describing the components of an ecosystem, their inter-relationships, and their evolution in the language of mathematics. For example, a detailed hydro-mechanical description, using the mathematics of fluid dynamics, of a system of sluices that controls flows within a water distribution network.
- **Executability**: describing the components of an ecosystem, their inter-relationships, and their evolution in languages that can be interpreted and executed by machines. For example, A computer program that simulates the effects of excess rainfall within the watershed of a river system, demonstrating graphically the expected extent and duration of flooding.

We explain our interpretation of the properties and their qualitative nature and provide some directions regarding the importance of the framework outside its use for classification.

In Sect. 4, we explain how models are constructed within the context of the triangle framework and how the rôle of co-design, within a translation zone for the different stakeholders in the modelling process, is central to the use of the framework.

In Sect. 5, we explain how ideas we are suggesting play out in the setting of security modelling. In particular, we report on how the triangle framework gives an account of the modelling that can be found in a wide array of papers in a diverse range of security conferences. Our choice of security for empirical analysis is at once both specific and generic: although the papers considered deal with specific security problems, the topic of security can be seen as providing a generic perspective on the behaviour of systems.

In Sect. 6, we consider the implications of using our framework for validating models, especially in the context of modelling large-scale ecosystems.

Finally, in Sect. 7, we summarize our contribution and briefly consider some directions for developing further the ideas we have introduced.

2   Philosophical Aspects of Models

There are predominantly two traditions on the nature of models, logical empiricist and relativist, dating back to the rationalist and empiricist schools of thought of the 16th century, and being further developed during the 19th and 20th century philosophical split between continental and analytical philosophy.

- *Logical empiricism.* Models are understood as an objective and absolute representations of systems. Validation is a process that is formal, algorithmic, and focussed on the accuracy of both the structure and outputs of the model. A single structural misrepresentation is enough to invalidate the model, regardless of its outputs. The overall modelling process is believed to reveal the truth if performed adequately.
- *Relativism.* Models are subjective; that is, they are just singular instantiations from a continuum of possible representations of the system. Validation is semi-formal, 'a gradual process of building confidence in the usefulness of a model' [6]. Such models do not attempt to reveal absolute truth, but rather produce a useful model given the modeller's goals.

Neither of these two views can solely be used for constructing diverse enough models for ecosystems security. Some of the reasons for this derive from some quite basic problems with, or objections to, each of these views.

Problems with Logical Empiricism. Theoretically, Logical Empiricism is struggling to overcome the epistemic and methodological implications of Kuhn's description of the acceptance of scientific theories and Popper's theory of falsification. Both the acceptance of Kuhn's thesis—stating that scientific progress is not achieved through the accumulation of knowledge but rather subjective community paradigm shifts—and Popper's view that scientific advancement can only be achieved through falsification rather than proving absolute truths, greatly reduce the focus on truth that logical empiricism held of a highest importance. Additionally, some of its practical caveats come from the difficulty of working with knowledge elements that have not been fully proven, completely accepted by the research community or that are yet unquantifiable because the underpinning theoretical work is not mature enough.

In the specific case of security, the most common such elements are related to the uncertainty introduced by human actors—either attackers or non-malicious actors—or the discovery of new technical attack vectors.

Also, logical empiricism requires an extremely powerful validation process which is not always possible in the case of complex cyber-physical systems. Particularly the structural representation criterion can lead to the invalidation of models that are producing seemingly viable results, which can be considered a quality upper bound, but certain phenomenons introduced by humans do not fit this type of approach because they lack the theoretical certainty.

In the best case scenario, a purely logical empiricist model can be used in well defined and seemingly stable conditions, for example when used to determine the trajectory of a rocket given the precise atmospheric conditions, but in today's cyber-physical ecosystems, this is rarely the case.

Problems with Relativism. Under a different set of circumstances, relativist stances hold the figuratively theoretic high ground in modern philosophy of science, in the sense that the subjectivity of knowledge and truth and the social construction of reality are well established notions.

However, this interpretative way of viewing reality also suffers from multiple caveats when singularly employed as paradigm for model construction.

First of all an ecosystemic model is composed of a high number of sub-models, each with their own primary goal, resources, processes, etc. To be able to obtain the relativistic notion of knowledge about those sub-systems, lengthy processes of data collection—interviews, debates—must be carried out by the modeller for the better understanding of the reality as seen by all the parts involved in the system under study. Although methodologically this might not be considered an actual problem, we must consider the fact that models are used today for tackling real world issues in reduced time-frames. The early usage of predictive models at the start of the Covid pandemic can be seen as a relevant example.

Secondly, and possibly the strongest advantage of this method, its openness, can also be its biggest problem in practice. If each sub-model is constructed with a different understanding of reality (the ones of the actors involved in it)—this can be seen in studies about the formal and alternative power structure of organisations—their integration becomes a serious issue. Albeit not directly concerned with models constructed based on a relativist philosophy of science, works such as [13, 14] or [11] provide a practical approach of this issue by using interfaces to specify the desired type of output moving between sub models without trying to alter the underlying notions of knowledge that led to the production of that output.

Thirdly, models constructed in this paradigm are complicated to use when trying to determine why certain decisions have been taken. Applying a simple root cause analysis method on a decision taken by such a model might lead either to a return to the real world simulated actors—if they are humans—for further explanations or to uncertainty.

On one hand, although methodologically sound, returning to the simulated actors is a lengthy process that can end up greatly delaying model implementation and should only be used in cases where there exists an evidence of a lack of understanding.

On the other hand, a model whose decisions cannot be certainly explained will hardly be accepted by decision makers who might prefer to use their own understanding of the system because it manifests a smaller degree of uncertainty. Studying which method would outperform the other is not the goal of this paper.

A New Perspective is Needed. As seen above, neither logical empiricism nor relativism alone offer a suitable methodology for modelling the dynamical systems of today. In a certain sense, the former approach places models under a set of too-powerful constraints, whereas the latter presents difficulties in choosing a set of constraints or quality measures usable in practice.

The logical empiricist perspective can provide speed and trace-ability by structure and method where the available system knowledge is suitable: the main phenomenons to be included in the model have been previously studied by the scientific community and an accepted theory has been formulated, and the phenomenons can be translated to quantifiable data types.

On the other hand, the relativist perspective provides better descriptive power and increases the overall comprehensibility of the model. Therefore, we believe that the need of a modelling framework that balances both views is justifiable.

In the next section, we introduce the Triangle Framework.

3   The Triangle Framework

The development of the logical empiricist and relativist views of models was driven by a desire to understand the nature, method of obtaining and validation of scientific truth. These perspectives were developed before the advent of computational modelling, which includes approaches to understanding dynamical systems such as discrete event modelling and Monte Carlo simulation.

Although computational models exhibit aspects of both logical empiricist and relativist views, we argue that their executable aspects give rise to a distinct perspective. As a result, we propose a new framework—the triangle framework—in which the perspective provided by executable models stands alongside that provided by the logical empiricist and relativist views of models with equivalent significance.

The triangle framework, as depicted in Fig. 1, identifies the key or core components of models, and the relationships between them, in terms of three qualities: conceptuality, mathematicality, and executability.

- *Conceptuality*—Aligned with the cognitive science perspective, we define concepts as mental representations of phenomena. The conceptuality of a model then refers to the degree to which its core components and the relationships between them exist and are directly expressed as such representations, through rigorous natural language, pictures, or diagrams, for example. In relation to the other qualities, the degree of conceptuality decreases as the key components of the model are expressed in an increasingly mathematical or executable way.

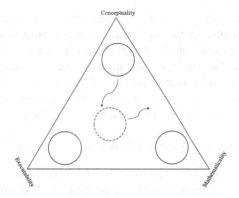

Fig. 1. The triangle framework

- *Mathematicality*—This refers to the degree to which the elements and relationships of a model are expressed using mathematical constructs. For example, models might be expressed as systems of equations or logical formulae.
- *Executability*—This represents the degree to which the elements and relationships of a model are simulated in a physical or computational environment.

These qualities can exist in combination models may have components that exhibit characteristics of all three. They also trade off against one another; that is, a highly conceptual model will be less mathematical and executable, or a highly executable one will be less conceptual and mathematical. Although we talk about degree, we don't mean a strict measure—there are no units of mathematicality, executability, or conceptuality, and they are quantified subjectively. However, these qualities, and the triangle framework more generally, give us a language for organizing and talking about models. Fig. 1 illustrates how we think of these three types of model and their relationships: in a given model, the relative significance of each of the components determines, by proximity, the position of the model within the triangle; furthermore, the position of the model may change as it evolves during its construction.

We explore empirically the appropriateness of these qualities for describing the components of models, in the setting of security, in Sect. 5.

We suggest that the importance of our proposed framework goes beyond its use for categorization, and hence understanding the relationships between, extant models and types of models. Specifically, we suggest that it can

- guide an on-going modelling process, helping the stakeholders to decide on what property to focus, to increase the chance of better representing the system, in accordance to their goals;
- reduce the risk of producing a model that cannot be practically used to achieve the goals of the modelling;
- can be used as common reference point during co-design: stakeholders from various domains will have a common point for their arguments; serves as a common language for structuring the process;

– offer a way of analysing a model through all the design and construction stages rather than just at the end and therefore, complement an agile testing methodology, providing the following advantages: reduced development time because both the customer and modeller have a common way of understanding how the model evolves and can offer focussed feedback or directions, easier for the customer to formulate requirements, constant focus on common quality metrics derived from the framework, ability to assess the model at any time; and
– lead to a way of comparing models based on the properties of sub-models.

We have mentioned again here the rôle of co-design in the modelling process and how the triangle framework serves to support it. We consider this issue in greater detail in Sect. 4.

4   Model Construction

Whereas the previous section was focussed on model description and interpretation according to a small subset of properties, the current one will examine the necessary methodological elements for the construction of ecosystem models.

Traditionally, in mathematical modelling, models have been constructed using the classical construction cycle depicted in Fig. 2. Succinctly, this represents an iterative process based on multiple stages:

– observing the phenomenon domain,
– constructing a candidate model based on the observations,
– deducing the mathematical consequences of the model,
– interpreting the consequences of the model in the domain, and
– comparing, for validation, the correspondence between these interpretations and the observed reality of the domain.

These stages are repeated until a criterion of adequacy for the intended purpose of the model, often determined by the judgement of the modellers, is passed and the model is considered to be a good enough representation of the system under study. Classical examples of this modelling approach can be observed in [5] as an application for global supply chain management, [46] as a tool for analysing credit scoring or [23] production scheduling.

The efficacy of this modelling process depends on certain key, usually unstated, assumptions about the modelling task:

– The structure and behaviour of the domain is clearly understood in conceptual or engineering terms. For example, the corrosion over time of a metal piston inside a diesel engine is a well-researched phenomenon attributed to the formation of sulphuric acid at the contact between low-grade fuels and water. Such a phenomenon is a good candidate for mathematical modelling, perhaps in the context of testing different materials for the construction of engine parts.

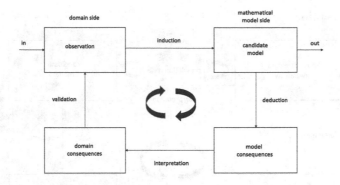

Fig. 2. The classical mathematical modelling cycle (see, e.g., [33])

- The data that can be collected about the domain is essentially unambiguously identified. For example, modelling an organization's employees productivity levels for the sake of improving them might prove an extremely complicated task for mathematical modelling since, essentially, employees might be motivated by extremely subjective concerns and the interpretation of those concerns might differ from person to person.
- The questions that the model is intended to address are identified independently of the detailed design choices required for the construction of a model. For example, building a model for the purpose of optimizing the production time of hardware components in a fully automated manufacturing environment is well suited for the traditional modelling methodology described above. Contrarily, simulating the same system for the purpose of understanding its behaviour and only then deciding what can be optimized—for example, for a reduction of costs—would be more suited to a different approach.

The ecosystems with which modellers in the modern world are presented pose much richer challenges for the form, design, and construction of models. Such ecosystems contain not only components that are clearly susceptible to mathematical modelling, but also include components—such as people and organizations, policies, and economic influences—which require models to have conceptual and computational (i.e., executable) components. In [39], Pidd puts this diversity of components on behalf of the design of human activity systems and Mingers [35] argues for a 'multimethodological' approach for the exploration of such systems. For example, one might imagine a model investigating the impact of malware infection on an organization's profits. However, the probability of infection of a machine is influenced both by the behaviour of the employees given a security policy and by technical elements such as the last installed patch on the machine. Furthermore, the malware spreading pattern heavily depends on network segmentation or existing countermeasures and the impact cannot be directly computed because of factors such as reputation loss. Therefore, one can easily observe that to understand the phenomenon of malware infection and its impact on an organization using a model requires distinct approaches for at least the above described components—employee behaviour, security policy, state of patching, network configuration, reputation loss.

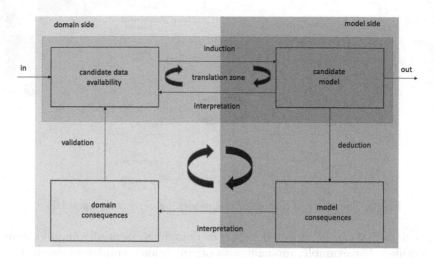

Fig. 3. Co-design in the translation zone

Moreover, it is in the very nature of such domains that the assumptions upon which the basic mathematical modelling cycle depends, as sketched above, do not necessarily hold:

- The structure and behaviour of the domain may depend on the behaviours of individuals and organizations, subject to incentives and policy constraints.
- It may be unclear what data is available for collection.
- It may be unclear, prior to the observation of the ecosystem, what questions can be properly formulated, depending on behaviours and the availability of data.

The key consequence is that a richer methodology of model construction is required in order to establish the cycle of model construction. A wide-ranging collection of articles on approaches to modelling and its challenges may be found in [19].

In the absence of such a priori foundations, we argue that a methodology that is grounded in the principles of co-design is required. What does this mean in the setting of ecosystems modelling? First, the classical modelling cycle, which need not be restricted to wholly mathematical models, should not be abandoned. Once a candidate model has been established, it provides the basis of the cycle of development that leads to an acceptable model. Second, it must, however, be adapted to account for the co-design process by which an initial candidate model is established.

Three key changes are required, all of which constitute proper generalizations of their counterparts in the basic modelling cycle. First, the observation of the domain involves essentially the discovery of the domain's structure and behaviour. Second, the initial postulation of candidate models is contingent upon this discovery process. Third, there is an induction-interpretation feedback loop between domain observation and candidate model postulation. This situation is depicted in Fig. 3.

In the literature regarding organizational learning, this type of problem-structuring as continuous exploration has been explored in works such as [4] or [29] and represents an important element of modelling methodologies such as Checkland's soft systems methodology [15], cognitive mapping [1, 18], or qualitative system dynamics [47].

These structural alterations to the methodology are not, however, sufficient alone. Whereas in the basic modelling cycle experts in the domain will have a relatively limited rôle of supplying information to the modellers, in the co-design sub-cycle their rôle is one of equal significance, forming a component of the modelling process, by identifying the structure and behaviour of the domain together with its policy constraints alongside the modellers' ability to model both the domain and its policies.

Thus, the cycle of domain observation and candidate model construction, as depicted in the upper half of Fig. 3, forms the *translation zone* of the dialogue between the domain experts and the modelling experts, which may have different perspectives and understandings of the domain and of models, and use different languages for expressing those perspectives. The translation zone enables the development of a shared understanding—in a controlled way that is focussed on the needs of the modelling project, managing the expectations of both the domain experts and model experts—as a consequence of the process.

Overall, this establishes a co-design process that

- ensures the participation of both modellers and domain experts, whose requirements are identified, characterized, and (possibly) modified according to the constraints of model design, construction, and deployment,
- identifies modelling objectives, including questions about the domain that are to be addressed, according to the identified requirements,
- designs and constructs appropriate models, and
- ensures that the available data that are identified during the process support the requirements of the models that are constructed.

As with the basic (mathematical) modelling cycle, as depicted in Fig. 2, the description of the co-design cycle—with a translation zone, as depicted in Fig. 3—does not specify the exit criteria for determining that a sufficiently accurate model has been constructed. In both cases, the criteria must be determined case-by-case, but always respecting a few key general considerations relative to which the notion of accuracy must be calibrated: remembering that 'the map is not the territory' [30]; appropriate level of detail; timeliness; and cost-effectiveness.

We argue that the triangle framework provides a conceptual setting within which the development of models through co-design in the translation zone can be characterized. First, the triangle offers the prospect of a common conceptual space—to some extent, even, a common language—to the domain and model experts. Second, while the three properties that anchor the corners of the triangle are difficult to quantify, the modeller, together with the domain expert, must nevertheless decide what spread of properties is required in order to deliver the objectives of the project: this is an essential aspect of modelling complex, socio-technical ecosystems, for which a model of one conceptual type is unlikely to be adequate in most situations. Third, as the co-design process via the translation zone proceeds, the choices presented in the initial model will, typically, evolve, thereby moving the model's location within the triangle.

A model's evolution during its construction can be seen as a sequence of configurations of the three qualities, with the evolution being driven by the co-design interaction of the stakeholders in the translation zone of Fig. 3.

As an example of this, recent (as yet unpublished [12]) work focuses on modelling the surge capacity of hospital emergency departments to help them prepare for major incidents, when a large number of seriously-injured patients arrive in a short amount of time. Building such a model requires the combined expertise of modellers and medical professionals and results in a model with conceptual, mathematical, and executable components. From the medical side, detailed knowledge of which procedures are needed by patients with different types of injuries and how teams of hospital staff with different skill sets are assembled (and reassembled, as patient flows evolve) to treat them is required. Gathering and using this information provide a good illustration of the translation zone and the way models change as they are constructed. Initially, largely conceptual 'paper-based' models were used in interviews with medical professionals, who explained their strategies for assigning teams of staff to treat patients. These were then codified initially into sets of rules and eventually embedded within executable models of the hospital emergency department. These rules and models—all considered candidate models—were presented to medical staff and evolved based on this feedback.

Some of these ideas will be illustrated in Sect. 5, where we consider a range of security examples.

5   Modelling in Security

In the previous sections, we have described the modelling triangle theoretically, and have explained how models move around the triangle during their construction.

In this section, we explore the modelling triangle in the concrete setting of security, exploring where different types of security models are placed within the triangle. We do this by looking at existing models published in recent security-related conferences and placing them on the triangle. This has several purposes: we want to get a sense of the types of models used in security, we want to understand if there is a relationship between the intended purpose of a model and its location on the triangle, and, lastly, we want to test the triangle approach.

5.1   Methodology

We select papers from five security conferences from 2020: BlackHat USA, NSPW, ACSAC, WEIS, and Gamesec. We select these conferences as they cover a range of topics and security traditions; we look at all the papers from each conference in 2020. In total, we look at 212 research papers encompassing a range of security topics: behavioral and security management, security policy, technical exploits, machine learning, economics, and more.

For each paper, we want to: (1) determine whether or not it contains a model; (2) understand the purpose and type of model; and (3) determine an appropriate location on the triangle for the model. As a methodological basis, we use a grounded theory approach. Grounded theory has two variants: one that focuses on the emergence of properties from the data coding process guided by a theoretical understanding of the domain of study and another that denies the need of any prior domain exploration. Kelle [28] illustrates both approaches. Since we did perform a prior domain-exploration by analysing the main philosophical positions regarding models and know the properties we are looking for—conceptuality, executability, mathematicality—we adopt the first method and perform the selective coding and classification processes with the properties described above in mind.

We have chosen this study methodology for a number of reasons:

1. Grounded theory is integrative as long as the coding process is consistent. This is extremely important, since it allows the analysis of models constructed using various methodologies. 'According to Ralph, Birks, and Chapman [42], grounded theory is "methodologically dynamic" in the sense that, rather than being a complete methodology, grounded theory provides a means of constructing methods to better understand situations humans find themselves in.'
2. Grounded theory provides ecological validity. This means that theory produced using this approach is representative of the underlying body of literature surveyed. Although not as powerful as when conducted through interviews with practitioners—since in that case additional questions about the subject of study could have been asked—the novelty of the papers shows the 'state of the art' in the security field at the moment.
3. Grounded theory maintains parsimony. Namely, in a situation where multiple hypothesis exist about a certain phenomenon, the one with the smallest amount of assumptions is preferred. This allows us to maintain a relatively small number of properties, since we aim to provide practical and simple explanations of complex phenomena by attempting to link those phenomena to abstract constructs and hypothesizing relationships among those constructs.
4. Although employing both qualitative and quantitative techniques, the nature of the analysis remains qualitative and facilitates the interpretation of conceptual aspects of the models under study.

We followed the following process. First, we analysed every paper to decide whether or not it contains a model, according to our definition from Sect. 1. We used a broad understanding of 'model' to ensure we captured conceptual as well as technical and formal models and as such were quite inclusive in the papers we accept. For example, papers that construct and reason about a structured representation of the phenomenon under study, even if descriptive, were considered models. Papers that did not include such a representation, such as those focussed on problem solving or tool building in a very specific and mostly technical focussed case were not included. Lastly, some papers included small models used for explanatory purposes, such as showing where their work fits within a system. These are also included in our analysis.

For the papers that contain models, we performed subjective coding focusing on the model description, the techniques employed in the model construction, the model purpose, and the topic. Since we wished to maintain some of the grounded theory ethos, we did not use a pre-established coding scheme in this step, and instead generated the codes as we went through the papers.

After that, we performed selective coding by linking the previously computed codes with our three primary categories—conceptuality, executability, mathematicality. At this point, we derived the 'triangle configuration' of the model under study, with the important note that we did not simply quantitatively analyse the size of the resulted categories. Deciding the relevance of the underlying codes with respect to the overall modelling goal remains a qualitative process and therefore the constructed configuration is subjective.

5.2 Findings

The intent of this study is to understand better the nature of the models employed in the information security field in 2020. Following the methodology described above, we discovered that 67% (142) of the total 212 surveyed papers did indeed employ models. The initial topic analysis and coding have produced 65 different topics that were further reduced to 35. For example, topic codes such as 'social behaviour', 'social engineering', 'community analysis', 'problem solving' or 'human oriented design' were included in the 'human oriented security' category. Table 1 illustrates the most encountered five topics for models in each conference, ranked by their total number of occurrences and having duplicates removed. Subsequently, the most encountered topics were 'attacks/exploits' and 'privacy'.

It is important to note that a model is not limited to a single topic: if one specifically focuses on attacks that affect user privacy, it would be assigned as having both the 'attacks/exploits' and 'privacy' topics. Also, the development of models for the purpose of better understanding machine learning in general can be seen as an interesting attempt at using descriptive models to understand other models.

By analysing the model's topic, goal, and construction procedure, we have produced triangle configurations for each of the surveyed conferences, which can be observed in Fig. 4. These configurations largely correspond to the publicly described conference tradition—for example, the models in Gamesec had a tendency towards mathematicality—with an interesting aspect identified in Blackhat: even though the models tackled many 'attacks/exploits' and 'hardware security' aspects—as it can be seen in Table 1—they are complemented by models with a tendency towards conceptuality that attempted to explain their functionality. Furthermore, we classified the models according to their construction method and modelling goal into five categories.

1. **Descriptive models:** Models in this category are mainly constructed using natural language descriptions, qualitative reasoning and sometimes graphs, charts or other means of visual representation. They construct a subjective representation of reality which can vary in complexity and can include both qualitative and quantitative studies as a starting point. Their primary goal is to simply describe or analyse phenomenons that are hard to quantify and therefore focus on topics such as 'human aspects of security', 'security management', 'philosophical aspects of security' or 'security policies'. However, the analysis process has revealed that such models can be used also for describing other models, not necessary phenomenons directly. As illustrated in Table 2 and Fig. 5a, models in this category represented roughly 21% of the total models encountered and had a strong tendency to be placed close to the upper corner of the triangle because of their highly descriptive nature.

2. **Simulation models:** This category contains two different types of models that have a common construction method—experimental simulations and practical demonstrations. They are comprised of interpretative executable code, constructed manually by a developer and reflecting a human interpretation of a certain phenomenon. With respect to their goal, they can either be used for experimentation, such as simulation based models coming from the dynamic systems tradition, attack demonstrations or enforcing qualitative reasoning. They focus on topics such as 'IoT', 'network security', 'software security', 'operation systems emulation', 'malware' or 'attacks/exploits' because the phenomenon under study can be quantified and represented using graph-like structures. As illustrated in Table 2 and Fig. 5b, models in this category represented roughly 26% of the total models encountered—the largest category—and were placed closer to the center of the triangle. They did not manifest a higher tendency towards the left corner because the model construction was manual and in some cases, the model was run a single time to illustrate that a certain attack was possible.

3. **Statistical models:** Models in this category are constructed using executable code that includes statistical algorithms, data science techniques, natural language processing, and even some traditional machine learning techniques not including deep learning. They construct a complex, stochastic interpretation of reality, usually employed for better understanding or making predictions about a phenomenon that is either extremely complex or would take too much time or analysis power to be understood individually. Furthermore, their most relevant aspect is that their method of producing results can be traced back and understood, with the important note that the results do not directly lead to some automated real world consequence, but require additional interpretation. The most relevant topics to this category were 'privacy', 'security management', 'economics' and 'human oriented security'. As shown in Table 2, statistical models represent almost 20% of the total surveyed models and Fig. 5e depicts them as having balanced triangle configurations, with some slight tendencies towards either conceptuality or mathematicality based on the nature of their input data. For example, a model employing natural language processing and principal component analysis techniques over qualita-

tive data obtained from interviews was placed closer to the conceptuality corner, whereas a Bayesian analysis of security investments was placed closer to the mathematicality corner.

4. **Deep Learning models:** Models in this category are constructed using deep learning and neural networks approaches and they construct a representation of reality that is similarly to statistical models, with the primary difference being the difficulty of interpreting or justifying the produced results. Because of this, they tend to be used for automated problem solving in areas such as offensive security or threat detection. Their triangle placement can be similar to that of simulation models, as Fig. 5d with the important difference that they do not manifest the slight conceptuality tendency since their phenomenon interpretation is particularly hard to understand. However, they do manifest the strongest tendency towards executability, and represent almost 20% of the total models surveyed. However, taken into account the current focus on the development of artificial intelligence explainability methods, we could observe a significant amount of models moving from the deep learning category to the statistical models one.

5. **Game-theoretic models:** This category is primarily comprised of mathematical models constructing game-theoretic interpretations of phenomena. Some of the observed models did produce analytical solutions for solving the represented games, whereas others were simply used for problem setting. In the second case, other types of model were used to produce the desired strategies in the game setting. They were usually employed in areas such as 'network security', 'risk' or 'attacks/exploits', but mostly provided the theoretical setting for another type of model to interpret. We observed the interpretation they produced was used as a setting for either deep learning or simulation models. For example, a game theory model was used to formalise the concept of cyber deception as a multi-party stochastic game and then a simulation model was used to illustrate a successful winning strategy. However, another approach was to construct a deep reinforcement learning model of the involved parties and execute it in multiple epochs such that the actors could develop increasingly better strategies while learning from their own mistakes. As Table 2 and Fig. 5c illustrate, these models can have both balanced triangle configurations and heavy tendencies towards mathematicality and represent roughly 13% of the models surveyed.

Moreover, some additional observations can be drawn when analysing the average and complete model types placement on the triangle in Figs. 6a and 6b. For example, the conceptual, deep learning and game-theoretic models can be seen as having the strongest manifested tendencies towards the triangle's corners. Subsequently, the simulation and statistics models manifested the most balanced configurations for two different reasons: simulation models had the most open approach and used internal sub-models that would have been assessed differently in isolation—for example a stochastic module for agent behaviour or an economics module for determining the risk of an actor's action—but produced balanced overall models, whereas statistical models used extremely varied input data that introduced an additional degree of conceptuality to the mathematical methods used.

However, Fig. 6b clearly shows that the model categories are not entirely delimited by their triangle configuration: for example, models in Kaczmarczyck et al. [27], Noor et al. [34] and Xiao et al. [48] have similar, central triangle placements even though they are members of the deep learning, statistical and respectively simulation categories. Furthermore, even though their topics are also different, namely automated malware family identification, illustrating a mechanism for key distribution on automotive networks and analysing the forensic validity of approximated audit logs, they all obtain a more balanced configuration by introducing qualitative reasoning about their inner workings.

We believe that this balancing process leads to models that are easier to understand, and therefore that become more suitable for security decision-making, but that requires further work to be validated. However, at the end of this exploration of the information security domain, we can draw several conclusions.

1. Models are an important tool for information security today.
2. Usually, models remain focussed on very specific problems.
3. Some models directly interact with or complement other models. This raises the question of how should models communicate with one another.
4. Some meta-modelling attempts exist, but only at theoretical level. For example, highly mathematical or conceptual models of machine learning algorithms.
5. Simulation models seem to provide a good base for constructing models with components of different types.

Table 1. Top 5 topics per conference

	Blackhat	Nspw	ACSAC	WEIS	GameSec	Total
Attacks/Exploits	19	1	12	2	3	37
Privacy	5	3	17	1	2	28
IoT	5	0	14	1	3	23
Human oriented security	7	5	5	3	2	22
Network Security	7	0	8	1	6	22
Economics	1	0	4	12	3	20
Policy	6	2	7	2	1	18
Hardware Security	10	0	3	0	4	17
Software Security	5	2	8	0	1	16
Machine Learning (as topic)	6	2	6	0	1	15
Theoretical Security	0	0	2	1	10	13
Systems architecture	6	0	2	0	4	12
Risk	2	0	4	4	1	11
Management	2	0	3	5	0	10
Game Theory	1	0	0	0	8	9

Table 2. Model types per conference

	Blackhat	Nspw	ACSAC	WEIS	GameSec	Total per type
Simulation Models	8	1	25	2	1	37
Descriptive Models	21	6	1	2	0	30
Statistical Models	2	0	15	11	1	29
Deep Learning Models	6	1	15	0	6	28
Game Theory Models	0	0	0	0	18	18
Total per conference	41	8	58	15	26	142

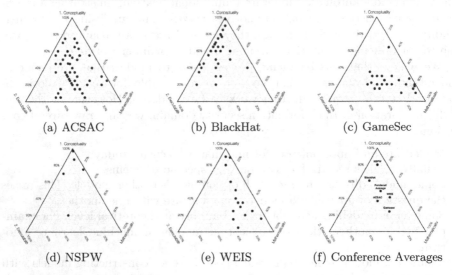

(a) ACSAC   (b) BlackHat   (c) GameSec

(d) NSPW   (e) WEIS   (f) Conference Averages

Fig. 4. Positions of papers from different conferences on the triangle

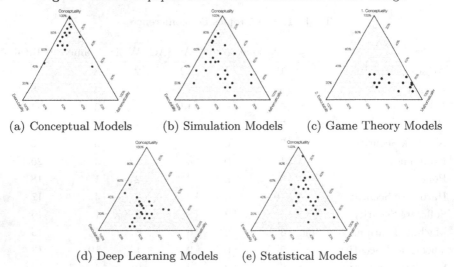

(a) Conceptual Models   (b) Simulation Models   (c) Game Theory Models

(d) Deep Learning Models   (e) Statistical Models

Fig. 5. Positions of different model types on the triangle

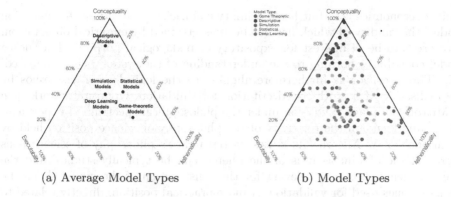

(a) Average Model Types

(b) Model Types

Fig. 6. Positions of different model types on the triangle

6 Implications for Validation

In the previous sections, we have focussed on constructing an integrated modelling framework for characterizing models according to three primary properties—conceptuality, mathematicality, and executability—that are directly linked to the relevant philosophical and modelling literature. We have described how these properties change during the model-construction cycle and have attempted to use this approach to explore a part of the present-day space of information security models. In the sequel, we seek to understand some of the implications that our vision might have on the ongoing debate regarding the validation of models, especially in the case of modelling large-scale ecosystems.

The validation of a model, at a general level, consists in the deployment of a set of processes that is used for testing that the model performs according to its original goal. As expressed in [6], models can be separated into at least three categories according to their primary goal: modelling for the purpose of improving a certain performance indicator of a system, modelling for testing a scientific theory, and modelling for the sake of understanding or learning about a certain system.

However, it is not the goal alone that determines the type of model to be constructed, but also the nature of the system or phenomenon under study and the available input data types and their collection process. These elements—the goal, the available data and the nature of the phenomenon under study—corroborated with the underlying philosophical implications illustrated in Sect. 2—have led to the development of different and sometimes opposing model validation methodologies in disparate domains of science. To illustrate some of these differences, we present some arguments from the economics, management science, and system dynamics literature that are of great importance for an information security context.

Starting with the management science domain, it can easily be observed that a singular position with respect to validation does not exist. For example, Naylor et al. [37] argue for a validation process that combines rationalist, empiricist and positive economics [21], but has a primary empiricist assumption: 'A simulation model, the validity of which has not been ascertained by empirical observation, may prove to be of interest for expository or pedagogical purposes, but such a model contributes nothing to the understanding of the system being simulated' [37]. Their position is furthermore aligning to the logical empiricist ethos by the utilisation of a truth based criterion for validation. Oppositely, work such as Mitroff [36] place validation under the philosophical spectrum of experimentalism and focus on the relativity of the philosophy of science position held by the modeller. As Mitroff [36] states, 'a researcher's philosophy of science is as characteristic of him as it is of the phenomena he typically studies' and the same elements chosen as relevant for the construction of the model should be the same ones used for validation. A more practical position, directly related to the need of validating large scale models in a reasonable amount of time can be seen in House and McLeod [24]. There, the authors follow Friedman's principle [21] that assumptions can serve as scientific hypotheses even if 'unrealistic' as long as they can produce significant predictions and focus on the utility of a model rather than its relationship with truth. In the authors' own words 'A businessman cannot afford to discount a "hoped-for" infinite return as the result of an unknown expenditure for a near perfect model today. Our business world exists in the present, so the businessman will be satisfied to buy a somewhat less than a perfect model for a known cost.'

The same heterogeneity of positions with respect to validation can be seen in the economics literature. As already described, Friedman's position with respect to the need of validation for scientific hypothesis is of great importance. In the author's view, scientific assumptions do not need to be verified since they can only be validated by their own predictive power. Since models can be considered a preliminary step in the formation of scientific theories—see Grim and Rescher [22] for a more detailed discussion—Friedman's assumption has been translated to models. A subtle distinction from this criterion of predictive power can be seen in the work of Cyert and Grunberg [16]. Following Popper's falsification thesis [40], the authors believe that a model's predictive power does not necessary validate its position as scientific truth. Therefore modelers should rather focus on constructing models with high descriptive power. Nevertheless, different variations of these criteria can be found in comprehensive literature overviews such as Dhrymes et al. [17] or Radzicki [41]. Of a particular relevance is the conclusion of Dhrymes et al.: 'validation becomes a problem-dependent or decision-dependent process, differing from case to case as the proposed use of the model under consideration changes' [17].

Last but not least, we discuss some of the validation approaches employed in the system dynamics literature. Compared to management science or economics, the system dynamics literature is much more comprehensive in its attempts to tackle philosophical aspects of model validation. An important starting point is the work of Forrester [20], which can be seen as a relativist take on system dynamic validation that was primarily done in a logical empiricist fashion before him. Forrester makes the claim that 'the validity of a model should not be separated from the validity and the feasibility of its goals' [20], and since the feasibility of the goals cannot be determined through a formal process, validation becomes 'a problem of social discussion' [7]. Furthermore, following a thesis similar to Kuhn's [31], he argues that 'Any "objective" model validation procedure rests eventually at some lower level on a judgment or faith that either the procedure or its goals are acceptable without any objective proof.' [20] and that qualitative model validation techniques must be used in practice, given the fact that 'a preponderant amount of human knowledge is in non quantitative for' [20]. However, Forrester's position was contested by works such as Ansoff & Slevin [3] or Nordhaus [38] that deem it unscientific on a logical empiricist basis and ask questions such as 'Does it represent the judgmental approach of a particular scientist?' [3]. Furthermore, Ansoff & Slevin [3] point out that Forrester does not clearly states a clear criterion of validity or a specific degree of correspondence between the model and the represented system. Additional details about this philosophical debate in the system dynamics field can be found in [2,9,10,43,44] or [45].

As seen above, the fields of economics, management science and system dynamics have been encountering this philosophical debate on model validation for a long period of time, and yet a singular integrative approach has not been designed. What is more interesting is that economic, management science and system dynamics models have been consistently used in information security without the necessary debate about validation.

The field of information security manifests, as shown in Sect. 5, the diversity of encompassing all these different types of models, with respect to both goals and method. For example, Yeo et al. [49] construct a system dynamics model for the sake of reducing the negative impact of security policies on the effectiveness of operations in ports, conceptual work such as Inglesant and Sasse [25] complemented by the modelling in Beautement et al. [8] has informed the theory that cyclic password ageing techniques lead to increased password security and the executable, language based model of Jachim et al. [26] can be used for understanding the behaviour changes of Twitter trolls during the Covid-19 pandemic.

Although a handful of examples, these are already enough to manifest different approaches on validation: [49] uses a system dynamics paradigm and both structural and behavior oriented validation techniques, [8] construct a model that can be placed in between the economics and management science traditions but admits the need of further validation stemming from the subjectivity of the input data obtained from interviews and [26] uses traditional machine learning validation metrics such as k-fold cross-validation.

However, none of the above examples are truly about ecosystems. One can imagine the need of constructing an information security model that combines multiple of the above described directions. Efforts in producing a practical, modular modelling approach that is both open to qualitative interpretation and at the same time constructed on a rigorous mathematical foundation can be seen in [13] or [14]. The relevant aspect of the method presented is that sub modules can be constructed using significantly different philosophical assumptions as long as the produced output is standardised by the use of interfaces.

Nevertheless, validating a model with sub-modules built according to different philosophic assumptions will not be a trivial task. Given the researched streams of literature concerning validation, it is a plausible assumption to make that such a process will not be unitary in nature. Therefore, the model description offered by the framework described in Sect. 3 and Sect. 4 becomes a roadmap for the selection of validation techniques on a case by case basis—[6,32,44] offer comprehensive overviews of practical validation tests. Therefore, our position is close to Dhrymes et al. [17], with the addition that the model description given by our framework can be used for guiding the selection of validation tests. In a certain sense, Mingers' 'multimethodology' [35] idea is being translated to the issues of validation. Additionally, this can facilitate the construction of validation loops from the early model design and implementation phases, thus bringing the advantages of an agile testing methodology. Furthermore, our belief is that the analysis procedure required to construct the model description and the process of choosing validation tests according to it can increase the believability in the usefulness of the constructed model, by design.

However, the modularity offered by this method comes with a need of using both sub-module validation and overall model validation. The selection of validation tests for sub-modules is guided by the description offered by the above presented framework. When considering overall validation, more experimentation with the framework is required for an attempt to derive a criterion. Nonetheless, our belief is that such a criterion should take into account both descriptive power and believability and cannot be purely based on logical empiricism.

7   Concluding Discussion

As the world has evolved to become ever more dependent on complex ecosystems of large interacting systems, it has become ever more important to be able to reason rigorously about the design, construction, and behaviour not only of individual systems—which may include aspects related to all of people, process, and technology—but also of their assembly into ecosystems. In such complex situations, it is inevitable that no one type of model—such as mathematical models of dynamical systems, logical models of languages, or discrete event simulation models—will be sufficient to describe all of the aspects of ecosystems about which rigorous reasoning is required.

We have proposed here a meta-theoretical framework, the 'triangle framework', within which different types of models may be categorized and their interactions, especially during the construction of models, can be understood. Specifically, we have identifed three qualities of models—conceptuality, mathematicality, and executability—and have explained how in practice models typically have all of these qualities to varying extents. We have conducted an empirical study of the models deployed in a range of security conference papers and have classified these models according to the framework.

We have also discussed how the triangle framework supports an analysis of how models can be co-designed by their various stakeholders within an identified translation zone within the process of model construction. We have explored how our ideas play out in the concrete setting of models that we find in range of security papers, drawn from a diverse collection of security conferences. Lastly, we have started the much needed debate on validation methods that the information security field has been avoiding for far too long.

Much further work is suggested, including on the following:

- the structure of the triangle and its component models;
- the evolution of models within the triangle as they are developed, especially in respect of the rôles of the stakeholders;
- the structure of the translation zone, again, especially in respect of the rôles of the stakeholders; and
- empirical studies of the co-design process in the context of the triangle and the rôles of the stakeholders.

Moreover, as we have already discussed, we hope to produce practical results such as correlations between a model's goals, the types of knowledge it employs, the means of design in its translation zone, its triangle configuration, and its success of implementation and deployment in the real world.

The results of these studies should be expected to inform a reformulation of the triangle, the co-design process, and their integration.

References

1. Ackermann, F., Eden, C., Cropper, S.: Getting started with cognitive mapping. Banxia Software (1992)
2. Andersen, D.F.: How differences in analytic paradigms can lead to differences in policy conclusions. In: Elements of the System Dynamics Method, pp. 61–75 (1980)
3. Ansoff, H.I., Slevin, D.P.: An appreciation of industrial dynamics. Manag. Sci. 14(7), 383–397 (1968)
4. Argyris, C.: Productive and counterproductive reasoning processes. The Executive Mind: New Insights on Managerial Thought and Action, Jossey-Bass, San Francisco, CA, pp. 25–58 (1983)
5. Arntzen, B.C., Brown, G.G., Harrison, T.P., Trafton, L.L.: Global supply chain management at digital equipment corporation. Interfaces 25(1), 69–93 (1995)
6. Barlas, Y.: Formal aspects of model validity and validation in system dynamics. Syst. Dyn. Rev. 12, 183–210 (1996)
7. Barlas, Y., Carpenter, S.: Philosophical roots of model validation: two paradigms. Syst. Dyn. Rev. 6(2), 148–166 (1990)
8. Beautement, A., Sasse, M.A., Wonham, M.: The compliance budget: managing security behaviour in organisations. In: Proceedings of the 2008 New Security Paradigms Workshop, NSPW '08, pp. 47–58. Association for Computing Machinery, New York (2008). https://doi.org/10.1145/1595676.1595684
9. Bell, J.A., Bell, J.F.: System dynamics and scientific method. In: Elements of the System Dynamics Method, pp. 3–22 (1980)

10. Bell, J.A., Senge, P.M.: Methods for enhancing refutability in system dynamics modeling. TIMS Stud. Manag. Sci. **14**(1), 61–73 (1980)
11. Caulfield, T., Pym, D.: Improving security policy decisions with models. IEEE Secur. Priv. **13**(5), 34–41 (2015)
12. Caulfield, T., Fong, K., Pym, D.: Systems modelling for surge capacity in emergency medicine [working title] (2021, in preparation)
13. Caulfield, T., Pym, D.: Modelling and simulating systems security policy. In: SIMU-TOOLS 2015: 8th EAI International Conference on Simulation Tools and Techniques, ICST (2015)
14. Caulfield, T., Pym, D., Williams, J.: Compositional security modelling. In: Tryfonas, T., Askoxylakis, I. (eds.) HAS 2014. LNCS, vol. 8533, pp. 233–245. Springer, Cham (2014). https://doi.org/10.1007/978-3-319-07620-1_21
15. Checkland, P.B.: Soft systems methodology. Human Syst. Manag. **8**(4), 273–289 (1989)
16. Cyert, R.M., Grunberg, E.: Assumption, prediction, and explanation in economics. Behav. Theory Firm **298**, 311 (1963)
17. Dhrymes, P.J., et al.: Criteria for evaluation of econometric models. In: Annals of Economic and Social Measurement, vol. 1, no. 3, pp. 291–324. NBER (1972)
18. Eden, C.: Cognitive mapping. Eur. J. Oper. Res. **36**(1), 1–13 (1988)
19. Pidd, M. (ed.): Systems Modelling: Theory and Practice. Wiley, Hoboken (2004)
20. Forrester, J.W.: Industrial dynamics. J. Oper. Res. Soc. **48**(10), 1037–1041 (1997)
21. Friedman, M.: The methodology of positive economics. Essays in Positive Economics (1953)
22. Grim, P., Rescher, N.: How modeling can go wrong: some cautions and caveats on the use of models. Philos. Technol. **26**(1), 75–80 (2013). https://doi.org/10.1007/s13347-012-0082-7
23. Hendry, L., Fok, K., Shek, K.: A cutting stock and scheduling problem in the copper industry. J. Oper. Res. Soc. **47**(1), 38–47 (1996). https://doi.org/10.1057/jors.1996.4
24. House, P.W., McLeod, J., McLeod, J.: Large-Scale Models for Policy Evaluation. Wiley, New York (1977)
25. Inglesant, P.G., Sasse, M.A.: The true cost of unusable password policies: password use in the wild. In: Proceedings of the SIGCHI Conference on Human Factors in Computing Systems, CHI '10, pp. 383–392. Association for Computing Machinery, New York (2010). https://doi.org/10.1145/1753326.1753384
26. Jachim, P., Sharevski, F., Treebridge, P.: Trollhunter [evader]: automated detection [evasion] of twitter trolls during the COVID-19 pandemic. In: New Security Paradigms Workshop 2020, NSPW '20, pp. 59–75. Association for Computing Machinery, New York (2020). https://doi.org/10.1145/3442167.3442169
27. Kaczmarczyck, F., et al.: Spotlight: malware lead generation at scale. In: Annual Computer Security Applications Conference, ACSAC '20, pp. 17–27. Association for Computing Machinery, New York (2020). https://doi.org/10.1145/3427228.3427273
28. Kelle, U.: "Emergence" vs. "forcing" of empirical data? A crucial problem of "grounded theory" reconsidered. Historical Social Research/Historische Sozialforschung. Supplement, pp. 133–156 (2007)
29. Kolb, D.A.: Problem management: learning from experience. The executive mind 28 (1983)
30. Korzybski, A.: Science and Sanity: An Introduction to Non-Aristotelian Systems and General Semantics. Institute of GS (1958)

31. Kuhn, T.S.: The Structure of Scientific Revolutions. University of Chicago press, Chicago (2012)
32. Martis, M.S.: Validation of simulation based models: a theoretical outlook. Electron. J. Bus. Res. Methods **4**(1), 39–46 (2006)
33. McColl, J.: Probability. Butterworth-Heinemann/Elsevier, Oxford (1995)
34. Michael, N., Mink, J., Liu, J., Gaur, S., Hassan, W.U., Bates, A.: On the forensic validity of approximated audit logs. In: Annual Computer Security Applications Conference, ACSAC '20, pp. 189–202. Association for Computing Machinery, New York (2020). https://doi.org/10.1145/3427228.3427272
35. Mingers, J.: Multimethodology. In: Wiley Encyclopedia of Operations Research and Management Science (2010)
36. Mitroff, I.I.: Fundamental issues in the simulation of human behavior: a case in the strategy of behavioral science. Manag. Sci. **15**(12), B-635 (1969)
37. Naylor, T.H., Finger, J.M., McKenney, J.L., Schrank, W.E., Holt, C.C.: Verification of computer simulation models. Manag. Sci. **14**(2), B92–B106 (1967). http://www.jstor.org/stable/2628207
38. Nordhaus, W.D.: World dynamics: measurement without data. Econ. J. **83**(332), 1156–1183 (1973)
39. Pidd, M.: Tools for thinking–modelling in management science. J. Oper. Res. Soc. **48**(11), 1150–1150 (1997)
40. Popper, K.: The Logic of Scientific Discovery. Routledge, London (2005)
41. Radzicki, M.J.: Institutional dynamics: an extension of the institutionalist approach to socioeconomic analysis. J. Econ. Issues **22**(3), 633–665 (1988)
42. Ralph, N., Birks, M., Chapman, Y.: The methodological dynamism of grounded theory. Int. J. Qual. Methods **14**(4), 1609406915611576 (2015). https://doi.org/10.1177/1609406915611576
43. Richardson, G.P., Pugh, A.L., III.: Introduction to system dynamics modeling with DYNAMO. J. Oper. Res. Soc. **48**(11), 1146–1146 (1997)
44. Senge, P.M., Forrester, J.W.: Tests for building confidence in system dynamics models. Syst. Dyn. TIMS Stud. Manag. Sci. **14**, 209–228 (1980)
45. Sterman, J.D.: The growth of knowledge: testing a theory of scientific revolutions with a formal model. Technol. Forecast. Soc. Chang. **28**(2), 93–122 (1985)
46. Thomas, L., Banasik, J., Crook, J.: Recalibrating scorecards. J. Ope. Res. Soc. **52**(9), 981–988 (2001)
47. White, A.S., et al.: Qualitative system dynamics as a tool in accessible design. J. Softw. Eng. Appl. **4**(01), 69 (2011)
48. Xiao, Y., Shi, S., Zhang, N., Lou, W., Hou, Y.T.: Session key distribution made practical for CAN and CAN-FD message authentication. In: Annual Computer Security Applications Conference, ACSAC '20, pp. 681–693. Association for Computing Machinery, New York (2020). https://doi.org/10.1145/3427228.3427278
49. Yeo, G.T., Pak, J.Y., Yang, Z.: Analysis of dynamic effects on seaports adopting port security policy. Transp. Res. Part A: Pol. Pract. **49**, 285–301 (2013). https://doi.org/10.1016/j.tra.2013.01.039. https://www.sciencedirect.com/science/article/pii/S0965856413000463

Modelling Organizational Recovery

Adrian Baldwin[1], Tristan Caulfield[2(✉)], Marius-Constantin Ilau[2],
and David Pym[2,3]

[1] HP Labs, Bristol, UK
[2] University College London, London, UK
{t.caulfield,marius-constantin.ilau.18,d.pym}@ucl.ac.uk
[3] Institute of Philosophy, University of London, London, UK

Abstract. Organizations today face a significant set of sophisticated information security threats, including rapidly spreading malware that can affect many devices across the organization. The impacts of such attacks are amplified by customers' rising expectations of high-quality and rapid delivery of products and services, as well as by organizational attempts to increase demand artificially. This leads to the development of defence mechanisms that prioritize availability and integrity for the sake of reducing the overall time of organizational recovery. However, such mechanisms and strategies around recovery must suit the organization that deploys them. Each organization will have different priorities in terms of budget, speed of recovery, and priority of services or devices, and all of these will be impacted by the architecture of the organization and its networks. In this paper, we show how modelling can play a role in helping organizations understand the consequences of the different recovery mechanisms and strategies available to them. We describe a rigorous modelling framework and methodology grounded in mathematical systems modelling and simulation, and present as an example a comparative analysis of recovery strategies and mechanisms on a medium-scale organization.

Keywords: Distributed systems · Malware · Modelling · Recovery · Compositionality · Interfaces · Organizations

1 Introduction

The problem of maintaining the integrity of data and availability of services of an organization represents, in today's transactional economy, an issue at least as important as the optimization of internal operations for the reduction of cost.

This work has been partially supported by the UK EPSRC research grant EP/R006865/1.

D. Jiang and H. Song (Eds.): SIMUtools 2021, LNICST 424, pp. 284–314, 2022.
https://doi.org/10.1007/978-3-030-97124-3_23

This can arise, for example, as a side-effect of sales strategy, focussed on producing short-term bursts of extremely high-volume of sales by artificially increasing customer demand around so-called 'sales events', such as Black Friday, Cyber Monday, and others. Even though not every organization is cost-oriented, the same concept of high operational demand in a short period of time can be understood according to the business' primary goal. For example, an online retailer during a sales event, a hospital during a pandemic, or a border control force the day after significant legislation has been introduced all may face possibly existential threats when confronted with poor service or even loss of service availability when most needed.

In such cases, the organizational loss increases because of a trust violation between the supply and demand and additional reputational 'recovery' measures may be needed, in the sense described in [13]. However, this impact varies across industries: in their comparative study of stock performance post cyber-breach, Tweneboah et al. [47] show that the healthcare industry in particular lacks resilience, the technology industry is somewhat neutral, in that the stock price remains fairly stable, and the financial industry actively manages to increase stock value, even post-breach.

In this context, the security professional can interpret such events as single points of failure for the business: the impact of a loss of availability of services during such an event is significantly higher than during business-as-usual times. This motivates the organizational need for mechanisms for quickly restoring service availability to a state in which data integrity is maintained. Such mechanisms are not limited to defensive purposes. They can provide valuable time optimizations in non adversarial contexts, such as recovery needed because of 'WinRot' [17] phenomenona—registry corruption, mismanagement of DLL libraries, or disk fragmentation—or scheduled patching, where the same mechanism used for recovery is used to deploy pre-updated system images.

Threats to availability and integrity come in many forms: malware, denial of service, faulty patch updates, disgruntled employees, database query mistakes, and so on. Summarizing, they arise from both malicious and non-malicious actions, internal or external. Active defense against such threats is possible, but dependent not only on technical measures and controls, but also on policy compliance and employee behaviour. Therefore, particularly in situations where the loss of business continuity even for small time periods can lead to acute organizational damage, the risk of employing solely active countermeasures against possible attacks is not enough. Following the defence in depth principle, we focus on a practical second-line control mechanism that can tackle both inside and outside threats with respect to availability and integrity: a recovery mechanism. The development of such mechanisms marks a shift from traditional defence strategy that focuses on practically countering attacks to economic-based deterrence that seeks to reduce the impact of attacks until they eventually become economically infeasible.

As might be expected, multiple approaches to recovery exist and a subset of interest will briefly be outlined and explored in Sect. 2. However, their positive impact on a company depends on the nature of the attack tackled, spread, size, recovery time, cost of deployment, existing policies, and employee knowledge and behaviour. Therefore, the problem of recovery in the context of a heterogeneous organization is complex, but particularly suitable for comparative modelling of solutions.

Relevant examples of how a simulation-based methodology has been used to assess and improve organizational supply chains can be found in [15] and [23]. Furthermore, analytical approaches can be found with respect to modelling the impact of cyber-attacks on web sales. For example [16], clearly shows the impact of lengthy cyber-attacks on organizational costs, and although the authors do not suggest it, a recovery solution would serve as a good mitigation in the described scenario.

In this paper, our primary aim is to demonstrate how a modelling and simulation approach, based on rigorous mathematical foundations, can be used to help organizations understand the problem and the consequences of different recovery choices for their organization, and help them make better decisions about this challenging problem. In addition to different preferences, different organizations will have different requirements, structure, and architectures: the number of employees, their travel patterns, the size and number of different offices, the devices used, the value of the information on different devices, and the network structure will all vary between organizations. A compositional modelling approach provides the flexibility required to create models that can be adapted to capture all of these differences between organizations. We will demonstrate this approach by using examples to explore the relationship between the impact of different deployment strategies under varying cyber-attack conditions and the recovery time in different scenarios, and discuss how the models can be adapted to different organizations, and extended to cover different scenarios and recovery strategies.

In Sect. 2, we describe some of the practical implications that modern destructive malware techniques have brought into the organizational recovery space and list some of the recovery strategies and mechanisms that organizations can choose from when attempting to manage this risk. Section 3 focuses on explaining the basic functional and methodological concepts behind our modelling approach, with references to the relevant literature that further develops these concepts. Building on top of Sect. 3, Sect. 4 describes the conceptual model of organizational recovery. Section 5 explains the discrete event simulation models of the recovery scenarios including the parameter space and choices, the results obtained, and validation. Lastly, Section 6 attempts to offer some organizational guidelines based on the results of the prior section while also illustrating some of the further work considerations that could be pursued in the future.

A systematic comparison of our modelling approach with other approaches is beyond the scope of this short, introductory paper. Such a comparative study is deferred to another occasion.

2   The Recovery Problem

In June 2017, the NotPetya ransomware [18] spread across the world and caused considerable disruption for enterprises because of its destructive capabilities. For example, Maersk's IT systems, including 49000 laptops and 3500 servers, were destroyed—effectively wiping out its ability to operate. The malware was introduced to the world through an update to an accounts package, but included the Eternal Blue library (also used in WannaCry [25]), which used vulnerabilities in the SMBv1 protocol to spread quickly between connected computers, particularly within enterprises. NotPetya not only encrypted files on the victims computer, but also overwrote the master boot record [43], hence stopping Windows from booting. More recently, human operated ransomware campaigns have been becoming an increasing threat to businesses [29,46]. Here, after an initial infection, the ransomware spreads using a variety of lateral movement techniques, usually based on acquiring accessed to privileged accounts and using system management tools such as WMI or powershell to spread throughout the enterprise. Such attacks often leave backdoors in infected systems, making reimaging necessary. Such a process can take a well-prepared organization weeks to recover from—and months for larger organizations or those without good backups and IT support. The details of the process and how organizations often end up paying ransoms rather than rebuilding their systems are described in [48].

It is not just ransomware that spreads over networks necessitating recovery at scale. Malware families, such as Emotet [10], also have mechanisms to spread rapidly through email. Spreading patterns have evolved to include WiFi [5], and can make it hard to clean corporate systems without taking everything offline. Some malware can be cleaned by Anti-Virus systems, but it can be hard to guarantee and trust that systems are clean; hence, easing the re-imaging process can become an essential part of a company's response to malware and attacks. For example, the SANS incident-responder's handbook recommends re-imaging of systems' hard drives to ensure malware is eradicated [24], with recent surveys showing incident response processes often leading to re-imaging [8].

Companies are becoming aware that they must start planning for both large-scale and smaller scale outages in order to get their and systems staff back up and functioning as soon as possible [14]. There are, of course, various products and approaches to backup, re-imaging and restoration. However, there are a lack of tools to help IT decision-makers decide on the most appropriate strategy and assess whether they have the necessary tools and infrastructure in place. This is the problem that we look at within this paper, showing how modelling and simulation can be used to aid the decision-makers in the choices they make.

2.1   Image Management and Recovery

There are several approaches that companies use in order to maintain and re-image client systems. Underlying these approaches there are three basic choices:

Full System Backups. Some companies will have backup systems that keep a full system backup of each client. Restoration will then happen by reinstalling this full backup. The backup vendor would support this restoration process with a typical reinstall process involving the download of a Windows PE agent along with the full system backup, placing this onto a bootable USB stick, and then, through the BIOS menus, booting into this cut-down version of Windows, which will reinstall from the full backup. Taking full backups is becoming less common as it means keeping copies of many standard system files and there are advantages to re-imaging to a clean up-to-date OS image.

Re-imaging to a Corporate Image. A more common scenario is for companies to have a standard corporate image along with a data backup strategy. For example, a company will often create a Windows image containing corporate management tools—such as a management agent for a system such as Microsoft's Endpoint Configuration Manager—and its security software, both AV and EDR systems, such that when a client image installation happens the system is secure and manageable [42]. Microsoft provide a management deployment toolkit [31] that describes and supports this overall deployment process. The management tools will then typically help install other applications as required. Such images will be updated regularly—quarterly or half yearly, say—to include the latest version of Windows, patches, and software.

Data backup may be through backup software to an enterprise server or the cloud, although companies are increasingly using synchronized cloud-based storage such as OneDrive, where data is stored on the cloud with local copies cached on the endpoint.

From a recovery perspective, as a user decides they need to re-image a system they get hold of a bootable image on a USB stick (or occasionally a DVD) and boot into this to re-image the system. In an office environment, where there is IT support, the IT engineers will maintain a set of current OS images on bootable media. In smaller offices, or where there are home workers, the OS image can be downloaded and there will be instructions for the user to create the bootable media and reinstall. Such instructions can be complex for a typical user and require access to a USB stick that can be wiped and reformatted. If a user is at home they would need a functioning computer to use to download the image.

IT support labs will also often have a PXE boot set-up to make re-imaging easier [30]. They have an image hosted on a local server and use PXE boot to point the system to that image to install. This can ease the problem of setting up larger numbers of client systems, although it requires staff and infrastructure.

Modern Management. There is an increasing move towards the use of modern management systems (Uniform Endpoint Management), such as Microsoft's InTune System [28]. This approach allows the use of a standard Windows image, such as that initially placed on the computer, rather than a specially maintained corporate image. During the install process, the management infrastructure will push critical security patches, AV signatures, Windows domain policies (Group policy objects), and necessary software. This produces a similar effect to having a corporate image, but removes the need to maintain custom images.

Typically, after a new image has been installed, an out-of-the-box experience (OOBE) process runs, the user will be lead through configuration screens, and will login using their corporate email. The login directs the system to a cloud-based management server, so that the enterprise configurations can be found and installed, and the computer added to the enterprise domain. This process can be simplified further using Microsoft's AutoPilot [32], where a computer is preregistered as belonging to a company, and user interactions and configurations can be simplified and reduced.

The re-imaging process still requires that the user can get hold of a clean Windows install image. However, the company does not need to maintain and host its own Windows image. Instead, a user can download the latest OS copy from either the PC manufacturer or from Microsoft. Companies using these mechanism will typically used cloud-synced storage, discussed above, to provide data resilience and, as the system is re-imaged and added to the corporate domain, data will gradually be synced back to the client.

Re-imaging Mechanisms. Re-imaging will typically involve booting from an ISO image and installing this onto a drive, or via a reduced version of Windows, such as WinRE or WinPE, which can install Windows from WIM files. Windows itself also includes a number of repair processes [27]—for example, allowing rollbacks to previous snapshots using Shadow Volume Copy. However, malware such as ransomware often disables volume shadow copy and delete snapshots, so making recovery and the retrieval of older files hard. Incident responders often recommend a clean install to ensure malware is eradicated.

Re-imaging processes require a boot into a system rather than the normal OS. The boot process is controlled by the BIOS, which will have a defined boot order and set of devices that can be used to boot the system. Thus, many systems will boot from an attached USB device or PXE boot before the main disk, making re-imaging easy—but with no controls. Early in the boot cycle, users can get into the BIOS menu and boot to an alternative device. Some enterprises will lock down the BIOS with passwords and ensure the system boots only from the internal disk and, in this case, re-imaging will require an IT support engineer who knows the BIOS password.

HP has built a bare metal recovery system (HP 'Sure Recover' [21]) into the BIOS in order to simplify the re-imaging process. The Endpoint Security Controller (EpSC) holds a configuration containing the location of image-servers, which may be either HP's servers for standard Windows images or other servers specified by the enterprise. The configuration also contains public keys of the authority allowed to sign the Windows image to be installed and, in this way, an enterprise can guarantee the image being installed has integrity and has been approved. Recovery can be triggered by the user at boot time through the BIOS recovery option or it can trigger automatically when the system fails to boot—such as with NotPetya. When triggered, the BIOS gets this configuration information and uses it to download a recovery agent, which then downloads the full OS image and re-images the system. Both recovery agents and the full image are signed and the signature is validated as part of the recovery process ensuring authenticity of the recovered image. The process simplifies recovery for the user as they no longer need to be able to find where to obtain the OS image and do not need an available USB stick. From the enterprise perspective, it allows the enterprise to lock the BIOS without support engineers doing rebuilds, as well as guaranteeing that the image installed is correct.

Enterprise Recovery Choices. The descriptions above show that there is a wide range of choices available to the enterprise as it looks to implement an image management and recovery strategy; for example:

- Maintain a corporate image or use a standard image. There is a choice as to how often the image is updated. After recovery, patches will need installing and updating images more often will reduce the need and time taken for post re-image patching. When a company maintains its own OS images, they must maintain servers to support the download of images. Download speeds may depend on the location of these servers, or how they are distributed over the world, the location of users, and the network bandwidth available in an office or to a home or travelling user. The volume of traffic to these servers will depend on the recovery scenario—in terms of the numbers of users likely to be recovering at a given time.
- How much IT support is needed and how much in each office? Many companies are looking to reduce IT costs, and this often creates pressure to centralize help-desks and remove support from offices. However, a lack of local support and locally kept OS images can delay recovery times. At the same time, the enterprise will need to plan for remote workers either working from home or as they travel.
- Control over the re-imaging process can bring various choices with which the enterprise may wish to lock down its client platforms, but this adds a considerable burden in recovery.
- There are many different data backup strategies, from the use of cloud synced drives through to full system backups. Each will have an impact on the ease of recovery and potential user data loss.
- The different re-imaging techniques, such as using a USB stick or PXE boot, in comparison to having recovery mechanisms such as HP 'Sure Recover' built into the system—whether with an image stored locally or downloaded.

3   The Modelling Technique

The growth of interconnected networked systems led to the development of the concept and theory of distributed systems in computer science. This paradigm views systems as collections of components, in different locations, that work together to perform tasks—that is, deliver services—and communicate by sending information or messages over network connections.

While the origin of this view is very specific to its focus on computer systems, its concepts can be taken more generally to provide a useful metaphor for understanding all types of systems and, finally, ecosystems. The models we use in this paper are executable models, implemented in Julia code, and constructed using a modelling framework designed around this distributed systems perspective [7]. The framework itself is built on a rigorous mathematical foundation—see, for example, [1,11,12,39]—which gives an understanding of the components and operation of distributed systems. There are three key components upon which we draw:

- *Location*—Distributed systems naturally have a concept of different locations, which are connected to each other. In the CS view, components are present at different locations and connected by a network. In the more general view, locations can be physical (e.g., a room, a container), logical (e.g., an address in computer memory), or abstract (e.g., the location where a semaphore exists). Mathematically, we require a topological structure that supports the concept of connected places. In many examples, found widely in the complex systems modelling literature, *directed graphs* are quite sufficient. Generalized notions of graph, as well as more exotic topological structures, can also be considered. The implementation uses a directed graph structure: locations have links to other locations, which constrain how resources may be moved from one location to another.
- *Resource*—Resources exist at locations and can move between them according to the locations' connections. In the general view, they can represent anything, including physical objects, people, and information.
  Mathematically, we start from the basic observation that resource elements can be combined and compared. This leads us to consider *ordered monoids*—and collections thereof—of resource elements. In some circumstances, slightly more complex structures may be required [1,11,12]. Examples of such structures include $(\mathbb{N}, +, 0, \leq)$—that is, the natural numbers—and computer memory cells, combined by concatenation and ordered simply by equality, as used in Separation Logic [22,41] and its many variants.
  Resources are implemented as instances of objects. Different types of resource are defined by declaring different types in the code. Each location has a collection of resources that are present at that location.
- *Process*—Processes execute relative to resources at locations and manipulate resources as they do so.
  Mathematically, we work employ a calculus of processes that is closely related to Milner's *Synchronous Calculus of Communicating Systems (SCCS)* [33,34]. The implementation of processes in code is based around a discrete event scheduler. Processes are written as functions whose execution can be interrupted by `hold` statements, which pause a process for some specified amount of (simulation) time, and `claim` statements, which pause a process until specified resources become available at specified locations.
  The first statement, `hold`, allows processes to model the passage of time—a real-world process that takes some amount of real-world time can be modelled

by a model process using `hold` statements to simulate the passage of time.
The second statement, `claim`, is how processes manipulate resources and how
processes interact with each other. Once a process has claimed a resource it
can move it from location to location, or remove it. When a process has finished manipulating a resource, it should `release` it. Only one process can
claim a resource at any given time. If a process tries to claim resources that
are not present (or are claimed by other processes) in the specified locations,
it will pause until the resources are released.

It is easy to see how complex models can be built using these simple constructs. For example, a process that represents a door opening can't continue
until the resource representing the key is present; or a process of a file download might move a resource from a server location to a client location, after
pausing for the length of time the download takes; or, if two processes are
representing cars trying to park, only one will be able to claim the resource
that signals a particular parking space is free. This shows how processes communicate and coordinate.

These concepts can be used to build a representation of a system's structure and
operation, but there is one more concept required: the environment in which the
system operates.

- *Environment*—Environments capture the world outside of the system of interest and how the two interact. We think of this in terms of events that happen
  at the boundary of the model and cause an action to occur in the model
  itself.

  Mathematically, we capture the incidence of events at the boundary of a
  model—be they inbound, originating outwith the model, or outbound, originating within the model, using probability distributions. For example, an
  arrival rate for requests to a server may have a negative exponential distribution.

  The concept of environment is implemented in code as a collection of environment processes—distinct from the processes in the model itself—which create
  resources or start other processes in the actual model. These can incorporate
  probability distributions to model the delay between events.

Overall, models are based on a transition system with evolutions of states—
with location L, resources R, and process, E—the form

$$L, R, E \xrightarrow{a} L', R', E'$$

read as 'the process E executing with access to resources R at location L evolves
by the action a to be the process E' executing with access to resources R' at
location L'.

Such evolutions are defined by an operational semantics that is structured
by the process combinators described above. Equality between states L, R, E
and L', R', E', denoted $L, R, E \sim L', R', E'$, is given by bisimulation equivalence
[1, 11, 12]. We sometimes denote states by $\mathcal{S}, \mathcal{T}$, and so on.

Along with the transition system comes a logic of states. In logical terms, states L, R, E form the worlds, in the sense of Kripke models, of a model of language of propositional assertions—see, for example, [1,11,12,19,19,33,34,44]. We write

$$L, R, E \models \phi$$

to denote that the property ϕ is true of the process E executing with resources R at location L. In modelling ecosystems, such logical properties can be used to specify the properties that required of the interfaces of two models in order for the models to be composable.

This generalization of the idea of a distributed system, together with its mathematical tools, provides concepts that can be used to model essentially any type of system, from physical to logical, or systems that incorporate both. We note also that these concepts are scale-free—they can be used at any level of abstraction or representation. However, we have not actually defined what it means to *build* a model using this distributed systems approach. This, too, is very flexible. Models can be largely conceptual, and use the ideas of location, resource, and process as a means to help think about the structure and behaviour of a system. Or distributed systems models can be mathematical, as we will show in the next section. Finally, this metaphor can be used to build executable models, in the spirit of Birtwistle's Demos [6], where a programmatic description of the system (in terms of locations, resources, and processes) is run to simulate the behaviour of the system [7,9,11,45].

An early implementation of these ideas, Gnosis [11], has been used in significant commercial applications [2–4] derived from an industry-based research project [20]. The current framework, the Julia SysModels package ([7]) is an improved, more modern implementation of these ideas that includes new capabilities such as composition of models.

The ability to compose models is important for modelling larger systems and ecosystems. During modelling, these systems can be decomposed into smaller parts, which can be modelled separately and then recombined, and which helps manage complexity. How does composition work in the distributed systems approach?

We start with interfaces. These define, for a model, the locations, resources, and processes involved in a composition. For a composition of two models to be valid, the interfaces in both models must match. Figure 1 depicts three models which compose together. When models with interfaces are not composed, the environment generates the events expected by the interface; when composed, the environment is replaced by a model. Also shown is an example of substitution: Model C can be substituted for Model B as the interfaces of the two models match; this allows a modeller to refine or increase detail in parts of a larger model.

Interfaces and composition naturally support the concept of local reasoning. Such an account of reasoning requires a mathematical conception of the distributed systems metaphor on top of which interfaces and composition can be defined.

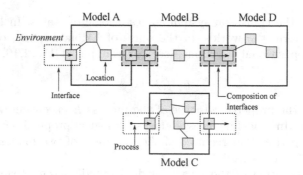

Fig. 1. Interfaces, composition, and substitution

We can identify here a local reasoning principle, or *frame rule* [22,37–39,49]. We begin by setting up some notation for the states of the various component models depicted in Fig. 2. The details of this set up may be found in [45]. Here, we denote the composition of two models M_1 and M_2, via interfaces I_1 and I_2, respectively, as

$$M_1 {}_{I_1}|_{I_2} M_2$$

Then, we can make the following assumptions:

- let the model $M = M_1{}_{I_1}|_{I_2}M_2$ have state $\mathcal{S}$;
- let the component models (of the composition of interest) M_i have states $\mathcal{S}_i$, respectively;
- let the submodels N_i have states $\mathcal{U}_i$, respectively; and
- let the interfaces I_i have states $\mathcal{I}_i$, respectively.

Now we assume the following, writing ∘ for composition of states, for $i = 1, 2$:

- $\mathcal{S}_i \sim \mathcal{U}_i \circ \mathcal{I}_i$, $\mathcal{S} \xrightarrow{a} \mathcal{T}$, and $\mathcal{I}_i \xrightarrow{a} \mathcal{J}_i$
- $a\#N_i\backslash I_i$; that is, that the action a is 'separated from' that part of the model N_i that is not coincident with the interface I_i in that the execution of a does not affect N_i.

Now, suppose that $\mathcal{U}_i \models \phi_i$, for $i = 1, 2$, and $\mathcal{J}_i \models \psi_i$. for $i = 1, 2$. Then we have the following frame rule:

$$\frac{\mathcal{J}_1 \models \psi_1 \quad \mathcal{J}_2 \models \psi_2}{\mathcal{T} \models (\phi_1 * \psi_1) * (\psi_2 * \phi_2)} \quad \begin{array}{l} \text{-} \ \mathcal{S} \xrightarrow{a} \mathcal{T} \text{ and } \mathcal{I}_i \xrightarrow{a} \mathcal{J}_i \\ \text{-} \ a\#N_i\backslash I_i \end{array}$$

This rule is sound with respect to bisimulation equivalence.

Milner [35,36] considers the concept of interface from the point of view of a quite abstract graphical theory of processes. Our notion is more directly grounded in the concept of a distributed system, but we conjecture that the approaches can be understood comparatively. Our approach is more directly concerned with the logical concept of local reasoning. Our notion of interface is also related to Lynch and Tuttle's input/output automata [26].

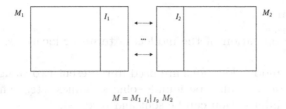

$$M = M_1 \, {}_{I_1}|\, {}_{I_2} \, M_2$$

Fig. 2. Local reasoning and the frame property

At the end of Sect. 4, after we have explained the set-up of the specific model we use in this paper, we discuss briefly its compositional structure and how this would facilitate local reasoning about the components of the model.

4 The Model

We wish to build a model that can help organizations understand the consequences of different device recovery technology and strategy choices in the presence of various kinds of attacks. Different organizations will be of different sizes, have different structures, use different technologies, place different values on their information and system assets, and have different understandings of what a successful recovery looks like. Because we want this modelling approach to be useful to a wide range of organisations, we focus on constructing a generic model that captures the systems, structures, and behaviours necessary for thinking about organizational recovery, and which can be parametrized and configured to create a model of a chosen organization.

Figure 3 illustrates the high-level architecture of our model, in the configuration used for this paper. It consists of three models which are composed together: a device model, a network model, and a server model. Each of these models can be configured differently to represent different organizations, and, because of the compositional structure, additional models could be substituted or added if the current models do not capture the necessary details of a particular system.

Device Model—The device model is the most complex model of the three. It is designed to be able to represent the devices (essentially, computers in the form of laptops and desktops) used by an organization, the locations these devices may be in (such as offices, homes, hotels, and so on), the movement of devices between these locations, and the different ways devices at each of these locations can recover.

Network Model—This models computer networks over which information can be sent. It is configurable; different network topologies can be constructed, with different bandwidths available on different segments. When segments are overloaded, transfers through them are throttled.

Server Model—This is the simplest of the three models. The server model listens for requests for operating system images sent by devices and responds by transmitting the OS image to the requesting device back across the network.

4.1   Operation

We describe the operation of the models in terms of locations, resources, and processes.

In the device model, locations are used to represent two things: the physical locations where devices may be found—offices, homes, etc.—and the network endpoints where information can be sent and received.

Resources are used to represent devices, which can be moved around the physical locations, and things used in the various recovery processes: USB sticks, OS images, and image requests and responses which are sent and received over the network. Resources are also used to represent the *availability* of network endpoints. When a device moves to a location, it obtains use of a network endpoint so it can send and receive data on the network by claiming one of these availability resources; when it leaves, it releases that availability resource so another device may use that endpoint later.

Each device in the model has its own process. This process is responsible for all of the device's behaviour, from movement, to recovery, to sending and receiving data on the network. As part of the configuration of the model, each device is set up with: a movement pattern (the sequence of physical locations to move to, and probability distributions determining the length of time it stays in each one), a method of recovery to use, whether or not the device should recover, and, if so, at what time.

These last two can be varied to model different intensities of attacks. More devices recovering in a shorter time period models a more intense attack—for example, faster-spreading malware. Fewer devices, possibly over a longer period of time models a less intense attack.

With these parameters, the device process executes. It moves the device resource from physical location to physical location according to the sequence, remaining in each one for a certain amount of time. If a particular device should recover, the device process initiates this at the appropriate time.

In this paper, we look at three recovery methods. USB recovery, where devices install a fresh OS from a USB stick; network recovery, where devices request and receive an OS image over the network from an image server; and, embedded recovery, where devices have a built-in storage capability that is used to hold an OS image for recover.

To model embedded recovery, the device process simply waits for the amount of time (as measured on real-world devices) it takes to restore from the embedded storage. For network recovery, the process has a few more steps. It starts by creating a request to download the recovery agent and moving it to the network endpoint so it can be sent to the server; it then waits for the response by claiming a response resource at the network endpoint. After receiving this, the process creates a request for the OS image, moves it to the endpoint, and waits for the response. For USB recovery, the device process tries to claim a USB stick resource with the OS image on it; if none are available, it tries to claim a blank USB; if no USBs of either type are available, and none *become* available, the recovery process fails. If a blank USB is obtained, the process must download the OS image by sending a request and waiting for the response, and writing it to the USB. This destroys a blank USB resource and creates a new USB stick resource with the image on it. Throughout all these steps in the process are time delays modelling the length of time it takes to, for example, verify an image after download, or copy an image to disk, or run the installer.

In the network model, locations are used to represent each of the network endpoints with one additional location representing data resources in transit. This model has one process, which claims resources that arrive at the endpoints, moves them to the transit location, and, after a delay suitable for the size of the data and the speed of the network segments it would traverse, moves them to the destination endpoint and releases them. If transfers are already ongoing when more resources are claimed or released, the process recalculates the time when the transfers will finish based on how throttled the network segments are.

The server model is the most simple. It has a network endpoint location, and a process which waits for requests to arrive from the network and sends responses back.

4.2   Composition

These three models compose together to form a model of device recovery in which OS images can be obtained from an image server over a network. As discussed in Sect. 3, composition of models occurs at interfaces. In this case, interfaces are defined at each network endpoint. The network model becomes the glue that sticks the server model and the device model together. The server model composes with the network model at an endpoint; the device model composes with the network model at *many* endpoints. After this, a request moved into the endpoint by the device model will be sent over the network by the network model, received by the server model, and the response sent back over the network model to the device model.

The compositional approach to the design of these models facilitates the ability to reason locally about the underlying components, providing two primary advantages: modularity, for further extension, and the ability to focus the analysis on a singular model component without the need to reason about its relationships with other components.

These ideas are important for future extensions to this modelling approach. The network model does not know anything about the type of data resources being transmitted over it; it only knows that when it receives a resource at one interface, it should deliver it to another. Additional models could easily be composed with the network model, too. For example, another server model could be used to store data backups received from devices, or a model of attacks, that transmits resources representing malware to devices. These examples and the existing device and server models work when composed without knowing how the other models function because of the well-defined interfaces between them. Knowing the specification of the interface between the models allows reasoning— that is, *local reasoning*, as explained in Sect. 3—about the components of these models in a similar fashion, without the fear of the arguments being invalidated by specific cases of interaction between the two models.

5   Scenarios, Parameters, and Validation

We describe a given recovery scenario and show how the model can be used to reason about different recovery choices including where to place recovery images and what recovery mechanisms, or mix of mechanisms, to support. The model currently covers the generic aspects of the recovery mechanisms, such as network bandwidth and other resource contention, but we discuss—informally for now— how local reasoning in the model can be used to model specific enterprise IT processes to produce more tailored results.

Here, we explore attack scenarios where fast spreading malware hits the enterprise to explore how such wide scale attacks will stress the enterprises recovery processes. From the model we measure two aspects, recoverability and the time to recover and these need to be placed along side deployment, support costs and security as the enterprise makes deployment choices. The scenarios and configurations we present here are examples to illustrate the modelling approach; when deploying this approach in a real organization, a different range of scenarios and recovery mechanisms may be required.

5.1   Recovery Mechanisms

Section 2 described the broader recovery space. Here, we consider a subset of these enterprise choices and address one of the first questions that an enterprise will need to tackle: what mechanisms should be used for re-imaging? We compare the use of USB sticks with different options of using the bare-metal recovery (network and embedded) provided by HP 'Sure Recover'. These basic recovery mechanisms cover the way in which a fresh Windows image gets onto the disk. We have included timings up to the point at which the new image has booted and the OOBE starts, and the user configures the system. In our scenario, this is the same process and timings in each recovery scenario.

USB Stick. USB stick recovery can be used when the OS is no longer trusted and would typically be used in an enterprise that manages its own bespoke Windows images. Here, we consider the USB sticks with and without images as a resource that can become limited as the number of devices in a given location need to recover. The process can be somewhat more complex as good security practice means disabling USB boot and only re-enabling it through the BIOS on recovery. Where companies follow good practice and lock down the BIOS settings with passwords or other mechanisms, this can create support requirements as administrators will need to perform the re-imaging tasks. This is a two stage recovery process.

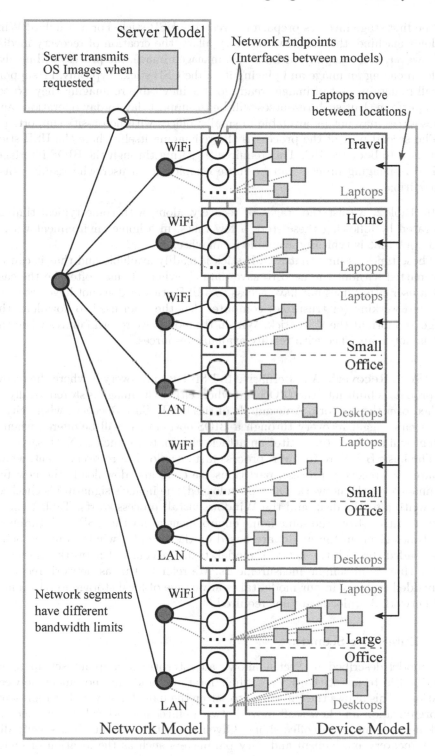

Fig. 3. Model of organizational recovery

1. The first stage involves preparing a recovery USB stick. For a standard Windows machine, the Windows recovery allows the creation of recovery media. However, in a company with its own managed image, the process will involve downloading an image and placing it on the USB stick. Typically, IT support will maintain a set of images ready for the inevitable re-imaging they expect to perform. But such resources will be to support day-to-day operations and resources may not be available in smaller offices with no on-site support.
2. The second part of the process is the re-imaging itself, where the USB stick is used to boot the PC. This requires triggering through the BIOS interface. The re-imaging process can be more complex for a user who requires disk partitioning.

In Table 2, we list the stages of recovery, along with some typical timings generated by following these steps a few times, in a home environment with a USB stick that is typically available in an office.

These times assume that a USB stick is readily available and that it can be reformatted without the need to save data elsewhere. It may often be the case that a user either does not have access to a USB stick or does not have access to a second working (or trustable) computer that they can used to download the image and format the USB stick. Within the model, we record failures when the user is not in an office with readily available resources.

HP 'Sure Recover'. An alternative to USB-based recovery is where the recovery process is built into the BIOS and where either the image is stored locally or fetched over the network. An example of this is HP 'Sure Recover', where either a user can trigger recovery through a BIOS option or it will be offered when a system will not boot (e.g., after an attack with malware such as NotPetya).

The basic HP 'Sure Recover' process first downloads a recovery agent, which initiates the recovery process, partitions the disk, and downloads the new full OS image over the network. Once downloaded, the image's signature is checked, it is written to the disk, and the Windows install process starts. Table 1 shows recovery times (from the same home environment as for the USB stick timings). The times given in the model are based on the size of a windows image being downloaded through the network model, taking account of network contention rather than from sample measurements. We refer to this as network recovery. Embedded recovery in our model takes advantage of local storage for the image and network downloads are not required.

5.2 Enterprise Scenario

The model described in Sect. 4 allows an enterprise's endpoint set-up to be described in terms of the devices, their locations, and any movement between locations. This allows the enterprise to set up the model in a way that represents its organization and how staff move between offices and other locations such as working at home or in coffee shops. Given this set-up we can then specify different recovery mechanism and vary parameters such as the location of image servers, the numbers of available USB sticks, and the network speeds in offices. Finally, we can set up a variety of failure scenarios, such as rapidly spreading destructive malware or just random infections and failures, that drive the need for recovery. This set-up allows the enterprise to compare different recovery options and parameters in a range of conditions and then combine this with other information about recovery, such as a security analysis, to aid decision-making.

We create a basic scenario, as depicted in Fig. 3, in which we have a large office with 40 desktops (systems that typically stay in the office) and 40 mobile workers who have movement profiles taking laptops between home, the office, and cafés (which represent other non-office locations). Within this office, we assume some level of IT support and when using USB based recovery the availability of some USB sticks with current images as well as a number of spare USB sticks. The large office is also well connected to the internet and has the possibility of having servers to host recovery images. We then have two smaller offices, each having slower internet connectivity and fewer users (10 fixed (desktop) and 10 mobile (laptops)). We assume minimal IT support and, in the case of USB stick recovery, that we do not have prepared images (but USB sticks are available).

In each of the offices, the mobile workers spend most of their day in the office, but will also move to other locations such as the home and cafés. We have a group of 20 travelling workers who move between a variety of networks such as airports and hotels, as well as appearing in the office. The public networks (airport, cafe, hotel) are assumed to be quite slow, with the homes having good home broadband speeds. In addition, we assume that as staff are mobile or working at home they do not have ready access to spare USB sticks.

We look at four recovery approaches.

- *USB*. USB stick recovery with the availability of USB sticks with and without images as set out above.
- *Network*. Network only based recovery for example using HP's 'Sure Recover'
- *Embedded*. A mix of laptops (mobile workers) HP's 'Sure Recover Embedded' (with images stored on devices) and the desktops just having HP's network based 'Sure Recover'.
- *30% Embedded*. 30% of the office workers laptops and all travelling staff having HP's 'Sure Recover' Embedded with the rest relying on HP's 'Sure Recover' for network-based recovery.

It is worth noting that the model captures the active elements of the different approaches but does not represent the security of the different approaches. Here, we should consider the 'Sure Recover'-based mechanisms as secure in that they check the signature of the image, thus validating that the image is correct and as intended by the enterprise—for example, with the chosen enterprise AV systems installed. USB-based recovery has no validation of the image and either requires administrators who know BIOS admin passwords to initiate the installation or requires the computer to be kept in an insecure state—allowing USB boot or boot with no BIOS password.

We add in an additional scenario to demonstrate the advantages that can come with planning where network images are located and, in this case, add an image server into the large office.

We test recovery under quite extreme attack scenarios assuming rapidly spreading destructive malware. We have spread-rates running a spread over a 2, 6, and 12 h time periods, with an increasing percentage of devices being hit by the malware. Such attack rates could correspond to automated fast-spreading ransomware, such as NotPetya, and could also correspond to more modern human-operated ransomware. For example, in [40] an attack scenario is described in which an attack using Ryuk takes about five hours to complete, with most of the spread happening in the final hour using RDP from the domain controller. Other attacks use mechanisms like empire powershell, which may be detected by AV systems. Hence, within our attack model, we include both the speed of attack and the chance of success, which will relate to device configurations such as allowing RDP or AV signatures.

Given our intention to comparatively analyse the recovery techniques described in a meaningful way for real organizations, we now focus on a set of verification and validation methods for ensuring that the model is representative of the scenarios illustrated. We briefly summarize our verification and validation steps procedures.

When considering verification, we employed a mix of anti-bugging—if-clauses and counters that ensure the program workflow is not invalidating primary constraints, such as minimum and maximum possible speed on the network—model prototyping and simplified and structured walk-through iterations to continuously check that the model results match expected knowledge and expectations about the system, deterministic and non-deterministic variable assignation to flag possible unexpected behaviour, and event-tracing in the form of both time- and location-based logging.

Regarding validation, we based our model on two primary approaches: continuous validation via expert knowledge at every stage of the design development cycle and the use of real-world data manually gathered—additional information about the timings used can be found in Appendix A.

5.3   Results

Factors within the model such as when recovery is triggered and the movement of devices between locations are sampled from stochastic variables representing the environment. As such, each variant of the model (recovery scenario, attack scenario, and success of the attack) is run 100 times and the graphs show the average performance, along with error bars showing the variability between the runs. The combination of these parameter ranges gives 144 different parameter configurations, each of which is run 100 times, resulting in a total of 14400 executions of the model. To obtain the results more quickly, we ran these across a number of computer cluster nodes. Most jobs completed successfully with a 3 GB memory limit; for the busiest scenarios, a 5 GB limit was sufficient.

Figure 4 shows how recovery speeds vary between the different methods under the different attack scenarios. We should expect that the network to saturate as mass recovery happens and hence slow recovery down. However, the model is showing that the recovery times are quite stable across the slower attack scenarios and recovery speeds only slow down with the fastest attacks. Even in this case, the recovery times increase gradually and, even with a severe attack, remain at a manageable speed.

The effectiveness of the USB-based recovery strategy is perhaps somewhat surprising, but the model assumes very good co-ordination within an office, with good availability of USB sticks, as well as good knowledge of how to use the process (which is less automated than HP 'Sure Recover'). These factors will depend on the preparedness and skill levels of the staff and hence would represent further enterprise-driven model parameters. The other factor with USB recovery comes from the availability of suitable equipment—Fig. 7 shows recovery failure rates between 5 and 40 systems, depending on the success of the attack (rather than speed).

As would be expected, HP 'Sure Recover Embedded' recovery is the quickest and most reliable mechanism. Having the embedded recovery within the mobile devices not only makes recovery of these devices quick it also significantly reduces the network load hence reducing the overall recovery times for the desktops dependent on the network even under the fast attacks. Even at a mix of 30% Mobile devices supporting HP 'Sure Recover Embedded' recovery the overall network load for mass recovery is significantly reduced. Suggesting considerable overall value for embedded recovery beyond just regular travellers.

The appendix contains a number of graphs showing how network contention affects different parts of our enterprise scenarios. Figures 8, 9, 10, 11, 12, 13 show considerable contention and slowdown with fast attacks on the office LAN. One question we wanted to show we can address using the model is the location of the recovery images. Figure 6 shows the results of placing an image server on the LAN within the large office as compared to Fig. 5 where all downloads go through the office internet connection. Given the speed of the LAN this leads to a massive improvement for the LAN connected desktops (the bottom line). The laptops recovery is slowed by the WiFi bandwidth limitations. Having the local image-server reduces recovery times significantly below those of the optimistic USB model, suggesting that a relatively cheap investment can significantly enhance recovery speeds (and without the security issues relating to USB based recovery).

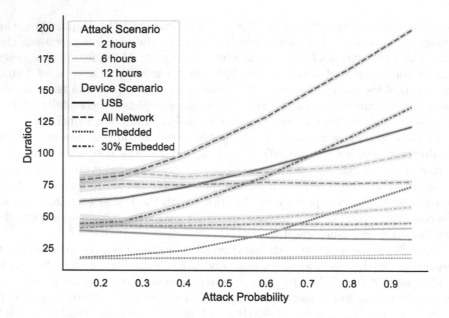

Fig. 4. All scenarios

5.4 Extending the Model

Within our the organizational model, we have a simple set-up in terms of recovery, in which we model recovery being triggered and the process happening, but do not consider the extent of the supporting management processes. These can be quite different for different enterprises. For example, in managing the USB-based recovery, some companies will have locked down the BIOS and will need administrators to be available to initiate recovery whereas others will allow users to perform these tasks. In addition, the skills and experience of users in different companies varies, as does the means to provide support, whether via help-desks or online.

The local reasoning concepts discussed in Sect. 4 talk about the ability to add resources and actions to the internal structure of a composed model whilst retaining the same interfaces. We can, for example, add additional actions and resource constraints to help handle USB recovery and have a smaller number of administrators who initiate USB recovery, and model the resource contention. We could have additional actions in which some users call help-desks and have additional resources to model help-desk operatives. Ideally, the latter would be based on either help-desk data or user studies to capture the resourcing required to support different likelihoods, under different modelled circumstances, that users will need help, given the desired times needed to help them.

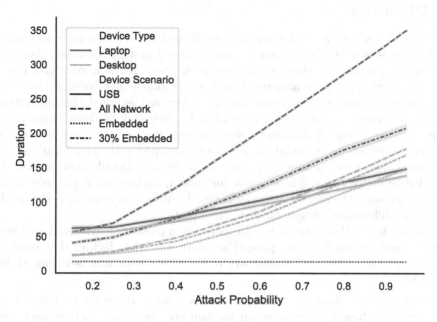

Fig. 5. Laptop vs Desktop; mean duration of recovery with remote image server; 2 h attack.

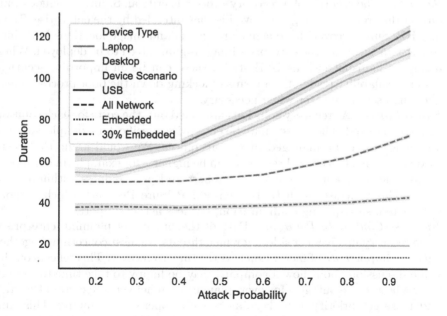

Fig. 6. Laptop vs Desktop; mean duration of recovery with local image server; 2 h attack.

6   Discussion

The time to recover—and whether recovery is even possible in a given location—are key measures for the success of any recovery system. However, from the enterprise's perspective the real concern is the cost of the impact and how a recovery solution can help mitigate those costs. It may be, for example, that costs of disruption to staff who are travelling are higher, as they need working systems to do sales presentations; or certain staff and offices may be doing time-critical tasks such as scheduling shipments. Such impacts can be very company-specific, but the model allows endpoint devices to be grouped with their locations and movements and with the need to recover to be defined. Detailed traces show the recorded recovery times. Thus, using the model, an enterprise can add value-information onto the overall recovery time information in order to compare the roll out of different strategies on disruption costs.

The model itself captures what happens when recovery is triggered over multiple systems within the enterprise. But there are other factors that must be taken into account for a full assessment of a recovery system to be deployed. For example:

- *Support During Recovery*—Critical aspects of recovery are the usability of any mechanism, how users know about mechanisms, and how easy they are to use. In Sect. 5.4, we discussed how extending the model with local reasoning can be used to model these further aspects. Here, evidence from usability studies will help in validating the model.
- *Security*—The security of a recovery process is critical. Security includes validating that recovery image deployed is that intended by the enterprise. Tools like HP 'Sure Recover' have signature checks and image locations built into the system such that the enterprise image is guaranteed to be deployed. When using mechanisms such as USB sticks, there can be an important security-versus-availability trade-off, in terms of locking down the boot process versus allowing users to recover when necessary.
- *Support costs*—As recovery solutions are rolled out, the costs for each solution must be assessed. These costs may be enterprise-specific; for example, support and images may be managed in various offices. We would argue that costs associated with USB based recovery can be higher—for example, in our model we assume a certain amount of IT support and preparedness within a large office. This contrasts with tools such as HP 'Sure Recover', which is more automated, so requiring configuration, but less active support.
- *Business Continuity Planning*—Part of the process of planning enterprise-scale recovery involves considering which threats are most concerning together with the importance of factors such as the time to recover. This reflects on the value discussion about how a company may be happy to take time to recover after a large scale outage. However, planning can help ensure certain key staff and tasks get priority, thus keeping essential operations running. This can, for example, be accomplished by having embedded recovery built into the laptops of travelling staff along with careful management of the placement of images in critical facilities.

These factors, and others, must be considered by system managers when making decisions about the recovery strategies and technologies to deploy. One way this might be achieved is by using a multi-attribute utility approach, where the preferences of system managers for various attributes—e.g. cost, time to recovery, information loss, and other measures of system performance—are used to determine a utility from the behaviour of the model (cf. [45]). The various policy and strategy choices can then be explored using the model, to determine which results in the greatest utility.

In this paper, we have modelled the re-imaging aspect of recovery, considering a case aimed at an enterprise managing its own image. In Sect. 2, we have outlined a wider space, including options for the enterprise to use modern management techniques and standard images. Such processes can be compared within our modelling framework; for example, varying image download times and changing the Windows install times to reflect differences in how users configure the system. Getting a user back and running also involves recovering applications and data. This can lead to additional network load as users download applications and data. However, cloud-synced storage devices, such as One Drive, will often configure file indexes and then download data as needed. The model can easily be extended to represent such additional network loads, but such loads will be very solution-dependent, and setting up the model requires careful planning.

7   Conclusion

Organizations are increasingly hit by malware, including rapidly spreading malware, which necessitates recovery strategies to eradicate the problems. Yet there are few tools that help enterprise decision-makers to understand recovery technologies and how they will react under such attack scenarios.

We have demonstrated how a modelling approach can help exercise critical aspects of the recovery problem, such as understanding network contention under different rapidly spreading malware attacks. Such tools can—for example, as demonstrated in the results—allow an enterprise to make choices about the placement of recovery images and about the value of having devices with embedded recovery support, both in recovering anywhere and reducing network load. This becomes possible because the modelling techniques allow models of different aspects of the IT stack to be composed. The local reasoning this enables will allow customization to match enterprise scenarios.

Further work will explore these issues—especially compositionality and local reasoning—theoretically, pragmatically, and empirically.

A   Recovery Timings

In this section, we report some recovery times for the various methods used in our experimental section. These were generated from a few recovery runs within a single home environment (given the Covid 19-related restrictions prevalent in the UK at the time). These runs both helped inform parameters within the model and are presented to give the reader a feel for the different recovery techniques.

Table 1. HP 'Sure Recover' times for both the network-based recovery and embedded recovery. Times are given in seconds and are based on a number of recovery cycles.

Recovery steps	'Sure Recover'	'Embedded'
Initialize Recovery	40	30
Copy from embedded	N/A	20
Download and verify Recovery Agent	100	N/A
Boot to recovery agent	15	25
Initialize Drive	25	N/A
Download Imaged	1130	N/A
Verify Image	50	40
Extract Image	180	145
Install Drivers	60	80
Windows Installer to Config Screen	480	480

Table 2. USB Based Recovery times. The first part of the table shows the steps in using a recovery tool to create a bootable windows installer. The second section shows times for the install from the USB stick. Again, times are quoted in seconds.

USB step	Time
Create Bootable USB	
Download recovery tool	60
Run Tool	45
Partition USB	35
Download Imaged	1260
Extract Image to USB	3120
Install from USB	
Boot USB to Installer	120
Partition Disk	60
Install Windows and Drivers to disk	780
Windows Installer to Config Screen	480

B Additional Graphs

B.1 Recovery performance

USB-based recovery requires that users have a clean system to download an image, along with an available USB stick. Hence, within the model, we make assumptions around the levels of availability during recovery. Figure 7 shows the rate at which recovery is not possible under these assumptions with the different attack scenarios.

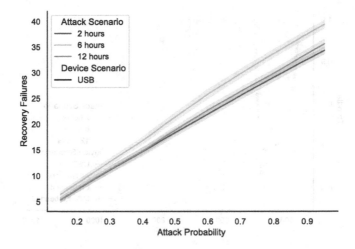

Fig. 7. USB failures

B.2   Network performance

Network contention is a large factor in recovery solutions, particularly when downloading images from the internet. Figs. 8 through 13 show the effective slow-down of the network because of contention. It is clear that where attacks happen quickly and with the attack happening within a two-hour period, the network load caused by recovery is significant. As attacks slow and become more gradual—say, as malware is distributed through email—then the network contention is reduced as the recovery load is spread over more time.

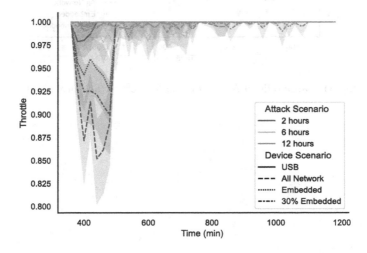

Fig. 8. Large office LAN throttling for 15% attack probability.

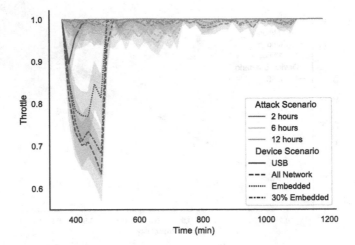

Fig. 9. Large office LAN throttling for 25% attack probability.

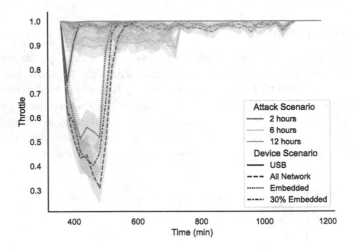

Fig. 10. Large office LAN throttling for 40% attack probability.

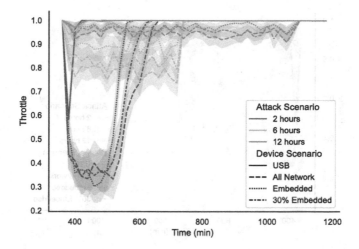

Fig. 11. Large office LAN throttling for 60% attack probability.

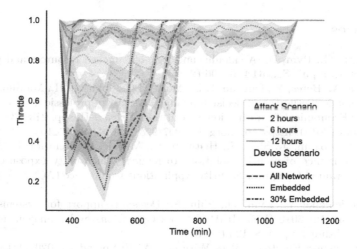

Fig. 12. Large office LAN throttling for 80% attack probability.

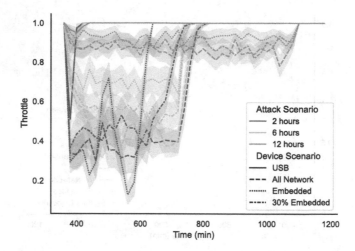

Fig. 13. Large office LAN throttling for 95% attack probability.

References

1. Anderson, G., Pym, D.: A calculus and logic of bunched resources and processes. Theoret. Comput. Sci. **614**, 63–96 (2016)
2. Baldwin, A., Beres, Y., Duggan, G.B., Mont, M.C., Johnson, H., Middup, C., Shiu, S.: Economic methods and decision making by security professionals. In: Schneier, B. (ed.) Economics of Information Security and Privacy III, pp. 213–238. Springer, New York (2013). https://doi.org/10.1007/978-1-4614-1981-5_10
3. Beres, Y., Griffin, J., Shiu, S., Heitman, M., Markle, D., Ventura, P.: Analysing the performance of security solutions to reduce vulnerability exposure window. In: 2008 Annual Computer Security Applications Conference (ACSAC), pp. 33–42 (2008)
4. Beresnevichiene, Y., Pym, D., Shiu, S.: Decision support for systems security investment. In: 2010 IEEE/IFIP Network Operations and Management Symposium Workshops, pp. 118–125 (2010)
5. Binary Defense: Emotet Evolves With new Wi-Fi Spreader (2020). https://www.binarydefense.com/emotet-evolves-with-new-wi-fi-spreader/. Accessed 28 June 2021
6. Birtwistle, G.: Demos—Discrete Event Modelling on Simula. Macmillan (1979)
7. [blinded]: SysModels Julia Package. Accessed 10 May 2021
8. Bromiley, M.: SANS 2019 Incident Response(IR) Survey: It's Time for aChange. SANS (2012). https://www.sans.org/reading-room/whitepapers/analyst/2019-incident-response-ir-survey-time-change-39070. Accessed 28 June 2021
9. Caulfield, T., Pym, D.: Modelling and simulating systems security policy. In: Proceedings of SimuTools (2015)
10. cisa: Emotet Malware (2017). https://us-cert.cisa.gov/ncas/alerts/aa20-280a. Accessed 28 June 2021
11. Collinson, M., Monahan, B., Pym, D.: A Discipline of Math. Systems Modelling. College Publns (2012)
12. Collinson, M., Pym, D.: Algebra and logic for resource-based systems modelling. Math. Struct. Comput. Sci. **19**, 959–1027 (2009)

13. Dietz, G., Gillespie, N.: Recovery of trust: case studies of organisational failures and trust repair, vol. 5. Institute of Business Ethics London (2012)
14. Parizo, E.: Maersk CISO Says NotPeyta Devastated Several Unnamed US firms (2019). https://www.darkreading.com/threat-intelligence/maersk-ciso-says-notpeyta-devastated-several-unnamed-us-firms/a/d-id/1336558?page_number=2. Accessed 28 June 2021
15. Frazzon, E.M., Silva, L.S., Hurtado, P.A.: Synchronizing and improving supply chains through the application of cyber-physical systems. IFAC-PapersOnLine **48**(3), 2059–2064 (2015)
16. Gelenbe, E., Wang, Y.: Modelling the impact of cyber-attacks on web based sales (2019, Submitted for Publication)
17. Gibbs, M.: Your top it hates. Netw. World Canada **24**(8), N_A (2008)
18. Greenburg, A.: The Untold Story of NotPetya, the Most Devastating Cyberattack in History (2018). https://www.wired.com/story/notpetya-cyberattack-ukraine-russia-code-crashed-the-world/. Accessed 28 June 2021
19. Hennessy, M., Milner, R.: On observing nondeterminism and concurrency. In: de Bakker, J., van Leeuwen, J. (eds.) ICALP 1980. LNCS, vol. 85, pp. 299–309. Springer, Heidelberg (1980). https://doi.org/10.1007/3-540-10003-2_79
20. Hewlett-Packard Laboratories: Security Analytics. https://www.hpl.hp.com/news/2011/oct-dec/security_analytics.html. Accessed 10 May 2021
21. HP: HP SureRecover. HP (2021). https://www8.hp.com/h20195/v2/GetPDF.aspx/4AA7-4556ENW.pdf. Accessed 28 June 2021
22. Ishtiaq, S., O'Hearn, P.: BI as an assertion language for mutable data structures. In: Proceedings of POPL (2001)
23. Jung, J.Y., Blau, G., Pekny, J.F., Reklaitis, G.V., Eversdyk, D.: A simulation based optimization approach to supply chain management under demand uncertainty. Comput. Chem. Eng. **28**(10), 2087–2106 (2004)
24. Kral, P.: The Incident Handlers Handbook. SANS (2012). https://www.sans.org/reading-room/whitepapers/incident/incident-handlers-handbook-33901. Accessed 28 June 2021
25. LogRhythm Labs: A Technical Analysis of WannaCry Ransomware (2017). https://logrhythm.com/blog/a-technical-analysis-of-wannacry-ransomware/. Accessed 28 June 2021
26. Lynch, N.A., Tuttle, M.R.: An introduction to input/output automata. CWI Quart. **2**, 219–246 (1989)
27. Microsoft: Windows Recovery Environment (Windows RE). Microsoft (2017). https://docs.microsoft.com/en-us/windows-hardware/manufacture/desktop/windows-recovery-environment-windows-re-technical-reference. Accessed 28 June 2021
28. Microsoft: Apply features and settings on your devices using device profiles in Microsoft Intune. Microsoft (2020). https://docs.microsoft.com/en-us/mem/intune/configuration/device-profiles. Accessed 28 June 2021
29. Microsoft: Microsoft Digital Defense Report - Sept 2020. Microsoft (2020), https://query.prod.cms.rt.microsoft.com/cms/api/am/binary/RWxPuf/. Accessed 08 Aug 2021
30. Microsoft: Deploy Windows 10 using PXE and Configuration Manager. Microsoft (2021). https://docs.microsoft.com/en-us/windows/deployment/deploy-windows-cm/deploy-windows-10-using-pxe-and-configuration-manager. Accessed 28 June 2021

31. Microsoft: Microsoft Deployment Toolkit. Microsoft (2021). https://docs.microsoft.com/en-us/windows/deployment/deploy-windows-mdt/get-started-with-the-microsoft-deployment-toolkit. Accessed 28 June 2021
32. Microsoft: Overview of Windows Autopilot. Microsoft (2021). https://docs.microsoft.com/en-us/mem/autopilot/windows-autopilot. Accessed 28 June 2021
33. Milner, R.: Calculi for synchrony and asynchrony. Theor. Comput. Sci. **25**(3), 267–310 (1983)
34. Milner, R.: Communication and Concurrency. Prentice Hall, New York (1989)
35. Milner, R.: The Space and Motion of Communicating Agents. Cambridge University Press, Cambridge (2009)
36. Milner, R.: Bigraphs as a model for mobile interaction. In: Corradini, A., Ehrig, H., Kreowski, H.-J., Rozenberg, G. (eds.) ICGT 2002. LNCS, vol. 2505, pp. 8–13. Springer, Heidelberg (2002). https://doi.org/10.1007/3-540-45832-8_3
37. O'Hearn, P.: Resources, concurrency, and local reasoning. Theor. Comput. Sci. **375**(1–3), 271–307 (2007)
38. O'Hearn, P., Reynolds, J., Yang, H.: Local reasoning about programs that alter data structures. In: Fribourg, L. (ed.) CSL 2001. LNCS, vol. 2142, pp. 1–19. Springer, Heidelberg (2001). https://doi.org/10.1007/3-540-44802-0_1
39. Pym, D.: Resource semantics: logic as a modelling technology. ACM SIGLOG News **6**(2), 5–41 (2019). https://doi.org/10.1145/3326938.3326940
40. Report, T.D.: Ryuk in 5 Hours. The DFIR Report (2020). https://thedfirreport.com/2020/10/18/ryuk-in-5-hours/. Accessed 08 Aug 2021
41. Reynolds, J.: Separation logic: a logic for shared mutable data structures. In: Proceedings of LICS (2002)
42. Rhodes, C., Bettany, A.: Windows Installation and Update Troubleshooting. Apress, New York (2016)
43. Hurley, S., Sood, K.: NotPetya Technical Analysis Part II: Further Findings and Potential for MBR Recovery (2017). https://www.crowdstrike.com/blog/petrwrap-technical-analysis-part-2-further-findings-and-potential-for-mbr-recovery/. Accessed 28 June 2021
44. Stirling, C.: Modal and Temporal Properties of Processes. Springer, Heidelberg (2001). https://doi.org/10.1007/978-1-4757-3550-5
45. Caulfield, T., Pym, D.: Improving security policy decisions with models. IEEE Secur. Priv. **13**(5), 34–41 (2015)
46. M.D.T.I. Team: Human-operated ransomware attacks: a preventable disaster. Microsoft (2021). https://www.microsoft.com/security/blog/2020/03/05/human-operated-ransomware-attacks-a-preventable-disaster/. Accessed 08 Aug 2021
47. Tweneboah-Kodua, S., Atsu, F., Buchanan, W.: Impact of cyberattacks on stock performance: a comparative study. Inf. Comput. Secur. (2018)
48. Vynck, G.D., Lerman, R., Nakashima, E., Alcantara, C.: The anatomy of a ransomware attack. Washington Post (2021). https://www.washingtonpost.com/technology/2021/07/09/how-ransomware-attack-works/?itid=mr_innovations_1. Accessed 08 Aug 2021
49. Yang, H., O'Hearn, P.: A semantic basis for local reasoning. In: Nielsen, M., Engberg, U. (eds.) FoSSaCS 2002. LNCS, vol. 2303, pp. 402–416. Springer, Heidelberg (2002). https://doi.org/10.1007/3-540-45931-6_28

Experimental Comparison of Open Source Discrete-Event Simulation Frameworks

Oskar Skak Kristiansen, Ulrik Sandberg, Casper Hansen, Morten Skovgaard Jensen, Jonas Friederich[✉], and Sanja Lazarova-Molnar

Mærsk Mc-Kinney Møller Institute, University of Southern Denmark, Campusvej 55, 5000 Odense, Denmark
jofr@mmmi.sdu.dk

Abstract. Simulation is a growing and very relevant field today. With many application domains and increasing computational power, simulations are solving an increasing number of real-world problems in a safe and efficient manner. The aim of this study is to make an experimental comparison among popular open-source discrete-event simulation frameworks, selected through a thorough survey. The experimental comparison considers numerous parameters, the most important of which were studied via an operational experiment of performance, as well as a survey of surface level characteristics and usability. We initially surveyed 50 frameworks for high-level parameters relating to corresponding implementations, filtered by the generality of domain, license, popularity, etc. As a result, we shortlisted five frameworks, which we then performance-tested in an operational experiment. We discovered significant performance differences under the given loads. We also completed a usability survey to provide a holistic impression of the frameworks, further identifying key differences.

Keywords: Discrete-event simulation · Open source · Performance comparison

1 Introduction

Simulation is a growing and very relevant field today. With many application domains and increasing computational power, simulations are solving an increasing number of real-world problems in a safe and efficient manner [1, 2]. Simulation is often used to conduct experiments where a real-world model would be either impractical or even impossible to make, saving on both cost and/or time. This enables analysts, engineers and stakeholders to communicate, verify and understand concepts and ideas concerning complex systems [3].

In the current literature, we have not identified a comprehensive comparison of open-source simulation frameworks in terms of the parameters that we investigated, i.e., performance, lines of code (LOC) for minimal implementation, community engagement, etc. [4]–[8]. In this article, we share our findings from investigating and comparing various open-source libraries available for discrete-event simulation (DES). Furthermore, we use a classical simulation model case study to experimentally perform the comparison.

D. Jiang and H. Song (Eds.): SIMUtools 2021, LNICST 424, pp. 315–330, 2022.
https://doi.org/10.1007/978-3-030-97124-3_24

While no similar comparison is available, there are numerous comprehensive studies comparing simulation frameworks in different specific or even more general contexts [6, 8, 9]. With this, we add to the current literature a quantitative comparison of several state-of-the-art open-source simulation frameworks in a more experimental and practical manner.

Being a relatively large field of study, it is obvious that choosing the right simulation tool for the job is one of the initial important decisions with high impact on the results. This is emphasized by performance as well as functionality required by the researcher often being a limiting factor for selection of tools. As many libraries exist, choosing the right one is not trivial.

As noted, the aim of this study is to compare among popular open-source simulation libraries in an experimental way. The purpose of this comparison is to provide researchers that need to use open-source DES frameworks, a guidance for a more informed choice. The study will seek to answer the following research questions: 1) What open-source modelling and simulation libraries exist? 2) How do these open-source libraries compare on specific parameters related to the quality attributes described within the field of software engineering and related categorical differences?, and 3) Which frameworks perform the best during run-time in regards to performance and related quantitative measures? In answering these questions, we aim to provide simulation practitioners with insight in the open-source modelling and simulation frameworks included in this study.

The paper is structured as follows. In Sect. 2, we examine the existing literature related to open-source DES frameworks. We present the overall research methodology involved in Sect. 3. This includes the search process that we used to identify articles and frameworks relevant to the context of open-source simulation frameworks. In the same section we also present the primary research method used in this project. In Sect. 4 we present and discuss the results of the operational experiment and the usability survey. We discuss whether a recommendation can be made from the investigated frameworks in Sect. 5, and lastly conclude in Sect. 6.

2   Related Work

The field of simulation is, while growing, already widely used throughout many disciplines. As a consequence, many studies comparing existing frameworks in different, and often quite specific contexts have been done.

To identify articles, similar in nature to our point of interest, we utilized scholarly database querying, which we further detail in Sect. 3.2. While no exact duplication in topic and context could be found, many related works exist. This includes works such as that of Franceschini et al., which is quite similar in nature to this project, except for its inclusion of proprietary simulation frameworks whereas we limit our investigation to open-source frameworks as well as the parameters included in the comparison, such as the ease of use comparison as well as some performance measures [5]. Other works include those by Majid et al. that has a similar methodology and purpose, with the significant difference of comparing frameworks on the accuracy parameter instead of performance, as well as the work by Dagkakis and Heavy, which focuses on operations research, and Knyazkov and Kovalchuk, which while similar in methodology, limits its scope to interactive virtual environments [4, 6, 7]. Further, analyses of single frameworks are quite exhaustive, including Göbel et. al., which focuses on DESMO-J, and Barlas and Heavy, whose focus is on the Knowledge Extraction Tool, all of which are quite useful in informing about the available frameworks themselves, but does not constitute the comparison between frameworks this study attempts to lay out [8, 10].

As implied above, while much published research in the field of modelling and simulation exists, they all differ in their primary focus, such as comparing frameworks on another criteria than performance, or in their criteria for inclusion in the comparison, such as not focusing exclusively on open source frameworks. This is noted in the aforementioned Dagkakis and Heavey journal, wherein they suggest future work should include a weighted comparison of open source DES frameworks (that is, the objective of this paper) [4]. Beyond the differing focus and chosen parameters of related works, another important aspect of these works is the time period in which they were conducted. Per the nature of the ever-evolving open source landscape, particularly in such an active field, new analysis of frameworks is needed intermittently, as any attempt of illuminating the state of the art landscape will quickly be partially outdated if not entirely deprecated. Lastly, we should note the field of study is simply too big as for any project to include all related existing research in its analysis. This is not of major concern in regard to the novelty of this project, as the methodology is quite specific, and the emphasis on the various parameters is almost sure to be unique. Further, although the environment is very controlled, different algorithmic comparisons will yield vastly different results in regard to performance of the selected frameworks, meaning the resulting comparison is sure to contribute to existing material.

3 Research Methodology

In this section we describe the research methodology for our survey, including the experiment but also the formulation of the evaluation criteria and the subsequent filtering of the numerous simulation frameworks under initial consideration.

3.1 Search Process

For the purpose of identifying related works and potential gaps in the existing literature, we utilized slightly broad search terms in the Web of Science academic research database. We narrowed down the search through additional constraints, including time, relevance, number of citations, etc., to identify articles relating to the relatively broad problem definition of this study. From these articles, we identified potential candidates for the technical comparison of open source DES frameworks through either direct mention in the given articles, or through references. With this methodology, we extracted 50 candidates for potential testing. We filtered out the candidates that are no longer actively supported in combination with additional filter: "LastUpdated $\geq 2018 - 01 - 01$". The result was the 13 frameworks shown in Table 1.

Table 1. Framework classification.

Name	Year	Domain	OS	Language	Ext	Lic	Vis	Engagement
SimPy	20	3	3	Python	1	3	–	26 (26s + 0f)
SimJulia	19	3	3	Julia	1	3	–	138 (22s + 106f)
OMNeT	19	3	3	C++	2	2	3D	277 (226s + 51f)
JaamSim	20	3	3	Java	2	3	3D	100 (77s + 33f)
NS-3	20	1	3	C++	2	2	3D	578 (202s + 376f)
Facsimile	20	2	3	Scala	1	3	–	26 (20s + 16f)
JavaSim	20	3	3	Java	1	3	–	36 (20s + 16f)
J-Sim	20	3	3	Java	1	3	2D	2 (1s + 1f)
Root-Sim	19	3	1	C	1	2	–	28 (13s + 15f)
TerraME	20	1	3	Lua	1	3	2D	41 (27s + 14f)
SSJ	18	3	3	Java	1	3	–	101 (68s + 33f)
VLE	19	3	3	C++	1	2	3D	34 (14s + 20f)
ADevs	20	3	2	Java	1	3	–	11 (4s + 7f)

The reasoning for excluding frameworks not updated before the specified date is that software frameworks need to update often, if not for functional reasons, then at least as a response to the ever-changing meta environment of the different operating systems, protocols of communication, etc. [11]. After the filtering on dates, we researched the remaining 13 frameworks and identified the most important characteristics, to give a more holistic impression of the overall collection. We summarize our findings in Table 1. For the domain ('Dom'), we gave a 1–3 score with 1 being very domain specific, 2 allowing generic use, and 3 decidedly generic in its domain. The OS columns refers to how many of the three most common operating systems (Microsoft, Mac OS and Linux-based) the frameworks are directly integrated into (meaning the frameworks can function without extensive custom configuration, usage of virtual machines, etc.). For the extension category ('Ext'), we denoted frameworks with only manual custom extension with 1, and frameworks with specific mechanisms for extension, such as offering virtual extension methods on existing modules which allows for modification without changing the underlying architecture or offering convenient ways of defining new options, data structures, etc., with 2. With license ('Lic') we denote frameworks with 1 if no distribution is allowed, 2 if only non-commercial distribution allowed, and 3 if the license is completely open. The Engagement category shows the GitHub star (s) and forking (f) score of the framework repositories.

To arrive at the five chosen frameworks, the following filters were used: (Domain-Score $==3$) $\wedge$ (LicenseScore $==3$) $\wedge$ (Max(Engagement)). There are several reasons for the choice of these filters. First, all 13 frameworks are recently updated and have decent possibilities in terms of development environments This means the filtering must be done on other criteria. Parameters, such as a graphical user interface (GUI) environment for development, documentation and integrated extension possibilities cannot be said to be objective measures of suitability, since their importance is almost entirely dependent on the context. Domain (as defined in the summation above), however, is obviously quite important in this context as the aim is to analyse generic frameworks. Further, licensing is of vital importance, as whatever the technical benefits of a framework might be, if the licensing is not permissive enough the framework is simply not usable in many cases. In the last filter the frameworks with the greatest level of engagement are chosen. From the sequential filtering, five frameworks were chosen to be included in the experiment. Each framework will be introduced below.

SimPy is based on standard Python, and can be described as a domain specific library. It is specifically designed for DES, but can obviously be extended to include continuous simulation through custom extension in Python [12]. It is distributed under the open MIT license, meaning all modifications and extensions are allowed, and maintains an active and widely engaged community.

SimJulia differs from SimPy in that continuous event processing is directly integrated, along with discrete event processing which is what we are interested in, in this context. It is technically quite similar to SimPy, in that the API modelling imitates that of SimPy [13]. Its documentation and community engagement are extensive, and the licensing is identical to that of SimPy.

JaamSim differs from SimPy and SimJulia in its method of simulation implementation, in that developers can use its IDE (Integrated Development Environment) and integrated graphical input functionality. Beyond that, it is quite similar in supported functionality and like SimPy, focuses directly on DES [14]. The functionality offered in the IDE is quite extensive, but potential users should still realize that many third-party opportunities are perhaps better integrated in the CLI (Command Line Interface) style development frameworks described above.

SSJ (Stochastic Simulation in Java) is, as the name suggests, a Java-based simulation framework, whose primary focus is on DES [15]. As such, SSJ includes the expected tools and methods for developing standard DES simulations. SSJ supports both continuous and hybrid simulation, and allows developers to implement models in a variety of general purpose languages, as well as simulation specific languages [15].

JavaSim is described as an 'object-oriented, discrete event simulation toolkit' [16], directly integrated with the general purpose Java language despite the specific paradigm, with a focus on flexibility, extensibility and efficiency. The specific simulation paradigm supported by JavaSim is 'continuous time-discrete event', which means it includes the expected tools relating to the context of this paper and allowed for relatively straightforward implementation of the chosen model.

3.2 Method Formulation

The primary research method in this study is experimental, specifically, a controlled experiment within the domain of Software Engineering, as described in "A Survey of Controlled Experiments in Software Engineering" [17]. The definition of a controlled experiment in this context is operational, and relates quite closely to the quasi-experimental method in classic scientific terminology, in that it involved conducting software engineering tasks to observe and compare processes, methods, etc. [17]. This definition and related procedures follows the stated purpose more closely than the different classical definitions, as there obviously is no need to introduce control groups or randomization in order to assess the chosen parameters [18], as the experiment can be directly controlled in a relatively precise manner. The experiment will be used to test parameters related to the performance of the included frameworks, specifically computational time under given loads as well as CPU usage, which are of significant importance within the field of simulation, given its resource intensive nature.

Beyond the primary method of experimentation, an arguably significant part of the comparison involves the characteristics described in Sect. 3.1, as well as the unstructured usability survey described in Sect. 3.5. As is evident, the procedure of this study will be exploratory and descriptive, as is commonplace in this context [19].

3.3 Experimental Simulation Model

We designed the simulation model to contain elements that are typical for discrete stochastic models. The simulation model used for the experiment emulates a street food like scenario, with three important aspects, namely customers are able to order multiple times, there is a limited amount of customers that can be in the street food at once and they pay before they leave.

In the simulation, agents "arrive" at the street food according to an exponential distribution. Following arrival, customers queue for a table, after which they decide to either order food or drinks immediately. If they decide to order food, they will distribute over three different food stands, namely burger, pizza or Chinese with an equal probability. For each food stand there is an associated probability distribution with both waiting for the food, as well as eating it afterwards. If a customer chooses to order a drink instead of food, he/she will immediately queue at the drink stand. Once served, he/she will decide if he/she also wants to order food. If he/she again decides to order food, he/she will proceed through the food order flow described earlier. When a customer is done eating or drinking, he/she has a final decision, he/she can either repeat the entire flow and thus order food/drinks again or leave the street food through a checkout process.

The model is formulated to be simple enough to not introduce errors or disputes in implementation across different frameworks, while still containing several of the elements which are ordinarily used in DES, such as limited relative resource usage, concurrency and generation of values from commonly used distributions.

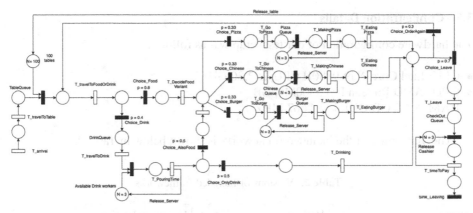

Fig. 1. Stochastic Petri Net of the experimental simulation model.

3.4 Framework Testing

We use the primary exploratory experiment, as described above, to compare the performance of the selected simulation frameworks during what could be described as normal use within the context of DES. That is to say, the model described above means to mirror a typical relatively low level task, albeit likely less intensive. However, since there is a variety of factors that can potentially influence the performance parameter, such as spikes in resource usage of background tasks or scheduled processes occurring, even within the relatively controlled environment, measures were taken to minimize influences external to the experiment itself. Since the complexity of the tested frameworks is of a relatively high degree, it is not necessarily the case that a fair comparison can be made with derived generic conclusions if the input to the simulation model is the same across all tests. Reasons for this include, as an example, the benefits obtained from overhead in a framework potentially being helpful when processing a resource intensive task, but has a negative trade-off in terms of comparison if the load is small, since such optimizations potentially would not outweigh their cost if the runtime is small. To avoid judging on a biased foundation, the simulation model described above is ran with an increasing input load from 25,000 to 500,000 customers (n), increasing by 25,000 per interval. Further, to reduce the variation in results as a consequence of environmental factors (such as the various background processes, services, etc.) each input interval is replicated ten times. To validate the summarized results, each individual run duration was inspected, ensuring no outliers would significantly diverge the summed results. The CPU usage percentage as well as computational time for each interval was recorded in order to properly analyse the performance of each framework. The tests were ran in a stable and as close to identical environment as possible to make the results quantitatively comparable. Each test can be seen in the projects repository [20], along with the implementation of the model in each of the tested frameworks.

3.5 Configuration Details

The hardware configuration of our test setup was as follows:

- CPU: Intel Core™ i9-9880H CPU @ 2.30 GHz
- GPU: AMD Radeon Pro 5500M 4 GB
- RAM: 8 * 2 GB DDR4 @ 2667 MHz

The versioning of the included frameworks is shown below in Table 2.

Table 2. Versions of included frameworks

Name	Version	Language Version
Javasim	2.3	15.0.2 (java)
JaamSim	2021.01	15.0.2 (java)
SSJ	3.3.1	15.0.2 (java)
Simply	4.0.1	2.7.16 (python)
SimJulia	1.2	15.0.2 (java)

3.6 Usability Comparison

The usability comparison was done in a relatively informal manner, since the primary focus of the applied research methodology was to test the performance and other naturally quantifiable aspects. We still feel, however, that even a subjective usability assessment is useful to include, since it can be helpful to potential users. While there are formalized quantifiable measures for usability, we found many of the methodologies presented were not fully applicable and did not necessarily give a fair picture given the experience gained in the sequential process of developing the model in each framework. We deemed it best to simply reflect on important parameters regarding usability and derive a 'score' which was relative to the other frameworks, and simulation frameworks in general. Specifically, each developer filled a simple survey asking them to judge the given parameters within an interval from one to five, and then generalize the results. The specific parameters are presented in Sect. 4.1 along with how each parameter scores.

4 Results

In this section we present and analyse the data gathered from the aforementioned tests. This includes the results of the performance tests, but also a more usability focused analysis of the utilization of the different frameworks based on the experience of working with the frameworks in this project. Lastly, we will discuss the results and explore aspects related to the observed differences in performance and usability.

4.1 Performance Comparison

As mentioned in Sect. 3.4, each framework was tested under increasing load in the interval from n = 25,000 to n = 500,000, with each interval having a range of 25,000, meaning 20 individual results per framework were gathered. Further, each interval was repeated ten times to ensure the results would not be overly biased by outliers. In Fig. 2, the averaged computational times are shown.

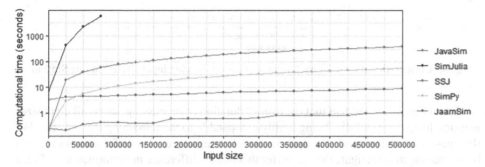

Fig. 2. Computational time for each framework given varying input size.

As is evident, the difference in performance under the given conditions and environment is very significant. Note, that due to time constraints and the very evident degradation in performance under increasing loads, the tests for SimJulia were halted after the tests with input size equal to 75,000. While JaamSim, SimPy, JavaSim and SSJ frameworks are somewhat comparable in performance, and follow a clearly evident linear progression under increasing load, SimJulia has a lot of variance between results internally, and is vastly slower under the recorded range of loads. Since SimJulia presents such a difference in both overall results and internal variance, further investigation of the framework was performed. Here, we focus on its difference to SimPy (a comparison with the other frameworks will be further explored below). As mentioned, SimJulia is written after the specification of the SimPy API. This means the internal processing is expressed syntactically very similar between SimJulia and SimPy. While this is convenient when attempting to perform functionally identical tests, it also means the possibility of human errors introduced in the test definition is quite low, since the given functionality needs only minimal translation to be functional in either environment. Further, to ensure the very significant difference and internal variance is not due to factors in the external environment, SimJulia's test was replicated numerous times in the environment, with similar results each time. While mistakes are always possible, the relative simplicity of the simulation model, along with the syntactic and functional similarity between SimJulia and SimPy, leads us to conclude that SimJulia likely simply performs far below the level of the other frameworks. This is further backed up by the large degree of popularity and extensiveness of the remaining frameworks relative to SimJulia. Simulation processing under a relatively large load is obviously quite complicated, and it seems SimJulia simply is not as fine-grained in its performance under increasing loads, as the other frameworks under consideration.

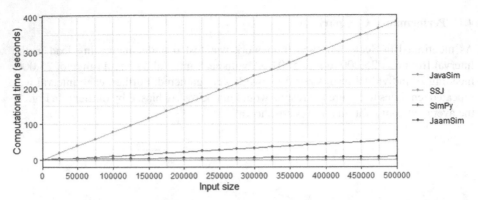

Fig. 3. Computational time for each framework given varying input size excluding SimJulia.

From Fig. 2, it is evident that the overall duration of processing across all input sizes is much longer in SimJulia, being hardly comparable to the remaining frameworks. For this reason, we will exclude SimJulia in the following discussion. In future work it could be interesting to investigate the reason for this drastic difference in performance. In Fig. 3 we show test results of the remaining frameworks.

As is evident, while all frameworks produce processing times which clearly have linear relationships to the loads, JaamSim and SSJ have a significantly smaller rate of growth. Practically, this means JaamSim and SSJ produce very similar processing times under the initial (and relatively light) load, but that the difference between the frameworks grows linearly, and JaamSim and SSJ outperforms SimPy and JavaSim increasingly significantly while the load increases. In future work, it could be interesting to explore if the exponential relationship between the graphs means SimPy actually has better performance with loads below the initial interval used here (that is, 25,000), as is loosely implied by the growing difference. Specifically, if the graph followed the implied relationship, it appears SimPy could outperform JaamSim in loads with input size slightly below the lower bounds in the experiment of 25,000.

In Fig. 4, the average CPU usages, in percentage, across the tested input intervals are shown. It is obvious from the graph, that JaamSim occupies a substantially greater percentage of the CPU for the lower input sizes, before gradually decreasing until it is around the level of the remaining frameworks. This is expected, given the nature of the JaamSim framework. While the remaining frameworks are integrated directly into general purpose programming languages, and could be described as a simulation library in the given languages, JaamSim is a standalone framework. One reason for the greater CPU usage could be attributed to the overhead of the standalone framework, even if it is compiled into an executable jar, similar to JavaSim and SSJ. This is supported by the development of the graph, since the overhead, if associated with the start-up of the framework, obviously would be a smaller part in the latter intervals, and the CPU usage, therefore, remains steady once the cost of the overhead is factored out by the larger overall cost of the framework running in steady use. In Fig. 5, we can see the CPU usage of JaamSim in the interval where input size equals 32,500, that is, the interval before the drop-off to a steady usage is found. Examining the graph, it is evident that a substantial percentage of the CPU is utilized by JaamSim in its beginning stages of execution, which drops off, in this case, after about 18 s (note that the run depicted shows 10 replications of the simulation).

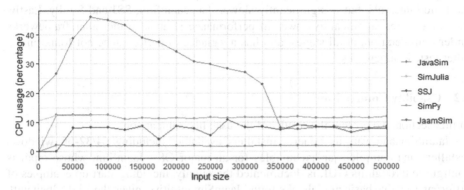

Fig. 4. Average CPU usage percentage across varying input sizes.

The trend identified in the CPU usage of JaamSim is not found in any of the CLI styled frameworks, which all remain relatively steady in their CPU usage throughout execution, despite the load. To conclude, it is evident that JaamSim is quite resource heavy in its beginning execution, which then tampers off during continuous use. Further JavaSim allocated substantially fewer resources than any other framework, which makes sense given its relatively slower execution across all tested intervals. SSJ and SimPy are quite similar in their CPU usage throughout the intervals, indicating there must be another reason for the significant difference in computational time needed to complete the simulations. Finally, SimJulia, for the few tested input sizes, is comparable to the other CLI styled frameworks in its CPU usage, meaning a lack of resource allocation is evidently not the reason for the reduced performance in comparison to the other frameworks.

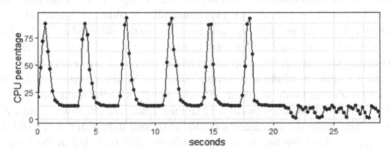

Fig. 5. JaamSim's CPU usage during runtime with n = 32,500.

To conclude, as is readily evident in the gathered results, there is a clear difference in performance between the frameworks, with SSJ outperforming the other frameworks in all tests within the given range. JaamSim is slightly behind SSJ on this parameter but follow relatively closely. This difference grows at an exponential rate in comparison to JavaSim and SimPy, meaning JaamSim and SSJ performs relatively better under increasing loads. SimPy is only slightly behind in the initial intervals but is slower throughout the range. JavaSim has a linear development in computational time across the tested intervals, but is significantly slower than JaamSim, SSJ and SimPy. Lastly, SimJulia scores significantly lower in performance relative to the other frameworks under consideration, at all stages, and has a variance in performance not found in the other tested frameworks.

4.2 Usability Comparison

In this section, we present the results of the usability comparison.

JaamSim had various generic installers available, including 64/32-bit windows installers and compiled jar executables for all major OSs. JaamSim, whose input is configured through its GUI, is documented thoroughly, including start-up examples of different available basic models. We found JaamSim intuitive, given the GUI, albeit with relatively poor debugging opportunities. Documentation and community engagement seems to be very limited on the more specific issues.

SimPy does not have a dedicated installer, given its integration in standard Python. This means the installation is specific to the given users' context, such as IDE integration, pip, etc. As a non-GUI framework, the documentation felt extra critical in order to facilitate an efficient workflow. Fortunately, both core concepts of the framework as well as DES vocabulary had been maintained throughout the documentation. It also featured blogs, examples and start-up walk-through guides. Effectively, this meant that the chosen simulation model was implemented easily. Besides the documentation, another aspect which felt beneficial and greatly impacted the feeling of "ease of use" was that we were free to extend, modify and structure the code as it optimally fitted our needs.

We found SimJulia had a far greater barrier to entrance than the other frameworks. Like SimPy, SimJulia is CLI based. It was quite difficult to use, relative to other frameworks. Setting up the correct SimJulia environment proved to be very difficult. The official documentation was incomplete and deprecated. Navigating to the projects' GitHub page resulted in conflicting results, as it recommended an older version of Julia than the documentation. This change, however, did not solve the documented examples. Very little community guidance exists, and we had to look to the SimJulia repositories test suite for the particular versioning. Once up and running, the model was easier to implement, however this was more a tribute to the completeness of SimPy's documentation and the fact that SimJulia's had modelled their API after SimPy's implementation.

The initial installation and setup of JavaSim was quite straightforward and well documented. Further, while documentation could not be said to be extensive, it did include some examples to illustrate the most basic tools of DES included in the framework. These examples were not as fully illustrative as would be ideal, but they were a good starting point. The framework did require more than surface level knowledge of Java, since things like parallelism, which is obviously vital to performance in simulation, were mostly left up to the developer to manage.

SSJ, like the other CLI based frameworks, does not come with an integrated installer, but is available through most of the common package managers such as Maven, Gradle, etc. The documentation was extensive, easy to understand and included examples. Additionally, a lot of examples were also provided in the repository which gave intuitive examples to work with. An important aspect of SSJ was its emphasis on using the object oriented paradigm. When compared to the more scripting oriented languages, SSJ felt a lot more structured and making more complicated models in SSJ feels facilitated better in comparison to the remaining frameworks. In Table 3 the score of the chosen parameters of usability is summarized.

Table 3. Ease of use comparison.

	SimJulia	JaamSim	SimPy	SSJ	JavaSim
Startup documentation	1	5	4	4	3
Best practice examples	1	3	5	5	3
Extension options	3	4	3	3	3
Errors during development	1	3	4	4	2
Time to implement	2	3	4	4	1
Lines of code to simulate	4(66)	5(6)	4(62)	1(504)	1(614)
Overall ease of use	12	23	24	21	13

Note, that each score is given within a one to five interval. For all parameters five is the best possible score. We will briefly address each parameter which is not intuitively understandable. Startup documentation refers to the 'get started' type of documentation often found within the documentation of development frameworks. Extension options refers to the intuitiveness and availability of methods to extend the framework with custom implementation. Lines of code shows the actual lines it took to implement the model depicted in Fig. 1, denoted within parenthesis after the respective scores (the JaamSim count refers to the script initializing and timing of the JAR (Java Archive) executable). From the gathered parameters an overall ease of use score was given by weighing each parameter equally. Note that JaamSim LoC, while not directly comparable given its different interface, has gotten the highest score since there is no code to write or manage. Another significant aspect of usability in the context is the framework language. Java and python are both very popular languages, and it could be argued that the choice of language would have a greater impact of overall usability. However, since it is very hard to quantify the difference in usability between two high level languages, this has not been directly included in the comparison

5   Discussion

In this section we will briefly discuss some of the most obvious questions in regard to the results of this paper. This includes whether a clear recommendation of a specific framework can be made and a discussion concerning the validity of the testing methodology utilized.

5.1   Comparison

An obvious subject to discuss is whether a concrete recommendation can be made, after evaluating the results. First, it is obvious that if the given load is comparable to the range tested in this project, and the performance parameter is of primary importance, JaamSim could be recommended if the GUI-styled builder is preferable in the given context. Further, SSJ could be recommended if the CLI-styled interface would be preferable, and performance is of greatest importance. However, performance is obviously not the only relevant parameter when choosing a framework. The other parameters tested in this paper related to usability or ease of use can be, depending on the context, at least equally important or even more so than performance. This includes what one could denote as more technical ease of use, such as the extension options and best practice examples (since the user in question in this case is an at least reasonably experienced developer). While it can certainly be argued that the results are of a subjective nature, it will still be of relevance to the aim of this study. The biggest discrepancy between the types of frameworks is in their integration in high level, widely used languages. It could be argued that this is a major advantage of the CLI based frameworks, as the extension and modification opportunities are endless. However, it is not necessarily relevant, depending on the issue at hand. Because of this, no generic conclusion can be drawn, but it is certainly an impactful precursor to an outright recommendation. Lastly, individual developers will obviously have differing preferences in terms of language used, interface, paradigm, etc. In conclusion, no clear recommendation can be made. However, if evaluating from the criteria examined in this article alone, it could be argued that a recommendation could be made for JaamSim if performance is of primary importance and the GUI builder is acceptable, or SSJ if integration directly in the environment of one of the most popular high-level languages would be preferable.

5.2   Test Validity

One almost universal criticism that can be levied in this context of testing a quantifiable parameter such as performance, is that the implementation is subjective, especially since the technologies used are of relatively high complexity. Specifically, the argument could be made that the frameworks performance is directly dependent on the individual implementation. This includes aspects such as integrated parallelization and opportunities for extension (one example of this could be the lower-level language integration in Python for performance-critical modules). This is a valid concern, but we would argue it is not directly applicable in the context of this project. The reason for this lies in the aim of the project, since the evaluation and comparison are geared towards informing on the aspects of these frameworks under what we loosely classify as normal work. While it is hard to quantify as a term, we can be specific in the methodology used to achieve that aim. First, all implementations follow the 'best practice' implied by their respective documentation, meaning effort was given to implement the tests in the way recommended by the framework's creators. Second, the simulation model was kept quite simple. Lastly, given the holistic nature of the desired results in this project, each test was implemented in a largely similar context to the expected use of the conclusions, meaning a developer with at least basic knowledge of simulation theory and programming methodologies, but with no specific knowledge regarding the given framework.

6 Conclusion

The aim of this study was to identify open-source modelling and simulation libraries and compare them on parameters related to performance and usability. 50 frameworks were initially considered, identified from the semi-structured material collection, which were filtered down on the basis of the following parameters: nature of domain, openness of license, popularity and how recently optimizing or modifying updates were released. After the filtering, five frameworks were extracted for further testing: JaamSim, SimPy, SimJulia, SSJ and JavaSim. JaamSim is a GUI based simulation builder as opposed to SimPy, SSJ, JavaSim and SimJulia which are CLI based, and integrated in Python, Julia and Java respectively.

SSJ was found to perform the best across all intervals in terms of computational time, while utilizing a relatively high percentage of the CPU. Closely following was JaamSim, which also took up a large average percentage of the CPU, especially at smaller input sizes. SimPy was comparable to the aforementioned frameworks for smaller input sizes, but was found to have a higher rate of change in regard to increasing input sizes, scoring significantly lower for the larger input sizes, albeit with a lower percentage of the CPU utilized. JavaSim was found to be significantly slower across all input sizes, but utilized a much lower percentage of the CPU. All aforementioned frameworks were found to have a linear development in the relationship between increasing input sizes and the time needed to process them, but with varying rates. Further, each frameworks' utilization of the CPU and their respective performance on the tested input sizes was found to be corresponding, with the exception of JaamSim in the smaller intervals, likely given the increased overhead of the framework. In the usability comparison SimPy scored the highest, with JaamSim being slightly behind. Lastly, SimJulia scored the lowest in both performance and usability. It was much slower under the given load range and showed worrying internal variation in its performance. Further, SimJulia's documentation was often incomplete and/or outdated, leading to a challenging user experience in implementing the selected model. JavaSim scores only slightly higher in usability, given especially the LoC it took to implement the model.

While much literature pertaining to the subject of this study exists, the landscape of simulation frameworks is so vast and ever evolving that we believe that studies of this type would be relevant to simulation practitioners. However, many of the frameworks that we 'filtered out', as well as frameworks not included in the first place, could be definitely be investigated further, since the parameters we chose to filter on might differ for other researchers. Namely, our focus was on well-supported, open-source and general simulation frameworks.

References

1. Maclay, D.: Simulation gets into the loop. IEEE Rev. **43**(3), 109–112 (1997)
2. Sarkar, N., Halim, S.: Simulation of computer networks: simulators, methodologies and recommendations, presented at the 5th International Conference on Information Technology and Applications, ICITA 2008, January 2008
3. Banks, J., Carson II, J.S., Nelson, B., Nicol, D.: Discrete-Event System Simulation, 5th edition. Upper Saddle River: Pearson (2009)
4. Dagkakis, G., Heavey, C.: A review of open source discrete event simulation software for operations research. J. Simul. **10** (2015). https://doi.org/10.1057/jos.2015.9
5. Franceschini, R., Bisgambiglia, P.-A., Touraille, L., Bisgambiglia, P., Hill, D.: A survey of modelling and simulation software frameworks using discrete event system specification, **43** (2014)
6. Majid, M.A., Aickelin, U., Siebers, P.-O.: Comparing simulation output accuracy of discrete event and agent based models: a quantitative approach. SSRN J. (2009). https://www.ssrn.com/abstract=2830304. Accessed 09 Mar 2021
7. Knyazkov, K.V., Kovalchuk, S.V.: Modeling and simulation framework for development of interactive virtual environments. Procedia Comput. Sci. **29**, 332–342 (2014)
8. Göbel, J., Joschko, P., Koors, A., Page, B.: The discrete event simulation framework DESMO-J: review, comparison to other frameworks and latest development, 100–109 (2013)
9. Mualla, Y., Bai, W., Galland, S., Nicolle, C.: Comparison of Agent-based simulation frameworks for unmanned aerial transportation applications. Procedia Comput. Sci. **130** (2018). https://trid.trb.org/view/1509849. Accessed 09 Mar 2021
10. Barlas, P., Heavey, C.: KE tool: an open source software for automated input data in discrete event simulation projects. In: 2016 Winter Simulation Conference (WSC), pp. 472–483, December 2016
11. Jayatilleke, S., Lai, R.: A systematic review of requirements change management. Inf. Softw. Technol. **93**, 163–185 (2018)
12. SimPy Documentation: 'Overview—SimPy 4.0.2.dev1+g2973dbe documentation' (2021). https://simpy.readthedocs.io/en/latest/. Accessed 09 Mar 2021
13. SimJulia Documentation: Welcome to SimJulia!—SimJulia documentation. https://simjuliajl.readthedocs.io/en/stable/welcome.html. Accessed 09 Mar 2021
14. Jaamsim Documentation: 'JaamSim Free Discrete Event Simulation Software' (2021). https://jaamsim.com/. Accessed 09 Mar 2021
15. L'Ecuyer, P.L., Meliani, L., Vaucher, J.: SSJ: a framework for stochastic simulation in Java, **1**, 234–242 (2003)
16. JavaSim Documentation: 'nmcl/JavaSim', *GitHub* (2021). https://github.com/nmcl/JavaSim. Accessed Mar 2021
17. Sjøberg, D., et al.: A survey of controlled experiments in software engineering. Softw. Eng. IEEE Trans. **31**, 733–753 (2005)
18. Creswell, J.W., Creswell, J.D.: Research Design: Qualitative, Quantitative, and Mixed Methods Approaches. SAGE Publications (2017)
19. Dodig-Crnkovic, G.: Scientific methods in computer science. In: Proceedings of the Conference for the Promotion of Research in IT at New Universities and at University Colleges in Sweden, Skövde, Suecia. https://www.academia.edu/35111214/Scientific_methods_in_computer_science. Accessed 24 Jun 2021
20. Project Repository: SDU-SimulationFrameworkReviews/SimulationFrameworks. SDU-SimulationFrameworkReviews (2021). https://github.com/SDU-SimulationFrameworkReviews/SimulationFrameworks. Accessed 09 Apr 2021

Dynamic and Static Performance Analysis of SiC MOSFET with PWM Control

Yue Qiu[1], En Fang[1,2(✉)], and Delu Li[3]

[1] School of Electrical and Control Engineering,
Xuzhou University of Technology, Xuzhou 221018, Jiangsu, China
fangen@cumt.edu.cn
[2] Jiangsu Key Construction Laboratory of Large Engineering Equipment Testing and Control
Technology, Xuzhou 221018, Jiangsu, China
[3] Jiangsu Vocational Institute of Architecture Technology, Xuzhou 221018, Jiangsu, China

Abstract. The superior electrical and thermal properties of silicon carbide (SiC) power electronic devices, compared with silicon (Si) devices, lead to high efficiency and low volume in power converter designs. In this paper, the simulation model of the SiC MOSFETs is built, and the dynamic and static performance is obtained. The switching loss of SiC devices for AC motor control with pulse width modulation is calculated and analyzed.

Keywords: SiC MOSFET · Switching loss

1 Introduction

In the development of power electronic technology, power electronic devices (power devices) are the decisive factors to promote the development of power electronic technology. Although the value of power electronic devices in the whole machine is not high (10%–30%), the quality of power electronic devices directly determines the performance of the entire device. It can be said that the performance index of power electronic devices directly determines the performance index of equipment.

Since the first electron tube came out in 1904, the technology for power conversion has existed. It was not until 1957 that GE developed the first thyristor, which marked the birth of power electronics technology and the first technological revolution in the electrical age. In the 60 years since then, the power electronic technology has been continuously improved, and the performance of power devices has been gradually improved.

1.1 Development of Power Electronic Devices

The development of power semiconductor devices has experienced three stages.

The First Generation: SCR and Its Derivatives. The thyristor is a semi-controlled device, which can be turned on but not off by controlling the gate. The control mode

D. Jiang and H. Song (Eds.): SIMUtools 2021, LNICST 424, pp. 331–341, 2022.
https://doi.org/10.1007/978-3-030-97124-3_25

of the thyristor circuit is mainly phased control mode. The thyristor is used to realize large capacity current control in low-frequency phase control. However, the working frequency of the thyristor is limited by dv/dt and di/dt, so thyristor is mainly used at a low switching frequency.

At present, in the field of superpower (voltage above 3.3 kV, capacity within 1–45 MW), thyristors and other power devices have a considerable market. Thyristors of 6-inch substrate with 8.5 kV/5 kA have been commercialized in the world. ABB and other companies in Switzerland have developed IGCT products with asymmetric structure, reverse conduction or reverse resistance. As 4.5 kV and 6 kV series products have been commercialized in the market, and 6.5 kV/6 kA series products have been supplied, the 9 kV/6 kA series products are researched and developed.

Second Generation: Power MOSFETs. In the late 1970s, GTO, BJT, and MOSFET devices developed rapidly. Through the control of the gate (base, gate) to turn it on or off. Especially for MOSFET, its driving circuit is simple, and it needs small driving power, fast switching speed, and high working frequency. Therefore, power MOSFET can work at a higher frequency and has a much wider safe working area than thyristor.

However, power MOSFET has a small current capacity and low withstand voltage, so there are not many applications of power MOSFET in large capacity and high power environments. In the field of medium and small power (below 900V), power MOSFET is still the device with the largest market capacity and the fastest-growing demand. The new structure device represented by super junction is the critical development direction of the device.

At the same time, since the 1990s, technology-leading enterprises have focused on wide bandgap semiconductor devices represented by SiC and GaN.

The Third Generation: IGBTs. GTO and other bipolar devices have a solid current capacity, but the switching speed is slow. The driving power required is enormous, and the driving circuit is complex. The switching speed of power MOSFET is fast, and the driving power is small. And the driving course is simple. Therefore, in 1982, GE proposed designing and developing a fully controlled power device, i.e., insulated gate bipolar transistor, which has the advantages of both MOSFET and bipolar device.

Due to the excellent characteristics of IGBT, it has become the leading device of medium and high power (voltage 1200 V–6.5 kV) for power electronic equipment. At present, IGBT devices have covered the field of 300 V–6.5 kV and 2 A–3600 A.

1.2 Development and Application of SiC Materials

Since the first generation of power devices, Si and Ge have been widely used as semiconductor materials. With the rapid development of technology, power devices based on Si, GaAs, and other traditional semiconductor materials have been developed. The corresponding technology has reached its limit. However, traditional materials such as Si and GaAs are facing severe challenges when working in extreme environments. Firstly, the low dielectric breakdown field of Si limits the maximum operating voltage of power devices, and the narrow bandgap and low thermal conductivity of Si lower the maximum operating temperature of power devices. Therefore, people urgently need a new type of material that can work stably at high temperature, high frequency, high power, intense radiation, and other extreme conditions.

Development of SiC Materials. In 1824, Swedish scientist Berzelius observed SiC in the process of synthetic diamond, which marked the beginning of SiC research. In 1885, Acheson first produced SiC crystal by hand and found that the crystal had high hardness and a high melting point. SiC material was hoped to be used as abrasive material, and the method of artificial preparation of SiC crystal was also named as Acheson method. In 1891, industrial SiC was successfully developed and became the earliest man-made abrasive. In 1907, a British engineer named Round produced the first light-emitting diode made of SiC, marking the formal application of SiC in electronics. In 1920, SiC single crystal was used as a detector in the early radio receiver. In 1959, Lely improved the manufacturing process, which laid the foundation for the development of SiC. This new method of producing SiC also became Lely method. In 1978, Russian scientists Tairov and Tsvetkov improved the Lely method to obtain SiC growth technology with larger crystals. In 1979, SiC blue LED was successfully manufactured. In 1981, Matsunami invented the technology of growing single-crystal SiC on Si substrate. In 1991, Cree produced 6H-SiC wafers by the improved Lely method. In 1994, Cree obtained 4H-SiC wafers. In 1997, Cree realized the marketization of 2-inch 6H-SiC wafers. In 2000, Cree accomplished the marketization of 4-inch 6H-SiC wafers. In 2007, Cree released a commercial 100 mm SiC substrates with zero microtubes. In 2010, Cree displayed high-quality 150 mm SiC wafers. In 2013, Cree developed 6-inch SiC single crystal products. So far, Cree and Rohm have developed SiC MOSFET products with voltage levels ranging from 650V to 1700V, and the maximum single-chip current exceeds 50A. All series of SiC power module products within 1200V/300A and 1700V/225A are developed.

Physical Properties of SiC Materials. SiC, as one of the third core generation semiconductor materials, has the advantages of the wide bandgap, high thermal conductivity, small thermal expansion coefficient, high electron saturation drift rate, strong insulation breakdown field, and good wear resistance compared with Si and GaAs. Therefore, SiC can be used for manufacturing high temperature, high frequency, high power density, and radiation-resistant power electronic devices. In addition, SiC materials can form oxide layer SiO_2 on the surface naturally, which is very beneficial to MOS devices.

The third-generation wide bandgap semiconductor materials have the following advantages compared with the first generation of traditional Si materials:

(1) The gap width of SiC and Gan materials is three times that of Si materials. The large bandgap width significantly reduces the leakage current of SiC devices. SiC and Gan devices have radiation resistance properties, which can improve the service life in extreme environments. Secondly, different crystalline states have other band gaps, which can be used as luminescent materials of various colors.

(2) SiC materials are of high thermal conductivity, which leads to excellent heat dissipation, and helps to improve the power density and integration of the devices. In addition, the high-temperature resistance of SiC materials also makes it have a unique advantage in a high-temperature environment. Theoretically, the junction temperature of SiC devices can work around 600 °C, which is far greater than the operating temperature range of Si.

(3) The insulation breakdown field of SiC is higher than that of Si material, which dramatically improves the voltage withstand capacity and current density of SiC devices. At the same time, the on-resistance of power semiconductors is inversely proportional to the cubic of the breakdown field strength, so the on-resistance of SiC is smaller, and the conduction loss is lower.

(4) The electron drift rate of SiC is twice as high as that of Si. SiC devices have excellent microwave characteristics and can work at higher frequencies and meet particular environments such as aerospace.

It can be seen that the wide bandgap semiconductor material has the incomparable advantages of Si materials. The power devices made by wide bandgap material can meet particular environmental requirements and meet the development needs of power electronic devices better, such as high temperatures, high voltage, and high-power density.

2 Characteristic Analysis of MOSFETs Based on SiC

Based on the advantages of SiC materials, the SiC semiconductor devices have the benefits of low on-resistance, high breakdown voltage, and high limit operating temperature. By comparing the output characteristics and switching characteristics of Si devices and SiC devices, the advantages of SiC devices are analyzed and compared.

2.1 Essential Characteristics of Power MOSFETs

Static Characteristic. The relationship between drain DC I_D and gate-source voltage U_{GS} reflects the relationship between the input voltage and output current, also known as the transfer characteristics of MOSFET, as shown in Fig. 1. And the slope of the curve is defined as the transconductance G_{FS} of MOSFET.

$$G_{fs} = \frac{dI_D}{dU_{GS}}$$

Figure 2 shows the volt-ampere drain characteristics of power MOSFET, i.e., output characteristics. Like a thyristor, the power MOSFET also has three working regions: cut-off, unsaturated, and saturated regions. In the saturated area, the drain current does not increase with the increase of drain-source voltage, while in the unsaturated region, the drain current increases with the rise of drain-source voltage. The working state of MOSFET switches back and forth between the cut-off region and the unsaturated region.

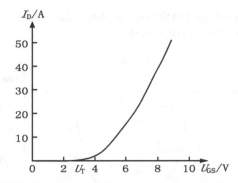

Fig. 1. Transfer characteristics of power MOSFETs.

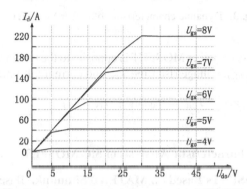

Fig. 2. Output characteristics of power MOSFETs.

Dynamic Characteristics. Figure 3 shows the dynamic characteristics of power MOS-FET, which is the voltage and current waveforms during switching. There is inter junction capacitance in power MOSFETs, so when the rising edge of the switching pulse comes, the gate-source voltage U_{GS} will rise exponentially. When the U_{GS} rises to threshold voltage U_{th}, the drain current I_D appears. After that, the drain current I_D increases with the rise of gate-source voltage U_{GS}. When the drain current rises to the steady-state, the gate voltage rises to U_{gsp}, and the drain voltage U_{DS} begins to decline. During the process of the drain voltage U_{DS} falling, the grid voltage U_{GS} will be maintained at the value of U_{gsp} and form a platform called the Miller platform. It will not continue to rise to the steady-state value in exponential form until the end of the drain voltage drop.

Miller platform is formed because the gate signal reversely charges the capacitance between gate-drain during voltage drop time, and the size of U_{gsp} is related to the steady-state value of I_D.

The opening delay time of power MOSFET is described as follows.

$$T_{on} = T_{d(on)} + T_{ri} + T_{fv}$$

Where, the turn-on delay time T_{on} refers to the time from the gate-source voltage U_{GS} from 0 to the drain current I_D. T_{ri} is the current-rise time, which refers to how long the drain current I_D rises from 0 to the steady-state value. T_{fv} refers to the time during which the drain voltage begins to drop to 0.

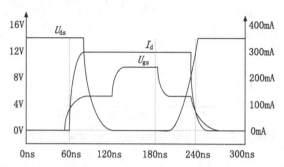

Fig. 3. Dynamic characteristics of power MOSFETs.

The turn-off process of power MOSFET is opposite to the turn-on process, including turn-off delay time $T_{d(off)}$, voltage rise time T_{rv}, and current fall time T_{fi}.

$$T_{off} = T_{d(off)} + T_{rv} + T_{fi}$$

2.2 Modeling and Characteristic Analysis of SiC MOSFET

Modeling of SiC MOSFETs Based on MATLAB/Simulink. Based on the equivalent structure of SiC MOSFETs mentioned above, the physical model can be comparable to the circuit in Fig. 4.

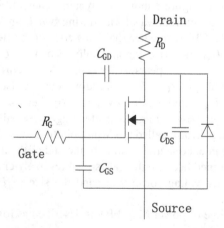

Fig. 4. Equivalent circuit of SiC MOSFETs.

The switching process of SiC MOSFET is modeled by MATLAB/Simulink. There is already a model of MOSFET in the Simulink library, but the model is an ideal model, and the characteristics of the switching process of the device can not be observed. Therefore, the equivalent simulation model of SiC MOSFET is rebuilt according to the identical circuit model, as shown in Fig. 5.

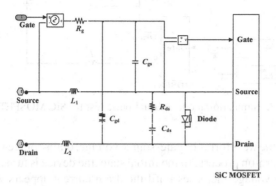

Fig. 5. Equivalent simulation model of SiC MOSFETs.

In this simulation model, the inter-electrode capacitance is modeled by three capacitor modules, and the body diode is modeled by a diode. For the on-off characteristics of MOSFET, the reverse layer is modeled by a controllable current source, as shown in Fig. 6.

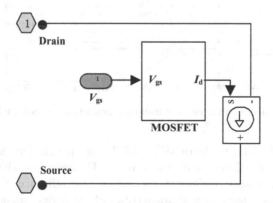

Fig. 6. Equivalent simulation model of the inversion layer in SiC MOSFETs.

The input of the module is gate-source voltage, and the output is the drain current. The output current is directly converted into the ideal current, which is output by a controllable current source, and its transfer function is written as follows.

$$I_d = K_n(V_{GS} - V_{DS})^2$$

The whole simulation model is shown in Fig. 7. The MOSFET model is placed in the half-bridge, and a diode replaces the upper half-bridge device. The switching characteristics of SiC MOSFET model are analyzed by the dual-pulse test method.

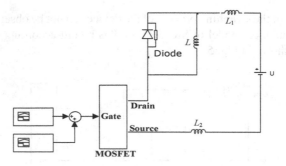

Fig. 7. Simulation model of dual-pulse test for SiC MOSFETs.

Figure 8 shows the waveforms of gate-source voltage, drain-source voltage, and drain current during the turn-on process. In the initial state, the device is turned off. When 2.59 ns, the gate-source voltage increases until the drain current appears when the driving voltage is higher than the threshold voltage. At this time, the drain current increases exponentially, and the corresponding drain voltage decreases rapidly. This process is the turn-on process of MOSFET.

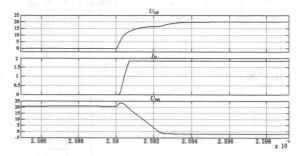

Fig. 8. Simulation waveforms of turn-on characteristics of SiC MOSFETs.

Although the MOSFET model of SiC is built by an equivalent model, the simulation waveforms are similar to the theoretical waveforms. The comparison between the model and the actual model is still insufficient, for example, the influence of junction temperature and shell temperature on the characteristics of the device can not be reflected in this model. Therefore, to observe the opening features of SiC MOSFET, it is necessary to use other software to simulate it more accurately.

3 Analysis of Dynamic Loss of SiC MOSFETs

3.1 Influence of Parasitic Inductance on Dynamic Parameters of Switching Process

Considering all the parasitic parameters in the current path, the whole loop inductance can be equivalent to three lumped inductors.

(1)   The parasitic inductance L_g is formed by the gate current circuit, which mainly includes the inductance L_{g1} brought by the device packaging and the inductance L_{g2} of the external gate path of the device, which can be expressed as $L_g = L_{g1} + L_{g2}$.

(2)   The parasitic inductance L_d of the power circuit is formed by the drain current path. It mainly includes MOS tube package inductor L_{d1}, PCB wiring inductor L_{d2}, upper half-bridge turn-on package inductor L_{d3}, positive and negative bus inductors L_{b1} and L_{b2}, which can be expressed as $L_d = L_{d1} + L_{d2} + L_{d3} + L_{b1} + L_{b2}$.

(3)   The common source inductance L_S, which exists in two loops, connects the grid and power loops.

Influence of Parasitic Inductance of Grid Circuit on Switching Process. The gate loop inductor has only a slight effect on the switching characteristics of SiC MOS-FET, and the overshoot of voltage and current remains unchanged. For the switching loss, the increase of L_g hardly affects the switching loss. Figure 9(a) shows the turn-on waveform when $L_g = 0.1\text{nH}$, and Fig. 9(b) shows the turn-off waveform when $L_g = 0.1\text{nH}$.

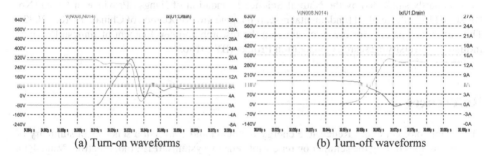

(a) Turn-on waveforms   (b) Turn-off waveforms

Fig. 9. Drain- source voltage and drain current waveforms when $L_g = 0.1$ nH.

The overshoot voltage ratio calculated from the turn-off waveform is $\sigma_1 = 7.2\%$ and for current is $\sigma_2 = 171\%$ when the device is turned on. The turn-on loss is $E_{on} = 51.585\ \mu\text{J}$. And the turn-off loss is $E_{off} = 7.791\ \mu\text{J}$.

4   Conclusion

The 1.2 kV SiC MOSFET in a three-phase inverter is studied in this paper by simulation with MATLAB/Simulink in order to evaluate the loss and efficiency under different switching frequencies.

At the low switching frequency, conduction loss is the primary source of total converter loss. Even at the lowest switching frequency, the performance of SiC MOSFET is better than that of Si IGBT.

With the increase of switching frequency, the advantage of using SiC MOSFET becomes more apparent because it has lower switching loss than Si IGBT. According to the switching resistance R_g, the switching loss of Si in inverters is 1.55 to 4.79 × (25 °C) and 3.5 to 8.6 × (125 °C) that of SiC. Therefore, the switching frequency of the inverter can be increased by 1.56 to 5 times for the same output power by using SiC power devices.

The switching phenomenon of MOSFET is almost independent of the operating temperature, while the temperature dependence of Si IGBT is strong. The simulation results show that the efficiency difference between inverters can reach 5.47% when the switching frequency is 100 kHz, and the junction temperature is 25 °C. Significantly, the reverse recovery current of Si diode and the trailing current of IGBT deteriorate with the increase of temperature.

Therefore, there are many ways to optimize the circuit design to reduce the switching loss, such as improving the efficiency and reducing the cooling requirements. Most importantly, by increasing the operating frequency, the size of passive components can be reduced to improve the power density of the system.

Acknowledgements. The authors acknowledge the Jiangsu University Natural Science Research Project (18KJB470024) and Provincial Construction System Science and Technology Project of Jiangsu Provincial Housing and Urban-Rural Construction Department (2018ZD088). This work is partly supported by the Natural Science Foundation of Jiangsu Province of China (No. BK20161165), the applied fundamental research Foundation of Xuzhou of China (No. KC17072). The authorized patents for invention are also the research and development of Jiangsu Province Industry-University-Research Cooperation Project (BY2019056).

References

1. Spagnuolo, G., et al.: Renewable energy operation and conversion schemes: a summary of discussions during the seminar on renewable energy systems. IEEE Ind. Electron. Mag. 4(1), 38–51 (2010)
2. Zuk, P.C., Odekirk, B.: SiC impacts greening of power - understanding the differences between Silicon Carbide (SiC) and Silicon (Si) for power electronics. Power Syst. Des. Eur. 3436 (2008)
3. Wrzecionko, B., Biela, J., Kolar, J.W.: SiC power semiconductors in HEVs: Influence of junction tem- perature on power density, chip utilization and efficiency. In: 35th Annual Conference of IEEE Industrial Electronics, pp. 3834–3841 (2009)
4. Evans, T., Hanada, T., Nakano, Y., Nakamura, T.: Development of SiC power devices and modules for au- tomotive motor drive use. In: 2013 IEEE International Meeting for Future of Electron Devices, pp. 116–117 (2013)
5. Skibinski, G., Braun, D., Kirschnik, D., Lukaszewski, R.: Development in hybrid Si-SiC power modules (2006)
6. Zhang, Z., Wang, F., Tolbert, L.M., Blalock, B.J., Costinett, D.J.: Evaluation of switching performance of SiC devices in PWM inverter-fed induction motor drives. IEEE Trans. Power Electron. 30(10), 5701–5711 (2015)
7. Zhao, T., Wang, J., Huang, A.Q., Agarwal, A.: Comparisons of SiC MOSFET and Si IGBT based motor drive systems. In: 42nd IAS Annual Meeting. Conference Record of the 2007 IEEE Industry Applications Conference, pp. 331–335 (2007)
8. Rice, J., Mookken, J.: Economics of high efficiency SiC MOSFET based 3-ph motor drive. In: Proceedings of International Exhibition and Conference for Power Electronics, Intelligent Motion, Renewable Energy and Energy Management, pp. 1–8 (2014)

9. Tiwari, S., Midtgård, O.-M., Undeland, T.M., Lund, R.: Experimental performance comparison of six- pack SiC MOSFET and Si IGBT modules paralleled in a half-bridge configuration for high temperature applications. In: 2015 IEEE 3rd Workshop on Wide Bandgap Power Devices and Applications (WiPDA), pp. 135–140 (2015)
10. Tiwari, S., Abuishmais, I., Undeland, T., Boysen, K.: Silicon carbide power transistors for photovoltaic applications. In: 2011 IEEE Trondheim PowerTech, pp. 1–6 (2011)
11. Tiwari, S., et al.: Design considerations and laboratory testing of power circuits for parallel operation of sili-con carbide MOSFETs. In: 17th European Conference on Power Electronics and Applications (EPE 2015 ECCE-Europe), pp. 1–10 (2015)
12. Agarwal, A., Singh, R., Ryu, S.-H., Richmond, J., Capell, C., Schwab, S., et al.: 600 V, 1- 40 A, schottky diodes in sic and their applications (2002)
13. Heer, D., Bayoumi, A.K.: Switching characteristics of modern 6.5kV IGBT/Diode. In: Proceedings of International Exhibition and Conference for Power Electronics. Intelligent Motion, Renewable Energy and Energy Management, pp. 1–8 (2014)
14. Cree, Inc.: SiC MOSFET Isolated Gate Driver, CPWR-AN10 Rev. C (2014)

Predictive Current Control of the Three-Level Four-Leg Active Filter Based on In-Phase Carrier Modulation

Li Delu[1]([⊠]) [ⓘ], Fang En[2], Liu Zhijian[1], and Zhang Kailiang[2]

[1] Jiangsu Vocational Institute of Architectural Technology, Xuzhou, China
[2] Jiangsu Province Key Laboratory of Intelligent Industry Control Technology, Xuzhou University of Technology, Xuzhou, China

Abstract. To reduce the complex calculation of three-level spatial vector modulation (SVPWM) in practical applications, improve the compensation performance of active filters (AF), and combine with the same-phase carrier modulation strategy, a predictive current control strategy based on the same-phase carrier is proposed. The strategy outputs a small voltage harmonic component and reduces the computational complexity of the modulation strategy. The effectiveness of the modulation strategy proposed in this paper is verified by simulation experiments.

Keywords: Electric electronics · In-phase carrier modulation · Predictive current

1 Introduction

Multilevel converter technology reduces voltage stress in the main power device and has less harmonic content in the output voltage by using a mature low-voltage device stacking combination to become a high-voltage converter [1–4]. Because of these characteristics, three-level AF are widely used [3, 5–9].

Three-level four-leg (TF) is one of the common active filter structures, and its modulation strategy has been widely concerned. Common modulation methods include phase-shifted carrier PWM method (PS-PWM), voltage space vector modulation (SVPWM) method, and phase disposition PWM method (PD-PWM).

Because the phase-shifted carrier PWM method has the same reference voltage and carrier frequency, the output energy and switching losses distribution of each unit is more even, which is beneficial to device selection and thermal design. Because of its simple realization and the advantages of power balance between units, it has been widely used in industry [8, 10, 11]. SVPWM strategy needs to be located in a specific triangle in voltage vector space before selecting spatial vector synthesis. This method has many voltage redundancy vectors, complex calculation and selection, and does not take into account the power balance distribution between the units when selecting spatial vectors. phase disposition PWM method has a better harmonic output effect than carrier shift phase modulation, but its carrier is distributed vertically, resulting in uneven power between units, which makes it rarely used in practice [5].

D. Jiang and H. Song (Eds.): SIMUtools 2021, LNICST 424, pp. 342–358, 2022.
https://doi.org/10.1007/978-3-030-97124-3_26

There are eight switch tubes in the TF active filter, which makes the carrier and modulation wave of three-level modulation technology more than two levels, more than one. And each carrier and modulation wave have multiple degrees of control, including frequencies, modulation amplitude values, modulation waves and carrier offsets. The different combinations of degrees of freedom have produced a variety of carrier PWM technology and based on the in-phase carrier modulation technology developed at two levels, a in-phase carrier prediction current control strategy for TF AF is proposed. The strategy is easy to implement, has a clear physical meaning, greatly reduces computing time, and better adapts to the rapid response requirements of harmonic compensation.

2 Carrier Modulation Strategy for Three-Level Four-Leg Active Filter

2.1 Basic Principles of Three-Level Four-Leg Active Filter

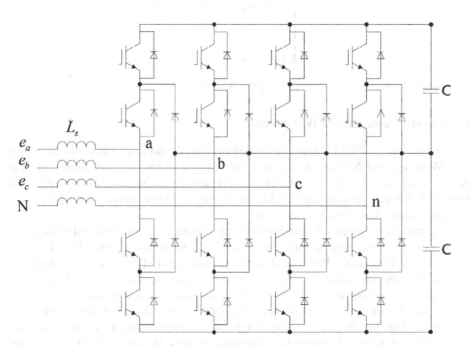

Fig. 1. Three levels Four-leg topology

In the above figure, the midline connecting inductor is selected to be consistent with the three-phase connecting inductor, and L_s is the connecting inductor, where the internal resistance of the inductor is ignored. i_{sa}, i_{sb}, i_{sc}, i_{sn} represent grid-side current. i_{la}, i_{lb}, i_{lc}, i_{ln} represent nonlinear load current (including midline current), which can be decomposed into fundamental component i i_{fa}, i_{fb}, i_{fc}, i_{fn} and harmonic component i_{ha}, i_{hb}, i_{hc}, i_{hn}, $i_{la} = i_{fa} + i_{ha} i_{lb} = i_{fb} + i_{hb} i_{lc} = i_{fc} + i_{hc} i_{ln} = i_{fn} + i_{hn}$. The compensation current generated by APF is expressed as i_{ca}, i_{cb}, i_{cc} and i_{cn}. The PWM inverter is controlled to make the following:

$$\begin{cases} i_{ca} = -i_{ha} \\ i_{cb} = -i_{hb} \\ i_{cc} = -i_{hc} \\ i_{cn} = -i_{hn} \end{cases} \tag{1}$$

So

$$\begin{cases} i_{sa} = i_{la} + i_{ca} = i_{fa} \\ i_{sb} = i_{lb} + i_{cb} = i_{fb} \\ i_{sc} = i_{lc} + i_{cc} = i_{fc} \\ i_{sn} = i_{ln} + i_{cn} = i_{fn} \end{cases} \tag{2}$$

The above is the basic principle of parallel APF.

2.2 Carrier Lamination PWM Method

Carrier Lamination PWM control technology is directly developed from the two-level SPWM, usually, for N-level carrier modulation, the need for (N-1) amplitude and frequency of the same triangular carrier, two sets of carriers distributed in the positive and negative half-week, divided into two layers of upper and lower cascades, modulation of the same modulation wave, so the name.

According to the phase relationship between carriers, the control method of the three-level midpoint clamp-type inverter can be divided into in-phase carrier PWM control and reversed-phase carrier PWM control, that is, with a pair of amplitude and frequency equivalent triangular carriers stacked up and down, distributed in the modulation wave of the positive and negative half wave. When the modulation wave is larger than the upper triangular carrier on the positive half axis, the output is high, when the modulation wave is smaller than the lower triangular carrier on the negative half axis, and when the modulation wave is between two triangular carriers, the output level is 0. In sine modulation waves, for example, Fig. 2 shows reversed-phase carrier PWM control, and Fig. 3 shows in-phase carrier PWM control.

Reversed-Phase Carrier PWM Control

Taking the three-phase single-phase bridge arm as an example, the reversed-phase carrier PWM control principle as shown in Fig. 2, U_A for the sine modulation wave of the A-phase bridge arm, U_P and U_N for the triangular carrier distributed in its upper and lower half waves.

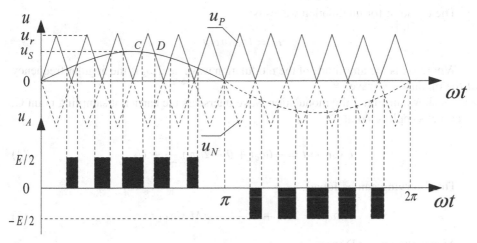

Fig. 2. Reversed-phase carrier PWM control

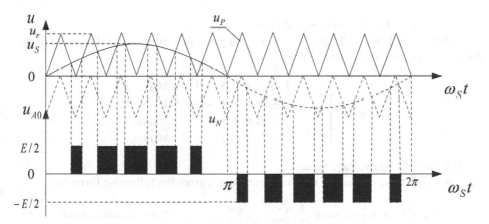

Fig. 3. In-phase carrier PWM control

The modulation wave U_A is compared with the triangular carrier U_P and U_N, respectively. In the positive half wave, $|U_A| \geq |U_P|$, the positive PWM pulse is triggered, so that the upper arm is turned on and the output level is 1. In the negative half wave, $|U_A| \leq |U_N|$, the negative PWM pulse is triggered to make the lower bridge arm turn on and output level -1. In a modulation wave period, the carrier is oddly symmetric about π.

$$U_P = \begin{cases} -(\omega_c t + \theta - 2k\pi)\frac{U}{\pi} + U, & 2k\pi - \theta \leq \omega_c t \leq 2k\pi + \pi - \theta \\ (\omega_c t + \theta - 2k\pi)\frac{U}{\pi} + U, & 2k\pi + \pi - \theta \leq \omega_c t \leq 2k\pi + \pi - \theta \end{cases} \quad (3)$$

Where U is the amplitude of the carrier, θ is the initial phase angle of the triangular carrier, and ω_c is the angular frequency of the carrier.

The equation for modulation waves is:

$$u_A = U_S sin\,\omega_s t$$

Where U_S is the amplitude of the modulation wave, and ω_s is the angular frequency of the modulation wave.

As shown in Fig. 2 the modulation wave intersects the carrier at sampling point C, D, and at sampling point C:

$$U_S sin\,\omega_s t = -(\omega_c t + \theta - 2k\pi)\frac{U_r}{\pi} + U_r \tag{4}$$

The following can be found:

$$\omega_c t = 2k\pi + \pi - \theta - \pi M\,sin\,\omega_s t \tag{5}$$

At sampling point D there is:

$$\omega_c t = 2k\pi + \pi - \theta + \pi M\,sin\,\omega_s t \tag{6}$$

Where $M = U_S/U_r$ is the modulation.

When $w_c t \in [2k\pi + \theta, 2k\pi + \pi + \theta]$, you get a time function for the output of the three-level single-bridge arm SPWM:

$$U_{AO} = \begin{cases} 0\;\omega_c t \begin{cases} < 2k\pi + \pi - \theta - \pi Msin\omega_s t \\ \geq 2k\pi + \pi - \theta + \pi Msin\omega_s t \end{cases} \\ \frac{E}{2}\;\omega_c t \begin{cases} < 2k\pi + \pi - \theta + \pi Msin\omega_s t \\ \geq 2k\pi + \pi - \theta - \pi Msin\omega_s t \end{cases} \end{cases} \tag{7}$$

E is the DC side voltage value.

Analysis of the formula (7) with Fourier stages gives the following formula:

$$U_{AO}(\omega_c t, \omega_s t) = \frac{1}{4}MEsin\omega_s t + \frac{E}{2m\pi}\sum_{n=1,2,\cdots}^{\infty}\sum_{n=\pm 1, \pm 3,\cdots}^{\pm\infty} e^{-jma}J_n(mM\pi)sin[(mF+n)\omega_s t] \tag{8}$$

The above shows that the DC component is zero in the voltage of the carrier inverted PWM control output, and the amplitude of the base wave component is 1/4ME.

In-Phase Carrier PWM Control

In-phase carrier PWM control principle as shown in Fig. 3, two sets of triangular carriers U_P and U_N phases are the same, its carrier waveform is asymmetrical to the x-axis, The same as reversed-phase carrier PWM control, the modulation wave U_A is compared with the triangular carrier U_P and U_N, respectively. In the positive half wave, $|U_A| \geq |U_P|$, the positive PWM pulse is triggered, so that the upper arm is turned on and the output level is 1. In the negative half wave, $|U_A| \leq |U_N|$, the negative PWM pulse is triggered to make the lower bridge arm turn on and output level -1. The difference is to write out two carrier expressions:

$$U_P = \begin{cases} (\omega_c t - 2k\pi)\frac{U_r}{\pi}, & 2k\pi \leq \omega_c t \leq 2k\pi + \pi \\ -(\omega_c t - 2k\pi)\frac{U_r}{\pi} + 2U_r, & 2k\pi + \pi \leq \omega_c t \leq 2k\pi + 2\pi \end{cases} \tag{9}$$

$$U_{s1} = \begin{cases} U_S \sin \omega_s t, 0 \leq \omega_s t \leq \pi \\ 0, \pi \leq \omega_s t \leq 2\pi \end{cases} \tag{10}$$

$$U_N = \begin{cases} (\omega_c t - 2k\pi)\frac{U_r}{\pi} - U_C, 2k\pi \leq \omega_c t \leq 2k\pi + \pi \\ -(\omega_c t - 2k\pi)\frac{U_r}{\pi} + U_r, 2k\pi + \pi \leq \omega_c t \leq 2k\pi + 2\pi \end{cases} \tag{11}$$

$$U_{s2} = \begin{cases} U_S \sin \omega_s t, \pi \leq \omega_s t \leq 2\pi \\ 0, 0 \leq \omega_s t \leq \pi \end{cases} \tag{12}$$

Where U_r for the amplitude of the carrier, ω_c for the angular frequency of the carrier, U_S for the amplitude of the modulation wave, ω_s for the angular frequency of the modulation wave.

Referring to the method of retrieving the reversed-phase PWM control expression, From the expression of in-phase carrier PWM control method, phase voltage output U_{AO1} and U_{AO2} can be obtained, then analyzed by Series of Fourier, and the output formula is:

$$U_{AO}(\omega_c t, \omega_s t) = \frac{1}{4} ME\sin\omega_s t \pm \frac{2E}{m\pi^2} \sum_{m=1,3,\cdots}^{\infty} \sum_v^{\infty} \frac{1}{2l-1} J_{2l-1}(mM\pi)cosmF\omega_s t \pm$$
$$\frac{2E}{m\pi} \sum_{m=2,4,\cdots}^{\infty} \sum_{n=\pm1,\pm3,\cdots}^{\pm\infty} J_n(mn\pi)\sin[mn\pi]sin[(mF+n)\omega_s t] \tag{13}$$

The above shows that in the voltage of the carrier's phase PWM control output, the DC component is zero, the base wave component amplitude is 1/4ME, the presence of m is even, n is an odd carrier up and down frequency harmonics, and the carrier and the odd carrier harmonics are included.

Simulation Comparison Under MATLAB/Simulink

In MATLAB/Simulink environment, the carrier phase PWM control and carrier inverter PWM control were simulated and compared, and the carrier ratio was set to 40, and the sine modulated wave line voltage amplitude was 380V and the frequency was 50 Hz.

Figure 4 is the line voltage U_{AB} waveform output by reversed-phase carrier PWM control, and Fig. 5 is the line voltage U_{AB} waveform output by in-phase carrier PWM control.

From Fig. 6 and Fig. 7, the line voltage output during in-phase carrier control contains less harmonic content than reversed-phase carrier control. After double Fourier analysis and simulation comparison, it can be concluded that: the output phase voltage of the two carrier lamination PWM methods does not contain a constant component. In the phase voltage of the carrier phase control method output, the harmonic energy is mainly concentrated in the carrier frequency, and the other harmonics are mainly integer multiple carrier frequency as the center of the edge band harmonics, the magnitude is smaller. In the phase voltage output of the reversed-phase carrier control method, there is an edge band harmonic centered on the integer carrier frequency, with a larger magnitude. At the same time, the line voltage waveform effect of the in-phase carrier PWM control output of the same phase stack is better than that of the reversed-phase carrier PWM control, and this paper will use the in-phase carrier PWM control to control the TF active filter.

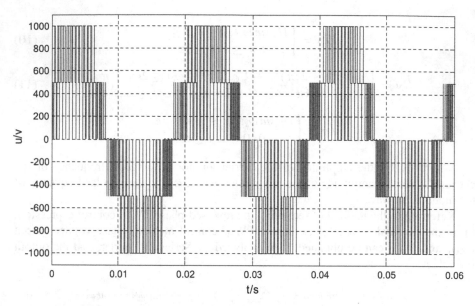

Fig. 4. Reversed-phase carrier PWM method controls the output line voltage.

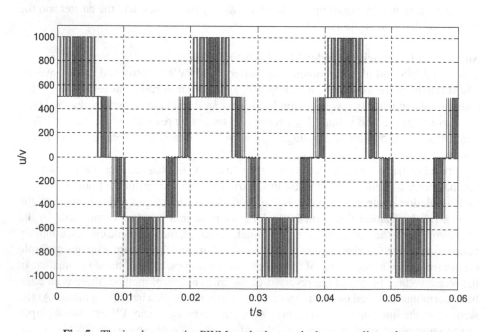

Fig. 5. The in-phase carrier PWM method controls the output line voltage.

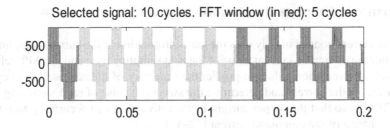

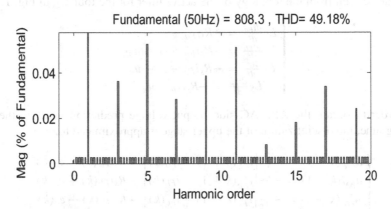

Fig. 6. FFT analysis of the inverted carrier control output line voltage (Color figure online)

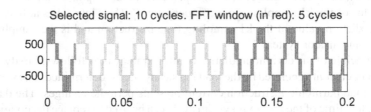

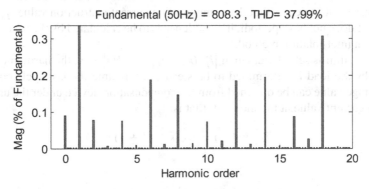

Fig. 7. FFT analysis of the output line voltage with phase carrier control (Color figure online)

3   Harmonic Current Prediction Control

Predictive current control mainly uses the state information of the current sampling time to calculate the command current value of the next sampling time and the APF reference output voltage prediction value, to predict the trajectory of the next sampling cycle to compensate for the current and determine the switching pulse of each switching device of the TF APF, so that the output current of the active filter can accurately and quickly track the change of the command current [12–15].

As can be seen from the topology of the active filter for the four-leg in Fig. 1.

$$\begin{cases} L_S \frac{di_{Fa}}{dt} = -R_s i_{Fa} + e_a - u_{aN} \\ L_S \frac{di_{Fb}}{dt} = -R_s i_{Fb} + e_b - u_{bN} \\ L_S \frac{di_{Fc}}{dt} = -R_s i_{Fc} + e_c - u_{cN} \\ L_S \frac{di_{Fn}}{dt} = -R_s i_{Fn} - u_{nN} \end{cases} \tag{14}$$

In order to obtain the APF AC side output voltage prediction value at the next sampling time, the discretization of the upper stage is approximated to:

$$\begin{cases} u_{aN}^*(k+1) = -\frac{L_S}{T_S}\left[i_{Fa}^*(k+1) - i_{Fa}(k)\right] - R_s i_{Fa}(k) + e_a(k) \\ u_{bN}^*(k+1) = -\frac{L_S}{T_S}\left[i_{Fb}^*(k+1) - i_{Fb}(k)\right] - R_s i_{Fb}(k) + e_b(k) \\ u_{cN}^*(k+1) = -\frac{L_S}{T_S}\left[i_{Fc}^*(k+1) - i_{Fc}(k)\right] - R_s i_{Fc}(k) + e_c(k) \\ u_{nN}^*(k+1) = -\frac{L_S}{T_S}\left[i_{Fn}^*(k+1) - i_{Fn}(k)\right] - R_s i_{Fn}(k) \end{cases} \tag{15}$$

Where $u_{xN}^*(k+1)$(x takes a, b, c, n) represents the three-phase output voltage prediction value of the k1 sampling time compensator, $i_{Fx}^*(k+1)$(x takes a, b, c, n) is the current prediction value of the k1 sampling time instruction and is the sampling cycle of the T_s compensator system.

The principle of the current predictive control strategy is as follows. Firstly, whether the harmonic current generated by the load is a steady state is determined. The steady state means that the harmonic instruction current presents periodic changes. The data at the corresponding time of the previous system cycle can be used to replace the compensation current instruction value $i_{Fx}^*(k+1)$ at $k+1$. If the harmonic current generated by the load is transient, it indicates that the compensation current instruction value $i_{Fx}^*(k+1)$ at time $k+1$ does not have periodicity, and it needs to be calculated by the second-order extrapolation interpolation method.

The error limit is set ε here, when $\left|i_{Fx}^*(k) - i_{Fx}^*(k-N)\right| < \varepsilon$, the harmonic current generated by the load is determined to be steady, at this time the last cycle command current storage value can be obtained from the compensation device under the use of the instruction current value at the moment, that is:

$$i_{Fx}^*(k+1) = i_{Fx}^*(k-N+1) \tag{16}$$

Where N is the number of sampling points for an industrial frequency cycle, when the compensator system samples at 10 kHz. $N = 0.02 \times 10^4 = 200$.

When $|i_{Fx}^*(k) - i_{Fx}^*(k - N)| \geq \varepsilon$ established, the harmonic current generated by the load is determined to be transient, at which time the load current changes greatly, and the instruction current value of the next sampling time of the compensator is predicted by using the Lagrange interpolation method, i.e.:

$$i_{Fx}^*(k + 1) = 3i_{Fx}^*(k) - 3i_{Fx}^*(k - 1) + i_{Fx}^*(k - 2) \tag{17}$$

According to the above command current prediction method, we can quickly get the command current prediction value of the TF APF at the next sampling moment, it can be $i_{Fx}^*(k + 1)$. Replaced it by Eq. (15) to obtain the next sampling moment APF AC side output voltage reference value $u_{xN}^*(k + 1)$, and finally use the same phase stack sine PWM modulation algorithm to produce a turn-off pulse of the TF APF power switch device, so as to accurately and quickly track the change of command current, to achieve the purpose of rapid compensation harmonics.

4 Predictive Control Simulation Based on Same-Phase Carrier Modulation

4.1 Simulation Model

The principle of predictive control has been discussed separately in the previous section, where a simulation model of TF AF using voltage-free sensor $p - q - r$ harmonic detection, predictive current control, and phase carrier modulation is established. The system simulation diagram is as follows (Fig. 8):

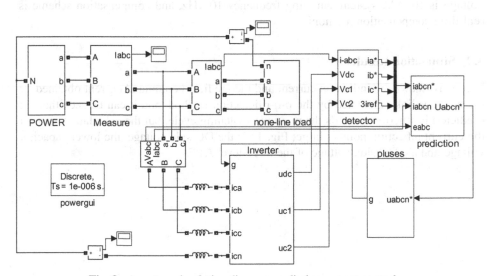

Fig. 8. A system simulation diagram predicting current control.

The simulation system consists of a power supply module, a nonlinear load module, a harmonic detection module, a predictive current control module and a TF with phase carrier module. The carrier module is shown in Fig. 9, and the main power tube switch states of the three levels of power level are represented by the bridge arm output, respectively, in the figures of 1100, 0110, and 0011.

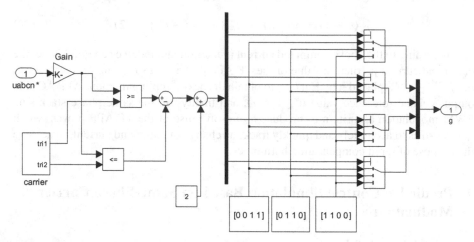

Fig. 9. Three-level four-leg carrier modulation module

The simulation conditions are as follows: grid voltage 380 V, 50 Hz, the nonlinear load is three-phase non-controlled rectifier bridge and A-phase single-phase noncontrolled rectifier bridge, APF access point network inductive value is 1mH, DC side voltage is 1000 V, system sampling frequency 10 kHz, and compensation scheme is real-time compensation harmonics.

4.2 Simulation Results

Figure 10 shows the induction current and the predicted command current obtained by the advance link calculated by the p-q-r detection method, and it can be seen that the predicted instruction exceeds the previous switching cycle, but the calculation error of the current inflection point is large; Fig. 11 is the DC side voltage, the lower capacitor voltage and the DC side voltage of the three-level APF.

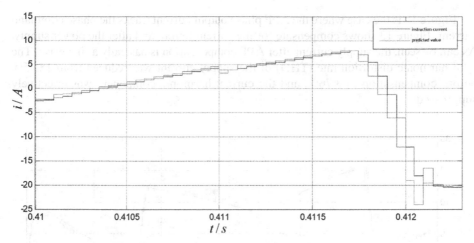

Fig. 10. Instruction current and its predicted value

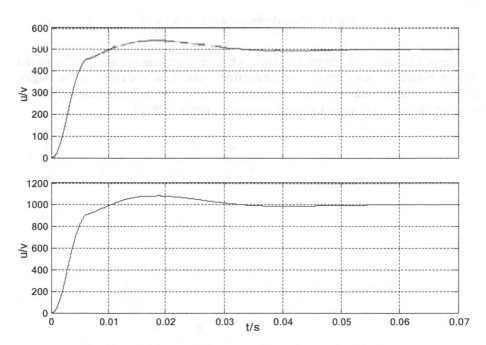

Fig. 11. DC side up and down capacitive voltage and total voltage

354   L. Delu et al.

Figure 12 is the case where the APF phase output current tracks the phase command current. Figure 13 shows compensate for the current before and after the power supply. As can be seen, the supply current after APF compensation is basically a sine wave. The total harmonic distortion rate (THD) of the supply current was reduced from 18.45% before compensation to 3.76%, and the current harmonic component was effectively suppressed.

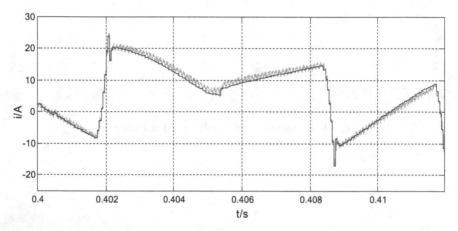

Fig. 12. Phase A command current tracking

Figure 14 is the APF Fourth Leg Output Current Tracking the Midline Command Current. Figure 15 shows compensate for the front and rear midline currents. The magnitude of the midline current before compensation is 20 A, and the magnitude and energy of the medium line current after compensation is greatly reduced.

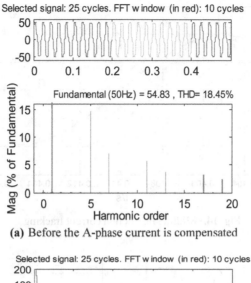

(a) Before the A-phase current is compensated

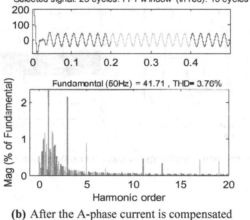

(b) After the A-phase current is compensated

Fig. 13. 1analysis before and after phase a current compensation

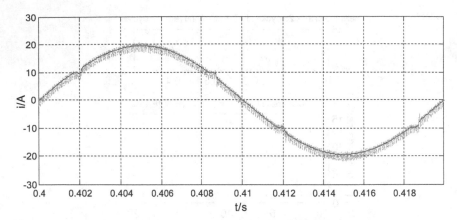

Fig. 14. Midline instruction current tracking

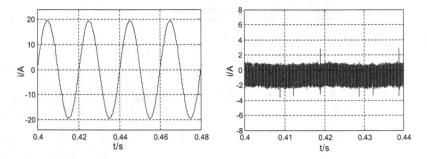

Fig. 15. Front and rear waveforms for current compensation for the midline

5   Conclusion

Through the analysis of carrier lamination PWM method strategy, a predictive current control strategy based on the same phase carrier modulation is proposed. Applying this strategy, the theoretical analysis and simulation of the active filter control system of the four-leg of the three levels are carried out. The simulation results show that:

1) The same-phase carrier modulation strategy output voltage harmonic performance is better. The harmonic component content is smaller.
2) Compared with the SVPWM modulation strategy, based on the predictive current control strategy of the same phase carrier, the physical significance is clear, the calculation time is greatly reduced, and the rapid compensation of harmonics can be realized.

Acknowledgement. The authors acknowledge the Jiangsu University Natural Science Research Project (18KJB470024) and Funding Project for Professional Leaders of Higher Vocational Colleges in Jiangsu Province (2020GRGDYX070). This work was supported by Scientific Research Project of Jiangsu Vocational Institute of Architectural Technology in 2019 (JYA319–13).

References

1. Wang, B.F., Liu, M., Yuan, T.L., Zhang, Z.H.: Study on topological structure of medium voltage active power filter. Dianli Zidonghua Shebei/Electr. Power Autom. Equip. **26**(6) (2006)
2. Waware, M., Agarwal, P.: Performance investigation of multilevel inverter based active power filter in distorted high voltage supply system (2010). https://doi.org/10.1109/ICSET.2010.5684961
3. Madhukar, W., Agarwal, P.: Comparison of control strategies for multilevel inverter based active power filter used in high voltage systems (2010). https://doi.org/10.1109/PEDES.2010.5712440
4. Waware, M., Agarwal, P.: Use of multilevel inverter for elimination of harmonics in high voltage systems. In: 2010 The 2nd International Conference on Computer and Automation Engineering, ICCAE 2010, vol. 2 (2010). https://doi.org/10.1109/ICCAE.2010.5451518
5. Hasim, A.S.B.A., Dardin, S.M.F.S., Ibrahim, Z.B., Azid, A.B.A., Ishak, A.M.B.: Comparative study; different types of PWM control scheme in three-phase four-wire shunt Active Power Filter (APF) topology (2019). https://doi.org/10.1109/ICECOS.2018.8605234
6. Dai, G., Zhao, D., Lin, P., Zhang, C.: Study of control strategy for active power filter based on modular multilevel converter. Dianli Xitong Baohu yu Kongzhi/Power Syst. Prot. Control, **43**(8) (2015)
7. Ziani, A.C., Llor, A.M., Fadel, M.: Geometrical approach of current predictive control for four-leg converters (2011). https://doi.org/10.1109/ISIE.2011.5984430
8. Li, J., Hu, C., Wang, L., Zhang, Z.: APF based on multilevel voltage source cascade converter with carrier phase shifted SPWM. In: IEEE Region 10 Annual International Conference, Proceedings/TENCON, vol. 1 (2003)
9. Geethalakshmi, B., DelhiBabu, K.: An advanced modulation technique for the cascaded multilevel inverter used as a shunt active power filter (2011). https://doi.org/10.1109/IICPE.2011.5728123
10. Li, J.L., Li, J., Wang, L.Q., Zhao, D.L., Zhang, Z.C., Xu, H.H.: Carrier phase shifted SPWM and its applications in shunt APF. Dianli Xitong Zidonghua/Autom. Electric Power Syst. **30**(9) (2006)
11. Sun, Y.Q., Yin, Q., Sheng, J., Pan, W.T.: Variable-frequency carrier bands PWM (VFCB-PWM) and its applications in shunt APF. Dianli Xitong Baohu yu Kongzhi/Power Syst. Prot. Control, **38**(10) (2010)
12. Du, G., Li, J., Liu, Z.: The improved model predictive control based on novel error correction between reference and predicted current. In: Conference Proceedings - IEEE Applied Power Electronics Conference and Exposition - APEC, March 2018. https://doi.org/10.1109/APEC.2018.8341528
13. Yu, J., Teng, Z., Zhang, J., Hu, K.: Predictive current control and stability analysis of active power filter. Diangong Jishu Xuebao/Trans. China Electrotechnical Soc. **24**(7) (2009)

14. Li, G., Zhao, C., Zhou, M., Li, G., Chen, Z.: A predicted control scheme of single phase active power filter in electric traction system. In: IEE Conference Publication, **478** I (2001). https://doi.org/10.1049/cp:20000372
15. Usama, M., Jaehong, K.: Simplified Model Predicted Current Control Method for Speed Control of Non-Silent Permanent Magnet Synchronous Motors (2020). https://doi.org/10.1109/iCoMET48670.2020.9073884

Harmonic Detection Method of Three-Phase Four-Wire APF Based on p-q-r Without Voltage-Sensor

Li Delu[1]($\boxtimes$) (iD), Liu Zhijian[1], Zhang Kailiang[2], and Hao Shaolong[1]

[1] Jiangsu Vocational Institute of Architectural Technology, Xuzhou, China
[2] Jiangsu Province Key Laboratory of Intelligent Industry Control Technology, Xuzhou University of Technology, Xuzhou, China

Abstract. The harmonic detection method based on $p - q - r$ defines the instantaneous power of zero-order current under the new spatial coordinate system, which can eliminate the midline current independently. This paper introduces the principle of the detection method and puts forward the $p - q - r$ method of harmonic detection without voltage sensors. The capacitive midpoint active filter is modeled and simulated to prove that when the voltage of the grid is unbalanced and distorted, the method based on $p - q - r$ do not require a voltage sensor to accurately carry out harmonic detection and fully compensate for the current harmonic components.

Keywords: Filter · Capacitor midpoint · Harmonic detection

1 Introduction

The three-phase four-wire (TF) active filter mainly has a four-leg or capacitive midpoint topology [1]. The four-leg structure has a group of bridge arms more than the capacitive midpoint structure, which is designed to compensate for the midline current, and the compensation effect is better [2]. The small number of switching devices used in the capacitor midpoint has attracted much attention in the small and medium capacity system [3–5], and the medium-line compensation and control strategy for the structure has been the focus of research [6, 7].

The $i_p - i_q$ method based on instantaneous reactive power theory usually introduces a zero-axis decomposition current perpendicular to p, q planes, resulting in only active components in the zero-order component, which conflicts with the usual power understanding [6, 8]. The $p - q - r$ method decomposes the voltage and current space vectors under the p, q, r space coordinate system, defines the active and reactive power of the zero-order components under the TF system, and the various power definitions coincide with the traditional power definitions, while the three power components are completely independent of each other and can be flexibly compensated without the need for energy storage components [3, 9–11]. The effect of midline compensation is improved and the application of the midpoint structure of the capacitor is promoted.

D. Jiang and H. Song (Eds.): SIMUtools 2021, LNICST 424, pp. 359–371, 2022.
https://doi.org/10.1007/978-3-030-97124-3_27

2 Detection Principle of p-q-r

Under the condition of three-phase grid voltage asymmetry, the grid voltage under the a-b-c plane coordinate system is transformed to the three-phase orthogonal α-β-0 spatial coordinate system.

From the Fig. 1

$$e_S = \sqrt{e_\alpha^2 + e_\beta^2 + e_0^2} \tag{1}$$

$$e_{sd} = \sqrt{e_\alpha^2 + e_\beta^2} \tag{2}$$

Voltage synthesis vector e_S is a spatial quantity whose projection on the α-β plane is e_{sd}. Fixed the 0-axis in Fig. 1 (a) to rotate the $\alpha - \beta$ coordinate system counterclockwise angle θ so that the axis α coincides with e_{sd} to obtain axis α_{sd}. The axis β also rotates θ angle to get the q axis, as shown in Fig. 1 (b). Fix the axis q, rotate the $0 - \alpha_{sd}$ coordinate system counterclockwise ϕ so that the axis α_{sd} coincides with the axis e_S to get the axis p and axis r, where the axis q is perpendicular to the $p - q - r$ plane, as shown in Fig. 1(c).

After two coordinate rotations, the spatial $\alpha - \beta - 0$ coordinate system is transformed into a spatial $p - q - r$ coordinate system, transforming matrix A as Eq. (3). After the three-phase current is transformed by matrix A, there is a current component on $p - q - r$ the shaft, such as formula (4). Obviously, in the new spatial coordinate system, the grid voltage space vector is directed to the axis p, and the axis q and axis r do not have a voltage component, so the axis p is an active current axis, the axis q, r is a reactive current axis.

$$A = \frac{1}{e_s} \begin{bmatrix} e_0 & e_\alpha & e_\beta \\ 0 & -e_s e_\beta / e_{sd} & e_s e_\alpha / e_{sd} \\ e_{sd} & -e_0 e_\alpha / e_{sd} & -e_0 e_\beta / e_{sd} \end{bmatrix} \tag{3}$$

$$\begin{bmatrix} e_p \\ e_q \\ e_r \end{bmatrix} = A \begin{bmatrix} e_0 \\ e_\alpha \\ e_\beta \end{bmatrix}, \quad \begin{bmatrix} i_p \\ i_q \\ i_r \end{bmatrix} = A \begin{bmatrix} i_0 \\ i_\alpha \\ i_\beta \end{bmatrix} \tag{4}$$

As can be seen in Fig. 1 (c), the components of the midline current on the axis p and axis r reflect the distribution of the active and reactive components of the midline current. To fully compensate for the midline current, the midline current components on the shaft p and axis r should be offset, i.e.

$$i_{rf} = -i_p tan(\theta_2) = -\frac{e_0}{e_{\alpha\beta}} i_p \tag{5}$$

The current on the p, q shaft is filtered through a low pass, and the resulting DC component corresponds to each phase-based wave component. Therefore, in the three-phase, four-wire harmonic compensation system, the compensation instructions for each axis should be:

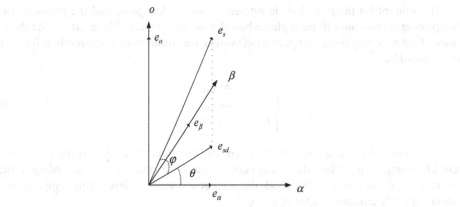

(a) The $\alpha - \beta - 0$ coordinate system

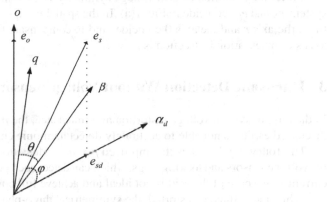

(b) The $\alpha_d - q - 0$ coordinate system

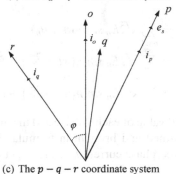

(c) The $p - q - r$ coordinate system

Fig. 1. The formation of a spatial $p - q - r$ coordinate system

The current on the p, q shaft is filtered through a low pass, and the resulting DC component corresponds to each phase-based wave component. Therefore, in the three-phase, four-wire harmonic compensation system, the compensation instructions for each axis should be:

$$\begin{cases} i_{pc} = i_{pac} \\ i_{qc} = i_{qac} \\ i_{rc} = i_r + \frac{e_0}{e_{\alpha\beta}} i_{pdc} \end{cases} \tag{6}$$

In formula (6), i_{pac} is the active current AC component and i_{pdc} is the active current DC component. When the system compensates for reactiveness, according to the advantages of the $p - q - r$ method, the q shaft and shaft r current full compensation can completely compensate for reactive.

Under the condition of grid voltage symmetry, $e_0 = 0$ in the $\alpha - \beta - 0$ coordinate system e_S and e_{sd} coincide in Fig. 1(a). In the spatial $p - q - r$ coordinate system at this time, the axis r and the axis 0 coincide, and to compensate for the midline current, the axis's compensation instruction is $i_{rc} = i_r$.

3   Harmonic Detection Without Voltage Sensor

In the case of system voltage distortion and imbalance, the $p - q - r$ detection method discussed earlier is not able to accurately detect harmonic current.

The following describes the improved $p - q - r$ detection method without the need for voltage sensors and locking rings, which can detect each phase harmonic and midline current in the case of the grid is not ideal and achieve full compensation.

When the voltage is distorted, the symmetrical three-phase grid voltage is:

$$\begin{cases} e_a = \sum\limits_{n=1}^{\infty} \sqrt{2} E_n \sin(nwt + \theta_n) \\ e_b = \sum\limits_{n=1}^{\infty} \sqrt{2} E_n \sin[n(wt - \frac{2\pi}{3}) + \theta_n] \\ e_c = \sum\limits_{n=1}^{\infty} \sqrt{2} E_n \sin[n(wt + \frac{2\pi}{3}) + \theta_n] \end{cases} \tag{7}$$

Where E_n, θ_n are the valid value of each voltage and the initial phase angle is $\theta_1 = 0$. The coordinates are transformed and brought in formula (3) in the event of voltage distortion. Transform the three-phase current i_a, i_b, i_c to get i_α, i_β, i_0, into formula (4), there is:

$$\begin{aligned} i_p &= (e_\alpha i_\alpha + e_\beta i_\beta + e_0 i_0)/e_p \\ i_q &= (e_\alpha i_\beta - e_\beta i_\alpha)/e_{\alpha\beta} \end{aligned} \tag{8}$$

Since e_α, e_β, e_0 all contain 3k harmonics, so that the DC components of i_p and i_q also contain higher secondary harmonics. After the low-pass filter and $C^- A^-$ transformation, i_p and i_q are no longer the fundamental current components of each phase. When the voltage distortion is large, the detection error produced by the $p - q - r$ method is large.

The core of the $p - q - r$ detection method is that E_p in the transformation matrix should represent the positive sequence component of the grid voltage when the vector coordinate transformation is performed. Considering that the point can replace the actual result of power grid voltage detection with a three-phase frequency sine unit vector under the environment of grid voltage distortion, the distortion asymmetric current expression is

$$\begin{bmatrix} i_0 \\ i_\alpha \\ i_\beta \end{bmatrix} = \begin{bmatrix} \sum\limits_{n=1}^{\infty} I_{an} \sin(nwt + \theta_{an}) \\ \sum\limits_{n=1}^{\infty} I_{bn} \sin(nwt + \theta_{bn}) \\ \sum\limits_{n=1}^{\infty} I_{cn} \sin(nwt + \theta_{cn}) \end{bmatrix} \tag{9}$$

In the formula, I_{an} denotes the effective value of a-phase n-th harmonic current, θ_{an} denotes the initial phase angle of a-phase n-th harmonic current. The improved A transform can be obtained (Fig. 2):

$$\begin{aligned} i_p &= \sqrt{3/2} \sum_{n=1}^{\infty} I_{1n} \cos[(nw - w_1)t + \theta_{1n} - \phi] - \sqrt{3/2} \sum_{n=1}^{\infty} I_{2n} \cos[(nw + w_1)t + \theta_{2n} + \phi] \\ i_q &= \sqrt{3/2} \sum_{n=1}^{\infty} I_{1n} \cos[(nw - w_1)t + \theta_{1n} - \phi] + \sqrt{3/2} \sum_{n=1}^{\infty} I_{2n} \cos[(nw + w_1)t + \theta_{2n} + \phi] \end{aligned} \tag{10}$$

In the case of a small system voltage frequency offset, given that the unit voltage is distributed according to the three-phase frequency sine, then only the base wave component will be included in the DC component of i_p i_q,

$$\begin{bmatrix} i_0 \\ i_\alpha' \\ i_\beta' \end{bmatrix} = C^{-1}A^{-1} \begin{bmatrix} i_{pdc} \\ i_{qdc} \\ i_r \end{bmatrix} = \begin{bmatrix} I_{11} \sin(wt + \theta_{11}) \\ I_{11} \sin(wt - 2\pi/3 + \theta_{11}) \\ I_{11} \sin(wt + 2\pi/3 + \theta_{11}) \end{bmatrix} a \tag{11}$$

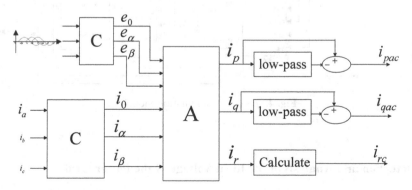

Fig. 2. The improved p-q-r method of detection

4 Simulation Analysis

The $i_p - i_q - i_0$ method is the classical $i_p - i_q$ method in the TF system expansion, The difference between it and the $p-q-r$ method is more reasonably divided from the active and reactive components in the midline current. Both have their own improved models to cope with voltage distortion and asymmetry when the grid voltage is not idealized. Here is the $p - q - r$ method and its improved type as the main research object. The simulation model is established by MATLAB. Figure 3 shows $i_p - i_q - i_0$ method and the simulation model of $p - q - r$ method is shown in Fig. 4.

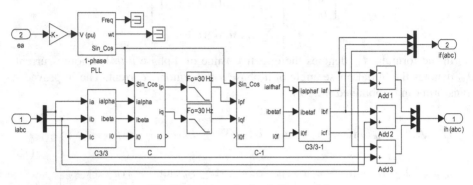

Fig. 3. $i_p - i_q - i_0$ simulation model

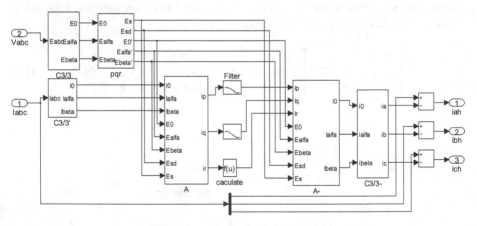

Fig. 4. $p - q - r$ simulation model

4.1 Detection and Analysis of the Ideal Voltage of the Power Grid

The nonlinear load in the simulation is a three-phase non-controlled rectifier bridge, the DC side is connected with two 4 Ω resistors, the middle line is drawn from the midpoint

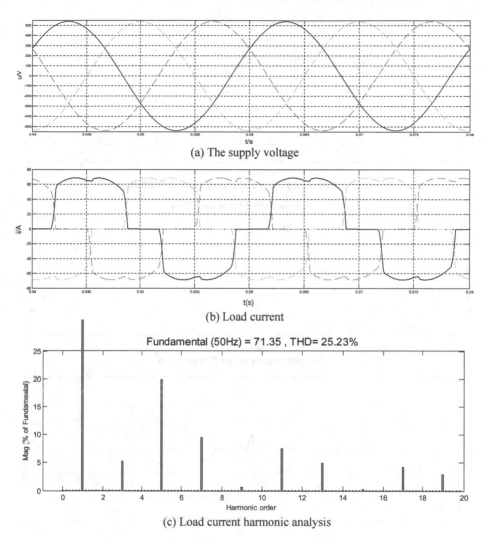

(a) The supply voltage

(b) Load current

Fundamental (50Hz) = 71.35 , THD= 25.23%

(c) Load current harmonic analysis

Fig. 5. Voltage and load current without distortion of the supply voltage

of the DC side, and the inductance of the AC side of the DC bridge is connected by 0.2 mH.

When the grid voltage is free of distortion, the voltage and current of the load are shown in Fig. 5, which shows that the load current is severely distorted and unbalanced, containing a large number of $6k \pm 1$ harmonic.

$i_p - i_q - i_0$ **Detection method**.

$p - q - r$ **Detection method**.

The positive sequence current of the load fundamental detected by $i_p - i_q - i_0$ method and the harmonic current to be compensated are shown in Fig. 6. The positive sequence current of the load fundamental detected by $p - q - r$ and the harmonic current to be compensated are shown in Fig. 7.

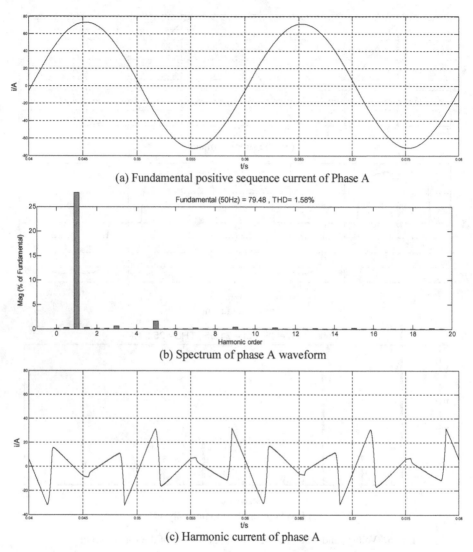

(a) Fundamental positive sequence current of Phase A

(b) Spectrum of phase A waveform

(c) Harmonic current of phase A

Fig. 6. Results of the $i_p - i_q - i_0$ detection method when the supply voltage is free of distortion

The positive current of the load base wave detected by the $i_p - i_q - i_0$ method and the harmonic current to be compensated are shown in Fig. 6. The positive sequential current of the load base wave detected by $p - q - r$ and the harmonic current to be compensated are shown in Fig. 7. The spectrum analysis of the positive current of the base wave captured by the two detection algorithms shows that the distortion rate of the positive sequential current of the a-phase-based wave detected by the $i_p - i_q - i_0$ method is 1.58%, and the distortion rate of the positive-order current of the a-phase-based wave detected by the $p - q - r$ method is 1.50%, which shows that under the ideal condition of the

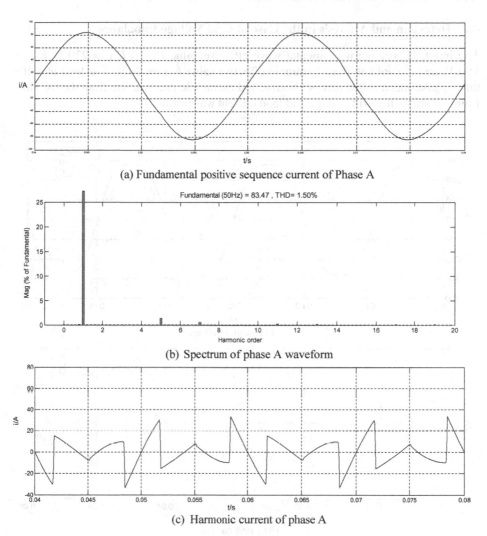

(a) Fundamental positive sequence current of Phase A

Fundamental (50Hz) = 83.47 , THD= 1.50%

(b) Spectrum of phase A waveform

(c) Harmonic current of phase A

Fig. 7. Results of the $p - q - r$ detection method when the supply voltage is free of distortion.

power grid voltage, both the $i_p - i_q - i_0$ method and the $p - q - r$ method can accurately detect the positive current of the base wave, and the effect is not much different.

4.2 Detection and Analysis in the Case of Grid Voltage Imbalance

The input AC voltage fundamental wave effective value $E_{a1} = E_{c1} = 220$ V, $E_{b1} = 150$ V, and the voltage third harmonic effective value $E_{x3} = 30$ V. The load is still a three-phase uncontrolled rectifier bridge, and the middle line is drawn from the DC side. Figure 8 shows the grid voltage and load current waveforms.

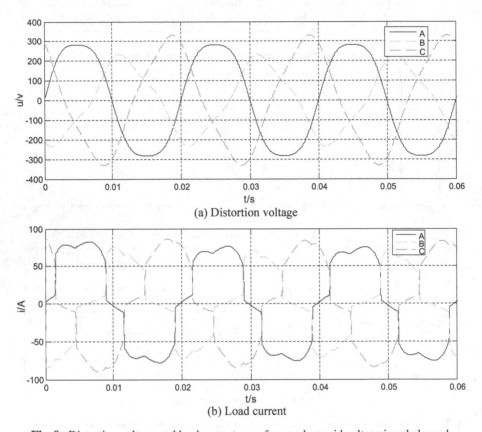

(a) Distortion voltage

(b) Load current

Fig. 8. Distortion voltage and load current waveforms when grid voltage is unbalanced.

In the case of grid voltage imbalance, the improved $p - q - r$ method uses unit sine signal instead of the real-time grid voltage detected by the voltage sensor, and the resulting a-phase and b-phase-based wave spectrum is shown in Fig. 9(b) and (c), which can detect harmonic currents in real-time. Figure 10 is the application of $p - q - r$ harmonic detection method to compensate for the front and rear waveforms of the midline current, indicating that the method is good for the midline current compensation effect.

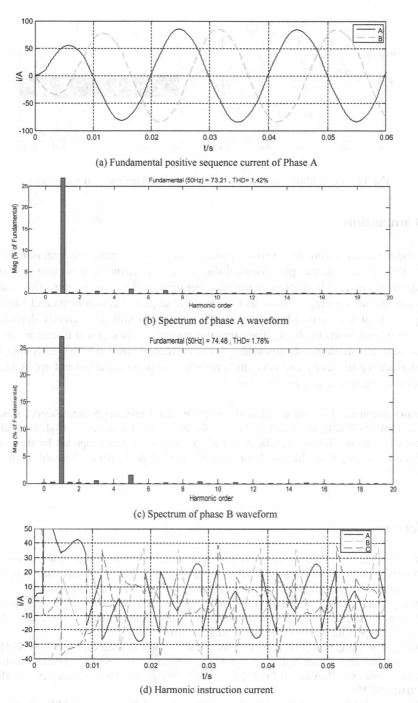

(a) Fundamental positive sequence current of Phase A

(b) Spectrum of phase A waveform

(c) Spectrum of phase B waveform

(d) Harmonic instruction current

Fig. 9. The results of the $p - q - r$ detection method when the voltage of the power grid is unbalanced.

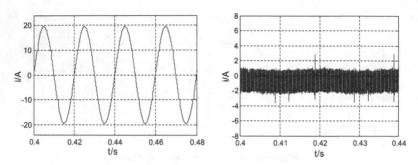

Fig. 10. The midline current compensates for the front and rear waveforms

5 Conclusion

This paper mainly introduces the basic principle of $p - q - r$ harmonic detection method under the TF system, and puts forward the $p - q - r$ harmonic detection method of voltage-free sensor. Simulation proves that the improved $p - q - r$ detection method does not require a voltage sensor, and the positive sequence components and harmonic components of the current-based wave of the grid can still be correctly detected in the case of uneven grid voltage. The capacitor midpoint active power filter uses the harmonic detection method to compensate the midline current well, which greatly simplifies the engineering difficulty and cost, and promotes the popularization and application of capacitive structure active power filter.

Acknowledgement. The authors acknowledge the Jiangsu University Natural Science Research Project (18KJB470024) and Funding Project for Professional Leaders of Higher Vocational Colleges in Jiangsu Province (2020GRGDYX070). This work was supported by the practice and innovation project of Jiangsu Vocational Institute of Architectural Technology in 2019 (JYSCZ19-10).

References

1. Beres, R.N., Wang, X., Liserre, M., Blaabjerg, F., Bak, C.L.: A review of passive power filters for three-phase grid-connected voltage-source converters. IEEE J. Emerg. Sel. Top. Power Electron. **4**(1), 54–69 (2016). https://doi.org/10.1109/JESTPE.2015.2507203
2. Wang, X.Q., Zhao, J.W., Wang, Q.J., Li, G.L., Zhang, M.S.: Improved three-phase four wire harmonic detection method. Dianji yu Kongzhi Xuebao/Electr. Mach. Control **24**(9), 84–94 (2020). https://doi.org/10.15938/j.emc.2020.09.010
3. Kang, Y.K., Jung, H.G., Lee, K.B.: Control method in a wind turbine driven by 3-parallel back-to-back converters using PQR power transformation. In: 2010 International Power Electronics Conference - ECCE Asia -, IPEC 2010, pp. 2562–2568 (2010). https://doi.org/10.1109/IPEC.2010.5542356
4. Hasim, A.S.B.A., Dardin, S.M.F.S., Ibrahim, Z.B., Azid, A.B.A., Ishak, A.M.B.: Comparative study; different types of PWM control scheme in three-phase four-wire shunt active power filter (APF) topology (2019). https://doi.org/10.1109/ICECOS.2018.8605234

5. Ben Braiek, M.L., Fnaiech, F., Al-Haddad, K., Yacoubi, L.: Comparison of direct current control techniques for a three-phase shunt active power filter. In: IEEE International Symposium on Industrial Electronics, vol. 4 (2002). https://doi.org/10.1109/isie.2002.1025963
6. Li, D.: Study on control strategy and application of a new harmonic detection method in three-phase four-wire APF. Concurr. Comput. **31**(10), e4853 (2019). https://doi.org/10.1002/cpe.4853
7. Bao, L., Xia, J., Dong, Z., Deng, Y., Lu, Y., Yang, Y.: An improved three-phase four-wire harmonic detection algorithm based on multi-synchronous rotating frame transformation. In: IECON Proceedings (Industrial Electronics Conference), vol. 2019, pp. 2115–2120 (2019). https://doi.org/10.1109/IECON.2019.8927561
8. Wang, G., Chang, W., Bak, C.L., Zhou, M., Hao, Z.: Control strategy for combined co-phase power supply system based on theory of control without harmonic detection and selective harmonic compensation. Dianli Zidonghua Shebei/Electr. Power Autom. Equip. **37**(12), 130–137 (2017). https://doi.org/10.16081/j.issn.1006-6047.2017.12.018
9. Yuniantoro, I., Gunawan, R., Setiabudy, R.: The PQR-coordinate in the mapping matrices model of Kim-Akagi on power transformation based on Euler angle rotation method. In: 2013 International Conference on Quality in Research, QiR 2013 - In Conjunction with ICCS 2013: The 2nd International Conference on Civic Space, pp. 121–126 (2013). https://doi.org/10.1109/QiR.2013.6632549
10. Lee, S.J., Kim, H., Sul, S.K., Blaabjerg, F.: A novel control algorithm for static series compensators by use of PQR instantaneous power theory. IEEE Trans. Power Electron. **19**(3), 814–827 (2004). https://doi.org/10.1109/TPEL.2004.826499
11. Kim, H., Lee, S.J., Sul, S.K.: Reference wave generation in dynamic voltage restorers by use of PQR power theory. In: Conference Proceedings - IEEE Applied Power Electronics Conference and Exposition - APEC, vol. 3, pp. 1452–1457 (2004). https://doi.org/10.1109/apec.2004.1296055

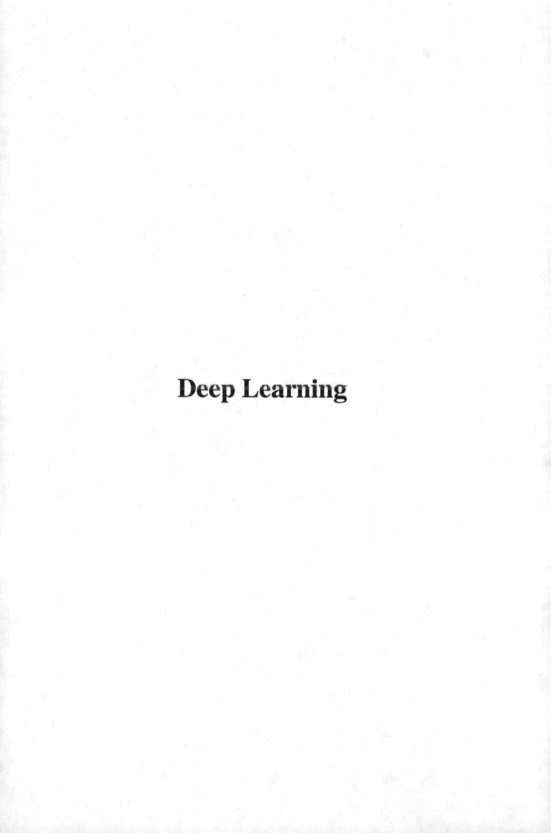

Deep Learning

Effective WiTech Identification Using Deep Transfer Learning with SNR as an Additional Feature

Sachin Nayak[1]([✉]), Amitesh Singh Sisodia[2], and Subrahamanya Swamy Peruru[2]

[1] University of Washington, Seattle, WA 98195, USA
sachinn@uw.edu
[2] Indian Institute of Technology Kanpur, Kanpur 208016, Uttar Pradesh, India
{amiteshs,swamyp}@iitk.ac.in

Abstract. Efficient sensing of wireless technology is critical in today's congested wireless ecosystem for effective utilization of limited resources. This paper presents a novel approach to wireless technology identification using deep transfer learning techniques, which are known to outperform conventional methods. A thorough study is required to understand the format of the data which is best suited for the task of technology identification, since wireless technology data is available in multiple formats like time-domain and frequency-domain representation. More importantly, which neural network architecture works best for each of these representations is to be studied. In this work, we show that fully connected neural networks and convolutional neural networks work best for classifying frequency-domain data and long short-term memory networks for time-domain data. Further, wireless signals with different signal-to-noise ratios (SNRs) may require a different strategy for efficient classification. In particular, a model that works well with signals having a high SNR may not perform well on signals that have low SNR. In this work, we study how the concept of transfer learning can be leveraged to design neural networks that work across different SNRs. In particular, we study questions like whether a neural network pre-trained on high-SNR data can improve the performance on low-SNR data? Our experimental results show that leveraging transfer learning can give additional gains of 4 to 20% in accuracy, depending on the SNR of the signal.

Keywords: Deep learning · Wireless technology identification · Signal to noise ratio · CNNs · LSTMs · FCNs

1 Introduction

In today's world, the spectrum is congested due to the presence of many devices communicating simultaneously [15]. This happens at both public locations like

Supported by University of Washington and the Indian Institute of Technology, Kanpur.

metro stations, streets and industrial locations like factories. Spectrum is sensed by both user devices such as mobile phones & laptops and industry devices, as well as mobile network operators (MNOs) at base stations that communicate to them. Mobile phones sense spectrum as belonging to 2G/3G/4G/5G on the setup as part of a process called initial access and are always on the lookout for Wi-Fi and Bluetooth channels. Wi-Fi devices and industrial devices sense signals in the unlicensed spectrum in order to communicate in the unused white spaces in between occupied spectrum and maximize spectrum usage. MNOs at base stations sense the licensed spectrum to allocate the spectrum with the least interference to its users, as well as to dynamically share spectrum with each other using a switching process.

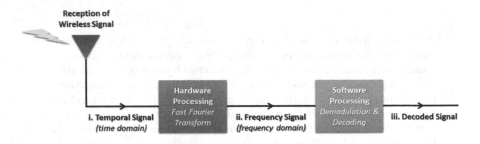

Fig. 1. Down link data processing after signal reception

Dynamic spectrum sharing is another application envisioned by the new 5G standard that requires sensing and switching spectrum [6,16]. In the process of mobile network operators switching from 4G to standalone 5G networks, 5G networks should be operated in non-standalone mode over existing 4G networks over the same frequency band to meet the requirements of spectrum sensing. Rapid spectrum sensing for demand-driven spectrum allocation between 4G and 5G is an essential part of this rollout process [5].

Spectrum sensing could be performed at various stages of the down link data processing, as shown in Fig. 1. Radio signal sensing for technology identification can be done either at acquisition as a temporal signal, after hardware processing as a frequency domain signal, or after software processing as the decoded signal. This is done conventionally at the end of the pipeline by decoding the signal but could be sped up significantly using deep learning algorithms, saving a large amount of energy. Another important aspect of sensing radio signals is that they appear at different signal-to-noise ratios (SNRs) based on the noise level and device density. A model designed for a particular SNR may not work for a different SNR. Hence, SNR is an important feature to consider while designing a model for wireless technology identification.

To meet the need for spectrum sensing for various applications, this paper describes an efficient and effective method to sense spectrum using deep learning. We focus on the unlicensed spectrum consisting of Wi-Fi, Bluetooth, and Zigbee signals since real signals are easy to capture for those technologies.

1.1 Related Work

Apart from detecting the wireless technology from the decoded signal as in Fig. 1, conventional methods for detecting wireless signals include energy detection [2] and standard machine learning [11] approaches. Most classification tasks focus on data for modulation schemes [8,12] rather than complex wireless technology standards like 4G, Wi-Fi, Bluetooth etc. Most data sets for classification purposes contain data obtained by simulations in MATLAB [13] or GNU Radio [9,17] due to the unavailability of real wireless signal data. Whenever real data was used or experimental studies were performed for data of wireless standards, the focus is one detecting one specific type of signal as in the following applications: Wi-Fi signal detection for LTE-WiFi Coexistence [4], detection of Bluetooth signals for frequency hopping [1] and detection of radar signals [7]. To the best of our knowledge, a combined study involving joint sensing of different wireless technologies by a single neural network has not been attempted in the past. Moreover, SNR is never considered as an input to any of the existing spectrum sensing algorithms. Hence, this study is unique as we trained a single neural network to sense a variety of wireless technology signals as well as adapting it across SNRs.

1.2 Our Contributions

In this work, we study the application of deep neural networks for wireless technology classification. We make the below contributions.

Matching Neural Networks to Wireless Signal Formats. Wireless technology data is available in both time domain and frequency domain, and can be represented in a variety of formats such as real & imaginary, phase & linear magnitude etc., for the same snapshot. The complexity and the accuracy of the classification task critically depends on the particular format of the signal and the architecture of the neural network that we choose, and therefore a thorough study is required to understand these dependencies. To that end, we identify the neural network architecture that works best for each format of wireless signals by studying their various characteristics. In particular, we observe that LSTMs work best for time domain data, FCNs & CNNs for frequency domain data. We also notice that the depth of the neural networks used for obtaining good accuracy on wireless signals is limited to 5–6 layers.

Using the Additional Feature of SNR in Wireless Signals. Wireless signals can appear at different SNRs based on the noise level and device congestion. We investigate whether the knowledge of this detected SNR of a signal can be effectively utilized to improve the performance. To that end, we propose a transfer learning based approach that improves the classification accuracy at certain SNRs, for which the neural network was performing poorly. In particular, we observe that transfer learning results in gains of 4 to 5% in accuracy for SNRs above −12 dB, and 20% improvement for SNRs below −12 dB. This shows the adaptivity of neural networks for wireless technology classification across SNRs.

1.3 Organization

The rest of the paper is organized as follows. We start with Sect. 2 on understanding the nature of wireless technology data. Section 3 discusses our process of selecting neural network architectures for different wireless signal formats. Section 4 discusses simulation results across specific SNRs and the use of transfer learning to improve performance. Section 5 highlights the unique insights derived from our simulation study for the purpose of applying neural networks to wireless signals sensing, followed by a short conclusion. The appendix describes the experimental environment used for the simulation study in detail.

2   Nature of Wireless Technology Data

Wireless technology data is available as time domain representation and frequency domain representation for the same snapshot. Conversion to the frequency domain signal requires additional processing at the hardware side and hence is more time-consuming. In addition, the wireless signal in time/frequency domain can be represented as real, imaginary, phase, linear magnitude, decibel magnitude data series or a combination of them, so the best format needs to be selected for classification purposes. The SNR is a time varying feature in wireless technology data that provides an additional degree of freedom.

This section starts with a short description of the dataset, followed by the possible format of wireless signal data and finally a short section on the unique feature of SNR in the wireless signal classification.

2.1   Description of Dataset Used

We focus on radio signal classification of real wireless signal data for the unlicensed spectrum belonging to the Wi-Fi, Bluetooth, and Zigbee standards using the 'owl/interference' dataset [14] from the CRAWDAD database [3] that was established to share data sets collected from real networks. The 'owl/interference' dataset contains traces of IEEE 802.11b/g (Wi-Fi), IEEE 802.15.4 (Zigbee) and Bluetooth packet transmission with varying SNRs in the baseband as shown in Fig. 2. Additionally, different frequency offsets were added in the baseband to reflect different channels of the wireless technologies. The data is in the form of 128 sample IQ snapshots. 15 labels (Bluetooth CH20-29, Wi-Fi CH3-5 and ZigBee CH15-16) and 21 SNRs (−20 dB, −18 dB, . . . 0 dB, 2 dB, 4dB, . . . 20 dB) are possible as indicated by Fig. 2 and Fig. 4 respectively. The dataset is equally distributed in terms of labels and SNRs with 715 snapshots for each label and SNR combination.

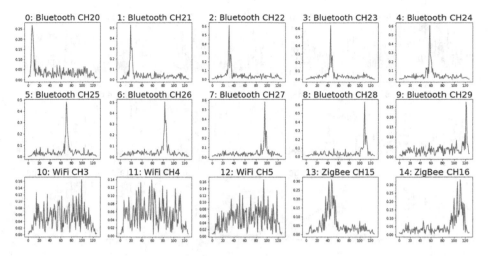

Fig. 2. FFT magnitude snapshots for each label (128 samples across X-axis at 0 dB SNR)

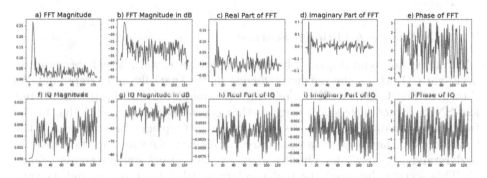

Fig. 3. 10 possible representations for the same wireless signal (128 samples across X-axis for snapshot of Bluetooth CH20 at 0 dB SNR)

2.2 Format of Wireless Signal Data

The time domain IQ representation of a signal can be converted to its frequency domain representation by performing an FFT. Both the time and frequency domain representations are complex vectors with imaginary and real parts that can be converted to phase/magnitude representations with the appropriate transforms. Thus, wireless signal data can be represented by 10 different data series for the same snapshot, as enumerated in Fig. 3.

A combination of these can also be used for any classification purposes, especially with CNNs and LSTMs that can extract features from multidimensional inputs. Popular combinations include the following: i. FFT IQ data in 2D form and ii. IQ Time Series in 2D form.

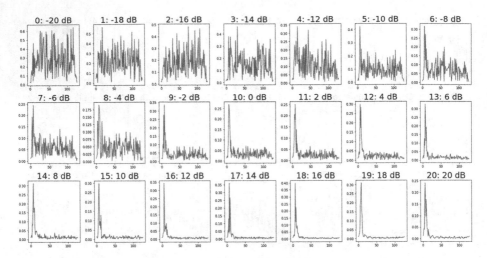

Fig. 4. Bin features become across SNR for the same frequency domain signal (128 samples across X-axis for snapshot of Bluetooth CH20)

2.3   SNR as an Additional Feature

SNR is an additional degree of freedom in wireless signals. This is because the SNR varies both as the hardware device moves spatially and temporally. As shown in Fig. 4, higher SNRs are easily classifiable having sharp features but low SNRs do not have sharp features that can be applied across SNRs. In the frequency domain, these features appears across frequency bins whereas in the time domain, they appear as time bursts. This fact plays an important part in understanding transfer learning to adapt neural network weights across SNRs.

This section discussed the real wireless signal dataset in use and its various representations, and finally the important additional dimension of SNR in wireless signals. The next section details the process of selecting neural network architectures for different wireless signal formats through a systematic simulation methodology.

3   Selecting Neural Network Architectures for Wireless Data Formats

The type of neural network that would suit each data type varies from the ones available in literature. We begin our simulation study by understanding the various formats of wireless signal data in relation to neural networks by classifying them with a simple baseline FCN. The details of the simulation environment used is described in the Appendix. Based on the results obtained regarding the nature of wireless data series, we expand into multi-layered FCNs, LSTMs and then CNNs.

Table 1. Baseline FCN structure

Layer type	Input size	Parameters	Activation function
Fully connected layer	128	15 neurons	SoftMax

3.1 Types of Neural Networks

Neural networks are used to learn complex non-linear functions from inputs to outputs for performing powerful tasks like classification or regression. The neural network architecture that would work best for each wireless signal format needs to be matched from the popular types of long-short term memory (LSTM), convolutional neural network (CNN) and fully connected network (FCN). LSTMs are well-suited for classifying, processing and making predictions based on time series data, since there can be lags of unknown duration between important events in a time series. FCNs would work well for frequency domain representations, as the data is compartmentalized into bins. CNNs are expected to work the best with IQ signal data series in the frequency domain, as they expect 2 dimensional inputs. CNN have been used rigorously for image classification tasks and are being recently extended to the wireless signal domain [10].

The complexity in terms of number of layers and neurons needs to determined as well. The higher the complexity of the neural network, the higher the accuracy, but the time required for classification also increases. A balance of these needs to be achieved to ensure the practical applicability of the neural networks that are trained.

3.2 Selecting Neural Network Architectures for Wireless Data Formats

We identify which format of data works with FCNs best by training the baseline FCN in Table 1 to classify the data formats mentioned in Sect. 2.3. The best classification score is for the 'FFT Magnitude' since most wireless technology features are evidenced by the frequency bins. Since 'FFT Magnitude' works best, we continue our exploration with that format for FCNs by varying the number of hidden layers & neurons and training to obtain the results in Table 3 and the final 2-layer FCN in Table 4.

Moving down the rows of Table 2, we observe that the real and imaginary parts of the FFT lead to very low accuracies of $\approx 20\%$ implying they don't contain sufficient information for classification by themselves. The accuracy for the phase part of FFT is almost 1/15 (remember our dataset has 15 labels) implying that it is uniformly distributed over labels and is least useful for classification out of the 5 FFT data series. We can infer that the information in a frequency domain signal is mainly represented by its magnitude and not its phase.

Looking at the second half of Table 2 containing the time domain data series representations, we notice that the accuracies are extremely low. These are better classified with LSTMs and not FCNs as LSTMs can model temporal correlations

Table 2. Accuracies across wireless signal data series for baseline FCN

Data Type	Accuracy (%)	Data type	Accuracy (%)
FFT Magnitude in dB	85.90	IQ Magnitude in dB	9.85
FFT Magnitude	88.90	IQ Magnitude	7.63
Real Part of FFT	20.58	Real Part of IQ	16.48
Imaginary Part of FFT	20.20	Imaginary Part of IQ	16.04
Phase Part of FFT	7.78	Phase Part of IQ	14.31

Table 3. Accuracies across different FCNs for 'FFT Magnitude' data series

Model	Accuracy (in %)
Baseline Model (No hidden layer but trained for 500 epochs)	85.90
One Hidden Layer with 60 neurons	88.53
One Hidden Layer with 80 neurons	88.90
Two Hidden Layers with 80 & 48 neurons	88.99
One Hidden Layer with 80 neurons, dropout = 0.2	88.90
One Hidden Layer with 80 neurons, dropout = 0.2	88.90
Two Hidden Layers with 80 & 48 neurons, dropout = 0.2 on first layer	89.12
Two Hidden Layers with 80 & 48 neurons, dropout = 0.2 on second layer	88.64
Two Hidden Layers with 80 & 48 neurons, dropout = 0.2 on both layers	89.20

Table 4. Proposed FCN structure

Layer type	Input size	Parameters	Activation function
Fully connected layer	128	80 neurons, dropout = 0.2	LeakyReLU
Fully connected layer	80	48 neurons, dropout = 0.2	LeakyReLU
Fully connected layer	48	15 neurons, dropout = 0.2	SoftMax

better. This also indicates that when a 2D convolutional neural network is to be used, the FFT data in the IQ form or phase/magnitude form would work best over IQ time series data as CNNs are not be able to capture temporal relations well. Another important observation we make is that now the magnitude part of the IQ data (as compared to the phase part) is uniformly distributed, implying that the information in a time domain signal is mostly represented by its phase and not magnitude.

Table 5. Proposed LSTM model

Layer type	Input size	Parameters	Activation function
Unidirectional LSTM Layer	128 × 2	256 neurons, dropout = 0.6	Tanh
Unidirectional LSTM Layer	128 × 256	256 neurons, dropout = 0.6	Tanh
Fully connected layer	256	15 neurons	SoftMax

Table 6. Structure of CNN2 [10]

Layer type	Input size	Parameters	Activation function
Convolutional layer	2 × 128	256 filters, filter size 1 × 3 dropout = 0.2	ReLU
Convolutional layer	256 × 2 × 128	80 filters, filter size 2 × 3 dropout = 0.6	ReLU
Fully connected layer	10240 × 1	256 neurons, dropout = 0.6	ReLU
Fully connected layer	256 × 1	15 neurons	SoftMax

Table 7. Performance Comparison for LSTM, CNN, and FCN models for different SNR scenarios [P: Precision; R: Recall; F1: F1-Score; High SNR: ≥ 0 dB; Low SNR: <0 dB]

Model	All SNR			High SNR			Low SNR		
	P	R	F1	P	R	F1	P	R	F1
LSTM	0.96	0.96	0.96	0.96	0.92	0.94	0.83	0.83	0.81
CNN	0.96	0.96	0.96	0.99	0.97	0.98	0.84	0.86	0.84
FCN	0.94	0.94	0.94	0.95	0.94	0.94	0.88	0.87	0.87

On experimenting with LSTMs of different lengths for our dataset, we arrive at the LSTM in Table 5 with 2 layers. The input to this LSTM is the IQ time series with both the real and imaginary components. In addition, we just choose CNN2, reproduced in Table 6, that was shown to give very high accuracies for modulation recognition [10] with input as the FFT IQ data format. On fully training these three models for the entire dataset for High (≥ 0 dB) and Low SNR (< 0 dB) splits of the dataset, we summarize the results as in Table 7. We note that the CNN and LSTM models perform slightly better than the FCN model due to the larger size of their inputs, enabling them to use all the information about the snapshot. Note that for each neural network type, i.e., LSTM, CNN and FCN, a different model (with different weights) is learned for each of the 3 splits of the dataset, i.e., i. All SNR, ii. Low SNR (< 0 dB) and iii. High SNR (≥ 0 dB), resulting in 3 models for each type.

The results from Table 7 shows that accuracies for the low SNR split differ from that of high SNR split by over 10% implying that SNR has an influence on wireless signal classification. For example, the accuracy changes from 83% for Low SNR to 96% for All SNR. The next section showcases simulation results for each SNR to understand this more deeply, and then elucidates the innovation of applying transfer learning for wireless signal classification.

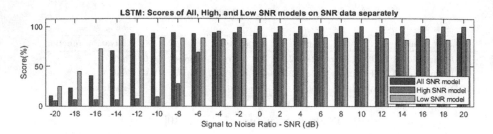

Fig. 5. Accuracies across SNR for LSTM models trained with different splits

4   Simulation Results on Specific SNRs and Use of Transfer Learning

In depth investigations are performed at each SNR specifically to truly under-stand the nature of wireless signal data and the adaptability of neural networks across this new dimension of wireless signals. This results in an understanding that transfer learning across SNRs can give large gains, as the accuracies across SNRs vary by large margins. Hence, our last subsection showcases the utility of transfer learning to adapt neural network weights across SNRs.

4.1   Investigating the Performance on Specific SNRs

SNR has a significant impact on the performance of the deep learning models, as models trained at low SNRs would not work as well as those trained at high SNRs. Moreover, a given trained deep learning model is more likely to perform better for high SNR inputs over low SNR inputs. To further analyze the variability of SNR influence on models trained with the three different splits: i. All SNR, ii. High SNR and iii. Low SNR, we visualize the accuracies for each SNR separately for LSTM as in Fig. 5 and make the below observations.

- As expected, the accuracies at lower SNR is lower with the values starting to drop beginning with 0 dB, i.e., for negative values. There is a drastic drop in accuracy at −12 dB.
- Models trained on the low SNR split seem to work reasonably at the higher SNRs, but models trained on the high SNR split work poorly at low SNRs and break down below −12 dB.
- For the lowest SNRs of ≤−12 dB, the models trained on the low SNR split seem to work better than the models trained over all SNRs implying the need to train models specifically for these lowest SNRs.

The reason behind these observations is that deep learning models can learn more generalized patterns at low SNRs but only specific patterns from high SNR data. The fact that specific models need to be trained to detect lowest SNRs of ≤−12 dB means that these SNRs do not contain enough information, and most of the information in the lower SNR split comes from the range of −8 dB to

0 dB. This calls for the need to learn specific weights or models to improve the performance of neural networks for specific SNRs which we do through the process of transfer learning described in the next section.

4.2   Leveraging Transfer Learning across the SNR Feature

Motivated by the need to improve deep learning performance for specific SNRs and inspired by the fact that neural networks pretrained at low SNRs can learn generalized features, we turn to transfer learning. Transfer learning is a machine learning method where a model learned for a given task is reused for a second task, using it as the starting or base model. It enables one to reuse or transfer information from previously learned tasks for the learning of new tasks.

We use transfer learning to improve the performance of deep learning models in the previous section in relation to specific SNRs. For a given neural network type, say LSTM, we have 3 models trained for the 3 splits of All SNR, Low SNR and High SNR respectively. We perform transfer learning to each SNR for each of the 3 models for the given network type. We perform the same for all 3 network types to result in the accuracies illustrated by Fig. 6. The results for SNR >-2 dB are not shown, as their accuracies without transfer learning are almost 100%. We make the below observations regarding applying transfer learning to improve the performance of our models for specific SNRs.

– Transfer learning improves accuracies across all the SNRs in Fig. 6 for all pre-trained models by modest values of 4 to 5% showing that transfer learning is effective in improving the performance of deep learning for wireless signals.
– Transfer learning seems to be most effective with LSTMs followed by CNNs and FCNs.
– The gains increase to 10 to 20% for the lowest SNRs for all the three models. In particular, when pretrained LSTMs are used, additional gains of 10% are witnessed.
– In general, neural networks pre-trained on the low SNR split give the best performance with transfer learning.
– However, FCNs are different in the manner that pretraining on the all SNR split gives larger gains over the low SNR split, showing that LSTM and CNN can learn generalized patterns due to their more complex structure.

Transfer learning works well with wireless signals for specific SNRs because any given wireless signal (say Bluetooth CH20) has the same features across SNRs. For example, we can look back at Fig. 4 to notice that the frequency peak appears at the same location across SNRs. Pretraining on the low SNR splits gives the best gains as neural networks can learn the most generalized features from them due to the presence of noise, which makes it robust to overfitting. Additional experiments were tried regarding transfer learning from the low SNR split to the high SNR split (or between any two splits) rather than specific SNRs, but they did not show good results, showing that transfer learning works only for a narrow SNR range.

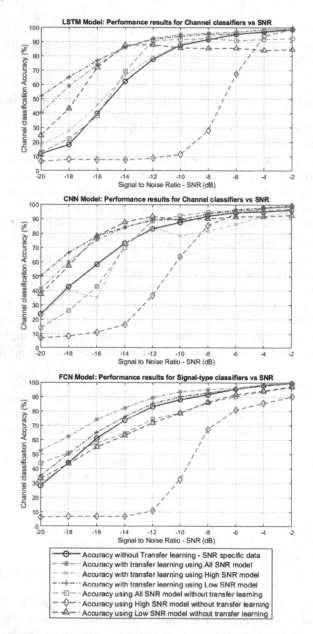

Fig. 6. Performance of Models on SNR specific data with and without transfer learning with Accuracy as performance parameter [Detailed information is present in the Legend]

This subsection emphasized the innovation of transfer learning as applied to wireless signal classification using deep learning. The next section summarizes all such insights obtained along this study for future research purposes.

5   Summary of Insights

This section discusses the unique insights derived from our simulation study across different types of neural networks, data formats and SNRs for the purpose of deployment of neural networks for wireless signal sensing, whether in consumer devices or industrial devices that control the network themselves like base stations. We make the below findings.

Information in Various Wireless Signal Formats. In wireless signals, the information in the frequency domain is represented mainly by the magnitude different from the phase in the time domain. The real and imaginary parts by themselves do not carry enough information and need to be input together for any deep learning applications. However, training neural networks solely using the 'FFT Magnitude' (as we did for the FCN we proposed) or 'IQ Phase' is less effective than using both the real and imaginary parts as input (as we did for the proposed LSTM and CNN2).

Neural Networks Selected for Various Wireless Signal Formats. One requires LSTMs or other forms of RNNs to represent the temporal structure of time domain signals in order to classify them as compared to FCNs or CNNs for frequency domain signals. As indicated by Fig. 1, frequency domain signals are obtained at a later stage in the down link processing pipeline and would require higher latencies to process. The neural networks we ended up choosing after thorough experimentation had reasonable length of a couple of layers, implying that neural networks can be feasibly implemented for hardware applications.

Insights on Using SNR as an Additional Feature. Neural networks are able to learn more generalized patterns at low SNRs and specific patterns from higher SNRs. However, the lowest SNRs do not have enough information in them, implying the need to train neural networks specifically for them. When applied to a narrow SNR range, transfer learning improves the performance of neural networks. The gains obtained are in the range of 4 to 5%. The gains increase to > 20% for the lowest SNRs.

6   Conclusion

Application of deep learning to wireless technology identification is not well researched due to the unavailability of real wireless signal data. This study started with understanding the nature of real wireless signal data using deep learning to arrive at the point that using FCNs/CNNs for FFT data and LSTMs for IQ time-series data is suitable. Further investigation showed that the performance of the neural network varies across the SNR of the wireless signal in question, calling for the need to study this additional dimension of wireless signals. We propose a transfer learning based approach to improve the accuracies at

SNRs for which the models were performing poorly. For signals with poor SNRs (<-12 dB), the proposed transfer learning approach improves the accuracies by 20%. In general, for other SNRs, we observe gains of 4 to 5%. The gains in speed and accuracy would make deep learning a strong choice for wireless technology identification.

Appendix- Details of Training and Analysis

Implementation Details. The neural networks are implemented using the Keras framework, an open-source software library that provides a Python interface for building artificial neural networks. It has a simple and highly modular interface, which makes it easier to create complex neural network models. Colab, a Google's free notebook environment, is used for training the models using GPUs.

Training Details. The whole dataset is partitioned into training, validation, and test splits in [60:20:20] ratio The labels y_data is converted into One-hot vectors for classification using Keras library. The input X_data for each model is normalized to have a train_mean of 0 and a standard deviation of 1. This removes bias in the data for better training, improves the stability of the model, and speeds up the training process. All the models are trained for a maximum of 200 epochs and the batch_size is 1024 for all the models, unless mentioned. Categorical loss is used along with Adam optimizer. EarlyStopping Technique is used for checking the problem of overfitting using validation accuracy as the monitor (parameters: min_delta = 0.001, patience = [LSTM:15; CNN:60; FCN:60]).

Analysis Details. Test accuracy is used as the main indicator for model performance in this paper because it is the accuracy achieved by the model on unseen data and hence is the optimal choice for checking robustness for practical applications. Performance of a classification model is quantified in terms of the precision (Π), recall (Ψ) and F1-score performance metrics. The precision metric quantifies how many positive results are actually positive, the recall provides information on how much true positives are identified correctly as positive, and F1-score gives an overall measure for the accuracy of a classifier model since it is the harmonic average of precision and recall. These metrics are calculated as below.

$$\Pi = \frac{\xi}{\xi + \nu}, \Psi = \frac{\xi}{\xi + \mu}, F_1 - Score = 2 \times \frac{\Pi \times \Psi}{\Pi + \Psi},$$

where ξ, ν, and μ denote the numbers of true positive, false positive, and false negative, respectively.

References

1. Bitar, N., Muhammad, S., Refai, H.H.: Wireless technology identification using deep convolutional neural networks. In: 2017 IEEE 28th Annual International Symposium on Personal, Indoor, and Mobile Radio Communications (PIMRC), pp. 1–6 (2017). https://doi.org/10.1109/PIMRC.2017.8292183

2. Cabric, D., Tkachenko, A., Brodersen, R.W.: Experimental study of spectrum sensing based on energy detection and network cooperation. In: Proceedings of the First International Workshop on Technology and Policy for Accessing Spectrum, TAPAS '06, p. 12-es. Association for Computing Machinery, New York (2006). https://doi.org/10.1145/1234388.1234400

3. CRAWDAD a community resource for archiving wireless data at dartmouth. https://crawdad.org/about.html. Accessed 13 June 2021

4. Dziedzic, A., Sathya, V., Rochman, M.I., Ghosh, M., Krishnan, S.: Machine learning enabled spectrum sharing in dense LTE-U/Wi-Fi coexistence scenarios. IEEE Open J. Veh. Technol. 1, 173–189 (2020)

5. A new standard for dynamic spectrum sharing. https://www.ericsson.com/en/blog/2019/6/dynamic-spectrum-sharing-standardization. Accessed 15 June 2021

6. Kaltenberger, F., Knopp, R., Danneberg, M., Festag, A.: Experimental analysis and simulative validation of dynamic spectrum access for coexistence of 4g and future 5g systems. In: 2015 European Conference on Networks and Communications (EuCNC), pp. 497–501 (2015). https://doi.org/10.1109/EuCNC.2015.7194125

7. Lees, W.M., Wunderlich, A., Jeavons, P., Hale, P., Souryal, M.: Deep learning classification of 3.5-GHZ band spectrograms with applications to spectrum sensing. IEEE Trans. Cogn. Commun. Netw. 5, 224–236 (2019)

8. Meng, F., Chen, P., Wu, L., Wang, X.: Automatic modulation classification: a deep learning enabled approach. IEEE Trans. Veh. Technol. 67(11), 10760–10772 (2018). https://doi.org/10.1109/TVT.2018.2868698

9. O'Shea, T., West, N.: Radio machine learning dataset generation with gnu radio. In: Proceedings of the GNU Radio Conference, vol. 1, no. 1 (2016). https://pubs.gnuradio.org/index.php/grcon/article/view/11

10. O'Shea, T.J., Corgan, J.: Convolutional radio modulation recognition networks. CoRR (2016). http://arxiv.org/abs/1602.04105

11. O'Mahony, G.D., Harris, P.J., Murphy, C.C.: Detecting interference in wireless sensor network received samples: a machine learning approach. In: 2020 IEEE 6th World Forum on Internet of Things (WF-IoT), pp. 1–6 (2020). https://doi.org/10.1109/WF-IoT48130.2020.9221332

12. Peng, S., Jiang, H., Wang, H., Alwageed, H., Yao, Y.D.: Modulation classification using convolutional neural network based deep learning model. In: 2017 26th Wireless and Optical Communication Conference (WOCC), pp. 1–5 (2017). https://doi.org/10.1109/WOCC.2017.7929000

13. Riyaz, S., Sankhe, K., Ioannidis, S., Chowdhury, K.: Deep learning convolutional neural networks for radio identification. IEEE Commun. Mag. 56(9), 146–152 (2018). https://doi.org/10.1109/MCOM.2018.1800153

14. Schmidt, M., Block, D., Meier, U.: CRAWDAD dataset owl/interference (v. 2019-02-12) (2019). https://crawdad.org/owl/interference/20190212

15. Taylor, G., Middleton, C., Fernando, X.: A question of scarcity: spectrum and Canada's urban core. J. Inf. Pol. 7, 120–163 (2017). http://www.jstor.org/stable/10.5325/jinfopoli.7.2017.0120

16. Wan, L., Guo, Z., Chen, X.: Enabling efficient 5G NR and 4G LTE coexistence. IEEE Wirel. Commun. 26, 6–8 (2019). https://doi.org/10.1109/MWC.2019.8641417

17. Ziegler, J.L., Arn, R.T., Chambers, W.: Modulation recognition with GNU Radio, Keras, and HackRF. In: 2017 IEEE International Symposium on Dynamic Spectrum Access Networks (DySPAN), pp. 1–3 (2017). https://doi.org/10.1109/DySPAN.2017.7920747

A Neural Network Algorithm of Learning Rate Adaptive Optimization and Its Application in Emitter Recognition

Jihong Jiang[1], Yan Gou[1,2], Wei Zhang[1,3], Jian Yang[4], Jie Gu[3], and Huaizong Shao[1,4(✉)]

[1] University of Electronic Science and Technology of China, Chengdu 611731, Sichuan, People's Republic of China
hzshao@uestc.edu.cn
[2] Southwest China Institute of Electronic Technology, Chengdu 610036, Sichuan, People's Republic of China
[3] Science and Technology on Electronic Information Control Laboratory, Chengdu 610036, People's Republic of China
[4] Peng Cheng Laboratory, Shenzhen 519012, Guangdong, People's Republic of China

Abstract. The setting of the learning rate in neural network training is very important. A too low learning rate will reduce the network optimization speed and prolong the training time while a too high learning rate is easy to exceed the optimal value, leading to the difficulty of model convergence. To solve this problem, based on the analysis of two common learning rate strategies, the attenuating learning rate and the adaptive learning rate, combined with the Adam algorithm, this paper proposes an adaptive learning rate algorithm based on the value of the current loss function and the previous one, and verifies the effectiveness of the algorithm by using the actual radiation source signal. The experimental results show that compared with the Adam algorithm, the number of network training iterations is reduced by 45.5% and the recognition accuracy has increased by 3.6%, which effectively improves the learning speed and reduces the training time.

Keywords: Neural network · Learning rate · Algorithm optimization · Emitter recognition · Application

1 Introduction

At present, the combination of deep learning and emitter identification is more and more closely. The realization of the recognition system is usually based on the construction and training of deep learning network model, and its goal is to minimize the loss function. The existing methods to improve the performance of deep learning systems are as follows: one is to optimize the network model structure, such as increasing the number of network

Supported by National Natural Science Foundation of China: NSFC61871092

D. Jiang and H. Song (Eds.): SIMUtools 2021, LNICST 424, pp. 390–402, 2022.
https://doi.org/10.1007/978-3-030-97124-3_29

layers, replacing simple neuron units with complex LSTM neurons [1]; the second is to optimize the initialization mode of the model to ensure that the early gradient has some beneficial properties [2], or has a lot of sparsity [3]. The third is to choose a better learning algorithm.

Gradient Descent algorithm [4] is a relatively simple and commonly used learning rate algorithm in machine learning. On this basis, researchers gradually put forward some extended methods, such as the Batch Gradient Descent algorithm [5], Stochastic Gradient Descent algorithm (SGD) [6], Mini-batch Gradient Descent algorithm [7], and Stochastic Gradient Descent with Momentum [8–10]. The Stochastic Gradient Descent algorithm with Momentum includes classical Momentum method and acceleration gradient algorithm based on momentum variation. In some basic gradient descent algorithms, the parameters are usually updated by a given global learning rate. It is difficult to optimize all variables to the minimum due to the different dependence of the variables to be optimized on the objective function. To solve this problem, researchers gradually optimize the method of updating the learning rate, and finally, the adaptive learning rate algorithm is born. For example, Jhon Duchi (2011) proposed AdaGrad algorithm [11], Tieleman, T. and Hinton, G. (2012) proposed RMSProp algorithm [12], Zeiler (2012) proposed AdaDelta algorithm [13], Kingma (2014) proposed Adam [14] algorithm, Timothy, D. (2016) proposed Nadam [15] algorithm, GH Wei et al. (2018) proposed ANGD algorithm [16].

This paper mainly analyzes the learning rate attenuation methods such as piecewise constant attenuation, exponential attenuation and cosine attenuation, as well as adaptive learning rate algorithms such as AdaGrad, RMSProp, and Adam. Combined with Adam algorithm, an algorithm of adaptive adjustment of learning rate based on the value of the current loss function and the previous one is proposed. Finally, the effectiveness of the algorithm is verified by the actual emitter signal.

2 Common Learning Rate Strategies in Neural Networks

At present, the learning rate strategies in deep learning are mainly divided into attenuation learning rate and adaptive change learning rate. The attenuation learning rate mainly includes piecewise constant attenuation, exponential attenuation, cosine attenuation and so on. Adaptive learning rate mainly includes AdaGrad algorithm, RMSProp algorithm, and Adam algorithm.

2.1 Attenuating Learning Rate

In the process of neural network training, the learning rate strategy, which decreases with the number of iterations, mainly includes piecewise constant attenuation, exponential decay, cosine attenuation, and so on [10].

1) Piecewise constant decay: Different learning rates are set at the defined training interval. The attenuation curve is shown in Fig. 1 (a). In the figure, the total number of training iterations is 50, and the learning rate constant is updated every 10 iterations.
2) Exponential decay: The learning rate is updated by exponential decay, and the update rules are as follows,

$$DLr = Lr \times Dr^{Gstep/Dstep} \tag{1}$$

where DLr is the learning rate after attenuation, Lr is the initial learning rate, Dr is the attenuation coefficient, $Gstep$ is the current number of training steps, $Dstep$ is the decay period. The attenuation curve is shown in Fig. 1(b). In the figure, the red line represents the ladder-type exponential decay. The green one is the standard exponential decay. The Lr is 0.5, the Dr is 0.9, and the $Dstep$ is 10.
3) Polynomial decay: It set an initial learning rate and a minimum learning rate. According to the polynomial attenuation rule, the learning rate gradually decreases from the initial value to the minimum value. When the learning rate decreases to the minimum value, the minimum value can be maintained for continuous training, otherwise the learning rate can be increased again to particular value, and then attenuated to the minimum value. The polynomial attenuation rules are as follows,

$$Gstep = minGstep, Dstep \tag{2}$$

$$DLr = Lr - ELr \times 1 - \frac{Gstep^p}{Dstep} + ELr \tag{3}$$

where ELr is the minimum learning rate. The default value is 0.0001, p is the polynomial power, the default value is 1.

If the learning rate decreases to the minimum value, continue to repeat the ascending and descending process, and the update formulas are as follows.

$$Dstep = Dstep \times ceil(Gstep/Dstep) \tag{4}$$

$$DLr = Lr - ELr \times 1 - \frac{Gstep^p}{Dstep} + ELr \tag{5}$$

The polynomial attenuation curve of the learning rate is shown in Fig. 1 (c). In the figure, the Lr is 0.1, the ELr is 0.01, the $Dstep$ is 50, and the p is 0.5.

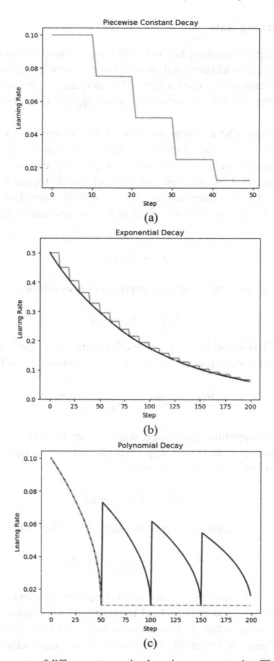

Fig. 1. Learning rate curve of different attenuating learning rate strategies: The abscissa represents the steps, and the ordinate represents the learning rate. The red line indicates that the learning rate does not rise after it decays to ELr and remains unchanged. The green line indicates that the learning rate will rise and fall after it decays to ELr. (a) piecewise constant decay; (b) exponential decay; (c) polynomial decay. (Color figure online)

2.2 Adaptive Learning Rate

The basic idea of adaptive learning rate is to make the learning rate automatically adapt to the parameters of the model through dynamic changes in the process of neural network model training. The commonly used adaptive learning rate algorithms mainly include the AdaGrad algorithm, RMSProp algorithm, Adam algorithm, and so on.

1) AdaGrad algorithm: The learning rate strategy in the algorithm is suitable for data with sparse features. For data with sparse features, it uses a higher learning rate to update parameters; for data with non-sparse features, it uses a lower learning rate to update parameters. It is assumed that in the classical stochastic gradient descent algorithm, any network parameters are updated with the same learning rate η. In the tth training update, the gradient $g_{t,i}$ of the objective function to the parameters θ_i is as follows.

$$g_{t,i} = \nabla_\theta J(\theta_i) \tag{6}$$

The updating equation of network parameters is as follows.

$$\theta_{t+1,i} = \theta_{t,i} - \eta g_{t,i} \tag{7}$$

In the AdaGrad algorithm, each network parameter is updated with a different learning rate. The updating equation of network parameters is as follows,

$$\theta_{t+1,i} = \theta_{t,i} - \frac{\eta}{\sqrt{G_{t,i} + \varepsilon}} \cdot g_{t,i} \tag{8}$$

where ε is a smoothing parameter, which generally takes e^{-8}, η is the global learning rate and needs to be set manually. $G_{t,i}$ represents the cumulative square gradient of the previous t-step parameter θ_i.

$$G_{t,i} = G_{t-1,i} + g_{t,i}^2 \tag{9}$$

The vector representation of network parameter update rules is as follows.

$$\theta_{t+1} = \theta_t - \frac{\eta}{\sqrt{G_t + \varepsilon}} \odot g_t \tag{10}$$

Although the AdaGrad algorithm can accelerate the gradient descent when dealing with sparse data, it is easy to lead to premature and excessive attenuation of the learning rate due to the continuous accumulation of the gradient square value of parameters from the beginning of training, so it cannot effectively update the network parameters.

2) RMSProp algorithm: RMSProp is an improved AdaGrad algorithm. Aiming at the problem that the learning rate of AdaGrad algorithm decays too fast, RMSProp introduces the attenuation coefficient. It improves the cumulative gradient sum of squares into an exponential decay moving average, which weakens the influence of

the historical gradient on the current learning rate. The exponential attenuation of the square of the gradient is calculated as follows,

$$E\left[g^2\right]_t = \gamma E\left[g^2\right]_{t-1} + (1 - \gamma)g_t^2 \tag{11}$$

where t is the number of update iterations, g^2 is the gradient square value of network parameters, γ is the attenuation coefficient, which is generally taken as 0.9. The size of γ determines the influence of the historical gradient value on the current learning rate. The update rule of network parameter θ is as follows,

$$\theta_{t+1} = \theta_t - \frac{\eta}{\sqrt{E\left[g^2\right]_t + \varepsilon}} \odot g_t \tag{12}$$

where η is the global learning rate, the recommended value is 0.001, and g_t is the gradient of network parameters in the tth iteration.

3) Adam algorithm: The basic idea of this algorithm is to calculate the first and second moment estimates of gradient, so that the learning rate can automatically adapt to the parameters of the network model. The gradient attenuation mode of Adam algorithm is as follows,

$$m_t = \beta_1 m_{t-1} + (1 - \beta_1)g_t \tag{13}$$

$$v_t = \beta_2 v_{t-1} + (1 - \beta_2)g_t^2 \tag{14}$$

where m_t is the weighted average of the gradient, v_t is the weighted biased difference of the gradient, and the initialization value is 0. Both β_1 and β_2 are attenuation factors. When β_1 and β_2 approach to 1, m_t and v_t approach to 0. The bias correction of m_t and v_t is as follows.

$$\hat{m}_t = \frac{m_t}{1 - \beta_1^t} \tag{15}$$

$$\hat{v}_t = \frac{v_t}{1 - \beta_2^t} \tag{16}$$

The renewal equation of network parameter θ is as follows, where t is iteration times, η is the global learning rate, and ε is the smoothing parameter.

$$\theta_{t+1} = \theta_t - \frac{\eta}{\sqrt{\hat{v}_t + \varepsilon}}\hat{m}_t \tag{17}$$

3 Learning Rate Algorithm Based on Loss Function

The piecewise constant attenuation strategy has higher requirements on artificial parameter adjustment. The learning rate strategies such as exponential attenuation and cosine attenuation have some problems such as slow convergence speed, serious time-consuming and easy to cross the optimal value. The AdaGrad algorithm is easy to lead to learning rate attenuation too fast and lack of certain robustness. The Adam algorithm usually needs to combine with the attenuation learning rate for model training, only using the default learning rate, the model cannot achieve the optimal convergence effect. Aiming at some existing problems, this paper proposes a learning rate algorithm.

3.1 Algorithm Design

At the beginning of training, the network parameters deviate from the optimal value greatly, and its loss function value is large. At this time, the higher learning rate can be used to accelerate the convergence speed of the model. In the later stage of training, the value of the loss function is close to the optimal value, and the value of the learning rate should be gradually reduced to avoid exceeding the optimal value. Therefore, this algorithm introduces a loss function on the basis of exponential attenuation, and adjusts the step factor of learning rate based on the current loss value and the previous loss value, so as to achieve the purpose of training optimization. The adaptive learning rate update formula is as follows,

$$lr(t) = p^t \beta_0 sigmoid[L(t)L(t-1) - d] \tag{18}$$

where t is the number of training iterations of deep convolution neural network, $lr(t)$ is the learning rate of the tth iteration, p is the attenuation factor, β_0 is the initial amplitude, $L(\cdot)$ is the loss function, $sigmoid(\cdot)$ is the sigmoid function, d is the unit number of sigmoid function right translation, where the value is 8. The sigmoid function curve and the curve after right translation are shown in Fig. 2.

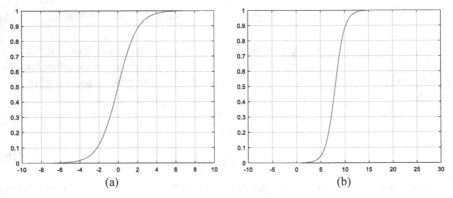

Fig. 2. Function image comparison: (a) sigmoid function curve; (b) sigmoid function curve after translation.

When the neural network is used to solve the classification problem, the loss function $L(t)$ selects the cross entropy loss function $H(p, q)$, and its expression is as follows,

$$H(p, q) = -\sum_x p(x) \log q(x) \tag{19}$$

$$L(t) = H(p, q) \tag{20}$$

where $p(x)$ is the probability distribution of the standard results, $q(x)$ is the probability distribution of the prediction results of the current network model, and x is the corresponding input of the current network model.

When the neural network is used to solve the regression problem, the loss function $L(t)$ usually adopts the mean square error $MSE(y, y')$, and its expression is as follows,

$$MSE(y, y') = \frac{1}{n} \sum_{i=1}^{n} (y_i - y_i')^2 \tag{21}$$

$$L(t) = MSE(y, y') \tag{22}$$

where y_i represents the correct result of the ith data in a batch data, and y_i' is the predicted value of the output of the neural network.

3.2 Parameter Updating of Neural Network

In the emitter recognition problem, the feature extraction function of Convolution Neural Network greatly simplifies the tedious engineering of constructing signal features under traditional conditions. In the training process of the convolutional neural network, the adaptive learning rate can effectively update the parameters of the convolutional neural network and accelerate the convergence of the network model. Note that the partial derivative of the loss function to the net input is $\partial L/\partial u = \delta$. The specific update process is as follows.

In the convolution layer, according to formulas (23) to (26), the variation of convolution kernel parameter Δk and addition bias Δb_a can be obtained respectively, and then the convolution kernel parameters and addition bias can be updated.

$$\frac{\partial L}{\partial K_{ij}^l} = \sum_{u,v} \left(\delta_j^l \right)_{uv} \left(p_i^{l-1} \right)_{uv} \tag{23}$$

$$\frac{\partial L}{\partial b_j^l} = \sum_{u,v} \left(\delta_j^l \right)_{uv} \tag{24}$$

$$\Delta k = -lr(t) \frac{\partial L}{\partial k_{ij}^l} \tag{25}$$

$$\Delta b = -lr(t) \frac{\partial L}{\partial b_j^l} \tag{26}$$

The i is the input neuron, j is the output neuron, l is the network layer number, u and v are the position coordinates of convolution or pooling operation in the input characteristic graph, δ is the partial derivatives of the loss function to net input, $lr(t)$ is the current learning rate, p represents the local region in the input characteristic graph that participates in convolution operation each time. The dot product of the partial derivative of the loss function to the net input of the jth output neuron in layer l and the characteristic graph of the input of the ith input neuron in layer $l - 1$ is as follows.

$$\sum_{u,v} \left(\delta_j^l \right)_{uv} \left(p_i^{l-1} \right)_{uv} \tag{27}$$

In the pooling layer, according to formulas (28)–(31), the variation of multiplication bias $\Delta\beta$ and addition bias Δb can be obtained respectively, and then the multiplication bias and addition bias of the pooling layer can be updated. The formulas are as follows,

$$\frac{\partial L}{\partial \beta_j^l} = \sum\nolimits_{u,v} \left(\delta_j^l \circ down\left(x_j^{l-1}\right) \right)_{uv} \tag{28}$$

$$\frac{\partial L}{\partial b_j^l} = \sum\nolimits_{u,v} \left(\delta_j^l \right)_{uv} \tag{29}$$

$$\Delta\beta = -lr(t)\frac{\partial L}{\partial \beta_j^l} \tag{30}$$

$$\Delta b = -lr(t)\frac{\partial L}{\partial b_j^l} \tag{31}$$

Where the x is the characteristic graph, $down(\cdot)$ is the down sampling function, the symbol $\circ$ is the dot product.

In the fully connected layer, according to the formula (32)–(35), the change of the weight Δw and bias Δb can be obtained respectively, and then the w and b can be updated.

$$\frac{\partial L}{\partial w^l} = \delta^l x^{l-1} \tag{32}$$

$$\frac{\partial L}{\partial b^l} = \delta^l \tag{33}$$

$$\Delta w = -lr(t)\frac{\partial L}{\partial w^l} \tag{34}$$

$$\Delta b = -lr(t)\frac{\partial L}{\partial b^l} \tag{35}$$

If the parameters of each layer in the deep convolution neural network model reach the convergence goal, the training of the neural network model is completed. Otherwise, the learning rate is updated by the adaptive learning rate algorithm.

4   Experimental Analysis of Actual Radiation Source Data

In this paper, the experimental verification of adaptive learning rate adjustment algorithm based on loss function is completed on the actual signal of the emitter. At the same time, the convergence performance of different learning rate algorithms for the emitter identification model is compared and analyzed in terms of recognition accuracy, training iterations, and convergence value of loss function.

4.1 Experimental Description

Experimental Data Set. The original data consists of two batches of signal data generated by five communication stations in different environments. Among them, the first batch of data is used as the training set and the second batch of data is used as the test set. Each communication station contains 5 kinds of center frequencies and data of 5 transmission rates are collected at each center frequency. Therefore, a communication station contains 25 data files, and 5 sources provide 125 data files. The center frequency and transmission rate of each communication station are shown in Table 1.

Table 1. Description of center frequency and transmission rate of each radio station

Communication station ID	Center frequency (MHz)	Transmission rate (kbps)
1, 2, 3, 4, 5	225	64
	300	128
	380	192
	450	512
	512	1024

Data Processing. The original communication radio signal is one-dimensional signal in time domain. After preprocessing such as denoising, frame detection and effective data segment extraction, the two-dimensional time-frequency diagram is obtained by short-time Fourier transform. In this paper, the number of FFT points is 512, and the number of overlapping windows is 89. After STFT transformation, two channel time-frequency map is obtained, with the size of $257 \times 257 \times 2$. Then, the depth self-encoder is used for feature extraction and dimensionality reduction to obtain a $128 \times 128 \times 2$ time-frequency map. Finally, it is input into Convolutional Neural Network for feature extraction and classification recognition, and the classification results are output.

Network Model. The neural network model is the convolution neural network which includes 12 convolution layers and 6 pooling layers. The whole network model uses 3×3 convolution kernel. For the convolution layer in the middle, the same padding is used, the convolution layer close to the input and output adopts the valid padding, and the optimization algorithm adopts the Adam algorithm.

Parameter Setting of Learning Rate. In the adaptive adjustment algorithm of the learning rate based on loss function, it is recommended to set the parameters as $p = 0.99$, $\beta_0 = 1$, $b = 8$, which can be adjusted according to the actual training objectives.

4.2 Comparing with Other Learning Rate Algorithm

The algorithm proposed in this paper is compared with the RMSProp algorithm, Adam algorithm, and exponential decay learning rate combined with the Adam algorithm. Under different learning rate algorithms, the change of emitter individual recognition accuracy with iteration times is shown in Fig. 3.

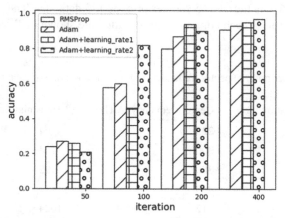

Fig. 3. Comparison of recognition accuracy of communication stations under four learning rate algorithms: the four learning rate algorithms are RMSProp, Adam, Adam with *learning_ rate1* and Adam with *learning_ rate2*.

Among them, *learning_ rate1* stands for exponential decay, *learning_ rate2* represents the learning rate based on the loss function. In the RMSProp algorithm, the attenuation coefficient is 0.9 and the global learning rate is 0.001. In the exponential decay learning rate algorithm, the initial learning rate is 0.001, the attenuation speed is 100, and the attenuation coefficient is 0.9. Among the four learning rate algorithms, the combination of learning rate based on loss function and Adam algorithm improves the recognition accuracy fastest, and finally achieves the highest recognition accuracy of emitter. The convergence performance of neural network model under different learning rate algorithms is shown in Table 2.

When the neural network model tends to converge, the training iterations needed by this algorithm are the least, which is 152 times, and the recognition accuracy is the highest, which is 97.48%. Experiments show that the convergence performance of the model is optimal under the learning rate algorithm. Compared with exponential decay learning rate algorithm, the number of iterations is reduced by 78 times and the recognition accuracy is improved by about 1%. Compared with the Adam algorithm, the number of training iterations is reduced by 127 times, and the recognition accuracy is improved by 3.6%. The results show that our algorithm can effectively improve the performance of the emitter individual identification model, which proves that the algorithm has a fast convergence speed and high recognition accuracy.

Table 2. Comparison of convergence performance of different learning rate algorithms for neural network model

Learning rate algorithm	Convergence performance		
	Epoch	Loss	Accuracy (%)
RMSProp	410	0.31	91.68
Adam	279	0.26	93.82
Adam + learning_ rate1	230	0.12	96.67
Adam + learning_ rate2	152	0.092	97.48

5 Conclusion

In this paper, the performance optimization of the learning rate algorithm for emitter identification is studied. Based on the analysis of attenuation learning rate and adaptive learning rate, a learning rate adaptive adjustment algorithm based on loss function is proposed. The algorithm aims to derive the size of step factor of current learning rate by calculating the value of the current loss function and the previous step one, so as to realize the fine control of the learning rate size by the loss function, and effectively adjust the change of the learning rate. Finally, the effectiveness of the algorithm is verified by the actual emitter signals. The experimental results show that our algorithm can improve the model convergence speed of the emitter individual identification tasks and reduce the training time.

References

1. Shi, X., Chen, Z., Wang, H., et al.: Convolutional LSTM network: a machine learning approach for precipitation nowcasting. In: Advances in Neural Information Processing Systems, pp. 802–810 (2015)
2. Glorot, X., Bordes, A., Bengio, Y.: Deep sparse rectifier neural networks. In: International Conference on Artificial Intelligence and Statistics, vol. 15, pp. 315–323 (2012)
3. Le, Q.V., Jaitly, N., Hinton, G.E.: A simple way to initialize recurrent networks of rectified linear units. Computer Science (2015)
4. Nesterov, Y.: Introductory lectures on convex optimization. Appl. Optim. **87**, xviii, 236 (2004)
5. Meng, X., Bradley, J., Yavuz, B., et al.: MLlib: machine learning in apache spark. J. Mach. Learn. Res. **17**, 1235–1241 (2015)
6. Guenter, B., Dong, Y., Eversole, A., et al.: Stochastic gradient descent algorithm in the computational network toolkit (2013). Research.microsoft.com
7. Khirirat, S., Feyzmahdavian, H.R., Johansson, M.: Mini-batch gradient descent: faster convergence under data sparsity. In: 2017 IEEE 56th Annual Conference on Decision and Control (CDC). IEEE (2017)
8. Srinivasan, V., Sankar, A.R., Balasubramanian, V.N.: ADINE: an adaptive momentum method for stochastic gradient descent (2017)
9. Shang, F., Liu, Y., Cheng, J., et al.: Fast stochastic variance reduced gradient method with momentum acceleration for machine learning (2017)

402   J. Jiang et al.

10. Li, S., Lu, X.: Static restart stochastic gradient descent algorithm based on image question answering. J. Comput. Res. Dev. **56**, 1092 (2019)
11. Duchi, J., Hazan, E., Singer, Y.: Adaptive subgradient methods for online learning and stochastic optimization. J. Mach. Learn. Res. **12**, 257–269 (2011)
12. Tieleman, T., Hinton, G.: Lecture 6.5—RMSProp, COURSERA: Neural Networks for Machine Learning. Technical report (2012)
13. Zeiler, M.D.: ADADELTA: an adaptive learning rate method (2012)
14. Kingma, D., Ba, J.: Adam: a method for stochastic optimization (2014)
15. Timothy, D.: Incorporating Nesterov momentum into Adam (2016)
16. Wei, W.G.H., Liu, T., Song, A., et al.: An adaptive natural gradient method with adaptive step size in multi-layer perceptrons. In: Chinese Automation Congress, pp. 1593–1597 (2018)

Agricultural Hyperspectral Image Classification Based on Deep Separable Convolutional Neural Networks

Yangyang Liang[1], Yu Wu[2], Gengke Wang[2,3]($\boxtimes$), and Lili Zhang[2]

[1] Henan University, Kaifeng 475004, China
[2] Chinese Academy of Sciences, Beijing 100094, China
wanggk@aircas.ac.cn
[3] University of Chinese Academy of Sciences, Beijing 100049, China

Abstract. Due to the high computational complexity of traditional convolutional neural networks, the execution time is long and the computational cost is too high. In this paper, we propose a deep separable convolutional neural network with attention mechanism added to improve the classification accuracy and generalization ability of hyperspectral images. The network uses separable convolution combined with residual connections to construct residual units with fewer parameters and adds an attention mechanism layer at the end of the network, which helps to improve the overall performance of the model. So this model has stronger generalization ability now, shorter computation time, and stronger network performance. Finally, the overall accuracy of the model in this paper is 98.48%, 99.1% and 97.40% on the Salinas dataset and the more newly proposed Wuhan Longkou and Wuhan Hanchuan datasets, respectively. It proves that the model has better generalization ability and can complete the calculation in a shorter time. Improving the classification accuracy of hyperspectral images like the Wuhan Longkou dataset is important for agricultural development.

Keywords: Residual Network · Separable convolution · Convolutional neural network · Attention mechanism · Agricultural hyperspectrum

1 Introduction

Hyperspectral images are generally images with hundreds or even more spectral bands composed. Hyperspectral images are not only rich in spectral information, but also have more spatial information, and only reasonable and sufficient use of these two parts can maximize the classification accuracy of hyperspectral images. At the same time, the computational cost should be taken into account. In conclusion, the classification of hyperspectral images is beneficial to many industries such as environment, agriculture, and atmosphere.

From the development of convolutional neural network (CNN), since AlexNet [1] won the ImageNet Large Scale Visual Recognition Challenge (ILSVRC) competition in

D. Jiang and H. Song (Eds.): SIMUtools 2021, LNICST 424, pp. 403–420, 2022.
https://doi.org/10.1007/978-3-030-97124-3_30

2012, the convolutional neural network has entered a rapid development stage. Firstly, the AlexNet network model deepens the previous neural network depth and integrates multiple transformation layers, which improves the classification accuracy and introduces regularization in CNNs again. This improvement directly reduced the ginger error rate from 25.8% to 16.4% compared to traditional ML techniques. Since then, CNNs have become more and more widely used in the field of computer vision (CV), and people have slowly started to try to improve the performance of CNNs by reducing the computational cost while maintaining the computational accuracy. Therefore, each new convolutional neural network will try to overcome the shortcomings of the previous networks. In 2013 and 2014, most of the efforts of experts working in this field were spent on the optimization of parameters, hoping to accelerate the computational speed of CNNs with increasing computational complexity. In 2013, Zeiler and Fergus [2] created a mechanism that is a filter that can be visualized for each layer of convolution. The method was designed to improve feature extraction by reducing the size of the convolutional kernel. Subsequently, a related group at Oxford University proposed the famous VGG network [3] in 2014, which was the runner-up in the ILSVRC competition that year. VGG reduces the perceptual field and expands the volume compared to the classical AlexNet, where the feature map after each layer of convolution in VGG gradually increases the number of channels. In the same year, GoogleNet [4], which won the ILSVRC competition, not only reduces the computational cost by improving the structure of the network, but also widens the channels of the feature map according to the depth of the network structure. The real major performance improvement of CNNs in the neural network domain is the residual network (ResNet) [5], both the very famous residual links or jump links, proposed by Kaiming He et al. in 2015. This design made it possible to design deep networks that greatly improved the classification accuracy of hyperspectral images. Zhang Lei et al. proposed a privacy protection scheme for data considering the security protection aspect of the computational process, again based on the verification tree as well as the signature mechanism to make security protection [6, 7].

In 2016 researchers in this field have explored mainly the width of the network with the hope of improving feature learning [8]. In addition there were no more prominent architectures proposed, almost always using a mixture of already emerged network structures and adding some newly researched mechanisms used to improve the overall network performance. This event gives the impression that for improving the performance of CNNs, in addition to proposing new network models, grid cells can also be properly assembled, and this practice can also be an important factor for improving the network performance. Therefore, Hu et al. in 2017 identified the role played by the grid representation in the whole training process of convolutional neural networks. They also introduced the idea of feature graph development, while pointing out that a small amount of information and domain-independent features may affect the performance of the network to a greater extent. Using this idea, a new network architecture called "Squeeze and Excite Network (SE-Network) [9]" was proposed. This network is designed to exploit the spectral information by designing a dedicated SE module that assigns weights to each feature map according to its role in class recognition. This idea has been further investigated by many researchers in the field who have shifted attention to important regions by exploiting spatial and feature map (channel) information [10]. The model in this paper also incorporates the attention mechanism. In 2018, Khan et al. introduced a new idea of channel boosting [11]. The performance of CNN can be effectively improved by learning various features, and by using the already learned features through TL concept.

In fact, since 2012, many improvements on CNN network models have appeared one after another. Regarding the advancement of convolutional neural networks, the research in recent years has focused on designing new residual modules, performing deep convolutional operations, enhancing the network performance by means of feature maps and adding artificial channels. Zhang L, Huang Z and other researchers used the study of hyperspectral images for weather radar echo prediction [12, 13] and achieved better results.

Regarding the research on hyperspectral image classification, in the early days of hyperspectral feature extraction (HSIFE), the focus of classification was on the extraction of spectra, recognition of objects by spectra, and other spectral-based methods. The main methods include principal component analysis (PCA), independent component analysis (ICA), linear discriminant analysis, etc. [5, 14]. These methods mainly apply linear transformations to extract the features of the input data, but in the natural world natural objects and complex light scattering mechanisms, and hyperspectral data are inherently nonlinear [15], which makes these linear-based transformations not very suitable for analyzing hyperspectral data.

With the development of imaging technology, hyperspectral sensors are again hungry for higher spatial resolution, and the spatial information we obtain is becoming more and more detailed in hyperspectral data. In [16], a method that combines the use of morphological operators and support vector machines (SVM) was introduced, which unfortunately significantly improves the classification efficiency. However, traditional image classification methods including support vector machine support vector machine (SVM) [17], 3D wavelet transform [18], Gaussian mixing, etc. all use band selection and feature extraction methods, which can reduce the dimensionality of hyperspectral images, however, it destroys the overall think of the data, and the related deficiencies can lead to unsatisfactory classification accuracy of images. Wei Huang et al. contributed to image preprocessing using dense networks for reconstruction of hyperspectral compressed images [19], and then went on to classify hyperspectral images using local binary patterns and superpixel multicores [20].

In recent years, it is obvious that convolutional neural networks (CNNs) have an excellent performance in the field of image classification, and researchers related to the field of hyperspectral image classification have also used CNNs for hyperspectral image classification. hu et al. first used convolutional neural networks for hyperspectral image classification in [21]. In the paper he and his team used principal component analysis (PCA) to reduce the image dimensionality, followed by using two-dimensional convolution to extract the spatial features of the input data, and then one-dimensional convolution to extract the spectral features of each pixel, and then combining the results of both convolutions to obtain higher accuracy classification results [22]. It is not difficult to find that the method can destroy the continuity of the spectrum. With the development of convolutional neural networks, people began to extract the spatial spectral information of HSI more fully, and due to the small data set, in order to achieve more accurate classification in a limited sample, related researchers proposed more godly and lighter complex network models, among which Lee et al. proposed an Inception-based deep CNN model (DC-CNN) [23], after Zhong et al. proposed a hyperspectral image classification by 3D convolution operation and proposed a spatial-spectral residual network (SSRN) [24], which can extract spatial and spectral features more completely. Later Wang et al. used 1×1 and 3×3 convolution kernels to extract spatial-spectral features of hyperspectral images by density linking, which can also be classified effectively [25]. Paoletti et al. [26] proposed a newer pyramidal residual network, mainly by stacking pyramidal bottleneck residual units [27] to construct a residual network (pResNet), which obtained a high classification accuracy.

However, it is important for agricultural hyperspectral classification, which can detect the nutrient and water content of each crop at any time, monitor the rise of crops, and further estimate the yield, so as to make corresponding countermeasures in advance and reduce unnecessary losses.

2 Analysis of the Model

2.1 Attention Mechanism

The whole attention mechanism acts to integrate global information (including the a priori information already obtained earlier) to extract important and useful information for the present features to adjust the corresponding weights. In this paper, we combine spatial attention and channel-wise attentiveness in a multilayer feature application. attentiveness is essentially the training of a weight that can then be used to select a channel or superimposed on each pixel of a feature map [28].

Spatial attention: each pixel of the current feature map is assigned a weight value for each pixel, which is a two-dimensional matrix; Channel-wise: a weight is assigned to each channel in terms of the feature map, so this weight is a vector.

The below figure is a diagram of one layer of SCA-CNN (see Fig. 1.), which takes the classical encoder-decoder structure and mainly contains two parts: CNN network (encoder) and LSTM network (decoder). The spatial attention can be understood as a unit of each pixel of the feature map, and each pixel of the feature map is assigned a weight value, so this weight value should be a matrix; the channel wise attention is a unit of the feature map, and each channel is assigned a weight value. The channel wise attention is assigned to each channel as a unit of feature map, so the weight value should be a vector.

Principles of attentional mechanisms:

Where $x \in R^{C \times N}$, A 1×1 convolution of x (the input to the previous layer) yields f, g, h. This changes the number of channels from C to C*.

$$f(x) = W_f x, g(x) = W_g x, h(x) = W_h x \tag{1}$$

These weights are called "attention maps" and essentially quantify the "importance" of pixel j relative to pixel i in the image. Since these weights (β) are computed over the

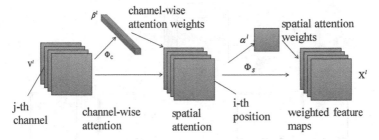

Fig. 1. A diagram of one layer of SCA-CNN.

entire height and width of the feature set, the receptive field is no longer limited to the size of the small kernel.

$$\beta_{j,i} = \frac{\exp(s_{ij})}{\sum_{i=1}^{N} \exp(s_{ij})}, s_{ij} = f(x_i)^T g(x_j) \tag{2}$$

The output of the self-attentive layer is calculated as:

$$o_j = v\left(\sum_{i=1}^{N} \beta_{j,i}(x_i)\right), v(x) = W_v x, W_v \in R^{C \times C^*} \tag{3}$$

Usually set $C^* = \frac{C}{8}$, As a final step, the input feature x is added to the output weighting (γ is another scalar parameter that can be learned):

$$y_i = \gamma o_i + x_i \tag{4}$$

2.2 Deep Separable Convolution

There are two main types of separable convolution: depth separable convolution and spatial separable convolution.

Deeply separable convolution means that the input of $N \times H \times W \times C$ is divided into C groups, Then each group does the corresponding convolution operation so that the spatial features of each Channel are collected, Depth-wise features (see Fig. 2).

Spatially separable convolution means making k ordinary $1 \times 1 \times C$ convolutions of the input of $N \times H \times W \times C$, which is equivalent to collecting the features of each point features, Pointwise features. Usually the W and H of the convolution kernel are 1 (see Fig. 3).

The advantage of separable convolution is mainly that it reduces the number of parameters and thus the number of computations. The computational burden of the model is alleviated.

The number of parameters for the regular convolution operation is: $H \times W \times C \times k$;

The number of parameters of the separable convolution operation is: $H \times W \times C + 1 \times 1 \times C \times k$.

Deeply separable convolution changes the previous ordinary convolution operation to consider both channels and regions (convolution first considers only regions and then channels), and achieves the separation of channels and regions.

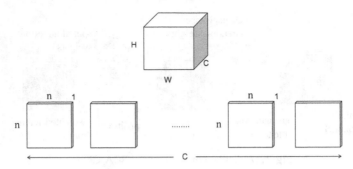

Fig. 2. Deeply separable convolution.

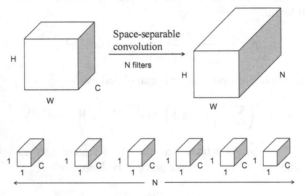

Fig. 3. Spatially separable convolution.

By separating the regions and channels, it is equivalent to compressing the computational effort of ordinary convolution is:

$$\frac{\text{depthwise} + \text{pointwise}}{conv} = \frac{H \times W \times C \times 3 \times 3 + H \times W \times C \times k}{H \times W \times C \times 3 \times 3} = \frac{1}{k} + \frac{1}{3 \times 3}$$

(5)

Depthwise: number of parameters for depth-separable convolution, pointwise: number of parameters for spatially separable convolution, conv: number of parameters for traditional convolution methods, k: number of convolution kernels.

2.3 Residual Unit

The residual unit in this paper consists of four BN (Batch Normalization) layers, three separable convolutions, and two ReLU activation layers (see Fig. 4).

The input hyperspectral image of $9 \times 9 \times 38$ is normalized and then subjected to separable convolution, which, as introduced in the previous section, reduces the number of parameters and thus the computation time. The separable convolution can effectively extract the spectral spatial information from the hyperspectral image, and after several such residual modules, the spectral spatial information of each region of the hyperspectral

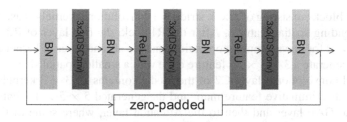

Fig. 4. Residual Unit is proposed.

image can be fully obtained. The final output after several residual modules is a matrix of shape $5 \times 5 \times 86$. This process uses a pyramidal type of residual units.

The pyramidal residual cell is a simple structure that increases the number of channels of the same feature map with each passing residual cell. This design approach can reduce the number of parameters and computational cost of the network model more significantly. Unlike the traditional pyramidal residual unit, the final ReLU layer is not used in this paper [29], and it is noteworthy that the data need to be normalized first when just entering the interior of the residual unit, i.e., first passing through the BN layer [30], and when passing through all residual units completely, the output will present a long strip-like feature map with smaller length and width and a larger number of channels. The most important thing is to replace the conventional convolution layer for each residual cell with a separable convolution. This can reduce the model parameters. In short, the core part of the network model proposed in this paper is composed of such units. The parameters do not increase significantly as the network is progressively deepened, resulting in the construction of a lightweight residual classification model.

2.4 HSI Classification Models

A depth-separable convolutional neural network model is built as shown below. The model first performs 1×1 convolutional dimensionality reduction on the HSI data cube after data pre-processing to extract the corresponding spectral information. Then, the output of the convolutional dimensionality reduction is put into the residual module as input to continuously extract the spatial contextual features and spectral features of the data cube, as shown in the figure below, each residual unit is composed of a BN layer, a ReLU layer and a 1×1 separable convolutional layer, and then, it enters a 1×1 convolutional layer with a global average pooling (GAP) layer, and finally, it passes through the attention mechanism module, which does not change the data structure, but modifies the weights of the corresponding pixel points to prepare for the next data processing, which can converge faster and complete the final classification.

In addition, taking Wuhan Hanchuan data set as an example, this paper proposes a new network model, as shown in the figure below (see Fig. 5).

First, the processed 3D hyperspectral data with the shape of $9 \times 9 \times 274$ (274 is the number of data channels) is input into this network model. In C1, the channel information of the input data is reorganized by 38 1×1 convolutional kernels, at which point the processed shape is $9 \times 9 \times 38$.

Than R1 block consisting of 3×3, stride $= 1$ convolutional kernels is used to extract the corresponding spatial features. After the R1block, the first layer of R2 is a 3×3 filter, stride $= 2$ for downsampling operation, and the second layer of kernel uses a step size of 1 to generate a $3 \times 3 \times 86$ feature cube with a smaller spatial size.

The final convolutional layer C2 of the model contains 16 3×3 kernels for compressing the discriminative feature map, and the generated $5 \times 5 \times 16$ feature map is passed to the GAP layer and then to the Attention layer, where some of the weights are strengthened by back propagation of the model, and then the shape of the space is transformed into a 1×16 one-dimensional vector. The more detailed model flow are shown in Table 1.

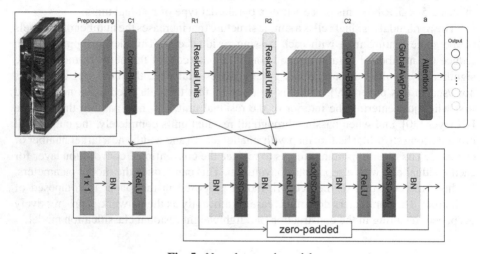

Fig. 5. Neural network model.

3 Detailed Design

The HSI has a continuum property and the data are relatively scattered in each waveform. To speed up the convergence and reduce the training time of the model, the input data cubes are first zero-averaged before being fed into the network. The standardized computational equation is defined as:

$$X_{m,n}^{a} = \frac{X_{m,n}^{a} - \overline{X}^{a}}{\sigma^{a}} (1 \leq m \leq W, 1 \leq n \leq H, 1 \leq a \leq N) \qquad (6)$$

$X_{m,n}^{a}$ denotes the pixel value of the mth row and nth column in the ath band of the HSI, $\overline{X}$ is the mean value of all pixels in the ath band, and σ is the standard deviation of pixels in the ath band; W, H, and N denote the width, height, and total number of channels of the input HSI, respectively.

Considering the numerous spectral bands of HSI data, the Hughes phenomenon is easily generated [31]. That is, with hundreds of spectral bands and a small amount of

Table 1. Model flow details.

Layer	Output size	Kernel size	Stride	Padding
Input	$9 \times 9 \times 274$			
C1	$9 \times 9 \times 38$	1×1	1	0
R1	$9 \times 9 \times 62$	3×3	1	1
	$9 \times 9 \times 62$	3×3	1	1
	$9 \times 9 \times 62$	3×3	1	1
R2	$5 \times 5 \times 86$	3×3	2	1
	$5 \times 5 \times 86$	3×3	1	1
	$5 \times 5 \times 86$	3×3	1	1
C2	$5 \times 5 \times 16$	1×1	1	1
GAP	$1 \times 1 \times 16$			
a	$1 \times 1 \times 16$			

data, this is prone to overfitting, so we use 1×1 convolution in the first layer of the model, which is used to reduce the number of channels of the hyperspectral data and does not change the spatial size. This approach not only ensures the spatial integrity of the data, but also effectively utilizes the multispectral information of the data, which in turn avoids the occurrence of overfitting phenomena. As shown in the above network structure, two residual network modules (R1, R2) can fully extract the spectral spatial information of the processed HSI data. Both modules use a 3×3 convolutional kernel. The value of stride in R1 is 1 and the value of padding is also 1 to ensure that the input and output data have the same size and the edge features of the data can be fully preserved. In R2, the value of stride is 2 and the value of padding is 1. This is designed to further reduce the size of the feature map and facilitate the final one-dimension visualization of the feature map, and then the second layer of convolution uses a design with both stride and padding of 1, which is designed to ensure that the input and output sizes are the same. Both residual blocks are connected with a jump with zero padding [32], so that the features of the data can be more fully utilized.

For the traditional convolution operation, to ensure that the output and input feature maps are of the same size, the Padding method is used to expand the edges of the feature maps, which undoubtedly increases the parameters and increases the computational cost of the computer. And it also increases the number of channels of the output feature map, while the pyramid residual structure used in this paper is an ordered small step to increase the number of channels of the output feature map, and this method reduces the number of parameters. The equations for the output channels of each residual module are as follows:

$$D_i = \mathrm{D_i} = \begin{cases} C; \mathrm{i} = 1 \\ \mathrm{D_{i-1}} + \frac{\alpha}{\mathrm{R}}; \mathrm{i} > 1 \end{cases} \tag{7}$$

Where D_i is the number of output channels of the ith residual cell and C the initial number of channels of the first residual cell. In this paper that is the number of output channels after the C1 layer, R is the number of residual cells, and α is an integer greater than zero.

After the residual block, the data enters the 1×1 convolution and global average pooling layer, which uses fewer parameters than the traditional fully connected layer and provides mitigation of the overfitting problem and accelerates the convergence of the network [33]. Moreover, the attention mechanism is added at the end of the model, and the role of adding the attention mechanism layer is to adjust the relevant weights of the pixel points in the data as soon as possible to highlight the characteristics of the crops we are concerned about, such as variety, growth, and pests, which is more likely to meet the practical needs of our related work, and also plays the same role of accelerating the convergence of the network model.

4 Experimental Procedure

In this paper, we use publicly available datasets from Wuhan University: the Wuhan Longkou dataset and the Wuhan Hanchuan dataset [27, 34, 35], in addition to the international publicly available dataset Salinas. The following Table 2 is a basic introduction to these three types of datasets.

Table 2. Three kinds of data sets are used in this paper.

	Salinas	WHHC	WHLK
Type of Sensor	AVIRIS	Aibot X6	DJI matrix 600 Pro (DJI M600 Pro)
Spatial Size	512×217	1217×303	550×400
Spectral Range	400–2500 nm	400–1000 nm	400–1000 nm
Spatial Resolution	3.7 m	0.109 m	0.463 m
Bands	204	274	270
Num. Of Classes	16	16	9

The experimental design of this paper is roughly as follows. Four experiments are set up in this paper, which are the model in this paper, the model in this paper without adding the attention mechanism, changing the separable convolution of the model in this paper to the ordinary two-dimensional convolution, and the last one changing the residual module in this paper to the classical residual module structure. The overall experimental results are measured by three parameters, which are overall classification accuracy (OA), average classification accuracy (AA) and Kappa coefficient (K). To ensure the accuracy of the experimental results, each experiment is done five times, and the final average is taken as the final experimental result.

5 Experimental Results

The results of the neural network model training and testing experiments in this paper is:

The below figure shows, from left to right, the Salinas dataset, the Wuhan Hanchuan dataset and the Wuhan Longkou dataset (see Fig. 6.), and the experimental results in the model experiments of this paper are shown in the following Table 3:

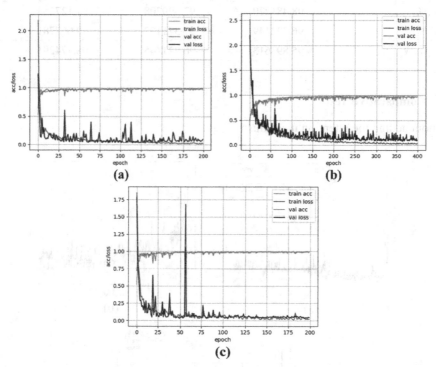

Fig. 6. Experimental results of the proposed model on Salinas dataset (a), Wuhan Hanchuan dataset (b), Wuhan Longkou dataset (c).

The model in this paper obviously has a better classification effect for Wuhan Longkou.

Table 3. Experimental results of the proposed model on three data sets are presented.

	Salinas	WHHC	WHLK
Train time (ms)	332.5548	452.1498	228.7295
Test time (ms)	12.5837	62.8690	66.1033
Test loss (%)	0.109	0.277	0.0307
Test Accuracy (%)	96.33	91.32	99.06
AA (%)	98.481220	97.399308	99.127253
OA (%)	96.332149	97.371132	99.067781
Kappa (%)	95.893613	96.921145	98.774291

5.1 Comparative Test

Without adding the attention mechanism:

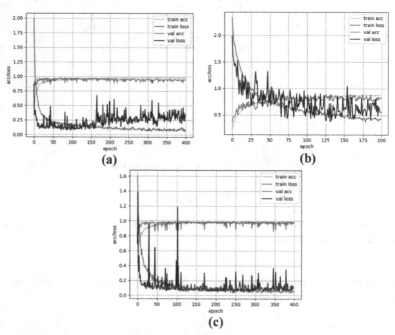

(a)

(b)

(c)

Fig. 7. Experimental results of the proposed model and delete the attention mechanism on Salinas dataset (a), Wuhan Hanchuan dataset (b), Wuhan Longkou dataset (c).

The above figure shows, from left to right, the Salinas dataset (a), the Wuhan Hanchuan dataset (b) and the Wuhan Longkou dataset (c) (see Fig. 7.), and their experimental results in the experiments without the inclusion of the attention mechanism are shown in the following Table 4:

Table 4. Experimental results of the proposed model and delete the attention mechanism on three datasets are presented.

	Salinas	WHHC	WHLK
Train time (ms)	2816.7585	1434.8909	862.5844
Test time (ms)	223.7624	159.9729	198.8493
Test loss (%)	0.206	0.277	0.061
Test Accuracy (%)	93.78	91.32	98.17
AA (%)	97.658851	88.729316	98.566262
OA (%)	93.787430	91.327016	98.179953
Kappa (%)	93.064872	89.846760	97.614027

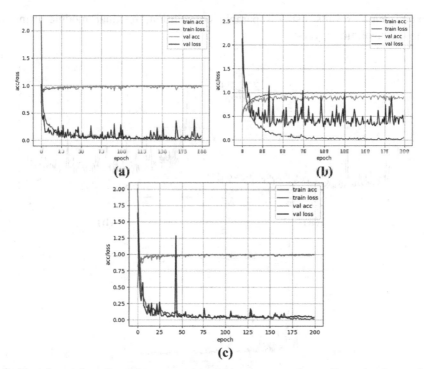

Fig. 8. Experimental results of the proposed model but use normal two-dimensional convolution on Salinas dataset (a), Wuhan Hanchuan dataset (b), Wuhan Longkou dataset (c)

Instead of separable convolution, a normal two-dimensional convolution is used:

The above figure shows, from left to right, the Salinas dataset (a), the Wuhan Hanchuan dataset (b) and the Wuhan Longkou dataset (c) (see Fig. 8.), and their experimental results in the experiments without the use of separable convolution are shown in the following Table 5:

Table 5. Experimental results of the proposed model but use normal two-dimensional convolution on three datasets are presented.

	Salinas	WHHC	WHLK
Train time (ms)	423.6212	471.5599	271.3779
Test time (ms)	10.2761	60.9518	52.6547
Test loss (%)	0.127	0.249	0.037
Test Accuracy (%)	95.47	93.34	99.15
AA (%)	98.253737	92.452533	98.961172
OA (%)	95.472128	93.348799	99.086524
Kappa (%)	94.934475	92.220816	98.798554

Experimental results using separable convolution, residual module using two separable convolution layers:

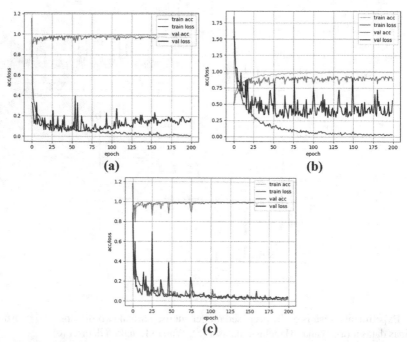

Fig. 9. The experimental result graph of each residual element of the proposed model using two separable convolution layers is presented on Salinas dataset (a), Wuhan Hanchuan dataset (b), Wuhan Longkou dataset (c)

The above figure shows, from left to right, the Salinas dataset (a), the Wuhan Hanchuan dataset (b) and the Wuhan Longkou dataset (c) (see Fig. 9.), and their experimental results are shown in the following Table 6:

Table 6. The experimental result graph of each residual element of the proposed model using two separable convolution layers is presented on three data sets are presented.

	Salinas	WHHC	WHLK
Train time (ms)	225.1533	255.6815	150.1188
Test time (ms)	9.2854	61.8522	39.6964
Test loss (%)	0.129	0.375	0.034
Test Accuracy (%)	96.11	91.62	98.95
AA (%)	98.485236	93.688709	99.192328
OA (%)	96.108308	93.916565	99.051504
Kappa (%)	95.645520	92.886840	98.753314

Through the above experimental comparisons, it is easy to conclude that the proposed deep separable convolutional neural network with added attention mechanism in this paper reduces the model parameters and shortens the training time while ensuring high classification accuracy for hyperspectral datasets.

6 Conclusion

In this paper, a new deeply separable convolutional neural network model for HSI classification is proposed, and an attention mechanism is added to the model, which is experimentally proven to have the advantages of high accuracy and fast convergence.

This lightweight model uses a 1 × 1 convolution kernel from the first layer to reorganize the channels of the hyperspectral data to reduce the number of spectral channels for further processing later. Then it enters the residual module to fully extract the spatial spectral features of the hyperspectral data through the residual unit. This is followed by a layer of 1 × 1 filters and a global average pooling to classify the data. The attention mechanism is added in the last layer to adjust the weights of the pixel points in the data without changing the execution results of the previous layer, and the weights of the pixel points where we are more concerned about the crop-related information are adjusted upward, which can effectively enhance our attention to the crop and also accelerate the convergence of the data.

The separable convolution used in the residual block of the model not only ensures the accuracy of the classification, but also further reduces the number of parameters of this model, decreases the load on the machine, and helps the model to classify more quickly. During the experimental comparison, we clearly see that the model used in this paper has the highest accuracy and the shortest operation time at the same time. This indicates that the model has a strong generalization ability and is fully capable of performing the classification task of HSI data excellently.

Therefore, in summary, the model proposed in this paper has high accuracy and fast speed, and is highly feasible for the task of classifying HSI data again. In the future research, I will devote myself to the classification of hyperspectral images, using 3D convolution, or adding density connection and other methods, and continue to work deeply in this field. I will strive to build a better network model.

Funding. This research was funded by Civil space technology advance research project (D040401), Highly differentiated Earth surface system science research (E1K503010M), Key Technologies for Collaborative Processing and Joint Verification of Quantitative Remote Sensing Basic Common Products for "One Belt and One Road (E0BD030404), Evaluation of Space Integration Satellite Application Technology (Y7k00100kJ).

References

1. Alom, M.Z., Taha, T.M., Yakopcic, C., et al.: The history began from AlexNet: a comprehensive survey on deep learning approaches, arXiv preprint arXiv:1803.01164 (2018)
2. Zeiler, M., Fergus, R.: Visualizing and understanding convolutional networks. In: Fleet, D., Pajdla, T., Schiele, B., Tuytelaars, T. (eds.) Computer Vision – ECCV 2014: 13th European Conference, Zurich, Switzerland, September 6-12, 2014, Proceedings, Part I, pp. 818–833. Springer, Cham (2014). https://doi.org/10.1007/978-3-319-10590-1_53
3. Simonyan, K., Zisserman, A.: Very deep convolutional networks for large-scale image recognition. arXiv preprint, pp. 1409–1556 (2014)
4. Szegedy, C., Liu, W., Jia, Y., et al.: Going deeper with convolutions. In: Proceedings of the IEEE Conference on Computer Vision and Pattern Recognition, pp. 1–9 (2015)
5. He, K., Zhang, X., Ren, S., et al.: Deep residual learning for image recognition. In: Proceedings of the IEEE Conference on Computer Vision and Pattern Recognition, pp. 770–778 (2016)
6. Zhang, L., Huo, Y., Ge, Q., et al.: A privacy protection scheme for IoT big data based on time and frequency limitation. Wirel. Commun. Mobile Comput. Article ID 5545648, 10 p (2021)
7. Han, D., Chen, J., Zhang, L., et al.: A deletable and modifiable blockchain scheme based on record verification trees and the multisignature mechanism. CMES-Comput. Model. Eng. Sci. **128**(1), 223–245 (2021)
8. Cheng, H.T., Koc, L., Harmsen, J., et al.: Wide & deep learning for recommender systems. In: Proceedings of the 1st Workshop on Deep Learning for Recommender Systems. ACM (2016)
9. Jie, H., Li, S., Gang, S., et al.: Squeeze-and-excitation networks. IEEE Trans. Pattern Anal. Mach. Intell. 99 (2017)
10. Wang, X., Girshick, R., Gupta, A., et al.: Non-local neural networks. In: Proceedings of the IEEE Conference on Computer Vision and Pattern Recognition, pp. 7794–7803 (2018)
11. Khan, N., Afaq, F., Saleem, M., et al.: Targeting multiple signaling pathways by green tea polyphenol epigallocatechin-3-gallate. Can. Res. **66**(5), 2500–2505 (2006)
12. Zhang, L., Huang, Z., Liu, W., et al.: Weather radar echo prediction method based on convolution neural network and long short-term memory networks for sustainable e-agriculture. J. Clean. Prod. **298**, 126776 (2021)
13. Zhang, L., Xu, C., Gao, Y., et al.: Improved Dota2 lineup recommendation model based on a bidirectional LSTM. Tsinghua Sci. Technol. **25**(6), 712–720 (2020)
14. Licciardi, G., Marpu, P.R., Chanussot, J., et al.: Linear versus nonlinear PCA for the classification of hyperspectral data based on the extended morphological profiles. IEEE Geosci. Remote Sens. Lett. **9**(3), 447–451 (2012)
15. Mou, L., Bruzzone, L., Zhu, X.X.: Learning spectral-spatial-temporal features via a recurrent convolutional neural network for change detection in multispectral imagery. IEEE Trans. Geosci. Remote Sens. **57**, 1–12 (2018)

16. Chen, P.H., Lin, C.J., Schlkopf, B.: A tutorial on ν-support vector machines. Appl. Stoch. Model. Bus. Ind. **21**(2), 111–136 (2005)
17. Luts, J., Ojeda, F., Plas, R., et al.: A tutorial on support vector machine-based methods for classification problems in chemometrics. Anal. Chim. Acta **665**(2), 129–145 (2010)
18. Zhu, Z., Jia, S., He, S., et al.: Three-dimensional gabor feature extraction for hyperspectral imagery classification using a memetic framework. Inf. Sci. **298**, 274–287 (2015)
19. Huang, W., Xu, Y., Hu, X., et al.: Compressive hyperspectral image reconstruction based on spatial-spectral residual dense network. IEEE Geosci. Remote Sens. Lett. **17**(5), 884–888 (2020)
20. Wei, H., Yao, H., Hua, W., et al.: Local binary patterns and superpixel-based multiple kernels for hyperspectral image classification. IEEE J. Sel. Top. Appl. Earth Observ. Remote Sens. **13**, 4550–4563 (2020)
21. Hu, W., Huang, Y., Wei, L., et al.: Deep convolutional neural networks for hyperspectral image classification. J. Sens. **2015** (2015)
22. Zhang, H., Li, Y., Zhang, Y., et al.: Spectral-spatial classification of hyperspectral imagery using a dual-channel convolutional neural network. Remote Sens. Lett. **8**(4–6), 438–447 (2017)
23. He, M., Li, B., Chen, H.: Multi-scale 3D deep convolutional neural network for hyperspectral image classification. In: 2017 IEEE International Conference on Image Processing (ICIP), pp. 3904–3908. IEEE (2017)
24. Zhong, Z., Li, J., Luo, Z., et al.: Spectral–spatial residual network for hyperspectral image classification: a 3-D deep learning framework. IEEE Trans. Geosci. Remote Sens. **56**(2), 847–858 (2017)
25. Wen, J.W., Shu, G.D., Zhong, M.J., et al.: A fast dense spectral-spatial convolution network framework for hyperspectral images classification. Remote Sens. **10**(7), 1068 (2018)
26. Gao, H., Yang, Y., Li, C., Zhang, X., Zhao, J., Yao, D.: Convolutional neural network for spectral–spatial classification of hyperspectral images. Neural Comput. Appl. **31**(12), 8997–9012 (2019). https://doi.org/10.1007/s00521-019-04371-x
27. Zhong, Y., Hu, X., Luo, C., et al.: WHU-Hi: UAV-borne hyperspectral with high spatial resolution (H2) benchmark datasets and classifier for precise crop identification based on deep convolutional neural network with CRF. Remote Sens. Environ. **250**, 11–20 (2020)
28. Chen, L., Zhang, H., Xiao, J., et al.: SCA-CNN: spatial and channel-wise attention in convolutional networks for image captioning. In: 2017 Proceedings of the IEEE Conference on Computer Vision and Pattern Recognition, pp. 5659–5667 (2017)
29. Nair, V., Hinton, G.E.: Rectified linear units improve restricted Boltzmann machines. In: Proceedings of the 27th International Conference on International Conference on Machine Learning (ICML), Haifa, Israel, USA, 21–24 June 2010, pp. 807–814. Omnipress, Madison (2010)
30. Ioffe, S., Szegedy, C.: Batch normalization: accelerating deep network training by reducing internal covariate shift. In: Proceedings of the 32nd International Conference on International Conference on Machine Learning, Paris, France, 6–11 July 2015, pp. 448–456 (2015)
31. Donoho, D.L.: High-dimensional data analysis: the curses and blessings of dimensionality. AMS Math Challenges Lect. 1–32 (2000)
32. He, K., Zhang, X., Ren, S., et al.: Deep residual learning for image recognition. In: 2016 IEEE Conference on Computer Vision and Pattern Recognition (CVPR), pp. 770–778 (2016)
33. Lin, M., Chen, Q., Yan, S.: Network in network. Comput. Sci. (2013)

34. Zhong, Y., Wang, X., Xu, Y., et al.: Mini-UAV-borne hyperspectral remote sensing: from observation and processing to applications. IEEE Geosci. Remote Sens. Mag **6**(4), 46–62 (2018)
35. Lv, L., Zheng, C., Zhang, L., et al.: Contract and Lyapunov optimization-based load scheduling and energy management for UAV charging stations. IEEE Trans. Green Commun. Network. **5**(3), 1381–1394 (2021)

Deep Reinforcement Learning Based Mimicry Defense System for IoT Message Transmission

Zhihao Wang, Dingde Jiang[✉], Jianguang Chen, and Wei Yang

University of Electronic Science and Technology of China, Chengdu 611731, China

Abstract. With the development of 5G and Internet of Everything, IoT has become an essential network infrastructure. The connection between massive devices brings huge convenience and effectiveness, also introducing more security threats and vulnerabilities that compromise the security, privacy and trust problem of the IoT data, devices and users or service providers. Traditional security approaches are mostly based on the analysis of attack characteristics, seeking vulnerabilities, or patching systems. Independent from prior knowledge or specific defense method, the mimic defense can realize a built-in security system through heterogeneity, redundancy, and dynamic. In this paper, to address the security problem of the IoT communication protocol MQTT, a DRL based mimicry defense system for IoT message transmission is proposed. We conduct mimic transformation on the MQTT broker, with functionally equivalent but structural dissimilar variants. To refine the determining accuracy of basic mimic ruling mechanism, namely majority voting, an intelligent ruling mechanism based on deep Q network is proposed. Finally, the simulation results demonstrate the security and effectiveness of the proposed scheme.

Keywords: Mimicry defense · Deep reinforcement learning · IoT

1 Introduction

With the growth of Internet technology, the capability and capacity of network could accommodate massive devices to assess the network. Internet of Everything is also a typical characteristic of 5G. One of the essential infrastructures 5G is the Internet of Things (IoT). The connection between massive devices brings convenience and effectiveness. Every household electrical appliance, the wearable device can be connected by IoT, collecting data for further advanced data analysis and functionalities. High connectivity and massive devices also introduce more vulnerabilities, which severely compromise the security and privacy of the IoT users or service providers [1], especially the M2M (Machine to Machine) message transmission protocol, the MQTT (Message Queuing Telemetry Transport) protocol. The security of MQTT plays a crucial role in the security of IoT architecture, which faces various threats including replay attacks, MITM (Man-in-the-Middle Attack) [2], data confidentiality threats, authentication threats [3], etc. Therefore, many endeavors are paid to study novel approaches enhancing the security of

D. Jiang and H. Song (Eds.): SIMUtools 2021, LNICST 424, pp. 421–431, 2022.
https://doi.org/10.1007/978-3-030-97124-3_31

the MQTT protocol. A novel MQTT communication structure based on broker bridging is proposed to enhance the overall security of IoT system, along with the secure authentication and authorization scheme [4]. Liao et al. propose an improved attribute-based encryption scheme for MQTT, combined with chaos synchronization, which enhances the security of resource-constrained IoT devices [5].

With the extensive application of AI (Artificial Intelligence), many researchers employ machine learning techniques to address network security problems [6], including random forest, support vector machine, deep neural network, etc. Deep reinforcement learning integrates deep learning and reinforcement learning, which could learn from the interaction with the environment. The reward and punishment to the agent make it behave more like a human. Remarkable achievements in network security fields have been realized using DRL approaches [7]. Jiadai et al. propose an attack-tolerance scheme in Internet of Vehicles utilizing the DRL to defense the topology poisoning attack and enable the self-recovery capability of vehicular edge network [8]. Giovanni et al. propose a DRL-based framework for botnet detectors against the adversarial attack, which also could prevent several unforeseen evasion attacks [9].

Traditional network defense techniques are mostly passive, developing targeted defense approaches based on the characteristics of specific attacks. If the network attack does not have specificity or is an unknown type, the traditional defense techniques will lose effectiveness. Besides, single-system architecture is easily affected by the single point of failure problem. Therefore, to secure the system from built-in or the attacked system perspective, active cyber defense approaches are proposed. The active cyber defense is to launch early warning before the attack is implemented, using big data analysis and AI technology. Typical active cyber defense approaches include data encryption, access control, intrusion detection [10], moving target defense [11], etc. The mimic defense is another type of active cyber defense approach, which is realized through DHR (Dynamic Heterogeneous Redundancy) structure, to address the unknown threats caused by the vulnerability, backdoor with uncharted characteristics [12]. Our previous work also focuses on the mimic transformation of smart grid system [13]. Several variants with distinct internal structures but with identical external functionalities are equipped in the mimic defense system to increase the uncertainty of internal structure [14]. The mimic defense system provides external uniform interfaces for system users, which makes the internal structure invisible to them. It has been demonstrated that the cost of attacking all variants in a short time is tremendous and scarcely possible, due to the various structure and implementation of the variants. Besides, the peculiar mimic ruling mechanism is capable to sense the abnormal variants with inconsistent output vectors, to further detect the non-cooperative attacks [15]. After detecting the abnormal variants, the negative feedback mechanism will force the abnormal variants to shut down and reconstruct. Backup variants will succeed the operation of invalid variants, with state synchronization. Based on the above analysis, the mimic defense system has attack tolerance and fault tolerance capability, which means even part of variants art attacked, the system is still secure and credible [16]. Besides, the uncertainty of the internal structure of mimic system can endow it with invisibility characteristic, which effectively confuses the attackers. Our previous work includes routing and distribution [17, 18, 21], security and networking [19, 20].

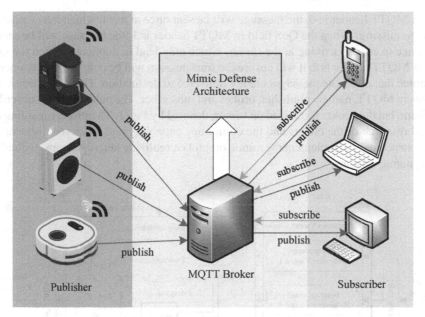

Fig. 1. MQTT structure

In this paper, to address the security problems of IoT system, a DRL-based mimic defense system for IoT message transmission is proposed to address the vulnerability of the single static architecture. By introducing the dynamic, redundancy, and heterogeneity characteristics into traditional IoT message transmission system, namely the MQTT protocol, the communication broker can maintain normal operation even there are network attacks. The mimic ruling mechanism improves the security and stability by validating the credibility of each variant and restructuring the problematic variants. Besides, to improve the effectiveness and accuracy of the ruling mechanism, the DRL approach is employed to realize intelligent mimic ruling, further improving the reliability of the system. A Deep Q Network (DQN) model is utilized to assess the credibility of the message from the variant. Finally, the simulation results demonstrate the security enhancement brought to the IoT communication broker.

2 System Architecture

2.1 MQTT Protocol

MQTT protocol is the most widely used communication protocol of IoT, a lightweight protocol based on the publish-subscribe model. MQTT works on the TCP/IP protocol, thereby it is feasible to extract the packet header to identify the packet type, which is employed in this paper to distinguish the correctness. It requires little code memory space, and a small amount of bandwidth, which makes it suitable for communication in resource-limited, low-bandwidth, high-latency, and unreliable networks. Besides, the QoS support of MQTT is flexible and applicable to a variety of scenarios. When the QoS field in MQTT header is 0, the message will be sent once at most, which may cause the message missing. When the QoS field in MQTT header is 1, the message will be sent at least once to ensure arriving at the server, which may lead to duplicate. When the QoS field in MQTT header is 2, it will ensure the transmission will be conducted only once to guarantee that duplicate messages are not delivered to destination. There are three kinds of roles in MQTT, namely publisher, broker and subscriber. The publisher and subscriber are client, but the broker is realized on server, denoted by Fig. 1. Therefore, regarding the limited resource of the clients and the computing capability and space requirements of mimic structure, we implement the mimic on broker, realizing heterogeneous, redundant and dynamic variants.

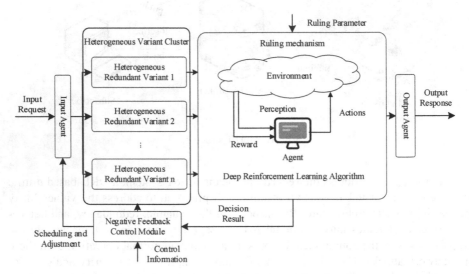

Fig. 2. Overall structure of mimicry defense system

2.2 Mimic Defense IoT System

To enhance the security of IoT system, based on the structure of MQTT communication protocol, a mimic defense architecture is equipped to the IoT system to realize a mimic MQTT broker. The overall structure of the mimic defense IoT system is shown in Fig. 2. Main components include input agent, heterogeneous variant cluster, ruling mechanism, negative feedback and output agent. First, once there are messages from the publisher, the input agent will reproduce the message to all variants that are functionally equivalent and have a uniform input interface. All the variants will process the message individually, extracting the packet header and matching the destination. After the variants yield outputs to the ruling mechanism, we utilize the DRL algorithm to determine the credibility of each message, through the decision-making of DRL model. A most credible message will be selected and transmitted to the output agent, which will further deliver it to corresponding subscribers. Meanwhile, the ruling result will also be duplicated and sent to the negative feedback control module, where the variant with inconsistent output vector will be located and killed. Before the abnormal variant offline, a new variant will be constructed and the corresponding state will be synchronized to it, which will replace the running problematic variant. After the problematic variant is replaced, cleaning and reconstruction will be conducted on it to prevent further damage to the system. Attacks with unknown features, random faults, vulnerabilities can be normalized into an inconsistency output vector problem, which can be handled by the cleaning and reconstruction mechanism. All the data flow or information flow in the mimic IoT system is unidirectional, which significantly avoids network intrusion.

3 DRL Ruling Mechanism

3.1 Deep Reinforcement Learning

In this paper, the DRL model we employed is Deep Q Network (DQN), a typical value-based DRL method. DQN combines the basic Q-learning and deep learning, fitting the value function with DNN. Besides, the experience replay mechanism is employed, to sample the history record for training the Q network. Target value mechanism is also utilized to train Q network. In basic Q-function, the action taken by the agent is always fixed, causing the exploration-exploitation dilemma. The agent will continuously choose the specific action with good reward rather than exploring the action space. Hence, we introduce the Epsilon Greedy (ε-greedy) strategy to force the agent to explore unknown actions with a small probability, denoted as (1):

$$a = \begin{cases} \arg\max_a Q(s, a), \text{ with probability } 1 - \varepsilon \\ random, \quad otherwise \end{cases} \tag{1}$$

where Q means the Q-function, and s is the current state, and a represents the action. In DQN, two Q network is exploited, namely the Q and $\hat{Q}$, which are the same at first. In each training episode, the agent interacts with the environment through obtaining a state s and selecting action (ε-greedy) a. Then the environment will feedback a reward r to agent along with a new state s'. Hence, a quadruple is obtained, as (s, a, r, s'), which will be further stored in the experience replay buffer. To train the Q and $\hat{Q}$, a batch of records from experience replay buffer will be extracted to calculate the target value with $\hat{Q}$, defined as (2):

$$y = r + \max_a \hat{Q}(s', a) \tag{2}$$

where action a is to maximize the $\hat{Q}$. Then we will update parameters in Q to make $Q(s, a)$ approach to target y as much as possible. Besides, an interval is set to synchronize $\hat{Q}$ with Q. The parameter updating method of Q network is the same as DNN. After a certain degree of exploration and training, the agent can take reasonable actions according to the given state of the environment.

Table 1. DRL-based Mimic Ruling Mechanism

Algorithm 1. DRL-based Mimic Ruling Mechanism
Input: Training Message Dataset Msg_T , Real Message group Msg_R .
Output: Mimic Ruling Result.
1   Conduct Min-Max normalization on $Msg_T.X$
3   Train the DQN :
4   **for** each message m in Msg_T :
5   Input $m.X$ to DQN as a state s
6   DQN take action a
7   **if** $a = m.y$ **then** reward $r = 1$
8   **else** $r = -1$
9   **end if**
10   Store the record and update network parameter
11   **end for**
12   Employ trained DQN for ruling:
13   Initialize result list R
14   **for** each message g in Msg_R
15   Normalize $g.X$ with parameter in step 1
16   Input $g.X$ to DQN as a state s
17   DQN take action a
18        $R = R \cup a$
19   **end for**
20   **return** $Msg_R[\arg\max(R)]$

3.2 DRL-Based Ruling Mechanism

The traditional mimic ruling mechanism is based on the majority voting, which could adapt to most scenarios. However, once the attackers have strong enough attack intensity and time to manipulate more than half of the variants in mimic system, the voting ruling will be invalid and untrustworthy. Therefore, to refine the accuracy of the ruling mechanism and further enhance the system security, a DRL-based mimic ruling mechanism is proposed in this paper. The decision-making ability is employed to distinguish the normal message from the outputs of heterogeneous variants, through analogizing the variants as the agent. First, a set of training message samples is utilized to train the DRL model, where the state is a feature of messages, and the action is to determine the correctness of the message. Once the agent takes action, the verification will be conducted to determine feedback, namely reward or punishment. The DRL model will update the parameters of deep neural network to take more correct decisions gradually. After training, the DRL model is employed to realize mimic ruling, verifying the correctness of the given messages. The messages judged to be normal will be taken as the ruling result. For faster training and convergence of deep neural network, the sample message data should be preprocessed, dimension removing and data normalization, which we employed in this paper is the Min-Max Normalization. Each message in the training message dataset contains the features and label, denoted as X and y. Overall procedure of the DRL-based mimic ruling mechanism is depicted in Table 1, where DQN indicates the employed deep Q network model.

4   Simulation Result

4.1   Experiment Setup

In this section, several experiments are conducted to verify the security enhancement brought to single-structure IoT communication broker and the performance of the proposed DRL-based ruling mechanism. First, we establish a simple MQTT simulation scenario, including message subscribing and publishing, to generate a validation dataset. Main features of the obtained MQTT messages are consisted of ControlPacketType, Flags, RemainingLength, PacketIdentifierMSB, PacketIdentifierLSB, PayloadLength. And an artificial-annotated label is utilized to represent the validity of the message. Then the message dataset will be processed by a single MQTT broker that takes the original message as output, a three-variant mimic broker with voting ruling mechanism, and the proposed DRL-based mimic broker with DRL ruling algorithm. We exploit the evaluation metrics in the machine learning classification task to validate the performance of three systems in environments with different attack intensities, namely the precision, recall, f1-score and accuracy.

4.2   Security Enhancement

To validate the security enhancement of the proposed DRL-based mimic IoT message transmission system, we first compare the performance with a certain attack intensity, which means every variant in the system has the same probability of failure or attack. The principal goal of MQTT broker is to deliver the messages safely. Hence, we input the messages into the systems, and validate the output of the broker. The judgment principle is given a normal message, to compare the correctness of the output message. The comparison result is shown in Fig. 3. It is obvious that the recall value of abnormal message of all three approach is 1, which means a very extreme situation that all three systems are attacked. The precision value of a normal message represents a totally secure system with no variants attacked. Apart from the above two useless metrics, the rest metrics all demonstrate that the proposed DRL-based mimic broker exceeds the single broker and basic mimic broker. For the abnormal message, the precision indicates that the DRL-Mimic broker could prevent more normal messages from being misjudged as abnormal messages with part of variants attacked. The recall value of a normal message represents the capability of extracting normal message from all outputs of the variants, measuring the security performance. For single structure broker, once the broker is attacked, the output message will be manipulated easily. The basic mimic structure broker could distinguish normal output from three variants to some extent, but it will misjudge when there are more than half of the variants with abnormal output. The DRL-based mimic broker could effectively improve this problem by selecting the most credible variant and utilizing its output. The f1-score is a comprehensive measurement index of precision and recall, which also demonstrates the superiority of the proposed scheme. Therefore, from the above analysis, compared with single-structure MQTT broker and basic mimic broker, the proposed DRL-based mimic defense IoT message transmission system has obvious security enhancement in the experiment scenario.

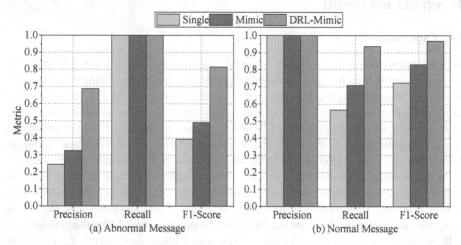

Fig. 3. Security enhancement validation.

4.3 Performance Analysis

To estimate the performance of three MQTT structures, we conduct the message transmission experiments with different attack intensity, which means every broker instance or variant is attacked with a certain probability and the transmitted message has a certain probability to be manipulated. Obviously, once the broker is attacked, the message in the single-structure MQTT broker could be easily manipulated. However, due to the redundancy of variant and the ruling mechanism, the mimic system has attack tolerance. Even part of variants is attacked, the mimic system still can function properly and self-recover. We take the accuracy and the recall value of normal message to validate the performance of three systems, the result of which is shown in Fig. 4. In (a), the accuracy metric is exploited to verify the effectiveness of the proposed scheme. It is obvious that the DRL-Mimic outperforms the other two approaches under all attack intensity conditions, which could maintain a relatively stable accuracy. The fluctuating of the other two schemes is because the calculating rule of accuracy is to validate whether the broker could output original results from publishers, the IoT devices. Therefore, before the attack intensity reaches 0.5 or 0.6, the ruling accuracy of single and mimic scheme drops at a nearly linear speed, and rises rapidly afterward. Because, once the attack intensity is higher than 0.5, the abnormal message takes the dominant position and accuracy will increase then. Different from the accuracy, the recall of normal message can truly reflect the security performance of the MQTT broker with different attack intensities, expressed as Fig. 4 (b). At the initial stage with no attack, all the systems are secure. With the increment of attack intensity, the recall value, indicating the ruling security performance of the broker, is getting lower gradually. The Single and Mimic system drop almost linearly. However, the descending speed or trend of DRL-Mimic system is significantly slower than the other two, keeping above 90%, which means even the attack intensity is huge, the proposed DRL-Mimic system could effectively determine the normal variants. The intelligent ruling mechanism address the simplicity and inaccuracy problem of the traditional majority voting approach. When the attack intensity comes to 1.0, all the recall values drop to zero, the reason of which is that each instance will certainly be attacked and there is no normal message that can be output. Even the mimic defense structure could improve the security of MQTT broker to some extent, the protection ability will decrease rapidly as the attack intensity increases. In summary, compared to the single-structure MQTT broker and basic mimic defense structure, the proposed DRL-based mimic defense IoT communication scheme can effectively improve the security of message transmission, with stability under different attack intensity.

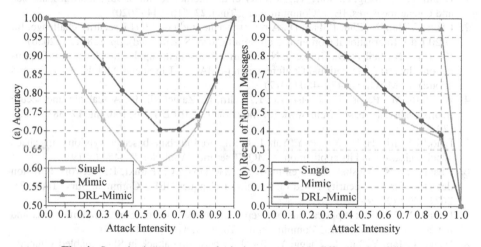

Fig. 4. Security improvement of mimic system with different algorithms.

5 Conclusion

As an essential infrastructure of 5G and future network, IoT is an important way to realize the Internet of Everything. MQTT is the most widespread transmission protocol in IoT, which is lightweight and space-saving. However, the massive devices and huge transmission operations bring tremendous vulnerabilities. To enhance the security of the IoT message transmission protocol, MQTT, a DRL-based mimic defense system is proposed in this paper. We employ equivalent but structural dissimilar variants to handle the same transmission task. The output of the variants will be distinguished and determined by the proposed DRL ruling mechanism, where the variant with inconsistent output will be reconstructed. The uncertain and dynamic internal structure will effectively mislead the attackers and enhance the security. The simulation results also reveal the security

430   Z. Wang et al.

improvement brought to the MQTT broker and the reliability and effectiveness of the proposed scheme.

Acknowledgements. This work was supported in part by the National Natural Science Foundation of China (No. 61571104), the Sichuan Science and Technology Program (No. 2018JY0539), the Key projects of the Sichuan Provincial Education Department (No. 18ZA0219), the Fundamental Research Funds for the Central Universities (No. ZYGX2017KYQD170), the CERNET Innovation Project (No. NGII20190111), the Fund Projects (Nos. 2020-JCJQ-ZD-016-11, 61403110405, 315075802, JZX6Y202001010161), and the Innovation Funding (No. 2018510007000134). The authors wish to thank the reviewers for their helpful comments.

References

1. Butun, I., Österberg, P., Song, H.: Security of the internet of things: vulnerabilities, attacks, and countermeasures. IEEE Commun. Surv. Tutor. **22**, 616–644 (2020)
2. Chen, F., Huo, Y., Zhu, J., Fan, D.: A review on the study on MQTT security challenge. In: 2020 IEEE International Conference on Smart Cloud (SmartCloud), pp. 128–133 (2020)
3. Swamy, S.N., Jadhav, D., Kulkarni, N.: Security threats in the application layer in IoT applications. In: 2017 International Conference on I-SMAC (IoT in Social, Mobile, Analytics and Cloud) (I-SMAC), pp. 477–480 (2017)
4. Amoretti, M., Pecori, R., Protskaya, Y., Veltri, L., Zanichelli, F.: A scalable and secure publish/subscribe-based framework for industrial IoT. IEEE Trans. Ind. Inf. **17**, 3815–3825 (2021)
5. Liao, T.-L., Lin, H.-R., Wan, P.-Y., Yan, J.-J.: Improved attribute-based encryption using chaos synchronization and its application to MQTT security. Appl. Sci. **9**, 4454 (2019)
6. Chaabouni, N., Mosbah, M., Zemmari, A., Sauvignac, C., Faruki, P.: Network intrusion detection for IoT security based on learning techniques. IEEE Commun. Surv. Tutor. **21**, 2671–2701 (2019)
7. Luong, N.C., et al.: Applications of deep reinforcement learning in communications and networking: a survey. IEEE Commun. Surv. Tutor. **21**, 3133–3174 (2019)
8. Wang, J., Tan, Y., Liu, J., Zhang, Y.: Topology poisoning attack in SDN-enabled vehicular edge network. IEEE Internet Things J. **7**, 9563–9574 (2020)
9. Apruzzese, G., Andreolini, M., Marchetti, M., Venturi, A., Colajanni, M.: Deep reinforcement adversarial learning against botnet evasion attacks. IEEE Trans. Netw. Serv. Manag. **17**, 1975–1987 (2020)
10. Wang, Z., Jiang, D., Huo, L., Yang, W.: An efficient network intrusion detection approach based on deep learning. Wirel. Netw. (2021)
11. Wang, S., Shi, H., Hu, Q., Lin, B., Cheng, X.: Moving target defense for internet of things based on the zero-determinant theory. IEEE Internet Things J. **7**, 661–668 (2020)
12. Hu, H., Wu, J., Wang, Z., Cheng, G.: Mimic defense: a designed-in cybersecurity defense framework. IET Inf. Secur. **12**, 226–237 (2017)
13. Wang, Z., Jiang, D., Wang, F., Lv, Z., Nowak, R.: A polymorphic heterogeneous security architecture for edge-enabled smart grids. Sustain. Cities Soc. **67**, 102661 (2021)
14. Li, G., Wang, W., Gai, K., Tang, Y., Yang, B., Si, X.: A framework for mimic defense system in cyberspace. J. Signal Process. Syst. **93**, 169–185 (2021)
15. Wu, J.: Cyberspace Mimic Defense. Springer, Heidelberg (2020)
16. Wang, Y.-W., Wu, J.-X., Guo, Y.-F., Hu, H.-C., Liu, W.-Y., Cheng, G.-Z.: Scientific workflow execution system based on mimic defense in the cloud environment. Front. Inf. Technol. Electron. Eng. **19**(12), 1522–1536 (2018). https://doi.org/10.1631/FITEE.1800621

17. Jiang, D., et al.: AI-assisted energy-efficient and intelligent routing for reconfigurable wireless networks. IEEE Trans. Netw. Sci. Eng. (2021). https://doi.org/10.1109/TNSE.2021.3075428
18. Jiang, D., et al.: QoE-aware efficient content distribution scheme for satellite-terrestrial networks. IEEE Trans. Mob. Comput. (2021). https://doi.org/10.1109/TMC.2021.3074917
19. Wang, Z., et al.: A polymorphic heterogeneous security architecture for edge-enabled smart grid. Sustain. Cities Soc. (2020)
20. Jiang, D., et al.: A performance measurement and analysis method for software-defined networking of IoV. IEEE Trans. Intell. Transp. Syst. (2020). https://doi.org/10.1109/TITS.2020.3029076
21. Jiang, D., et al.: Energy-efficient heterogeneous networking for electric vehicles networks in smart future cities. IEEE Trans. Intell. Transp. Syst. (2020). https://doi.org/10.1109/TITS.2020.3029015

Research on Website Traffic Prediction Method Based on Deep Learning

Rong Bao[1], Kailiang Zhang[1(✉)], Jing Huang[1], Yuxin Li[1], Weiwei Liu[2], and Likai Wang[2]

[1] Jiangsu Province Key Laboratory of Intelligent Industry Control Technology, Xuzhou University of Technology, Xuzhou 221018, China
zhangkailiang@xzit.edu.cn
[2] Traffic Police Detachment, Xuzhou Police Bureau, Xuzhou 221002, China

Abstract. Accurate prediction of website traffic can improve network management, improve service quality, and improve the end user experience. Using the neural network learning and memory function, we can predict the time series of network traffic flow. Based on short - and long-term memory, we design the structure of data and neural network model and select the nonlinear activation function. The experimental results show that the proposed prediction method obtains the higher accuracy, which can effectively predict the traffic of visiting websites. At the same time, this method can effectively reduce the training time. By accurate traffic prediction, the network manager can adjust scheduling strategy to guarantee the user experience.

Keywords: Network traffic prediction · Bidirectional LSTM · Deep learning · Activation function · Automatic polling

1 Introduction

With the development of emerging technologies such as artificial intelligence, big data, and 5G, some emerging network technologies and communication methods have been proposed [1, 2], and the quality and experience of the network are constantly improving [3, 4]. The WEB data is advancing the development of big data technology [5, 6]. Based on data mining, we can predict the network flow and reconstruct the traffic flow [7–10]. The machine learning is adopted to improve network scheduling and experience of end user [11]. Based on these emerging technologies, we can deploy new scheduling strategies in base station and mobile nodes to improve the energy efficiency [12–15]. By predicting future website visiting, grasping the network operation status in the future and taking more measures, the pressure of network congestion can be alleviated. According to the prediction results of website traffic, network resources are scheduled and allocated. Abnormal website traffic can also reflect the situation of network intrusion. If an abnormal phenomenon is detected in some key nodes on the website traffic, it is likely to have illegal behavior, and the administrator only needs to issue an alert, Taking preventive measures will ultimately protect user privacy, improve security and reliability,

D. Jiang and H. Song (Eds.): SIMUtools 2021, LNICST 424, pp. 432–440, 2022.
https://doi.org/10.1007/978-3-030-97124-3_32

and maintain a stable operating environment. Establish a suitable prediction model and use it to predict the size of website visits. Using the prediction results as a guideline can effectively reduce network congestion, prevent network attacks, maintain the normal operating environment of the website, reduce the possibility of failure, and improve security mechanism. From a higher perspective, it can have a very positive effect on website management and service performance.

2 Introduction

Information technology era, the Internet technology brought further changes to our lives, the network traffic as the amount of data transferred on the network, the actual situation of network indicators, through the website of network traffic analysis and forecasting, in network planning, network security, user experience, etc. have not kill the practical significance. In recent years, many methods and studies have emerged. In Literature [16], traffic prediction models are built in terms of text targets based on the characteristics of ever-growing pattern for attendance websites and business process objects. However, these models are relatively simple and their accuracy needs to be improved. In Literature [17], a network transmission point process based on deep mechanism is proposed to simulate network traffic characteristics, which can be used for effective mode prediction. It is suitable for large institutions such as data centers and has a good performance improvement. However, its architecture is complex and the actual application scenarios are limited. In Literature [18], based on layered network traffic, an efficient algorithm HTSIMPUTE was developed. In the time series of multivariable network traffic, the eigenvalues were predicted more accurately and had consistency constraints. The prediction model developed in literature [19] is enhanced by the general adaptive conditional scoring model, and can effectively deal with various load fluctuations by using the characteristics of regression. Its accuracy has been improved, and its practicability remains to be studied. Some scholars [20, 21] proposed a method based on request statistics and used vector machine classification to better predict traffic. In the face of the pattern and its statistical characteristics, an incremental learning method was proposed to improve the performance in terms of accuracy. Some scholars [22] also mark the characteristics of samples through a semi-unsupervised method, aiming at the abnormal HTTP traffic, providing a good foundation for the future development trend of traffic. The classification accuracy of traffic is improved [23, 24], which is conducive to reducing data resampling and improving the generalization ability of the system. By using Internet domain and sandbox analysis, logs can be correctly interpreted and weak supervision can be realized. Accurate detection channels can be obtained to provide a stable platform environment for improving prediction accuracy. Literature [25] evaluates the performance of eight machine learning algorithms in classification applications and traffic prediction, and compares the differences between different algorithms and models. Literature [26] proposes a network traffic encryption prediction method based on OQE, which has certain effect on the future expectation of video users. It further improves the model and analyzes the cause and time of the prediction error. In addition, the adaptive algorithm is studied. Therefore, from the perspective of experience quality, valuable insights are provided on the logical direction of strategy selection. This approach is also of certain significance for improving the future QoE algorithm and enhancing the core competitiveness. Scholars [27] estimate the future trend of network security problems by using the dark web crawling method of routers, and predict and evaluate high risk traffic. The model idea of this research is helpful to improve the accuracy of website traffic. Literature [28] proposed a TC engine, from the perspective of training and characteristics, the selection module and classifier, through the data plane, offline, to accurate classification of data packets, and then sent to the control plane, the effective mark packets implement resources and queue management, defined by the software point of view, the development trend of flow and main mark characteristic has the very good revelation function, however, the accuracy of future expected effect in site visits, needs further research. The traffic identification model in Literature [29] can automatically learn the nonlinear relationship between the original input and the predicted output, and it can effectively predict the traffic through classification and recognition. The method proposed in Literature [30] can provide abnormal interpretation of Web traffic, cope with traffic dynamics and future explosion, and the dimension-reduction technology based on neural network can extract the effective trend model of Web access data.The fuzziness and chaos of network traffic limit the precision of SVM prediction model. Wang et al. proposed a method to optimize model parameters, which improved the precision of SVM prediction model [31]. Literature [32] introduces the actual traffic data of enterprise network access points, and the temporal and spatial analysis of network traffic during actual operation. The results show that LSTM can effectively improve the prediction performance of access points. However, it is slightly insufficient in terms of versatility and cannot achieve the best results. In [33], for the 5G core network, a mechanism for predicting traffic load changes through LSTM is proposed, which can realize traffic load prediction. The results show that the scalability mechanism based on prediction is superior to other solutions in terms of responsiveness and resource integration. However, the choice of threshold needs to be improved. To sum up, in the field of web site network traffic prediction, a variety of methods and models, are put forward and continue to improve, to establish a suitable prediction model, and use it to predict the future, the size of the network traffic to improve network security, network management and network performance and so on can generate a very positive role, especially in the aspect of improving the end user experience, has a huge potential value.

3   Data Processing

The processing of website traffic-related data requires standardized processing to improve the accuracy of forecasts. The current predictive evaluation system often contains multiple indicators, among which the nature of the dimensions and the order of magnitude is different, resulting in huge differences. Such differences will cause poorer expected results. Therefore, in order to reduce this difference and ensure the standardization of traffic prediction related data and the rapid characteristics of cost function optimization, the original data of the training set and the test set are standardized here. In the training process, the use of dimensionless data features can improve the running speed of the model, and at the same time can avoid the influence of outliers on the overall calculation, improve the accuracy of the model, and ensure the reliability of the results.

Transform the sequence $P = \{p_1, p_2, p_3 \cdots p_n\}$ to obtain the dimensionless sequence $Q = \{q_1, q_2, q_3 \cdots q_n\}$, and the model is shown in Formula (1).

$$q_i = \frac{p_i - \min_{1 \le j \le n} \{p_j\}}{\max_{1 \le j \le n} \{p_j\} - \min_{1 \le j \le n} \{p_j\}} \tag{1}$$

In Eq. (1), $\min_{1 \le j \le n} \{p_j\}$ is the minimum value in the sequence and $\max_{1 \le j \le n} \{p_j\}$ is the maximum value in the sequence, then the new sequence $Q = \{q_1, q_2, q_3 \cdots q_n\}$ is dimensionless. We selected a data set to carry out normalization processing on the data, and made images before and after normalization, as shown in Fig. 1 and Fig. 2.

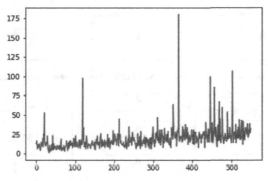

Fig. 1. Before regression.

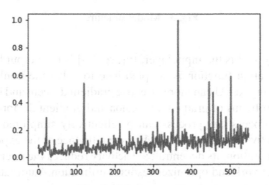

Fig. 2. After regression.

Figure 1 shows the data graph before regression, and Fig. 2 shows the data graph after regression. It can be seen that the shapes of the two graphs tend to show the same, and the range of the longitudinal axis is narrowed by regression processing, limiting it to 0–1. After data standardization processing, all indicators of the original data are in the same order of magnitude, which is suitable for comprehensive comparative evaluation. Among them, the most typical is the normalization of data processing.

4 Model

The input data of a one-way LSTM is unique, and these training data include the information of visited user. Bidirectional LSTM uses input data to run in two ways, one is from the past to the future, and the other one is from the future to the past. The difference between the two methods is that in the feedback operation, the future information is retained in both directions and the information before and after can be saved at any point in time. Bidirectional LSTM is composed of two LSTM cyclic layers with opposite information transmission. The two cyclic layers transmit information in time order and reverse order respectively, and the output results are calculated in combination with consideration of two directions. The model structure is shown in Fig. 3.

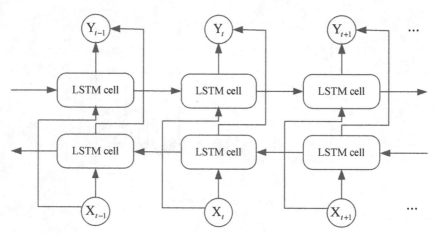

Fig. 3. Model structure.

In Fig. 3, $\{x_1, x_2, \cdots\}$ is the input layer, $\{y_1, y_2, \cdots\}$ is the output layer.

The ReLU activation function is adopted here to solve the nonlinear problem of neural networks. Using ReLU can more effective gradient descent and back propagation, thus avoiding the problems of gradient explosion and gradient disappearance. In terms of the calculation process, the process can be effectively simplified and the negative influence of other activation functions, such as the influence of the exponential function, can be shielded. In addition, its decentralized activity reduces the overall computational cost of the neural network and optimizes resource utilization. Automatic polling verifies universality, as shown in Table 1.

Table 1. Automatic polling algorithm.

Automatic algorithm
Input:Range1,Range2,Step
Output:figures
//Random generated parameter and run the model
for K=1 to Step.size do
P1 = random(Range1)
P2 = random(Range2)
Result.figures=LSTM(P1,P2)
end for
return Result.figures

In Table 1, an automated method is proposed to automatically poll and traversal the target, saving time cost and ensuring the comprehensiveness of data evaluation.

5 Assessment

In this case, the use of CUDNNLSTM acceleration is specifically implemented for CUDA parallel processing and can only be implemented in a GPU environment, otherwise it will not run. The faster execution time is due to the parallelism. Train_rmse and test_rmse values are obtained and plotted. It can be found that although the look_back value has changed, test_rmse and train_rese are basically stable. In order to prove the superiority of bidirectional LSTM in time series forecasting, the stacked and bidirectional LSTM are compared by error criteria, and RMSE (rootmeansquarederror) is selected for judgment, as shown in formula (2).

$$\text{RMSE} = \sqrt{\frac{\sum (y - y')^2}{n}} \tag{2}$$

In formula (2), y is the real result, y' is the predicted result, and n is the size of the data set. The evaluation index can unify the error, and the dimensions of the original data and the target data, compared with MAE (mean absolute error), make up for the defects of non-direction at some points. Randomly select 40 articles, use the bidirectional and stacked LSTM models to make predictions, and compare the RMSE of the results of the two models, as shown in Fig. 4.

It can be seen from Fig. 4 that the RMSE of the bidirectional LSTM is generally small, which is more suitable for time series forecasting analysis.

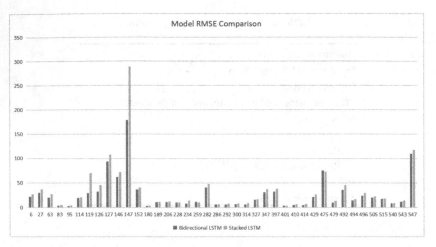

Fig. 4. Rmse comparison.

6 Assessment

This paper adopts neural network learning and memory function to predict website traffic. According to the time series of network traffic forecasting, we design a method to optimize the data structure. The nonlinear activation function of the enhanced neural network model is adopted, and automatic polling traversal is proposed to access the site prediction data of the specified target. The experimental results show that the method has certain practical value. On the other hand, the acceleration function can effectively reduce the running time of the model and save costs. Accurate website traffic forecasting can help better network management, improve service quality, optimize resource allocation, and improve user experience.

Acknowledgment. This work is partly supported by Jiangsu technology project of Housing and Urban-Rural Development (No. 2018ZD265) and Xu Zhou Science and Technology Plan Project (No. KC21309).

References

1. Zhang, K., Chen, L., An, Y., Cui, P.: A QoE test system for vehicular voice cloud services. Mob. Netw. Appl. **26**(2), 700–715 (2019). https://doi.org/10.1007/s11036-019-01415-3
2. Chen, L., Jiang, D., Bao, R., Xiong, J., Liu, F., Bei, L.: MIMO scheduling effectiveness analysis for bursty data service from view of QoE. Chin. J. Electron. **26**(5), 1079–1085 (2017)
3. Chen, L., et al.: A lightweight end-side user experience data collection system for quality evaluation of multimedia communications. IEEE Access **6**(1), 15408–15419 (2018)
4. Chen, L., Zhang, L.: Spectral efficiency analysis for massive MIMO system under QoS constraint: an effective capacity perspective. Mob. Netw. Appl. **26**(2), 691–699 (2020). https://doi.org/10.1007/s11036-019-01414-4
5. Jiang, D., Huo, L., Song, H.: Rethinking behaviors and activities of base stations in mobile cellular networks based on big data analysis. IEEE Trans. Netw. Sci. Eng. **7**(1), 80–90 (2020)

6. Jiang, D., Wang, Y., Lv, Z., Qi, S., Singh, S.: Big data analysis based network behavior insight of cellular networks for industry 4.0 applications. IEEE Trans. Ind. Inform. **16**(2), 1310–1320 (2020)
7. Jiang, D., et al.: A performance measurement and analysis method for software-defined networking of IoV. IEEE Trans. Intell. Transp. Syst. (2020). https://doi.org/10.1109/TITS.2020. 3029076
8. Jiang, D., Wang, W., Shi, L., Song, H.: A compressive sensing-based approach to end-to-end network traffic reconstruction. IEEE Trans. Netw. Sci. Eng. **7**(1), 507–519 (2020)
9. Yang, B., Bao, W., Huang, D.S., Chen, Y.: Inference of large-scale time-delayed gene regulatory network with parallel mapreduce cloud platform. Sci. Rep. **8**(1) (2018). https://doi.org/ 10.1038/s41598-018-36180-y
10. Yang, B., Wenzheng, B.: Complex-valued ordinary differential equation modeling for time series identification. IEEE ACCESS **7**(1) (2019). https://doi.org/10.1109/ACCESS.2019.290 2958
11. Boutaba, R., et al.: A comprehensive survey on machine learning for networking: evolution, applications and research opportunities. J. Internet Serv. Appl. **9**(1), 1–99 (2018). https://doi. org/10.1186/s13174-018-0087-2
12. Jiang, D., et al.: AI-assisted energy-efficient and intelligent routing for reconfigurable wireless networks. IEEE Trans. Netw. Sci. Eng. (2020)
13. Jiang, D., et al.: Energy-efficient heterogeneous networking for electric vehicles networks in smart future cities. IEEE Trans. Intell. Transp. Syst. (2020). accepted, https://doi.org/10. 1109/TITS.2020.3029015
14. Jiang, D., Wang, Y., Lv, Z., Wang, W., Wang, H.: An energy-efficient networking approach in cloud services for IIoT networks. IEEE J. Sel. Areas Commun. **38**(5), 928–941 (2020)
15. Jiang, L. Huo, Z. Lv, H. Song, W. Qin.: A joint multi-criteria utility-based network selection approach for vehicle-to-infrastructure networking. IEEE Trans. Intell. Transp. Syst. **19**(10), 3305–3319 (2018)
16. Pasichnyk, R., Susla, M., Honchar, L., Avhustyn, R.: Mathematical models of websites attendance and methods of its improvement. In: 2017 14th International Conference The Experience of Designing and Application of CAD Systems in Microelectronics (CADSM), pp. 375–377. Lviv (2017).https://doi.org/10.1109/CADSM.2017.7916154
17. Saha, A., Ganguly, N., Chakraborty, S., De, A.: Learning network traffic dynamics using temporal point process. In: IEEE INFOCOM 2019–IEEE Conference on Computer Communications, pp. 1927–1935. Paris, France (2019). https://doi.org/10.1109/INFOCOM.2019. 8737622
18. Liu, Z., Yan, Y., Yang, J., Hauskrecht, M.: Missing value estimation for hierarchical time series: a study of hierarchical web traffic. In: 2015 IEEE International Conference on Data Mining, pp. 895–900. Atlantic City, NJ (2015). https://doi.org/10.1109/ICDM.2015.58
19. Adegboyeg, A.: A dynamic bandwidth prediction and provisioning scheme in cloud networks. In: 2015 IEEE 7th International Conference on Cloud Computing Technology and Science (CloudCom), pp. 623–628. Vancouver, BC (2015). https://doi.org/10.1109/CloudCom.201 5.45
20. Punitha, V., Mala, C.: Traffic classification in server farm using supervised learning techniques. Neural Comput. Appl. **33**(4), 1279–1296 (2020). https://doi.org/10.1007/s00521-020-05030-2
21. Salman, O., Elhajj, I.H., Kayssi, A., Chehab, A.: A review on machine learning–based approaches for Internet traffic classification. Ann. Telecommun. **75**(11–12), 673–710 (2020). https://doi.org/10.1007/s12243-020-00770-7
22. Kozik, R., Choraś, M., Renk, R., Hołubowicz, W.: Semi-unsupervised machine learning for anomaly detection in HTTP traffic. In: Burduk, R., Jackowski, K., Kurzyński, M., Woźniak,

M., Żołnierek, A. (eds.) Proceedings of the 9th International Conference on Computer Recognition Systems CORES 2015. Advances in Intelligent Systems and Computing, vol. 403. Springer, Cham (2016). https://doi.org/10.1007/978-3-319-26227-7_72

23. Liu, Z., Wang, R., Tao, M.: SmoteAdaNL: a learning method for network traffic classification. J. Ambient. Intell. Humaniz. Comput. **7**(1), 121–130 (2015). https://doi.org/10.1007/s12652-015-0310-y

24. Franc, V., Sofka, M., Bartos, K.: Learning detector of malicious network traffic from weak labels. In: Bifet, A., et al. (eds.) Machine Learning and Knowledge Discovery in Databases. ECML PKDD 2015. LNCS, vol. 9286, pp. 85–99. Springer, Cham (2015). https://doi.org/10.1007/978-3-319-23461-8_6

25. Fowdur, T.P., Baulum, B.N., Beeharry, Y.: Performance analysis of network traffic capture tools and machine learning algorithms for the classification of applications, states and anomalies. Int. J. Inf. Technol. **12**(3), 805–824 (2020). https://doi.org/10.1007/s41870-020-00458-0

26. Orsolic, I., et al.: A machine learning approach to classifying youtube qoe based on encrypted network traffic. Multimed. Tools Appl. **76**, 22267–22301 (2017). https://doi.org/10.1007/s11042-017-4728-4

27. Gokhale, C., Olugbara, O.O.: Dark web traffic analysis of cybersecurity threats through South African internet protocol address space. SN Comput. Sci. **1**(5), 1–20 (2020). https://doi.org/10.1007/s42979-020-00292-y

28. Audah, M.Z.F., Chin, T.S., Zulfadzli, Y., Lee, C.K., Rizaluddin, K.: Towards efficient and scalable machine learning-based qos traffic classification in software-defined network. In: Awan, I., Younas, M., Ünal, P., Aleksy, M. (eds.) MobiWIS 2019. LNCS, vol. 11673, pp. 217–229. Springer, Cham (2019). https://doi.org/10.1007/978-3-030-27192-3_17

29. Guo, L., Wu, Q., Liu, S., Duan, M., Li, H., Sun, J.: Deep learning-based real-time VPN encrypted traffic identification methods. J. Real-Time Image Proc. **17**(1), 103–114 (2019). https://doi.org/10.1007/s11554-019-00930-6

30. Atienza, D., Herrero, Á., Corchado, E.: Neural analysis of HTTP traffic for web attack detection. In: Herrero, Á., Baruque, B., Sedano, J., Quintián, H., Corchado, E. (eds.) International Joint Conference. CISIS 2015. Advances in Intelligent Systems and Computing, vol. 369. Springer, Cham (2015). https://doi.org/10.1007/978-3-319-19713-5_18

31. Wang, Q.M., Fan, A.W., Shi, S.H.: Network trac prediction based on improved support vector machine. Int. J. Syst. Assur. Eng. Manag. **8**(3), 1976–1980 (2017)

32. Sone, S.P., Lehtomäki, J.J., Khan, Z.: Wireless traffic usage forecasting using real enterprise network data: analysis and methods. IEEE Open J. Commun. Soc. **1**, 777–797 (2020). https://doi.org/10.1109/OJCOMS.2020.3000059

33. Alawe, I., Ksentini, A., Hadjadj-Aoul, Y., Bertin, P.: Improving traffic forecasting for 5G core network scalability: a machine learning approach. IEEE Netw. **32**(6), 42–49 (2018). https://doi.org/10.1109/MNET.2018.1800104

Network Simulations

An Online Algorithm for Effective Capacity Estimation

Lei Chen[✉] and Ping Cui

Jiangsu Province Key Laboratory of Intelligent Industry Control Technology, Xuzhou University of Technology, Xuzhou 221018, China
chenlei@xzit.edu.cn

Abstract. Effective Capacity is an important metric to measure the capacity of a wireless channel. However, the estimation algorithm cost a lot of computation time. The current estimation algorithm thus cannot predict the real-time Effective Capacity for online service. An online estimation algorithm is proposed to reduce computation time cost in this paper. A simulation is designed with QoS constraint. The simulation results illustrate that the proposed algorithm save a lot of computation time.

Keywords: Effective capacity · Wireless channel · Quality of service

1 Introduction

In 5G networks, some methods of routing and network measurement [1–3] are proposed. In core network and edge network, a number of traffic characteristic extraction schemes [4–7], scheduling policies are proposed to improve the quality of experience (QoE) [8–11], raise resources utilization [12–15] and energy efficiency [16–18]. To evaluate these new methods, researchers reconstruct traffic in test bed [19–21]. At the edge of 5G network, more antennas are used to improve the quality of signal. With limited channel resource, the spectral efficiency (SE) is critical to support a huge number of end devices [22–25]. To utilize spectral efficiency, the traffic prediction [2, 26, 27] and effectively scheduling resource are premises for QoS guarantee [28–30].

To design a QoS-aware system, it is necessary to model the wireless channel with a QoS constraint. By considering the probability of delay constraint in wireless networks, Wu and Negi proposed a concept of effective capacity (EC) [31]. This concept is the duality of the effective bandwidth. The EC is defined as the maximum constant arrival rate that the system is able to afford meeting a fixed delay constraint. Based on the EC model, we can adjust the scheduling strategy to meet the QoS constraint with perfect knowledge of the instantaneous channel state information (CSI) at the transmitter. Unfortunately, the estimation algorithm cost a lot of computation time. The current estimation algorithm thus cannot predict the real-time Effective Capacity for online service. This high cost prevents the real-time QoS aware scheduling. We proposed an online estimation algorithm to save the computation time. The simulation is carried out for a massive

D. Jiang and H. Song (Eds.): SIMUtools 2021, LNICST 424, pp. 443–451, 2022.
https://doi.org/10.1007/978-3-030-97124-3_33

MIMO case [32, 33]. Our simulation results demonstrate that the proposed algorithm is able to obtain high prediction precision within less time.

The paper is divided into five sections. In Sect. 2, we introduce the effective capacity model and its off-line estimation algorithm. In the Sect. 3, we give the online estimation algorithm. We give our simulation results in Sect. 4 and conclude in Sect. 5.

2 Effective Capacity Model

For a stable channel, the main issue of QoS guarantee is the relationship between the envelope of source rate and the capacity of the system for stable transmission, namely effective bandwidth. For the bursty data services, we can describe the QoS constraint by a threshold of SINR at each time slot. However, in the emerging 5G services, the mobile station experiences a strong channel state fluctuation. For the transmissions of the new services, such as speech recognition cloud and real-time remote control, we need to consider the time-varying channel because of fast-moving mobile station. The key issue for QoS guarantee is to predict the probability of the varying channel rate meeting the delay constraint with special arrival rate. The EC model is a function of source rate with the probability of delay violation. In many mobile scenarios, this model is more suitable for the delay violation probability analysis in a time-varying channel [34–38].

In the EC model, let $Q(t)$ is the queue length, the queue length constraint can be written as [31].

$$P_r(\max Q(0) > B) \leq \epsilon. \tag{1}$$

According to inequality (1), let B denotes a large buffer, given a queue length violation constraint ϵ and selecting $\theta = -\log(\epsilon)/B$, the QoS guarantee problem can be formulated as an EC problem:

$$r^{(c)}(\theta) = \frac{1}{\theta} \lim_{n \to \infty} \frac{-1}{n} \ln E\left(e^{-\theta \sum_{t=1}^{n} r(t)}\right) \tag{2}$$

For a smaller buffer size, the queue length probability can be estimated by

$$\sup_t \Pr\{Q(t) \geq B\} \approx \gamma(r) \times e^{-\theta(r) \times B} \tag{3}$$

If we consider the delay violation problem, the approximation can be rewritten as

$$\sup_t \Pr\{D(t) \geq D_{max}\} \approx \gamma(r) \times e^{-\theta(r) \times r \times D_{max}}, \tag{4}$$

where $\gamma(r)$ is the probability of a nonempty queue, $\theta(r)$ is a solution of $\alpha(\theta) = r$, the $\alpha(\theta)$ is a function of accumulated transmitted bit length $S(t)$ and θ:

$$\alpha(\theta) = \frac{\lim_{t \to \infty} \frac{-1}{t} \ln E\left(e^{-\theta S(t)}\right)}{\theta}, \quad \forall \theta \geq 0 \tag{5}$$

If we employ a fluid model, the $\theta(r)$ can be obtained by taking a number of samples [31],

$$\hat{\gamma} = \frac{1}{N} \sum_{n=1}^{N} S_n \quad S_n \in \{0, 1\} \tag{6}$$

$$\hat{q} = \frac{1}{N} \sum_{n=1}^{N} Q_n \tag{7}$$

$$\hat{\theta} = \frac{\hat{\gamma} \cdot r^c}{\hat{q}} \tag{8}$$

where S_n indicates whether a packet is in transmission. And Q_n is the length of queue. The subscript n is sequence number of time slot.

The conventional binary search algorithm estimating effective capacity is illustrated in Fig. 1 [31].

3   Online EC Estimation Algorithm

This algorithm searches the suitable source rate from a wide range. Actually, the time-varying channel state does not changing so fast. Therefore, the effective capacity won't change in a wide range. The initial value of service rate is also usually far deviate from the aim value. By using the previous effective capacity, we can reduce significantly the searching range.

Let the expected service rate is equal to access probability times channel capacity. The proposed algorithm is illustrated in Fig. 2.

The QoS metric estimation algorithm is illustrated in Fig. 3. The empirical value of sample number K is set as 10^5 times the expected transmitted bits in 1 time slot.

In our proposed algorithm, we use previous EC estimation value as initial value to reduce the computation time. Because the channel state fluctuation is limited, we expect that this method is able to reduce the iterations.

algorithm 1	
1	Initialize the error estimation parameters. Set lower bound and upper bound of sustainable service rate;
2	While error estimation is higher than bias
3	If the source rate is lower than that of service rate can support
4	If the bias is higher than constraint
5	Lower bound = source rate
6	Set new service rate=1/2(lower bound + upper bound);
7	endif
8	else
9	upper bound = source rate
10	Set new source rate=1/2(lower bound + upper bound);
11	endif
12	Based on new source rate, estimate QoS metric;
13	Compute new error estimation;
14	End while

Fig. 1. Off-line effective capacity estimation algorithm

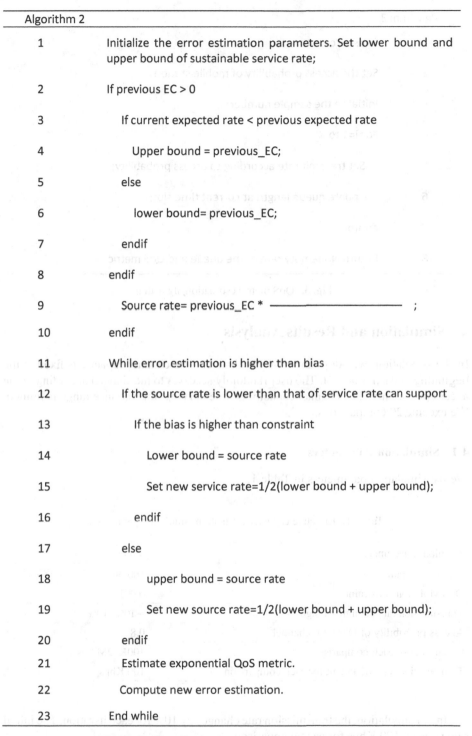

Algorithm 2	
1	Initialize the error estimation parameters. Set lower bound and upper bound of sustainable service rate;
2	If previous EC > 0
3	If current expected rate < previous expected rate
4	Upper bound = previous_EC;
5	else
6	lower bound= previous_EC;
7	endif
8	endif
9	Source rate= previous_EC * ——————————— ;
10	endif
11	While error estimation is higher than bias
12	If the source rate is lower than that of service rate can support
13	If the bias is higher than constraint
14	Lower bound = source rate
15	Set new service rate=1/2(lower bound + upper bound);
16	endif
17	else
18	upper bound = source rate
19	Set new source rate=1/2(lower bound + upper bound);
20	endif
21	Estimate exponential QoS metric.
22	Compute new error estimation.
23	End while

Fig. 2. Online effective capacity estimation algorithm

Algorithm 3	
1	Set source rate
2	Set the access probability of mobile station
3	Initialize the sample number K;
4	For i=1 to K
5	Set transmit rate according to access probability;
6	update queue length at current time slot;
7	endfor
8	Return Nonempty rate of the queue and QoS metric

Fig. 3. QoS metric estimation algorithm

4 Simulation and Results Analysis

In the simulation, we adopt an ON-OFF channel. The channel capacity is fixed at the beginning of each time slot. The user randomly accesses to the channel according to the access probability. The channel capacity is time-varying, the variance range is limited. We execute 20 comparisons.

4.1 Simulation Parameters

We list simulation parameters in Table 1.

Table 1. Effective capacity estimation simulation parameters

Simulation parameter	Value
Delay constraint	100 ms
QoS violation constraint	0.001
Transmission rate changing range	$-10\%-10\%$
Access probability of ON-OFF channel	0.8
Initial rate for each comparison	100K–2M bps
Transmission rate increment for each comparison	100 Kbps

In our simulation, the transmission rate changes by 10% for each iteration. The initial rate rises by 100 Kbps for each comparison.

4.2 Simulation Results

Our simulation results are showed in Fig. 4. The traditional algorithm and our proposed online algorithm can both obtain exact EC value. Moreover, the online algorithm uses much less iterations than that of traditional algorithm.

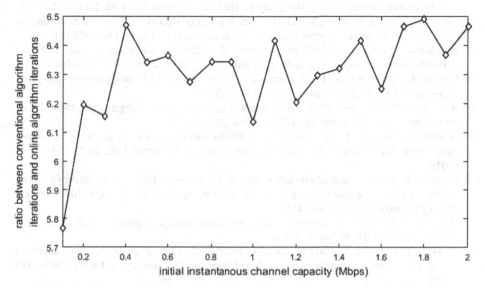

Fig. 4. Ratio between iterations between conventional algorithm and online algorithm

5   Conclusion

In this paper, we discuss the lower cost online effective capacity algorithm for QoS prediction of online services. By using iterative strategy, the proposed estimation algorithm can make an accurate prediction of the effective capacity of wireless channel. This algorithm can monitor the QoS and scheduling communication resource.

Acknowledgement. This work was supported in part by Xu Zhou Science and Technology Plan Project (Grant No. KC21309).

References

1. Wang, F., Jiang, D., Qi, S.: An adaptive routing algorithm for integrated information networks. China Commun. **7**(1), 196–207 (2019)
2. Huo, L., et al.: An intelligent optimization-based traffic information acquirement approach to software-defined networking. Comput. Intell. **36**(1), 151–171 (2020)
3. Zhang, K., Chen, L., An, Y., Cui, P.: A QoE test system for vehicular voice cloud services. Mob. Netw. Appl. **26**(2), 700–715 (2019). https://doi.org/10.1007/s11036-019-01415-3

4. Chen, L., Jiang, D., Bao, R., Xiong, J., Liu, F., Bei, L.: MIMO Scheduling effectiveness analysis for bursty data service from view of QoE. Chin. J. Electron. **26**(5), 1079–1085 (2017)
5. Jiang, D., et al.: Big data analysis-based network behavior insight of cellular networks for industry 4.0 applications. IEEE Trans. Ind. Inform. **16**(2), 1310–1320 (2020)
6. Jiang, D., Huo, L., Song, H.: Rethinking behaviors and activities of base stations in mobile cellular networks based on big data analysis. IEEE Trans. Netw. Sci. Eng. **1**(1), 1–12 (2018)
7. Chen, L., et al.: A lightweight end-side user experience data collection system for quality evaluation of multimedia communications. IEEE Access **6**(1), 15408–15419 (2018)
8. Barakabitze, A.A., et al.: QoE management of multimedia streaming services in future networks: a tutorial and survey. IEEE Commun. Surv. Tutor. **22**(1), 526–565 (2020)
9. Orsolic, I., Skorin-Kapov, L.: A framework for in-network QoE monitoring of encrypted video streaming. IEEE Access **8**, 74691–74706 (2020)
10. Song, E., et al.: Threshold-oblivious on-line web QoE assessment using neural network-based regression model. IET Commun. **14**(12), 2018–2026 (2020)
11. Seufert, M., Wassermann, S., Casas, P.: Considering user behavior in the quality of experience cycle: towards proactive QoE-aware traffic management. Commun. Lett. **23**(7), 1145–1148 (2019)
12. Chen, L., Zhang, L.: Spectral efficiency analysis for massive MIMO system under QoS constraint: an effective capacity perspective. Mob. Netw. Appl. **26**(2), 691–699 (2020). https://doi.org/10.1007/s11036-019-01414-4
13. Wang, F., et al.: A dynamic resource scheduling scheme in edge computing satellite networks. Mob. Netw. Appl. **26**, 597–608 (2021)
14. Jiang, D., Huo, L., Lv, Z., et al.: A joint multi-criteria utility-based network selection approach for vehicle-to-infrastructure networking. IEEE Trans. Intell. Transp. Syst. **19**(10), 3305–3319 (2018)
15. Jiang, D., Zhang, P., Lv, Z., et al.: Energy-efficient multi-constraint routing algorithm with load balancing for smart city applications. IEEE Internet Things J. **3**(6), 1437–1447 (2016)
16. Wiatr, P., Chen, J., Monti, P., Wosinska, L.: Energy efficiency versus reliability performance in optical backbone networks [invited]. IEEE/OSA J. Opt. Commun. Netw. **7**(3), A482–A491 (2015)
17. Jiang, D., Li, W., Lv, H.: An energy-efficient cooperative multicast routing in multi-hop wireless networks for smart medical applications. Neurocomputing **220**(2017), 160–169 (2017)
18. Jiang, D., Wang, Y., Lv, Z., Wang, W., Wang, H.: An energy-efficient networking approach in cloud services for IIoT networks. IEEE J. Sel. Areas Commun. **38**(5), 928–941 (2020)
19. Jiang, D., Wang, W., Shi, L., et al.: A compressive sensing-based approach to end-to-end network traffic reconstruction. IEEE Trans. Netw. Sci. Eng. **5**(3), 1–12 (2018)
20. Jiang, D., Huo, L., Li, Y.: Fine-granularity inference and estimations to network traffic for SDN. Plos One **13**(5), 1–23 (2018)
21. Wang, Y., et al.: A new traffic prediction algorithm to software defined networking. Mob. Netw. Appl. **26**, 716–725 (2021)
22. Lee, Y., Kim, Y., Park, S.: A machine learning approach that meets axiomatic properties in probabilistic analysis of LTE spectral efficiency. In: 2019 International Conference on Information and Communication Technology Convergence (ICTC), pp. 1451–1453. Jeju Island, Korea (South) (2019)
23. Ji, H., Sun, C., Shieh, W.: Spectral efficiency comparison between analog and digital rof for mobile fronthaul transmission link. J. Lightwave Technol. **38**(20), 5617–5623 (2020)
24. Hayati, M., Kalbkhani, H., Shayesteh, M.G.: Relay selection for spectral-efficient network-coded multi-source D2D communications. In: 2019 27th Iranian Conference on Electrical Engineering (ICEE), pp. 1377–1381. Yazd, Iran (2019)

25. You, L., Xiong, J., Zappone, A., Wang, W., Gao, X.: Spectral efficiency and energy efficiency tradeoff in massive MIMO downlink transmission with statistical CSIT. IEEE Trans. Signal Process. **68**, 2645–2659 (2020)
26. Qi, S., Jiang, D., Huo, L.: A prediction approach to end-to-end traffic in space information networks. Mob. Netw. Appl. **26**, 726–735 (2021)
27. Huo, L., et al.: An SDN-based fine-grained measurement and modeling approach to vehicular communication network traffic. Int. J. Commun. Syst. 1–12 (2019, early access). https://doi.org/10.1002/dac.4092
28. Tan, J., Xiao, S., Han, S., Liang, Y., Leung, V.C.M.: QoS-aware user association and resource allocation in LAA-LTE/WiFi coexistence systems. IEEE Trans. Wirel. Commun. **18**(4), 2415–2430 (2019)
29. Wang, Y., Tang, X., Wang, T.: A unified QoS and security provisioning framework for wiretap cognitive radio networks: a statistical queueing analysis approach. IEEE Trans. Wirel. Commun. **18**(3), 1548–1565 (2019)
30. Hassan, M.Z., Hossain, M.J., Cheng, J., Leung, V.C.M.: Hybrid RF/FSO backhaul networks with statistical-QoS-aware buffer-aided relaying. IEEE Trans. Wirel. Commun. **19**(3), 1464–1483 (2020)
31. Wu, D., Negi, R.: Effective capacity: a wireless link model for support of quality of service. IEEE Trans. Wirel. Commun. **2**(4), 630–643 (2003)
32. Gao, X., Edfors, O., Rusek, F., Tufvesson, F.: Massive MIMO performance evaluation based on measured propagation data. IEEE Trans. Wirel. Commun. **14**(7), 3899–3911 (2015)
33. Björnson, E., Larsson, E., Debbah, M.: Massive MIMO for maximal spectral efficiency: how many users and pilots should be allocated? IEEE Trans. Wirel. Commun. **15**(2), 1293–1308 (2016)
34. Guo, C., Liang, L., Li, G.Y.: Resource allocation for low-latency vehicular communications: an effective capacity perspective. IEEE J. Sel. Areas Commun. **37**(4), 905–917 (2019)
35. Shehab, M., Alves, H., Latva-aho, M.: Effective capacity and power allocation for machine-type communication. IEEE Trans. Veh. Technol. **68**(4), 4098–4102 (2019)
36. Cui, Q., Gu, Y., Ni, W., Liu, R.P.: Effective capacity of licensed-assisted access in unlicensed spectrum for 5G: from theory to application. IEEE J. Sel. Areas Commun. **35**(8), 1754–1767 (2017)
37. Xiao, C., Zeng, J., Ni, W., Liu, R.P., Su, X., Wang, J.: Delay guarantee and effective capacity of downlink NOMA fading channels. IEEE J. Sel. Top. Signal Process. **13**(3), 508–523 (2019)
38. Björnson, E., Larsson, E.G., Debbah, M.: Massive MIMO for maximal spectral efficiency: how many users and pilots should be allocated? IEEE Trans. Wircl. Commun. **15**(2), 1293–1308 (2016)

Space Vector Modulation Strategy and Related Improvement Technology of Matrix Converter

Li Delu[1]([⊠]) [iD], Liu Zhijian[1], and Zhang Kailiang[2]

[1] Jiangsu Vocational Institute of Architectural Technology, Xuzhou, China
[2] Jiangsu Province Key Laboratory of Intelligent Industry Control Technology, Xuzhou University of Technology, Xuzhou, China

Abstract. Based on the modeming strategy, the paper studies the influence of three different pulse output modes on the input and output performance of matrix converter (MC) and obtains the result analysis by simulation results: Pulse output mode II is better in output low frequency and high frequency, and the pulse output mode II is selected as the pulse output mode of spatial vector modulation strategy in the process of impedance load experiment. Experiments verify the correctness of control policies.

Keywords: Matrix converter · Spatial vector modulation strategy · Pulse output

1 Introduction

Three-phase - Three-phase MC space vector modulation (SVM) strategy by Yugoslav scholar L. Professor Huber D. Borojevic proposed in 1989, this modulation method will be the traditional concept of spatial vector pulse wide modulation for MC control, simple and easy to implement, greatly reducing the requirements of the control circuit, the use of this method does not need to introduce low-frequency harmonics in the output phase voltage, the MC voltage utilization rate can reach a maximum of 0.866, to achieve arbitrary control of the input current phase difference.

MC SVM through the introduction of vector concept to achieve the control of output voltage and input current, not directly using instantaneous voltage, current to calculate the duty-to-duty ratio of each switch, so in the case of interference with the input voltage source control effect is slightly inferior. In the process of MC industrial application, there is imbalance of industrial power supply and interference factors such as harmonics, coupled with the MC input side for filtering out the high-level harmonics in the input current, there is a second-order low-pass filter, the input voltage of the switch matrix must have a certain degree of asymmetrical harmonic distortion. Therefore, it is necessary to analyze the operating performance of the MC when the input grid voltage is abnormal and adopt the corresponding control strategy to ensure the normal operation of the transformer load equipment.

The operating performance of the MC under the conditions of input voltage imbalance, non-sine, and instantaneous drop is analyzed respectively, and the abnormal conditions have a serious effect on the input, output performance, and load equipment of the

D. Jiang and H. Song (Eds.): SIMUtools 2021, LNICST 424, pp. 452–472, 2022.
https://doi.org/10.1007/978-3-030-97124-3_34

MC. A SVM control strategy of spatial vector modulation is adopted to keep the output voltage of the MC as normal by compensating for the change of virtual DC voltage, and the simulation and experiment verify the correctness and effectiveness of the SVM control strategy.

2 Topology and Modulation Principle of 3-Phase to 3-Phase Matrix Converter

2.1 The Topology of a Three-Phase-Three-Phase Matrix Converter

As a new type of interchange-interchange converter, the MC transforms the sine wave of the AC utility grid constant frequency amplitude into a sine wave of the variable frequency amplitude, and its topology is shown in Fig. 1, wherein S11toS33 these nine bidirectional switches form a 3 × 3 switch matrix. MC in the process of operation, the switching device's on-off state constantly changes, three-phase output through a two-way switch can be connected to any one-phase input, according to a certain strategy to control S11to S33 these 9 bidirectional switches, you can get the frequency and amplitude are continuously adjustable sine wave.

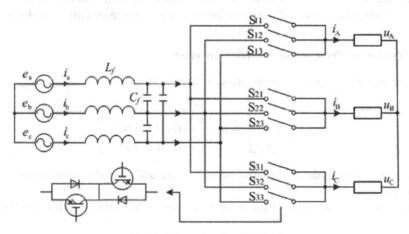

Fig. 1. The main circuit of MC

In the figure, e_ a, e_ b, e_ C is the three-phase input phase voltage, I_ a, i_ b, i_ C is the current of three-phase input phase, l_ f, C_ F is the filter inductance and the filter capacitance of the input filter; u_ A, u_ B, u_ C is the three-phase output phase voltage, I_ A, i_ B, i_ C is the current of three-phase output phase. First, define switch S_ The control function of JK is:

In the figure, e_a, e_b, e_c is the three-phase input phase voltage, i_a, i_b, i_c is the three-phase input phase current, respectively, L_f, C_f is the filter inductor and filter capacitor of the input filter; u_A, u_B, u_C is the three-phase output phase voltage. i_A, i_B, i_C is the current of three-phase output phase. First, define switch S_{jk}, the control function of S_{jk} is:

$$S_{jk}(t) = 1 \ or \ 0, j \in \{1, 2, 3\}, \ k \in \{1, 2, 3\} \tag{1}$$

When $S_{jk}(t) = 1$, indicates that the switch is closed; $S_{jk}(t)S_{jk}(t) = 0S_{jk}(t)$.

The voltage source characteristics of the MC power supply require that the input side cannot be shorted, and the perceptic characteristics of the load require that the output side cannot open, so that at any one time, the three bidirectional switches connected to each output must have and only one switch is closed, which can be expressed as:

$$\sum_{k=1}^{3} S_{jk} = 1, j \in \{1, 2, 3\} \tag{2}$$

Under these constraints, there are 27 combinations of MC switches that meet the requirements, given in Table 1. The three output phases in Group 1 are connected to three different inputs, consisting of six switch combinations, the three outputs in Group 2 are connected to two different inputs, containing 18 switch combinations, and the three outputs in Group 3 are short with only one input, consisting of three switch combinations.

2.2 Modulation Principle of Matrix Converter

The three-phase input power supply phase voltage of the MC is:

$$U_{iPh} = \begin{bmatrix} e_a \\ e_b \\ e_c \end{bmatrix} = U_{im} \begin{bmatrix} cos(\omega_i t) \\ cos(\omega_i t - 120^\circ) \\ cos(\omega_i t + 120^\circ) \end{bmatrix} \tag{3}$$

U_{im} is the magnitude of the input phase voltage and ω_i is the input voltage angle frequency.

The base wave sine value of the three-phase output line voltage of the desired MC is:

$$U_{oL} = \begin{bmatrix} u_{AB} \\ u_{BC} \\ u_{CA} \end{bmatrix} = \sqrt{3} U_{om} \begin{bmatrix} cos(\omega_o t - \phi_o + 30^\circ) \\ cos(\omega_o t - \phi_o + 30^\circ - 120^\circ) \\ cos(\omega_o t - \phi_o + 30^\circ + 120^\circ) \end{bmatrix} \tag{4}$$

U_{om} is the magnitude of the output phase voltage, ω_o is the output voltage angle frequency, and ϕ_o is the phase shift angle of the output voltage relative to the input voltage.

Table 1. The switching combinations of MC

Grouping	Switch connection status	Output line voltage			Enter the phase current		
	$S_{11}S_{12}S_{13}S_{21}S_{22}S_{23}S_{31}S_{32}S_{33}$	u_{AB}	u_{BC}	u_{CA}	i_a	i_b	i_c
1	1 0 0 0 1 0 0 0 1	e_{ab}	e_{bc}	e_{ca}	i_A	i_B	i_C
	1 0 0 0 0 1 0 1 0	$-e_{ca}$	$-e_{bc}$	$-e_{ab}$	i_A	i_C	i_B
	0 1 0 1 0 0 0 0 1	$-e_{ab}$	$-e_{ca}$	$-e_{bc}$	i_B	i_A	i_C
	0 1 0 0 0 1 1 0 0	e_{bc}	e_{ca}	e_{ab}	i_C	i_A	i_B
	0 0 1 1 0 0 0 1 0	e_{ca}	e_{ab}	e_{bc}	i_B	i_C	i_A
	0 0 1 0 1 0 1 0 0	e_{cb}	e_{ba}	e_{ac}	i_C	i_B	i_A
2–1	1 0 0 0 0 1 0 0 1	$-e_{ca}$	0	e_{ca}	i_A	0	$-i_A$
	0 1 0 0 0 1 0 0 1	e_{bc}	0	$-e_{bc}$	0	i_A	$-i_A$
	0 1 0 1 0 0 1 0 0	$-e_{ab}$	0	e_{ab}	$-i_A$	i_A	0
	0 0 1 1 0 0 1 0 0	e_{ca}	0	$-e_{ca}$	$-i_A$	0	i_A
	0 0 1 0 1 0 0 1 0	$-e_{bc}$	0	e_{bc}	0	$-i_A$	i_A
	1 0 0 0 1 0 0 1 0	e_{ab}	0	$-e_{ab}$	i_A	$-i_A$	0
2–2	0 0 1 1 0 0 0 0 1	e_{ca}	$-e_{ca}$	0	i_B	0	$-i_B$
	0 0 1 0 1 0 0 0 1	$-e_{bc}$	e_{bc}	0	0	i_B	$-i_B$
	1 0 0 0 1 0 1 0 0	e_{ab}	$-e_{ab}$	0	$-i_B$	i_B	0
	1 0 0 0 0 1 1 0 0	$-e_{ca}$	e_{ca}	0	$-i_B$	0	i_B
	0 1 0 0 0 1 0 1 0	e_{bc}	$-e_{bc}$	0	0	$-i_B$	i_B
	0 1 0 1 0 0 0 1 0	$-e_{ab}$	e_{ab}	0	i_B	$-i_B$	0
2–3	0 0 1 0 0 1 1 0 0	0	e_{ca}	$-e_{ca}$	i_C	0	$-i_C$
	0 0 1 0 0 1 0 1 0	0	$-e_{bc}$	e_{bc}	0	i_C	$-i_C$
	1 0 0 1 0 0 0 1 0	0	e_{ab}	$-e_{ab}$	$-i_C$	i_C	0
	1 0 0 1 0 0 0 0 1	0	$-e_{ca}$	e_{ca}	$-i_C$	0	i_C
	0 1 0 0 1 0 0 0 1	0	e_{bc}	$-e_{bc}$	0	$-i_C$	i_C
	0 1 0 0 1 0 1 0 0	0	$-e_{ab}$	e_{ab}	i_C	$-i_C$	0
3	1 0 0 1 0 0 1 0 0	0	0	0	0	0	0
	0 1 0 0 1 0 0 1 0	0	0	0	0	0	0
	0 0 1 0 0 1 0 0 1	0	0	0	0	0	0

As shown in Table 1 and Fig. 1, the relationship between three-phase output line voltage U_{oL} of the MC and the three-phase input phase voltage U_{iPh} is:

$$U_{oL} = \begin{bmatrix} u_{AB} \\ u_{BC} \\ u_{CA} \end{bmatrix} = \begin{bmatrix} S_{11} - S_{21} & S_{12} - S_{22} & S_{13} - S_{23} \\ S_{21} - S_{31} & S_{22} - S_{32} & S_{23} - S_{33} \\ S_{31} - S_{11} & S_{32} - S_{12} & S_{33} - S_{13} \end{bmatrix} \begin{bmatrix} e_a \\ e_b \\ e_c \end{bmatrix} \tag{5}$$

The relationship between the input phase current and the output phase current is:

$$i_{iPh} = \begin{bmatrix} i_a \\ i_b \\ i_c \end{bmatrix} = \begin{bmatrix} S_{11} & S_{21} & S_{31} \\ S_{12} & S_{22} & S_{32} \\ S_{13} & S_{23} & S_{33} \end{bmatrix} \begin{bmatrix} i_A \\ i_B \\ i_C \end{bmatrix} \tag{6}$$

According to the high-frequency synthesis theory, when the switching frequency f_s is high enough, the high-frequency components of variables in formulas (5) and (6) can be ignored, and the remaining low-frequency components are represented as the average of the variables in a switching cycle T_s. The average of a switching cycle of a switch function is the duty cycle of the switch S_{jk}, which can be reworded as d_{jk}:

$$U_{oL} = \begin{bmatrix} u_{AB} \\ u_{BC} \\ u_{CA} \end{bmatrix} = \begin{bmatrix} d_{11} - d_{21} & d_{12} - d_{22} & d_{13} - d_{23} \\ d_{21} - d_{31} & d_{22} - d_{32} & d_{23} - d_{33} \\ d_{31} - d_{11} & d_{32} - d_{12} & d_{33} - d_{13} \end{bmatrix} \begin{bmatrix} e_a \\ e_b \\ e_c \end{bmatrix} = T_{PhL} U_{iPh} \tag{7}$$

$$i_{iPh} = \begin{bmatrix} i_a \\ i_b \\ i_c \end{bmatrix} = \begin{bmatrix} d_{11} & d_{21} & d_{31} \\ d_{12} & d_{22} & d_{32} \\ d_{13} & d_{23} & d_{33} \end{bmatrix} \begin{bmatrix} i_A \\ i_B \\ i_C \end{bmatrix} = T_{PhPh}^T i_{oPh} \tag{8}$$

In the formula, the upper angle label T represents transpose, T_{PhL} is the switch transfer function matrix from the MC input side phase variable to the output sideline variable, and T_{PhPh} is the switch transfer function matrix from the MC input side phase variable to the output side phase variable. $T_{PhL} T_{PhPh}$ is also known as the duty-ratio matrix, each element represents the instantaneous duty-to-duty ratio of the corresponding switches in the main circuit of the MC, reflecting the control method of the MC. According to the duty-ratio matrix T_{PhL}, T_{PhPh}, the determination method is different, then the MC can get a variety of different modulation strategies.

Depending on the formula (3), (4), and (7), the duty-to-duty matrix T_{PhL} of the MC can be selected as:

$$\overline{T}_{PhL} = m \begin{bmatrix} cos(\omega_o t - \phi_o + 30^\circ) \\ cos(\omega_o t - \phi_o + 30^\circ - 120^\circ) \\ cos(\omega_o t - \phi_o + 30^\circ + 120^\circ) \end{bmatrix} \begin{bmatrix} cos(\omega_i t - \phi_i) \\ cos(\omega_i t - \phi_i - 120^\circ) \\ cos(\omega_i t - \phi_i + 120^\circ) \end{bmatrix}^T \tag{9}$$

m is the modulation coefficient of the MC, $0 \le m \le 1$; and ϕ_i is the phase difference between the input phase voltage and the phase current. (3), (4), (9) need to satisfy (7), and the relationship between the input phase voltage amplitude and the output phase voltage amplitude is:

$$U_{om} = \frac{\sqrt{3}}{2} U_{im} \, m \, cos(\phi_i) \tag{10}$$

It can be seen from Eq. (10) that when the modulation coefficient $m = 1$, the input power factor $cos(\phi_i) = 1$, i.e. input phase difference $\phi_i = 0$, the voltage transfer rate of MC will reach the maximum value $\sqrt{3}/2$, which is 0.866.

Because the load in a MC system is typically an inductive device, the output phase current waveform is also a sine and can be represented as:

$$i_{oPh} = \begin{bmatrix} i_A \\ i_B \\ i_C \end{bmatrix} = I_{om} \begin{bmatrix} cos(\omega_o t - \phi_o - \phi_L) \\ cos(\omega_o t - \phi_o - \phi_L - 120°) \\ cos(\omega_o t - \phi_o - \phi_L + 120°) \end{bmatrix} \tag{11}$$

I_{om} is the amplitude of the output phase current and ϕ_L is the phase difference between the output phase voltage and the phase current, i.e. the load phase difference.

Similar to the output voltage, the base wave value of the three-phase input phase current of the MC you want is:

$$i_{iPh} = \begin{bmatrix} i_a \\ i_b \\ i_c \end{bmatrix} = I_{im} \begin{bmatrix} cos(\omega_i t - \phi_i) \\ cos(\omega_i t - \phi_i - 120°) \\ cos(\omega_i t - \phi_i + 120°) \end{bmatrix} \tag{12}$$

In the formula, I_{im} is the input phase current amplitude, and the formula (11), (12) needs to satisfy (8), thus obtaining:

$$I_{im} = \frac{\sqrt{3}}{2} I_{om} \, m \cos(\phi_L) \tag{13}$$

The duty-to duty matrix T_{PhL} shown in the formula (9) can be represented as the product of two matrices:

$$\overline{T}_{PhL} = \overline{T}_{VSI}(\omega_o) \overline{T}_{VSR}^T(\omega_i) \tag{14}$$

$\overline{T}_{VSR}(\omega_i)$ is virtual rectifier matrix on the input side and $\overline{T}_{VSI}(\omega_o)$ is virtual rectifier matrix on the output side. Take $\overline{T}_{VSR}^T(\omega_i)$ by multiplying with the input phase voltage formula (3), a constant voltage is obtained as follows:

$$\overline{T}_{VSR}^T(\omega_1) U_{iPh} = \frac{3}{2} U_{im} \cos(\varphi_i) = constant \tag{15}$$

(15) can be used to represent how a voltage source rectifier works, multiplying the constant voltage obtained in formula (15) by the matrix $\overline{T}_{VSI}(\omega_o)$, and representing the operation of a voltage source inverter. Thus, a MC can theoretically be equivalent to a series connection between a virtual rectifier and a virtual inverter, as shown in Fig. 2, which records the intermediate virtual DC voltage as U_{pn}.

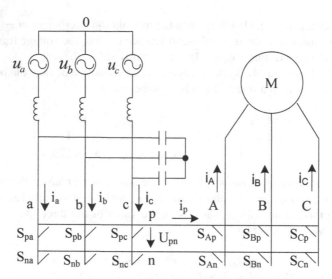

Fig. 2. Equivalent topology of MC VSR and VSI in series

3 Traditional Matrix Transformer Space Vector Modulation Strategy of Matrix Converter

According to the analysis of Sect. 2.2, the MC can be equivalent to a virtual voltage source rectifier (VSR) and a virtual voltage source inverter (VSI) series connection as shown in Fig. 2, which is the basis of the MC indirect spatial vector modulation strategy. According to this equivalent circuit model, the traditional SVM technology is applied to the virtual rectifier and virtual inverter respectively, the virtual rectifier is fed phase current SVM, the virtual inverter is output line voltage SVM, and then the intermediate DC link is eliminated, and finally, the SVM strategy of the MC is integrated.

3.1 Input Phase Phase Current Space Vector Vector Modulation of VSR

The circuit of the virtual rectifier of the MC is shown in Fig. 3. In the figure, only one of the three switches connected with positive and negative buses is closed, and six switches have nine combined states, corresponding to nine current basic space vectors I_0–I_8. Among them, I_1–I_6 is the effective basic vector, and the corresponding switch states are (a, c), (b, c), (b, a), (c, a), (c, b) and (a, b), respectively. The phase difference between adjacent effective vectors is 60; I_0, I_7, I_8 is the zero vector, and the corresponding switch states are (a, a), (b, b) and (c, c) respectively. By I_1–I_6 get a regular hexagon of switch vector, and the zero vector is located in the center of the regular hexagon. The spatial position and relationship of each vector are shown in Fig. 4.

In the spatial vector modulation of virtual rectifiers, a new current space vector can be generated by a linear combination of 9 basic current vectors. The spatial vector that defines the reference input phase current is:

$$I_{\text{ref}} = \frac{2}{3}\left(i_a + i_b \cdot e^{j120°} + i_c \cdot e^{-j120°}\right) = I_{\text{im}} \cdot e^{j(\omega_i t - \phi_i)} \tag{16}$$

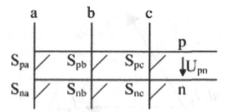

Fig. 3. VSR conversion part of MC

The spatial vector modulation of the input phase current can be performed in each sector of the space vector positive hexagon, and the input phase current reference space vector I_{ref} can be synthesized by two valid current vectors I_μ and I_γ zero vectors I_0 in the sector at a certain time, as shown in Fig. 5, the expression of the input phase current reference space vector is:

$$I_{ref} = d_\mu I_\mu + d_\gamma I_\gamma + d_{0c} I_0 \tag{17}$$

where

$$\begin{cases} d_\mu = T_\mu/T_s = m_c sin(60° - \theta_{sc}) \\ d_\gamma = T_\gamma/T_s = m_c sin(\theta_{sc}) \\ d_{0c} = T_{0c}/T_s = 1 - d_\mu - d_\gamma \end{cases} \tag{18}$$

In Eq. (2–18), m_c is the SVM coefficient of input phase current, $0 \le m_c \le 1$; T_s is the switching period; T_μ, T_γ And T_{0c} is the current vector I_μ, I_γ And I_0, d_μ, d_γ And d_{0c} is the corresponding duty cycle; θ_{sc} is the phase angle of the reference current vector in its sector.

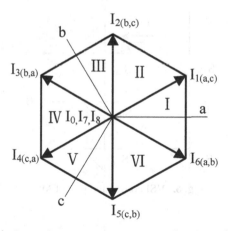

Fig. 4. Input phase current space vector hexagon of VSR

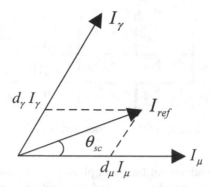

Fig. 5. Input phase current space vector synthesis of VSR

3.2 Virtual Inverter Output Line Voltage Space Vector Vector of VSI

The circuit diagram of the virtual inverter of the MC is shown in Fig. 6. In the figure, only one of every two switches connected from the positive and negative buses to the three-phase outputs of A, B and C is closed. Six switches have eight combined states, corresponding to eight voltage basic space vectors $U_0–U_7$. Where, $U_1–U_6$ is the effective basic vector, and the corresponding switch states are (p, n, n), (p, p, p, n), (n, p, n), (n, p, n), (n, p, p, p), (n, n, p), and (p, n, p) respectively. The phase difference between adjacent effective vectors is 60°; U_0 and U_7 is the zero vector, and the corresponding switch states are (n, n, n) and (p, p, p) respectively. By $U_1–U_6$ get a regular hexagon of switch vector, and the zero vector is located in the center of the regular hexagon. The spatial position and relationship of each vector are shown in Fig. 7.

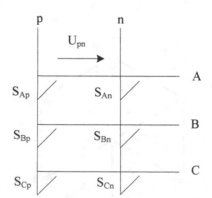

Fig. 6. VSI conversion part of MC

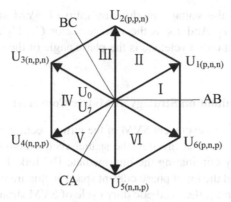

Fig. 7. Output line voltage space vector hexagon of VSI

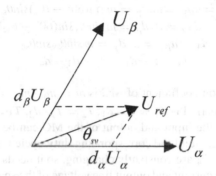

Fig. 8. Output line voltage space vector synthesis of VSI

In the spatial vector modulation of virtual inverters, a new voltage space vector can be produced by a linear combination of 8 basic voltage space vectors. The desired output line voltage space vector is defined as:

$$U_{ref} = \frac{2}{3}\left(u_{AB} + u_{BC} \cdot e^{j120^\circ} + u_{CA} \cdot e^{-j120^\circ}\right) = \sqrt{3}U_{om}e^{j(\omega_o t - \phi_o + \frac{\pi}{6})} \quad (19)$$

The spatial vector modulation of the output line voltage can be performed in each sector of the space vector positive hexagon, and at some point the output line voltage reference space vector U_{ref} can be synthesized by two effective voltage vectors, $U_\alpha U_\beta$ and zero vectors U_0 in the sector, as shown in Fig. 8. The expression of the composited output line voltage reference space vector is:

$$U_{ref} = d_\alpha U_\alpha + d_\beta U_\beta + d_{0v} U_0 \quad (20)$$

Where

$$\begin{cases} d_\alpha = T_\alpha/T_s = m_v sin(60^0 - \theta_{sv}) \\ d_\beta = T_\beta/T_s = m_v sin(\theta_{sv}) \\ d_{0v} = T_{0v}/T_s = 1 - d_\alpha - d_\beta \end{cases} \quad (21)$$

In Eq. (21), m_v is the voltage modulation ratio of SVM strategy, $0 \leq m_v = \sqrt{3}U_{om}/U_{pn} \leq 1$; T_α, T_β And T_{0v} is the voltage vector U_α, U_β And U_0, d_α, d_β And d_{0v} is the corresponding duty cycle; θ_{sv} is the phase angle of the reference line voltage vector in its sector.

3.3 Space Vector Modulation Strategy of Matrix Converter

By combining the input phase current SVM of the virtual rectifier and the voltage SVM of the output line of the virtual inverter, the spatial vector modulation strategy of the MC can be obtained by eliminating the intermediate DC link. If both the output line voltage space vector and the input phase current space vector are in sector I, then in one switching period Within T_s, the synthetic duty cycle of SVM strategy is:

$$
\begin{aligned}
d_1 &= d_{\alpha\mu} = d_\alpha d_\mu = m\,sin(60° - \theta_{sv})sin(60° - \theta_{sc}) \\
d_2 &= d_{\alpha\gamma} = d_\alpha d_\gamma = m\,sin(60° - \theta_{sv})sin\theta_{sc} \\
d_3 &= d_{\beta\mu} = d_\beta d_\mu = m\,sin\theta_{sv}sin(60° - \theta_{sc}) \\
d_4 &= d_{\beta\gamma} = d_\beta d_\gamma = m\,sin\theta_{sv}sin\theta_{sc} \\
d_0 &= 1 - d_1 - d_2 - d_3 - d_4
\end{aligned}
\tag{22}
$$

Where, the modulation coefficient of MC is $m = m_v \cdot m_c = \frac{2}{\sqrt{3}} \cdot \frac{U_{om}}{U_{im}} \cdot \frac{1}{cos\phi_i}$. The duty cycle time of each period is $T_1 = T_s \cdot d_1$, $T_2 = T_s \cdot d_2$, $T_3 = T_s \cdot d_3$, $T_4 = T_s \cdot d_4$ and $T_0 = T_s \cdot d_0$. Since the input and output of the MC can be set to AC of different frequencies, the duty cycle, and the corresponding duty cycle time t are calculated for each switching cycle T_0–T_4 are constantly changing, so it needs real-time calculation.

Since the input phase current and output line voltage of the spatial vector modulation strategy each have six effective spatial vectors, there may be 36 combined states, each corresponding to one of the 27 switch combinations, as shown in Table 2. The three letters in the table represent the connection state of the output phase to the input phase, such as acc indicating that output A is connected to input a, output B is connected to input c, and output C is connected to input c.

Table 2. 36 Kinds of switching combinations.

Current vector → Voltage vector ↓	I_1	I_2	I_3	I_4	I_5	I_6
U_1	acc	bcc	baa	caa	cbb	abb
U_2	aac	bbc	bba	cca	ccb	aab
U_3	cac	cbc	aba	aca	bcb	bab
U_4	caa	cbb	abb	acc	bcc	baa
U_5	cca	ccb	aab	aac	bbc	bba
U_6	aca	bcb	bab	cac	cbc	aba

The vector combination in different sectors is different, so it is necessary to judge the combination of the sectors in real-time. Taking virtual rectifier and virtual inverter working in sector I as an example, the space vector used to synthesize input phase current is I_6, I_1 and I_0, the space vector used to synthesize the output line voltage is U_6, U_1 and U_0, so the synthesis process of input phase current vector and output line voltage vector has $I_6 - U_6$, $I_6 - U_1$, $I_1 - U_6$, $I_1 - U_1$ and $I_0 - U_0$. The duty cycle of each combination is the product of the duty cycle of each vector in the combination.

4 Study on the Mode of Output Pulse on Space on Vector Modulation Strategy

In each spatial vector switch cycle T_s, the duty cycle of the five vector combinations involved in the synthesis is calculated, and the control switch switching in some vector sequence can be used to achieve control of the MC. The sequence of vector action within each switching cycle and the position of the zero vector in the vector sequence affect the switching loss and input and output waveform quality of the MC. Depending on the location of the zero vector in the vector sequence, it can be divided into three different pulse output modes. The first vector sequence, within each switching cycle, starts with zero vector and ends with zero vector, called pulse output mode I; This section analyzes and compares the input and output waveforms and the spectrum obtained by the simulation to select the ideal pulse output mode.

4.1 Mode I of Output Pulse

In each switching cycle, the selection of vector action sequence follows two principles: one is the principle of minimum switching loss, that is, only one switching device is switched to minimize the switching loss each time the switching state is switched; The second is the symmetry principle, that is, in each switching cycle, the vector sequence is symmetrically distributed and the vector action time is evenly distributed, so that the harmonic content of input and output waveforms is less.

Assuming that the reference input phase current space vector and the reference output line voltage space vector are in the first sector, the effective vector combination is: $I_6 U_1$, $I_6 U_6$, $I_1 U_6$ and $I_1 U_1$. The corresponding switch combination is: abb, aba, aca, acc. According to the principle of minimum switching loss and symmetry, the switch combination sequence is: abb–aba–aca–acc–aca–aba–abb. According to the pulse output mode I, if the zero vector is inserted at the beginning and end of the switch combination sequence, the switch combination sequence is bbb–abb–aba–aca–acc–aca–aba–abb–bbb, and the corresponding vector action sequence is $I_0 U_0$–$I_6 U_1$–$I_6 U_6$–$I_1 U_6$–$I_1 U_1$–$I_1 U_6$–$I_6 U_6$–$I_6 U_1$–$I_0 U_0$. The vector action sequences of other sectors can be obtained by the same method.

Let I be the effective vector of the sector where the reference vector of the input phase current of the MC is located I_μ And I_γ, The effective vector of the sector where the output line voltage reference vector is located is U_α And U_β. Then the five vector combinations of SVM are: $I_\mu U_\alpha$ (abbreviation $\mu\alpha$), $I_\mu U_\beta$ (abbreviation $\mu\beta$), $I_\gamma U_\alpha$ (abbreviation $\gamma\alpha$),

$I_\gamma U_\beta$ (abbreviation γβ) And $I_0 U_0$ for short. Considering the optimization strategy of reducing switching loss, the general vector sequence in a switching cycle is obtained as follows:

When the sum of current sector number and voltage sector number is even, 0–μβ–μα–γα–γβ–γα–μα–μβ–0; When the sum of current sector number and voltage sector number is odd, 0–μα–μβ–γβ–γα–γβ–μβ–μα–0.

When the SVM of MC is in the combination of I-I sectors, the pulse waveform of three output phases in a switching cycle is shown in Fig. 9. In the figure, level 1 indicates that the output phase is connected with input a, level 2 indicates that the output phase is connected with input b, level 3 indicates that the output phase is connected with input c, and the time constant $T_1 = T_0$, $T_2 = T_{\mu\beta}$, $T_3 = T_{\mu\alpha}$, $T_4 = T_{\gamma\alpha} = T\_{\gamma\beta}$ and $T_5 = T_{\gamma\beta}$.

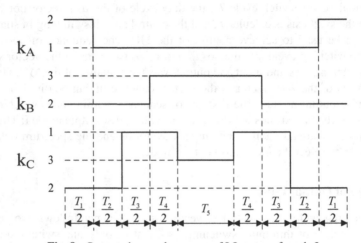

Fig. 9. Output phase pulse waves of I-I sector of mode I

4.2 Mode II of Output Pulse

According to the pulse output mode II, the zero vector is inserted in the middle of the switch combination sequence. When the reference input phase current vector and the reference output line voltage vector are in the first sector, the switch combination sequence in a switching cycle is: abb–aba–aca–acc–ccc–acc–aca–aba–abb, and the corresponding vector sequence is: I_6U_1–I_6U_6–I_1U_6–I_1U_1–I_0U_0–I_1U_1–I_1U_6–I_6U_6–I_6U_1. By synthesizing the vector sequence of each sector combination, the general vector sequence in a switching cycle can be obtained.

When the sum of current sector number and voltage sector number is even, μβ–μα–γα–γβ–0–γβ–γα–μα–μβ; When the sum of current sector number and voltage sector number is odd, μα–μβ–γβ–γα–0–γα–γβ–μβ–μα.

When the SVM of MC is in the combination of I-I sectors, the pulse waveform of three output phases in a switching cycle is shown in Fig. 10, and the time constant $T_1 = T_{\mu\beta}$, $T_2 = T_{\mu\alpha}$, $T_3 = T_{\gamma\alpha}$, $T_4 = T_{\gamma\beta}$ And $T_5 = T_0$.

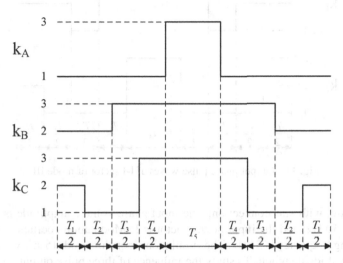

Fig. 10. Output phase pulse waves of I-I sector of mode II

4.3 Mode III of Output Pulse

According to the pulse output mode III, a zero vector is inserted in the middle of the first half and the second half of the switch combination sequence. When the current vector of the reference input phase and the voltage vector of the reference output line is in sector I, the switch combination sequence in a switching period is: abb–aba–aaa–aca–acc–aca–aaa–aba–abb, and the corresponding vector sequence is: I_6U_1–I_6U_6–I_0U_0–I_1U_6–I_1U_1–I_1U_6–I_0U_0–I_6U_6–I_6U_1. By synthesizing the vector sequence of each sector combination, the general vector sequence in a switching cycle can be obtained.

When the sum of current sector number and voltage sector number is even, $\mu\beta$–$\mu\alpha$–0–$\gamma\alpha$–$\gamma\beta$–$\gamma\alpha$–0–$\mu\alpha$–$\mu\beta$; When the sum of current sector number and voltage sector number is odd, $\mu\alpha$–$\mu\beta$–0–$\gamma\beta$–$\gamma\alpha$–$\gamma\beta$–0–$\mu\beta$–$\mu\alpha$.

When the SVM of MC is in the combination of sector I-I, the pulse waveform of three output phases in a switching period is shown in Fig. 2–11, and the time constant $T_1 = T_{\mu\beta}$, $T_2 = T_{\mu\alpha}$, $T_3 = T_0$, $T_4 = T_{\gamma\alpha}$ And $T_5 = T_{\gamma\beta}$.

4.4 Simulation Analysis

The input and output performances of the MC in three pulse output modes are simulated by Matlab/Simulink. The simulation parameters are input filter $L_f = 5\,\text{mH}$, $C_f = 10\,\mu\text{F}$, $R_f = 15\,\Omega$; Three phase symmetrical resistive load, $R = 11\,\Omega$, $L = 5\,\text{mH}$

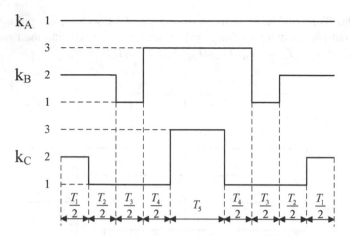

Fig. 11. Output phase pulse waves of I-I sector of mode III

for each phase, with star connection; The input phase voltage amplitude is 100 V, the frequency is 50 Hz, and the input power factor is 1; Modulation coefficient $m = 0.75$; The switching frequency is 5 kHz; The simulation algorithm is ode15 s; Two-way switch is composed of ideal switch. To study the influence of three pulse output modes on the input and output performance of MC at high frequency and low frequency of output voltage, the simulation is carried out when the expected output voltage frequency is 30 Hz and 80 Hz respectively. The simulation model is shown in Fig. 12.

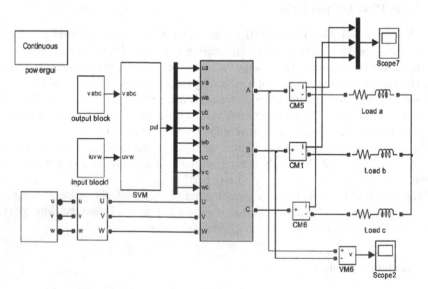

Fig. 12. The Matlab/Simulink simulation model of MC

Due to the limited space, only the simulation waveform with an output frequency of 30 Hz is given. Figure 13 shows the expected output frequency of 30 Hz. The current waveform of three-phase output phase and the spectrum of phase an output current of MC is respectively adopted in three pulse output modes; Fig. 14 shows the input current waveform and spectrum of MC under three pulse output modes with an expected output frequency of 30 Hz; Fig. 15 shows the output line voltage u_{AB} waveform and spectrum of MC under three pulse output modes with an expected output frequency of 30 Hz.

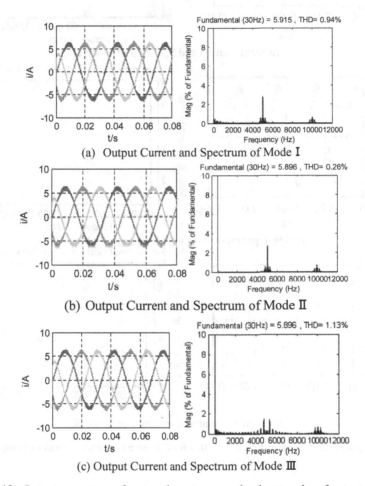

(a) Output Current and Spectrum of Mode I

(b) Output Current and Spectrum of Mode II

(c) Output Current and Spectrum of Mode III

Fig. 13. Output current waveforms and spectrums under three modes of output pulse

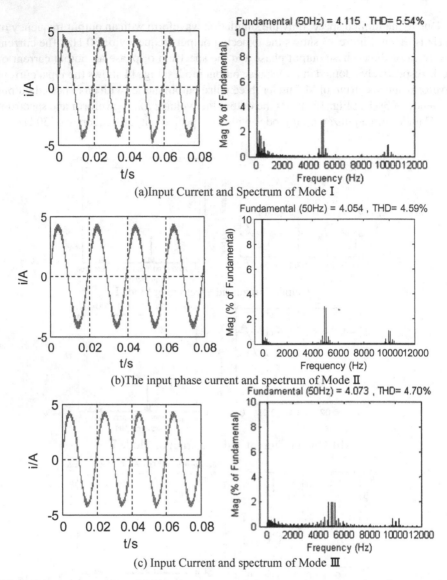

(a)Input Current and Spectrum of Mode I

(b)The input phase current and spectrum of Mode II

(c) Input Current and spectrum of Mode III

Fig. 14. Input current waveforms and spectrums of phase a under three modes of output pulse

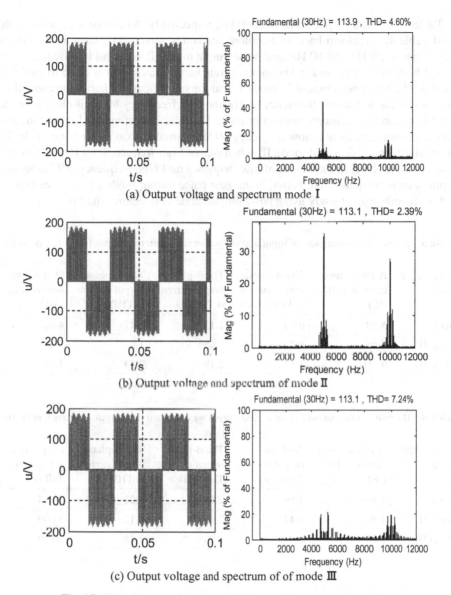

(a) Output voltage and spectrum mode I

(b) Output voltage and spectrum of mode II

(c) Output voltage and spectrum of of mode III

Fig. 15. Waveforms and spectrum in three pulse output u_{AB} modes

Table 3 and Table 4 list 30 Hz and 80 Hz, respectively. As can be seen from Table 3 and Table 4, waveform harmonic content and better waveform quality in the output frequencies of 30 Hz and 80 Hz, and pulse output mode III is output low-frequency 30 Hz and high-frequency 80 Hz The input current harmonic content is close to mode II, less than the harmonic content in mode I, and the output current harmonic content of pulse output mode I at low frequency 30 Hz and high frequency 80 Hz is close to mode II and less than the harmonic content of mode III. Pulse output mode II the output line voltage harmonic content at low frequency 30 Hz is smaller than mode I and mode III, but greater than mode I and mode III when output high frequency 80 Hz. In general, pulse output mode II in the output of low frequency and high frequency, MC input and output waveform quality are better, is the best pulse output mode of the three typical modes, the subsequent study using pulse output mode II to control the MC.

Table 3. Harmonic comparison of input and output waves when the output frequency is 30 Hz

Pulse output mode	A Phase input current THD (%)	The A-phase output current is THD (%)	The B-phase output current is THD (%)	The C-phase output current is THD (%)	Output line voltage u_{AB} THD (%)
Mode I	5.54	0.94	2.13	2.47	4.60
Mode II	4.59	0.26	1.65.	1.83	2.39
Mode III	4.70	1.13	2.19	2.53	7.24

Table 4. Harmonic comparison of input and output waves when the output frequency is 80 Hz

Pulse output mode	A Phase input current THD (%)	A-phase output current THD (%)	The B-phase output current THD (%)	The C-phase output current is THD (%)	Output line voltage u_{AB} THD (%)
Mode I	5.10	1.56	2.56	3.22	30.54
Mode II	4.56	1.47	2.46	3.12	34.09
Mode III	4.73	1.93	2.86	3.48	30.30

5 Experimental Results

With dSPACE hardware real-time simulation platform as the main control unit, the experimental device of MC is designed. Experimental parameters: input filter $L_f = 5$ mH, $C_f = 6\,\mu$F, $R_f = 15\,\Omega$; Three phase symmetrical resistive load, $R = 12\,\Omega$, $L = 5$ mH for each phase, with star connection; The effective value of input line voltage is 120 V, the frequency is 50 Hz, and the input power factor is 1; The modulation coefficient $m = 0.75$, and the expected output line voltage frequency is 30 Hz; The sampling frequency is 5 kHz. Figure 2, 3, 4, 5, 6, 7, 8, 9, 10, 11, 12, 13, 14, 15 and 16 shows the experimental waveform of SVPWM strategy using pulse output mode II, in which Fig. 16 (a) is the three-phase output current waveform of MC, Fig. 16(b) is the output PWM line voltage waveform, and Fig. 16 (c) is the A-phase input current waveform. It can be seen that the quality of input and output waveforms of MC is better with pulse output mode II.

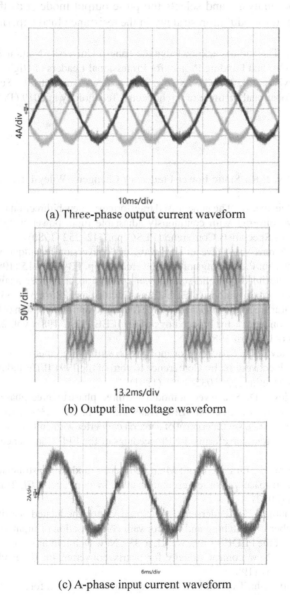

(a) Three-phase output current waveform

(b) Output line voltage waveform

(c) A-phase input current waveform

Fig. 16. Experimental waveforms of mode II of output pulse based on SVM strategy

6 Conclusion

This paper analyzes the principle of the spatial vector modulation strategy of the MC, studies the influence of three different pulse output modes on the input and output performance of the MC, obtains the pulse output mode II as the ideal pulse output mode through simulation analysis, and selects the pulse output mode II as the pulse output mode of spatial vector modulation strategy in the resistance load experiment.

Acknowledgement. The authors acknowledge the Jiangsu University Natural Science Research Project (18KJB470024) and Funding Project for Professional Leaders of Higher Vocational Colleges in Jiangsu Province (2020GRGDYX070). This work was supported by Scientific Research Project of Jiangsu Vocational Institute of Architectural Technology in 2019 (JYA319-13).

References

1. Gyugyi, L., Pelly, B.R.: Static Power Frequency Changers. Wiley-Interscience, New York (1976)
2. Venturini, M., Alesina, A.: The generalised transformer: a new bidirectional sinusoidal waveform frequency converter with continously adjustable input power factor. In: 1980 IEEE Power Electronics Specialists Conference PESC, pp. 242–252 (1980)
3. Venturini, M.: A new sine wave in sine wave out conversion technique which eliminates reactive elements. In: Proceedings of the Powercon 7, pp. E3–1-E3–15 (1981)
4. Alesina, A., Venturini, M.: Solid-state power conversion: a Fourier analysis approach to generalized transformer synthesis. IEEE Trans. Circuit Syst. **28**(4), 319–330 (1981)
5. Alesina, A., Venturini, M.: Intrinsic amplitude limits and optimum design of 9-switches direct PWM AC–AC converters. In: Proceedings of the IEEE PESC 1988, vol. 2, pp. 1284–1291. Kyoto, Japan, 11–14 April 1988
6. Huber, L., Borojevic, D.: Space vector modulation with unity input power factor for forced commutated cycloconverters. In: Conference Record of the 1991 IEEE Industry Applications Society Annual Meeting, pp. 1032–1041 (1991)
7. Huber, L., Borojevic, D.: Space vector modulated three-phase to three-phase matrix converter with input power factor correction. IEEE Trans. Ind. Appl. **31**, 1234–1246 (1995)
8. Casadei, D., et al.: Space vector control of a matrix converter with unity input power factor and sinusoidal input/output waveforms. In: Proceedings of the EPE Conference, vol. 7, pp. 170–175 (1993)
9. Casadei, D., Serra, G., Tani, A., et al.: Matrix converter modulation strategies: a new general approach based on space-vector representation of the switch state. IEEE Trans. Ind. Electron. **49**(2), 370–381 (2002)
10. Nielsen, P., Blaabjerg, F., Pedersen, J.K.: Space vector modulated matrix converter with minimized number of switching and feedforward compensation of input voltage unbalance. In: Proceedings of the PEDES 1996, vol. II, p. 833. New Delhi, India-839, 8–11 January 1996
11. Oyama, J., et al.: New control strategy for matrix converter. In: IEEE PESC Conference Record, pp. 360–367 (1989)
12. Ishiguro, A., Furuhashi, T., Okuma, S.: A novel control method for forced commutated cycloconverters using instantaneous values of input line-to-line voltages. IEEE Trans. Ind. Electron. **38**(3), 166–172 (1991)
13. Watanabe, E., et al.: High performance motor drive using matrix converter. In: Advances in Induction Motor Control, IEEE Seminar, pp. 1–7 (2000)

Research on Weighing Method Innovation and Device Development for On-Board Sensors of Logistics Vehicle

En Fang[1,2(⊠)], Yuchao Zhou[1], and Delu Li[3]

[1] School of Electrical and Control Engineering,
Xuzhou University of Technology, Xuzhou 221018, Jiangsu, China
fangen@cumt.edu.cn

[2] Jiangsu Key Construction Laboratory of Large Engineering Equipment Testing and Control Technology, Xuzhou 221018, Jiangsu, China

[3] Jiangsu Vocational Institute of Architecture Technology, Xuzhou 221018, Jiangsu, China

Abstract. In this paper, both ends of the on-board weighing devices are not fixed simultaneously to prevent the force constraints from affecting the measurement accuracy of the sensor. According to the test results with analysis and the market feedback on small batch production and sales of prototype, a weighing method innovation and device development for on-board sensors of logistics vehicles are proposed The base end of the sensor is fixed with the axle, and the other end can work in two states with a safety device. The safety device can be lifted in the upper position to keep the sensors off the carriage without weighing for safe transportation. In the lower place, the carriage and the on-board sensors are in uniform contact to realize weighing without restriction. The influence of random interference factors is eliminated, and the bottleneck problem of on-board dynamic weighing technology is solved.

Keywords: Weighing with on-board sensor · Weighing method innovation · Research and development of weighing device

1 Research on Weigh-in-Motion at Home and Abroad

The foreign dynamic weighing system research was focused on in some developed countries in the 20th century. The United States has been studying the dynamic weighing technology of vehicles since the mid-19th century because of the earlier situation of over-limit transportation. In 1974, the earliest research on vehicle dynamic weighing was the earliest reference of vehicle dynamic weighing system (Gvvacs Company) at IMEK0/TC3 conference in Hungary, which laid a solid foundation for developing dynamic measurement technology. At present, due to the different use of the dynamic weighing system, the average error of the world's advanced dynamic weighing system for axle weight measurement can be controlled within 30%, and its confidence can reach 90%. The most advanced dynamic weighing system can handle the error of axle weight

D. Jiang and H. Song (Eds.): SIMUtools 2021, LNICST 424, pp. 473–487, 2022.
https://doi.org/10.1007/978-3-030-97124-3_35

measurement within 5%, and the confidence degree reaches 90%. Because of its high cost, it can only be used on some special occasions.

The first research on the dynamic weighing system in China was done by the research institute of highway science of Chongqing. They have developed a new dynamic vehicle weighing technology, which was applied in model SM2000 and SM3000 sensors. Later, Shanxi Institute of Measurement and Testing cooperated with Taiyuan institute of engineering to research axle-metering weighing devices for vehicles. Especially in recent years, the demand for dynamic weighing of vehicles has been dramatically increased in the domestic industry. Many manufacturers and companies have launched their dynamic weighing products, taking BDZ-AE portable dynamic axle weight tester produced by Defeng Precision Machinery Co., Ltd as a typical example. With the improvement of science and technology, China has developed various dynamic weighing systems for many years. It is mainly used in weight calculation and law enforcement inspection, which plays an essential role in highway traffic management.

The sensor weighing is divided into dynamic weighing and static weighing. The static weighing accuracy mainly depends on the sensor itself. The accuracy of dynamic weighing results is related to the precision of sensors and the installation and using methods, working conditions, and other factors of sensors. If the improper installation or operating approach is adopted, the impact of interference on the system is difficult to detect and estimated in advance. And it is challenging to realize error compensation through algorithms and improve measurement accuracy. The crucial problem of dynamic weighing technology is inaccurate results. The weighing error exceeds while the average error should generally be controlled within 30%. Dynamic weighing can be divided into direct dynamic weighing and indirect dynamic weighing. Vehicle weighing is divided into weighing with the vehicle and weighing on the platform (ground weighing).

2 Research and Development Background

There are some problems with the dynamic weighing devices of logistics vehicles using sensors. At present, when using sensors to weigh heavy objects in the market, the connecting threaded holes at both ends of the sensor structure are commonly provided. Thus, both ends are fixed with threads. One end is connected with the vehicle bridge through the mounting base of the sensor device, and the other end is associated with the carriage or the weighing objects. After joining, the weighing products, carriage, sensor, mounting base, and axle become whole through connection. Because two ends of the sensor are fixed with threads, the restrictions on both ends of the sensor device increase. The interference factors are random and unpredictable. Under the effect of gravity, which acts not only through the weighing center, the bending moment also deviates from the center, which directly affects the weighing accuracy. The crucial problem feedback from the market of dynamic weighing devices for logistics vehicles is inaccurate. The carriage weighing results measured by sensors at different positions are inconsistent. The difference between the weighing result and the actual weight is too significant. The reason is that in theory, only when the resultant force of the gravity of the object and the supporting power of the thread on both ends of the sensor connected by screw thread is vertically downward and passes through the weighing center, the bending moment generated by the resultant force vanishes to zero. Thus, the weighing results can be accurate, which is impossible to realize in practice.

Therefore, we get a new research idea which is described as follows. The two ends of the on-board dynamic weighing sensors should not be fixed with thread simultaneously.

In principle, it can be divided into two states. One is that the carriage and the weighing object works in the vehicle transportation state. In this state, the weighing products, carriage, sensor, mounting base, and axle are connected into a piece of equipment with high rigidity to ensure safe transportation. The other is to descend in the weighing state. In this state, the car stops, and the weighing devices of the logistics vehicle fall without restrictions of forces outside the vertical direction. The weight or carriage contacts with the upper end of the sensor by the spherical point in the center of the weighing communication. The weight is weighed in a free state of being affected by gravity and support. The lower end of the sensor device is fixed or welded with the axle through the sensor mounting base. That is to say, the pan or dish of a steelyard is specified. The weighing object and the carriage are not connected with the upper end of the sensor by a thread. And there is no restriction on the upper end of the sensor to realize weighing. There are two possibilities for these weighing devices with poor accuracy. One is that the weight's center of gravity exceeds the weighing area (rollover phenomenon may occur). And the other is that the sensor has problems.

To innovate and discover the use methods of the on-board sensors of logistics vehicles solves the bottleneck problem of on-board weighing problems in principle. Because the weighing time of the on-board weighing device is relatively short compared with the whole working time, the weighing sensors are disconnected in the transportation state, which effectively improves the service life of the sensor weighing device.

3 Weighing Method Innovation and Device Development for On-Board Sensors of Logistics Vehicle

Independent weighing method innovation and device design for on-board sensors of small and medium-sized logistics vehicles are studied in this paper. Also, the weighing sensor protection device and control method are discussed. The principle of the on-board weighing device is that the gravity of the weighing object acts on the sensor body and is transferred to the internal chip to produce micro elastic deformation. The gravity is always vertical downward, and the micro elastic deformation of the sensor chip is one-dimensional linear. According to the micro elastic deformation, the stress and strain are calculated. The signal is collected, processed, amplified, and calculated. The weight value is sent to the display instrument of the vehicle terminal and then to the system management server through mobile communication. According to the test report "Beijing Institute of Aerospace Metrology and Testing Technology (authorized by the state administration of science, technology and industry for national defense, authorized certificate No.: National Defense Military Industry-JLJG-1-003) - Certificate No.: TJ1C2019-04-07386, calibration certificate of force sensor FYXZ-07" for the force sensor of Xuzhou university of engineering, the calibration results meet the technical requirements of JJG 455-2000 (verification regulation of working dynamometer). In this report, if the test pressure value of the sensor is 500N, the measured value is 500.1. The indication error is –0.20%, and the repeatability is 0.01. If the test pressure value of the sensor is 7000N, the measured value is 7000.1. The indication error is –0.01%, and the repeatability is 0.01. The weighing accuracy of the sensor device is high enough to meet the weighing requirements on logistics vehicles.

The weighing test and analysis during prototype trial production are as follows.

(1) Start the weighing system and adjust the sensor output to zero when the car is empty.
(2) Stand with the same person in different positions (such as middle or four corners) of the carriage and observe and record the results displayed by the instrument.
(3) Stand with varying weights in different positions (such as middle and four corners) of the carriage, and observe and record the results displayed by the instrument (Table 1).

Table 1. Prototype test weighing results.

Tester	Position				
	Upper Left	Upper Right	Center	Lower Left	Lower Right
A	55.0	56.5	57.5	52.5	54.0
B	60.0	61.0	62.5	62.0	59.5
C	70.5	71.5	75.0	72.0	72.5

The test found that when the same weight load is applied to different parts of the car, the instrument output will display different weight values. The test results show that the sensor's installation mode, orientation, and load distribution have other effects on the measurement results. The following problems can also be found after the market research.

(1) The connection between the sensor and the car is rigid. During the installation of the sensor, the fixing bolt will add a specific interference force to the sensor in the non-gravity direction. In principle, four sensors should be in the same plane. Ideally, the flat surface should be perpendicular to the gravity direction. Limited by the installation conditions, it is difficult for the four sensors to be in the same plane after installation. Even if there is no load in the car, there will be a particular output signal of the sensor under the action of the mounting bolt, forming a "zero correction error". When the loads are in different positions in the car, the interference force of the fixed bolt on the sensor will also change, so an unstable "system error" is formed. Zero adjustments cannot solve the unstable system error.

(2) It is found that the supporting frame of the experimental car body is not entirely rigid. When the vehicle load is in different positions, the structure drives the load cell to shift. At the same time, the stress of the weighing system is changed, which makes the stress of the load cell extremely complex. The load is no longer the only factor affecting the output of the load cell. Therefore, the weighing is not accurate.

The analysis of on-board weighing test is consistent with the feedback information of market users, which is described as that the error of weighing value exceeds the limit. The scientific research found that both ends of the sensor of the on-board sensor weighing device can not be fixed with thread at the same time.

The load cell structure is designed, and the technology of sticking stress-strain sensor chip is used flexibly. The weighing accuracy of the on-board weighing device is improved by testing and calibrating data on the prototype many times. Design and enhance the connection stiffness of the sensor weighing device of logistics vehicles in the transportation state. The safety device can lock and protect the weighing device in the transportation state. The development of intelligent controller and supporting software includes the design and debugging of controller development board, information interaction among sensors, controllers, network terminals and human-computer interaction interface, terminal display and control software design, etc. The system solves the problems of logistics vehicle weighing, vehicle terminal displaying net weight and total weight, mobile communication video monitoring in material transportation. It is suitable for logistics transportation and storage, large wholesale market, both sides of commercial trade, and self-proof reading of Expressway weight charge.

4   Structural Innovation Technology I: Innovation of Weighing Device and Method for Medium and Small Logistics Vehicles

The on-board sensor weighing device and method innovation of small and medium-sized logistics vehicles are as follows. In the small and medium-sized logistics transportation vehicle without a hydraulic transmission system, the on-board sensor weighing device is designed. The carriage and weighing object are lowered to the weighing position when weighing. A thread fixedly connects the connecting end of the sensor and the mounting base. The other end of the sensor is in an unrestricted free state so that the weighing object can be weighed freely without any restriction. When weighing is not needed or the vehicle is in transportation, the carriage and the weighing thing rise to the vehicle transportation state. The carriage and the weighing object are connected with the vehicle bridge through the vehicle weighing device to form a highly rigid body to ensure vehicle transportation safety.

The working principle of the on-board weighing device for medium and small logistics vehicles is shown in Fig. 1 and Fig. 2.

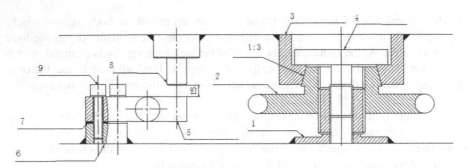

Fig. 1. Upper lifting position - vehicle transportation status.

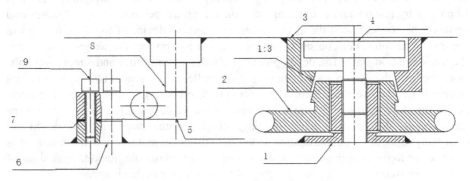

Fig. 2. Lower lifting position - weighing status.

1-bolt base, 2-lifting handwheel, 3-cars with a tapered hole, 4-up limit plate, 5-bar sensor, 6-sensor connection base, 7-assembly adjustment pad, 8-weighing contact, 9-hexagon bolt.

(1) The weighing device for medium and small logistics vehicles is composed of: the axle is connected with bolt base 1, the upper end of lifting handwheel 2 is provided with a tapered shaft, and the taper of 1:3 is used to match with the connecting plate of cars with a tapered hole 3. up limit plate 4, bar sensor 5, sensor connection base 6, assembly adjustment pad 7, weighing contact 8, hexagon bolt 9.

(2) Principle: when the carriage and the weighing object are in the lower position, they can be weighed without any restrictions to realize free weighing; There is no gap between the tapered shaft and the taper hole, and the automatic alignment can be realized; The lifting thread is self-locking under the action of the vertical downward force of the weight, and the thread lifting thrust is significant when the lifting handwheel is rotated; When the vehicle is in the transportation state, the tapered shaft and hole are matched without clearance, and the bolt is fastened with double safety.

(3) Working process:
The working process in the upper lifting position is shown in Fig. 1. When vehicles are in transportation status, the lifting handwheel is rotated clockwise to loosen the

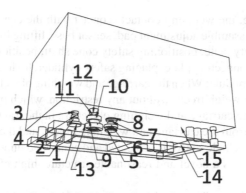

Fig. 3. Layout of 4 groups of on-board weighing devices for medium and small logistics vehicles between axle and carriage.

clamping from top to bottom. The lifting hand wheel continues to be turned, and the carriage will descend with the weighing object. When descending 15 mm is obtained, the weighing contact (the spherical point in the center of the weighing contact) will encounter the strip sensor. When the lifting handwheel continues to be rotated and another descending 15 mm is reached, there is a 10 mm gap between the tapered shaft and the tapered hole in the diameter direction. The lower lifting position is achieved in the weighing state, as shown in Fig. 2.

The working process in the lower lifting position is shown in Fig. 2. When the vehicles are in weighing status, the lifting handwheel is rotated counterclockwise from top to bottom to rise 15mm. And then, the tapered shaft contacts with the tapered hole and the position is automatically aligned. The lifting handwheel continues to be rotated to drive the carriage and the weighing object to rise. When it rises 15 mm again, it meets the rising limit plate. The lifting handwheel continues to be rotated to achieve clamping. The gravity will press down more and more tightly. The upper lifting position is performed in vehicle transportation status, as shown in Fig. 1.

As shown in Fig. 3, four groups of on-board weighing devices for small and medium-sized logistics vehicles are arranged between the two axles and the carriage pad, and the weighing center and weighing area are delimited in the carriage.

5   Structural Innovation Technology II: G2152 [Australia] Load Cell Protection Device and Control Method of for Logistics Vehicle (International Patent)

The invention independently innovates and designs the weighing device and method innovation of the logistics vehicle on the logistics vehicle with a hydraulic transmission system. The invention discloses the protection device of the weighing sensor of the logistics vehicle, including the axle, the lifting cylinder, the cylinder connecting plate, the lifting and lowering center cone shaft, the lifting and lowering center cone hole, the carriage backing plate, the weighing contact (contact with the center spherical point), the weighing sensor Assemble adjustment pad, sensor base, lifting limit plate, reinforcement, positioning safety plate, positioning safety cone shaft, positioning guide support, positioning cylinder connecting plate, placing safety cylinder, hydraulic control module and electrical control module; When the carriage and weighing object are in the weighing state, the load cell can weigh freely without any restriction, which improves the weighing accuracy; When the carriage and weighing object are in the transportation state, the load cell is separated from the carriage and weighing object, and the load cell weighing device of the logistics vehicle sensor is protected and controlled under the transportation condition. The device has a novel and reasonable structure, high efficiency, and broad application scope.

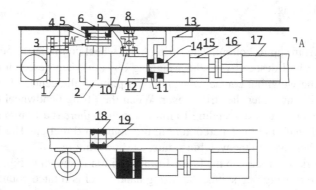

Fig. 4. Transportation status diagram of load cell protection device of logistics vehicle.

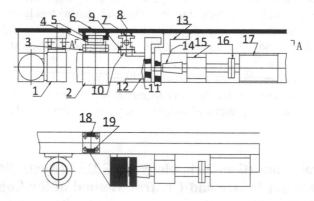

Fig. 5. Weighing status diagram of load cell protection device of logistics vehicle.

As shown in Fig. 4 and 5, the invention provides a load cell protection device for logistics vehicles, which includes: axle 1, lifting oil cylinder 2, oil cylinder connecting plate 3, lifting centering cone shaft 4, lifting centering cone hole 5, carriage base plate 6, weighing contact 7, weighing sensor 8, assembly adjustment pad 9, sensor base 10, lifting limit plate 11, reinforcing rib 12, positioning safety plate 13, positioning safety cone shaft 14, positioning guide mount 15, positioning oil cylinder connecting plate 16, positioning safety oil cylinder 17, oil cylinder hydraulic control module 18 and electric control module 19. The lifting cylinder 2 is welded and fixed with the outside of axle 1. The cylinder connecting plate 3 is associated with the piston rod end of the lifting cylinder 2. The cylinder connecting plate 3 and the lifting centering cone shaft 4 are fixed and secured by bolts. The taper of the lifting centering cone shaft 4 and the lifting centering cone hole 5 is 1:3, and the base of the lifting centering cone hole 5 is welded and fixed with the carriage base plate 6. The weighing contact 7 is welded and fixedly connected with the carriage base plate 6. The sensor base 10 is placed on the axle 1 and welded and the assembly adjustment pad 9 is installed between the weighing sensor 8 and the sensor base 10 by bolts. The lifting limit plate 11 is welded and fixed with the outside of the axle 1 and fastened with the reinforcing rib 12. The positioning safety plate 13 is welded and settled with the carriage base plate 6. The lifting limit plate 11 and the positioning safety plate 13 have taper holes with a taper of 1:12. The positioning safety oil cylinder 17 is welded and fixedly connected with the outside of axle 1. The piston rod end of the positioning safety oil cylinder 17 is provided with a positioning oil cylinder connecting plate 16. The push rod of the positioning safety cone shaft 14 is associated with the positioning oil cylinder connecting plate 16 through the positioning guide mount 15. The taper of the positioning safety cone shaft 14 is 1:12, and the lifting limit plate 11 and the positioning safety plate 13 are fixed by the lock.

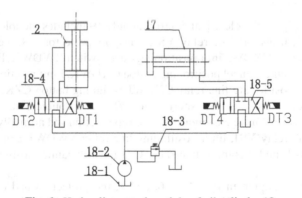

Fig. 6. Hydraulic control module of oil cylinder 18.

Further, as shown in Fig. 6, the hydraulic control module 18 of the oil cylinder includes: oil tank 18–1, oil pump 18–2, relief valve 18–3, three-position four-way electromagnetic directional valve 18–4, three-position four-way electromagnetic directional valve 18–5, first electromagnetic coil dt1, second electromagnetic coil DT2, third electromagnetic coil DT3, and fourth electromagnetic coil DT4. The oil pump 18–2 supplies pressure oil to the oil cylinder system through the relief valve 18–3. The first solenoid coil dt1 and the second solenoid coil DT2 of the three-position four-way solenoid directional valve No.1 18–4 control the piston rod of the lifting oil cylinder 2 to move up and down. The third solenoid coil DT3 and the fourth solenoid coil DT4 of the three-position four-way solenoid directional valve 18–5 control the piston rod of the positioning safety oil cylinder 17 to move left and right.

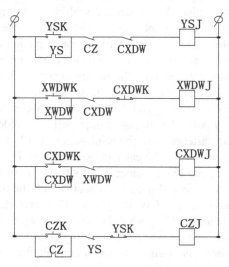

Fig. 7. Electrical control module 19.

As shown in Fig. 7, the electrical control module 19 includes: double contact transport button YSK, transport line relay YSJ, transport protector YS, weighing switch CZ, cancel positioner CXDW, limit positioning travel switch XWDWK, limit positioner XWDW, double contact cancel positioning button CXDWK, limit positioning line relay XWDWJ, cancel positioning line relay CXDWJ Weighing button CZK, weighing line relay CZJ; The double contact transport button YSK and double contact cancel positioning button CXDWK have customarily closed connection and normally open contact. The transport line relay YSJ, limit positioning line relay XWDWJ, cancel positioning line relay CXDWJ, and weighing line relay CZJ have dynamic closing and breaking contact.

Furthermore, as shown in Fig. 4, 5, 6, and 7, the protection and control method of the device is as follows. When the carriage and the weighing object are in the up and down position, which means the vehicles are in the transportation state, the double contact transport button YSK is pressed down. The normally closed contact of the double contact transport button YSK first cuts off the weighing line. Then its normally open contact is closed and stays for 2 s. The transport line relay YSJ receives the electric signal and makes the dynamic contact of the transport line relay YSJ close. The transport line relay YSJ is powered on and self-locking; The oil pump 18–2 is started. The relief valve 18–3 sets the pressure value of the system pressure oil and supplies the pressure oil to the system. The first solenoid coil DT1 of the three-position four-way solenoid directional valve 18–4 is energized, the right position of the three-position four-way solenoid directional valve 18–4 is in the working state, and the pressure oil enters the lower chamber of the lifting cylinder 2 through the right position of the three-position four-way solenoid directional valve 18–4. At the same time, the pressure oil in the upper chamber of lifting cylinder 2 flows back to the oil tank 18–1 through the right position of the three-position four-way solenoid directional valve 18–4. The piston rod of the lifting cylinder 2 moves up, and through the cylinder connecting plate 3, the lifting centering cone shaft 4 moves up and meets the lifting centering cone hole 5. The lifting centering cone hole 5 is aligned. When the positioning safety plate 13 touches the lifting limit plate 11, the resistance of the lifting cylinder 2 increases again. When the system pressure increases to the set value, the pressure is maintained, and the lifting stops. At this time, the limit positioning travel switch XWDWK on the lifting limit plate 11 is pressed. The limit positioning line relay XWDWJ receives the electric signal and makes the dynamic contact of the limit positioning line relay XWDWJ close. The limit positioning line relay XWDWJ is powered on and self-locking. At the same time, the third electromagnetic coil DT3 of the three-position four-way solenoid directional valve 18–5 is powered on, and the right position of the three-position four-way solenoid directional valve 18–5 is in the working state. The pressure oil enters the right chamber of the positioning safety oil cylinder 17 through the right position of the three-position four-way solenoid directional valve 18–5, and pushes the piston rod of the positioning safety oil cylinder 17 to move to the left. Through the connecting plate 16 of the positioning oil cylinder and the positioning guide mount 15, the positioning safety cone shaft 14 moves left to the cone hole on the positioning safety plate 13 and the lifting limit plate 11. When there is no clearance between 13 and 14, the left movement stops. The set positioning safety oil pressure value is maintained, and the taper of 1:12 in the horizontal direction is adopted so that it has a self-locking function in the vertical direction, which plays a protective and control role for the logistics vehicle load cell in the transportation state.

After transportation, when the carriage and the weighing objects are in the lower lifting position, that is, in the weighing state, the double contact cancel positioning button CXDWK should be pressed. In the process of moving down, the normally closed contact of the double contact cancel positioning button CXDWK cuts off the position limit and then closes the normally open connection. After staying for 2 s, the cancel positioning line relay CXDWJ received the electrical signal. At the same time, the fourth solenoid coil DT4 of the three-position four-way solenoid directional valve 18–5 is energized. The left position of the three-position four-way solenoid directional valve 18–5 is in working state, and the pressure oil enters the left chamber of the positioning safety oil cylinder 17 through the left position of the three-position four-way solenoid directional valve 18–5. The piston rod of positioning safety oil cylinder 17 is pushed to the right. At the same time, the pressure oil in the right chamber of positioning safety oil cylinder 17 flows back to the oil tank 18–1 through the reversing valve. The piston rod of positioning safety oil cylinder 17 moves to the right. Through the connecting plate 16 of the positioning oil cylinder and the positioning guide mount 15, the positioning safety cone shaft 14 moves to the right to the beginning of the stroke. The weighing button CZK is pressed, and then, the weighing line relay CZJ is powered on and self-locking. The dynamic contact is closed. At the same time, the second solenoid coil DT2 of the three-position four-way solenoid directional valve 18–4 is charged. The left position of the three-position four-way solenoid directional valve 18–4 is working. The pressure oil enters the upper chamber of lifting cylinder 2 through the left part of the three-position four-way solenoid directional valve 18–4. The piston rod of the lifting oil cylinder 2 is pushed to make the cylinder connecting plate 3. The centering cone shaft 4 and centering cone hole 5 are lifted. The carriage base plate 6 moves downward. At the same time, the pressure oil in the lower chamber of the lifting oil cylinder 2 flows back to the oil tank 18–1 through the left of the three-position four-way electromagnetic directional valve 18–4. The carriage and the weighing body move downward under the vertical downward gravity. The weighing contact 7 is in connection with the upper end of the weighing sensor 8 and then the carriage and the weighing object stop moving down. Weighing is carried out without any restriction. And the piston rod of the lifting oil cylinder 2, the oil cylinder connecting plate 3 and the lifting centering cone shaft 4 continue to move down to the original position. In the weighing state, there is enough clearance in the diameter direction between the tapered shaft of the lifting centering tapered shaft 4 and the lifting centering tapered hole 5, and a certain amount of allowance in the horizontal direction.

The base end of on-board load cell is connected with the fixed thread of the vehicle bridge, and the other end is free to weigh without restriction. It is unnecessary to make a connecting thread hole so as to avoid mistakes in using methods. The problem of inaccurate weighing in on-board weighing is solved in principle, and the dynamic weighing sensors are detached. Thus, the service life is effectively improved. The device has a reasonable and compact structure, novel technology and wide application range.

6   Innovation

(1) It is found that the two ends of the load cell can not be connected with a screw simultaneously through scientific research. The end of the load cell base is fixed with the axle by bolts. The other end is recommended that no connection screw holes be made and two working states are used. The weighing device of the vehicle sensor is lifted to the upper position to realize safe transportation. The force on the sensors turns from pressure to tension. The carriage and weighing object are free to contact the upper end of the sensor through the weighing contact to realize free weighing without any restrictions. In principle, the interference and random factors are eliminated, and the bottleneck problem of inaccurate weighing with logistics vehicles is solved.

(2) Apply for Australian international patent "G2151 [Australia] one vehicle weighing device" and "G2152 [Australia] logistics vehicle weighing sensor protection device and control method". The patent of "one-dimensional angular, linear weighing method of multi-support weighing system ZL201810280073.9" is authorized.

(3) Innovative design of small and medium-sized logistics vehicle weighing device and method innovation is accomplished. The logistics vehicle weighing sensor protection device and two sets of weighing machines are obtained for testing. The experimental results show the correctness and reliability of the research.

(4) The conclusion can be seen in Scientific and technological novelty Report No.: 2017-036. In the current situation and with the development trend of dynamic weighing and force measurement technology, the research and development of key technologies of the one-dimensional linear dynamic weighing device in this project have not been reported.

(5) The calibration results meet the technical requirements of JJG 455-2000 standard force measuring instrument verification regulation, which is proved in the test report of Beijing Institute of measurement and testing technology (authorized by the state defense science and Technology Industry Bureau, authorization certificate No.: National Defense military industry-JLJG-1-003). The Certificate No. is TJ1C9019-04-07386 for force sensor FYXZ-07.

7 Application Examples

7.1 One Dimensional Angle Linear On-Board Dynamic Weighing Device for Logistics Vehicles

Jiangsu Zongshen Automobile Industry Co., Ltd. and Xuzhou University of technology bring their respective industrial and technological advantages into play. The college and enterprise alliance is formed with research cooperation. Through the joint research and development of a new sensor device for 12-point position 12-point force video display, one-dimensional linear wireless sensor network node positioning method and other system software and hardware, multi-support weighing system unified dimension linear weighing method, and so on, scientific and technological achievements are obtained with obvious social and economic benefits. The application demonstration of on-board weighing technologies with patents, such as the utility model relating to a dual-signal and dual-screen cross-type vehicle terminal for logistics vehicles (ZL201310434153.2), non-contact detection device system for mixture parameters of vehicle terminal interaction (ZL201310740127.2), and so on, gains remarkable results and feedback. In Huaihai Economic Zone, 90% of Shunfeng express logistics vehicles and 40% of Jingdong logistics vehicles are provided by Jiangsu Zongshen Automobile Industry Co., Ltd. According to the applicable certificate of Xuzhou Haipai Technology Co., Ltd., Jiangsu Zongshen Automobile Industry Co., Ltd., and Xuzhou Daoge Information Technology Co., Ltd., the total amount of new-increased profit from 2018 to 2020 is 107.44 million yuan. The new-increased tax is 16.885 million yuan. The foreign exchange income is 18.22 million US dollars, and the total expenditure is 40.47 million yuan.

7.2 Video Monitoring Device with Visual Vehicle Terminal for Mobile Communication

Xuzhou Haipai Technology Co., Ltd., as an application and promotion enterprise of scientific and technological achievements, is engaged in the development, sales, use and maintenance of software and hardware of on-board terminal and handheld terminal XGZS001. The technologies of vehicle networking visualization vehicle terminal software, Internet of things parking service and management fees, overload of passenger and freight vehicles on the highway, mobile communication visualization, on-board terminal video monitoring device achieve astonishing results. From 2018 to 2020, the new-increase profit is 3.29 million yuan. The new-increase tax is 435000 yuan. The foreign exchange income is 3.02 million US dollars, and the total expenditure is 1.86 million yuan.

In May 2018, Xuzhou Daoge Information Technology Co., Ltd. introduced the XGHP001 system software and hardware, which was researched and developed by Xuzhou Institute of engineering, and carried out the application demonstration of scientific research achievements. In the past three years, it has increased profits by 7.15 million yuan and taxes of 910000 yuan. A foreign exchange of 310 US dollars was generated, and a total of 3.86 million yuan was saved. Remarkable social and economic benefits have been achieved.

7.3   Benefits from Core Patented Technology Transfer

In 2019, To realize the transformation of science and technology into productivity and the promotion and application of patented technology, the authorized invention patent rights of the core key technologies were transferred, namely "a dual-signal and dual-screen cross-type vehicle terminal for logistics vehicles (ZL201310434153.2)" and "non-contact detection device system for mixture parameters of vehicle terminal interaction (ZL201310740127.2)", to Jiangsu Zongshen Automobile Industry Co., Ltd.

Acknowledgements. The authors acknowledge the Jiangsu University Natural Science Research Project (18KJB470024) and Provincial Construction System Science and Technology Project of Jiangsu Provincial Housing and Urban-Rural Construction Department (2018ZD088). This work is partly supported by the Natural Science Foundation of Jiangsu Province of China (No. BK20161165), the applied fundamental research Foundation of Xuzhou of China (No. KC17072). The authorized patents for invention are also the research and development of Jiangsu Province Industry-University-Research Cooperation Project (BY2019056).

References

1. Xi, J.: Parking information interaction of global internet of things based on the timer and elastic pressure switch sensor combination. Appl. Mech. Mater. **614**, 497–502 (2014)
2. Xi, J., Han, C.: Parking navigation system based on the double signal double display intersection vehicle terminal and automobile internal information. Appl. Mech. Mater. 803–808 (2014)
3. Xi, J.: Global internet of things garage system wite parking information release of timer control. Meas. Control Technol. **33**(9), 128–130 (2014)
4. Xi, J.: Self-organizing IOV technology oriented vehicle driving and parking service using vehicle terminal. J. Comput. Sci. Technol. **41**(11A), 466–467 (2014)
5. Xi, J.: Parking information release and booking park equipment for garage system on the Internet of things. J. Comput. Appl. **34**(S1), 306–308 (2014)
6. Wang, L., Xi, J., Han, C., Qiao, S.: One dimensional angle linear weighing method for multi fulcrum weighing system. CN108489578A (2018)
7. Huang, W., et al.: Node localization method for wireless sensor networks in one dimensional linear region. CN104703277B (2018)
8. Han, C., Xi, J.: Vehicle terminal space labyrinth module. CN103522963B (2017)
9. Xi, J., Daihong, J., Han, C.: A crossover vehicle terminal with dual channel and double screen. CN103528594B (2017)
10. Liu, A., Xi, J.: Non contact detection system of mixture parameters based on vehicle terminal interaction. CN103674776B (2017)

11. Wang, S., et al.: A logistics dynamic weighing sorting integrated device. CN110252678A (2019)
12. Wang, L., et al.: A dynamic weighing equipment for logistics transportation. CN209727234U (2019)
13. Yu, J., et al.: An electronic driving scale with stable installation and anti-collision. CN110260960A (2020)
14. Fang, E., et al.: A dynamic weighing device. CN210375366U (2020)
15. Wang, L., et al: A kind of vehicle weighing equipment. CN212363390U (2021)
16. Xuzhou University of Technology: Weighing in motion self-calibration algorithm software. 2018SR670312 (2018)
17. Xuzhou University of Technology: Dynamic electronic weighing system software. 2018SR632550 (2018)
18. Xuzhou University of Technology: Intelligent weighing dynamic memory management system. 2019SR1078748 (2019)
19. Xuzhou University of Technology: Dynamic digital weighing automatic management system. 2019SR1078732 (2019)
20. Xuzhou University of Technology: Calibration and optimization software for vehicle weigh in motion. 2019SR1141072 (2019)
21. Xuzhou University of Technology: Key technology research and development of one dimensional linear dynamic weighing electronic device. Science and Technology Novelty Search Report 2017-036, Xuzhou science and Technology Information Institute of Jiangsu Province (2017)
22. Xuzhou University of Technology: Load cell test report. Beijing Institute of aerospace metrology and testing technology (authorized by the State Administration of science, technology and industry for national defense, Certificate No.: National Defense industry-JLJG-1-003), Certificate No.: TJ1c2019-04-07386, Calibration certificate of load cell FYXZ-07 (2019)

Short Video Service Evaluation System Design from the Viewpoint of QoE

Wan Chen, Lei Chen[⊠], Tian Zhou, Jiayi Zhu, and Ping Cui

Jiangsu Province Key Laboratory of Intelligent Industry Control Technology, Xuzhou University of Technology, Xuzhou 221018, China
chenlei@xzit.edu.cn

Abstract. The main purpose of this study is to understand the short video industry, guide the short video provider to improve the service quality of short video. In this study, literature method, questionnaire survey method, interview method, statistical analysis method and analytic hierarchy process were used, and SPSSAU data analysis was employed. A total of 106 questionnaires were collected in this survey, and the main respondents were young people. Survey, according to the results of the weight for the primary index reflects the users more attention to the safety and reliability, we conclude that primary index can help improve the value-added services, because in some service products research, found a lot of products are set up members value-added services, users can buy them to enhance personal experience.

Keywords: Short video · Questionnaire · SPSSAU · Evaluation index · Quality of experience

1 Introduction

In recent years, with the rapid development of network technology, the short video industry in China has been developing for 10 years. So far, there are numerous short video platforms in the market, and the domestic short video market is becoming increasingly fierce [1]. Our research is mainly to analyze several popular short video platforms in the market, find out the advantages and disadvantages of different short videos, and put forward suggestions for improvement. User experience [2] is based on the users in the use of products in the process of a purely subjective feeling, the user experience is the main part of the user, the object is the product, find products through the user's user experience, the advantages and disadvantages of improve the quality of the product development and promote the development of products for the better, so the quality of the user experience is very important.

General evaluation application will release questionnaire to study the user's experience, our study also used the questionnaire survey method, after the collected data using SPSSAU data analysis it is concluded that the weight of indicators and secondary indicators, comprehensive weight, index of RI values, consistency check, etc., an analysis of the different short video platform user experience satisfaction; In the selection of

D. Jiang and H. Song (Eds.): SIMUtools 2021, LNICST 424, pp. 488–500, 2022.
https://doi.org/10.1007/978-3-030-97124-3_36

indicators, we use the SERVPERF (Quality of Service) model as the basis, and use the questionnaire survey combined with the previous scholars' research to get the indicators.

2 Investigation Methods

In this study, literature method, questionnaire survey method, interview method, statistical analysis method and analytic hierarchy process [3] were adopted, and SPSSAU data was used for analysis. In the selection of indexes, the principles of usability [4], objectivity and practicability are followed to ensure the authenticity and effectiveness of indexes. For the selection of first-level indicators, we refer to the SERVPERF model [5]. The short video service based on user experience provides users with online services through the Internet, mobile phones, tablet computers and other terminal devices. In addition, short video service has certain particularity compared with other services. In the process of researching user's short video business in the mobile Internet market, it is found that short video has established value-added business, and users can obtain personalized services different from ordinary users by purchasing value-added business. According to the SERVPERF model, the quality of service [6] is analyzed, and the following indicators are finally selected as the main indicators, including reliability, assurance, security, use experience and functionality. If the order n of the judgment matrix is greater than 2, it will bring some difficulties to obtain the consistency result of the constructed judgment matrix. Therefore, conformance testing is necessary. First, the formula is:

$$\lambda \max = \frac{1}{n} \sum\nolimits_{i=1}^{n} \frac{(A * w)}{wi} \tag{1}$$

The maximum eigenroot of the judgment matrix A of order λmax-n is calculated, and the relative weight vector of the judgment matrix A of order W-n is given in the formula. Then calculate the maximum characteristic root λ Max of each judgment matrix, and then calculate the magnitude of the consistency index $CI = \frac{(\lambda \max - n)}{n-1}$ by the following formula:

$$CI = \frac{(\lambda \max - n)}{n - 1} \tag{2}$$

By introducing the $RI = CI/CR$ value of the index, the consistency of the judgment matrix is verified by checking the Ri value of the corresponding order. When the order of the judgment matrix is 1 or 2, the judgment matrix has strong consistency. When the order of the judgment matrix is greater than 2, the consistency index $CI = \frac{(\lambda \max - n)}{n-1}$ of the judgment matrix is equal to the average value of the random consistency index Ri of the same order.

In this preliminary survey, the coefficient of variation and the arithmetic mean of each indicator will be calculated based on the results of user evaluation to determine the extent of user adjustment and the consistency of user opinions. The smaller the arithmetic mean, the lower the perception of the metric in the eyes of some users, so it can be deleted. The degree of coordination is inversely proportional to the coefficient of variation, the greater the coefficient, the greater the divergence of users, and vice versa.

The degree of users' opinions $My = \frac{1}{my}\sum_{x-1}^{mx} Cxy$ can be calculated by the following formula:

$$My = \frac{1}{my}\sum_{x-1}^{mx} Cxy \ y = 1, 2, 3 \ldots \ldots, n \tag{3}$$

$My == \frac{1}{my}\sum_{x-1}^{mx} Cxy$ is the arithmetic average value of the score of Y index. M and CXY respectively represent the number of users and the score of the index. The larger the value of MY is, the more important the index is in the evaluation of short video service by users.

For the coordination degree of users' opinions, $Vy = \frac{\beta y}{My}$ can be calculated by the following method. First, the standard deviation of the evaluation result of Y index can be calculated by the following formula:

$$\beta y = \sqrt{\frac{\sum_{x-1}^{mi}(Cxy - My)^2}{my - 1}} \ \ y = 1, 2, 3, 4 \ldots \ldots, n \tag{4}$$

Then the coefficient of variation of Y index score is calculated as follows:

$$Vy = \frac{\beta y}{My} \ y = 1, 2, 3, 4 \ldots \ldots, n \tag{5}$$

Analytic Hierarchy Process (AHP) is a kind of decision evaluation method which can determine the weight of evaluation index. It can analyze the evaluation problem of multi-level and multi-dimensional index efficiently. The construction of judgment matrix is to determine the importance degree of each index, according to the judgment matrix can calculate and obtain the weight of evaluation index, and the comprehensive weight of the index can be calculated to order the importance degree of indicators. The key point of the selection of the two indicators is obviously different from the selection of the first level indicators. The two level indicators are integrated again on the basis of the first level indicators. The selection of secondary indicators is mainly based on the literature method and interview method. The information in the literature is combined with relevant theories, and then the indicators are modified and improved through the interview results of users. After selecting the indicators, the indicators are explained to the users so that they can understand the indicators and answer their doubts. Finally, the interview results are analyzed in order to obtain more effective information. According to the understanding of literature and relevant theories, combined with the interview content, a preliminary evaluation index of short video service based on user experience is constructed. Finally, five first-level indicators are selected (Table 1), among which each first-level indicator contains three second-level indicators (Table 2).

3 Result Analysis

3.1 Indicator Analysis

Through consistency test, the index is analyzed, and the AHP results of the index are obtained: the feature vector of the security of the first level index is 2.174, and the weight value is 43.476%; The eigenvector of first-level index reliability is 1.307, and the weight value is 26.138%. The feature vector of the first-level indicator user experience is 0.299, and the weight value is 5.973%. The feature vector of first-level index functionality was 0.451, and the weight value was 9.022%. The characteristic vector of the guarantee of the first-level index is 0.770, and the weight value is 15.390%. The maximum eigenvalue was 5.426 and CI was 0.106. Through the first-level index weight consistency test, $\lambda = 5.426$ and CR = 0.095 were obtained, which passed the consistency test.

Table 1. First level indicators.

The overall goal	Level indicators
Research on Evaluation Index System of Short Video Service Based on User Experience	Security
	Reliability
	Usage experience
	Functional
	Guarantee

For the weight results of secondary indicators, the weight value of privacy protection of secondary indicators of primary index security is 0.405, the weight value of identity information and authorization security is 0.479, and the weight value of market regulation is 0.115. The weight of system stability, disaster recovery strategy and sustainability is 0.600, 0.200 and 0.200 respectively. The weight of mobile demand, humanized experience and recommendation preference is 0.633, 0.260 and 0.106, respectively. The weight of backup synchronization is 0.600, the weight of feature function is 0.200, and the weight of resource search and sharing is 0.200. The weight of compensatory index is 0.655, the weight of version update is 0.186, and the weight of product brand and strength is 0.157. According to the results of consistency test, the random consistency ratio CR was all less than 0.10, so the indicators passed the consistency test.

For the comprehensive weight of indicators at all levels, in the study, the comprehensive weight is the weight factor of each second-grade rating indicator in the overall goal. Among them, the product of the weight distribution of the second-level index in the first-level evaluation index, the weight distribution of the first-level evaluation index in the overall objective evaluation and the weight distribution of the price index is the combined weight of the second-level evaluation index. And the calculation tells us.

Table 2. Secondary indicators.

Level indicators	The secondary indicators
Security	Privacy protection
	Identity information and authorization security
	Market regulation
Reliability	System stability
	Disaster strategy
	Persistent
Usage experience	Mobile demand
	Humanized experience
	Be fond of the recommended
Functional	Backup synchronization
	Features
	Resource search and sharing
Guarantee	Compensatory
	Version update
	Product brand and strength

The weight of criterion layer factor security is 0.434, the weight of dimension layer factor privacy protection is 0.405, and the comprehensive weight is 0.175. The weight of criterion layer factor security is 0.434, the weight of dimension layer factor identity information and authorization security is 0.479, and the comprehensive weight is 0.208. The weight of safety factor in criterion layer is 0.434, the weight of market regulation factor in dimension layer is 0.115, and the comprehensive weight is 0.050. The weight of reliability of criterion layer factor is 0.261, the weight of stability of dimension layer factor is 0.600, and the comprehensive weight is 0.157. The weight of reliability of criterion layer factor is 0.261, the weight of disaster recovery strategy of dimension layer factor is 0.200, and the comprehensive weight is 0.052. The weight of criterion layer factor reliability is 0.261, the weight of dimension layer factor persistence is 0.200, and the comprehensive weight is 0.052. The weight of the criterion layer factor's use experience is 0.059, the weight of the dimension layer factor's mobile demand is 0.633, and the comprehensive weight is 0.037. The weight of criterion layer factor's use experience is 0.059, the weight of dimension layer factor's humanization experience is 0.260, and the comprehensive weight is 0.015. The weight of use experience of criterion layer factor is 0.059, the weight of preference recommendation of dimension layer factor is 0.160, and the comprehensive weight is 0.009. The weight of criterion layer factor functionality is 0.091, the weight of dimension layer factor backup synchronization is 0.600, and the comprehensive weight is 0.054. The functional weight of criterion layer factor is 0.091, the characteristic synchronization weight of dimension layer factor is 0.200, and the comprehensive weight is 0.018. The weight of criterion layer factor functionality is

0.091, the weight of dimension layer factor resource search and sharing is 0.200, and the comprehensive weight is 0.018. The guarantee weight of criterion layer factor is 0.153, the compensatory weight of dimension layer factor is 0.655, and the comprehensive weight is 0.100. The guarantee weight of criterion layer factor is 0.153, the version update weight of dimension layer factor is 0.186, and the comprehensive weight is 0.028. The weight of assurance of criterion layer factor is 0.153, the weight of product brand and strength of dimension layer factor is 0.157, and the comprehensive weight is 0.024.

As for the research on the degree of unity of user opinions and the degree of coordination of user opinions, the preliminary survey results show that the degree of unity of user opinions of all indicators is greater than 4.0. The above data indicates that the evaluation index system of short video service based on users is highly approved. Preliminary research in the first round of the users of coordination degree, all user coordinate degree not greater than 0.2, the mean evaluation index differences in team for the first round of preliminary research is relatively small, so all data, according to the established evaluation index system of short video services based on user is of high rationality, the index can be used in later research.

Reliability analysis is used to study quantitative data. First, analyze the X coefficient. If this value is higher than 0.8, it indicates high reliability. If the value is between 0.7 and 0.8, the reliability is good. If the value is between 0.6 and 0.7, then the reliability is acceptable. If this value is less than 0.6, it indicates poor reliability. If CITC value is lower than 0.3, this item can be deleted; If the value of "the deleted alpha coefficient of the item" is significantly higher than the alpha coefficient, then the item can be deleted and re-analyzed.

Table 3. Questionnaire reliability test α value.

The dimension	Cronbach alpha coefficient	N of Items
Security	0.949	3
Reliability	0.959	3
Usage experience	0.932	3
Functional	0.910	3
Guarantee	0.935	3
The overall questionnaire	0.980	15

It can be seen from Table 3 that Cronbach α value of each indicator is greater than 0.8, and the overall questionnaire is greater than 0.9, so it can be verified that the reliability of the indicator system is high.

Table 4. Cronbach validity analysis.

Name	Correction Total correlation (CITC)	Item deleted α factor	Cronbachα coefficient
Privacy Protection	0.865	0.978	0.980
Identity Information and Authorization Security	0.818	0.978	
Market supervision	0.880	0.978	
System stability	0.894	0.978	
Disaster tolerance strategies	0.877	0.978	
Continability	0.903	0.978	
Mobile requirements	0.854	0.978	
Humanized experience	0.911	0.978	
Favorable Experience	0.886	0.978	
Backup synchronization	0.798	0.979	
Features Features	0.864	0.978	
Resource Search and Sharing	0.886	0.978	
Compability	0.847	0.979	
Version Update	0.827	0.979	
Product brand and strength	0.869	0.978	

Standardization Cronbach α coefficient: 0.980

As can be seen from Table 4, the reliability coefficient value is 0.980, greater than 0.9, indicating that the reliability quality of the research data is very high. For the "coefficient with deleted items", the reliability coefficient will not increase significantly after any item is deleted, so it indicates that the item should not be deleted.

For the "CITC value", the CITC value of the analysis items is all greater than 0.4, indicating that there is a good correlation between the analysis items and a good reliability level. In conclusion, the reliability coefficient value of the research data is higher than 0.9, which comprehensively indicates that the reliability quality of the data is high and can be used for further analysis.

Table 5. Validity analysis is the result.

Name	Factor load factor	Common degree (common factor variance)
	Factor 1	
Privacy Protection	0.884	0.782
Identity Information and Authorization Security	0.844	0.712
Market supervision	0.898	0.806
System stability	0.911	0.830
Disaster tolerance strategies	0.896	0.802
Continability	0.918	0.843
Mobile requirements	0.875	0.766
Humanized experience	0.925	0.856
Favorable Experience	0.902	0.813
Backup synchronization	0.822	0.675
Features Features	0.883	0.779
Resource Search and Sharing	0.901	0.811
Compability	0.864	0.747
Version Update	0.847	0.717
Product brand and strength	0.886	0.784
Eigenvalue (before rotation)	11.725	–
Variance interpretation% (before rotation)	78.168%	–
Accumulated variance interpretation% (after rotation)	78.168%	
KMO value	0.934	–
Bart spherical value	2182.027	–
df	105	–
p value	0.000	–

Table 6. KMO and Bartlett.

KMO and Barlett values		
KMO value	0.934	
Barlett sphericity test	Apcard square	2182.027
	df	105
	p value	0.000

As can be seen from Table 5 and Table 6, the corresponding common degree values of all the research items are all higher than 0.4, indicating that the research item information can be effectively extracted. In addition, the KMO value is 0.934, greater than 0.6, indicating that the data has validity. The variance interpretation rate values of the other 1 factor were 78.168%, and the cumulative variance interpretation rate after rotation was 78.168% > 50%. It means that the information of research items can be extracted effectively.

3.2 QoE Analysis

This time, three representative short videos, Douyin, Kuaishou and People's Short Video, were selected as the research objects. After the sample is determined, each second-level indicator is judged and scored. The evaluators of this questionnaire are mainly college students. 106 questionnaires will be released to conduct the survey and ensure its validity. In the selection of secondary indicators, the literature information and the information improved by the interviewees were integrated. Table 7 shows the information of the interviewees.

In qualitative index of the evaluation, the score of each secondary index is 5 points, score from 1 to 5 is expressed as "very dissatisfied, not satisfied, in general, satisfied and very satisfied", participants according to their own understanding, each index of the degree of satisfaction and the sample rate, and the reference description, it is concluded that each index of the score, then multiplied by the weight of the index finally concluded that the overall score, The score of each index is calculated by weighting the score results of 106 surveyors, and then multiplied by the weight of the corresponding index to get the score of each index. Finally, the comprehensive score is summarized (Table 8).

Table 7. Interviewee information.

Number	Age	Sex	Education	Way	Frequency	Usage time
1	21	Woman	Undergraduate course	Face to face	Occassionally	Half a year
2	20	Woman	Undergraduate course	Face to face	Every day	Two years
3	21	Woman	Undergraduate course	Face to face	Every day	A year and a half
4	20	Man	Undergraduate course	Face to face	Often	A year
5	21	Man	Undergraduate course	Face to face	Occassionally	Half a year
6	21	Man	Undergraduate course	Face to face	Every day	Two years

Table 8. Statistical table of study sample scores.

Level indicators	The secondary indicators	The total weight	Douyin	Kuaishou	Quanmin
Security A 0.434	Privacy protection A1	0.175	4.5	4.3	4.2
	Identity information and authorization securityA2	0.208	4.2	3.8	4.1
	Market regulationA3	0.050	4.2	4.1	4.0
Reliability B 0.261	System stabilityB1	0.157	4.3	4.2	4.2
	Disaster strategyB2	0.052	4.1	3.9	3.9
	PersistentB3	0.052	3.6	3.8	3.9
Usage experience C 0.059	Mobile demandC1	0.037	4.3	4.0	3.9
	Humanized experience	0.015	3.8	4.1	4.0
	Be fond of the recommendedC3	0.009	4.0	4.1	3.9
Functional D 0.091	Backup synchronizationD1	0.054	4.1	4.2	3.9
	FeaturesD2	0.018	3.8	4.0	4.0
	Resource search and sharing	0.018	4.1	4.0	3.8
Guarantee E 0.153	CompensatoryE1	0.100	4.0	4.1	3.9
	Version updateE2	0.028	4.2	4.2	4.0
	Product brand and strengthE3	0.024	3.9	4.2	4.1

According to the index level design of the user-based index system of short video service, and combined with the weight calculation results of A1–E3, the first-level index is calculated and shown in Table 9:

Table 9. Statistical table of A–E results for primary indicators.

	Douyin	Kuaishou	Quanmin
Security A	1.870	1.747	1.787
Reliability B	1.075	1.058	1.064
Usage experience C	0.253	0.246	0.239
Functional D	0.363	0.321	0.351
Guarantee E	0.612	0.629	0.600
Composite scores	4.173	4.001	4.041

Based on the collated data set, the score of each secondary index of the sample product is firstly calculated, and then the weighted score is calculated for the total score. Other sample products are calculated according to this method, and Table 10 is obtained:

Table 10. Statistical table of A1–E3 score of secondary indicators.

The secondary indicators	The total weight	Douyin	Kuaishou	Quanmin
A1	0.175	0.787	0.752	0.735
A2	0.208	0.873	0.790	0.852
A3	0.050	0.210	0.205	0.200
B1	0.157	0.675	0.659	0.659
B2	0.052	0.213	0.202	0.202
B3	0.052	0.187	0.197	0.203
C1	0.037	0.160	0.148	0.144
C2	0.015	0.057	0.061	0.060
C3	0.009	0.036	0.037	0.035
D1	0.054	0.221	0.227	0.211
D2	0.018	0.068	0.072	0.072
D3	0.018	0.074	0.072	0.068
E1	0.100	0.400	0.410	0.390
E2	0.028	0.118	0.118	0.112
E3	0.024	0.094	0.101	0.098

4   Conclusion

So far, there have been many short video platforms in the market, so our research on short video service platform is mainly to understand the development status of short video and users' satisfaction with some service indicators of short video platform, further improve product quality, and maximize the advantages of short video platform. Comprehensively, we have carried out a careful study on the safety, reliability, experience, functionality and assurance of five level 1 indicators of short video. In the process of building and applying the user-based evaluation index system for short video service, it is found that there are still many deficiencies in short video and great room for improvement. The evaluation results of samples will be analyzed in the following sections. Through the analysis of sample data results can be concluded that compared to the market the same kind of short video services, douyin occupy a certain advantage in the market, get appreciated and welcomed by the masses [7], this is because the douyin convenient features, attracts more users to use, its search share function is very powerful, and to provide users open live entertainment and commercial activities, convenient and quick. Therefore, users have high requirements for the safety and reliability of short video platform, so the later maintenance in this aspect is very worthy of in-depth research. Secondly, in terms of user experience and functionality, all short video platforms are virtually the same, so there is not much difference in user experience in this aspect. Therefore, in view of our experimental results, we also put forward some suggestions, hoping to provide effective information for the study of short videos.

Acknowledgements. This work was supported in part by Xu Zhou Science and Technology Plan Project (Grant No. KC21309).

References

1. Shao, T., Wang, R., Hao, J.: Visual destination images in user-generated short videos: an exploratory study on douyin. In: 2019 16th International Conference on Service Systems and Service Management (ICSSSM), pp. 1–5 (2019). https://doi.org/10.1109/ICSSSM.2019.888 7688
2. Wehner, N., Wassermann, S., Casas, P., Seufert, M., Wamser, F.: Beauty is in the eye of the smartphone holder a data driven analysis of youtube mobile QoE. In: 2018 14th International Conference on Network and Service Management (CNSM), pp. 343–347 (2018)
3. Zeng, L., Liu, D.: A study on the model of furniture aesthetic value based on fuzzy AHP comprehensive evaluation. In: 2010 Seventh International Conference on Fuzzy Systems and Knowledge Discovery, pp. 1173–1175 (2010). https://doi.org/10.1109/FSKD.2010.5569152
4. Zeng, Y., Lou, Z.: The new PCA for dynamic and non-Gaussian processes. In: 2020 Chinese Automation Congress (CAC), pp. 935–938 (2020). https://doi.org/10.1109/CAC51589.2020. 9327354
5. Pinasthika, S.J., Bukhori, S., Prasetyo, B.: Hybrid lean SERVPERF-WebQual-IPA for measuring IT service quality. In: 2019 International Conference on Computer Science, Information Technology, and Electrical Engineering (ICOMITEE), pp. 13–18 (2019). https://doi.org/10. 1109/ICOMITEE.2019.8921252

6. Gong, Q.: Notice of retraction: quality, satisfaction and loyalty: a comparison of SERVQUAL and SERVPERF for educational service in China. In: 2010 International Conference on Management and Service Science, pp. 1–7 (2010). https://doi.org/10.1109/ICMSS.2010.557 6967
7. Wei, B., Chenxi, L.: Study on the win-win strategy of douyin and its users. In: 2020 IEEE 3rd International Conference on Information Systems and Computer Aided Education (ICISCAE), pp. 183–186 (2020). https://doi.org/10.1109/ICISCAE51034.2020.9236835

Research on QoE Evaluation Index of Online Music Service

Rong Chen, Lei Chen$^{(\boxtimes)}$, Jing He, Wenlin Li, Yvxing Yang, and Ping Cui

Jiangsu Province Key Laboratory of Intelligent Industry Control Technology, Xuzhou University of Technology, Xuzhou 221018, China
chenlei@xzit.edu.cn

Abstract. Online music service is one of the most popular kinds of online services. To analyze the quality of end user experience, we investigate the quality of experience (QoE) index of these services. Based on the SERVPERF model, we collect data from college students and obtain weights of key factors. A hierarchical QoE index system is proposed in this paper. Using this QoE index system, we comparing several popular online music services, and give some improvement suggestion to these services.

Keywords: Online music · Quality of experience · Quality evaluation

1 Introduction

With the rapid development of network technology, the transmission mode of music works has also changed. The music industry has ushered in the Internet era and the network music platform has gradually become the main way for people to listen to music [1–3]. Nowadays, online music copyright is gradually becoming standardized, and the market competition of online music platform is becoming increasingly fierce. In this case, the performance of the network music platform service is very important, it may affect the user stickiness [4]. In the performance of online music platform, there are mainly six important performances, namely assurance, security, reliability, use experience, value-added services, and functionality. These six important properties can be refined again. The study found that the network music platform needs to pay attention to strengthen its security and guarantee, and expand its functionality. Through these studies, we can promote each network music platform to enhance its value and development potential to improve the competitiveness. On this basis, college students account for a large proportion of users, and the performance they pay attention to becomes particularly important [5]. Therefore, it is of great practical significance to study the service evaluation index system of music platform service for college students.

Common methods of user experience evaluation mainly include subjective evaluation method, behavioral data method, interview method, literature method, questionnaire method and physiological method [6]. By using the above methods, we can know all the

D. Jiang and H. Song (Eds.): SIMUtools 2021, LNICST 424, pp. 501–510, 2022.
https://doi.org/10.1007/978-3-030-97124-3_37

feelings of users when using the network music platform. In the process of establishing the index system, it is necessary to design a set of index system first, and then the index system can be obtained after expert rating and analysis [7]. In this study, interview method, literature method, questionnaire survey method and analytic hierarchy process were adopted to conduct a sampling survey with college students as the sample population. Through literature, interviews and analysis, 6 first-level indicators and 17 s-level indicators were finally established, which made the index system more objective and reasonable. Reliability analysis, validity analysis, consistency analysis, determination of index weight and other calculation and analysis were carried out on the questionnaire results. Reliability analysis makes the research results stable and reliable, validity analysis reflects the effectiveness of the research results [8, 9], and consistency complex analysis and the determination of index weight make the results authentic and accurate. The analytic hierarchy process (AHP) provides a scientific basis for the research results. Through the above methods, relatively accurate research results can be obtained [10].

It can be seen from the results of this survey that college students pay more attention to the security, assurance and functionality of music platforms when they use them. The network music platform can improve these three aspects to enhance the user's service experience and user stickiness. This survey provides future improvement directions for all online music platforms, provides reference for promoting the development of online music platforms to meet the multi-level personalized users, and promotes the positive circular development of platform ecosystem.

2   Investigation Methods

The service of online music platform is different from the SERVPERF model, so according to the model, some experiential perception indicators are discarded, and some networked first-level indicators are added according to the particularity of online music platform and user needs. Then through the literature method and interview method to the primary index characteristics of more comprehensive addition. In this paper, six college students with inconsistent frequency of using online music were carefully selected for face-to-face interviews to collect better and reasonable indicators based on user needs. For preliminary build a platform for the online music service evaluation index, design questionnaire, please users according to their own understanding, in accordance with the indicators on the importance of the network music platform service indicators, to rate and the correlation of evaluation system, in this preliminary investigation, according to user's evaluation result to calculate the variation coefficient of each index and arithmetic mean, To determine the degree of user adjustment and user opinion uniformity. The smaller the arithmetic mean is, the lower the perception of this indicator is in the user's eyes, so it can be deleted. The degree of coordination is inversely proportional to the coefficient of variation, the greater the coefficient, the greater the divergence of users, and vice versa. Uniformity of user opinion M_y:

$$M_y = \frac{1}{m_y} \sum_{x-1}^{m_x} C_{xy} \quad y = 1, 2, 3, \ldots\ldots, n. \tag{1}$$

M_y is the arithmetic mean of the score of y indicator. m and C respectively represent the number of users and the rating of indicators. The larger the value of M_y, the more important the indicator is in the evaluation of online music platform services, and the smaller the value of M_y, the smaller the influence of the indicator on the evaluation of online music platform services. For the coordination degree of users' opinions V_y, the coefficient of variation β_y of the index score was calculated first:

$$\beta_y = \sqrt{\frac{1}{m_y - 1} \sum_{x-1}^{m_i} (C_{xy} - M_y)^2} \quad y = 1, 2, 3, \ldots\ldots, n \tag{2}$$

M_y and β_y to calculate the user opinion coordination degree V_y:

$$V_y = \frac{\beta_y}{M_y} \quad y = 1, 2, 3, \ldots\ldots, n. \tag{3}$$

If the users' consensus degree M_y is more than 4.0, it means that the overall evaluation index system of online music platform service has a high degree of recognition. In the degree of coordination of users' opinions V_y, all indicators are lower than 0.2, which means that there are few divergent opinions on various indicators. After investigation, this index system has a higher rationality.

If the order n of the judgment matrix is greater than 2, it will bring some difficulties to obtain the consistency result of the constructed judgment matrix, so it is necessary to carry out consistency test. First, the maximum Eigen root of λ_{max-n} order judgment matrix A is calculated by the formula:

$$\lambda_{max} = \frac{1}{n} \sum_{i=0}^{n} \frac{(A \cdot W)}{Wi}. \tag{4}$$

Wi is the weight of each index. Find the magnitude of CI:

$$CI = \frac{(\lambda_{max} - n)}{n - 1}. \tag{5}$$

The smaller the CI, the greater the consistency. Considering that the deviation of consistency may be caused by random reasons, it is necessary to compare CI with the average random consistency index RI to get the test coefficient CR when testing whether the judgment matrix has satisfactory consistency CR:

$$CR = \frac{CI}{RI}. \tag{6}$$

The random consistency ratio CR, that is, when $CR < 0.10$, the judgment matrix passes the consistency test.

Indicator specified processing process is shown in the following table (Figs. 1 and 2):

Step 1	Based on the SERVPERF model, six first-level indexes are selected in combination with the particularity of online music platform services and user needs.
Step 2	Six college students who have been using online music platforms for a long time were carefully selected for face-to-face interviews to understand their feelings about using online music platforms and discuss the most important performance of online music platforms in their opinion.
Step 3	The main views obtained from the interview were summarized and classified into secondary indicators under the primary indicators by combining with literature, and 17 secondary indicators were obtained.

Fig. 1. Indicators specify the process flow

Step1	Questionnaires were designed according to Likert 5-point scale, with scores set at 1-5, respectively representing "very unimportant, unimportant, average, important and very important".[11]
Step2	Six college students using online music platform were selected to score the indicators of online music platform.
Step3	According to the score data collected, the index of user opinion uniformity degree M_y and user opinion coordination degree V_y were calculated by formulas (1), (2) and (3), which were compared with the standard value to analyze whether it was reasonable.
Step4	Based on the reasonable results, the established index system will be adjusted. After the adjustment, the quality investigation will be conducted until all the indicators are reasonable, and the evaluation index system of online music platform service will be obtained.
Step5	89 preliminary questionnaires were released and recovered. SPSS 22.0 was used to conduct reliability analysis and validity analysis on the evaluation index system to check whether the index system reached the standard.
Step6	The 1-9 scale method proposed by T.L. SSSTY was used to carry out comparative analysis among various indicators, and questionnaires were designed, 6 copies were issued and recovered, and the weight of indicators at all levels was calculated.[12]
Step7	Consistency test was carried out through (4), (5) and (6) to check the degree of coordination among various indicators.

Fig. 2. Quality investigation flow

The final evaluation index of online music platform service (Table 1):

Table 1. Key evaluation index of online music platform service

Level indicators	The secondary indicators
Security A	Security of downloading stored music A1
	Security of identity information and authorization A2
	Market Regulation A3
Reliability B	System stability B1
	Disaster strategy B2
	Persistent B3
Interaction experience C	Mobile demand C1
	The user interface C2
	Response and transmission speed C3
Value-added features D	Function of privilege D1
	Privacy D2
Functionality E	Music search and share E1
	Backup synchronization E2
	Features E3
Guarantee F	Compensatory F1
	Version update F2
	Product brand and strength F3

3 Results Analysis

3.1 Indicator Analysis

According to the suggestion of Tinsley (1987), 85 samples will be considered in this paper, as the ratio between the number of questions and the number of samples is about 1:5–1:10. The created questionnaires will be distributed to full-time students through electronic questionnaires and other means. There are 89 questionnaires collected this time, all of which are valid. The results of the questionnaire were imported into SPSS 22.0 for reliability analysis and validity analysis. Reliability analysis is to determine the stability of the questionnaire by calculating the obtained data results and output data results. The evaluation results of the same survey object on the same index reflect the strength of the consistency trend. Cronbach α coefficient of the first-level indexes are respectively 0.972 for safety, 0.971 for reliability, 0.968 for use experience, 0.960 for value-added services, 0.975 for functionality and 0.973 for assurance. If the values of all indicators are greater than 0.9 and the overall questionnaire is also greater than 0.9, it can be verified that the reliability of the indicator system is extremely high. Validity, also known as validity, means the use of certain measurement methods and tools to measure the accuracy of the detected things. Each index in this paper is directly measured, and the main test is the content validity and structure validity of the questionnaire. KMO value is used to judge validity; common degree value is used to exclude unreasonable research items; variance interpretation rate value is used to illustrate the level of information extraction; factor loading coefficient is used to measure the corresponding relationship between factor (dimension) and item. KMO value is 0.744, greater than 0.6, indicating that data has validity. Therefore, the indexes determined in this paper are reasonable.

Secondly, the judgment matrix of evaluation index of network music platform is constructed, and the 1–9 scaling method proposed by T.L.ssty is used to conduct comparative analysis among various indicators. The weight of each indicator is shown in the table, and the CR value of consistency test is lower than 0.1, indicating good consistency.

Finally, it calculates the weight distribution of the second-level index in the first-level evaluation index and the weight distribution of the first-level evaluation index in the overall objective evaluation index. The product is the combined weight of the second-level evaluation index, as shown in the table, to determine the final weight of each index in the evaluation (Table 2).

Table 2. The weight of each level of indicators.

Level indicators	Weight right	The secondary indicators	Weight right	The comprehensive weights
A	0.33325	A1	0.14286	0.047608095
		A2	0.42857	0.142820953
		A3	0.42857	0.142820953
B	0.15462	B1	0.42857	0.066265493
		B2	0.14286	0.022089013
		B3	0.42857	0.066265493
C	0.06927	C1	0.2605	0.018044835
		C2	0.10616	0.007353703
		C3	0.63335	0.043872155
D	0.04619	D1	0.25	0.0115475
		D2	0.75	0.0346425
E	0.21993	E1	0.14286	0.0314192
		E2	0.42857	0.0942554
		E3	0.42857	0.0942554
F	0.17673	F1	0.42857	0.075741176
		F2	0.42857	0.075741176
		F3	0.14286	0.025247648

3.2 QoE Analysis

In the modern music dissemination way change trend, the expansion of market exploded, each big manufacturer began to flock to enter the market, and the competition is fierce, the manufacturers in order to fight for market limited customer successively introduced each has its own characteristic service, in order to stand out in a wave of music network platform. However, the features of these online music platforms are often very similar in functionality, which makes it difficult for consumers to choose between them in a chaotic and complex market.

In this paper, the representative online music platforms in China are netease cloud, QQ music and Kugou music. This paper will study and analyze the four representative service providers of network music service platform, including netease cloud, QQ music, Kugou music and Kuwo music.

After determining the sample, it is followed by a judgment score for each secondary index. The evaluators of this questionnaire survey are mainly frequent users of online music platforms, almost college students. This paper will publish questionnaires for each sample to conduct investigation and ensure validity.

In qualitative index of the evaluation, five-point scale is adopted for each secondary index to describe five-level degree of importance, we ranked according to their own understanding, to sample each to the importance of the evaluation index, and the reference index, score of each index, and then multiplied by the weight of the index and then it is concluded that the overall score, The scoring results of each index were weighted by 15 surveyors, and then the scores of each index were obtained by multiplying the weights of the corresponding indexes. Finally, the comprehensive scores were summarized (Table 3).

Table 3. Collected values of indicators.

The secondary indicators	Netease cloud	QQ music	Kuwo music	Kugou music
A1	4.5	4.4	4.3	4.3
A2	4.6	4.3	4.3	4.2
A3	3.8	3.2	3.5	3.3
B1	4.5	4.3	4.3	4.4
B2	4.1	4.0	3.8	3.7
B3	4.2	3.9	3.7	3.8
C1	4.6	4.5	4.2	4.3
C2	4.7	4.5	3.9	3.9
C3	3.7	3.8	3.2	3.5
D1	4.5	4.3	4.0	3.9
D2	4.5	4.4	4.0	3.9
E1	4.5	4.3	3.8	3.9
E2	4.3	4.2	4.0	4.1
E3	4.6	4.1	3.8	3.8
F1	3.9	4.0	4.1	4.2
F2	4.6	4.5	3.8	3.7
F3	4.3	4.1	3.5	3.4

Based on the collated data set, the score of each secondary index of the sample product is firstly calculated, and then the total score is calculated by weighting the score. Other sample products shall be settled according to this calculation method (Table 4):

Table 4. The scores of each secondary indicators.

Secondary indicators	Score	Netease cloud	QQ music	Kuwo Music	Kugou music
A1	0.047608095	0.214236428	0.209476	0.204715	0.204715
A2	0.142820953	0.656976384	0.61413	0.61413	0.599848
A3	0.142820953	0.542719621	0.457027	0.499873	0.471309
B1	0.066265493	0.298194719	0.284942	0.284942	0.291568
B2	0.022089013	0.090564953	0.088356	0.083938	0.081729
B3	0.066265493	0.278315071	0.258435	0.245182	0.251809
C1	0.018044835	0.083006241	0.081202	0.075788	0.077593
C2	0.007353703	0.034562404	0.033092	0.028679	0.028679
C3	0.043872155	0.162326974	0.166714	0.140391	0.153553
D1	0.0115475	0.05196375	0.049654	0.04619	0.045035
D2	0.0346425	0.15589125	0.152427	0.13857	0.135106
E1	0.0314192	0.1413864	0.135103	0.119393	0.122535
E2	0.0942554	0.40529822	0.395873	0.377022	0.386447
E3	0.0942554	0.43357484	0.386447	0.358171	0.358171
F1	0.075741176	0.295390586	0.302965	0.310539	0.318113
F2	0.075741176	0.34840941	0.340835	0.287816	0.280242
F3	0.025247648	0.108564886	0.103515	0.088367	0.085842

According to the index hierarchy design of the network music platform service evaluation index system, combined with the weight calculation results of the secondary indexes A1–F3, the results of the first-level index of the six network music platform services are calculated (Table 5):

Table 5. Comprehensive score of four popular music services.

	Netease cloud	QQ music	Kuwo Music	Kugou music
Security A	1.413932433	1.280632766	1.318718	1.275872
Reliability B	0.667074742	0.631733095	0.614062	0.625106
Interaction experience C	0.279895619	0.28100761	0.244859	0.259825
Value-added features D	0.207855	0.20208125	0.18476	0.180141
Functionality E	0.98025946	0.98025946	0.917422	0.854585
Guarantee F	0.752364882	0.752364882	0.747315	0.686722
Composite scores	4.301382136	4.128079063	4.027137	3.882251

In terms of the final comprehensive score, the highest score was 4.301382136 for netease Cloud, followed by 4.128079063 for QQ Music and 3.882251 for Kugou Music. Regardless of the comprehensive score, the first three indicators of service evaluation of all online music platforms are the same, namely, security, functionality and assurance. According to the survey score, college students pay more attention to the security, assurance and functionality of music platforms, and netease Cloud has the highest comprehensive score among the four music platforms. In addition, the results of this survey can not only provide users with reference for choosing online music platforms, but also enable online music platforms to know the advantages and disadvantages of their products and clarify the optimization direction, as well as provide indicator system reference for the latter to investigate and evaluate online music platform services.

4 Conclusion

With the rapid development of new media, the digital music industry is thriving, and the online music platform has become a hot topic of attention. College students as the main force of the use of network music platform, their music platform service evaluation for the future improvement of network music platform has a great impact. Therefore, it is of great value to discuss and study the factors of online music platform service that college students are concerned about. It can provide reference for the development of network music platform in the future.

This research establishes a set of objective evaluation index system for online music platform services. Taking Yiyun, QQ Music, Kuwo music and Kugou music as examples, the samples are collected by sending questionnaires to college students. Then the analytic hierarchy Process is used to calculate and analyze the samples, and finally the service scores of each online music platform are obtained.

References

1. Rahimi, R.A., Park, K.-H.: A comparative study of internet architecture and applications of online music streaming services: the impact on the global music industry growth. In: 2020 8th International Conference on Information and Communication Technology (ICoICT), pp. 1–6 (2020)
2. Chang, J., Liu, S., Huang, H., Qi, D., Zhao, Z.: Study on online music business model innovation based on value chain theory. In: 2016 International Conference on Logistics, Informatics and Service Sciences, pp. 1–6 (2016)
3. Xu, C., Zhu, Y., Feng, D.D.: Content protection and usage control for digital music. In: Proceedings First International Conference on WEB Delivering of Music. WEDELMUSIC 2001, pp. 43–50 (2001)
4. Chen, M., Lin, K.C., Kung, C., Chou, C., Tu, C.: On the design of the semantic P2P system for music recommendation. In: International Symposium on Parallel and Distributed Processing with Applications, pp. 442–448 (2010)
5. Rui, S., Jiaji, Z.: Research on influencing factors of user satisfaction of interactive online music platform. Econ. Res. Rev. 32, 157–159 (2018). (in Chinese)
6. Yuling, F., Shengli, D., Lina, Y.: Research on comprehensive evaluation method of user experience in information interaction. J. Inf. Resour. Manag. 1, 38–43 (2015)

7. Kong, F., Liu, H.: Analysis of and improvement on ranking method for fuzzy AHP. In: 2006 6th World Congress on Intelligent Control and Automation, pp. 2498–2502 (2006)
8. Razali, S.N., Shahbodin, F.: Questionnaire on perception of online collaborative learning: measuring validity and reliability using rasch model. In: 2016 4th International Conference on User Science and Engineering (i-USEr), pp. 199–203 (2016)
9. Suradi, N.R.M., Kahar, S., Jamaludin, N.A.A.: Validation of a web-based integrated student assessment application questionnaire in public institution: a rasch analysis approach. In: 2020 6th International Conference on Interactive Digital Media (ICIDM), pp. 1–5 (2020)
10. Youssef, Y.B., Afif, M., Tabbane, S.: Novel AHP-based QoE factors' selection approach. In: 2016 IEEE/ACS 13th International Conference of Computer Systems and Applications (AICCSA), pp. 1–6 (2016)
11. Kai, Z.: Competitiveness analysis of O2O online group buying platform based on Likert scale and AHP. J. Kunming Cadre Acad. Natl. **2016**(10), 64 (2016). (in Chinese)
12. Tang Yuanyi, H., Qingfeng, L.Y.: A new scale method of analytic hierarchy process. J. Ezhou Univ. **2005**(6), 40–41 (2005)

Target Detection and Machine Learning

A Crop Disease Recognition Algorithm Based on Machine Learning

Yuchao Zhou, Kailiang Zhang$^{(\boxtimes)}$, Yi Shi, and Ping Cui

Jiangsu Province Key Laboratory of Intelligent Industry Control Technology,
Xuzhou University of Technology, Xuzhou 221018, China
zhangkailiang@xzit.edu.cn

Abstract. There are many related diseases in the process of crop planting, which reduces the quality and yield of crops. Faced with such a situation, the prevention of crop diseases has become a hot spot and has broad application prospects. This experiment uses the image recognition technology of machine vision to analyze and recognize crop diseases. Based on the features of machine vision that can capture details that cannot be observed by the human eye, with high accuracy and high efficiency, it provides accurate image recognition of crop diseases. In accordance with. In the process of selecting the SVM classifier for image classification, the kernel function and gamma parameters in the classifier were adjusted, and the kernel function and high accuracy parameter interval suitable for crop disease analysis were found.

Keywords: Machine learning · Crop disease recognition · Support vector machine

1 Introduction

Our country is the country with the largest population in the world and a large agricultural country. The quality and output of crops are related to my country's economic lifeline and the people's living foundation. However, crop diseases will lead to a decline in plant viability, thereby affecting yield. Traditional crop diseases mainly rely on manual field identification, which not only takes time and effort, but also has low accuracy. Without accurate and quantitative standards, manual identification requires accumulation of experience, and often cannot be accurate in time when crops have problems. To judge and deal with different situations locally, these shortcomings have seriously affected the development of agricultural modernization [1, 2]. As a relatively mature advanced technology, machine learning technology, combined with agricultural knowledge, uses image recognition technology to make accurate judgments of crop diseases, which can then be controlled and processed to increase crop yields [3–5].

SVM classifier is used as the main classification technology for image recognition. The investigation found that due to the huge difference between the image features automatically extracted by the computer and the semantics understood by humans, the

D. Jiang and H. Song (Eds.): SIMUtools 2021, LNICST 424, pp. 513–522, 2022.
https://doi.org/10.1007/978-3-030-97124-3_38

results of image retrieval are unsatisfactory. Relevant feedback methods have appeared in recent years [6]. Using SVM as the classifier, the positive and negative samples marked by the user are learned in each feedback, and retrieval is performed according to the learned model. Relevant researchers used an image library composed of 9918 images to conduct experiments, and the results showed that this method has a good generalization function in the case of limited training samples [7]. Because SVM is analyzed for the linearly separable situation. For the case of linear inseparability, the non-linearly inseparable samples in the low-dimensional input space are converted into high-dimensional feature spaces by using the nonlinear mapping algorithm to make them linearly separable, so that the linear algorithm is nonlinear to the samples in the high-dimensional feature space [8, 9]. It is possible to perform linear analysis of features. And based on the theory of structural risk minimization, it constructs the optimal classification surface in the feature space, so that the learner can get the global optimization, and the expected risk of the entire sample space meets a certain upper bound with a certain probability [10]. From the above two basic ideas, SVM does not use the traditional derivation process, which simplifies the usual classification and regression problems: a small number of support vectors determine the final decision function of the SVM, and the complexity of the calculation depends on the support vector, and Instead of the entire sample space, this can avoid the "curse of dimensionality". A small number of support vectors determine the final result, which not only helps us to grasp the key samples, but also destined that the method is not only simple in algorithm, but also has good "robustness".

In recent years, there have been some researches on crop disease identification. Literature [11] uses a variety of plant diseases and pests for analysis and research, and expands the practical field by modifying model parameters, saving time. However, the accuracy needs to be improved. Literature [12] studies image processing techniques for identifying and classifying symptoms of fungal diseases on different agricultural and horticultural crops. However, the early detection and classification of fungal diseases and their related symptoms need to be improved. Literature [13] studies, trains and tests a deep learning model with high accuracy. However, object-oriented is relatively large, and its wide popularization needs to be studied. In reference [14], a mechanism for dynamic analysis of disease images is provided, which is fast. However, the actual accuracy needs to be further tested. In literature [15], a customized efficient memory convolution neural network is proposed for automatic detection of rice grain diseases, with good classification and accuracy. However, the applicability of other crops needs to be studied. Some authors have also studied the expert system for identifying crop diseases [16] and the grading system for identifying diseases on a given image set [17], and achieved some results. However, the relevant model mechanism needs to be further improved. Some authors have proposed algorithms and mechanisms in the application of convolutional neural network to automatic identification of crop diseases [18, 19], but the accuracy and classification level need to be improved. During the image recognition process, it was found that different kernel function selections in SVM have an impact on feature description, and the relevant gamma parameters in the kernel function were experimentally studied. It was found that the RBF kernel function training obtained the highest matching degree in crop disease recognition [20]. And find out the parameter interval with high matching degree among the gamma parameters.

2 System Model

The experiment chooses the SVM classifier, which can segment the positive and negative examples in the sample set by finding the hyperplane of the sample set. SVM is developed from the optimal classification surface in the case of linear separability. The problems that can be solved are linear separable, approximately linear separable and nonlinear separable. Linear separability means that two types of samples can be completely separated with a linear function; in the case of non-linear separability, an adjustable error penalty coefficient c will be introduced to find the best classification hyperplane. However, in many classification situations, linear classifiers have limitations. Relaxation of constraints for nonlinear problems is prone to a large number of sample misclassification errors. Therefore, it is necessary to map the nonlinear problem to a linear in a high-dimensional space through nonlinear mapping. Improvement of separable problems. Therefore, the SVM with kernel function mapping is introduced SVM [21]. The four kernel function formulas of the classifier are as follows.

Linear function formula:

$$K(x, y) = x \cdot y \tag{1}$$

Polynomial kernel function:

$$K(x, y) = (\gamma(x \cdot y) + r)^d, d = 1, 2, \cdots, N \tag{2}$$

Radial basis (RBF) kernel function formula:

$$K(x, y) = \exp\left(-\gamma \|x - y\|^2\right) \tag{3}$$

Sigmoid kernel function formula:

$$K(x, y) = \tanh(\gamma(x \cdot y) + r) \tag{4}$$

Since the image recognition problem in this experiment is a two-classification problem, briefly describe the two-class SVM algorithm. The image sample training set is $D = \{(x_1, y_1), \cdots, (x_i, y_i), \cdots, (x_n, y_n)\}$, where $x_i \in \chi = R^d$, $y_i \in \gamma = \{-1, +1\}$, n are sample dimensions, d is the sample dimension, $x_i = (x_{i1}, x_{i2}, \cdots, x_{id})^T$ is the i-th sample, and y_i is the corresponding label:

Define hyperplane formula:

$$\omega^T + b = 0 \tag{5}$$

Where $\omega = (\omega_1, \omega_2, \ldots, \omega_d)^T$ is the normal vector of the hyperplane, b is the intercept. The classification decision function:

$$f(x_i) = sign\left(\omega^T x_i + b\right) \tag{6}$$

Where $sign()$ is the symbolic function:

Support vector machines are divided into two categories: linear and nonlinear. When linearly separable, the algorithm is as follows:

Normalize, set constraints:

$$y_i\left(\omega^T x_i + b\right) \geq 1, i = 1, \ldots, n \qquad (7)$$

Maximize the distance between classes is $\frac{2}{||\omega||}$:

$$\min_{\omega, b} \quad \tfrac{1}{2}||\omega||^2 \qquad (8)$$
$$\text{subject to } y_i(\omega^T x_i + b) \geq 1, i = 1, \ldots, n$$

Construct Lagrangian function, construct and solve convex quadratic programming problem:

$$L(\omega, b, a) = \frac{1}{2}||\omega||^2 + \sum_{i=1}^{n} \alpha_i \left[1 - y_i\left(\omega^T x_i + b\right)\right] \qquad (9)$$

Where $\alpha_i \geq 0$ is the Lagrange multiplier.
Take the derivative of $L(\omega, b, \alpha)$ with respect to ω and b and assign it to 0:

$$\begin{cases} \frac{\partial L}{\partial \varphi} = 0 \\ \frac{\partial L}{\partial b} = 0 \end{cases} \rightarrow \begin{cases} \omega = \sum_{i=1}^{n} \alpha_i y_i x_i \\ \sum_{i=1}^{n} \alpha_i y_i = 0 \end{cases} \qquad (10)$$

Finally, organize (4) into:

$$\max_{\alpha} \quad \sum_{i=1}^{n} \alpha_i - \frac{1}{2} \sum_{i=1}^{n} \alpha_i \alpha_j y_i y_j x_i^T x_j$$
$$\text{subject to } \sum_{i=1}^{n} \alpha_i y_i = 0$$
$$\alpha_i \geq 0, i = 1, \ldots, n \qquad (11)$$

Formula (7) has a unique solution $\alpha^* = (\alpha_1^*, \ldots, \alpha_n^*)^T$, get $\omega^* = \sum_{i=1}^{n} \alpha_i^* y_i x_i$ and $b^* = y_i - \sum_{i=1}^{n} \alpha_i^* y_i x_i^T x_j$
Get the final classification function:

$$f(x) = sign\left[\left((\omega^*)^T x + b^*\right)\right] = sign\left(\sum_{i=1}^{*} \alpha_i^* y_i x_i^T x + b^*\right) \qquad (12)$$

For nonlinear problems, nonlinear mapping is introduced to solve them. At this time, the sample does not satisfy the constraint conditions in the case of linear separability. The new constraint conditions are as follows:

$$y_i\left(\omega^T x_i + b\right) \geq 1 - \xi_i, i = 1, \ldots, n \qquad (13)$$

Constrained optimization:

$$\min_{\phi, b} \quad \frac{1}{2}||\omega||^2 + C \sum_{i=1}^{n} \xi_i$$
$$\text{subject to } y_i\left(\omega^T x_i + b\right) \geq 1 - \xi_i,$$
$$\xi_i \geq 0, i = 1, \ldots, n \qquad (14)$$

Among them, $C > 0$ is the penalty parameter, the larger the C value, the greater the cost.

Construct Lagrangian function, construct and solve convex quadratic programming problem, after introducing nonlinear mapping, the final classification function is:

$$\max_{\alpha} \sum_{i=1}^{n} \alpha_i - \frac{1}{2}\sum\sum \alpha_i\alpha_j y_i y_j K(x_i, x_j)$$
$$subject\ to\ \sum_{i=1}^{n} \alpha_i y_i = 0$$
$$0 \le \alpha_i \le C, i = 1, 2, \ldots, n \quad (15)$$

In the low-dimensional space, the inner product operation is completed through the kernel function, and the nonlinear classification function is obtained:

$$f(x) = sign\left[\left((\omega^*)^T \phi(x) + b^*\right)\right] = sign\left(\sum_{i=1}^{n} \alpha_i^* y_i K(x_i, x) + b^*\right) \quad (16)$$

3 Parameter Optimization

3.1 Key Parameter Analysis

The Gamma parameter is a parameter that comes with the function after selecting the RBF function as the kernel. It implicitly determines the distribution of the data after mapping to the new feature space. The larger the gamma, the fewer the support vectors, and the smaller the gamma value, the more support vectors. The number of support vectors affects the speed of training and prediction.

3.2 Optimization Experiment

We selected the diseases that tomatoes in the crops may suffer from during the cultivation process and tested them. Using the collected tomato diseases as a data set, we conducted training tests on different kernel functions, predicted the same disease map, and recorded the matching of each category. The greater the matching degree, the more consistent the feature points are (Tables 1, 2, 3, 4 and 5).

Table 1. Umbilical rot test data sheet

Serial number	Kernel function	Hollow fruit	Umbilical rot	Botrytis	Soft rot	Leaf mold	Result
1	LINEAR	−1.03413	−0.986507	−0.999999	−1.00081	−1	Correct
2	POLY	−1.0127	−0.99561	−1.00193	−1	−1.0021	Correct
3	RBF	−1.06445	−0.973202	−1	−1.00163	−1	Correct
4	SIGMOID	−0.97682	−1.02455	−0.985664	−1.01534	−0.987585	Wrong

Table 2. Leaf mold test data sheet

Serial number	Kernel function	Hollow fruit	Umbilical rot	Botrytis	Soft rot	Leaf mold	Result
1	LINEAR	−1.00965	−1.00383	−0.997917	−0.999992	−0.99505	Correct
2	POLY	−1.00345	−1.00166	−0.998995	−1	−0.998132	Correct
3	RBF	−1.01885	−1.00755	−0.996097	−0.999981	−0.990068	Correct
4	SIGMOID	−1.06562	−1.00243	−1.03528	−1.03178	−1.0364	Wrong

Table 3. Gray mold test data sheet

Serial number	Kernel function	Hollow fruit	Umbilical rot	Botrytis	Soft rot	Leaf mold	Result
1	LINEAR	−1.02671	−1.00132	−0.993519	−0.999949	−1.00033	Correct
2	POLY	−1.00978	−1.00077	−0.998458	−1	−1.00023	Correct
3	RBF	−1.0516	−1.00252	−0.986959	−0.999988	−1.00067	Correct
4	SIGMOID	−1.00465	−0.998737	−1.01102	−1.01893	−1	Wrong

Table 4. Hollow fruit test data sheet

Serial number	Kernel function	Hollow fruit	Umbilical rot	Botrytis	Soft rot	Leaf mold	Result
1	LINEAR	−0.993842	−0.997809	−1.00205	−1.00083	−1.00017	Correct
2	POLY	−0.999627	−0.998101	−1.00121	−1.00096	−1.00084	Wrong
3	RBF	−0.988151	−0.995578	−1.00411	−1.00196	−1.00027	Correct
4	SIGMOID	−1.26598	−1.04431	−1.04837	−1.08427	−1.069	Wrong

Table 5. Soft rot test data sheet

Serial number	Kernel function	Hollow fruit	Umbilical rot	Botrytis	Soft rot	Leaf mold	Result
1	LINEAR	−1	−1.00003	−0.999999	−0.998154	−1.00038	Correct
2	POLY	−1	−1	−1	−0.999891	−1.00006	Correct
3	RBF	−1	−0.999993	−1	−0.996123	−1.00043	Correct
4	SIGMOID	−1.1057	−1.03209	−1.03451	−1.08342	−1.04455	Wrong

From the results of testing and comparing the records of five different diseases, it is found that the kernel function LINEAR and the kernel function SIGMOID are still lacking in the accuracy rate, and the kernel function POLY and the kernel function RBF have a certain degree of accuracy. By comparing the matching degree of the kernel function POLY and the kernel function RBF in each disease, it is found that the matching degree obtained by using the RBF kernel function will be relatively accurate.

Then, in the research, it was found that the gamma parameter in SVM has a certain influence on the matching degree of RBF, and the parameter was tested and researched. The result of the research is shown in Fig. 1.

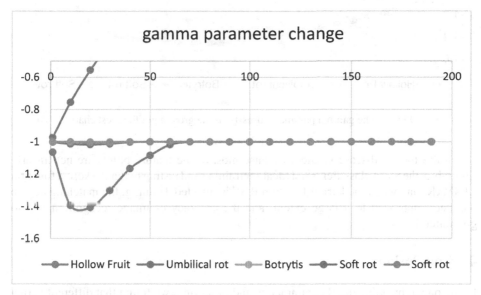

Fig. 1. The gamma parameter takes 1 as the growth gradient test chart

The selected research test picture is the tomato umbilical rot map. After a large number of data tests, it is found that the matching degree of this category is steadily increasing, and there is a significant gap with other categories. Through this test result, it is found that the greater the gamma parameter, the higher the matching degree. It can be inferred that when the gamma parameter approaches a certain value, the recognition result will be the most accurate. Furthermore, large-parameter research on gamma parameters is carried out, and the test data diagram is shown in Fig. 2.

Through the test, it is found that the larger the gamma parameter, the higher the matching degree, which is the same as the guess, but the improvement of the matching degree is not obvious when the parameter increases, and the gradual smoothing no longer has a significant improvement. The test found that the best parameter interval is 140 to 160. The gamma parameter in this interval will make the recognition of image recognition reach the best state, and it is found that there is a clear difference compared to other categories.

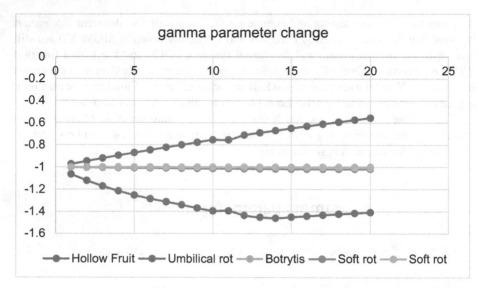

Fig. 2. The gamma parameter uses 10 as the growth gradient test chart

In the tomato disease studied, because most of the feature points are not linearly separable, the SVM classifier is not ideal for training and testing under the kernel function LINVAR, and when the kernel function RBF is selected Training, the matching degree has been improved to a large extent, and the accuracy of image recognition is also guaranteed.

4 Conclusion

In the paper, by adjusting the parameters and observing, we found that different kernel functions have an impact on the feature description of crop disease when training the model of the SVM classifier. After experiments, we found that the matching degree obtained by selecting the kernel function RBF is relatively accurate. However, in the process of understanding the kernel function RBF, it is found that the parameter gamma has a certain influence on the matching degree obtained by it, so the parameter is tested and studied.

After testing, it is found that under the training of the kernel function RBF, the effect of tomato disease recognition is the best, and it is found that when the gamma parameter is selected in the interval 140 to160, the accuracy of image recognition will be improved. In future research, we can also strengthen the preprocessing of disease images, taking into account the feature extraction of different attributes during image processing from multiple aspects, thereby improving the accuracy and efficiency of image recognition.

References

1. Kulkarni, O.: Crop disease detection using deep learning. In: International Conference on Computing Communication Control and Automation (ICCUBEA), pp. 1–4 (2018)

2. Zhu, S., Zhang, J., Shuai, G., Hongli, L., Zhang, F., Dong, Z.: Autumn crop mapping based on deep learning method driven by historical labelled dataset. In: IEEE International Geoscience and Remote Sensing Symposium, pp. 4669–4672 (2020)
3. Kalimuthu, M., Vaishnavi, P., Kishore, M.: Crop prediction using machine learning. In: International Conference on Smart Systems and Inventive Technology (ICSSIT), pp. 926–932 (2020)
4. Medar, R., Rajpurohit, V.S., Shweta, S.: Crop yield prediction using machine learning techniques. In: IEEE 5th International Conference for Convergence in Technology (I2CT), pp. 1–5 (2019)
5. Xu, Q., Zhang, J., Zhang, F., Zhu, S.: Develop large-area autumn crop type product using a deep learning strategy. In: IEEE International Geoscience and Remote Sensing Symposium, pp. 4673–4676 (2020)
6. Singh, J., Mahapatra, A., Basu, S., Banerjee, B.: Assessment of Sentinel-1 and Sentinel-2 satellite imagery for crop classification in Indian region during Kharif and Rabi crop cycles. In: IEEE International Geoscience and Remote Sensing Symposium, pp. 3720–3723 (2019)
7. Kumar, A., Sarkar, S., Pradhan, C.: Recommendation system for crop identification and pest control technique in agriculture. In: International Conference on Communication and Signal Processing (ICCSP), pp. 0185–0189 (2019)
8. Verma, G., Taluja, C., Saxena, A.K.: Vision based detection and classification of disease on rice crops using convolutional neural network. In: International Conference on Cutting-Edge Technologies in Engineering (ICon-CuTE), pp. 1–4 (2019)
9. Kang, J., Zhang, H., Yang, H., Zhang, L.: Support vector machine classification of crop lands using Sentinel-2 imagery. In: International Conference on Agro-geoinformatics (Agro-geoinformatics), pp. 1–6 (2018)
10. Chu, H., Zhang, D., Shao, Y., Chang, Z., Guo, Y., Zhang, N.: Using HOG descriptors and UAV for crop pest monitoring. In: Chinese Automation Congress (CAC), pp. 1516–1519 (2018)
11. Hu, H., Su, C., Yu, P.: Research on pest and disease recognition algorithms based on convolutional neural network. In: International Conference on Virtual Reality and Intelligent Systems (ICVRIS), pp. 166–168 (2019)
12. Pujari, J.D., Yakkundimath, R., Byadgi, A.S.: Identification and classification of fungal disease affected on agriculture/horticulture crops using image processing techniques. In: IEEE International Conference on Computational Intelligence and Computing Research, pp. 1–4 (2014)
13. Militante, S.V., Gerardo, B.D., Medina, R.P.: Sugarcane disease recognition using deep learning. In: IEEE Eurasia Conference on IOT, Communication and Engineering (ECICE), pp. 575–578 (2019)
14. Park, H., Eun, J., Kim, S.: Image-based disease diagnosing and predicting of the crops through the deep learning mechanism. In: International Conference on Information and Communication Technology Convergence (ICTC), pp. 129–131 (2017)
15. Emon, S.H., Mridha, M.A.H., Shovon, M.: Automated recognition of rice grain diseases using deep learning. In: International Conference on Electrical and Computer Engineering (ICECE), pp. 230–233 (2020)
16. Prashar, K., Talwar, R., Kant, C.: CNN based on overlapping pooling method and multi-layered learning with SVM & KNN for American cotton leaf disease recognition. In: International Conference on Automation, Computational and Technology Management (ICACTM), pp. 330–333 (2019)
17. Nikhitha, M., Roopa Sri, S., Uma Maheswari, B.: Fruit recognition and grade of disease detection using inception V3 model. In: Communication and Aerospace Technology (ICECA), pp. 1040–1043 (2019)
18. Ai, Y., Sun, C., Tie, J., Cai, X.: Research on recognition model of crop diseases and insect pests based on deep learning in harsh environments. IEEE Access **8**, 171686–171693 (2020)

19. Genaev, M., Ekaterina, S., Afonnikov, D.: Application of neural networks to image recognition of wheat rust diseases. In: Genomics and Bioinformatics (CSGB), pp. 40–42 (2020)
20. Liu, J., Lv, F., Di, P.: Identification of sunflower leaf diseases based on random forest algorithm. In: Automation and Systems (ICICAS), pp. 459–463 (2019)
21. Zhu, S., Xu, C., Wang, J., Xiao, Y., Ma, F.: Research and application of combined kernel SVM in dynamic voiceprint password authentication system. In: IEEE 9th International Conference on Communication Software and Networks (ICCSN), pp. 1052–1055 (2017)

Optimization of Loss Function for Pedestrian Detection

Shuo Zhang[1], Kailiang Zhang[1]($\boxtimes$), Yuan An[1], Shuo Li[1], Yong Sun[1], Weiwei Liu[2], and Likai Wang[2]

[1] Jiangsu Province Key Laboratory of Intelligent Industry Control Technology, Xuzhou University of Technology, Xuzhou 221018, China
zhangkailiang@xzit.edu.cn
[2] Traffic Police Detachment, Xuzhou Police Bureau, Xuzhou 221002, China

Abstract. The advanced intelligent driving assistance system has improved the current traffic congestion to a great extent and effectively reduced frequent traffic safety accidents. Pedestrian detection technology is the core of autonomous driving technology, and its accuracy, real-time and complexity will directly determine the safe operation of autonomous driving. In the case of heavy traffic, detecting a single pedestrian in a crowd is still a challenging problem. Considering the problem of mutual occlusion between pedestrians in dense crowds, an improved function algorithm based on YOLOv3 is proposed to optimize the loss function and increase the accuracy of detection by replacing the anchor frame. Experimental results show that this method can effectively reduce the missed detection rate, increase the average accuracy, and help improve the effectiveness of pedestrian occlusion detection, ensure accurate pedestrian detection in traffic congestion scenarios, and ensure driving safety.

Keywords: Computer vision · Deep learning · Pedestrian detection · Loss function

1 Introduction

With the development of urbanization, the density of urban population and vehicles continues to increase, and the frequency of traffic accidents is gradually increasing. Therefore, how to effectively reduce traffic accidents and ensure traffic safety has become an urgent social problem to be solved. Some new network technologies and communication methods have been proposed [1, 2], network quality and experience have been continuously improved [3, 4], and intelligent driving systems have also been continuously improved. In road traffic, pedestrians are a disadvantaged group because they are more casual and active than car driving. Reducing the driving pressure of drivers and ensuring the safety of pedestrians are important goals in the design of urban traffic systems and intelligent driving systems to ensure pedestrian safety and reduce the occurrence of traffic accidents. The information around the car is collected through multiple sensors. The smart routing technology can transmit this information in real time [5, 6]. After intelligent

D. Jiang and H. Song (Eds.): SIMUtools 2021, LNICST 424, pp. 523–531, 2022.
https://doi.org/10.1007/978-3-030-97124-3_39

analysis and big data processing in cloud platform [7–10], the key information of pedestrian dynamics will be detected and fed back to the system. Then the system accurately provides the driver with road condition information, so that the driver can accurately and timely grasp the pedestrian movement information, and avoid pedestrian collision accidents caused by negligence. Of course, in an emergency, the driver does not need to operate the intelligent driving system and take mandatory safety measures to ensure that dangerous accidents can be stopped in time. The scene of pedestrian detection is very complicated. First, compared with vehicles, the postures of pedestrians are diverse and uncertain. Current pedestrian detection methods cannot fully adapt to these changes. However, based on the energy efficient transmission approaches, the complex algorithm can be deployed in mobile devices [11–14]. In a busy traffic environment, interference factors such as the mutual influence between characters, occlusion and changes in ambient light perception need to improve the accuracy of detection and recognition, and the algorithm structure is usually more complicated. Pedestrian detection technology is an indispensable key part in the field of self driving. It is a solid foundation to ensure driving safety and promote the development of intelligent transportation, and has important practical significance.

2 Related Work

So far, pedestrian detection technology has been developed for many years, and many research institutions and industries have achieved many outstanding research results. Some scholars [15] proposed a depth separable convolution model from the perspective of large background changes, overlaps or serious obstacles, which are optimized using different single-shot detector frameworks and have good reliability. Some scholars [16] proposed an improved R-CNN pedestrian retrieval framework, optimized the distance function, constructed the network using regions, and improved the hybrid similarity distance function. The experimental results show that compared with traditional methods, the learning ability has been enhanced, and has a certain driving performance. Some scholars [17] studied a pedestrian detection and recognition method based on deep learning from the perspective of active safety, which improved the speed and efficiency. Literature [18] proposed an integrated learning method and used structured learning optimization. At the same time, a visual feature extraction method based on spatial pooling is proposed. In the case of continuous translation, some improvements have been made in robustness. However, this method is still in the laboratory verification stage, and its application in actual scenarios has not yet been developed. Literature [19, 20] based on the detection model of YOLO, the network structure is light and the computing power is low, the detection efficiency is guaranteed, and there is a certain anti-collision function display, but the interference effect in complex scenes needs to be improved. With the development of deep learning, more and more scholars have gradually improved pedestrian detection [21, 22]. Whether it is the detection of small and medium-sized SSDs or the optimized PVANet to generate function maps, it will further improve accuracy and optimize performance. Literature [23] proposed a multi-class pedestrian detection network based on the fast R-CNN neural network, which detects different types of targets. In the training phase, multiple classification layers are defined. However, laboratory conditions have certain limitations. The methods and models proposed in [24–26] are aimed at crowded pedestrian scenes. Pedestrian detection methods based on deep convolutional neural networks, Gaussian mixture models, HOG feature extraction and SVM classification can make full use of them. These methods continuously improve the performance of the model and can bring some optimization ideas, but they require constant running-in. The methods and models proposed by scholars [27, 28] have good performance in detection accuracy and processing speed. However, the impact of missed detection rate needs to be further optimized. In smart driving scenarios, pedestrian detection is an important task in applications such as monitoring driver assistance systems and autonomous driving. Detection and recognition models based on deep neural networks have been continuously proposed [24, 29]. In intelligent driving, an early warning mechanism needs to be established to ensure driving safety. In addition to the safety of the driver, pedestrians are also detected to ensure their safety. The efficiency of image processing and the accuracy of target detection are the first problems to be solved [30, 31]. In summary, a real-time and accurate pedestrian detection method is proposed, which is consistent with the development trend of intelligent driving. In particular, the security early warning mechanism in dense scenarios requires the higher recognition accuracy and lower time cost.

3   Model

The YOLO algorithm avoids the use of sliding windows for target detection. The feature is extracted through the Darknet-53 backbone network to obtain the image feature map with a size of N × N. YOLOv3 retrieves targets in three different scale feature maps. The range is determined to be 13 × 13 to detect large targets, the range is 26 × 26 to detect medium targets, and the range of 52 × 52 feature maps are responsible for searching and detecting other types. Through multiple detections of the target, the detection rate is improved. When predicting the bounding box, the dimensional cluster is used to anchor the box.

3.1   Darknet-53

The backbone network has been modified to Darknet-53, and its important feature is the use of Residual Network Residual. Its network structure is shown in Fig. 1.

It can be seen from Fig. 1 that there is only a convolutional layer in the model, and the size of the output feature map is controlled by adjusting the volume base layer step. There is no special restriction on the size of the input image. Using the idea of pyramid feature maps, small-size feature maps are used to detect large-size objects, while on the contrary, large-size feature maps are used to detect small-size objects. The output dimension of the feature map is N * N * [3 * (4 + 1 + 80)], where N * N is the number of grid points of the output feature map, there are three Anchor boxes, and each box has a 4-dimensional prediction box value, a 1-dimensional prediction box confidence, and the number of 80-dimensional object categories.

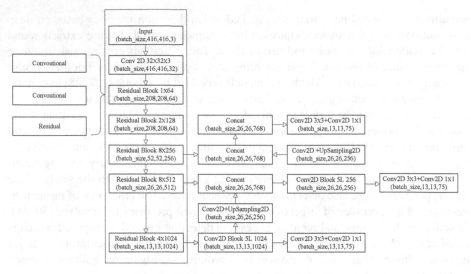

Fig. 1. Network Structure of Darknet-53.

3.2 Loss Function

In actual training, the loss function is lost by target positioning, position loss is used for translation operations, and size loss is used for retracting operations. For more pedestrians in dense scenes, Wang's team [37] can use the repulsive loss function to reduce the loss value, which refers to the characteristics of the magnet. $L = L_{Attr} + \gamma L_{RepGT} + \omega L_{RepBox}$ with L_{Attr} is to attract losses, said forecasting and loss between the real box, box with the real loss value is smaller that predict box the closer. In order to keep the prediction box as far away as possible from other target boxes and the prediction box of these target boxes which can affect it, the exclusion loss is proposed. The second part is the loss value produced by the prediction frame of the prediction frame and the adjacent real target, and the third part is the loss value produced by the prediction frame and the adjacent frame that are not predicting the same real target. Pass two correlation coefficients. Gamma and Omega are used to balance the loss of the second and third parts. γ and ω are the weight factors of repulsive force loss. The specific model is shown in Eq. (1).

$$L_{Attr} = \frac{\sum_{P \in P_+} Smooth_{L1}(B^P, G^P_{Attr})}{|P_+|} \tag{1}$$

In Formula (1), P represents candidate boxes, and represents all candidate boxes whose intersection with the real box is greater than the threshold value. G^P_{Attr} represents the real box with the maximum IOU with the candidate box, and B^P represents the prediction box regression from the candidate box. Finally, $Smooth_{L1}$ is used to establish the regression loss function, and the model is shown in Eq. (2).

$$L_{RepGT} = \frac{\sum_{P \in P_+} Smooth_{\ln}(IOG(B^P, G^P_{Rep}))}{|P_+|} \tag{2}$$

In Eq. (2), G^P_{Rep} and B^P represent the real box and prediction box of other surrounding targets respectively. When the overlap is larger, the function value is larger. If IOG is used in the overlap calculation; there is only one way to reduce the loss function, that is, to reduce the overlap value between the prediction box and other surrounding target boxes, so that the two boxes are as far away as possible. In general, the fewer methods, the better the function optimization.

4 Function Optimization

In order to optimize the detection performance of YOLOV3 in dense crowds, we add two exclusions to the original YOLOV3 loss function. Specifically, in the increased rejection loss, the available loss function is included in these three parts, mainly to improve the target positioning loss. The repulsion function is aimed at the target detection algorithm based on the area candidate frame. The target detection algorithm based on the anchor frame is adopted here. The anchor frame is obtained by comparing the training data clustering. The positioning loss of the two algorithms in the loss function it is consistent with the attraction loss of Repulsion in the loss function, that is, the purpose is to make the prediction of the frame close to the true value of the match. In the original Repulsion loss function refers to the real match on G^P_{Attr} box, matching the real box is expressed as $G^P_{Attr} = \arg\max_{G \in g} IOU(G, P)$ which P said candidate box, G said real box, $g = \{G\}$ said all of the real target box in A picture. In Yolov3, anchor boxes are used instead of candidate boxes. We introduce the repulsive force loss $L_R \text{ep} GT$ into the loss function of Yolov3, with the purpose of moving the prediction box away from the real box of the surrounding targets. In order to be better applied in the algorithm, the following improvements are made to the exclusion loss function as $G^P_{Attr} = \arg\max_{G \in g} IOU(G, P)$, the loss of Repulsion, P for candidates, and only exist in the YOLOv3 anchor box, according to the repulsive force loss function design idea, the anchor box is similar to the original candidate box in the loss function. When the candidate box is replaced with the anchor box, the target box in the attraction loss is represented as the true box with the largest IOU in the anchor box. The function model is shown in Eq. (3).

$$G^A_{Rep} = \mathrm{argmax}_{G \in g} IOU(G, A) \tag{3}$$

In Eq. (3), A is the anchor box, then the other surrounding real target boxes are expressed as $G^A_{Rep} = \arg\max_{G \in g\{G^A_{Attr}\}}$, so the new rejection loss function is shown in Eq. (4).

$$L_{RepGT'} = \frac{\sum_{A \in A_+} Smooth_{\ln}(IOG(B^A, G^A_{Rep}))}{|A_+|} \tag{4}$$

In Eq. (4), the anchor frame representing all matched true frames. If the rejection loss is designed in this way, the following situations will occur: the direction of the adjustment of the prediction box has a great relationship with the position of the anchor box, and the selection of other real targets around it will have a large probability of vote difference. In the intelligent driving dense crowd scene, matching the targets that

Fig. 2. Schematic diagrams of other real boxes around (Color figure online)

may exist around the anchor frame, this overlapping structure between them can be seen everywhere, and the result is shown in Fig. 2.

In Fig. 2, the green box is three real boxes, indicating that the red box matches the real target in the middle of the anchor box. If only the intersection of the anchor box and other real boxes is used to mark other real boxes, then the other real boxes on the right side of the pedestrian are the surrounding real boxes, so the exclusion loss can only be suppressed to intersect with the anchor frame on the right side of the box, but in the above case. The woman on the left side of the pedestrian frame will affect the reverse of the predicted frame, so the repulsive loss can only suppress the intersection with the anchor frame on the right side of the box.

5   Function Optimization

Caltech pedestrian data set is used in the training set, and the IOU threshold of the selected anchor frame is set to 0.5 during training. In which function $Smooth_{\ln}(x)$, parameter n = 1. The model trains 100 epochs. The trained models are tested in three subsets: Resonable, Occ = none and Occ = partical. In order to verify the effectiveness of the loss function, the original loss function is modified in different degrees. Firstly, the addition of the original loss function is the repulsive force loss of other real frames around the anchor frame that the prediction frame principle is close to the matched anchor frame, and the loss function is denoted as $L_{RepGT\_}tran01$; Secondly, the prediction box is added into the loss function, which is far away from and close to other real boxes around the match on the real, and the loss function is denoted as $L_{RepGT\_}tran02$; Finally, two repulsive force loss functions are added to the original loss function, denote as $L_{RepGT\_}tran$. LAMR(log average miss-rate) values are compared as shown in Table 1.

Table 1. Comparison of LAMR values.

Subset	LOYO v3	L_{RepGT}_tran01	L_{RepGT}_tran02	L_{RepGT}_tran
Resonable	32.36%	31.20%	29.61%	27.28%
Occ = none	30.24%	29.12%	27.73%	26.27%
Occ = Partical	47.14%	45.89%	41.72%	40.73%

It can be seen from Table 1 that a single repulsive force loss can also effectively reduce the miss rate. In addition, L_{RepGT}_tran02 is more effective than L_{RepGT}_tran01 in reducing the rate of missed detection, while using the two loss functions together on the basis of the original loss function can greatly reduce the rate of missed detection. It is shown that in the training process of the model, when the prediction box is close to the matched anchor box and the prediction box is close to the real box, the performance of the detection can be slightly improved by adding the maximum, which indicates that the new loss function can effectively reduce the missed detection rate in the case of occlusion, which is in line with the original intention of the loss function.

6 Conclusion

In this paper, aiming at the problem of mutual occlusion between pedestrians in dense crowds in self driving scenarios, an improved function algorithm based on YOLOv3 is proposed. By replacing anchor frames, the loss function is optimized and the detection accuracy is improved. Experimental results show that this method can effectively reduce the missed detection rate, improve the average accuracy, and help improve the effectiveness of pedestrian occlusion detection, ensuring accurate pedestrian detection under traffic jams, and ensuring driving safety. The advanced intelligent driving assistance system has greatly improved the current traffic congestion and effectively reduced frequent traffic safety accidents. Pedestrian detection technology is the core of self driving technology, and its accuracy, real-time and computation complexity will directly influence the safety of self driving.

Acknowledgment. This work is partly supported by Jiangsu technology project of Housing and Urban-Rural Development (No. 2019ZD040) and Xu Zhou Science and Technology Plan Project (No. KC21309).

References

1. Zhang, K., Chen, L., An, Y., et al.: A QoE test system for vehicular voice cloud services. Mob. Netw. Appl. **26**, 700–715 (2019)
2. Chen, L., Jiang, D., Bao, R., Xiong, J., Liu, F., Bei, L.: MIMO scheduling effectiveness analysis for bursty data service from view of QoE. Chin J. Electron. **26**(5), 1079–1085 (2017)
3. Chen, L., et al.: A lightweight end-side user experience data collection system for quality evaluation of multimedia communications. IEEE Access **6**(1), 15408–15419 (2018)

4. Chen, L., Zhang, L.: Spectral efficiency analysis for massive MIMO system under QoS constraint: an effective capacity perspective. Mob. Netw. Appl. (2020)
5. Jiang, D., Wang, Z., Huo, L., et al.: A performance measurement and analysis method for software-defined networking of IoV. IEEE Trans. Intell. Transp. Syst. (2020)
6. Jiang, D., Wang, W., Shi, L., Song, H.: A compressive sensing-based approach to end-to-end network traffic reconstruction. IEEE Trans. Netw. Sci. Eng. 7(1), 507–519 (2020)
7. Jiang, D., Huo, L., Song, H.: Rethinking behaviors and activities of base stations in mobile cellular networks based on big data analysis. IEEE Trans. Netw. Sci. Eng. 7(1), 80–90 (2020)
8. Jiang, D., Wang, Y., Lv, Z., Qi, S., Singh, S.: Big data analysis based network behavior insight of cellular networks for industry 4.0 applications. IEEE Trans. Ind. Inform. 16(2), 1310–1320 (2020)
9. Yang, B., Bao, W., Huang, D.-S.: Inference of large-scale time-delayed gene regulatory network with parallel MapReduce cloud platform. Sci. Rep. 8(1) (2018). https://doi.org/10.1038/s41598-018-36180-y
10. Yang, B., Bao, W.: Complex-valued ordinary differential equation modeling for time series identification. IEEE Access 7(1) (2019). https://doi.org/10.1109/ACCESS.2019.2902958
11. Jiang, D., Wang, Z., Wang, W., et al.: AI-assisted energy-efficient and intelligent routing for reconfigurable wireless networks. IEEE Trans. Netw. Sci. Eng. (2020)
12. Jiang, D., Huo, L., Zhang, P., et al.: Energy-efficient heterogeneous networking for electric vehicles networks in smart future cities. IEEE Trans. Intell. Transp. Syst. (2020). https://doi.org/10.1109/TITS.2020.3029015
13. Jiang, D., Wang, Y., Lv, Z., Wang, W., Wang, H.: An energy-efficient networking approach in cloud services for IIoT networks. IEEE J. Sel. Areas Commun. 38(5), 928–941 (2020)
14. Jiang, D., Huo, L., Lv, Z., Song, H., Qin, W.: A joint multi-criteria utility-based network selection approach for vehicle-to-infrastructure networking. IEEE Trans. Intell. Transp. Syst. 19(10), 3305–3319 (2018)
15. Ahmed, Z., Iniyavan, R., Madhan Mohan, P.: Enhanced vulnerable pedestrian detection using deep learning. In: 2019 International Conference on Communication and Signal Processing (ICCSP), Chennai, India, pp. 0971–0974 (2019). https://doi.org/10.1109/ICCSP.2019.8697978
16. Chen, E., Tang, X., Fu, B.: A modified pedestrian retrieval method based on faster R-CNN with integration of pedestrian detection and re-identification. In: 2018 International Conference on Audio, Language and Image Processing (ICALIP), Shanghai, pp. 63–66 (2018). https://doi.org/10.1109/ICALIP.2018.8455703
17. Song, H., Choi, I.K., Ko, M.S., Bae, J., Kwak, S., Yoo, J.: Vulnerable pedestrian detection and tracking using deep learning. In: 2018 International Conference on Electronics, Information, and Communication (ICEIC), Honolulu, HI, pp. 1–2 (2018). https://doi.org/10.23919/ELINFOCOM.2018.8330547
18. Paisitkriangkrai, S., Shen, C., van den Hengel, A.: Pedestrian detection with spatially pooled features and structured ensemble learning. IEEE Trans. Pattern Anal. Mach. Intell. 38(6), 1243–1257 (2016). https://doi.org/10.1109/TPAMI.2015.2474388
19. Lin, S., Lin, M., Hwang, Y., Fan, C.: Deep-learning based pedestrian direction detection for anti-collision of intelligent self-propelled vehicles. In: 2019 IEEE 8th Global Conference on Consumer Electronics (GCCE), Osaka, Japan, pp. 387–388 (2019). https://doi.org/10.1109/GCCE46687.2019.9015528
20. Lan, W., Dang, J., Wang, Y., Wang, S.: Pedestrian detection based on YOLO network model. In: 2018 IEEE International Conference on Mechatronics and Automation (ICMA), Changchun, pp. 1547–1551 (2018). https://doi.org/10.1109/ICMA.2018.8484698
21. Liu, S., Lv, S., Zhang, H., Gong, J.: Pedestrian detection algorithm based on the improved SSD. In: 2019 Chinese Control and Decision Conference (CCDC), Nanchang, China, pp. 3559–3563 (2019). https://doi.org/10.1109/CCDC.2019.8832518

22. Sun, W., Zhu, S., Ju, X., Wang, D.: Deep learning based pedestrian detection. In: 2018 Chinese Control and Decision Conference (CCDC), Shenyang, pp. 1007–1011 (2018). https://doi.org/10.1109/CCDC.2018.8407277
23. Zhang, J., Xiao, J., Zhou, C., Peng, C.: A multi-class pedestrian detection network for distorted pedestrians. In: 2018 13th IEEE Conference on Industrial Electronics and Applications (ICIEA), Wuhan, pp. 1079–1083 (2018)
24. Ghosh, S., Amon, P., Hutter, A., Kaup, A.: Reliable pedestrian detection using a deep neural network trained on pedestrian counts. In: 2017 IEEE International Conference on Image Processing (ICIP), Beijing, pp. 685–689 (2017)
25. Luo, S., Qin, S.: Pedestrian detection of occlusion based on multi-marker method. In: 2019 3rd International Conference on Electronic Information Technology and Computer Engineering (EITCE), Xiamen, China, pp. 1033–1037 (2019)
26. Liu, T., Cheng, J., Yang, M., Du, X., Luo, X., Zhang, L.: Pedestrian detection method based on self-learning. In: 2019 IEEE 4th Advanced Information Technology, Electronic and Automation Control Conference (IAEAC), Chengdu, China, pp. 2161–2165 (2019)
27. Kim, D., Park, S., Kang, D., Paik, J.: Improved center and scale prediction-based pedestrian detection using convolutional block. In: 2019 IEEE 9th International Conference on Consumer Electronics (ICCE-Berlin), Berlin, Germany, pp. 418–419 (2019)
28. Ayachi, R., Afif, M., Said, Y., Abdelaali, A.B.: Pedestrian detection for advanced driving assisting system: a transfer learning approach. In: 2020 5th International Conference on Advanced Technologies for Signal and Image Processing (ATSIP), Sousse, Tunisia, pp. 1–5 (2020)
29. Kulkarni, R., Dhavalikar, S., Bangar, S.: Traffic light detection and recognition for self driving cars using deep learning. In: 2018 Fourth International Conference on Computing Communication Control and Automation (ICCUBEA), Pune, India, pp. 1–4 (2018)
30. Kankaria, R.V., Jain, S.K., Bide, P., Kothari, A., Agarwal, H.: Alert system for drivers based on traffic signs, lights and pedestrian detection. In: 2020 International Conference for Emerging Technology (INCET), Belgaum, India, pp. 1–5 (2020)
31. Hbaieb, A., Rezgui, J., Chaari, L.: Pedestrian detection for autonomous driving within cooperative communication system. In: 2019 IEEE Wireless Communications and Networking Conference (WCNC), Marrakesh, Morocco, pp. 1–6 (2019)

Pollen Recognition and Classification Method Based on Local Binary Pattern

Haotian Chen[✉], Zhuo Wang, and Yuan An

Xuzhou University of Technology, Xuzhou 221018, China

Abstract. Aiming at the problem of low resolution and small sample size of pollen images, this paper proposes a pollen image classification method based on local binary mode. This method first performs preprocessing such as sharpening and normalization on the pollen image. For the preprocessed image, calculate the local binary pattern. Then extract the directional gradient histogram operator of the local binary pattern calculation result as the identification feature. And finally, use the SVM as the classifier for the classification and recognition of the three-dimensional pollen image. Through the experiment on the European Confocal standard pollen database, the results show that the recognition rate of this method can exceed 95% at the highest, and at the same time, it has better robustness to the proportion and pose changes of pollen images, and has better recognition effect than traditional methods.

Keywords: Local binary pattern · Texture feature · Pollen recognition

1 Introduction

In recent years, with the continuous improvement of environmental problems, the coverage of many plants that quickly release a large amount of highly allergic pollen has increased year by year, such as poplar, resulting in the incidence of pollen allergic diseases. At present, the environmental departments of many countries in the world are gradually developing air pollen. The monitoring and forecasting services of pollen species are also attempting related work in some cities in China. However, the current pollen classification and identification mainly rely on manual operation under a microscope. This method is inefficient compared with the use of computers to classify and identify pollen. It is time-consuming and labor-intensive and is affected by the operator's subjective experience, and the recognition rate is generally not high. The pollen images under the microscope have different morphologies. Different pollen images have a high degree of distinction in the structure and texture, so the computer is used Pollen recognition can effectively improve the accuracy and efficiency of pollen classification.

Many scholars have conducted in-depth research on pollen image recognition in recent years and have achieved specific research results. The Treloar team designed an automatic classification and recognition algorithm for pollen images based on the geometric features of pollen and achieved a 95% recognition rate on the best subset

D. Jiang and H. Song (Eds.): SIMUtools 2021, LNICST 424, pp. 532–539, 2022.
https://doi.org/10.1007/978-3-030-97124-3_40

of variables [1]. The Rodriguez-Damian team combined the texture features and shape features of the pollen. In the classification of Urticaceae pollen, a recognition rate of 89% was obtained. Da Silva's team combined machine learning and image classification and recognition algorithms, using wavelet transform (WT) for texture feature extraction, and achieved good recognition results. The Kong team designed an automated sub-recognition method (Combined Global Shape and Local Texture, GSLT) that matches the global shape feature on the image block with the local texture feature and has a good effect on recognizing the fossil pollen data set. The Daood team proposed a new idea, the classification and recognition method (MultitLayer Feature Decomposition, MLFD), which first divides the image into layers and then extracts each layer's texture and geometric features, achieved some results in recognition of ancient pollen samples [2].

At present, most texture feature extraction methods have a specific recognition ability for certain unique pollen textures. Still, they are not universal enough to be applied to the recognition of all pollen images. The method proposed by the Rodriguez-Damian team has high time complexity and feature dimensionality. The method proposed by the Treloar team has too many strict requirements on the shape and contour of the pollen. The Da Silva team only uses wavelet transform to extract the texture of the pollen image. The way of Kong's team is not effective in traditional pollen recognition. The technique used by the Daood team is not robust to the rotation of pollen.

This paper proposes a pollen image recognition method using local binary patterns to respond to the above problems. The process first performs preprocessing, such as sharpening and normalization of the pollen image. Then calculates the regional binary pattern for the preprocessed image. Finally, extract the results. The statistical histogram descriptor of the calculation results of the local binary mode is used as the identification feature, and finally, SVM is used as the classifier for the classification and recognition of the three-dimensional pollen image. Through experimental verification, the method proposed in this paper can achieve high recognition efficiency while retaining the complete information of pollen images [3].

2   Methods

2.1   Traditional Local Binary Pattern

This local binary pattern is defined in the neighborhood of a 3×3 matrix. The target image is convolved with this matrix as a calculation template. The pixel value of each district of the center pixel is binarized with the center pixel as the threshold: The position of the center pixel is more significant than code 1. Otherwise, it is coded to form a local binary numerical matrix. Obtain the values in the matrix clockwise from a given point to obtain a binary string, and convert the string to decimal. The number is used to mark the central pixel uniquely, then the LBP value defined at this point is expressed as:

$$LBP_R(x_c) = \sum_{n=0}^{R} 2^n s(x_n - x_c)$$

Where R is the neighborhood range, xn is all pixels contained in the neighborhood under this range, xc is the sampling center point, and s(x) is:

$$s(x) = \begin{cases} 1, & x \geq 0 \\ 0, & x < 0 \end{cases}$$

The simplest form of the LBP feature vector is established as follows:

(1) Divide the detection window into small blocks (such as 16 * 16 small blocks);
(2) For each pixel in the small block, compare its neighboring eight neighbors. Follow the pixels clockwise or counterclockwise along the circle;
(3) If the value of the center pixel is greater than the neighbor's value, write 0, otherwise write 1. This constructs an 8-digit number (usually, for convenience, it will be converted to a decimal);
(4) Calculate the frequency histogram of each "number" in a small block;
(5) The histogram can be standardized selectively;
(6) Connect all the small (normalized) histograms. This constitutes the feature vector of the entire window (Fig. 1).

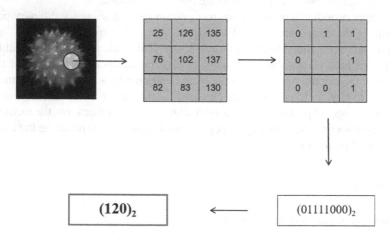

Fig. 1. Local Binary Pattern of pollen image

2.2 Extended Local Binary Pattern

To adapt to the texture features of different scales and meet the grayscale and rotation invariance requirements, Ojala made improvements, extending the 3×3 neighborhood to any neighborhood and replacing the square with a circular area.

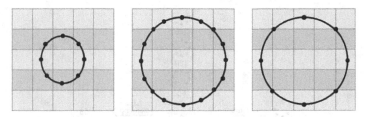

Fig. 2. Extended Local Binary Pattern of pollen image

Where, LBP_p^r Represents the LBP local coding with p sampling points in a circular area with r as the radius, for a given center point (x_c, y_c), its neighborhood pixel position is (x_p, y_p), $p \in P$, and its sampling point (xp, yp) is calculated as follows:

$$x_p = x_c + R \cos(\frac{2p\pi}{P})$$

$$y_p = y_c - R \sin(\frac{2p\pi}{P})$$

However, we will zoom in on the calculated coordinate position and assume that the image coordinates around the calculated position are from 0 to 1 or 1 to 0. The computed coordinates are not necessarily integers. How to determine its pixel value? In this case, we generally use interpolation calculation to calculate its reasonable pixel value. There are many interpolation methods at present, and the more widely used one is a bilinear interpolation. The formula for bilinear interpolation is as follows:

$$f(x, y) \approx \begin{bmatrix} 1 - x & x \end{bmatrix} \begin{bmatrix} f(0, 0) & f(0, 1) \\ f(1, 0) & f(1, 1) \end{bmatrix} \begin{bmatrix} 1 - y \\ y \end{bmatrix}$$

2.3 Uniform Local Binary Pattern

The LBP features already have gray and illumination invariance, but they do not yet have rotation invariance. To achieve rotation invariance, researchers have proposed a rotation invariance LBP feature. The main idea is rough: firstly, continuously rotate the LBP features in the circular neighborhood, obtain a series of LBP feature values according to the selection, and select the LBP feature with the smallest LBP feature value as the central pixel from these LBP feature values. The specific approach is shown in the figure below (Fig. 3):

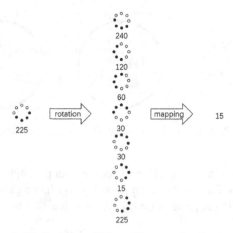

Fig. 3. Uniform Local Binary Pattern of pollen image

As shown in the figure, by rotating the obtained LBP features, a series of LBP feature values are obtained, and finally, the feature pattern with the smallest feature value is used as the LBP feature of the center pixel.

The statistical histogram of the LBP feature combines the LBP feature with the spatial information of the image. The LBP feature image is divided into m local blocks, and the histogram of each local block is extracted. Then these histograms are sequentially connected to form a statistical histogram of LBP features, that is, LBPH. The specific process of calculating LBPH for an image:

(1) Calculate the LBP feature image of the image;
(2) Divide the LBP feature image into blocks. Opencv divides the LBP feature image into eight rows, eight columns, and 64 areas by default;
(3) Calculate the histogram cell LBPH of the feature image of each area, normalize the histogram, and the histogram size is $1 * n$;
(4) Arrange the histogram of each area feature image calculated above into a row according to the spatial order of the blocks to form the LBP feature vector, the size is one $* (n * 64)$;
(5) Use this vector as the classifier's input to realize automatic classification of pollen images.

3   Experiential Results

The experimental environment of this paper is a PIV computer, 2.8 GHz CPU, and 8 GB memory. To verify the method's effectiveness, the pollen image of the experiment in this paper uses the Confocal data set. It currently includes most of the image data of allergic pollen detected in the air. The data set uses a laser scanning confocal microscope to ensure data concentration. In this paper, SVM is used to calculate the similarity between features. 20% of each type of pollen is selected as the training sample, and the rest are used as the experimental sample.

Before calculating the LBP feature value, the original image needs to be interpolated or down-sampled according to the resolution of the original image. And then, image filtering and other preprocessing are performed to improve the image quality. In the experiment, the accuracy rate Correct Recognition Rate (CRR), Recall Rate (RR), and Recognition Time (RT) verify the performance of the experiment.

3.1 Experiential Results on Confocal Pollen Dataset

It can be seen in Fig. 2 that in the Confocal pollen image with minor deformation and pollution, the pollen image particles have apparent edge contours. As well as transparent textures, most of them can be correctly identified and classified (Fig. 4).

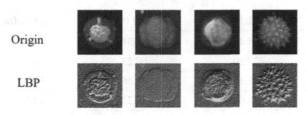

Fig. 4. Experiential results of proposed method

Table 1 shows the classification and recognition performance of six representative pollen images. From the experimental results, it can be seen that the recognition rate on the Confocal image database is generally higher. The correct recognition rate can reach more than 90%, and the recall rate can reach 95%. For pollen images with relatively poor quality, such as Juglans, it can also get about 80%. From the recognition results, it can be concluded that the recognition performance of pollen will be affected by the quality of pollen to a certain extent. The wrong classification is mainly caused by the noise or the unclear sampling. The experimental results show that the LBP is not the spatial geometric transformation of pollen images has good invariance.

Table 1. Experiential results on confocal pollen dataset

Category	CRR (%)	RR (%)	RT (s/frame)
Carpinus	89.25	82.75	0.35
Plantago	87.32	95.28	0.32
Rumex	90.18	79.26	0.31
Juglans	80.02	82.75	0.31
Taxus	84.35	81.00	0.32
Salix (Weide)	85.96	82.42	0.34

3.2   Results and Discussion

This paper compares the experimental results with the WT feature descriptor, GSLT feature descriptor, and MLFD feature descriptor. Because different types of pollen have various internal texture features such as thorns, nodules, rods, holes, nets, depending on the type of pollen, these features will become more evident in the three-dimensional pollen image. Hence, this article's LBP texture feature extraction has more vital discrimination ability, better recognition effect, and higher recognition efficiency. Table 2 shows the comparison results of this method's average recognition rate and recognition time and the other four methods.

Table 2. Comparison between PROPOSED METHOD and other methods

Method	CRR (%)	RR (%)	RT (s/frame)
PROPOSED	88.46	83.34	0.31
WT	73.50	69.23	2.01
GSLT	76.14	74.56	3.07
MLFD	86.04	74.22	6.12

It can be seen from the experimental results that compared with the other three methods, the average recognition rate can reach 88.46%, 9.9% higher than other similar methods on average. It is also superior to most methods in terms of computational efficiency. For example, compared with WT, the correct recognition rate of the method provided in this article is about 14.96% higher. Compared with GSLT, the method in this article has significantly reduced time and space complexity and improved recognition rate in the process of extracting 3D features. Compared with MLFD, the correct recognition rate of the method provided in this article is 2.42% higher. Experiments show that this method has a higher recognition rate and good geometric invariance than other texture feature extraction methods and is suitable for actual pollen classification and recognition.

4   Conclusion

This paper proposes an automatic classification method for pollen images based on local binary patterns. This method is based on the low-complexity LBP operator. It directly extracts the features of the image in the spatial domain, avoiding the processing of transforming the image to the frequency domain. The calculation step has high operating efficiency. This paper combines the gray change direction of the pollen image with the texture feature to extract the image feature with relatively low dimensionality and reasonable recognition rate and obtained in the experiment High pollen recognition rate. However, for partially occluded pollen images, especially pollen images in internal slice images of pollen images with a fuzzy texture. Experimental analysis shows that the classification method in this paper has strong pollen characteristics, representation ability, and distinguishability and has high robustness to illumination, rotation, and position changes of pollen.

In addition, due to the dimensionality reduction characteristics of the local binary mode in the calculation process of this paper, the local features of the source image are retained. At the same time, the computational efficiency is ensured so that the descriptor meets the requirements of real-time pollen classification. Further work will focus on how to solve the recognition problem of partially occluded pollen slice images and improve the recognition efficiency of pollen images.

Acknowledgements. This work is supported by the Youth Foundation of Xuzhou Institute of Technology (No. XKY2019204).

References

1. Ronneberger, O., Schultz, E., Burkhardt, H.: Automated pollen recognition using 3D volume images from fluorescence microscopy. Aerobiologia **18**(2), 107–115 (2002)
2. Xie, Y.H., Xu, Z.F., Burkhardt, H.: Spatial geometric constraints histogram descriptors based on curvature mesh graph for 3D pollen particles recognition. Chin. Phys. **23**(6), 060701 (2014)
3. Wang, Z., Bao, W., Lin, D., et al.: A local feature descriptor based on SIFT for 3D pollen image recognition. IEEE Access **7**, 152658–152666 (2019)

Prediction Protein-Protein Interactions with LSTM

Zheng Tao[1], Jiahao Yao[1], Chao Yuan[1], Ning Zhao[1], Bin Yang[2(✉)], Baitong Chen[3], and Wenzheng Bao[1]

[1] School of Information Engineering, Xuzhou University of Technology, Xuzhou 221000, China
[2] School of Information Science and Engineering, Zaozhuang University, Zaozhuang 277160, China
[3] Xuzhou No. 1 People's Hospital, Xuzhou 221000, China

Abstract. As the basis and key of cell activities, protein plays an important role in many life activities. Protein usually does not work alone. Under normal circumstances, most proteins perform specific functions by interacting with other proteins, and play the greatest role in life activity. The prediction of protein-protein interaction (PPI) is a very basic and important research in bioinformatics. PPI controls a large number of cell activities and is the basis of most cell activities. It provides a very important theoretical basis and support for disease prevention and treatment, and drug development. Because experimental methods are slow and expensive, methods based on machine learning are gradually being applied to PPI problems. We propose a new model called BiLSTM-RF, which can effectively predict PPI.

Keywords: Deep learning · Protein-protein interaction · LSTM

1 Introduction

In 2020, the outbreak of the COVID-19 epidemic ignited the enthusiasm of pharmaceutical companies for the protein [1, 2]. With the inactivation of domestic COVID-19 and the approval of adenovirus and recombinant protein vaccines, the progress of vaccine has become the focus of attention [3]. On November 9,2020, Pfizer of the United States announced that the mRNA novel coronavirus vaccine BNT162B2, developed in collaboration with BioNTech in Germany, is effective in healthy subjects not infected with 2020 and has contracted novel coronavirus and is more than 90% effective. This was followed by that, on November 16, 2020, novel researches released the results of phase 3 clinical experiments with the COVID-19 vaccine, mPROTEIN-1273, indicating that the vaccine has 94.5% protective efficacy [4–6]. In June 2021, the mRNA vaccine ARCov, developed by Amber Bio, is about to become the first mRNA vaccine in China to enter the phase 3 clinical stage. According to statistics, more than there are 200 COVID-19 vaccines in development worldwide, 48 of which have entered the clinical research stage. Now, PROTEIN therapy has become a hot investment spot of heavy capital bets, and more and

© ICST Institute for Computer Sciences, Social Informatics and Telecommunications Engineering 2022
Published by Springer Nature Switzerland AG 2022. All Rights Reserved
D. Jiang and H. Song (Eds.): SIMUtools 2021, LNICST 424, pp. 540–545, 2022.
https://doi.org/10.1007/978-3-030-97124-3_41

more academic research institutions and pharmaceutical companies are making efforts in this field [7–9]. Thus, protein has become a research direction that cannot be ignored in the current market.

Within organisms, protein has very important cellular functions, including synthetic proteins, catalytic reactions, regulating gene expression, regulating innate immunity, and sensing small molecules. On the one hand, protein is an important link of genetic information expression [10–12]. On the other hand, protein also modulates some important life activities. In recent years, with the researchers' research on PROTEIN structure, various scientific research achievements have come in. For example, scientists from institutions like the University of Toronto have developed a new technique called CHyMErA (Cas Hybrid for Multiplexed Editing and Screening applications) that is applied to any mammalian cells while systematically targeting DNA fragments at multiple sites. Professor Gao Caixa of the Institute of Genetic and Developmental Biology of the Chinese Academy of Sciences and his team optimized a guided editing system (prime editing system, PPE) to produce the required point mutations, insertions, and deletions in the two major cereal crops. The main components of the PPE system are the Cas9 incision ase-RT fusion protein and protein [13–16].

In this paper, a new prediction framework was constructed to predict different proteins according to their characteristic numbers. We compare the proportion of positive and negative samples, and test the accuracy of the proportion of positive and negative samples. The results show that, although the model has satisfactory prediction performance, it has some shortcomings, such as embedding more advanced super parameter selection scheme in the system, further optimizing the proposed deep learning framework, Deep learning methods are time-consuming, and need to pay more attention to deep learning methods based on PU and heterogeneous computing, which can be strengthened in future research.

2   Methods and Materials

The data should contain more characteristic values, and the total data should not be too small. In that case, the network of training is not fit well, and the classification effect will not be very good. The physical and chemical properties of the proteins can reflect the differences between different proteins and can be used as the characteristic number. Then the proteins are roughly divided into two categories, and the positive and negative labels are taken as the last column of the data. Finally, the characteristic number of proteins is 406, and 407 columns of data are obtained by adding tag column. For classification problems.

The performance of a model is determined by many things. One of the most important factors is feature selection. Extraction method. Feature extraction can change our Convert raw data into features that better represent the data. Improving the prediction accuracy of unknown data. It directly affects the prediction results of the model. At present, researchers have proposed many feature extraction methods which are dedicated to extracting the most effective features from data for classification and identification.

To minimize training errors, Gradient descent methods, such as applying a time series back-propagation algorithm, can be used to modify the weights of each time based on errors. The main problem with gradient descent in recurrent neural networks (RNN) was first discovered in 1991 when the error gradient disappeared exponentially with the length of time between events. When LSTM blocks are set, the error is also calculated backwards, from output to each gate in the input stage until the value is filtered out. Normal retransmitting nerves are therefore an effective way to train LSTM blocks to remember long-term values.

After obtaining a group of data with positive and negative sample labels, ten-layer cross validation is carried out to obtain the training set and test set, and then the labels and data are separated and processed respectively. Here, a group of positive and negative sample ratio of 1:10 is taken as an example. In order to get the best proportion of training, we test it from 1:1 to 1:7, and judge its accuracy by ACC value and ROC curve. Acc reflects the model's ability to classify positive samples correctly.

Therefore, training data should be converted to cell array, and training data label should be converted to category type.

The basic model structure of LSTM can be made with deep network designer in MATLAB. The characteristic number of the data is determined, and the corresponding parameters are written according to the model structure of LSTM. Based on this model structure, we can clearly see the internal structure and data function of LSTM at each layer. The parameters of each layer should be modified according to the actual data.

Sequence input layer (inputsize): sequence input layer, specify input dimensionlstm-Layer: Determine the number of LSTM hidden units.

Lstmlayer (numhiddenunits, 'outputmode', 'last'): bidirectional LSTM layer. It specifies the hidden node, and the output mode is 'last', that is, the last classification value is output.

Fully connected layer (numclasses): full connected layer, specifying the number of output classes.

Softmax layer: this layer outputs the probability of each category.

Classificationlayer: classification layer, which outputs the final classification results, similar to probability competition voting.

Determined the relevant parameters of training options, including optimization function, initial learning rate and iteration times. LSTM does not support multi-core operation, so in the running environment parameter, only CPU or GPU can be selected. But GPU support for convolutional neural networks requires a GPU device with compute capability 3.0 or higher.

The problem of fitting should be considered in the training process. If the correct rate of training is very high, but the correct rate applied to the test set is very low, then the practicability of this network will be very low, that is, there is the problem of over fitting.

Through the training set to get the network, and then put the test set into the network to test, get the final prediction result through the network, and compare the result with the label of the test set to get the correct rate. Adjust the proportion of relevant parameters and training set test set in time.

3   Results

The main analysis method of ROC is to draw this characteristic curve. The abscissa of the curve is the false positive rate (FPR), and N is the number of true negative samples, FP is the number of positive samples predicted by the classifier in n negative samples. The ordinate was true positive rate (TPR), P is the number of real positive samples, TP is the number of positive samples predicted by the classifier.

If we want to make a quantitative analysis of the model, we need to introduce a new concept, namely AUC (area under ROC curve). This concept is very simple, that is, the area under the ROC curve. To calculate the AUC value, we only need to integrate along the transverse axis of the ROC. In real scenes, the ROC curve is generally above this line, so the AUC value is generally between 0.5 and 1. The larger the AUC, the better the performance of the model (Table 1).

Table 1. The performances of each ratio of positive and negative data.

pos:neg	1:1	1:2	1:3	1:4	1:5	1:6	1:7	1:8
Acc	0.7451	0.7360	0.7690	0.7546	0.7806	0.7530	0.7879	0.7506

Through the ten layer cross validation method to divide the training set and test set can also effectively give the network sufficient data for training. It can be seen from the results that the classification effect of LSTM is mostly better. It can be seen that the ACC value is generally above 0.7, that is to say, the overall classification effect of LSTM is relatively good. Through the different proportion of positive and negative samples, we can find that the ACC value is the largest at 1:7, that is to say, the network classification effect is the best at 1:7. Of course, for the classification problem, the influencing factors are not only the positive and negative sample ratio, but also the number of features of the data. When the number of features is less, the classification result is poor. When the number of features is more, the classification result is good, but the running speed will become worse. Therefore, we need to find the appropriate positive and negative sample ratio and accurate data eigenvalues. The effect of LSTM classification of such data can best meet people's needs.

The shortcomings of LSTM. LSTM allows information to be stored across arbitrary time lags, and error signals to be carried far back in time. This potential strength, however, can contribute to a weakness in some situations: the cell states S often tend to grow linearly during the presentation of a time series (the nonlinear aspects of sequence processing are left to the squashing functions and the highly nonlinear gates). If we present a continuous input stream, the cell states may grow in unbounded fashion, causing saturation of the output squashing function, H. This happens even if the nature of the problem suggests that the cell states should be reset occasionally, e.g. at the beginnings of new input sequences (whose starts, however, are not explicitly indicated by a teacher). Saturation will make H derivative vanish, thus blocking incoming errors, and make the cell output equal the output gate activation, that is, the entire memory cell will degenerate into an ordinary BPTT unit, so that the cell will cease functioning as a memory.

The problem did not arise in the experiments reported by Hochreiter and Schmidhuber because cell states were explicitly reset to zero before the start of each new sequence.

4 Conclusions

In this paper, a new prediction framework was constructed to predict different proteins according to their characteristic numbers. We compare the proportion of positive and negative samples, and test the accuracy of the proportion of positive and negative samples. The results show that, although the model has satisfactory prediction performance, it has some shortcomings, such as embedding more advanced super parameter selection scheme in the system, further optimizing the proposed deep learning framework, Deep learning methods are time-consuming, and need to pay more attention to deep learning methods based on PU and heterogeneous computing, which can be strengthened in future research.

Acknowledgement. This work is supported by the fundamental Research Funds for the Central Universities, 2020QN89, Xuzhou science and technology plan project (KC19142), the talent project of 'Qingtan scholar' of Zaozhuang University, Jiangsu Provincial Natural Science Foundation, China (SBK2019040953), Youth Innovation Team of Scientific Research Foundation of the Higher Education Institutions of Shandong Province, China (2019KJM006), the Key Research Program of the Science Foundation of Shandong Province (ZR2020KE001), the PhD research startup foundation of Zaozhuang University (2014BS13) and Zaozhuang University Foundation (2015YY02), the Natural Science Foundation of China (61902337), Natural Science Fund for Colleges and Universities in Jiangsu Province (19KJB520016), Xuzhou Natural Science Foundation KC21047 and Young talents of science and technology in Jiangsu.

References

1. Brohee, S., Van Helden, J.: Evaluation of clustering algorithms for protein-protein interaction networks. BMC Bioinform. **7**(1), 1–19 (2006)
2. Sugaya, N., Ikeda, K.: Assessing the druggability of protein-protein interactions by a supervised machine-learning method. BMC Bioinform. **10**(1), 1–13 (2009)
3. Shen, J., et al.: Predicting protein–protein interactions based only on sequences information. Proc. Natl. Acad. Sci. **104**(11), 4337–4341 (2007)
4. Zhang, Q.C., et al.: Structure-based prediction of protein–protein interactions on a genome-wide scale. Nature **490**(7421), 556–560 (2012)
5. Wu, J., Vallenius, T., Ovaska, K., Westermarck, J., Mäkelä, T.P., Hautaniemi, S.: Integrated network analysis platform for protein-protein interactions. Nat. Methods **6**(1), 75–77 (2009)
6. De Las Rivas, J., Fontanillo, C.: Protein–protein interactions essentials: key concepts to building and analyzing interactome networks. PLoS Comput. Biol. **6**(6), e1000807 (2010)
7. Zhang, Y.P., Zou, Q.: PPTPP: a novel therapeutic peptide prediction method using physicochemical property encoding and adaptive feature representation learning. Bioinformatics **36**(13), 3982–3987 (2020)
8. Shen, Z., Lin, Y., Zou, Q.: Transcription factors–DNA interactions in rice: identification and verification. Brief Bioinform. **21**(3), 946–956 (2020)

9. Liu, G.H., Shen, H.B., Yu, D.J.: Prediction of protein–protein interaction sites with machine-learning-based data-cleaning and post-filtering procedures. J. Membr. Biol. **249**(1), 141–153 (2016)
10. Sato, T., et al.: Interactions among members of the BCL-2 protein family analyzed with a yeast two-hybrid system. Proc. Natl. Acad. Sci. **91**(20), 9238–9242 (1994)
11. Schwikowski, B., Uetz, P., Fields, S.: A network of protein–protein interactions in yeast. Nat. Biotechnol. **18**(12), 1257–1261 (2000)
12. Coates, P.J., Hall, P.A.: The yeast two-hybrid system for identifying protein–protein interactions. J. Pathol.: A J. Pathol. Soc. Great Br. Ireland **199**(1), 4–7 (2003)
13. Free, R.B., Hazelwood, L.A., Sibley, D.R.: Identifying novel protein-protein interactions using co-immunoprecipitation and mass spectroscopy. Curr. Protoc. Neurosci. **46**(1), 5–28 (2009)
14. Kim, Y., Subramaniam, S.: Locally defined protein phylogenetic profiles reveal previously missed protein interactions and functional relationships. Proteins: Struct. Funct. Bioinform. **62**(4), 1115–1124 (2006)
15. Zhang, S.W., Hao, L.Y., Zhang, T.H.: Prediction of protein–protein interaction with pairwise kernel support vector machine. Int. J. Mol. Sci. **15**(2), 3220–3233 (2014)
16. Burger, L., Van Nimwegen, E.: Accurate prediction of protein–protein interactions from sequence alignments using a Bayesian method. Mol. Syst. Biol. **4**(1), 165 (2008)
17. You, Z.H., Zhu, L., Zheng, C.H., Yu, H.J., Deng, S.P., Ji, Z.: Prediction of protein-protein interactions from amino acid sequences using a novel multi-scale continuous and discontinuous feature set. BMC Bioinform. **15**(15), 1–9 (2014)
18. Cui, G., Fang, C., Han, K.: Prediction of protein-protein interactions between viruses and human by an SVM model. BMC Bioinform. **13**(7), 1–10 (2012)
19. Bradford, J.R., Westhead, D.R.: Improved prediction of protein protein binding sites using a support vector machines approach. Bioinformatics **21**(8), 1487–1494 (2005)
20. Guo, Y., Yu, L., Wen, Z., Li, M.: sing support vector machine combined with auto covariance to predict protein–protein interactions from protein sequences. Nucleic Acids Res. **36**(9), 3025–3030 (2008)
21. Koike, A., Takagi, T.: Prediction of protein–protein interaction sites using support vector machines. Protein Eng. Des. Sel. **17**(2), 165–173 (2004)
22. Yi, H.C., You, Z.H., Wang, M.N., Guo, Z.H., Wang, Y.B., Zhou, J.R.: RPI-SE: a stacking ensemble learning framework for ncRNA-protein interactions prediction using sequence information. BMC Bioinform. **21**(1), 1–10 (2020)
23. Du, X., Sun, S., Hu, C., Yao, Y., Yan, Y., Zhang, Y.: DeepPPI: boosting prediction of protein–protein interactions with deep neural networks. J. Chem. Inf. Model. **57**(6), 1499–1510 (2017)
24. Sun, T., Zhou, B., Lai, L., Pei, J.: Sequence-based prediction of protein protein interaction using a deep-learning algorithm. BMC Bioinform. **18**(1), 1–8 (2017)
25. Zhang, L., Yu, G., Xia, D., Wang, J.: Protein–protein interactions prediction based on ensemble deep neural networks. Neurocomputing **324**, 10–19 (2019)
26. Kong, M., Zhang, Y., Xu, D., Chen, W., Dehmer, M.: FCTP-WSRC: protein–protein interactions prediction via weighted sparse representation based classification. Front. Genet. **11**, 18 (2020)
27. Ma, W., Cao, Y., Bao, W., Yang, B., Chen, Y.: ACT-SVM: prediction of protein-protein interactions based on support vector basis model. Sci. Program. **2020** (2020)

The Identifications of Post Translational Modification Sites with Capsule Network

Baitong Chen[1], Yujian Gu[2], Bin Yang[3(✉)], and Wenzheng Bao[2]

[1] Xuzhou No. 1 People's Hospital, Xuzhou 221000, China
[2] School of Information Engineering, Xuzhou University of Technology, Xuzhou 221000, China
[3] School of Information Science and Engineering, Zaozhuang University, Zaozhuang 277160, China

Abstract. Post-translational modification (PTM) is considered a significant biological process with a tremendous impact on the function of proteins in both eukaryotes, and prokaryotes cells. Malonylation of lysine is a newly discovered post-translational modification, which is associated with many diseases, such as type 2 diabetes and different types of cancer. In addition, compared with the experimental identification of propionylation sites, the calculation method can save time and reduce cost. In this paper, we combine principal component analysis with support vector machine (SVM) to propose a new computational model - Mal-prec (malonylation prediction). Firstly, the one-hot encoding, physicochemical properties and the composition of k-spacer acid pairs were used to extract sequence features. Secondly, we preprocess the data, select the best feature subset by principal component analysis (PCA), and predict the malonylation sites by SVM. And then, we do a five-fold cross validation, and the results show that compared with other methods, Mal-prec can get better prediction performance. In the 10-fold cross validation of independent data sets, AUC (area under receiver operating characteristic curve) analysis has reached 96.39%. Mal-pred is used to identify the malonylation sites in the protein sequence, which is a computationally reliable method. It is superior to the existing prediction tools that found in the literature and can be used as a useful tool for identifying and discovering novel malonylation sites in human proteins.

Keywords: Post translational modification · Malonylation · One-hot encoding · Principal component analysis · Support vector machine

1 Introduction

Post translational modifications play vital roles not only during biological processes but in various cell functions. They also work in the regulation of cellular plasticity and dynamics [1]. What's more, lysine is one of the most heavily modified residues of the 20 kinds of natural amino acids in proteins. Lysine is one of the essential amino acids for human beings and mammals [2]. The body cannot synthesize it by itself, so it must be supplemented from food. Lysine mainly exists in animal food and beans, but

D. Jiang and H. Song (Eds.): SIMUtools 2021, LNICST 424, pp. 546–554, 2022.
https://doi.org/10.1007/978-3-030-97124-3_42

lysine content in cereal food is very low. Lysine has positive nutritional significance in promoting human growth and development, enhancing body immunity, anti-virus, promoting fat oxidation, relieving anxiety and so on [3, 4]. At the same time, it can also promote the absorption of some nutrients, and cooperate with some nutrients to better play the physiological functions of various nutrients [5]. Recent studies have found multiple types of new protein lysine acylations, which have greatly deepened our understanding of the post translational modification sites of lysine. The structurally similarity of the three types of acidic lysine modifications and the potential to regulate different types of proteins in different pathways are determined since malony1, succiny1 and glutary1 groups have a negatively charged carboxy1 group. It is also proved that malonylation, succinylation, and glutarylation of lysine residues are deeply concerned with evolution and dynamic under various biological and cellular conditions, including stress response, genetic mutations and more [4, 6–8].

Because of the great effects of post translational modifications, distinguishing them from various modifications is quite necessary [9–11]. However, the huge amounts of features as well as simples make it really hard to distinguish between the modifications which are post translation or not.

In this paper, we do some efforts to solve the recognition of post translational modifications. Since our dataset consisted of weak classification features, we did a series of processing works, and try to improve its effect. What's more, we used the capsule to complete the classification. Since the dataset contains a lot of invalid features, various arrangements and combinations of different features are tried to discover the features which contribute more. After all, we deleted Interference terms, and the results witness the improvement of the final effect. We had additionally constructed LSTM classifier for comparing the predictive performance. Experimental results demonstrate that the model based on capsule and a series of processing works, which is used by us performs relatively better.

2 Methods and Materials

We first did some processing works to divide each features apart, and then reassembled them by the method of combination. After all, we got various new datasets which contains different features, and whose quantities of the features are diverse too. Then we did the classification through every single of the reassembled datasets, which aims to find out which features are beneficial to classification and which hinder the progress. In addition, we utilized AUC, AC to evaluate the performance of our models and the LSTM model utilized as a comparison.

2.1 Dataset

We used the database of numerical indices named AAindex representing various physicochemical and biochemical properties of amino acids [12–14]. The data consists of three sections: (1) AAindex1 including 566 properties for the amino acid index of 20 numerical values; (2) AAindex2 containing amino acid mutation matrix, and (3) AAindex3 with protein contact potentials. The data could be found at the following URL address https://www.genome.jp/aaindex/ [15–18]. In this paper, eight physical and chemical properties are used, which are hydrophilicity value, mean polarity, isoelectric point, refractivity, average flexibility indices, average volume of buried residue, transfer free energy to surface, and consensus normalized hydrophobicity. The length of each peptide is 17, so the physiochemical properties is 17 * 8-dimensional vector. The physical and chemical properties are shown in the table below (Table 1).

Table 1. Eight physicochemical properties.

Properties description	Reference
Hydrophilicity value	Hopp and woods
Mean polarity	Radzicka and wolfenden
Isoelectric point	Zimmerman et al.
Refractivity	Treece et al.
Average flexibility indices	Bhaskaran and Ponnuswamy
Average volume of buries residue	Chothia
Transfer free energy to surface	Bull and Breese
Consensus normalized hydrophobicity	Eisenberg

2.2 Reassemble Dataset

We divided each features apart from the dataset, and pair the post translational modifications with the none translational modifications. Since there are 1735 post translational modifications and 1735 none translational modifications, we get eight 1735 * 17 datasets for each single feature, and then reassemble them by the law of combination. At last, we get 28 different datasets consisted of 2 of the 8 features, 56 new datasets composed of 3 of the 8 features, 56 different datasets composed of 3 of the 8 features, 70 datasets made up of 4 of the 8 features, 56 datasets consisted of 5 of the 8 features, 28 datasets made up of 6 of the 8 features, 8 datasets made up of 7 of the 8 features and a dataset made up of 8 of the 8 features. In a word, we get various new datasets which contains different features, and whose quantities of the features are diverse too.

2.3 Classifier Construction

Convolutional neural network is very successful and popular. However, it is not suitable for all tasks. Due to some defects in the architecture, it cannot complete some tasks well. CNN extracts features from data and recognizes objects through feature learning. The bottom layer of the network learns general features. With the deepening of layers, the extracted features are more complex. Then, the network uses all the features it learns to make the final prediction. There is a drawback here: there is no available spatial information in CNN, and the pooling layer used for connection is actually very inefficient.

So, we used the capsule to avoid the problem above. The solution of capsule to the problem is to encode the spatial information and calculate the existence probability of objects. This can be represented by vector, the modulus of vector represents the probability of feature existence, and the direction of vector represents the attitude information of feature.

The working principle of capsule can be summarized into a sentence, that is, all the important information of the state of the feature in capsule detection will be encapsulated in the form of vector.

Capsule's network structure consists of parts named input layer, convolution layer, main capsule layer and digital capsule layer.

Take one sample from the dataset made up of 8 of the 8 features as an example. After the 8 * 17 sample scanned by 128 2 * 5 convolution kernels with 2 steps, we obtains a 4 * 9 * 128 feature map. This layer is a common convolutional neural network, and the next layer uses 8 groups of 2 * 2 * 16 convolution kernel with 2 steps convolution 8 times. Then, each feature map is expanded into one dimension, and the corresponding positions are combined. A total of 128 8-dimensional vector neurons, namely capsules, are obtained. Finally, the dynamic routing algorithm is used to get the digital capsule layer, and the module length of the digital capsule layer vector is the prediction result.

During the dynamic routing algorithm, it has 128 * 2 weights, and every weight is a 16 * 1 vector W_{ij}. And the capsules from the previous layer is u_{ij}. The update formula is as following:

$$u_{j|i} = W_{ij} * u_i + B_j \tag{1}$$

Then, we used the next formula to complete the vector compression. It is designed to combine the information of all capsules. C_{ij} is calculated by B_{ij} with softmax function.

$$s_j = \sum_i c_{ij} * u_{j|i} \tag{2}$$

The module length is compressed to 0–1 by the squashing function, the formula is as following:

$$v_j = squash(s_j) \tag{3}$$

$$squash(s) = \frac{||s||^2}{1 + ||s||^2} * \frac{s}{||s||} \tag{4}$$

And, the dynamic routing forward propagation has completed.

When it comes to loss function, it is constructed by 2 parts: the first part is the interval loss, and the second part uses the original 8 * 17 data minus the 8 * 17 data of reconstruction, Then square the result, and ride 0.005 at the same time.

2.4 Evaluation of the Predictor

In order to verify the reliability and stability of our model, we used 10-fold cross-validation to get the result. In this paper, we employ two evaluation indicators to evaluate the predictive performance of our proposed method, including accuracy (AC) and area under curve (AUC). Among them, AC reflects the model's ability to classify positive samples correctly. AUC is an evaluation index to measure the pros and cons of the binary classification model, which indicates the probability that the positive cases of prediction are in front of the negative ones. Their definitions are as follows:

$$AC = \frac{TP + TN}{TP + TN + FP + FN} \tag{5}$$

Where TP is the number correctly divided into positive samples, FP is the number incorrectly divided into positive samples, FN is the number incorrectly divided into negative samples, and TN is correctly divided into negative samples.

$$AUC = \frac{\sum\limits_{i \in positive\_class} rank_i - \frac{M*(M+1)}{2}}{M*N} \tag{6}$$

Where $\sum\limits_{i \in positive\_class}$ means add up the serial numbers of the positive samples, $rank_i$ represents the serial number of the i sample(The probability score is from small to large, ranking in the rank position), M, N is the number of positive samples and the number of negative samples.

3 Results and Discussions

3.1 Model Stability Analysis

K-fold cross-validation is widely utilized to compare the performance of different machine learning models on a specific dataset. The principle of k-fold cross-validation is to divide the dataset into equal k shares for k trainings and finally take the average of the K results. So we use 10-fold cross-validation to get the result, which can guarantee the stabilization of the result.

3.2 Model Performances

To verify the reliability of our proposed method, we constructed LSTM classifiers for comparison. We utilized 28 different datasets consisted of 2 of the 8 features, 56 new datasets composed of 3 of the 8 features, 56 different datasets composed of 3 of the 8 features, 70 datasets made up of 4 of the 8 features, 56 datasets consisted of 5 of the 8 features, 28 datasets made up of 6 of the 8 features, 8 datasets made up of 7 of the 8 features and a dataset made up of 8 of the 8 features. What's more, we also chose 10-fold cross-validation to evaluate the classifiers we constructed. The results are shown in the table following (Fig. 1):

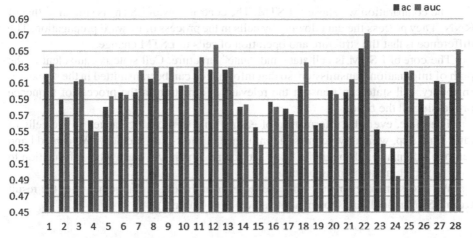

Fig. 1. The result gotten from 2 of the 8 features.

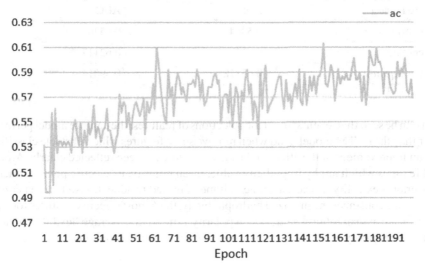

Fig. 2. The result gotten from the 8 features.

From the result gotten from 28 different datasets consisted of 2 of the 8 features, we noticed that the 22nd combination stands apart, which could mean that the mixture of 4th feature and the 7th feature contributes more to the classification, while the mixture of the 5th and 6th feature behaved relatively not well (Fig. 2).

From the result gotten from the datasets consisted of the 8 features, we can see that the result of not only AC but AUC rises in general, but fluctuated greatly. We thought the reason for it belongs to not only the weak classification features but the influence of interference term.

The comparation we chose is LSTM. The control flow of LSTM is similar to that of RNN. They process the data flowing by cells in the process of forward propagation. The difference is that the structure and operation of cells in LSTM change.

The core of LSTM is cell state and "gate" structure. Cell state is equivalent to the path of information transmission, so that information can be transmitted in the sequence. In theory, cell state can transmit the relevant information in the process of sequence processing all the time.

Therefore, even the information of earlier time step can be carried to the cells of later time step, which overcomes the influence of short-term memory. We can add and remove information through the "gate" structure, which will learn what information to save or forget in the training process.

We choose the best result from the experiment below, and together with the result from LSTM model, are shown in the table below (Table 2).

Table 2. The performances of each classification model.

Feature number	Acc	AUC
C_8^8 (lstm)	0.5364	0.5530
C_8^8 (capture)	0.61271	0.62117
$C_8^6\_14$ (capture)	0.65318	0.69013

It can be seen that, even without the selections of features, the capture model performs better than the LSTM model. And when remove some features which obstacle classification, an improvement of the effect of the classification has been reflected clearly. Among the 8 features which are hydrophilicity value, mean polarity, isoelectric point, refractivity, average flexibility indices, average volume of buried residue, transfer free energy to surface, and consensus normalized hydrophobicity, the 6 most effective features for classification are hydrophilicity value, mean polarity, refractivity, average flexibility indices, transfer free energy to surface, and consensus normalized hydrophobicity.

4   Conclusions

In recent years, studies about post translational modifications have grown more and more popular. Because of the great effects of post translational modifications, distinguishing them from various modifications is quite necessary. However, the huge amounts of features as well as simples make it really hard to distinguish between the modifications which are post translation or not. What's more, the features for classification are quite weak. So we did a dozen of works to improve its precision. We picked up the capsule as our initial model. The model behaves way better than the LSTM model, which is already a better model compared to the basic models like RNN. Then, we reassemble the database by the law of combination. As a result, we get 28 new datasets consisted of 2 of the 8 features, 56 new datasets composed of 3 of the 8 features, 56 different datasets composed of 3 of the 8 features, 70 datasets made up of 4 of the 8 features, 56 datasets consisted of 5 of the 8 features, 28 datasets made up of 6 of the 8 features, 8 datasets made up of 7 of the 8 features and a dataset made up of 8 of the 8 features. We put these datasets into the model for classification, and compared them among each other to found the feature combination which has better classification effect. The combination consists of features named hydrophilicity value, mean polarity, refractivity, average flexibility indices, transfer free energy to surface, and consensus normalized hydrophobicity behaved best. What's more, when it comes to the combinations consisted of different amount of features, we also picked some better ones, and pointed out the combinations which behaved bad. Apart from the features themselves, sometimes the right combination just helps a lot too.

Acknowledgement. This work is supported by the fundamental Research Funds for the Central Universities, 2020QN89, Xuzhou science and technology plan project (KC19142), the talent project of 'Qingtan scholar' of Zaozhuang University, Jiangsu Provincial Natural Science Foundation, China (SBK2019040953), Youth Innovation Teamof Scientific Research Foundation of the Higher Education Institutions of Shandong Province, China (2019KJM006), the Key Research Program of the Science Foundation of Shandong Province (ZR2020KE001), the PhD research startup foundation of Zaozhuang University (2014BS13) and Zaozhuang University Foundation (2015YY02), the Natural Science Foundation of China (61902337), Natural Science Fund for Colleges and Universities in Jiangsu Province (19KJB520016), Xuzhou Natural Science Foundation KC21047 and Young talents of science and technology in Jiangsu.

References

1. Molinie, B., Giallourakis, C.C.: Genome-Wide Location Analyses of N6-Methyladenosine Modifications (m6A-Seq), pp. 45–53. Humana Press (2017)
2. Nye, T.M., van Gijtenbeek, L.A., Stevens, A.G.: Methyltransferase DnmA is responsible for genome-wide N6-methyladenosine modifications at non-palindromic recognition sites in Bacillus subtilis. Nucleic Acids Res. **48**, 5332–5348 (2020)
3. O'Brown, Z.K., Greer, E.L.: N6-methyladenine: a conserved and dynamic DNA mark. In: Jeltsch, A., Jurkowska, R.Z. (eds.) DNA Methyltransferases - Role and Function. AEMB, vol. 945, pp. 213–246. Springer, Cham (2016). https://doi.org/10.1007/978-3-319-43624-1_10
4. Zhang, G., Huang, H., Liu, D.: N6-methyladenine DNA modification in Drosophila. Cell **161**(4), 893–906 (2015)
5. Janulaitis, A., Klimašauskas, S., Petrušyte, M.: Cytosine modification in DNA by BCNI methylase yields N4-methylcytosine. FEBS Lett. **161**, 131–134 (1983)
6. Unger, G., Venner, H.: Remarks on minor bases in spermatic desoxyribonucleic acid. Hoppe-Seyler's Zeitschrift fur physiologische Chemie **344**, 280–283 (1966)
7. Fu, Y.: N6-methyldeoxyadenosine marks active transcription start sites in Chlamydomonas. Cell **161**, 879–892 (2015)
8. Greer, E.L., Blanco, M.A., Gu, L.: DNA methylation on N6-adenine in C. elegans. Cell **161**, 868–878 (2015)
9. Wu, T.P., Wang, T., Seetin, M.G.: DNA methylation on N6-adenine in mammalian embryonic stem cells. Nature **532**, 329–333 (2016)
10. Xiao, C.L., Zhu, S., He, M.: N-methyladenine DNA modification in the human genome. Mol. Cell **71**, 306–318 (2018)

11. Zhou, C., Wang, C., Liu, H.: Identification and analysis of adenine N6-methylation sites in the rice genome. Nat. Plants **4**, 554–563 (2018)
12. Chen, W., Lv, H., Nie, F.: i6mA-Pred: identifying DNA N6-methyladenine sites in the rice genome. Bioinformatics 2796–2800 (2019)
13. Almagor, H.: A Markov analysis of DNA sequences. J. Theor. Biol. **104**, 633–645 (1983)
14. Borodovsky, M., Mclninch, J.D., Koonin, E.V.: Detection of new genes in a bacterial genome using Markov models for three gene classes. Nucleic Acids Res. **17**, 3554–3562 (1995)
15. Durbin, R., Eddy, S.R., Krogh, A.: Biological Sequence Analysis Probabilistic Models of Proteins and Nucleic Acids. Cambridge University Press, Cambridge (1998)
16. Ohler, U., Harbeck, S., Niemann, H.: Interpolated Markov chains for Eukaryotic promoter recognition. Bioinformatics 362–369 (1999)
17. Reese, M.G., Eeckman, F.H., Kulp, D.: Improved splice site detection in Genie. J. Comput. Biol. 311–323 (1997)
18. Wren, J.D., Hildebrand, W.H., Chandrasekaran, S.: Markov model recognition and classification of DNA/protein sequences within large text databases. Bioinformatics 4046–4053 (2005)

An SIR Epidemic Model with Birth Pulse and Pulse Vaccination on the Newborn

Airen Zhou(✉) and Jianjun Jiao

School of Mathematics and Statistics, Guizhou University of Finance and Economics, Guiyang 550025, People's Republic of China

Abstract. Pulse vaccination is an important strategy to eradicate an infectious disease. In this paper, we investigate an SIR epidemic model with birth pulse and pulse vaccination on the newborn. By using the discrete dynamical system determined by stroboscopic map, we obtain the condition for the global asymptotical stability of the disease-free periodic solution of the studied system. The permanent condition of the investigated system is also given. Numerical simulation is employed to illustrate our results. The result indicates that pulse vaccination rate on the newborn plays an important role in eradicating the disease. It provides a reliable tactic basis for preventing the disease from spreading.

Keywords: SIR epidemic model · Birth pulse · Global asymptotical stability · Permanence · Pulse vaccination

1 Introduction

Since last century, there has been a great deal of work in the mathematical theory of epidemics; for example, we can refer to the books, [1–4]. SIR (susceptible, infective, recovered) model is suitable for describing the transmission of infectious diseases with life long immunity, which is one of the most important epidemic models in epidemiology. In 1927, a classical SIR model was initially presented by Kermack and Mckendrick [5]. After that, lots of continuous SIR models with various transmission rates have been purposed, which have been investigated extensively and many threshold conditions have been obtained [6,7]. However, these models do not consider pulse vaccination, neither do they contain birth pulse, which is the novelty of our model in this present paper.

Supported by National Natural Science Foundation of China (11761019), Guizhou Science and Technology Platform Talents ([2017] 5736-019), Science and Technology Foundation of Guizhou Province ([2020]1Y001), and Guizhou Education Department Youth Science and Technology Talents Growth Project (Guizhou Jiaohe KY[2018]157), Guizhou Team of Scientific and Technological Innovation Talents (No. 20175658), Guizhou University of Finance and Economics Project Funding (No. 2019XYB11), Guizhou University of Finance and Economics Introduced Talent Research Project (2017).

D. Jiang and H. Song (Eds.): SIMUtools 2021, LNICST 424, pp. 555–563, 2022.
https://doi.org/10.1007/978-3-030-97124-3_43

Recently, pulse vaccination strategy, a new vaccination strategy against measles, has been proposed. Its theoretical study was started by Agur *et al.* in [8]. As far as pulse vaccination strategy are concerned, a lot of original work has been done in [9–13].

In the real world, individual members of many species experience two stages of life, immature and mature ones. Stage-structured population models have attracted great attention, and many stage-structured models have been studied in recent years [14–16].

Theories of impulsive differential equations have been introduced into population dynamics lately. Impulsive equations are found in almost every domain of applied science and have been studied in many investigations [17, 18]. They generally describe phenomena which are subject to steep or instantaneous changes.

Motivated by the above studies, our study is to investigate transmission dynamics of an SIR epidemic model with birth pulse and pulse vaccination. We assume full immunity of recovered individuals; that is to say, those individuals are no longer susceptible after they have recovered.

The present paper is to introduce birth pulse of the population and pulse vaccination into SIR epidemic model, and obtain some important qualitative properties for the investigated system. As a matter of fact, pulse birth and pulse vaccination on the newborn are used in an epidemic model. To the best of our knowledge, few research has been conducted.

2   The Model

In this paper, we consider an SIR epidemic model with birth pulse and pulse vaccination on the newborn:

$$
\begin{cases}
\begin{rcases}
\dfrac{dS_1(t)}{dt} = -(c+d_1)S_1(t) - \beta S_1(t)I(t), \\[2mm]
\dfrac{dS_2(t)}{dt} = cS_1(t) - d_2 S_2(t), \\[2mm]
\dfrac{dI(t)}{dt} = \beta S_1(t)I(t) - (r+d_3)I(t), \\[2mm]
\dfrac{dR(t)}{dt} = rI(t) - d_4 R(t),
\end{rcases} \quad t \neq n\tau, \quad t \neq (n+l)\tau, \\[10mm]
\begin{rcases}
\Delta S_1(t) = S_2(t)(a - bS_2(t)), \\[2mm]
\Delta S_2(t) = 0, \\[2mm]
\Delta I(t) = 0, \\[2mm]
\Delta R(t) = 0,
\end{rcases} \quad t = n\tau, \quad n = 1,2,\ldots, \\[10mm]
\begin{rcases}
\Delta S_1(t) = -\mu S_1(t), \\[2mm]
\Delta S_2(t) = 0, \\[2mm]
\Delta I(t) = 0, \\[2mm]
\Delta R(t) = \mu S_1(t),
\end{rcases} \quad t = (n+l)\tau, \quad n = 1,2,\ldots,
\end{cases}
\tag{1}
$$

where $S_1(t), S_2(t)$ represent the numbers of the immature and the mature of the susceptible. $I(t), R(t)$ represent the numbers of the infectious, and the recovered, respectively. c is called the rate of the immature susceptible turning into the mature susceptible. d_1, d_2, d_3, d_4, respectively denote the natural death rate of the immature susceptible, the mature susceptible, the infectious and the recovered. β is the average number of adequate contacts of an immature infectious individual per unit time. r stands for the recovery rate of the immature infectious individual. The mature susceptible is birth pulse with intrinsic rate of natural increase and density dependence rate of the mature susceptible denoted by a, b, respectively. The pulse birth and pulse vaccination occurs every τ period (τ is a positive constant). $\Delta S_1(t) = S_1(t^+) - S_1(t)$. $\mu(0 < \mu < 1)$ is the proportion of the successful vaccination which is called pulse vaccination rate, at $t = (n+l)\tau$, $0 < l < 1$, $n \in Z_+$. $S_2(t)(a - bS_2(t))$ represents the birth effort of the mature susceptible at $t = n\tau, n \in Z_+$.

In this work, we assume:

(i) The infection is not fully susceptible; that is to say, the disease is spread by the immature individual, the recovery from the disease will confer long lasting immunity.
(ii) The mature susceptible is immune to the disease; that is to say, the mature susceptible achieves lifetime immunity.

Since the first, second, and third equations do not include $R(t)$, we can simplify system (1) as follows:

$$
\begin{cases}
\left.\begin{array}{l}
\dfrac{dS_1(t)}{dt} = -(c + d_1)S_1(t) - \beta S_1(t)I(t), \\[2mm]
\dfrac{dS_2(t)}{dt} = cS_1(t) - d_2 S_2(t), \\[2mm]
\dfrac{dI(t)}{dt} = \beta S_1(t)I(t) - (r + d_3)I(t),
\end{array}\right\} t \neq n\tau, \quad t \neq (n+l)\tau, \\[6mm]
\left.\begin{array}{l}
\Delta S_1(t) = S_2(t)(a - bS_2(t)), \\
\Delta S_2(t) = 0, \\
\Delta I(t) = 0,
\end{array}\right\} t = n\tau, \quad n = 1, 2, \ldots, \\[6mm]
\left.\begin{array}{l}
\Delta S_1(t) = -\mu S_1(t), \\
\Delta S_2(t) = 0, \\
\Delta I(t) = 0,
\end{array}\right\} t = (n+l)\tau, \quad n = 1, 2, \ldots.
\end{cases}
\tag{2}
$$

This is equivalent to system (1).

3   Some Lemmas

Before discussing the main results, we will introduce some definitions, notations, and lemmas. Denote by $f = (f_1, f_2, f_3, f_4)^T$ the map defined by the right-hand side of system (1), the solution of (1), denoted by $z(t) = (S_1(t), S_2(t), I(t), R(t))^T$, is a piecewise continuous function $z : R_+ \to R_+^4$, where $R_+ = [0, \infty)$, $R_+^4 = \{z \in R^4 : z > 0\}$. $z(t)$ is continuous on $(n\tau, (n+l)\tau] \times R_+^4$ and $((n+l)\tau, (n+1)\tau] \times R_+^4$ ($n \in Z_+, 0 < l < 1$). According to [17, 18], the global existence and uniqueness of solutions of system (1) is guaranteed by the smoothness properties of f, the mapping defined by the right-hand side of system (1).

Let $V : R_+ \times R_+^4 \to R_+$. Then V is said to be belonged to class V_0 if:

(i) V is continuous in $(n\tau, (n+l)\tau] \times R_+^4$ and $((n+l)\tau, (n+1)\tau] \times R^4$, for all $z \in R_+^4$, $n \in Z_+$, and $\lim_{(t,y) \to ((n+l)\tau^+, z)} V(t, y) = V((n+l)\tau^+, z)$ and $\lim_{(t,y) \to ((n+1)\tau^+, z)} V(t, y) = V((n+1)\tau^+, z)$ exist.

(ii) V is locally lipschitzian in z.

Definition 3.1. If $V \in V_0$, then, for $(t, z) \in (n\tau, (n+l)\tau] \times R_+^4$ and $((n+l)\tau, (n+1)\tau] \times R_+^4$, the upper right derivative of $V(t, z)$ with respect to the impulsive differential system (1) is defined as

$$D^+V(t, z) = \lim_{h \to 0} \sup \frac{1}{h}[V(t + h, z + hf(t, z)) - V(t, z)].$$

Lemma 3.2. (see [17], Theorem 1.4.1) Let the function $m \in PC'[R_+, R]$ satisfy the inequalities

$$\begin{cases} m'(t) \le p(t)m(t) + q(t), \ t \ne t_k, \ k = 1, 2, \ldots, \\ m(t_k^+) \le d_k m(t_k) + b_k, \ t = t_k, \ t \ge t_0, \end{cases} \tag{3}$$

where $p, q \in C[R_+, R]$ and $d_k \ge 0$ and b_k are constants. Then

$$m(t) \le m(t_0) \prod_{t_0 < t_k < t} d_k \exp\left(\int_{t_0}^t p(s)ds\right) + \sum_{t_0 < t_k < t} \left(\prod_{t_k < t_j < t} d_j \exp\left(\int_{t_k}^t p(s)ds\right)\right) b_k$$

$$+ \int_{t_0}^t \prod_{s < t_k < t} d_k \exp\left(\int_s^t p(\sigma)d\sigma\right) q(s)ds, \quad t \ge t_0.$$

Lemma 3.3. There exists a constant $M > 0$ such that $S_1(t) \le M$, $S_2(t) \le M$, $I(t) \le M$, $R(t) \le M$ for each solution $(S_1(t), S_2(t), I(t), R(t))$ of system (1) with t large enough.

We choose the following notation:

$$\mu^* = \frac{ace^{-d_2\tau}(1 - e^{-(c+d_1-d_2)\tau}) - (c+d_1-d_2)(1-e^{-d_2\tau})(1-e^{-(c+d_1)\tau})}{ace^{-d_2\tau}(e^{-(c+d_1-d_2)l\tau} - e^{-(c+d_1-d_2)\tau}) + (c+d_1-d_2)(e^{-(c+d_1)\tau} - e^{-(c+d_1+d_2)\tau})}.$$

If $I(t) = 0$, then we have the following subsystem of (2):

$$
\begin{cases}
\left.
\begin{aligned}
\frac{dS_1(t)}{dt} &= -(c + d_1)S_1(t), \\
\frac{dS_2(t)}{dt} &= cS_1(t) - d_2S_2(t),
\end{aligned}
\right\} \quad t \neq n\tau, \quad t \neq (n+l)\tau, \\[2mm]
\left.
\begin{aligned}
\Delta S_1(t) &= S_2(t)(a - bS_2(t)), \\
\Delta S_2(t) &= 0,
\end{aligned}
\right\} \quad t = n\tau, \quad n = 1, 2, \ldots, \\[2mm]
\left.
\begin{aligned}
\Delta S_1(t) &= -\mu S_1(t), \\
\Delta S_2(t) &= 0,
\end{aligned}
\right\} \quad t = (n+l)\tau, \quad n = 1, 2, \ldots.
\end{cases} \tag{4}
$$

We easily obtain the analytic solution of system (4) between pulses as follows:

$$
\begin{cases}
S_1(t) = \begin{cases}
S_1(n\tau^+)e^{-(c+d_1)(t-n\tau)}, t \in (n\tau, (n+l)\tau], \\[2mm]
(1-\mu)S_1(n\tau^+)e^{-(c+d_1)(t-n\tau)}, t \in ((n+l)\tau, (n+1)\tau],
\end{cases} \\[6mm]
S_2(t) = \begin{cases}
e^{-d_2(t-n\tau)}\left[S_2(n\tau^+) + \frac{cS_1(n\tau^+)(1-e^{-(c+d_1-d_2)(t-n\tau)})}{c+d_1-d_2}\right], \quad t \in (n\tau, (n+l)\tau], \\[4mm]
\frac{ce^{-d_2(t-n\tau)}S_1(n\tau^+)}{c+d_1-d_2}\left[1 - \mu e^{-(c+d_1-d_2)l\tau} - (1-\mu)e^{-(c+d_1-d_2)(t-n\tau)}\right] \\[2mm]
\qquad\qquad + e^{-d_2(t-n\tau)}S_2(n\tau^+), t \in ((n+l)\tau, (n+1)\tau].
\end{cases}
\end{cases} \tag{5}
$$

Considering the fourth, fifth, seventh, and eighth equations of system (2), we have the stroboscopic map of (2)

$$
\begin{cases}
S_1((n+1)\tau^!) = \left[(1-\mu)e^{-(c+d_1)\tau} + \frac{ac\zeta}{c+d_1-d_2}\right]S_1(n\tau^+) + ae^{-d_2\tau}S_2(n\tau^+) \\[3mm]
\qquad\qquad -b\left[\frac{c\zeta}{c+d_1-d_2}S_1(n\tau^+) + e^{-d_2\tau}S_2(n\tau^+)\right]^2, \\[4mm]
S_2((n+1)\tau^+) = \frac{c\zeta}{c+d_1-d_2}S_1(n\tau^+) + e^{-d_2\tau}S_2(n\tau^+),
\end{cases} \tag{6}
$$

where $\zeta = e^{-d_2\tau}[(1-e^{-(c+d_1-d_2)l\tau}) + (1-\mu)e^{-(c+d_1-d_2)l\tau} - (1-\mu)e^{-(c+d_1-d_2)\tau}] > 0$. If we choose $A = (1-\mu)e^{-(c+d_1)\tau} + \frac{ac\zeta}{c+d_1-d_2} > 0$, $B = ae^{-d_2\tau} > 0$, $C = \frac{c\zeta}{c+d_1-d_2}$, $D = e^{-d_2\tau}$, $A < 1$, and $0 < D < 1$, the following two equivalence relations are found by calculation

$$
\mu < \mu^* \Leftrightarrow 1 - A - D + AD - BC < 0,
$$
$$
\mu > \mu^* \Leftrightarrow 1 - A - D + AD - BC > 0.
$$

The two fixed points of (6) are obtained as $G_1(0,0)$ and $G_2(S_1^*, S_2^*)$, where

$$
\begin{cases}
S_1^* = \dfrac{(1 - D - A + AD - BC)(-1 + D)}{bC^2}, & \mu < \mu^*, \\[4mm]
S_2^* = \dfrac{-(1 - D - A + AD - BC)}{bC}, & \mu < \mu^*.
\end{cases} \tag{7}
$$

Lemma 3.4. (i) If $\mu > \mu^*$, then the fixed point $G_1(0,0)$ is globally asymptotically stable. (ii) If $\mu < \mu^*$, then the fixed point $G_2(S_1^*, S_2^*)$ is globally asymptotically stable (The proof can refer to [19]).

Lemma 3.5. (i) If $\mu > \mu^*$, then the trivial periodic solution $(0,0)$ of system (4) is globally asymptotically stable.

(ii) If $\mu < \mu^*$, then the periodic solution $(\widetilde{S_1(t)}, \widetilde{S_2(t)})$ of system (4) is globally asymptotically stable, where

$$
\begin{cases}
\widetilde{S_1(t)} = \begin{cases} S_1^* e^{-(c+d_1)(t-n\tau)}, & t \in (n\tau, (n+l)\tau], \\ (1-\mu)S_1^* e^{-(c+d_1)(t-n\tau)}, & t \in ((n+l)\tau, (n+1)\tau], \end{cases} \\[2em]
\widetilde{S_2(t)} = \begin{cases} e^{-d_2(t-n\tau)}\left[S_2^* + \dfrac{cS_1^*(1-e^{-(c+d_1-d_2)(t-n\tau)})}{c+d_1-d_2}\right], & t \in (n\tau, (n+l)\tau], \\[1.5em] \dfrac{ce^{-d_2(t-n\tau)}S_1^*}{c+d_1-d_2}\left[1-\mu e^{-(c+d_1-d_2)l\tau} - (1-\mu)e^{-(c+d_1-d_2)(t-n\tau)}\right] \\[1em] \qquad\qquad\qquad\qquad +e^{-d_2(t-n\tau)}S_2^*, & t \in ((n+l)\tau, (n+1)\tau], \end{cases}
\end{cases} \tag{8}
$$

in which S_1^*, S_2^* are determined as in (7).

4   The Dynamics

In this section, for system (2) there obviously exists a disease-free periodic solution $(\widetilde{S_1(t)}, \widetilde{S_2(t)}, 0)$. First, we prove that the disease-free periodic solution $(\widetilde{S_1(t)}, \widetilde{S_2(t)}, 0)$ of system (2) is globally asymptotically stable. After that, we prove that system (2) is permanent.

Theorem 4.1. If

$$\mu < \mu^*$$

and

$$\mu > \frac{1-e^{-(c+d_1)\tau}}{e^{-(c+d_1)l\tau} - e^{-(c+d_1)\tau}} - \frac{(c+d_1)(r+d_3)\tau}{\beta S_1^*(e^{-(c+d_1)l\tau} - e^{(c+d_1)\tau})},$$

then the disease-free periodic solution $(\widetilde{S_1(t)}, \widetilde{S_2(t)}, 0)$ of system (2) is globally asymptotically stable, where S_1^*, S_2^* are defined by (7).

Definition 4.2. System (2) is said to be permanent if there are constants $m, M > 0$ (independent of initial value) and a finite time T_0, such that for all solutions $(S_1(t), S_2(t), I(t))$ with any initial values $S_1(0^+) > 0, S_2(0^+) > 0, I(0^+) > 0$, we have $m \leq S_1(t) \leq M, m \leq S_2(t) \leq M, m \leq I(t) \leq M$ for all $t \geq T_0$. Here T_0 may depend on the initial values $(S_1(0^+), S_2(0^+), I(0^+))$.

Theorem 4.3. If

$$\mu < \mu^*$$

and

$$\mu < \frac{1-e^{-(c+d_1)\tau}}{e^{-(c+d_1)l\tau} - e^{-(c+d_1)\tau}} - \frac{(c+d_1)(r+d_3)\tau}{\beta S_1^*(e^{-(c+d_1)l\tau} - e^{(c+d_1)\tau})}, \tag{9}$$

then system (2) is permanent, where S_1^*, S_2^* are defined by (7).

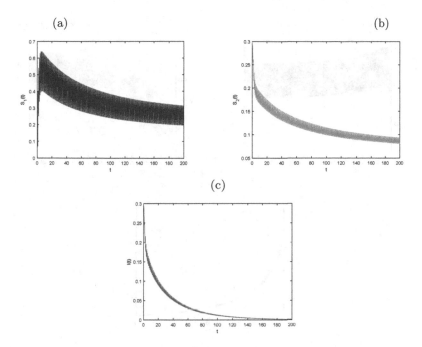

Fig. 1. Globally asymptotically stable disease-free periodic solution of System (1) with $S_1(0) = 0.1, S_2(0) = 0.3, I(0) = 0.3, a = 0.1, b = 0.2, c = 0.1, \beta = 0.2, \mu = 0.37, d_1 = 0.02, d_2 = 0.018, d_3 = 0.016, r = 0.15, \tau = 1, l = 0.25$. (a) Time-series of $S_1(t)$; (b) Time-series of $S_2(t)$; (c) Time-series of $I(t)$.

5   Conclusion and Simulation

In this work, we consider an SIR epidemic model with birth pulse and pulse vaccination on the newborn at different fixed moments. All solutions of system (1) are uniformly ultimately bounded. The condition for the global asymptotic stability of the disease-free periodic solution of system (1) is given, and the permanence of system (1) is also obtained.

According to the relevant statistical data of the National Health and Family Planning Commission, it is assumed that $S_1(0) = 0.1, S_2(0) = 0.3, I(0) = 0.3, a = 0.1, b = 0.2, c = 0.1, \beta = 0.2, \mu = 0.37, d_1 = 0.02, d_2 = 0.018, d_3 = 0.016, r = 0.15, \tau = 1, l = 0.25$, the conditions of the Theorem 4.1 are obviously satisfied, then the disease-free periodic solution of system (1) is globally asymptotically stable. (see Fig. 1). It is also assumed that $S_1(0) = 0.1, S_2(0) = 0.3, I(0) = 0.3, a = 0.1, b = 0.2, c = 0.1, \beta = 0.2, \mu = 0.1, d_1 = 0.02, d_2 = 0.018, d_3 = 0.016, r = 0.15, \tau = 1, l = 0.25$, the conditions of the Theorem 4.3 are obviously satisfied, then system (1) is permanent (see Fig. 2). The threshold dynamics about parameters l, τ can be also analyzed. If birth pulse and pulse vaccination are not considered in the traditional method, the disease of the system as a whole tends to be in a pandemic state. The results show that

(a)   (b)

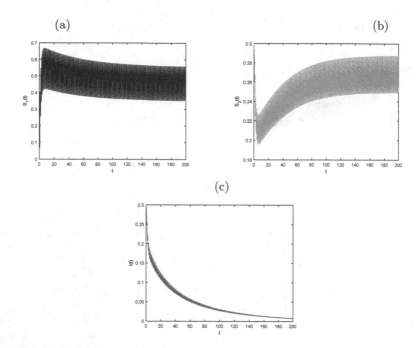

(c)

Fig. 2. The permanence for System (1) with $S_1(0) = 0.1, S_2(0) = 0.3, I(0) = 0.3, a = 0.1, b = 0.2, c = 0.1, \beta = 0.2, \mu = 0.1, d_1 = 0.02, d_2 = 0.018, d_3 = 0.016, r = 0.15, \tau = 1, l = 0.25$. (a) Time-series of $S_1(t)$; (b) Time-series of $S_2(t)$; (c) Time-series of $I(t)$.

the factors considered in this paper are more consistent with the actual situation. Our results indicate that pulse vaccination rate on the newborn plays an important role in eradicating the disease. It also provides a reliable tactic basis for preventing the disease from spreading.

References

1. Hoppenstaedt, F.: Mathematical Theories of Populations: Demographics. Genetics and Epidemics. Society for Industrial and Applied Mathematics, Philadelphia (1975)
2. Miller, E.: Population Dynamics of Infectious Diseases: Theory and Applications. Springer, New York (1983)
3. Hethcote, H.W.: Three basic epidemiological models. In: Levin, S.A., Hallam, T.G., Gross, L.J. (eds.) Applied Mathematical Ecology, vol. 18, pp. 119–144. Springer, Heidelberg (1989). https://doi.org/10.1007/978-3-642-61317-3_5
4. Allen, L.J., Brauer, F., Van den Driessche, P., Wu, J.: Mathematical Epidemiology. Springer, Berlin (2008)
5. Kermack, W.O., Mckendrick, A.G.: A contribution to the mathematical theory of epidemics. Proc. Roy. Soc. **115**(772), 700–721 (1927)
6. Buonomo, B., d'Onofrio, A., Lacitignola, D.: Global stability of an SIR epidemic model with information dependent vaccination. Math. Biosci. **216**(1), 9–16 (2008)

7. Jiao, J., Liu, Z., Cai, S.: Dynamics of an SEIR model with infectivity in incubation period and homestead-isolation on the susceptible. Appl. Math. Lett. 107 (2020). https://doi.org/10.1016/j.aml.2020.106442
8. Agur, Z., Cojocaru, L., Mazor, G., Anderson, R., Danon, Y.: Pulse mass measles vaccination across age cohorts. Proc. Natl. Acad. Sci. U.S.A. **90**(24), 11698–11702 (1993)
9. Shulgin, B., Stone, L., Agur, Z.: Pulse vaccination strategy in the SIR epidemic model. Bull. Math. Biol. **60**(6), 1123–1148 (1998)
10. Stone, L., Shulgin, B., Agur, Z.: Theoretical examination of the pulse vaccination policy in the SIR epidemic model. Math. Comput. Model. **31**(4), 207–215 (2000)
11. d'Onofrio, A.: On pulse vaccination strategy in the SIR epidemic model with vertical transmission. Appl. Math. Lett. **18**(7), 729–732 (2005)
12. Gao, S., Teng, Z., Xie, D.: Analysis of a delayed SIR epidemic model with pulse vaccination. Chaos Soliton Fract. **40**(2), 1004–1011 (2009)
13. Meng, X., Chen, L.: The dynamics of a new SIR epidemic model concerning pulse vaccination strategy. Appl. Math. Comput. **197**(2), 582–597 (2008)
14. Wang, W., Chen, L.: A predator prey system with stage-structure for predator. Comput. Math. Appl. **33**(8), 83–91 (1997)
15. Zhou, A., Sattayatham, P., Jiao, J.: Dynamics of an SIR epidemic model with stage structure and pulse vaccination. Adv. Difference Equ. **2016**(1), 1–17 (2016). https://doi.org/10.1186/s13662-016-0853-z
16. Jiao, J., Liu, Z., et al.: Threshold dynamics of a stage-structured single population model with non-transient and transient impulsive effects. Appl. Math. Lett. **97**, 88–92 (2019)
17. Lakshmikantham, V., Bainov, D.D., Simeonov, P.S.: Theory of Impulsive Differential Equations. World Scientific, Singapore (1989)
18. Bainov, D.D., Simeonov, P.S.: Impulsive Differential Equations: Periodic Solutions and Applications. Longman Scientific and Technical, New York (1993)
19. Jiao, J., Cai, S., Chen, L.: Analysis of a stage-structured predator-prey system with birth pulse and impulsive harvesting at different moments. Nonlinear Anal. RWA **12**(4), 2232–2244 (2011)

A Multi-objective Artificial Bee Colony Algorithm for Multiple Sequence Alignment

Ying Yu[1], Chen Zhang[1(✉)], Lei Ye[2], Ming Yang[3], and Changsheng Zhang[1]

[1] Software College of Northeastern University, Shenyang 110169, China
[2] College of Computer Science and Technology, Zhejiang University of Technology, Hangzhou 310000, China
[3] School of Information Network Security, People's Public Security University of China, Beijing 10038, China

Abstract. The multiple sequence alignment (MSA) problem is essential in biological research for finding specific relationship between the biologic sequences and their functions. This paper proposes a multi-objective artificial bee colony optimization algorithm for MSA (MOABC-MSA), which uses three kinds of searching to optimize a multi-objective MSA problem. The employed bee searching aims to make the solutions converge to the Pareto front (PF) of the problem; the onlooker bee accelerates the convergence speed; the scout bee facilitates the algorithm to avoid the local optimal. A comparative experiment is implemented on BAliBASE 3.0, a MSA benchmark. Experimental results show that the proposed algorithm has competitive performance with state-of-the-art metaheuristic algorithms.

Keywords: Multiple sequence alignment · Multi-objective optimization · Artificial bee colony optimization

1 Introduction

The multiple sequence alignment (MSA) problem aims to align three or more sequences simultaneously. MSA can help researchers to identify regions that exists same elements, which might contain valuable information.

The MSA problem has been proven to be a NP-complete problem with the sum-of-pairs (SP) metric [1], and NP-hard for most of existing metrics [2]. Different kinds of algorithms are developed to solve MSA problem.

Literature [3] finds six groups of approaches for MSA problem: (1) exact methods; (2) progressive methods; (3) consistency-based methods; (4) iterative methods; (5) evolutionary algorithms; (6) structure-based methods.

The mataheuristic algorithms have shown competitive performance in optimizing MSA problems. A hybrid multiobjective metaheuristic combining shuffled

D. Jiang and H. Song (Eds.): SIMUtools 2021, LNICST 424, pp. 564–576, 2022.
https://doi.org/10.1007/978-3-030-97124-3_44

frog-leaping algorithm with Kalgin algorithm is proposed in [3]. Literature [4] proposed a characteristic-based framework for MSA, which extracts the characteristics of input unaligned sequences and aligns the sequences with specific configuration according to the characteristics. A bi-objective evolutionary algorithm with a tree-based initialization method and a gap-re-inserting-based mutation operator is proposed in [1]. Literature [5] proposes a quantum-inspired heuristic optimization method for MSA. A multi-objective formulation for MSA is proposed in [9] for inferring the evolutionary history relating. ProbPFP [6] combines the partition function and the hidden Markov model (HMM), where the parameters is optimized by a particle swarm optimization (PSO). Literature [7] proposes an algorithm that employs sparse approximation to reduce computational cost for the relaxation. Literature [8] proposes a hybrid artificial bee colony optimization (ABC) algorithm for MSA, which performs a single-point crossover for employed bee phase and a multiple mutation operator that contains four kinds of mutations operators for onlooker bee phase.

Early literatures evaluates the alignments by one score function. However, when optimizing the MSA problem, researchers have more than one requirement for aligned sequences. To meet different requirements of researchers, the MSA problem is designed to contain multiple optimization objectives. [3] adopts the weighted sum-of-pairs function with affine gap penalties (WSP) and the number of total conserved columns (TC) score. [4] uses the Q-score (i.e., sum-of-pairs (SP) score) and total column (TC) score as the objective functions. In [1], the MSA problem is a bi-objective minimization problem, where the first objective function is the scoring function that minimizes the number of gaps, the second objective function is the opposite of SP function. Four objectives are proposed in [9]: non-gap columns for the calculation of entropy, the similarity of columns containing one or more gaps, the similarity of column containing no gap, and the number of consecutive gaps. [7] develops a relaxed formulation for the MSA problem based on a regression-coding framework.

This paper proposes a novel artificial bee colony optimization algorithm for MSA (MOABC-MSA). The employed bee stage achieves optimization for each sub-problem. The onlooker bees stage is based on a non-dominated ranking-based roulette wheel selection, which can obtain high-quality solutions with high diversity. The scout bee works could facilitate the algorithm in avoiding local optimums. The details of the MOABC-MSA is introduced in the third section of this paper.

The remainder parts of this paper is organized as follows. The second section introduces the definition of the multi-objective MSA problem. Section 3 describes the design and implementation of the proposed MOABC-MSA. Section 4 compares the MOABC-MSA with state-of-the-art metaheuristics on a benchmark MSA test suite. The last section summarizes the proposed work and predicts the research direction of metaheuristic algorithms for MSA.

2   Problem Definition

There are three objectives in the problem: single structure induced evaluation (STRIKE), percentage of totally conserved columns (%TC), and percentage of non-gaps (%nonGap). STRIKE aims to maximizing the accuracy of the alignment. Maximizing %TC ensures there are more columns that the residues are exactly the same, i.e., more conserved or special regions within an alignment. Maximizing the %nonGap encourages the aligner to reduce the number of gaps in the aligned sequences. The MSA problem is represented by the mathematical form shown in Eq. 1:

$$\text{maximize } F(S) = (STRIKE(S), \%TC(S), \%nonGap(S)) \tag{1}$$

Strike evaluates the accuracy of an alignment based on structural information of, at least, one sequence of the alignment. This structural information is commonly retrieved from the Protein Data Bank [10].

Using the structural information as a source for amino acid frequencies and contacts, a log-odds contact matrix is estimated by measuring the ratio between the frequency of each possible contact and its expectation, given the background frequency of each single amino acid. Given any pair of amino acids i and j, the score for their contacts can be estimated as:

$$M_{ij} = 10 \times \ln\left(\frac{f_{ij}}{f_i f_j}\right) \tag{2}$$

where f_{ij} is the frequency of contacts involving i and j across all observed *residue-residue* contacts, f_i and f_j are the single residue frequencies in the dataset considered.

%TC takes into account the number of columns that are fully aligned with exactly the same compound. TC is defined as shown in Eq. 3:

$$\%TC(S) = 100 \sum_{l=1}^{L} \frac{totalColumn(S_l)}{L} \tag{3}$$

where S_l is the lth column of S, $S_l = s_{il} \forall i = 1, ..., k$, and $totalColumn(S_l)$ is defined following Eq. 4:

$$totalColumn(S_l) = \begin{cases} 1, & \text{if } s_{il} = s_{1l} \forall i = 2, ..., k \\ 0, & \text{otherwise} \end{cases} \tag{4}$$

%nonGap measures the number of residues with respect to the number of gaps into the alignment. This objective function is shown in Eq. 5:

$$\%nonGap(S) = 100 \sum_{i=1}^{k} \sum_{j=1}^{L} \frac{isNotGap(s_{ij})}{k \times L} \tag{5}$$

where s_{ij} represents the symbol in the jth position of the ith sequence in the alignment S. The function *isNotGap* for a specific residue is defined in Eq. 6:

$$isNotGap(residue) = \begin{cases} 1, & \text{if } residue = \text{`` -- ''} \\ 0, & \text{otherwise} \end{cases} \tag{6}$$

3   MOABC-MSA

3.1   Representation of Individuals

This paper adopted a encoding strategy that records the positions of gaps for each sequence. The adopted representation uses the format $(begin, end)$ to store the position of a gap or several consecutive gaps. For example, if a sequence is {REDH-PDLIQ NAK-K-}, it is represented as: {(5,5), (11,14), (18,18), (20,21)}.

3.2   Crossover and Mutation Operators

This paper employs a single-point crossover operator [3]. There are three kinds of mutation operators adopted in the proposed algorithm: shift-closed gaps, non-gap group splitting, and adjacent gap groups merging [16].

3.3   Algorithm Overview

Algorithm 1 shows the framework of the proposed MOABC-MSA. First, the algorithm uses MUSCLE, a non-metaheuristic method, to initialize N random food sources that represents N candidate alignments. Meanwhile, an archive NA for storing non-dominated solutions is initialized as NULL. Then the algorithm executes searching procedures of employed bees, onlooker bees and scout bees. The MOABC-MSA repeats the searching behaviours of two kinds of bees until it meets the stop criterion. Finally, the algorithm outputs non-dominated solutions and their corresponding scores.

3.4   Employee

Algorithm 2 shows the execution process of the employed bee stage. Each employed bee is assigned a food source. Each bee performs single-point crossover operation. For the ith bee, the first individual of the crossover operation is the ith food source, the second individual is randomly selected. After the crossover, two new candidate alignments are generated. Then the proposed algorithm performs shift-closed gaps mutation operator on the newly-generated candidate alignments. The new solutions are evaluated by the objective functions and merged into the candidate solution set.

The non-dominated sorting-based selection [13] is adopted in employed bee stage. The candidate solutions in each iteration is divided into several levels. The first level is non-dominated solutions among all candidates. The second is

---

Algorithm 1: Algorithm framework of MOABC-MSA

Input: sequences to be aligned;
Output: aligned sequences;
1 initialize N random food sources;
2 initialize non-dominated set NA;
3 evaluate food sources;
4 **while** *termination criterion is false* **do**
5 | employed bees execute search behaviour;
6 | onlooker bees execute search behaviour;
7 | **for** *each sub-problem* **do**
8 | | **if** *is not updated for k iterations* **then**
9 | | | scout bee execute search behaviour;
10 | | **end**
11 | **end**
12 | update non-dominated set NA;
13 **end**
14 output non-dominated solutions;

---

non-dominated solutions among candidates except the first level. The rest of the food sources is sorted in the same manner. If the algorithm can obtain N optimal solutions by select certain levels of candidate solutions into the population of next generation, it goes into the next iteration; if not, assuming that the first s levels are selected, the algorithm associates solutions in the $(s+1)^{th}$ level with N uniformly distributed reference vectors (RVs), and choose $N - \sum_{i=0}^{s} |level_i|$ solutions into the population of next generation by niche-preservation method [13].

3.5   Onlooker

The onlooker bees prefer to exploit high-quality solutions founded by employed bees. Meanwhile, the bees should maintain diversity of food sources.

At this stage, each onlooker bees select food sources to search according to the solution quality. Inspired by the fast non-dominated sort method [12], the proposed algorithm divides the food sources into several ranks.

When selecting food sources, an onlooker bee first select a rank based on roulette wheel selection, which guarantees that the non-dominated food sources are more likely to be selected. Assuming that there are M ranks among the food sources, the selected probability of the ith rank is calculated according to Eq. 7:

$$p_i = \frac{M - i + 1}{\sum_{j=1}^{M} j} \tag{7}$$

Next, the onlooker bee selects a food source randomly from the selected rank.

Each onlooker bee performs a single-point crossover operation. Then it performs the shift-closed gaps mutation, non-gap group splitting mutation, and adjacent gap groups merging mutation in sequence.

The food sources are updated by the non-dominated and crowded-based sorting selection [12]. The onlooker bee stage is described in Algorithm 3.

Algorithm 2: Searching behaviour of employed bees

    Input: N food sources;
    Output: N new food sources;
1   initialize ω_1 to ω_N;
2   calculate neighborhood of each food source;
3   **while** *termination criterion is false* **do**
4   **for** *each employed bee* **do**
5   perform single-point crossover operation;
6   perform shift-closed gaps mutation operation;
7   **end**
8   evaluate new solutions;
9   merge food sources and new solutions;
10   non-dominated sorting;
11   **if** $N = \sum_{i=0}^{s} |level_i|$ **then**
12   select s levels as new food source;
13   **end**
14   **else**
15   select new food source using sorted levels and niche-perservation method;
16   **end**
17   update food sources;
18 **end**

Algorithm 3: Searching behaviour of onlooker bees

    Input: N food sources;
    Output: N new food sources;
1   perform fast non-dominated sorting;
2   calculate selected probability for each food source;
3   select a food source for each onlooker by roulette wheel selection;
4   **while** *termination criterion is false* **do**
5   **for** *each employed bee* **do**
6   perform single-point crossover operation;
7   perform shift-closed gaps mutation operation;
8   perform non-gap group splitting;
9   perform adjacent gap groups merging;
10   **end**
11   evaluate new solutions;
12   merge food sources and new solutions;
13   perform non-dominated and crowded-based sorting selection;
14   update food sources;
15 **end**

3.6   Scout Bee Phase

The scout bees work when the optimal solution of a sub-problem is not updated for more than k iterations. The scout bees performs the same crossover operator and mutation operator with the onlooker bees. Algorithm 4 shows the searching behaviour of scout bee.

Algorithm 4: Searching behaviour of scout bee

Input: sequences to be aligned;
Output: aligned sequences;
1   initialize N random food sources;
2   initialize non-dominated set NA;
3   evaluate food sources;
4   **while** *termination criterion is false* **do**
5   **for** *each sub-problem* **do**
6   **if** *the optimal solution is not updated for more than k iterations* **then**
7   perform single-point crossover operation;
8   perform shift-closed gaps mutation operation;
9   perform non-gap group splitting;
10   perform djacent gap groups merging;
11   **end**
12   **end**
13   evaluate new solutions;
14   merge food sources and new solutions;
15   find optimal solution of each sub-problem;
16   update food sources;
17 **end**

---

4   Experimental Result

This section proposed a comparison study. The performance of the proposed MOABC-MSA is compared with metaheuristics on benchmark dataset.

This paper uses the 3.0 version of Benchmark alignment database (BAliBASE) to test the proposed algorithm. There are 218 sets of sequences in BAliBASE 3.0, they are divided into six families: RV11, RV12, RV20, RV30, RV40, and RV50.

This experiment selects twenty-seven test cases from BAliBASE 3.0 to implement the comparative study between the proposed MOABC-MSA and other genetic and metaheuristic algorithms. The selected instances are: BB11001, BB11005, BB11018, BB11020 from RV11, BB12001, BB12013, BB12022, BB12035, BB12044 from RV12, BB20001, BB20010, BB20022, BB20033, BB20041 from RV20, BB30001, BB30008, BB30015, BB30022 from RV30, BB40001, BB40013, BB40025, BB40038, BB40048 from RV40, BB50001, BB50005, BB50010, BB50016 from RV50.

This paper compares MOABC-MSA with several state-of-the-art evolutionary or metaheuristic algorithms. The competitor algorithms includes: NSGA-II [18], MOEA/D [17], GAPAM [15], MO-SAStrE [16], and HMOABC [19]. The parameters of the peer algorithms are set according to their original literatures.

Table 1. Comparison on RV11

Test case		MOABC-MSA	HMOABC	NSGA-II	MOEA/D	GAPAM	MO-SAStrE
BB11001	STRIKE	**3.25**	3.07	2.94	2.98	2.79	2.88
	%TC	**7.89**	7.48	7.40	7.37	6.84	7.42
	%nonGap	**94.84**	89.46	93.75	92.98	90.57	91.44
BB11005	STRIKE	**3.14**	3.09	2.89	2.94	2.67	2.88
	%TC	**8.04**	6.90	6.59	6.54	6.38	6.52
	%nonGap	**93.68**	87.56	92.64	90.53	88.24	83.20
BB11018	STRIKE	**3.58**	3.07	2.75	2.84	2.39	2.58
	%TC	**8.44**	7.35	7.03	6.89	5.35	5.24
	%nonGap	**94.37**	87.36	92.58	92.46	90.45	91.85
BB11020	STRIKE	**3.38**	3.25	2.93	2.86	2.37	2.25
	%TC	**7.33**	7.28	7.29	7.25	7.32	7.30
	%nonGap	**93.53**	90.45	92.37	92.59	91.43	92.50

Table 2. Comparison on RV12

Test case		MOABC-MSA	HMOABC	NSGA-II	MOEA/D	GAPAM	MO-SAStrE
BB12001	STRIKE	**2.74**	2.52	2.60	2.58	2.47	2.35
	%TC	**3.79**	3.62	3.74	3.75	3.68	3.71
	%nonGap	**84.40**	80.43	82.13	81.37	78.48	79.63
BB12013	STRIKE	**2.07**	0.78	0.68	0.68	0.74	0.70
	%TC	**3.79**	2.59	3.62	3.55	2.98	2.82
	%nonGap	**84.03**	80.38	83.44	82.56	81.47	78.38
BB12022	STRIKE	**2.81**	2.63	2.72	2.69	2.54	2.60
	%TC	**3.66**	3.47	3.58	3.21	3.46	3.29
	%nonGap	**82.94**	80.65	82.56	81.53	82.08	81.32
BB12035	STRIKE	**2.76**	2.51	2.69	2.65	2.55	2.49
	%TC	**3.73**	3.50	3.71	3.68	3.41	3.59
	%nonGap	**82.30**	79.73	82.21	81.99	80.35	81.02
BB12044	STRIKE	**2.71**	2.46	2.58	2.59	2.32	2.44
	%TC	**3.74**	3.56	3.67	3.66	3.69	3.52
	%nonGap	**82.39**	79.93	81.95	80.61	78.16	77.08

4.1 Statistic Results

This section compares the statistical results of the algorithms on STRIKE, %TC, and %nonGap. Meanwhile, the executing times of the algorithms are recorded and compared. Each algorithm runs each test cases for 30 times to avoid the randomness. The termination criterion is set as 25,000 times of evaluation to guarantee the fairness of the experiment. For MOABC-MSA and HMOABC, both the number of employed bees and the number of onlooker bees are set to 20. For the other algorithms, the size of their populations is set to 20.

Table 3. Comparison on RV20

Test case		MOABC-MSA	HMOABC	NSGA-II	MOEA/D	GAPAM	MO-SAStrE
BB20001	STRIKE	**0.69**	0.67	0.54	0.58	0.42	0.51
	%TC	**0.21**	0.09	0.13	0.10	0.14	0.08
	%nonGap	**41.22**	38.85	40.06	39.57	38.30	36.94
BB20010	STRIKE	**0.48**	0.42	0.47	0.41	0.39	0.44
	%TC	**0.27**	0.22	0.25	0.23	0.18	0.20
	%nonGap	**40.18**	36.94	39.82	37.81	38.89	39.06
BB20022	STRIKE	**0.28**	0.24	0.26	0.25	0.25	0.24
	%TC	**0.21**	0.18	0.19	0.17	0.17	0.15
	%nonGap	**39.42**	38.22	38.57	38.26	37.26	37.01
BB20033	STRIKE	**0.56**	0.50	0.55	0.52	0.49	0.54
	%TC	**0.26**	0.19	0.24	0.22	0.17	0.21
	%nonGap	**41.27**	38.48	40.53	36.52	34.83	35.66
BB20041	STRIKE	**0.37**	0.32	0.34	0.35	0.29	0.31
	%TC	**0.20**	0.14	0.18	0.16	0.11	0.13
	%nonGap	**40.28**	36.53	39.39	34.55	32.17	33.68

Table 4. Comparison on RV30

Test case		MOABC-MSA	HMOABC	NSGA-II	MOEA/D	GAPAM	MO-SAStrE
BB30001	STRIKE	**1.75**	1.63	1.65	1.67	1.54	1.56
	%TC	**0.33**	0.29	0.32	0.30	0.25	0.22
	%nonGap	**50.77**	43.70	49.42	50.04	44.66	42.97
BB30008	STRIKE	**1.85**	1.68	1.74	1.77	1.63	1.66
	%TC	**0.33**	0.27	0.31	**0.33**	0.25	0.22
	%nonGap	**51.40**	42.34	50.06	50.56	49.28	44.30
BB30015	STRIKE	**2.44**	2.18	2.35	2.39	2.22	2.15
	%TC	0.35	0.34	0.35	**0.36**	0.29	0.28
	%nonGap	**49.07**	43.92	48.91	47.40	43.21	40.06
BB30022	STRIKE	**2.06**	1.74	1.93	1.95	1.86	1.88
	%TC	**0.41**	0.34	0.39	0.40	0.36	0.36
	%nonGap	**48.52**	46.03	47.60	47.88	42.52	43.94

Tables 1, 2, 3, 4, 5 and 6 shows the best value of STRIKE, %TC, and %non-Gap among solutions found by the tested algorithms for each test case. The bold number indicates the optimum. Table 1, 2 and 3 shows that for instances in RV11, RV12, and RV20, MOABC-MSA obtains the optimal STRIKE, %TC, and %nonGap on all test cases. For BB30008, both MOABC-MSA and MOEA/D obtain the optimal %TC. For BB30015 and BB50010, MOEA/D obtains the optimal %TC. For BB40048, results of NSGA-II obtain the best %nonGap. For the other test cases in RV30, RV40, and RV50, MOABC-MSA outperforms the compared algorithms in both the three objectives.

Table 5. Comparison on RV40

Test case		MOABC-MSA	HMOABC	NSGA-II	MOEA/D	GAPAM	MO-SAStrE
BB40001	STRIKE	**3.50**	2.99	3.45	3.47	3.09	3.14
	%TC	**0.42**	0.23	0.36	0.33	0.27	0.29
	%nonGap	**31.13**	27.62	30.75	30.90	28.84	27.56
BB40013	STRIKE	**3.79**	3.22	3.67	3.54	3.48	3.26
	%TC	**0.33**	0.21	0.29	0.27	0.20	0.26
	%nonGap	**31.01**	27.45	29.84	29.98	27.59	25.86
BB40025	STRIKE	**3.59**	3.44	3.53	3.58	3.32	3.17
	%TC	**0.38**	0.26	0.34	0.25	0.27	0.30
	%nonGap	**29.03**	25.34	28.77	27.40	24.59	22.05
BB40038	STRIKE	**3.33**	2.98	3.21	3.25	3.08	3.04
	%TC	**0.36**	0.28	0.35	0.35	0.33	0.29
	%nonGap	**29.88**	26.36	29.24	29.34	28.37	27.75
BB40048	STRIKE	**3.47**	3.05	3.36	3.42	3.06	3.11
	%TC	**0.27**	0.22	0.24	0.25	0.18	0.20
	%nonGap	29.97	26.58	**30.13**	28.44	27.93	26.55

Table 6. Comparison on RV50

Test case		MOABC-MSA	HMOABC	NSGA-II	MOEA/D	GAPAM	MO-SAStrE
BB50001	STRIKE	**2.11**	1.88	1.97	2.04	1.83	1.65
	%TC	**0.39**	0.27	0.35	0.33	0.28	0.31
	%nonGap	**70.05**	55.93	69.90	67.34	62.98	63.51
BB50005	STRIKE	**2.03**	1.48	1.95	1.88	1.57	1.62
	%TC	**0.35**	0.30	0.34	0.33	0.24	0.25
	%nonGap	**69.01**	62.48	68.45	63.44	61.50	60.24
BB50010	STRIKE	**1.89**	1.56	1.84	1.80	1.61	1.69
	%TC	0.36	0.26	0.36	**0.37**	0.25	0.32
	%nonGap	**63.33**	59.02	62.75	60.45	59.93	57.28
BB50016	STRIKE	**1.89**	1.37	1.88	1.67	1.34	1.42
	%TC	**0.32**	0.19	0.30	0.31	0.24	0.25
	%nonGap	**64.01**	58.99	63.90	61.52	59.31	60.04

4.2 Hypothesis Results

This paper uses the Wilcoxon signed-rank hypothesis test to investigate the difference between the performance of the MOABC-MSA and results of the competitors. The objective values of each solution is normalized to real number between zero and one, then the normalized solutions are evaluated by the IGD indicator [14]. The IGD indicator works out a scalarized score for each non-dominated solution set. Finally, the IGD value of each solution set is utilized in the hypothesis test. Table 7 shows the p-values between results of MOABC-MSA

Table 7. Comparison on BAliBASE test cases

Test case	HMOABC	NSGA-II	MOEA/D	GAPAM	MO-SAStrE
BB11001	0.005	0.005	0.005	0.005	0.005
BB11005	0.005	0.005	0.005	0.005	0.005
BB11018	0.005	0.005	0.005	0.004	0.05
BB11020	0.005	0.005	0.005	0.05	0.05
BB12001	0.05	0.005	0.05	0.05	0.05
BB12013	0.005	0.005	0.005	0.005	0.005
BB12022	0.005	0.003	0.004	0.005	0.005
BB12035	0.005	0.005	0.005	0.005	0.005
BB12044	0.005	0.005	0.005	0.005	0.005
BB20001	0.005	0.01	0.05	0.005	0.005
BB20010	0.005	0.05	0.01	0.01	0.01
BB20022	0.005	0.01	0.01	0.005	0.005
BB20033	0.005	0.05	0.01	0.005	0.005
BB20041	0.005	0.05	0.05	0.005	0.005
BB30001	0.005	0.005	0.01	0.005	0.005
BB30008	0.005	0.005	0.005	0.005	0.005
BB30015	0.005	0.01	0.01	0.005	0.005
BB30022	0.005	0.01	0.01	0.005	0.005
BB40001	0.005	0.05	0.05	0.005	0.005
BB40013	0.005	0.01	0.01	0.01	0.01
BB40025	0.01	0.05	0.0 5	0.005	0.01
BB40038	0.005	0.01	0.01	0.005	0.005
BB40048	0.01	0.01	0.10	0.01	0.01
BB50001	0.005	0.005	0.01	0.005	0.005
BB50005	0.005	0.01	0.05	0.005	0.005
BB50010	0.005	0.10	0.10	0.01	0.01
BB50016	0.005	0.05	0.10	0.005	0.01

and results of the peer algorithms. The significance level is set at 0.05 in this paper. If the p-value is less than 0.05, it indicates that the result of MOABC-MSA is significantly better than the result of the competitor. According to Table 7, except for BB40038, BB50010, and BB50016, MOABC-MSA outperforms all its competitors in the test cases.

Experimental results show that MOABC-MSA can obtain better solution on all objectives when optimizing the three-dimensional multi-objective MSA problem. This result means that MOABC-MSA not only obtains solutions that are close to the PF of the problems, but also obtains uniform solution distribution. In other words, MOABC-MSA achieves a good balance between convergence and diversity of solutions.

4.3 Further Analysis

The computation complexity of the employee phase and the onlooker phase is $O(N^2)$. Therefore, the computation complexity of the MOABC-MSA is $O(N^2)$.

Compared to other heuristic multi-objective algorithms, the proposed algorithm uses three kinds of searching strategies alternately. Therefore, MOABC-MSA can balance the convergence and diversity during the searching process. Different from existing ABC-based algorithms, MOABC-MSA uses a roulette wheel selection according to the performance in Pareto dominance relationship. The selection strategy uses the information of non-dominated solutions to accelerate the convergence to the PF.

5 Conclusion

This paper proposes MOABC-MSA, an artificial bee colony optimization algorithm for solving MSA problem. The proposed algorithm considers both the convergence performance and the distribution of the alignments. The employed bees not only make the food sources converge to the PF, but also ensure the distribution of the food sources can reflect the real shape of the PF. The onlooker bees of MOABC-MSA accelerates the converging of food sources by utilizing high-quality solutions. MOABC-MSA uses the scout bee to avoid the local optimum. The comparative study on BAliBASE 3.0 verifies that MOABC-MSA has competitive performance. For the future study, improving the efficiency is a tough task and promising research direction.

References

1. Zhu, H., He, Z., Jia, Y.: A novel approach to multiple sequence alignment using multiobjective evolutionary algorithm based on decomposition. IEEE J. Biomed. Health Inform. **20**(2), 717–727 (2015)
2. Ramakrishnan, R.K., Singh, J., Blanchette, M.: RLALIGN: a reinforcement learning approach for multiple sequence alignment. In: 2018 IEEE 18th International Conference on Bioinformatics and Bioengineering (BIBE), pp. 61–66. IEEE (2018)
3. Rubio-Largo, Á., Vega-Rodríguez, M.A., González-Álvarez, D.L.: A hybrid multiobjective memetic metaheuristic for multiple sequence alignment. IEEE Trans. Evol. Compu. **20**(4), 499–514 (2015)
4. Rubio-Largo, Á., Vanneschi, L., Castelli, M., Vega-Rodríguez, M.A.: A characteristic-based framework for multiple sequence aligners. IEEE Trans. Cybern. **48**(1), 41–51 (2016)
5. Giannakis, K., Papalitsas, C., Theocharopoulou, G., Fanarioti, S., Andronikos, T.: A quantum-inspired optimization heuristic for the multiple sequence alignment problem in bio-computing. In: 2019 10th International Conference on Information, Intelligence, Systems and Applications (IISA), pp. 1–8. IEEE (2019)
6. Zhan, Q., Wang, N., Jin, S., Tan, R., Jiang, Q., Wang, Y.: ProbPFP: a multiple sequence alignment algorithm combining partition function and hidden Markov model with particle swarm optimization. In: 2018 IEEE International Conference on Bioinformatics and Biomedicine (BIBM), pp. 1290–1295. IEEE (2018)

7. Doan, P.T., Takasu, A.: Sparse regression-based multiple sequence alignment. In: 2019 IEEE International Conference on Multimedia and Expo (ICME), pp. 1372–1377. IEEE (2019)
8. Altwaijry, N., Almasoud, M., Almalki, A., Al-Turaiki, I.: Multiple sequence alignment using a multiobjective artificial bee colony algorithm. In: 2020 3rd International Conference on Computer Applications & Information Security (ICCAIS), pp. 1–6. IEEE (2020)
9. Nayeem, M.A., Bayzid, Md.S., Rahman, A.H., Shahriyar, R., Rahman, M.S.: Multiobjective formulation of multiple sequence alignment for phylogeny inference. IEEE Trans. Cybern. (2020)
10. Burley, S.K., Berman, H.M., Kleywegt, G.J., Markley, J.L., Nakamura, H., Velankar, S.: Protein Data Bank (PDB): the single global macromolecular structure archive. In: Wlodawer, A., Dauter, Z., Jaskolski, M. (eds.) Protein Crystallography. MMB, vol. 1607, pp. 627–641. Springer, New York (2017). https://doi.org/10.1007/978-1-4939-7000-1_26
11. Zhang, Q., Li, H.: MOEA/D: a multiobjective evolutionary algorithm based on decomposition. IEEE Trans. Evol. Comput. **11**(6), 712–731 (2008)
12. Deb, K., Pratap, A., Agarwal, S., Meyarivan, T.A.M.T.: A fast and elitist multiobjective genetic algorithm: NSGA-II. IEEE Trans. Evol. Comput. **6**(2), 182–197 (2002)
13. Deb, K., Jain, H.: An evolutionary many-objective optimization algorithm using reference-point-based nondominated sorting approach, Part I: solving problems with box constraints. IEEE Trans. Evol. Comput. **18**(4), 577–601 (2014)
14. Sun, Y., Yen, G.G., Yi, Z.: IGD indicator-based evolutionary algorithm for many-objective optimization problems. EEE Trans. Evol. Comput. **23**(2), 173–187 (2018)
15. Naznin, F., Sarker, R., Essam, D.: Progressive alignment method using genetic algorithm for multiple sequence alignment. IEEE Trans. Evol. Comput. **16**(5), 615–631 (2012)
16. Ortuño, F.M., et al.: Optimizing multiple sequence alignments using a genetic algorithm based on three objectives: structural information, non-gaps percentage and totally conserved columns. Bioinformatics **29**(17), 2112–2121 (2013)
17. Huazheng, Z., He, Z., Jia, Y.: A novel approach to multiple sequence alignment using multiobjective evolutionary algorithm based on decomposition. IEEE J. Biomed. Health Inform. **20**(2), 717–727 (2016)
18. Kaiwartya, O., et al.: Multiple sequence alignment using genetic algorithm and Non-Dominant Sorting Genetic Algorithm-II (NSGA II) and variants. J. Bioinform. Intell. Control **3**(4), 294–299 (2014)
19. Zhang, H., Zhu, Y., Zou, W., Yan, X.: A hybrid multi-objective artificial bee colony algorithm for burdening optimization of copper strip production. Appl. Math. Model. **36**(6), 2578–2591 (2012)

Research on Parallel Attribute Exploration Algorithm Based on Unrelated Attribute and Intent Sets

Daojun Han[1,2], Wan Chen[1,2], and Xianyu Zuo[1,2(✉)]

[1] Henan Key Laboratory of Big Data Analysis and Processing, Henan University, Kaifeng, Henan, China
[2] School of Computer and Information Engineering, Henan University, Kaifeng, Henan, China
`http://cs.henu.edu.cn/`

Abstract. The attribute exploration algorithm is an important knowledge discovery tool for obtaining the stem basis and intent of a given formal context in formal concept analysis. However, when the scale of the formal context is large, the traditional attribute exploration algorithm and the improved attribute exploration algorithm still traverse the attribute sets in the lexicographical order, which leads to the calculation process of the algorithm is too time-consuming. It seriously hinders the promotion and application of the current big data era. The time-consuming bottleneck mainly exists in the link of "traversing attribute sets in the lexicographic order". To solve this problem, first, we construct a prefix dictionary tree in the inverse linear order of the attribute sets in the inter-layer cardinality order and use the irrelevant definition. Second, we propose and prove three theorems by the above definition and formal concept analysis. Third, according to these theorems, we put forward a new parallel attribute exploration algorithm based on attribute and intent sets. In the process of calculating intent and pseudo-intent sets, the algorithm skips the computing process of attribute sets which are intent sets and neither intent nor pseudo-intent sets with the help of these proposed theorems and reduces search space of the algorithm and the scale of implication calculation, so as to reduce the time complexity. Experimental results show that the worst time complexity of the algorithm is $O(M^2 \times \max(P, G))$. Compared with the improved algorithm, this algorithm has obvious time performance advantages.

Keywords: Formal concept analysis · Stem base · Intent · Parallel attribute exploration · Lexicographic order · Knowledge discovery

This work was supported by the Scientific and technological project of Henan Province (Grant No. 202102310340), Foundation of University Young Key Teacher of Henan Province (Grant No. 2019GGJS040, 2020GGJS027), and Key scientific research projects of colleges and universities in Henan Province (Grant No. 21A110005).

D. Jiang and H. Song (Eds.): SIMUtools 2021, LNICST 424, pp. 577–599, 2022.
https://doi.org/10.1007/978-3-030-97124-3_45

1 Introduction

Formal Concept Analysis (abbrev. FCA) [1] was proposed by Professor Wille in Germany in the early 1980s. It uses Galois connection to obtain common attributes and possessions of objects from a given formal context. These objects with common attributes are then summarized as formal concepts or concepts for short. According to the generalization-instancing relationship between formal concepts, concepts of the formal context are formed into a complete lattice, namely the Concept Lattice [2–4].

As the kernel data structure of FCA, concept lattice has attracted wide attention from an abundance of researchers. It has been widely used in data mining [5–8], rule extraction [9,10], knowledge discovery [11,12], access control [13,14], granular computing [15], and conceptual cognitive learning [16–18] and other fields [19–22].

Among them, for a given formal context, the attribute exploration algorithm [23] obtains the implication relationship between attributes in the formal context through interactive inquiry with the domain expert. This kind of implication relationship can express the knowledge contained in the formal context and is an important form of knowledge representation. Different from other existing methods of obtaining knowledge based on known data for statistics or induction, attribute exploration can actively interact with the domain expert to explore the implication relationship between attribute sets. The exploration process can be generalized as the following steps: firstly, we obtain attribute sets and its' lexicographical relationship according to the given formal context; secondly, according to the lexicographical order, it gradually asks the domain expert whether the implication relationship between attribute sets is valid; third, it is up to for the domain expert to judge whether these problems are true; fourth, if the implication relationship is not valid, the domain expert provides a counterexample from the formal context that refutes the implication relationship and adds it to the current formal context. If it is valid, then it adds the implication to the candidate stem base; fifth, we should find the next attribute set to be interacted with the domain expert according to the lexicographical order; finally, the algorithm can explore the implication relations between all attribute sets according to the lexicographical order, so as to it can acquire the stem base of the given formal context.

At present, the attribute exploration algorithm has been widely used in many fields. Borchmann [24] started from the exploration of classic attribute exploration algorithm, and retained the completeness, non-redundancy of classic attribute exploration algorithm, and asked the domain expert about the characteristics of the smallest number of implications, and proposed a general attribute exploration framework. The various variants of attribute exploration are regarded as an instance under this framework. Jäschke and Rudolph [25] proposed a method to support attribute exploration through Web information retrieval, and extended attribute exploration to the Web domain, and improved query efficiency. Potoniec and Rudolph [26] combined attribute exploration with machine learning to make the development and optimization of domain-specific ontology easier. Hanika and Zumbragel [27] proposed a collaborative concept exploration algorithm, which established a consortial expert based on a well-formed query to give multiple domain experts the initial ability to handle false acceptance implications. Codocedo and Baixeries [28] sampled the formal context through the attribute exploration algorithm and proposed a general method to convert the irreducible pattern structure to the representation formal context, which reduces the complexity of mining pattern structure.

However, the process is too time-consuming due to the completeness of the attribute exploration algorithm when calculating the implication. Ryssel [29, 30] used appropriate premises to improve the efficiency of attribute exploration, but this scheme improves efficiency while also causing the problem of not being able to obtain the minimum cardinality implication. Zhao [31] used the definition of correlation between attribute sets and the stem base to improve the traditional attribute exploration algorithm to a certain extent. On the basis of Zhao Xiaoxiang's improved attribute exploration algorithm, Shen [32] further proposed an irrelevant definition to further improve the algorithm after studying the attribute exploration algorithm between the two departments [35], but the algorithm still traverses attribute sets in lexicographic order, and the complexity is still high.

In fact, any algorithm that calculates the pseudo-intent of the formal context in lexicographical order has shown that it cannot obtain the stem base of the formal context [33] with the polynomial-time complexity. Therefore, for theoretically difficult problems, a popular method is to explore the possibility of parallelization of known algorithms. Kriegel [34] proposed a parallel attribute exploration algorithm, which reduces the overall time-consuming of the attribute exploration algorithm, but the algorithm still traverses too many attribute sets in lexicographic order, so it is still very time-consuming.

Different from the aforementioned schemes, we propose a new algorithm which focuses on finding less time-consuming algorithms as a whole, but also considers avoiding the inherent redundant calculation processes of the algorithm. Therefore, this paper proposes a new parallel attribute exploration under unrelated attribute and intent sets algorithm (PAEUIS), which constructs a prefix dictionary tree according to the attribute sets of the formal context in the interlayer cardinality order and the inverse linear order within the layer, and skips the attribute sets in the layer that are obviously intent sets and not related to the stem base, which achieves the pruning effect in the prefix dictionary tree layer, and reduces the search space of the algorithm, and calculates the implication expressions in parallel for the remaining pseudo-intents, and reduces the overall consumption of the algorithm time. Our approach achieves new state-of-the-art performances on randomly generated datasets in the field of attribute exploration.

2   Preliminaries

This section briefly illustrates some related fundamental notions of FCA [1,5, 23,24] used in this article as follows:

Definition 1. *A formal context $K = (G, M, I)$ is composed of two sets G and M and the relationship I between them, where G is the set of objects, M is an attribute set, and the relationship between them is $I \subseteq G \times M$. $(G, M) \in I$ or (gIm) means that the object g has an attribute m. We use $(g, m) \notin I$ to indicate that the object g does not possess the attribute m.*

Definition 2. *Let $K = (G, M, I)$ be a formal context, then define the following operations in the object subset $A \subseteq G$, and the attribute subset $B \subseteq M$:*

$$A^I = \{m \in B \mid \forall g \in A, (g, m) \in I\}$$
$$B^I = \{g \in A \mid \forall m \in B, (g, m) \in I\}$$

A^I refers to a collection of attributes shared by all objects in A, and B^I represents a collection of objects shared by all attributes in B. If for any $g \in G$, $m \in M$ there is, the formal context is said to be regular.

Definition 3. *Let $K = (G, M, I)$ be a formal context, then in the object subset $A \subseteq G$, and the attribute subset $B \subseteq M$, if A, B satisfies $A^I = B$, $B^I = A$, then we call the two-tuple (A, B) is a formal concept, abbreviated as a concept. Among them, A is the extent of the concept (A, B), and B is the intent of the concept (A, B).*

Definition 4. *Suppose $K = (G, M, I)$ is a formal context, then the concepts on the formal context $K = (G, M, I)$ has the following basic properties $(\forall\ A, A_1, A_2 \subseteq G, \forall\ B, B_1, B_2 \subseteq M)$:*

Property 1. $A_1 \subseteq A_2 \rightarrow A_1{}^I \supseteq A_2{}^I$, $B_1 \subseteq B_2 \rightarrow B_1{}^I \supseteq B_2{}^I$;

Property 2. $A \subseteq A^{II}$, $B \subseteq B^{II}$;

Property 3. $A = A^{III}$, $B = B^{III}$;

Property 4. $A \subseteq B^I \Leftrightarrow B \subseteq A^I$

Property 5. Both (A^{II}, A^I) and (B^I, B^{II}) are concepts.

Definition 5. *Suppose $K = (G, M, I)$ is a formal context, then $P \subseteq M$ is called the pseudo-intent in the formal context K and satisfies the following conditions:*

1. $P^{II} \neq P$;
2. For every pseudo-intent $Q \subsetneq P$ there is $Q^{II} \subseteq P$.

Definition 6. *Suppose $K = (G, M, I)$ is a formal context. Let $B_1, B_2 \subseteq M$, then any formula of the form $B_1 \rightarrow B_2$ is called an implication formula. If there exists $B_1{}^I \subseteq B_2{}^I$ is valid, then the implication formula $B_1{}^I \subseteq B_2{}^I$ is valid in the formal context K.*

Definition 7. *Suppose $K = (G, M, I)$ is a formal context, and the set of implication $Imp(K) = \{P \rightarrow P^{II} \backslash P \mid P \text{ is a pseudo–intent of } K\}$ is the Duquenne-Guigues Base on the formal context, referred to as the stem base.*

Definition 8. *Suppose $K = (G, M, I)$ is a formal context, and the set of implication $Imp(K)$ has the implication expression of $C \rightarrow D \in Imp(K)$. If there exists $C \nsubseteq T$ or $D \subseteq T$ for the attribute set $T \subseteq M$, then T is related to $C \rightarrow D$. If the attribute set T is related to all the implication expressions in $Imp(K)$, then it is said that T is related to $Imp(K)$.*

Definition 9. *Suppose $K = (G, M, I)$ is a formal context, the attribute set $M = m_1, \cdots, m_n$, if the basic linear order given on M is $(m_1 < m2 < \cdots < m_n)$, then for any $B_1, B_2 \subseteq M$ there exists $B_1 < B_2$ if and only if $m_i \in B_2 - B_1$ exists and $B_1 \cap \{m_1, \cdots, m_{i-1}\} = B_2 \cap \{m_1, \cdots, m_{i-1}\}$.*

Definition 10. *Suppose $K = (G, M, I)$ is a formal context, the attribute set $M = m_1, \cdots, m_n$, if the basic linear order given on M is $(m_1 < m2 < \cdots < m_n)$, then the lexicographical relationship $<$ of the attribute set in the formal context K is the linear order relationship of 2^M. According to the lexicographical relationship, the attribute set in the formal context can be tested one by one whether the attribute set is an intent or pseudo-intent.*

Definition 11. *Suppose $K = (G, M, I)$ is a formal context, and the set of implication $Imp(K)$ has the implication form $C \rightarrow D \in Imp(K)$. If there exists $C \subseteq T$ and $D \nsubseteq T$ for the attribute set $T \subseteq M$, then T and $C \rightarrow D$ are not related. If the attribute set T is not related to any one of the implication expression in $Imp(K)$, then it is said that T is not related to $Imp(K)$.*

Definition 12. *Suppose $K = (G, M, I)$ is a formal context, and $Imp(K)$ is the stem base of K. As for any one implication $C \rightarrow D \in Imp(K)$, if the attribute set T is not related to the implication $C \rightarrow D$, then T is neither an intent nor pseudo-intent in the formal context K.*

3 Research on Parallel Attribute Exploration Algorithm Based on Unrelated Attribute and Intent Sets

For a given formal context, the implication relationship between attribute sets, that is, the knowledge implied by the formal context can be represented by the inclusion relationship between attribute sets. Attribute exploration algorithm is a tool to obtain these inclusion relationships in FCA, and can find the intent and stem base of a given formal context.

The famous NextClosure algorithm proposed by Ganter can be used to obtain the intent and stem base of a given formal context. The mathematical idea behind the algorithm is mainly to traverse attribute sets in lexicographical order, and actively asks the domain expert whether the implication between attributes is valid, so as to calculate all the intent and pseudo-intent sets of a given formal context. The implications obtained from the pseudo-intent attribute sets constitute the stem base of the given formal context. One of the great advantages of this algorithm is that the next (pseudo) intent is uniquely determined, but it may require backtracking to find it. In addition, the algorithm is essentially in linear order, that is, it cannot be parallelized. In this paper, we find that linear order is not used, and layer the attribute sets in a set cardinal order, and hierarchically parallelize to determine whether the attribute sets are intents or pseudo-intents, and in the process of exploration, the intent sets and irrelevant pseudo-intent sets are skipped the implication judgment of the attribute sets can avoid a lot of redundant calculation, and then quickly calculate the stem base of a given formal context. Besides, since in the implementation of multiple threads, there is no communication between different threads, that is, the calculation of the implication formula of the attribute sets in each cardinality layer can be calculated in parallel.

3.1 Theoretical Basis

To facilitate the following explanation, this article first sets definitions as follows.

Definition 13. *Let $K = (G, M, I)$ be a formal context, attribute set $B, B^+ \subseteq M$, if $B < B^+$ and the interval $<B, B^+>$ is an empty set, then it is said that B^+ is only greater than B, which is recorded as $B^+ \succ B$.*

Definition 14. *Let $K = (G, M, I)$ be a formal context, the attribute set $B, D \subseteq M$ and $B < N$, $N \not\supseteq B$. If there is $T \supset B$ for any attribute set $T \in <B, N>$, then it is said that N is non-trivial and only greater than B, which is recorded as $B \precsim N$.*

Definition 15. *Let $K = (G, M, I)$ be a formal context and a Stem base $Imp(K)$ on K, any implication $C \to f(g(C)) - C \in Imp(K)$. If there is an attribute set B^+, $N \in M$ satisfies $B^+ > B$ and B^+ is not related to the Stem base $Imp(K)$, $B \precsim N$ and N is related to $Imp(K)$. Then in the interval $<B, \min(f(g(B)), N)>$, there is neither an intent nor pseudo-intent.*

Definition 16. *Suppose $K = (G, M, I)$ is a formal context, and the attribute set $M = m_1, \cdots, m_n$, if the basic reverse linear order given on M is $(m_1 > m2 > \cdots > m_n)$, then the lexicographic relationship $>$ of the attribute set is an inverse linear order relationship of 2^M in the formal context. According to the reverse lexicographical relationship, the attribute set in the formal context can be tested one by one whether the attribute set is an intent or pseudo-intent.*

Definition 17. *Let $K = (G, M, I)$ be a formal context, the attribute set $M = m_1, \cdots, m_n$, if the basic reverse linear order given on M is $(m_1 > m2 > \cdots > m_n)$, according to the reverse linear order, all the attribute sets of the formal context K can be constructed as a prefix dictionary tree (the attribute sets of the parent node is actually contained in the attribute sets of the child node and the sibling node follows the reverse linear order).*

Based on the above definitions, the following findings in this paper can be used as a theoretical basis for further improving the attribute exploration algorithm.

Theorem 1. *Let $K = (G, M, I)$ be a formal context, any one implication $C \to D \in Imp(K)$. If attribute set $T = C \cap D$, then T is an intent.*

Proof. Since $C \to D \in Imp(K)$, so by Definition 7, we know that $D = C^{II} - C$, then $T = C \cap D = C \cap \{C^{II} - C\} = C^{II}$. That is, $T = C^{II}$. From Definition 7, we can see that $T^{II} = C^{II^{II}} = C^{II} = T$.

Theorem 1 shows that if the attribute sets only composed of the antecedents and consequents of any one implication in the stem base, then these attribute sets must be an intent. Because in the process of attribute exploration, the stem base is only obtained by the implication of the pseudo-intent sets, so the attribute sets that satisfy Theorem 1 do not need to calculate the corresponding implications.

Theorem 2. *Let $K = (G, M, I)$ be a formal context, any one implication $C \to D \in Imp(K)$. According to Definition 16, the reverse linear order of the sub-nodes of C in the dictionary prefix tree is $C_1 > C_2 > \cdots > C_n$, if $D \subseteq <C_n, C_1>$, then the node between the largest child node C_1 to D (including the D node) is not related to $Imp(K)$, so it does not exist pseudo-intent and intent in the interval $<D, C_1>$.*

Proof. According to Definition 17, the sub-nodes of C can be set as $(C_1, C_2, \cdots, C_n) \subset C$ in the dictionary prefix tree. If $D \subseteq <C_n, C_1>$, so for any attribute set $T \subseteq <D, C_1>$ contains at least one antecedent and does not include the consequent of the implication $C \to D \in Imp(K)$, then it can be known that T is neither an intent nor pseudo-intent from Definition 12.

Theorem 2 shows that, in the prefix dictionary tree, if the attribute sets of this layer are contained in the interval between any one known implication subsequent and the largest child node of the implication antecedent in the stem base, then there are neither an intent nor pseudo-intent attribute sets in this interval. This provides a theoretical basis for skipping the calculation of these attribute sets when parallelly judging these attributes are intents or pseudo-intents in the inner layer of the prefix dictionary tree.

Theorem 3. *Suppose $K = (G, M, I)$ is a formal context, if $D = \emptyset$ for any one implication $C \to D$, then the implication $C \to D$ is must be valid in the formal context K, and the attribute set C must be an intent.*

Proof. For any one implication $C \to D$ and $D = \emptyset$, the implication $C \to D = C \to \emptyset$. And in the formal context $K = (G, M, I)$, there is $C^I \subseteq G = \emptyset^I$, so any one implication $C \to \emptyset$ is valid in the formal context K. And because the implication $C \to \emptyset$ holds in the formal context K, so $\emptyset = C^{II} - C$ namely $C^{II} = C$, so C must be an intent.

Theorem 3 shows that when judging implications in the formal context, if the consequents of any one implication is an empty set, then the implication must be valid in the given formal context, and the antecedents of the implication must be an intent. Because, the stem base is only obtained by implications of the pseudo-intent sets in the process of attribute exploration, so the implications that satisfy Theorem 3 do not need to be judged whether it is valid in the given formal context.

3.2 Algorithm

Based on the above definitions and theorems, according to the recursive definition of pseudo-intent, we designed a parallel attribute exploration algorithm based on pseudo-intent and intent sets (PAEUIS) which arranges attribute sets in a hierarchical cardinal order and skips irrelevant attribute and intent sets and only considers pseudo-intent sets. The algorithm description is shown in Algorithm 1.

At the beginning of the PAEUIS algorithm, the given formal context is known, the attribute set and the cardinality between attribute sets are known, and the stem base is an empty set. The algorithm first starts to obtain the empty attribute set and attribute sets for single attributes, then uses Definition 12 and Theorem 1 to skip implications that do not require the attribute set as the antecedent in the cardinal order of the attribute set between interlamination calculation. The specific steps of the algorithm are as follows:

Steps 2–9 in the PAEUIS algorithm, the algorithm judges whether these attributes of the single point layer are intents in parallel according to Definition 3. If the attribute set currently determined is an intent, then this attribute set is not required further calculations; otherwise, the attribute set currently determined must be a pseudo-intent. The corresponding implications are directly calculated for these pseudo-intent attribute sets and add them to the set of implication, and then wait for the end of parallel processes of all the attribute sets in the first layer, so far the calculation of the first layer attribute sets of the algorithm is completed. Step 12 of the algorithm means that after the implications of all pseudo-intent sets in the current layer are calculated, the algorithm needs to enter the next layer through the cardinal number auto-increment method to judge and calculate the implication for the attribute sets of the next layer. In steps 13–16 of the algorithm, according to Theorem 2, it judges parallelly whether the attribute sets in the current layer are contained in the interval of any one known implication subsequent and the largest child node of the antecedent, thereby skipping these attribute intervals. According to Definitions 11 and 12, Steps 17–19 are to judge the irrelevant relationship between the attribute sets in the current layer and the obtained implication set in parallel, so as to find the attribute sets in this layer that are not related to the stem base, and skip the judgment that takes these attribute sets as antecedent. In steps 20–25, according to Theorem 1, the algorithm judges in parallel whether the attribute set in the current layer is composed of any one known implication antecedent and subsequent and determines whether the attribute sets in the current layer in

---

Algorithm 1. PAEUIS

Input Formal context: $K(G, M, I)$.

Output Stem base: $Imp(K)$, Intent set: $C_{(}K)$.

1: $k = 1$, $B[k] = \{\emptyset\} \cup M[k]$, $Imp(K) = \emptyset$

2: **for** *all b in B[k] in parallel* **do**

3:     **if** $b^{II} == b$ **then**

4:         b is an intent, $C(K) = C(K) \cup \{b\}$, and skip the implication of attribute set b.

5:     **else**

6:         $Imp(K) = Imp(K) \cup \{b \rightarrow b^{II} - b\}$

7:     **end if**

8:     Wait for termination of all parallel processes in this layer.

9: **end for**

10: $Imp_{k-1}(K) = Imp(K)$, $C_{k-1}(K) = C_k(K)$

11: **while** $k < |M|$ **do**

12:     $k = k + 1$

13:     **for** *all b in B[k] in parallel* **do**

14:         **if** $b \subseteq \ <F, D_1>$, F is the consequent of any one implication $D \rightarrow F \in Imp_{k-1}(K)$, D_1 is the largest child node of D **then**

15:            b is neither an intent nor pseudo-intent, skip the calculation of attribute set b.

16:         **end if**

17:         **if** b is unrelated to $Imp_{k-1}(K)$ **then**

18:            b is neither an intent nor pseudo-intent, skip the calculation of attribute set b.

19:         **end if**

20:         **if** b is consisted of antecedent and consequent of any one implication $Imp_{k-1}(K)[i]$ in $Imp_{k-1}(K)$ **then**

21:            b is an intent, $C_k(K) = C_{k-1}(K) \cup \{b\}$, skip the calculation of attribute set b.

22:         **end if**

23:         **if** $b^{II} - b == \emptyset$ **then**

24:            b is an intent, $C_k(K) = C_{k-1}(K) \cup \{b\}$, skip the calculation of attribute set b.

25:         **end if**

26:         $Imp_k(K) = Imp_{k-1}(K) \cup \{b \rightarrow b^{II} - b\}$

27:         Wait for termination of all parallel processes in this layer.

28:     **end for**

29: **end while**

30: $Imp(K) = Imp_k(K)$, $C(K) = C_k(K)$

31: **return** $Imp(K)$, $C(K)$.

---

parallel are intents or not by Definition 3 and Theorem 3, thus skipping the judgment of this kind of attribute set as the antecedent implication. After these two judgments, the attribute sets that algorithm needs to calculate implications are all pseudo-intents sets. Step 26 is to calculate the corresponding implications for the pseudo-intent sets, and add the implications to the set of implication.

Step 27 is to wait for the end of all parallel processes in the current layer. Step 31 of the final algorithm directly outputs the set of implication Imp(K), namely the stem base and intent set of the given formal context.

Suppose the scale of the formal context is $G \times M$. In the PAEUIS algorithm, all attribute sets need to be divided into M layers, so the time complexity of the entire process layering is $O(M)$. When the algorithm calculates the first-layer attributes in parallel, it needs to traverse the formal context once for the first-layer attribute b in parallel and to calculate b^{II} once, so for the first-layer attribute sets, the time complexity is $O(G \times M)$. In each of the following layers, the irrelevance of any attribute set b to the implications in stem base is related to the scale of the stem base, because the scale of stem base is related to the scale of the formal context, but the relationship is not very clear. Therefore the scale of stem base can be set as P, then the complexity of calculating a single attribute set b unrelated to stem base in each layer is $O(M \times P)$. Similarly, for any one attribute set b in each layer, the time complexity of computing b is whether composed of any one implication antecedent and subsequent in stem base is $O(M \times P)$. Finally, for each layer of pseudo-intent set implication parallel calculation, it is still necessary to traverse the formal context once, that is, the time complexity is $O(G \times M)$. Therefore, the worst time complexity of the PAEUIS algorithm is $O(M \times \max(M \times P, \ M \times G))$. Although the time complexity of this algorithm is related to the scale P of stem base, compared with the best time complexity $O(M \times M \times G \times P \times P)$ of the AEUS algorithm, the time complexity of the algorithm in this paper is significantly less than that of the AEUS algorithm.

4   A Case Study of Attribute Exploration

This section uses an example to illustrate the running process of Shen Xiajiong's attribute exploration algorithm (AEUS) and the PAEUIS algorithm proposed in this article, and focuses on the comparison of the number of implications required in the attribute exploration process.

Example 1. Given a formal context $K = (G, M, I)$ as shown in Table 1, where $G = \{1, 2, 3, 4\}$, $M = \{a, b, c, d, e, f, g, h, i\}$ and the basic linear order on M is $a < b < c < d < e < f < g < h < i$.

4.1   An Example of AEUS Algorithm

The initial state of the formal context K is shown in Table 2, $K_0 = \emptyset$, intent set $C_0(K) = \emptyset$, stem base $Imp_0 = \emptyset$, and the first attribute set $B_0 = \emptyset$ according to the lexicographic order. Specific steps are as follows:

Table 1. The formal context of K

	a	b	c	d	e	f	g	h	i
1	0	0	1	1	1	1	1	0	0
2	0	0	0	0	0	0	1	0	1
3	0	0	1	1	1	0	1	0	0
4	1	1	1	1	0	0	0	1	0

Table 2. The formal context of K_0

a	b	c	d	e	f	g	h	i

1. In the formal context K_0, $\emptyset^{II} = \{abcdefghi\}$, we ask the domain expert whether the implication $\emptyset \to \emptyset^{II} - \emptyset = \emptyset \to \{abcdefghi\}$ is valid in the formal context K? In the formal context K, $\emptyset^I = \{1,2,3,4\}$, $\{abcdefghi\}^I = \emptyset$. And because $\{1,2,3,4\} \nsubseteq \emptyset$, the implication $\emptyset \to \{abcdefghi\}$ does not hold in the formal context K. We take a counterexample 1 from the formal context K to refute the implication $\emptyset \to \{abcdefghi\}$, and add it in the formal context K_0 to obtain the formal context K_1 as shown in Table 3, where $C_1(K) = C_0(K)$, $B_1 = B_0$, $Imp_1(K) = Imp_0(K)$.

Table 3. The formal context of K_1

	a	b	c	d	e	f	g	h	i
1	0	0	1	1	1	1	1	0	0

2. In the formal context K_1, $\emptyset^{II} = \{cdefg\}$, we ask the domain expert whether the implication $\emptyset \to \emptyset^{II} - \emptyset = \emptyset \to \{cdefg\}$ holds in the formal context K? In K, $\emptyset^I = \{1,2,3,4\}$, $\{g\}^I = \{1,2,3,4\}$. And since $\{1,2,3,4\} \nsubseteq \{1,2,3\}$, the implication $\emptyset \to \{g\}$ does not hold in K. We take a counterexample 2 from the formal context K to refute the implication $\emptyset \to \{abcdefghi\}$, and add it in the formal context K_1 to obtain the formal context K_2 as shown in Table 4, where $C_2(K) = C_1(K)$, $B_2 = B_1$, $Imp_2(K) = Imp_1(K)$.

3. In the formal context K_2, $\emptyset^{II} = \{g\}$, we ask the domain expert whether the implication $\emptyset \to \emptyset^{II} - \emptyset = \emptyset \to \{g\}$ holds in K? In K, $\emptyset^I = \{1,2,3,4\}$, $\{g\}^I = \{1,2,3,4\}$. And since $\{1,2,3,4\} \nsubseteq \{1,2,3\}$, the implication $\emptyset \to \{g\}$ does not hold in K. We take a counterexample 4 from the formal context K to refute the implication $\emptyset \to \{g\}$ and add it in the formal context K_2 to get the formal context K_3 as shown in Table 5, where $C_3(K) = C_2(K)$, $B_3 = B_2$, $Imp_3(K) = Imp_2(K)$.

4. In the formal context K_3, $\emptyset^{II} = \{\emptyset\}$, we ask the expert whether the implication $\emptyset \to \emptyset^{II} - \emptyset = \emptyset \to \{\emptyset\}$ holds in K? In K, $\emptyset^I = \{1,2,3,4\}$, $\{\emptyset\}^I =$

Table 4. The formal context of K_2

	a	b	c	d	e	f	g	h	i
1	0	0	1	1	1	1	1	0	0
2	0	0	0	0	0	0	1	0	1

Table 5. The formal context of K_3

	a	b	c	d	e	f	g	h	i
1	0	0	1	1	1	1	1	0	0
2	0	0	0	0	0	0	1	0	1
4	1	1	1	1	0	0	0	1	0

$\{1,2,3,4\}$. And since $\{1,2,3,4\} == \{1,2,3,4\}$, the implication $\emptyset \to \{\emptyset\}$ holds in K. And because $\emptyset^{II} = \emptyset$, $\emptyset$ is an intent, and add it in C_3. So $C_4(K) = C_3(K) \cup \emptyset$, $K_4 = K_3$, $Imp_4(K) = Imp_3(K)$, then we need to calculate B_4.

5. According to the lexicographic order, we know that the next attribute set of $\emptyset$ is $\emptyset^+ = \{i\}$. Since $\emptyset \subseteq \{i\}$, $\{i\}$ is related to $Imp_4(K)$, $B_4 = \{i\}$. In the formal context K_4, $\{i\}^{II} = \{gi\}$, we ask the domain expert whether the implication $\{i\} \to \{i\}^{II} - \{i\} = \{i\} \to \{g\}$ holds in the formal context K? In the formal context K, $\{i\}^I = \{2\}$, $\{g\}^I = \{1,2,3\}$. And because $\{2\} \subseteq \{1,2,3\}$, the implication $\{i\} \to \{g\}$ holds in K. And because $\{i\}^{II} = \{gi\} \neq \{i\}$, $\{i\}$ is a pseudo-intent, and add $\{i\} \to \{g\}$ in Imp_4. So $Imp_5(K) = Imp_4(K) \cup \{i \to g\}$, $K_5 = K_4$, $C_5(K) = C_4(K)$, then we need to calculate B_5.

6. According to the lexicographic order, we know that the next attribute set of $\{i\}$ is $\{i\}^+ = \{h\}$, because $i \not\subseteq \{h\}$ so $\{h\}$ is related to $Imp_5(K)$, $B_5 = \{h\}$. In the formal context K_5, $\{h\}^{II} = \{abcdh\}$, we ask the domain expert whether the implication $\{h\} \to \{h\}^{II} - \{h\} = \{h\} \to \{abcd\}$ is valid in the formal context K? In the formal context K, $\{h\}^I = \{4\}$, $\{abcd\}^I = \{4\}$. Since $\{4\} == \{4\}$, the implication $\{h\} \to \{abcd\}$ is valid in K. And because $\{h\}^{II} = \{abcdh\} \neq \{h\}$, $\{h\}$ is a pseudo-intent, and add $\{h\} \to \{abcd\}$ in Imp_5. So $Imp_6(K) = Imp_5(K) \cup \{h \to abcd\}$, $K_6 = K_5$, $C_6(K) = C_5(K)$, then we need to calculate B_6.

7. According to the lexicographic order, we know that the next attribute set of $\{h\}$ is $\{h\}^+ = \{hi\}$, because $\{i \cup h\} \subseteq \{hi\}$ and $\{g\} \not\subseteq \{hi\}$, $\{abcd\} \not\subseteq \{hi\}$, $\{hi\}$ is not related to $Imp_6(K)$, then we calculate $T = \{B_5\}^{II} = \{h\}^{II} = \{abcdh\}$. According to Definition 15, $N = \{g\}$, because $T > N$, $B_6 = N = \{g\}$. In the formal context K_6, $\{g\}^{II} = \{g\}$, we ask the domain expert whether the implication $\{g\} \to \{g\}^{II} - \{g\} = \{g\} \to \emptyset$ holds in the formal context K? In K, $\{g\}^I = \{1,2,3\}$, $\emptyset^I = \{1,2,3,4\}$. And since $\{1,2,3\} \subseteq \{1,2,3,4\}$, the implication $\{g\} \to \emptyset$ holds in K. And because $\{g\}^{II} = \{g\} == \{g\}$, $\{g\}$ is an intent and add it in C_6. So $C_7(K) = C_6(K) \cup \{g\}$, $K_7 = K_6$, $Imp_7(K) = Imp_6(K)$, then we need to calculate B_7.

8. According to the lexicographic order, we know that the next attribute set of $\{g\}$ is $\{g\}^+ = \{gi\}$, since $\{g \cup \emptyset\} \subseteq \{gi\}$ and $\{h\} \nsubseteq \{gi\}$, $\{gi\}$ is related to $Imp_7(K)$, $B_7 = \{gi\}$. In the formal context K_7, $\{gi\}^{II} = \{gi\}$, we ask the domain expert whether the implication $\{gi\} \rightarrow \{gi\}^{II} - \{gi\} = \{gi\} \rightarrow \emptyset$ holds in K? In K, $\{gi\}^I = \{2\}$, $\emptyset^I = \{1,2,3,4\}$. And since $\{2\} \subseteq \{1,2,3,4\}$, the implication $\{gi\} \rightarrow \emptyset$ holds in K. And because $\{gi\}^{II} = \{gi\} == \{gi\}$, $\{gi\}$ is an intent, and add it in C_7. So $C_8(K) = C_7(K) \cup \{gi\}$, $K_8 = K_7$, $Imp_8(K) = Imp_7(K)$, then we need to calculate B_8.

9. According to the lexicographic order, we know that the next attribute set of $\{gi\}$ is $\{gi\}^+ = \{gh\}$, because $\{h\} \subseteq \{gh\}$ and $\{adcd\} \nsubseteq \{gh\}$, $\{gh\}$ is not related to $Imp_8(K)$, then we need to calculate $T = \{abcdgh\}$. According to Definition 15, $N = \{f\}$, because $T > N$, $B_8 = N = \{f\}$. In the formal context K_8, $\{f\}^{II} = \{cdefg\}$, we ask the domain expert whether the implication $\{f\} \rightarrow \{f\}^{II} - \{f\} = \{f\} \rightarrow \{cdeg\}$ in the formal context K? In K, $\{f\}^I = \{1\}$, $\{cdeg\}^I = \{1,3\}$. And because $\{1\} \subseteq \{1,3\}$, the implication $\{f\} \rightarrow \{cdeg\}$ is valid in K. And because $\{f\}^{II} = \{cdefg\} \neq \{f\}$, $\{f\}$ is a pseudo-intent, and add $\{f\} \rightarrow \{cdeg\}$ in Imp_8. So $Imp_9(K) = Imp_8(K) \cup \{f \rightarrow cdeg\}$, $K_9 = K_8$, $C_9(K) = C_8(K)$, then we need to calculate B_9.

10. According to the lexicographic order, we know that the next attribute set of $\{f\}$ is $\{f\}^+ = \{fi\}$, because $\{f\} \subseteq \{fi\}$ and $\{cdeg\} \nsubseteq \{fi\}$, $\{fi\}$ is not relevant to $Imp_9(K)$, then we need to calculate $T = \{cdefg\}$. According to Definition 15, $N = \{e\}$, because $T > N$, $B_9 = N - \{e\}$. In the formal context K_9, $\{e\}^{II} = \{cdefg\}$, we ask the domain expert whether the implication $\{e\} \rightarrow \{e\}^{II} - \{e\} = \{e\} \rightarrow \{cdfg\}$ is valid in the formal context K? In the formal context K, $\{e\}^I = \{1,3\}$, $\{cdfg\}^I = \{1\}$. And since $\{1,3\} \nsubseteq \{1\}$, the implication $\{e\} \rightarrow \{cdfg\}$ does not hold in K. We take a counterexample 3 from the formal context K to refute the implication $\{e\} \rightarrow \{cdfg\}$ and add it in the formal context K_9 to get the formal context K_{10} as shown in Table 6, where $C_{10}(K) = C_9(K)$, $B_{10} = B_9$, $Imp_{10}(K) = Imp_9(K)$.

Table 6. The formal context of K_{10}

	a	b	c	d	e	f	g	h	i
1	0	0	1	1	1	1	1	0	0
2	0	0	0	0	0	0	1	0	1
4	1	1	1	1	0	0	0	1	0
3	0	0	1	1	1	1	0	1	0

11. In the formal context K_{10}, $\{e\}^{II} = \{cdeg\}$, we ask the domain expert whether the implication $\{e\} \rightarrow \{e\}^{II} - \{e\} = \{e\} \rightarrow \{cdg\}$ is valid in the formal context K? In K, $\{e\}^I = \{1,3\}$, $\{cdg\}^I = \{1,3\}$. Since $\{1,3\} == \{1,3\}$, the implication $\{e\} \rightarrow \{cdg\}$ is valid in K. And because

$\{e\}^{II} = \{cdeg\} \neq \{e\}$, $\{e\}$ is a pseudo-intent, and add $\{e\} \to \{cdg\}$ in Imp_{10}. So $Imp_{11}(K) = Imp_{10}(K) \cup \{e \to cdg\}$, $K_{11} = K_{10}$, $C_{11}(K) = C_{10}(K)$, then we need to calculate B_{11}.

12. The subsequent steps of the algorithm AEUS are shown in Table 7.

Table 7. The subsequent calculation process of the AEUS algorithm

Step B_i	B_i^+	$Imp_{i+1}(K)$	$C_{i+1}(K)$	Whether B_i^+ is not related to $Imp_{i+1}(K)$?	T	N	B_{i+1}	Whether $B_{i+1} \to \{B_{i+1}\}^{II} - \{B_{i+1}\}$ is valid in the formal context K?
(12) $B_{10}=\{e\}$	$B_{10}^+=\{ei\}$	$Imp_{11}(K)=Imp_{10}\cup\{e\to cdg\}$	$C_{11}(K)=C_{10}(K)$	$\{ei\}$ is not related to $Imp_{11}(K)$	$\{cdeg\}$	$\{d\}$	$\{d\}$	$\{d\}\to\{c\}$ is valid in K
(13) $B_{11}=\{d\}$	$B_{11}^+=\{di\}$	$Imp_{12}(K)=Imp_{11}\cup\{d\to c\}$	$C_{12}(K)=C_{11}(K)$	$\{di\}$ is not related to $Imp_{12}(K)$	$\{cdg\}$	$\{c\}$	$\{c\}$	$\{c\}\to\{d\}$ is valid in K
(14) $B_{12}=\{c\}$	$B_{12}^+=\{ci\}$	$Imp_{13}(K)=Imp_{12}\cup\{c\to d\}$	$C_{13}(K)=C_{12}(K)$	$\{ci\}$ is not related to $Imp_{13}(K)$	$\{cdg\}$	$\{cd\}$	$\{cd\}$	$\{cd\}\to\emptyset$ is valid in K
(15) $B_{13}=\{cd\}$	$B_{13}^+=\{cdi\}$	$Imp_{14}(K)=Imp_{13}$	$C_{14}(K)=C_{13}(K)\cup\{cd\}$	$\{cdi\}$ is not related to $Imp_{14}(K)$	$\{cdgi\}$	$\{cdg\}$	$\{cdg\}$	$\{cdg\}\to\emptyset$ is valid in K
(16) $B_{14}=\{cdg\}$	$B_{14}^+=\{cdgi\}$	$Imp_{15}(K)=Imp_{14}$	$C_{15}(K)=C_{14}(K)\cup\{cdg\}$	$\{cdgi\}$ is not related to $Imp_{15}(K)$	$\{cdeg\}$	$\{b\}$	$\{cdeg\}$	$\{cdeg\}\to\emptyset$ is valid in K
(17) $B_{15}=\{cdeg\}$	$B_{15}^+=\{cdegi\}$	$Imp_{16}(K)=Imp_{15}$	$C_{16}(K)=C_{15}(K)\cup\{cdeg\}$	$\{cdegi\}$ is related to $Imp_{16}(K)$			$\{cdegi\}$	$\{cdegi\}\to\{abfh\}$ is valid in K
(18) $B_{16}=\{cdegi\}$	$B_{16}^+=\{cdegh\}$	$Imp_{17}(K)=Imp_{16}\cup\{cdegi\to abfh\}$	$C_{17}(K)=C_{16}(K)$	$\{cdegh\}$ is not related to $Imp_{17}(K)$	$\{cdefg\}$	$\{b\}$	$\{cdefg\}$	$\{cdefg\}\to\emptyset$ is valid in K
(19) $B_{17}=\{cdefg\}$	$B_{17}^+=\{cdefgi\}$	$Imp_{18}(K)=Imp_{17}(K)$	$C_{18}(K)=C_{17}(K)\cup\{cdefg\}$	$\{cdefgi\}$ is not related to $Imp_{18}(K)$	$\{abcdefgh\}$	$\{b\}$	$\{b\}$	$\{b\}\to\{acdh\}$ is valid in K
(20) $B_{18}=\{b\}$	$B_{18}^+=\{bi\}$	$Imp_{19}(K)=Imp_{18}\cup\{b\to acdh\}$	$C_{19}(K)=C_{18}(K)$	$\{bi\}$ is not related to $Imp_{19}(K)$	$\{abcdh\}$	$\{a\}$	$\{a\}$	$\{a\}\to\{bcdh\}$ is valid in K
(21) $B_{19}=\{a\}$	$B_{19}^+=\{ai\}$	$Imp_{20}(K)=Imp_{19}\cup\{a\to bcdh\}$	$C_{20}(K)=C_{19}(K)$	$\{ai\}$ is not related to $Imp_{20}(K)$	$\{abcdh\}$		$\{abcdh\}$	$\{abcdh\}\to\emptyset$ is valid in K
(22) $B_{20}=\{abcdh\}$	$B_{20}^+=\{abcdhi\}$	$Imp_{21}(K)=Imp_{20}(K)$	$C_{21}(K)=C_{20}(K)\cup\{abcdh\}$	$\{abcdhi\}$ is not related to $Imp_{21}(K)$	$\{abcdegh\}$		$\{abcdegh\}$	$\{abcdegh\}\to\emptyset$ is valid in K
(23) $B_{21}=\{abcdegh\}$	$B_{21}^+=\{abcdeghi\}$	$Imp_{22}(K)=Imp_{21}(K)$	$C_{22}(K)=C_{21}(K)\cup\{abcdegh\}$	$\{abcdeghi\}$ is not related to $Imp_{22}(K)$	$\{abcdefghi\}$		$\{abcdefghi\}$	$\{abcdefghi\}\to\emptyset$ is valid in K

After the calculation of the above process, we can see that the intent set of this formal context set is $\{\emptyset, \{g\}, \{gi\}, \{cd\}, \{cdeg\}, \{cdefg\}, \{abcdh\}, \{abcdefghi\}\}$ and the stem base is $Imp(K) = \{i \to g, h \to abcd, f \to cdeg, e \to cdg, d \to c, c \to d, cdegi \to abfh, b \to acdh, a \to bcdh, abcdegh \to fi\}$. And from the above process, it can be seen that the AEUS algorithm skips a part of attribute sets based on the linear order, but the algorithm still calculates too many implications of attribute sets, and there are many repeated calculations when the subsequent is the empty set, and the existence of the redundant calculation of attribute sets which are composed of the antecedent and subsequent in the obtained implication sets in these implications.

4.2 Example Process of PAEUIS Algorithm

According to Definition 16, the inverse linear order of the attribute set of the formal context K shown in Table 1 is $a > b > c > d > e > f > g > h > i$, and according to the inverse linear order all the obtained attribute sets constitute a 9-layer prefix dictionary tree in the inter-layer attribute sets cardinality order and the inner-layer attribute sets reverse linear order. The initial state of the formal context K as shown in Table 1, the implication set $Imp(K) = \emptyset$, the intent set $C(K) = \emptyset$.

1. Then we need to calculate the first-layer attribute set of the formal context K, and the first-level attribute set is $B[1] = \{\emptyset \cup M[1]\} = \{\emptyset, a, b, c, d, e, f, g, h, i\}$. The parallel calculation of the attribute set b in $B[1]$ is $\emptyset^{II} =$

$\emptyset$, $\{a\}^{II} = \{abcdh\} \neq \{a\}$, $\{b\}^{II} = \{abcdh\} \neq \{b\}$, $\{c\}^{II} = \{cd\} \neq$ $\{c\}$, $\{d\}^{II} = \{cd\} \neq \{d\}$, $\{e\}^{II} = \{cdeg\} \neq \{e\}$, $\{f\}^{II} = \{cdefg\} \neq$ $\{f\}$, $\{g\}^{II} = \{g\}$, $\{h\}^{II} = \{abcdh\} \neq \{h\}$, $\{i\}^{II} = \{gi\} \neq \{i\}$. So $C(K) = \{\emptyset, g\}$, $Imp(K) = \{a \to bcdh, b \to acdh, c \to d, d \to c, e \to cdg, f \to cdeg, h \to abcd, i \to g\}$.

2. Then we need to calculate the second-layer attribute set of the formal context K. First, according to Theorem 2, Theorem 1, and $Imp(K)$, we can skip the attribute set range of this layer is all child nodes of a, all child nodes of b, and all child nodes of c except a node cd, all child nodes of d, all child nodes of e, all child nodes of f, all child nodes of h, and all child nodes of i. Then, the remaining attribute set, namely $\{gh, gi\}$, it is judged parallelly the correlation with $Imp(K)$ based on Definition 12. It can be seen that $\{gh\}$ is not related to $Imp(K)$, and according to Theorem 1, we can know $\{gi\}$ is an intent. So $C_2(K) = C(K) \cup \{cd, gi\}$, $Imp_2(K) = Imp(K)$.

3. Then we need to calculate the third-layer attribute set of the formal context K. First, according to Theorem 2 and $Imp_2(K)$, we can skip the attribute set range of this layer is all sub-nodes of a, all sub-nodes of b, and all sub-nodes of d, all sub-nodes of e, all sub-nodes of f. Then the remaining attribute set, namely $\{T \cup \{ghi\}| T \leq cde\}$, where $T \leq cde$ are elements of c's child nodes in the reverse linear order that are less than or equal to cde. According to Definition 12, the correlation between this attribute set and $Imp_2(K)$ is judged in parallel. It can be seen that $\{cde, cdf, T| T \leq cdh\}, ghi\}$ is not related to $Imp_2(K)$, and $\{cdg\}$ is not an intent by Definition 3. So $C_3(K) = C_2(K) \cup \{cdg\}$, $Imp_3(K) = Imp_2(K)$.

4. Then we need to calculate the fourth-layer attribute set of the formal context K. First, according to Theorem 2 and $Imp_3(K)$, we can skip the attribute set range of this layer is all sub-nodes of a, all sub-nodes of b, and all sub-nodes of d, all sub-nodes of e, all sub-nodes of f. Then the remaining attribute set, namely $\{T| T \leq cdef\}$, where $T \leq cdef$ are the elements of c in the reverse linear order which are less than or equal to $cdef$. According to Definition 12, then we need to judge the correlation between this attribute set and $Imp_3(K)$ in parallel. So we know $\{cdef, T| T \leq cdeh\}$ is not related to $Imp_3(K)$, and $\{cdeg\}$ is an intent by Theorem 1. Therefore $C_4(K) = C_3(K) \cup \{cdeg\}$, $Imp_4(K) = Imp_3(K)$.

5. Then we need to calculate the fifth-layer attribute set of the formal context K. First, according to Theorem 2, Theorem 1, and $Imp_4(K)$, we can skip the attribute set range of this layer is all sub-nodes of a except a node $abcdh$, all sub-nodes of b, all sub-nodes of d, all sub-nodes of e, all sub-nodes of f. Then the remaining attribute set i.e. $\{T| T \leq cdefg\}$, where $T \leq cdefg$ are the elements of c in the reverse linear order which are less than or equal to $cdefg$, and $\{cdefg\}$ is an intent by Theorem 1. According to Definition 12, we need to judge the correlation between this attribute set and $Imp_4(K)$ in parallel. Obviously, $\{cdegi\}$ is a pseudo-intent attribute set and the rest attribute sets are not related to $Imp_3(K)$. So $C_5(K) = C_4(K) \cup \{abcdh, cdefg\}$, $Imp_5(K) = Imp_4(K) \cup \{cdegi \to abfh\}$.

6. Then we need to calculate the sixth-layer attribute set of the formal context K. First, according to Theorem 2 and $Imp_5(K)$, we can skip the attribute set range of this layer is all sub-nodes of b and all sub-nodes of d. Then the remaining attribute set i.e. $\{T|\ T \leq abcdef \cup T \leq cdefgh\}$, where $T \leq abcdef$ are the elements of a in the reverse linear order which is less than or equal to $abcdef$, $T \leq cdefgh$ are the elements of c in the reverse linear order which are less than or equal to $cdefgh$. According to Definition 12, the correlation between this attribute set and $Imp_5(K)$ is judged in parallel. It can be seen that this attribute set is not related to $Imp_5(K)$. So $C_6(K) = C_5(K)$, $Imp_6(K) = Imp_5(K)$.

7. Then we need to calculate the seventh-layer attribute set of the formal context K. First, according to Theorem 2, Theorem 1, and $Imp_6(K)$, we can skip the attribute set range of this layer is all sub-nodes of b. Then the remaining attribute set i.e. $\{T \cup cdefghi|\ T \leq abcdefg\}$, where $T \leq abcdefg$ are the elements of a in the reverse linear order which are less than or equal to $abcdefg$. According to Definition 12, we need to judge the correlation between this attribute set and $Imp_6(K)$ in parallel and it is judged parallelly whether the attribute set exists intent set by Definition 3. It can be seen that $\{abcdegh\}$ is a pseudo-intent and the rest attribute sets are not related to $Imp_6(K)$. So $C_7(K) = C_6(K) \cup \{abcdegh\}$, $Imp_7(K) = Imp_6(K) \cup \{abcdegh \rightarrow fi\}$.

8. Then we need to calculate the eighth-layer attribute set of the formal context K. First, according to Theorem 2, Theorem 1, and $Imp_7(K)$, we can skip the attribute set range of this layer is all sub-nodes of a and b. Obviously, it can be seen that this attribute set is not related to $Imp_7(K)$. So $C_8(K) = C_7(K) \cup \{abcdegh\}$, $Imp_8(K) = Imp_7(K)$.

9. For the ninth-layer attribute set of the formal context K, that is, we need the attribute set $\{abcdefghi\}$ to calculate. According to Theorem 1, $\{abcdefghi\}$ is an intent. So $C_9(K) = C_8(K)$, $\{abcdefghi\}$, $Imp_9(K) = Imp_8(K)$.

After the calculation of the above process, we know that the intent set of this formal context is $\{\emptyset, \{g\}, \{gi\}, \{cd\}, \{cdeg\}, \{cdefg\}, \{abcdh\}, \{abcd\ efghi\}\}$ and the stem base of this formal context is $Imp(K) = \{i \rightarrow g, h \rightarrow abcd, f \rightarrow cdeg, e \rightarrow cdg, d \rightarrow c, c \rightarrow d, cdegi \rightarrow abfh, b \rightarrow acdh, a \rightarrow bcdh, abcdegh \rightarrow fi\}$. Compared with the AEUS algorithm, we know the PAEUIS algorithm is correct with the stem base. And in the PAEUIS algorithm, because all attribute sets of the formal context are constructed a prefix dictionary tree with the inter-layer attribute set in the cardinality order and the inner attribute sets in the inverse linear order, it can guarantee the completeness of the PAEUIS algorithm. And after we skip attribute sets that are not related to the stem base, then intent sets are eliminated by the definition of intent, and then all pseudo-intent sets are obtained, so the non-redundancy of the algorithm can be guaranteed.

By comparing the two processes, we can see that when calculating implications of the AEUS algorithm, it needs to judge whether the implication is valid in the formal context, and because there are many implications whose consequent is $\emptyset$, it causes the redundancy calculation of $\emptyset^I$, besides, there are many redundant calculations in which the implication antecedent is the attribute set composed of the antecedent and consequent in acquired implication set, and because the

AEUS algorithm is still serial, the search space of the algorithm is very large when M is getting larger. However, the PAEUIS algorithm does not use linear order, the attribute set of the formal context is calculated according to the inter-layer cardinality order and the inverse linear order within the layer is used to calculate the attribute set. So, many attribute set intervals that are not related to the stem base are skipped in the calculation process for the inner-layer attribute sets. In addition, the PAEUIS algorithm can skip some calculations that are obviously intent sets through Theorem 1. Then, the PAEUIS algorithm uses the parallel computing implication method to save the running time of the algorithm for the remaining pseudo-intent attribute sets in the inner-layer.

5   Experiments and Analysis

5.1   Experimental Setting

In order to assess the effectiveness of the new improved algorithm proposed in this paper, we use the random function in Java language MATH library to simulate and generate a set of test data as formal context. The algorithm proposed in this paper (PAEUIS) is compared with parallel attribute explo-ration (PAE) [34], Shen Xiajiong's improved unrelated attribute exploration algorithm [32] (AEUS), and the traditional attribute exploration algorithm [1] (TAE). All of above algorithms were performed on a machine with 3.3 GHz CPU, 16 GB main memory and the Windows 10 operating system. Note that all of above algorithms were implemented in IDEA and JDK9. The experimental design is divided into three aspects. The first aspect is to change the form context scale and observe the change of the stem base quantity. The second aspect is to change the form context scale and observe the change of intent quantity. Third, we change the formal context scale and observe the time-consuming changes of the above algorithms.

In the first set of experiments, we set the formal context with the same number of objects as 20, and the number of attributes range from 0 to 50 at an interval of 10 to test. The purpose of the test is to fix the number of objects to change the number of attributes, and observe the change of the number of stem base. The test results are shown in Fig. 1.

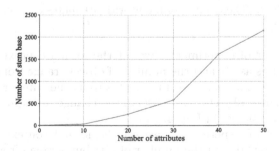

Fig. 1. The number of stem base with attributes change.

In the second set of experiments, we set the formal context with the same number of attributes as 20, and the number of objects range from 0 to 100 at an interval of 20 to test. The purpose of the test is to fix the number of attributes to change the number of objects, and observe the change of the number of stem base. The test results are shown in Fig. 2.

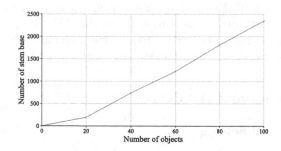

Fig. 2. The number of stem base with objects change.

In the third set of experiments, we set the formal context with the same number of objects as 20, and the number of attributes range from 0 to 50 at an interval of 10 to test. The purpose of the test is to fix the number of objects to change the number of attributes, and observe the change of the number of intent. The test results are shown in Fig. 3.

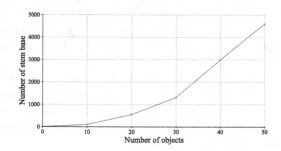

Fig. 3. The number of intent with attributes change.

In the fourth set of experiments, we set the formal context with the same number of attributes as 20, and the number of objects range from 0 to 100 at an interval of 20 to test. The purpose of the test is to fix the number of attributes to change the number of objects, and observe the change of the number of intent. The test results are shown in Fig. 4.

In the fifth set of experiments, we set the formal context with the same number of objects as 20, and the number of attributes range from 0 to 50 at an interval of 10 to test. The purpose of the test is to fix the number of objects to

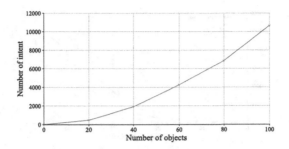

Fig. 4. The number of intent with objects change.

change the number of attributes, and observe the change of the time-consuming of above algorithms. The test results are shown in Fig. 5.

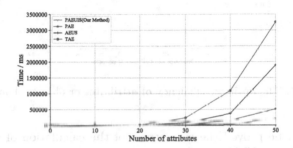

Fig. 5. The consuming-time of attributes change.

In the sixth set of experiments, we set the formal context with the same number of attributes as 20, and the number of objects range from 0 to 50 at an interval of 20 to test. The purpose of the test is to fix the number of attributes to change the number of objects, and observe the change of the number of above algorithms. The test results are shown in Fig. 6.

In the seventh experiment, we set an equal number of objects and attributes in the formal context. The number of objects range from 0 to 60 and were tested at an interval of 10. The purpose of the test is to change the scale of the formal context and observe the optimization efficiency of the PAEUIS algorithm. The test results are shown in Fig. 7.

5.2 Experimental Analysis

According to the first and second sets of experiments, it can be seen that the number of stem base will increase with the increase of the number of objects and attributes under the given formal context. At the same time, we compared the stem base obtained by PAE, AEUS and TAE algorithms, and found the results were consistent obtained by these four algorithms. Therefore, these two sets of

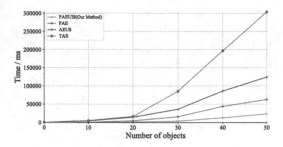

Fig. 6. The consuming-time of objects change.

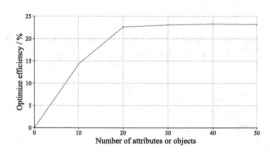

Fig. 7. The optimize efficiency of attributes or objects change.

experiments can be proved the correctness of the calculation of the stem base by the proposed PAEUIS algorithm.

According to the third and fourth sets of experiments, it can be seen that the number of stem base will increase with the increase of the number of objects and attributes under the given formal context. At the same time, we compared the intent obtained by PAE, AEUS and TAE algorithms, and found the results were consistent obtained by these four algorithms. Therefore, these two sets of experiments can be proved the correctness of the intent calculated by the PAEUIS algorithm proposed in this paper.

According to the fifth and sixth sets of experiments, it can be seen that the algorithm proposed in this paper takes less time than the three algorithms compared no matter how the number of objects is fixed and changed the number of attributes or the number of attributes is fixed and changed the number of objects. Moreover, the more the number of objects or attributes is, the more time would be saved by the algorithm proposed in this paper. Among them, in the fifth set of experiment, it can be seen that the PAEUIS algorithm only takes 18.9% time of AEUS algorithm when the number of attributes is 30. In the sixth set of experiment, it can be seen that the PAEUIS algorithm only takes 15.1% time of AEUS algorithm when the number of objects is 30. Furthermore, the seventh set of experiment shows that the PAEUIS algorithm can effectively reduce the scale of the implications calculated by the attribute exploration algorithm, and the number of implications reduced is about 23% compared with AEUS from an overall perspective.

The experimental results show that the proposed PAEUIS algorithm can effectively further reduce the time complexity of the attribute exploration algorithm.

6 Conclusion and Further Research

Based on the traditional attribute exploration algorithm and the improved attribute exploration algorithm under the unrelated set, first, this paper makes further research on the problem of high time complexity of the algorithm. This paper hopes that the algorithm skips some attribute sets that are neither intent nor pseudo-intent and certain intent to reduce the time complexity of the algorithm. Second, this article further summarizes three theorems based on the irrelevant definition of the AEUS algorithm, and makes a rigorous mathematical demonstration of the proposed theorems. Finally, a further improved attribute exploration algorithm (PAEUIS) is given based on these theorems. This algorithm constructs a prefix dictionary tree by taking all the attribute sets of the formal context according to the inter-layer cardinal order and the inverse linear order within the layer. With the help of the above theorems, it automatically jumps the attribute sets that are not related to the stem base and that are obviously intent sets in parallel when calculating the implications of the attribute set in attribute exploration. So the search space of the algorithm is further reduced, and then the implications of the pseudo-intent set are calculated in parallel, reducing the calculation scale of implication. Because attribute exploration can semi-automatically assist users in acquiring unknown knowledge, the next step is to combine attribute exploration with deep learning to further develop an automatic learning system using attribute exploration.

References

1. Ganter, B.: Formal Concept Analysis: Mathematical Foundations, 1st edn. Springer, Heidelberg (1999)
2. Li, J., et al.: Concept lattice theory and method and their research prospect. Pattern Recogn. Artif. Intell. **33**(7), 619–642 (2020)
3. Zhang, L., Zhang, H., Shen, X., Yin, L.: A bottom-up algorithm of vertical assembling concept lattices. Int. J. Data Min. Bioinform. **7**, 229–244 (2013)
4. Yang, J., Shen, X., Chen, W., Ge, Q., Zhang, L., Chen, H.: A model study on collaborative learning and exploration of RBAC roles. Wirel. Commun. Mob. Comput. (2021). https://doi.org/10.1155/2021/5549109
5. Shemis, E., Mohammed, A.: A comprehensive review on updating concept lattices and its application in updating association rules. Wiley Interdisc. Rev. Data Min. Knowl. Discov. **11**(2), e1401 (2021)
6. Shen, X., Yang, J., Zhang, L., Yang, G.: An interactive role learning and discovery model for multi-department RBAC building based on attribute exploration. J. Ambient Intell. Humaniz. Comput. (2020). https://doi.org/10.1007/s12652-020-02634-3

7. Zhang, L., Huang, Z., Liu, W., Guo, Z., Zhang, Z.: Weather radar echo prediction method based on convolution neural network and Long Short-Term memory networks for sustainable e-Agriculture. J. Clean. Prod. (2021). https://doi.org/10.1016/j.jclepro.2021.126776

8. Zhang, L., Xu, C., Gao, Y., Han, Y., Du, X., Tian, Z.: Improved Dota2 lineup recommendation model based on a bidirectional LSTM. Tsinghua Sci. Technol. **25**(6), 712–720 (2020)

9. Wei, L., Liu, L., Qi, J., Qian, T.: Rules acquisition of formal decision contexts based on three-way concept lattices. Inf. Sci. **516**, 529–544 (2020). https://doi.org/10.1016/j.ins.2019.12.024

10. Zhang, L., Tang, S., Lv, L.: An finite iterative algorithm for sloving periodic Sylvester bimatrix equations. J. Frankl. Inst. **357**(15), 10757–10772 (2020)

11. Hua, M., Zhen, Z., Xiaoqing, L.: A method for mining decision rules based on decision formal context. J. Hebei Univ. (Nat. Sci. Ed.) **9**(01), 1–6 (2021)

12. Ling, W., Siyu, Z.: Granules and knowledge structure in three-way concept analysis. J. Northwest Univ. (Nat. Sci. Ed.) **50**(04), 537–545 (2020)

13. Xueyan, Z.: Research on role updating technology based on concept lattices. Inner Mongolia University of Science and Technology (2020)

14. Jingyu, W., Junqing, L., Yuesheng, T.: Design of role based access control for triadic concept analysis. J. Harbin Univ. Sci. Technol. **25**(02), 31–37 (2020)

15. Tang, J., Wei, L., Ren, R., Zhao, S.: Granule description using possible attribute analysis. J. Shandong Univ. (Nat. Sci. Ed.) **56**(01), 75–82 (2021)

16. Mi, Y., Liu, W., Shi, Y., Li, J.: Semi-supervised concept learning by concept-cognitive learning and concept space. IEEE Trans. Knowl. Data Eng. (99), 11 (2020)

17. Huilai, Z., Li, Y.: Knowledge representation based on concept cluster. J. Northwest Univ. (Nat. Sci. Ed.) **50**(04), 529–536 (2020)

18. Yan, E., Yu, C., Lu, L., Hong, W., Tang, C.: Incremental concept cognitive learning based on three-way partial order structure. Knowl.-Based Syst. **220**(23), 106898 (2021). https://doi.org/10.1016/j.knosys.2021.106898

19. Li, J.H., He, J.J., Wu, W.Z.: Optimization of class-attribute block in multi-granularity formal concept analysis. J. Shandong Univ. (Nat. Sci.) **55**(05), 1–12 (2020)

20. Zhou, Y., Li, J.: Skill reduction and assessment in formal context. Comput. Sci. Explor. 1–10 (2021)

21. Lei, Z., Yu, H., Qiang, G.: A privacy protection scheme for IoT big data based on time and frequency limitation. Wirel. Commun. Mob. Comput. (3), 1–10 (2021)

22. Lv, L., et al.: Contract and Lyapunov optimization based load scheduling and energy management for UAV charging stations. IEEE Trans. Green Commun. Netw. https://doi.org/10.1109/TGCN.2021.3085561

23. Ganter, B., Obiedkov, S.: Conceptual Exploration. 1st edn. Springer, Heidelberg (2016)

24. Borchmann, D.: A general form of attribute exploration. ArXiv. vol. abs/1202.4824 (2012)

25. Jäschke, R., Rudolph, S.: Attribute exploration on the web. Computer Science (2013)

26. Potoniec, J., Rudolph, S., Lawrynowicz, A.: Towards combining machine learning with attribute exploration for ontology refinement. In: International Semantic Web Conference (2014)

27. Hanika, T., Zumbragel, J.: Towards collaborative conceptual exploration. ArXiv. vol. abs/1712.08858 (2018)

28. Codocedo, V., Baixeries, J., Kaytoue, M., Napoli, A.: Sampling representation contexts with attribute exploration. In: Cristea, D., Le Ber, F., Sertkaya, B. (eds.) ICFCA 2019. LNCS (LNAI), vol. 11511, pp. 307–314. Springer, Cham (2019). https://doi.org/10.1007/978-3-030-21462-3_20
29. Reppe, H.: Attribute exploration using implications with proper premises. In: Eklund, P., Haemmerlé, O. (eds.) ICCS-ConceptStruct 2008. LNCS (LNAI), vol. 5113, pp. 161–174. Springer, Heidelberg (2008). https://doi.org/10.1007/978-3-540-70596-3_11
30. Ryssel, U., Distel, F., Borchmann, D.: Fast algorithms for implication bases and attribute exploration using proper premises. Ann. Math. Artif. Intell. **70**(1-2), 25–35 (2013)
31. Xiaoxiang, Z., Ping, Q.: On attribute exploration algorithms. J. Front. Comput. Sci. Technol. (2009)
32. Xiajiong, S., Jiyong, Y., Lei, Z.: Attribute discovery algorithm based on unrelated attribute sets. Computer Science (2020)
33. Distel, F.: Hardness of enumerating pseudo-intents in the lectic order. In: Kwuida, L., Sertkaya, B. (eds.) ICFCA 2010. LNCS (LNAI), vol. 5986, pp. 124–137. Springer, Heidelberg (2010). https://doi.org/10.1007/978-3-642-11928-6_9
34. Kriegel, F.: Parallel Attribute Exploration. In: Haemmerlé, O., Stapleton, G., Faron Zucker, C. (eds.) ICCS 2016. LNCS (LNAI), vol. 9717, pp. 91–106. Springer, Cham (2016). https://doi.org/10.1007/978-3-319-40985-6_8
35. Shen, X., Yang, J., Zhang, L., Yang, G.: An interactive role learning and discovery model for multi-department RBAC building based on attribute exploration. J. Ambient Intell. Humaniz. Comput. (2020)

Life and Medical Sciences

Location Model of Overseas Warehouses of Japanese Cross-Border E-Commerce Based on Ant Colony Algorithm

Jingxian Huang[✉]

Guizhou Minzu University, Guiyang 550025, Guizhou, China

Abstract. The rapid development of overseas warehouses has brought new opportunities for cross-border e-commerce. Taking Japan's cross-border e-commerce as the research object, this paper expounds the development model of cross-border e-commerce and the concept of cross-border logistics. Extracting the characteristics of Japan's cross-border e-commerce development model, improve the cross-border payment environment, obtain the influencing factors of overseas warehouse location, predict the demand according to the past transaction data and future development trend, take the warehouse location as the variable, and construct the location decision model by using ant colony algorithm.

Keywords: Ant colony algorithm · Cross border e-commerce in Japan · Overseas warehouse · Transaction mode · Cross border logistics · Location decision model

1 Introduction

With the rapid development of science and technology and the Internet, digitization and informatization are constantly changing our lives. The originally scattered links in commercial trade, such as products, capital flow, logistics and other information are integrated on the platform. Since then, the traditional trade mode has been deeply changed. In addition, the restrictions and challenges of information, policy environment and other aspects are becoming greater and greater [1, 2]. And more advanced and complete logistics facilities are needed. However, the e-commerce environment involves many factors, it is a complex project, so it is difficult to consider all influencing factors comprehensively [3, 4]. Cross border e-commerce overseas warehouse refers to the warehouse established by cross-border e-commerce in countries or regions other than their own countries to facilitate overseas trade. It is a cross-border logistics mode to achieve high efficiency, that is, cross-border e-commerce uses bulk cargo transportation to transport products to target countries or regions, and uniformly manages products by building or renting local warehouses locally, It also provides consumers with a series of logistics services, including one-stop services such as product warehousing, sorting, secondary packaging and local delivery. As a new way of logistics, overseas warehouses have gradually produced

D. Jiang and H. Song (Eds.): SIMUtools 2021, LNICST 424, pp. 603–612, 2022.
https://doi.org/10.1007/978-3-030-97124-3_46

many problems due to the complex international trade environment in recent years, and different development models also have different problems. Overseas warehouses under the self built mode require a lot of capital investment from cross-border e-commerce, and the construction cycle is long. The pursuit of minimum cost and maximum benefit has always been the pursuit of enterprises. Therefore, providing effective overseas warehouse location scheme for cross-border e-commerce enterprises is an important problem encountered by enterprises in planning and building warehouses. Among the existing site selection methods, there is no mature theoretical guidance for overseas warehouse construction, and there is also a lack of open overseas warehouse construction experience. At this time, a set of overseas warehouse location scheme for enterprises to refer to is particularly important for multinational e-commerce enterprises. At present, the academic literature on the combination of ant colony algorithm and Japanese cross-border e-commerce overseas warehouse location model is not very rich and needs to be further discussed.

2   Overview of Cross-Border E-Commerce and Logistics

2.1   Main Modes of Cross-Border E-Commerce

Under the Internet-based mode, the subjects of both parties complete the purchase and payment of one party and the collection and delivery of the other party through the electronic information platform of PC or mobile terminal. Compared with traditional trade, the development of cross-border e-commerce has become a new growth point in import and export trade [5, 6]. In order to better study this new trade mode, cross-border e-commerce is artificially divided according to different standards. The mainstream standard is divided according to the transaction subject, which can be divided into B2B mode, B2C mode, C2C mode and B2G mode. B2B mode is a cross-border business mode between enterprises on the network platform. On the other hand, through the B2B transaction mode, both parties can complete the whole transaction process on the network platform, from establishing the initial purchase and sale intention of both parties, to users' multi-directional comparison of products, to negotiating price, placing orders, signing orders and delivery, and finally to after-sales services. B2B mode enables enterprises to avoid many transactional workflow and personnel costs in the transaction process, speeds up the work efficiency between enterprises, makes enterprises cross the constraints of time and space through network technology, makes enterprise development more convenient and cheaper across regions and borders. B2C mode, that is, the cross-border e-commerce mode between enterprises and consumers on the network platform. The advantage of this model is that manufacturers often face consumers directly, eliminating many intermediate links and price differences. C2C mode, that is, the online transaction mode between consumers. The cross-border e-commerce platform provides an online mall for trading subjects at home and abroad. The seller can publish the products to be traded through the online mall, and the buyer can buy the products they need by browsing the online mall. With the popularity of mobile Internet and mobile payment, C2C transaction mode is more convenient, and the price is more competitive than the traditional transaction mode. More and more consumers choose online shopping. According to the data of iResearch, Taobao, eBay and paipai account for more than 95% of the C2C market share in China. B2G mode, that is, the operation mode of transaction activities between enterprises and the government through the network. Its concept is that enterprises and government organs use the network platform to exchange trade information and conduct business with each other. This way is more concise and efficient than their usual offline office, and the whole transaction process is faster and more convenient. For example, through the informatization, networking and intelligence of network government affairs, the government office is more transparent and the government policy trend is more timely, so as to improve the service level of government affairs. For example, government departments publish bidding and procurement online and enterprises conduct online bidding.

2.2 Cross Border Logistics

The traditional cross-border logistics mode is mainly divided into postal parcel mode, international express mode and special line logistics mode [7]. Cross border logistics is very important for cross-border e-commerce. Cross border logistics determines whether the traded goods can be delivered to consumers accurately and safely. It is the final link of direct contact with customers and directly affects customers' consumption experience [1, 8]. Among them, the postal parcel channel is currently the mainstream mode of cross-border e-commerce delivery, and the overseas warehouse mode is a new cross-border logistics mode in recent years. The details of various cross border logistics modes are shown in Table 1 below.

It can be seen from Table 1 that various market entities such as e-commerce enterprises, e-commerce platform enterprises and third party logistics enterprises are also actively planning to build a cross-border logistics system to provide new development ways for cross-border logistics through "cross-border settlement" of overseas warehouses. And further integrate into the overseas circulation system by improving the level of logistics services, such as customs clearance efficiency of commodities, reducing logistics costs and improving distribution efficiency.

3   Location Model of Overseas Warehouses of Japanese Cross-Border E-Commerce Based on Ant Colony Algorithm

3.1   Extracting the Characteristics of Japan's Cross-Border E-Commerce Development Model

Japanese cross-border e-commerce enterprises choose online platforms to sell products and complete the steps of order processing. E-commerce enterprises will prepare goods in advance, first transport products from China to overseas warehouses, and store them in overseas warehouses for sale. Corresponding customs clearance business will be handled for products leaving the country. Corresponding customs entry business will also be handled when entering and leaving overseas warehouses. When the products enter the overseas warehouse, the customs clearance business will be completed according to the specified procedures of the location of the overseas warehouse, such as declaration and inspection, which can be said to be the "first customs clearance". When cross-border

Table 1. Main logistics modes of cross-border e-commerce

Cross border logistics model	Advantage	Disadvantage	Typical representative
Postal packet	Wide coverage and lowest cost	Poor timeliness, easy to lose parts and relatively imperfect service	China Post, Singapore Post, etc.
International express service	High timeliness, high reliability and safety, and can be tracked in the whole process	Higher cost	UPS, DHL, FEDEX, TNT etc.
Special line logistics	Effectively reduce the cost of trunk transportation, and the price is lower than that of international express	The timeliness is low. It usually needs to assemble goods with the goods of other shippers and sort them again	Russian special line, Middle East special line, American special line and European Special Line
Overseas warehouse	Reduce logistics costs, improve customer responsiveness and optimize after-sales service	There are some problems such as inventory backlog or shortage due to inaccurate sales forecast and market changes	FBA, SF overseas warehouse, China Post overseas warehouse, etc.

e-commerce enterprises receive orders, they guide overseas warehouse delivery through remote information management. When the goods are sent from overseas warehouses, the "second customs clearance" will be carried out, usually including taxation, inspection application, release, etc. As the "one-time customs clearance" has completed the reporting of some product information at the customs, the customs clearance time is relatively short during the "second customs clearance". If the customer is satisfied with the product after receiving the product order, the online electronic transaction is completed. If you are not satisfied and need to return and exchange the goods, the products will be returned to the overseas warehouse to complete the return and exchange. In terms of cross-border logistics, there are mainly four different stages. One is the domestic head-on transportation stage, that is, the transportation stage of exporting the products of cross-border e-commerce enterprises from the supply point to the domestic logistics hub. Goods can be directly transported to overseas warehouses abroad through domestic ports, airports and other transportation hubs. If there are multiple supply places in China, the goods can be collected in the collection warehouse at the logistics hub and transported to the overseas warehouse. Under normal circumstances, the collection warehouse and overseas warehouse will be located at or near the transportation hub. Second, in the trunk transportation stage, products are transported from China to overseas warehouses. The third is the end distribution stage of products, in which products are delivered from overseas warehouses to customers. On the other hand, export cross-border e-commerce enterprises sell products through online platforms. When receiving customer orders, goods are sent from overseas warehouses and distributed to customers [9, 10]. Generally speaking, most products have completed the whole logistics process of cross-border e-commerce logistics at this stage. For a few products, there is still a fourth stage, that is, the reverse logistics stage. When the customer needs to return and replace the goods, the goods are directly returned from the customer to the overseas warehouse for after-sales treatment. At this stage, Japanese payment enterprises have limited cooperation with foreign banks and financial institutions, covering less areas, and few foreign merchants adopt Japan's cross-border e-commerce payment platform. In addition, the Bank of Japan has not participated in many international third-party platform payment projects, resulting in less application in cross-border settlement, which has not been widely trusted and adopted by Japanese enterprises. We should actively guide the Bank of Japan's cross-border cooperation with international institutions, improve the cross-border payment environment, and spare no effort to support the upgrading and improvement of the cross-border payment and settlement system. For Japanese cross-border electricity the business enterprise, the first mock exam is that the long term logistics cost is low, the management autonomy is high, it is advantageous to control the quality of logistics service, and establish a good corporate image [11, 12]. The third-party overseas warehouse mode means that the overseas warehouse is constructed and operated by a third party other than in the process of cross-border e-commerce transactions. The third party here includes the third-party cross-border e-commerce platform, such as Amazon overseas warehouse, China Post overseas warehouse, etc. It also includes the main mode of non cross-border e-commerce transactions such as third-party cross-border logistics enterprises. The first mock exam is a high level of logistics professional standard. But the first mock exam is also difficult to provide personalized service. Japanese cross-border e-commerce enterprises lack autonomy in this mode. The fourth party overseas warehouse model can also be called one-stop overseas warehouse model. Its essence is the cross-border e-commerce logistics resource integration model with overseas warehouse as the core. It does not build overseas warehouses. It creates a one-stop cross-border logistics service platform for cross-border e-commerce enterprises by integrating resources such as third-party overseas warehouses, third-party logistics distribution enterprises, customs declaration enterprises, insurance enterprises and circulation processing enterprises, So as to realize resource co construction, sharing and win-win. The first mock exam can effectively integrate and optimize all kinds of resources, including information, capital and technology, which will help build a more perfect cross border logistics service system. Based on the above description, complete the steps of extracting the characteristics of Japan's cross-border e-commerce development model.

3.2   Obtaining Influencing Factors of Overseas Warehouse Location

Warehouse location is an important part of enterprise strategy. Therefore, location strategy plays an important role in enterprise operation. Unscientific location will bring long-term negative impact to enterprises. We must comprehensively consider various influencing factors in order to scientifically give correct analysis and decision-making methods for overseas warehouse location. The so-called warehouse location refers to that a certain scale enterprise determines the location of warehouse,once completed, it will be difficult to make changes in the short term. Overseas warehouse mode is a new modern logistics service mode that takes into account management, warehousing and distribution. It aims to provide the seller with one-stop supporting services and warehouse management at the place of sale [13, 14]. From the process of the whole overseas warehouse, the overseas warehouse mode mainly includes the seller's businesses transporting goods to the overseas warehouse in large quantities by sea and air [13, 15]. The seller remotely operates the level of overseas stored goods through the information management platform and manages the real-time inventory. And the localized distribution that the local staff use the local logistics resources to distribute the goods to the customers according to the order information. The flow chart of the whole overseas warehouse logistics mode is shown in Fig. 1.

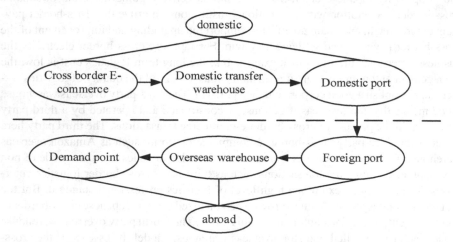

Fig. 1. Logistics service flow chart of cross-border e-commerce based on overseas warehouse mode

As can be seen from Fig. 1, the self built overseas warehouse mode refers to the way that cross-border e-commerce enterprises independently select, build and operate overseas warehouses. This mode has large investment and high threshold, and requires enterprises to have a certain level of logistics expertise. Therefore, it is not suitable for cross-border small and medium-sized enterprises, but only for cross-border e-commerce enterprises with large enterprise scale. Compared with the location of general storage facilities, the location of overseas warehouses should be considered in many aspects and all directions in the process of location selection because of its more complex logistics network system, wider scope and more diversified participants. Political factors, we need to focus on the policies and regulations implemented by domestic and foreign governments on overseas warehouses. On the one hand, the construction of overseas warehouses can be based in overseas countries and meet the requirements of local policies and regulations. On the other hand, the construction of overseas warehouses can make full use of all kinds of favorable support and preferential policies, such as tax reduction and exemption, in combination with the development needs of domestic and foreign countries. On the other hand, the construction cost, labor cost, logistics cost and other cost elements of the area where the overseas warehouse location is located shall be fully considered. At the same time, the relevant factors such as local transportation conditions and the development level of logistics industry are investigated. Natural environmental factors, fully consider the climate conditions, terrain and other natural environmental factors of the area where the overseas warehouse is located, so that the construction and operation of the overseas warehouse can achieve long-term sustainable development and avoid the external environmental impact of force majeure. Meso factors mainly refer to the development level of the industry, which refers to the development level of the logistics industry. The logistics level of the region where the overseas warehouse is located represents the local logistics efficiency to a certain extent, and can also reflect the logistics cost from the side. In particular, the development status and trend of express industry in the region should be fully considered, because it involves the cost of tail transportation. Micro factors are mainly from the cost of each link process in the cross-border logistics network where the overseas warehouse is located. The transportation cost also includes head-on transportation cost, trunk transportation cost and end distribution cost. Tax cost includes relevant tax cost, import value-added tax cost, etc. As the logistics node closest to customers, the location of overseas warehouse should also consider its subsequent operation, which can improve customer satisfaction to a greater extent. Therefore, the distribution timeliness and the reverse logistics cost caused by return and exchange services should also be considered. The cross-border logistics system where overseas warehouses are located has a large space span and a long time, which is greatly affected by uncertain factors. For cross-border e commerce enterprises, they can only predict the demand according to the past transaction data and future development trend, but they can not fully and accurately predict the local demand. For customers, different customers have different psychological expectations for products. In addition to product quality and price, the factors that measure customer satisfaction in cross-border e-commerce transactions, the receiving time of products is also very important, and the delivery time of products after receiving orders is affected by customs clearance and other links, so there is a certain degree of uncertainty. The time value of local satisfaction with product receipt is also affected by factors such as local logistics level, which is uncertain. Therefore, considering the influence of various factors in overseas warehouse location will be more practical. Based on this, complete the steps to obtain the influencing factors of overseas warehouse location.

3.3 Construction of Location Decision Model Based on Ant Colony Algorithm

Ant colony algorithm is a new bionic optimization algorithm, which comes from the foraging behavior of real ant colony. It is a heuristic optimization algorithm based on cluster intelligence [16–18]. According to the principle of ant colony algorithm, the location process of Japanese cross-border e-commerce overseas warehouse is designed. 1. Determine warehouse location objectives. Clarify the purpose and significance of establishing the warehouse, and take this as the premise to make preliminary preparations for site selection. 2. Analyze the constraints of warehouse location. During the selection of alternative warehouses, the geographical environment of the region shall be understood, and the man-made constraints shall be clarified in order to reduce the number of alternative warehouses. Generally, the constraints of site selection include capital, traffic environment, distribution of demand points, government policies, etc. 3. Collect and sort out data. The location of warehouse is generally calculated by cost, that is, the construction cost, transportation cost and operation cost involved in the location are formulated, the mathematical model is established according to the target formula and constraints, and the effective algorithm is used to solve it. Therefore, the basic data of various expenses in the model should be investigated to ensure the smooth solution of the model. 4. Quantitative analysis. Select the appropriate warehouse location model and calculation method, calculate according to the survey data, and get the optimal solution of the scheme. 5. Site selection scheme evaluation. Combined with market adaptability, land use nature and customer satisfaction, the results are evaluated to verify the feasibility of the implementation of the scheme. 6. Review results. Firstly, other non cost factors affecting site selection are analyzed, each factor is given a certain weight, and the weighted method is used to recheck the results. If it passes the review, the calculation result is the final scheme; otherwise, it shall be screened again. 7. Determine the site selection results. After the review is passed, the optimal result of the final calculation is obtained. The continuous model assumes that the candidate range is regarded as a plane, and the warehouse can be set at any point of the plane as the best position. Through the two-dimensional coordinate system, the balance among time, distance and demand is displayed. Taking the warehouse location as the variable, the objective function is obtained, as shown in formula (1):

$$\min G = \sum_{m=1}^{e} l_m \left[(\beta_m - \beta_e)^2 + (\delta_m - \delta_e)^2 \right]^{\frac{1}{2}} \tag{1}$$

In formula (1), β represents the demand node, l represents the weight of the demand node, δ represents the total number of demand nodes, m represents the transportation cost, and e represents the variable slight partial score. Assuming that the center of gravity of the demand node is taken as the initial coordinate of the warehouse, the constraint conditions of the objective function are obtained, as shown in formula (2):

$$H = \begin{cases} \sum_{p=1}^{D} h_{pq} = 1, q \in K \\ \sum_{p=1}^{D} t_p = y \\ h_{pq} \le t_p, q \in K, p \in D \end{cases} \tag{2}$$

In formula (2), D represents the maximum number of warehouses allowed to be built, K represents the set of candidate locations that can be used as warehouses in the plane, p represents the demand of the p demand point, q represents the set of demand points in the plane, and h represents the unit transportation cost from the warehouse to the demand point. According to the calculation result of formula (2), ensure that the requirements of each demand node are met by one warehouse, limit the number of alternative warehouses, and ensure that there are no requirements at demand points without warehouses. For Japanese cross-border e-commerce, enterprises have been pursuing profit maximization and cost minimization. In the decision-making of overseas warehouse construction, the problem can be simplified to the problem of minimum cost. Then the overseas warehouse location decision model can be expressed as:

$$R = \sum_{i=1}^{m} s_i w_i + \sum_{i=1}^{m} \sum_{j=1}^{n} FV_{ij} \tag{3}$$

In formula (3), s represents the fixed cost required to build the overseas warehouse, w represents the decision variable, F represents the shipping distance from the overseas warehouse i to the demand node j, V represents the linear penalty coefficient of the time penalty cost exceeding the time threshold, m represents the set of candidate locations of the alternative overseas warehouse, and n represents the air transportation cost per unit cargo. The three-tier cross-border logistics network with supply points, overseas warehouses and demand points as nodes is relatively simple and intuitive in structure. Cross border e-commerce enterprises adopting this logistics network structure generally have the following characteristics: the product supply point is located at or close to a large transportation hub and has the geographical location conditions to complete cross-border transportation. Products can be easily transported to overseas areas by shipping, air transportation or cross-border trains. The business development of cross-border e-commerce enterprises has a certain foundation, and the supply of goods is concentrated, which is generally the location of cross-border e-commerce enterprises. Most of the overseas warehouses selected by Japanese cross-border e-commerce enterprises are self built overseas warehouses. The e-commerce enterprise shall establish or lease overseas warehouses by itself, and the operation and management of overseas warehouses shall be the responsibility of the cross-border e-commerce enterprise itself. Cross border e-commerce enterprises hope to realize cross-border logistics services by controlling the independent management authority of overseas warehouses. Based on this, the steps of constructing the location decision model are completed.

4 Conclusion

In order to fit the actual situation better, based on the multi-objective location model of overseas warehouse considering market value and transportation conditions under the determined environment, this paper further puts forward the multi-objective location model under the conditions of random demand and uncertain warehouse building cost, and constructs the location decision model according to the variable distribution form. Due to the limited research conditions, the parameters of freight discount in overseas warehouses are not deeply studied in this paper, and such problems will be optimized in the future research.

References

1. Ren, S., Choi, T.M., Lee, K.M., et al.: Intelligent service capacity allocation for cross-border-E-commerce related third-party-forwarding logistics operations: a deep learning approach. Transp. Res. Part Logistics Transp. Rev. **134**, 101834 (2020)

2. Newmark, N.S.: Cross border state sales and use taxation after south Dakota v. wayfair: a new paradigm for e-commerce. Bus. Entrepreneurship Tax Law Rev. 3(1), 17–17 (2019)
3. Guo, A.: Cross-border e-commerce as the main force to stabilize foreign trade. China's Foreign Trade 581(05), 53–55 (2020)
4. Ma, S., Guo, X., Zhang, H.: New driving force for china's import growth: assessing the role of cross-border e-commerce. World Econ. 44(12), 3674–3706 (2021)
5. Ye, Z., Huang, L.: Research on the influence of China's cross-border e-commerce tax reform policy on microeconomic subjects World Sci. Res. J. 6(3), 210–216 (2020)
6. Song, B., Yan, W., Zhang, T.: Cross-border e-commerce commodity risk assessment using text mining and fuzzy rule-based reasoning. Adv. Eng. Inform. 40(APR.), 69–80 (2019)
7. Furuichi, M.: Cross-border logistics practices, policies, and its impact. Glob. Logistics Netw. Model. Policy, 47–69 (2021)
8. Sosorjav, N., Zhihua, H.U.: Mongolia's cross-border logistics system under the belt and road initiative and the development strategy. Bus. Econ. (2019)
9. Su, T.: Route planning method for cross-border e-commerce logistics of agricultural products based on recurrent neural network. Soft Comput. 1–10 (2021)
10. Abudureheman, A., Nilupaer, A.: Optimization model design of cross-border e-commerce transportation path under the background of prevention and control of COVID-19 pneumonia. Soft Comput. 1–9 (2021)
11. Chen, N., Yang, Y.: The impact of customer experience on consumer purchase intention in cross-border E-commerce——taking network structural embeddedness as mediator variable. J. Retail. Consum. Serv. 59, 102344 (2020)
12. Lynn, Y.: Cross-border e-commerce financing was on the rise. China's Foreign Trade. 577(01) 51–51 (2019)
13. Huang, Y.B., University, Z.W.: Public overseas warehouse services performance evaluation for export cross-border e-commerce in the view of value co-creation. J. Zhejiang Wanli Univ. (2019)
14. Zheng, Y., Chen, D., Sun, Y., et al.: Problems for the development of china's cross-border e-commerce overseas warehouses and the countermeasure. Bus. Econ. (2019)
15. Wen-Wen, A.N., Dai, H.W., Yi-Feng, W.U.: Research on the factors affecting the choice of overseas warehouses by small and medium-sized cross-border e-commerce. Value Eng. (2019)
16. Dahan, F.: An effective multi-agent ant colony optimization algorithm for QoS-aware cloud service composition. IEEE Access 9, 17196–17207 (2021)
17. Sudharson, D., Dr, P.: Hybrid software reliability model with Pareto distribution and ant colony optimization (PD–ACO). Int. J. Intell. Unmanned Syst. 8(2), 129–140 (2020)
18. Jin, X.: Deep mining simulation of unstructured big data based on ant colony algorithm Comput. Simul. 37(11) 329–333 (2020)

Study on Egg Freshness Detection Based on Inception and Attention

Min-lan Jiang[✉], Li-yun Mo, and Pei-lun Wu

College of Physics and Electronic Information Engineering, Zhejiang Normal University,
Jinhua 321004, China
xx99@zjnu.cn

Abstract. Egg freshness is an important economic index to measure egg quality, and it is also the main factor affecting egg sales. In this paper, aiming at the problem of small number of training and testing samples in current research, a sample collection device was set up, and 1173 pictures of egg samples with three different levels of freshness were collected, which greatly expanded the number of samples. On this basis, aiming at the problems of strong subjectivity and low accuracy of the obtained model when extracting features manually in the current research, the CBAM module is used in combination with the Inception module to construct a network model, and attention mechanism was introduced to assign adaptive weights to the collected multi-scale features, which further improved the accuracy of the network and the problem of network over-fitting, and establishes a high-precision egg freshness detection model. The test results showed that the average test accuracy of GoogLeNet-A reaches 94.05%, and the highest test accuracy reaches 98.44%. At the same time, compared with other existing deep learning models, the experimental results showed that the detection model proposed in this paper has the highest accuracy, which provided a new idea and method for egg freshness detection.

Keywords: Egg freshness classification · Inception · CBAM

1 Introduction

Eggs are one of the most frequently eaten eggs, which contain a large amount of vitamins and minerals and are a good source of dietary nutrition. According to the statistics of the World Food and Agriculture Organization, in 2018, there were more than 137 million metric tons of eggs produced globally. The output of the top five egg-laying countries accounted for 56% of the total demand, of which China ranked first in the world. If eggs can be classified according to freshness in the process of production and consumption, it will not only be helpful for producers and operators to adopt scientific management methods to ensure the quality of eggs and their by-products, but also safeguard the rights and interests of consumers and protect the health of consumers [1]. So how to select a good egg is one of the urgent problems to be solved. At present, the artificial selection method of observing the internal quality of eggs by using an egg illuminator

© ICST Institute for Computer Sciences, Social Informatics and Telecommunications Engineering 2022
Published by Springer Nature Switzerland AG 2022. All Rights Reserved
D. Jiang and H. Song (Eds.): SIMUtools 2021, LNICST 424, pp. 613–626, 2022.
https://doi.org/10.1007/978-3-030-97124-3_47

in a darkroom is widely used. This method is inefficient, and the results are based on the experience of workers, with strong subjectivity and low accuracy.

Since the beginning of the 21st century, many researches have been put forward by domestic and foreign scholars on the non-destructive detection of egg freshness. At present, the main research directions are: non-destructive detection based on machine vision [2–5], non-destructive detection based on acoustic impact characteristics [6, 7], non-destructive detection based on optical characteristics [8–10], non-destructive detection based on dielectric properties, etc. The non-invasive detection technology based on machine vision mostly uses extracting the inside and outside characteristics of eggs, such as egg weight, yolk size, air chamber diameter ratio, to detect the freshness of eggs. Wang Qiaohua et al. [11] Constructed the model of the Haugh value of eggs and the optical information parameters of eggs by using the BP network. The non-destructive detection and grading of the freshness of eggs were carried out, and the detection accuracy reached 89%. Li Xincheng et al. [12] separated four characteristic parameters from the egg light transmittance chart, which were yolk area ratio, air chamber area ratio, air chamber height ratio and air chamber diameter ratio, and used them as independent variables, and established a univariate regression model with the egg Haugh value to detect the egg freshness, in which the goodness of fit between the egg yolk area ratio and the Haugh value reached 0.62. Li Jiating et al. [13] established the relationship model between the electronic nose response signal and the physical and chemical indexes of eggs by using the BP network analysis method. The detection accuracy of egg freshness reached 90.19%. Liu Yan et al. [14] established a ternary model for egg freshness detection by extracting the three characteristics of the air chamber size, egg yolk size and ovality in the light transmission image of eggs. The model correlation coefficient R^2 reached 0.952.

The above studies show that it is feasible to establish an egg freshness detection model through the corresponding relationship between the characteristic parameters such as the ratio of chamber diameter in the egg translucent picture and the Haugh value. Current studies usually use the method of extracting the characteristics of egg translucency map manually, which is a complex image preprocessing method with a small number of samples and a strong subjectivity. With the development of deep learning in recent years, convolution neural network has made many breakthroughs in the field of image analysis and processing, avoiding the complex pre-processing of images. Convolution, pooling and filling replace the subjectivity of traditional machine learning in extracting image features manually. However, as the network depth increases, the network parameters increase exponentially, resulting in the disappearance of gradients, over-fitting, and so on.

Inception modular structure proposed by Christian Szegedy [15] et al. can further improve network performance within limited computing resources. Therefore, in order to improve the generalization ability and speed of operation, it is easy to overfit the artificial neural network. In this paper, the Inception module is used to optimize the network structure while enlarging the number of samples, and multiscale convolution is introduced to acquire the required convolution kernel size for autonomous learning of the input image features. At the same time, this paper introduces the attention mechanism to assign adaptive weights to it, which makes the network focus on the characteristics related to egg freshness, such as yolk size, air chamber diameter ratio, to further improve the accuracy of the network, and establishes a high-precision ICBAM egg freshness detection network model.

2 ICBAM Network Model

2.1 Inception Module

The performance improvement of convolution neural network depends on increasing the depth of the network and the number of hidden layer neurons, which will result in a larger network parameter space, making the network more prone to over-fitting, computational load, slow operation, and so on. Moreover, as the network depth increases, the gradient disappears during the model building process. The solution to this problem is to introduce the sparse nature and convert the full connection layer to sparse connection, even if convolution is used instead of full connection, but hardware optimization for dense matrices only results in inefficient computation of asymmetric sparse data in the network. Christian Szegedy et al. proposed an Inception module to solve the above problems. The convolution network is designed as an optimal local sparse structure, which can be implemented with existing density matrix computing hardware. This structure improves the performance of the network and guarantees the computational efficiency of the network.

The three Inception module structures used in this paper are shown in Figs.1, 2 and 3. These three modules contain multiple convolution core branches of $1 \times 1, 3 \times 3, 3 \times$

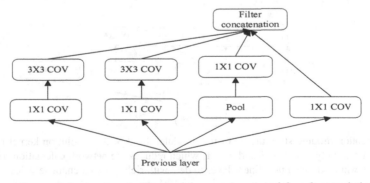

Fig. 1. Inception module structure 1. The module uses 1×1 and 3×3 convolution cores to extract image features.

1, 1 × 7, and 7 × 1. The multicore structure can extract and learn the features of different forms of eggs. At the same time, this multiscale convolution makes it unnecessary to design the convolution core size manually or to determine whether convolution and pooling layers need to be created in the module, which reduces the influence of human factors on the network.

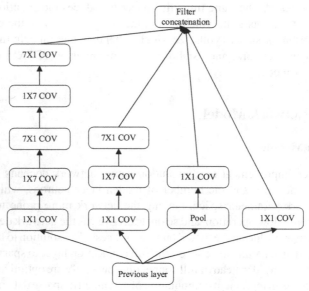

Fig. 2. Inception module structure 2. The module decomposes the 7 × 7 convolution kernel asymmetrically into 1 × 7 and 7 × 1, which greatly reduces the network calculation parameters and adds a non-linear layer to handle richer spatial characteristics.

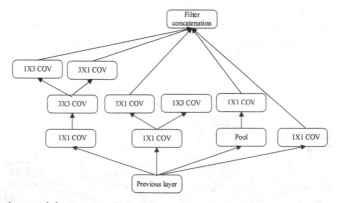

Fig. 3. Inception module structure 3. In this module, the 3 × 3 convolution kernel is decomposed asymmetrically into 1 × 3 and 3 × 1, which reduces the network calculation parameters significantly while adding a non-linear layer to deal with richer spatial characteristics.

2.2 CBAM (Convolutional Block Attention Module) Module

Attention Model, originally used for machine translation, has become an important concept in the field of neural networks. In the field of artificial intelligence, attention can better capture the visual structure by focusing on some scenes and selectively on the prominent parts, and has now become an important part of the structure of neural networks. Because convolution extracts information features by mixing cross-channel and spatial information, Sanghyun Woo et al. [16] used a CBAM module to infer attention mapping from two independent dimensions: channel and spatial order, and then multiplies the attention mapping into an input feature mapping with adaptive feature refinement, which improves the performance of the convolution neural network classification task.

Channel Attention Mapping compresses the convoluted image features on the channel dimension by averaging and maximizing the pooling of the image features, then using the same simple MLP network structure, and finally adding the corresponding elements of the features together as the channel Attention Mapping, as shown in Fig. 4.

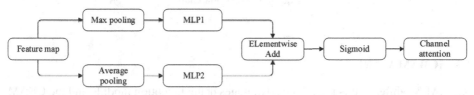

Fig. 4. Channel Attention Mapping

Sanghyun Woo et al. not only generated channel attention mappings on channels, but also established spatial attention mappings on image features in spatial dimensions. Sanghyun Woo et al. first compressed channel attention features using average pooling and maximum pooling, respectively, to get two two-dimensional features and stitch them together in channel dimensions. A 1×1 convolution layer is then used to convolute it, as shown in Fig. 5.

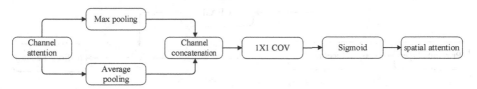

Fig. 5. Spatial Attention Mapping

Channel Attention and Spatial Attention solve the problem of equal processing of all image features by neural network models during training. Channel attention enables the neural network to distinguish what is meaningful in a sample picture, and spatial attention supplements the missing location information in channel attention. The CBAM module used in this paper learns channel attention and spatial attention separately while maintaining good network performance and reducing the amount of parameters used in calculating 3D feature maps. In the input feature map multiplied by the attention map, the network focus is on the features related to egg freshness, which reduces the impact of background on sample collection and improves network performance. The CBAM flowchart is shown in Fig. 6.

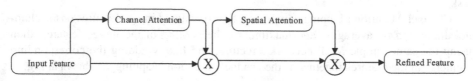

Fig. 6. CBAM flow chart

2.3 ICBAM Model

ICBAM Module. In this paper, the advantages of the Inception module and the CBAM module are used to combine the Inception module and the CBAM module. The Inception module was used to convolute the input egg freshness feature map with multi-scale, and the multi-scale image features were used as the input of CBAM. The CBAM module infers attention mapping from two independent dimensions, channel and space, and multiplies it by input features, which enables the whole network to selectively focus on the highlights and improves the accuracy of egg freshness classification tasks. The ICBAM module flow is shown in the dashed wireframe section of Fig. 7.

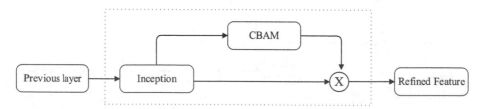

Fig. 7. ICBAM module structure

ICBAM Model Structure. The GoogLeNet-A network built in this paper has four ICBAM modules, six convolution layers, four Dropout layers and one softmax layer. The parameters required for convolution layer design are step (s), convolution kernel size (f), number of convolution cores (n), and activation function. The activation function selected in this paper is Relu, and the parameters for each convolution layer are shown in

Table 1. The sample collected in this paper is 1173. In the case of non-massive samples, dropout layer can effectively prevent over-fitting problem, so dropout layer is added after convolution layer in the ICBAM model structure for egg freshness detection in this paper. The GoogLeNet-A model is shown in Fig. 8.

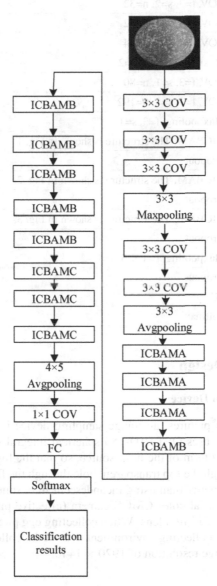

Fig. 8. GoogLeNet-A model

Table 1. Model structure diagram

Number of layers	Layer type	Enter dimension
1	Input layer	$144 \times 192 \times 3$
2	COV, f=3, s=2, n=32	$144 \times 192 \times 3$
3	COV, f=3, s=1, n=32	$71 \times 95 \times 32$
4	COV, f=3, s=1, n=64	$69 \times 93 \times 32$
5	Maxpooling, f=3, s=2	$69 \times 93 \times 64$
6	COV, f=3, s=1, n=80	$34 \times 46 \times 64$
7	COV, f=3, s=2, n=192	$32 \times 44 \times 80$
8	Maxpooling, f=3, s=1	$16 \times 22 \times 192$
9	3 ICBAM, The structure is shown in Fig. 1.	$16 \times 22 \times 288$
10	Dropout	
11	5 ICBAM, The structure is shown in Fig. 2.	$8 \times 11 \times 768$
12	Dropout	
13	3 ICBAM, The structure is shown in Fig. 3.	$4 \times 5 \times 1280$
14	Dropout	
15	Maxpooling, f=4 × 5, s=1	$4 \times 5 \times 1280$
16	Dropout	
17	FC	$1 \times 1 \times 3$
18	Softmax	$1 \times 1 \times 3$

3 Experimental Design

3.1 Image Acquisition Device

In order to collect eggs pictures, an image sampling device is designed as shown in Fig. 9. The light source uses OPT-RID-150 spherical integral light source, and a flat mirror is placed at the bottom of the light source, so that the light emitted by the light source is reflected through the top transparent hole through the flat mirror, and the light intensity on the eggs is better than using incandescent light source directly in previous studies, and select industrial color CMOS camera (effective pixel 2592×1944), the camera has 5 megapixels, 12 mm lens. When collecting egg pictures, you need to limit the light intensity of the collecting environment to 2–10 lx, collect RGB three-channel color image with an image resolution of 1920×1440.

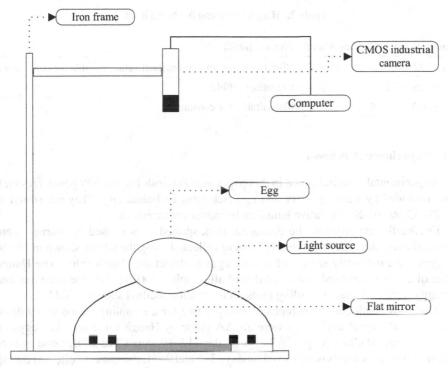

Fig. 9. Image acquisition device

3.2 Image Preprocessing

The color of egg picture collected in Fig. 9 is yellow to red, the chamber that can highlight the egg characteristics and the yolk color is dark red to black. The color contrast between them is not high. After color enhancement experiments, it is found that the G component in RGB space is easier to highlight the egg feature [17], so the G component in sample picture is enhanced four times. The interpolation algorithm is then used to reduce the G-enhanced image size to 1/10 of the original sample to meet the requirements of fast training and testing of CNN network models.

3.3 Determination of Haugh Value

The Haugh unit value is an index established by USDA to synthesize two factors, egg protein height and egg weight, to characterize the freshness of eggs. Fresh egg Haugh unit is usually between 70 and 82, and its formula is as follows:

$$Ha = 100 \times \lg\left(H + 7.57 - 1.7 \times w^{0.37}\right) \tag{1}$$

In formula H is the protein height in mm and W is the egg mass in g.

According to the relationship between egg freshness level and Haugh value in the domestic trade industry standard of the People's Republic of China (SB/T 10683–2011), the tested eggs are divided into three levels: AA, A, B, as shown in Table 2.

Table 2. Haugh value and freshness level

Haugh value	Freshness level	Protein stability
Ha ≥ 72	AA	High freshness, high nutritional value, suitable for consumers
60 ≤ Ha ≤ 72	A	Consumer edible
Ha ≤ 60	B	Not suitable for consumers

3.4 Experimental Process

The experimental materials used in this paper are 500 fresh Jingbai 939 powdered-shell eggs provided by Lanxi poultry and egg-rich farm in Jinhua city. They are stored at 26–28 °C and 70–80% relative humidity in indoor environment.

During the experiment, the damaged, dark-spotted eggs caused by storage were removed every day. All remaining eggs were collected using the device shown in Fig. 9. 20 eggs were randomly selected from the eggs to detect the Haugh value. The Haugh value of 20 eggs was used instead of that of all samples (500 eggs) on the same day and the eggs were classified according to the classification method shown in Table 2.

The above collection was repeated every 1 day for a sampling period of 19 days. The first and second day's eggs were all AA grade by Haugh value test. The eggs on days 6–8 were all Class A eggs. All eggs on days 12–19 were Class B. Because eggs of different freshness levels were mixed on days 3–5 and 9–11, the images collected during these two periods were not used in subsequent experiments.

After removing the samples with unclear images due to shooting and other problems, 366 AA grade samples, 402 A grade samples and 405 B grade samples were obtained. 43 (129 total) samples were selected from each freshness sample as test samples, and 1044 samples were all used as training samples. First, the training samples are pre-processed by quadrupling the channel and one-hot encoding is used to code the labels of three freshness levels. Then, the training samples and their labels are substituted into the ICBAM model in Sect. 2.4. The weights are updated by the random gradient descent algorithm to obtain the egg freshness detection model. The detection process is shown in Fig. 10.

4   Experimental Result

This paper is based on Python 3.7 programming environment. The deep learning framework is Tensorflow framework. 1044 training samples are used as input data of the model, and one-hot code of sample label is used as output data of the model. When each training starts, 64 samples are randomly selected from the training set as input data for one training, and 64 samples are labeled as output data for the model. When a training is completed, 64 samples from 129 test samples are randomly selected to test the trained model. The test accuracy and loss function are shown in Fig. 11 and Fig. 12.

It can be seen from Fig. 11 and Fig. 12, as the number of training iterations increases, the loss function of training decreases and tends to be stable, while the accuracy of training increases. This shows that the network model is continuously optimized during

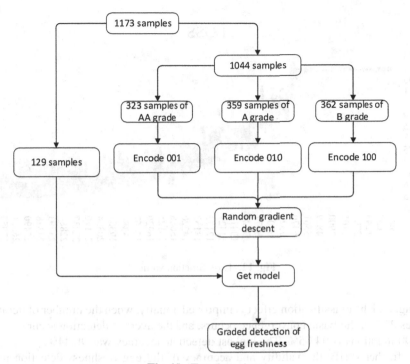

Fig. 10. Test flow chart

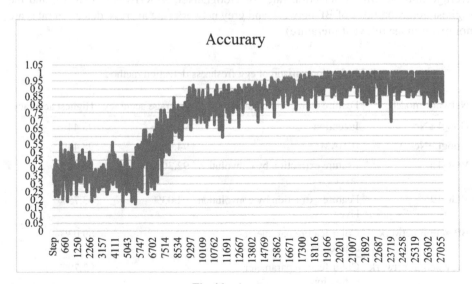

Fig. 11. Accuracy

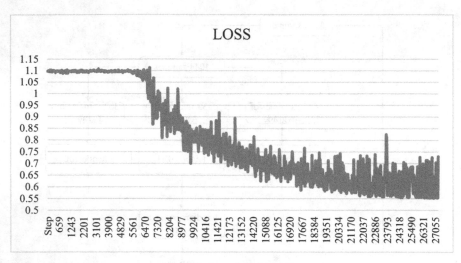

Fig. 12. Loss function value

training, and the classification effect is improved. Finally, when the number of iterations reaches 27037, the basic convergence occurs, and the average detection accuracy of the last 100 iterations is 94.05%. The highest detection accuracy was 98.44%.

To further verify the validity and accuracy of the egg freshness detection model proposed in this paper, three kinds of network models, GoogLeNet, VGG16 and VGG19, were introduced and compared with each other using the same dataset with the same experimental settings. The experimental results are shown in Table 3. Table 3 gives the average and maximum detection rates of GoogLeNet, VGG16 and VGG19, and the highest detection rates of BP network and grey network (the average detection rates are not given in the relevant literature).

Table 3. Comparison of egg freshness detection methods

Network model	Feature extraction method	Average accuracy	Highest accuracy
GoogLeNet	Inception	93.54%	98.44%
GoogLeNet-A	ICBAM	94.05%	98.44%
VGG16	Feature extraction by convolution layer	92.30%	96.88%
VGG19	Feature extraction by convolution layer	92.03%	93.75%
BP neural network	Color feature parameter extraction	/	89.03%
Grey neural network	Color feature parameter extraction	/	92.70%

The results from Table 3 show that the method of extracting egg freshness features by self-selection of the model is more accurate and comprehensive than the method of extracting egg freshness features by artificial network model. The highest accuracy of GoogLeNet, GoogLeNet-A, VGG16 and VGG19 networks using convolution neural network instead of manual selection of image features is higher than that of BP network and grey neural network using manual selection of image features. Among all the deep learning models tested, ICBAM module extracts the most comprehensive features with an average test accuracy of 94.05%. Extraction of multiscale features from GoogLeNet and GoogLeNet-A networks results in higher average and highest accuracy than VGG16 and VGG19 networks using a single convolution core. After introducing the attention mechanism, the focus of the network is more on the characteristics of egg freshness. The average accuracy of the GoogLeNet-A network is 0.49% higher than that of GoogLeNet under several tests, which verifies that GoogLeNet-A has better network performance and better stability in practical application.

5 Conclusion

Non-destructive grading of egg freshness can be used to detect the freshness level online without destroying the sample, which is of great significance in the process of actual sales, production and supervision. In previous studies, the method of extracting egg freshness characteristics manually is often used for egg freshness level classification, and then the classification model is built by machine learning. The precision of the model established by this method is limited, and only a few dozen or one or two hundred samples are used for training and testing. It is easy to fit the extracted features. In this paper, the training and testing samples are expanded first. 1173 samples collected by the collection device are used for model building and testing. At the same time, the model structure is improved. CBAM module is embedded after Inception module, and the extracted image features are weighted by attention mechanism. The average test accuracy of the model is increased to 94.05%, and the maximum test accuracy is increased to 98.44%. In comparison experiments, the accuracy of VGG16, VGG19 and GoogLeNet is not as good as that of GoogLeNet-A model using ICBAM module, which verifies the validity of the proposed model and has great significance for the economic benefits of actual production, sales and market supervision.

References

1. Zhang, W., Zhou, W., et al.: Research progress in detection of egg freshness. J. Human Univ. Sci. Technol. **32**(12), 54–56 (2011)
2. Wang, Q., Xiong, L., Ding, Y., et al.: Study on neural network detection system of egg freshness. J. Huazhong Agric. Univ. **24**(6), 630–632 (2005)
3. Wang, Q., Wen, Y., et al.: Correlation between morphological characteristics of transmitted light image and freshness of eggs. J. Agric. Eng. **24**(03), 179–183 (2008)
4. Zheng, L., Yang, X., Xu, G., et al.: Nondestructive detection of egg freshness based on computer vision. J. Agric. Eng. **25**(2), 335–339 (2009)
5. Wei, X., Wang, S.: Model and experiment of comprehensive nondestructive testing of egg freshness. J. Agric. Eng. **25**(3), 242–2479 (2009)

6. Wang, S., Wei, X.: Correlation between egg beating response characteristics and freshness. J. Huazhong Agric. Univ. **28**(3), 373–376 (2009)
7. Long, X., Li, Y., Luo, X.: Research and design of egg freshness nondestructive testing system. J. Comput. Dig. Eng. **38**(5), 155–158 (2010)
8. Lin, H., Zhao, J., Sun, L., et al.: Freshness measurement of eggs using near infrared (NIR) spectroscopy and multivariate data analysis. J. Innov. Food Sci. Emerg. Technol. **12**(2), 182–186 (2011)
9. Giunchi, A., Berardinelli, A., Ragni, L., et al.: Non-destructive freshness assessment of shell eggs using FT-NIR spectroscopy. J. Food Eng. **89**(2),142–148 (2008)
10. Kemps, B., Bamelis, F., Ketelaere, D., et al.: Visible transmission spectroscopy for the assessment of egg freshness. J. Sci. Food. Agric. **86**(9), 1399–1406 (2006)
11. Wang, Q., Reng, Y., Wen, Y.: Nondestructive detection method of egg freshness based on BP neural network. J. Agric. Mach. **37**(01), 104–106 (2006)
12. Li, X., Zhao, D., Shi, H., Yuan, Y.: Nondestructive testing method for egg quality based on machine vision. J. Food Saf. Qual . **10**(2), 408–493 (2019)
13. Li, J., Wang, J., Li, Y., Wei, Y.: Detection of egg freshness based on electronic nose. J. Mod. Food Sci. Technol. **33**(4), 300–305+188 (2017)
14. Liu, Y., Li, Q., Huang, X., et al.: Study on feature extraction and freshness detection model of egg transparency image. Sci. Technol. Eng. **15**(25), 72–77 (2015)
15. Szegedy, C., Liu, W., Jia, Y.Q., et al.: Going deeper with convolutions. In: IEEE Conference on Computer Vision and Pattern Recognition, Boston, MA, USA (2015)
16. Woo, S., Park, J., Lee, J., et al.: CBAM: convolutional block attention module. Computer Vision Foundation. ArXiv,1807.06521v2 (2018)
17. Li, X., Zhao, D., Shi, H.: Non-destructive testing method of egg quality based on machine vision. J. Food Saf. Qual. **10**(2), 408–493 (2019)

Real-Time Statistical Method for Marketing Profit of Japanese Cosmetics Online Cross-Border E-commerce Platform

Jingxian Huang(✉)

Guizhou Minzu University, Guiyang 550025, Guizhou, China

Abstract. In the cosmetics online cross-border e-commerce platform, the real-time statistics of marketing profits are very important. Taking the marketing profit of Japanese cosmetics online cross-border e-commerce platform as the research object, the development status and trend of Japanese cosmetics market are analyzed. Relying on the e-commerce platform to automatically evaluate the pledge value, the internal circulation of marketing profit is realized. The multi-level classification statistical analysis of marketing profit using the support vector machine in the SLS-SVM algorithm, and the real-time statistics of platform marketing profit are realized.

Keywords: Japanese cosmetics · Online cross-border e-commerce platform · Marketing profit · Real-time statistics · Principal component analysis · Support vector machine

1 Introduction

In recent years, online shopping has become a habit in people's daily lives and people's lives are being quietly changed by e-commerce. E-commerce platform is a platform for businesses or individuals to conduct transactions and communication. Both consumers and businesses can use e-commerce platforms to carry out business activities, but in the face of a large number of goods, the quality of goods on e-commerce platforms varies, so consumers need to spend time and effort to choose the quality goods they need [1, 2]. At this time, it is relatively difficult to meet the needs of consumers who pursue quality and efficiency at the same time. With the development of the country, the residents' consumption is developing in the direction of high quality and high quality. If the demand exists, the market exists, and with the upgrading of consumption, a large number of e-commerce businesses are also on the rise. Data research continues to grow in importance in business and finance, and because of the rich data environment that exists in the cross-border e-commerce market, data from economic and financial markets are more integrated and complete than ever before, and are gradually resulting in more systematic and accurate collection of data on a large number of variables, which, together with the rapid development of computer hardware and software, makes it possible to use statistical learning methods to deal with complex, high-dimensional data analysis. Cross-border

D. Jiang and H. Song (Eds.): SIMUtools 2021, LNICST 424, pp. 627–636, 2022.
https://doi.org/10.1007/978-3-030-97124-3_48

e-commerce is developed based on the Internet, and cyberspace is a new space relative to physical space, a virtual but objective world consisting of URLs and passwords [3–5]. The unique value standards and behavioral patterns of cyberspace profoundly affect cross-border e-commerce, making it different from traditional transaction methods and presenting its own characteristics. The network is a borderless media body with global and non-centralized characteristics. Cross-border e-commerce, which is dependent on the network, also has global and non-centralized characteristics. An important feature of e-commerce compared with traditional trading methods is that e-commerce is a borderless transaction, losing the geographical factor that traditional transactions have. Internet users do not need to consider crossing borders to submit their products, especially high value-added products and services, to the marketplace. The positive impact of the global nature of the Web is the maximum sharing of information, and the negative impact is that users must face risks arising from cultural, political and legal differences. Anyone with certain technical means can get information into the network at any time, anywhere, and connect with each other for transactions. In its fiscal report, the United States Department of the Treasury noted that taxing e-commerce activities based on globalized networks was difficult because: e-commerce was based on virtual computer space, losing the geographical element that was present in traditional trading methods; and manufacturers in e-commerce were prone to conceal their domicile, which was indifferent to consumers. For example, a very small Irish online company could sell its products and services over the Internet through a web page that could be clicked on and viewed by consumers around the world, provided that they had access to the Internet. It is difficult to define exactly within which country this transaction is taking place. The development of the Internet has led to the prevalence of digital transmission of products and services [6]. Digital transmission takes place through the concentration of different types of media, such as data, sound and images, in a globalized network environment, which appear as computer data codes in the network and are therefore intangible. The transmission of an e-mail message, for example, is first broken down by the server into millions of packets, which are then transmitted over different network paths to a destination server and reorganized for forwarding to the recipient according to the TCP/IP protocol, all in an instant over the network. For networks, the speed of transmission is independent of geographical distance [7–9]. In traditional transaction mode, information exchange methods such as letters, telegrams, faxes, etc., there is a time difference of different lengths between the sending and receiving of information. In contrast, the information exchange in e-commerce, regardless of the actual space time distance, one party sends information and the other party receives information almost simultaneously, just like face-to-face conversation in life. For certain digital products, transactions can also be settled instantly, and orders, payments and deliveries can all be completed in an instant.

The cosmetics market is constantly expanding, and consumer demand for various categories and grades of cosmetics is increasing dramatically. Many overseas cosmetic companies are using cross-border e-commerce platforms to expand their user markets. Many Japanese and Korean cosmetic brands not only occupy a place in the international cosmetic market, but are also popular in the Chinese market, where both brand culture and product quality are well received [10–12]. Shiseido, as the leading cosmetics group in Japan, has been ranked in the top ten in terms of market share of cosmetics in each country for the past decade. Japanese cosmetics are marketed through online cross-border e-commerce platforms, which not only facilitate consumers' purchasing behavior, but also effectively reduce the investment in offline counters and enhance the marketing profit of the company, and it is worthwhile to pay more attention to its experience in the development of online cross-border market. This study will analyze the issue of real-time statistics on the marketing profits of Japanese cosmetics online cross-border e-commerce platforms. This paper analyzes in detail the development mode of cross-border e-commerce platform, designs the route of the platform for supply chain enterprises at all levels to raise funds, and solves the financing difficulties of small, medium, and micro enterprises through three main lines: cooperation with core enterprises, financial industry and supply chain service platform. The innovation point is in the multi-level classification statistical analysis of marketing profits using the support vector machine in the SLS-SVM algorithm.

2 Overview of Japanese Cosmetics and Online Cross-Border E-commerce Platforms

2.1 Cross-Border E-commerce Platform Development Approach

In the specific market analysis, products with high-end positioning are developing at a faster pace than those with low- and mid-range positioning. Online sales platforms are increasingly valued by major cosmetic companies, which have all opened their own online flagship stores, such as Sephora, Guerlain and Skin Key, which have opened official online stores on the Tmall website. Compared to domestic brands, multinational cosmetic companies are still extremely competitive, such as building a better brand image and improving product quality, using strong research and innovation capabilities to develop products, and more effective marketing techniques. These have contributed to multinational cosmetic companies continuing to maintain their leading position in the cross-border market. The current main business models of cross-border e-commerce (export) can be divided into: B2B, B2C, B2B2C, C2M, O2O, etc.

(1) B2B model

B2B mode is Business-to-Business, refers to the online transaction mode between enterprises and enterprises, is one of the earliest cross-border e-commerce (foreign trade e-commerce) mode, and can be divided into platform mode and independent station mode. The platform model has a low entry barrier, relatively low investment, and can quickly use the platform's own traffic to obtain orders for conversion, the disadvantage is homogeneous competition and serious copying behavior. Under the price war of peers, the chances of small enterprises to obtain orders are getting smaller and smaller, and the head customers have established a more stable supply and demand relationship, it is not easy to break this balance [13]. Independent site model is relatively high cost of entry, need to spend costs to buy servers, space, domain names, and invest costs for website development, and the need for greater investment is the operation and promotion of the site, as a new independent site, traffic is zero, conversion is zero, trust is zero, all these need to spend a larger cost to obtain. And the advantages are obvious, the user traffic is very accurate, in the case of product cost-effective guarantee, the conversion rate is relatively high. And as a website independent of the platform, no dependence on the platform, relative to the annual fixed fee cost of the platform, it seems that the long-term cost of the independent site is lower.

(2) B2C model

The B2C model, Business-to-Customer, is a direct-to-consumer e-commerce model for merchants, and like B2B, B2C can also be divided into a platform model and an independent site model.

(a) B2C platform model: the current mainstream business model of cross-border e-commerce, of which Amazon, eBay, and Sotom are typical representatives of these platforms, merchants through the release of goods on these platforms, consumers place orders to buy after the formation of valid orders, through the unification of information flow and capital flow, logistics (some platforms build their own logistics) three flows, forming a complete closed loop of transactions.

(b) B2C independent site model: different from the platform model, independent site is a website with independent domain name, with online transaction function, not bound by the rules of the platform, generally focus on a certain product line or category [14]. Relatively speaking, the entry barrier of B2C platform business is relatively low, which is mainly reflected in many aspects such as products, registration, logistics, collection and traffic.

Product: Most of the platform sellers are still in the primary stage of "buying and selling", they mostly do not pay attention to the development of the product itself, to earn the price difference as the main way of profit. There are two typical phenomena: a) Through simple data analysis, they find a relatively popular product line and then adopt a swarm of follow-the-wind sales. They buy these products in bulk on some wholesale websites and post them on foreign B2C platforms for sale, using simple and brutal methods such as low prices and low quality standards, until they finally make a category into a red sea and then switch to another product line. b) Mass SKU method, that is, sellers upload a large number of products on the platform, but do not purchase these products themselves, and then go to the market to purchase goods and mail them to customers abroad after customers place orders on the platform. Both ways lack attention to the products themselves, and the quality of products varies.

Registration: Among the above-mentioned platforms, Amazon, which claims to have the strictest audit system, can also register multiple accounts through multiple personal information or business information, and the information required is only basic information such as photocopies of ID cards, utility invoices, company business licenses, and rental information. The account audit of eBay and Selling is more lenient [15–17]. Only niche vertical niche platforms such as Houzz and Wayfair need to have the requirement of a US registered company.

Logistics: From commercial express lines to dedicated logistics, many logistics service providers can provide a variety of options for cross-border logistics. Commercial express lines such as DHL, FedEx, etc. have high timeliness and generally take only 3–7 working days to arrive from China to the U.S., but the cost is higher; dedicated logistics can solve the delivery problems of certain specific markets, such as Australia, Northern Europe and other regions, and the cost is moderate, but the disadvantage is that the scale is smaller and the trust is lower.

Collection: Cross-border e-commerce collection has always been a concern for practitioners, and various platforms are launching their own collection policies and channels, such as eBay using its own PayPal for collection, but the 3% commission is expensive to start with; Selling is using Alipay as a collection tool; Amazon has opened up the collection channel, and companies with collection qualifications can be audited and adopted by platform sellers, such as Payoneer and WorldFirst. Amazon has opened up the collection channel, and companies with collection qualifications can be vetted and adopted by platform sellers, such as Payoneer, WorldFirst, etc. The fees range from 1% to 3%. However, since the money is first paid by the buyer to the platform, if there are complaints or serious problems with the account/store, the fees will be withheld or penalized by the platform.

Traffic: platform means a large number of users and the aggregation of traffic, to the Amazon U.S. site, for example, according to the 2015 statistics, the average daily visits up to 738 million, so huge traffic dividends. As long as good product image display, product copy, station advertising and a reasonable price range can bring a lot of traffic conversion, platform sellers do not need to focus on where to get customers from, more research on how to attract traffic and convert traffic, the platform comes with traffic can easily help sellers quickly achieve sales products to gain profits [18].

In general, B2C platform business work is easier, most sellers will choose to station in the B2C e-commerce platform as the starting point of cross-border e-commerce business. The three aforementioned Amazon, eBay, and Speedy Business have become the first choice for sellers to be stationed in the triad of cross-border e-commerce platform model. There are also some emerging platforms that also vigorously carry out investment promotion, such as Wish, a mobile shopping platform, Lazada, a Southeast Asian e-commerce platform, and Cdiscount, a French e-commerce platform, which have also achieved good performance. The mainstream model of export cross-border e-commerce B2B2C has a seamless connection between B2B and B2C business at its core. Using the B2B business experience accumulated for many years, the channel sinks to the C-terminus, solving the problem of being familiar with the target market and the target consumers, and realizing the integration of supply chain, channel and marketing, the cross-border e-commerce business can be made bigger and stronger.

2.2 Development Status and Trends of the Japanese Cosmetics Market

In the last five years, the Chinese cosmetics market has been dominated by foreign companies, such as the European and American giants of the daily chemical industry like P&G, L'Oreal and Unilever, as well as the Japanese Shiseido. Leaving aside local brands and European and American brands, Japanese and Korean cosmetic companies developing in China, led mainly by the Japanese company Shiseido, have been in the forefront all year round.

As can be seen from Table 1, the market share of Japanese Shiseido in China declined year by year from 2016 to 2019, and rebounded slightly in 2019, but in terms of all

Table 1. Top 7 Japanese cosmetic companies in terms of market share in China (Unit: %)

The company	Shiseido Co Ltd	ROHTO Pharmaceutical Co Ltd	Kao Corp	DHC Corp	Pigeon Corp	Fancl Corp	Kosé Corp
2016	3.64	0.54	0.74	0.69	0.27	0.46	0.39
2017	3.37	0.57	0.75	0.54	0.28	0.32	0.34
2018	3.21	0.65	0.59	0.44	0.26	0.33	0.27
2019	3.04	0.61	0.54	0.42	0.21	0.31	0.22
2020	3.15	0.63	0.52	0.37	0.24	0.27	0.25

Japanese and Korean companies developing in China, there are far more Japanese cosmetic companies than Korean ones, such as ROHTO, Japanese Kao, and Japanese DHC, all of which have reputable cosmetic companies in China.

3 Real-Time Statistical Methods for Platform Marketing Profits

3.1 Relying on E-commerce Platforms to Automatically Assess the Value of Pledges

The sharing economy is when one party with idle resources gives up the right to use them to another party for a fee. When the subject of the transfer is the right to use capital, the sharing economy becomes shared finance, and supply chain finance is a form of shared finance. One of the mainstream financing models of supply chain finance is the pledge financing of movable assets, in which the provider of funds gets the return and obtains the pledge right, and the financing enterprise gets the right to use the funds. Compared with real estate, movable assets have the characteristics of liquidity and difficulty in preserving value, and the price of movable assets is in constant fluctuation, which is prone to depreciation during the pledge period. In addition, in practice, affected by the wide variety of pledged items and opaque prices, it is difficult to judge the true market value of the financing enterprise if it only relies on the purchase contract and purchase and sale invoices issued by the financing enterprise. As commercial banks are not qualified to supervise movable assets, they are highly dependent on third parties for movable pledge financing, and their risk appetite is low, which makes them gradually raise the threshold of movable pledge, making movable pledge financing a "chicken and egg" business for banks [19]. However, MSMEs are the main force in choosing chattel financing, which leads to banks not being able to solve the problem of difficult and expensive financing. Actively establish user data; connect all the service scenarios online and offline, and build an e-commerce platform ecosystem, cross-border e-commerce purchase has a huge amount of SME customer resources, and holds the whole process transaction information of online and offline shops, covering real-time price information of multi-category products. The supply chain finance platform is fully connected with the information system in the whole ecosystem, realizing the "four streams" of business flow, capital flow, information flow and logistics, and forming a closed loop in the ecosystem and establishing a more complete database. The real-time transmission of supply chain finance data has efficiently solved the capital needs of upstream and downstream small and medium-sized enterprises in the supply, production and marketing chain [20]. In movable assets pledge financing, relying on data resources within the ecosystem, information technology such as artificial intelligence is used to grasp information on the value of movable assets at all stages of the financing business and realize real-time value assessment of pledges.

3.2 Internal Circulation of Marketing Profits

Through the multi-line layout, it allows internal and external enterprises at all levels to directly access the platform's marketing profit statistics, reaching out to multi-level enterprises in the internal and external supply chains, and using technologies such as big data and cloud computing to reduce the information asymmetry between the fund provider and the demand side and improve the financing efficiency of enterprises. Through star products such as chattel pledge financing, order financing, bill discounting and credit financing, it revitalizes various resources lying on the accounts of enterprises for a long time, accelerates the flow of funds between supply chains, and makes funds sink straight down to the bottom-level entity enterprises at all levels to meet their financing needs, as follows.

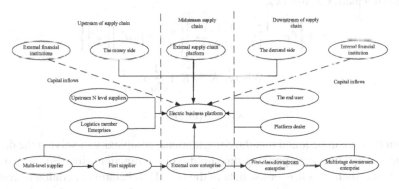

Fig. 1. Roadmap of the platform to help supply chain enterprises at all levels to raise finance

Through three lines of cooperation with core enterprises, financial peers and supply chain service platforms to solve financing problems for small, medium and micro enterprises. Line 1 provides financial services for enterprises and users at all levels upstream and downstream, solving the financing problems of its own upstream and downstream suppliers, distributors and users; Line 2 helps external core enterprises build supply chain financial services capabilities and helps enterprises outside the platform's own supply chain achieve financing. Line 3: Helps supply chain service platform connect the capital side with the demand side. Through strengthening the cooperation with internal and external financial institutions, we can obtain a continuous inflow of funds. It realizes the "internal circulation" of part of the capital flow and makes the parties form a substantial community of interests.

3.3 Multi-classification and Statistical Analysis of Marketing Profits

Through the performance analysis of e-commerce platform, the overall development trend and internal investment trend make some level of reference, combined with the latest basic theory of statistics, the current support vector machine based and e-commerce platform marketing profit characteristics of multi-classification and performance related problems are explored in depth. This part is based on the kernel function of principal component analysis and the least squares support vector machine theory of sparse matrices to explore in depth the statistical classification study of multi-classification rather than binary classification problems. According to the new classification method, it is necessary to make certain categorization and synthesis of various characteristic variables of listed companies and to train the research indexes practically according to the main theories of statistics. Considering the SLS-SVM as an iterative operation, first initialize the index sets A and B of all sample data SV, $A = B = \{1, 2, \ldots, l\}$, where the sets A and B are the index sets of non- SV and SV samples, respectively. The iterative operation of the SLS-SVM algorithm uses the back-fitting rule to add a new SV each time, thus giving the resulting solution sparsity. Since the support vector in the SLS-SVM algorithm increases with the number of iterations, we need to iteratively solve for the decision coefficient p and the corresponding threshold q of the function.

To simplify the computational difficulty, the pairwise problem is transformed into the form of a matrix as follows.

$$\min\left\{f = \frac{1}{2}\begin{bmatrix} q p^T \end{bmatrix}\begin{bmatrix} 0 & 1^T \\ 1 & \overline{K} \end{bmatrix}\begin{bmatrix} q \\ p \end{bmatrix} - \begin{bmatrix} q p^T \end{bmatrix}\begin{bmatrix} 0 \\ y \end{bmatrix}\right\} \tag{1}$$

$$\text{Where, } \overline{K} = K + \frac{1}{2\alpha}I \tag{2}$$

$$K_{ij} = k\left(m_i, m_j\right) \tag{3}$$

From this, it can be found that the computational complexity of solving the decision coefficient p and the corresponding threshold q of the function using Eq. (1) is $O(n^3)$. Suppose that when the s th exercise data of the $(n + 1)$ th iteration operation is treated as a support vector, to solve the decision coefficient p of the function and the corresponding threshold q, the inverse of the matrix is computed once again.

$$R^{n+1} = \begin{bmatrix} 0 & 1^T & 1 \\ 1 & \overline{K}_{AA} & \overline{k}_s \\ 1 & \overline{k}_s^T & \overline{K}_{ss} \end{bmatrix}^{-1} \tag{4}$$

According to the Sherman-Morrion equation, we can obtain the calculation of R^{n+1} and transform the calculation of R^{n+1} into an iterative calculation of R^n. Due to the greedy nature of backfitting, we need to find a reasonable condition for termination in the actual operation process, and first use the KPCA method to process the sample and its features, which is used to reflect the overall characteristics of the data and reduce the complexity of the operation. According to the previous principles of SVM model construction, Gaussian function is selected as the kernel function, and the optimal parameters are selected by interleaved experiments. SVMLS, on the other hand, the least squares support vector machine kernel function is selected to construct the model, as well as to finally obtain the best model parameters that can statistically represent the real characteristics and situation inside the data.

4 Conclusion

The platforming of cross-border e-commerce third-party services, as a cross-border e-commerce operation service provider, is only a very segmented part of the cross-border e-commerce industry chain, and with the emergence of more and more competitors, the industry gradually presents phenomena such as homogenization and price wars. Therefore, through the opening of its own resources and the integration of external resources, it is crucial to provide high-value and cost-effective quality services for the industry through the combination of breadth and depth. The above-mentioned content mainly focuses on the study of real-time statistical methods for marketing profits of Japanese cosmetics online cross-border e-commerce platforms, hoping to provide reference for the better and faster development of e-commerce platforms.

References

1. Santos, P.D., Zambroni de Souza, A.C., Bonatto, B.D., Mendes, T.P., Neto, J.A.S., Botan, A.C.B.: Analysis of solar and wind energy installations at electric vehicle charging stations in a region in Brazil and their impact on pricing using an optimized sale price model. Int. J. Energy Res. **45**(5), 6745–6764 (2020)
2. Eunyoung, C., Kun, C.L.: Effect of trust in domain-specific information of safety, brand loyalty, and perceived value for cosmetics on purchase intentions in mobile e-commerce context. Sustainability, **11**(22), 6257–6257 (2019)
3. Ma, Q., Chang, C., Lin, C.T.: Detecting the crisis of supply chain management on e-commerce for sustainability using q-technique. Sustainability, **13**(16), 9098–9098 (2021)
4. Gao, Y., Liang, H., Sun, B.: Dynamic network intelligent hybrid recommendation algorithm and its application in online shopping platform. J. Intell. Fuzzy Syst. **40**(5), 9173–9185 (2021)
5. France, B., Janine, S.H., Wanda, J.S.: Trustworthiness in electronic commerce: the role of privacy, security, and site attributes. J. Strat. Inf. Syst. **11**(3), 245–270 (2002)
6. Quan, H., Agbanyo, G.K., Caputo, F., Chin, T.: The role of value appropriation capability of chinese multinationals in operating cross-border business models. Sustainability, **13**(17), 9812–9812 (2021)
7. Taleizadeh, A.A., Cheraghi, Z., CárdenasBarrón, L.E., NooriDaryan, M.: Studying the effect of noise on pricing and marketing decisions of new products under co-op advertising strategy in supply chains: game theoretical approaches. Mathematics, **9**(11),1222–1222 (2021)
8. Chien, L., Tu, K.: Establishing merger feasibility simulation model based on multiple-criteria decision-making method: case study of taiwan's property management industry. Sustainability, **13**(5), 2448–2448 (2021)
9. Tsai, M.C.: Storytelling advertising investment profits in marketing: from the perspective of consumers' purchase intention. Mathematics **8**(10) 1704 (2020)
10. Aditya, R.K., Ashok, K.M., Joaquin, M., Stefan, H.: Choice of contract farming strategies, productivity, and profits: evidence from high-value crop production. J. Agric. Resource Econ. **45**(3), 589–604 (2020)

11. Gerard, H., Kathryn, A., Douglas, E., Kate, H.: Selling second best: how infant formula marketing works. Global. Health, **16**(1), 77–77 (2020)
12. Jiwen, G., Dorothee, H., Fransoo, J.C., Zhao, L.: Supplying to mom and pop: traditional retail channel selection in megacities. Manuf. Serv. Oper. Manage. **23**(1),19–35 (2020)
13. Li, G., Zhu, Z.H.: Estimation of flexible space tether state based on end measurement by finite element Kalman filter state estimator. Adv. Space Res. **67**(10), 3282–3293 (2021)
14. Vu Thanh, L.: Research on the influence of transportation services quality on purchasing intention of customer in e-commerce - evidence from purchasing intention of vietnamese consumer in cosmetic industry. Adv. Soc. Sci. **5**(7), 460–466 (2019)
15. Giuffrida, M., Mangiaracina, R., Perego, A., Tumino, A.: Cross-border B2C e-commerce to China: an evaluation of different logistics solutions under uncertainty. Int. J. Phys. Distrib. Logistics Manage. **47**(6), 355–378 (2019)
16. Guihe, H.: Enterprise e-commerce marketing system based on big data methods of maintaining social relations in the process of e-commerce environmental commodity. J. Organ. End User Comput. (JOEUC) **33**(6) 1–16 (2021)
17. Scott, L.N., et al.: Safety assessment of saccharide esters as used in cosmetics. Int. J. Toxicol. **40**(2_suppl), 52S–116S (2021)
18. Kristóf, G., Maciej, S., Michał, Z.: What drives price dispersion in the European e-commerce industry? Central Eur. Econ. J. **3**(50), 53–71 (2018)
19. İzmirli, D., Ekren, B.Y., Kumar, V.: Inventory share policy designs for a sustainable omni-chanel e-commerce network. Sustainability, **12**(23), 10022–10022 (2020)
20. Kanwar, N., Gupta, N., Niazi, K.R., Swarnkar, A., Abdelaziz, A.Y.: Day-ahead optimal scheduling of distributed resources and network reconfiguration under uncertain environment. Electric Power Comp. Syst. **48**(18), 1945–1954 (2020)

Audience Feature Extraction Method for Cross-Border Cosmetics Online Marketing in Japan

Jingxian Huang$^{(\boxtimes)}$

Guizhou Minzu University, Guiyang 550025, Guizhou, China

Abstract. In the context of economic globalization, combined with the development conditions of e-commerce, the trade between countries is becoming closer and closer. In recent years, cosmetics online marketing has become the focus of all sectors of society. Taking Japanese cross-border cosmetics as the research object, this paper makes an in-depth analysis on the characteristics of its online marketing audience. Through the definition of the concept of cross-border e-commerce and the analysis of the current situation of cross-border cosmetics in Japan, this paper comprehensively expounds the development status from two perspectives. Explore Japan's cross-border cosmetics market positioning, divide the market level of women's needs, control product quality risks, optimize the online marketing mode of e-commerce platform, identify audience preferences with hybrid recommendation algorithm, investigate the information recognition degree of women consumers, obtain users' comprehensive similarity, establish feature extraction mechanism, and finally realize the design of feature extraction method.

Keywords: Japanese cross-border cosmetics · Online marketing · Audience groups · Feature extraction · E-commerce platform · Electronic commerce

1 Introduction

With the development and popularization of high-tech information technology and Internet, e-commerce has gradually crossed the border and played a great role in the trade between countries. Traditional trade has a long time and high trade cost. Based on Internet technology, e-commerce can realize information interconnection and real-time communication. Using e-commerce to carry out cross-border trade has become an important form of transformation and upgrading of China's foreign trade industry. Cross border e-commerce is conducive to simplifying the transaction process, saving transaction costs, improving transaction efficiency, gradually becoming China's new economic growth point and foreign trade mode, and then changing the traditional world trade pattern [1–3]. At present, many foreign trade companies in China have introduced information systems and built information platforms to develop cross-border e-commerce and enhance their competitiveness [4, 5]. As a populous country, China's demand and consumption

D. Jiang and H. Song (Eds.): SIMUtools 2021, LNICST 424, pp. 637–647, 2022.
https://doi.org/10.1007/978-3-030-97124-3_49

of cosmetics are also amazing. At present, it ranks second in the global cosmetics consumption ranking, and under the development trend of the Internet era, it has widened the development channels for China's cosmetics industry, resulting in an increasing trend in cosmetics sales. In fact, during the period of reform and opening up in 1978, international cosmetics have poured into the Chinese market, and many enterprises have won certain market opportunities. Through the investigation of Chinese consumption demand and Asian skin characteristics, they have made certain achievements in cosmetics R & D and sales, and formed a certain brand effect, Of course, this success is based on a certain marketing strategy of market segmentation and distribution channels. Throughout the field of China's cosmetics market, European and American brands enjoy a certain position. P & G is a leader in China's cosmetics market, accounting for nearly 16% of the market, and L'Oreal also has nearly 11% of the market share. In addition to these company products, European and American cosmetics brands have also become popular in the Chinese market. It can even be said that Chinese cosmetics are led by European and American cosmetics to a certain extent, and have achieved considerable economic benefits. This successful development case has stimulated the investment attention of other international well-known brands all the time, and is eager to try for China's cosmetics market. It points out that the consumption characteristics of Chinese cosmetics are obviously reflected in the influence of brand power, while the varieties of Chinese local cosmetics industry are relatively single, The quality is in contradiction with the increasing demand of consumers. The enterprise's R & D is relatively backward and does not produce targeted products. Therefore, the development of enterprises is at a disadvantage, and there is no more international local brand for Chinese cosmetics in the international market, which is the lack of Chinese cosmetics market. Many products have the problem of imitation without actual innovation. Take product innovation as their own development characteristic advantage, and pay attention to multi-channel promotion and the driving role of stars and public figures. Cosmetics marketing can also be carried out through accurate market segmentation and positioning. This method also has reference significance for Japanese cross-border cosmetics companies developing in China to a certain extent. With the progress of the times and the continuous improvement of women's social status, women consumers have become the main force in the consumer market. At present, the academic research materials on the online marketing audience of cross-border cosmetics in Japan are not rich enough and need to be further discussed.

2 Development Status of Cross-Border E-commerce and Cosmetics

2.1 Definition of Cross Border E-commerce

In a broad sense, cross-border e-commerce can be regarded as foreign trade e-commerce to a certain extent. It refers to the trade entities belonging to different customs territories to achieve import and export trade activities by using e-commerce technology. Cross border e-commerce also involves data exchange, capital transfer, information transmission, etc. all international trade can be called cross-border e-commerce [6]. Electronic data exchange, which originated in the 1960s, is the predecessor of the development of cross-border e-commerce. Electronic data exchange abandons the traditional paper form and exchanges data directly through the network, which saves the time and economic cost of both sides and is welcomed by the market. Later, with the progress of technology, funds transfer, information service and payment security system other than data exchange were developed, and cross-border e-commerce activities had a certain scale. In a narrow sense, cross-border e-commerce refers to cross-border online retail. Cross border e-commerce can be divided into different forms according to different elements [7, 8]. According to different service objects, it can be divided into four types: business to business, business to consumer, business to government and consumer to consumer. Business to business mainly refers to trade between enterprises through information technology platform. Business to consumer means that enterprises provide products to users through cross-border e-commerce platforms. Enterprise to government means that the government purchases products or services operated by enterprises through the platform. Consumer to consumer transaction mode refers to individual goods trade and exchange through the platform. The cross-border e-commerce referred to in this paper mainly refers to the cross-border e-commerce at the narrow level. In 1999, Alibaba took the lead in opening the Internet transaction mode, using the Internet to connect domestic suppliers with overseas customers, resulting in the e-commerce of foreign trade in China. Since then, the Internet has gradually approached thousands of households in China, which has had a profound impact on the whole social economy. The number of people using computers to access the Internet is increasing all over the world, the number of enterprises using information systems is increasing, the data encryption technology is constantly updated, and the intelligent logistics system is also in the process of R & D and updating. Under this background, China's cross-border e-commerce has also achieved great development. Gradually realized the transformation and upgrading within the industry, as shown in Table 1:

According to Table 1, compared with cross-border B2C, the main body of cross-border trade has changed, and the trend of fragmentation and miniaturization is constantly emerging. The development of cross-border e-commerce has not only changed personal life, but also changed the development model of China's cosmetics industry.

2.2 Analysis on the Current Situation of Cross-Border Cosmetics in Japan

The marketing strategy of Japan's cross-border cosmetics market in China is based on certain segmentation principles. It is to divide the environmental observation of the Chinese market and the consumption concept of Chinese people of all ages, and adopt targeted marketing methods in the five market segments of top, advanced, medium and high, medium and low. Targeted sales of cosmetics needed by consumer groups and different grades of consumers' skin through market segments [9–11]. In terms of marketing channels, it is not difficult to find that Japan's top cosmetics representatives represented by CPB, the Ginza and pola are concentrated on the counters of major shopping malls, because this channel can better promote consumers' product experience, personally feel the use effect of products at the first time, and provide convenience for after-sales service, so as to increase the subsidiary value of products, This service itself is one of the selling points. China's cosmetics market structure is relatively complex. According to the purpose of use, it can be divided into cleaning, basic, beauty, curative effect, hair and other categories. From the recent China consumer's cosmetics concern

Table 1. Development history of cross-border E-commerce

Stage/development model	Budding period (1997–2007)	Development period (2008–2013)	Outbreak period (2014-so far)
Business Model	Online display, offline transactions, foreign trade information services, not involving transactions	Form an online trading platform to realize the electronization of all links of e-commerce and effectively open up the upstream and downstream supply chain. There are mainly two modes: B2C and B2B	Online service of the whole industry chain
Profit Model	Charge membership fee	Diversified Revenue: 1. Backward charge and commission 2. Obtain value-added income such as marketing promotion, payment service and logistics service	Diversified Revenue: 1. Backward charge and commission 2. Obtain value-added income such as marketing promotion, payment service and logistics service
Typical representative	Alibaba resource station, made in China	Lanting Jishi Express	Tmall global, Netease koala overseas shopping, Jumei premium products, ocean wharf, etc

category, people pay the most attention to skin care products, and secondly, the demand for make-up, the attention to hair care products and perfume. This shows that China's consumers have more concerns about the consumption characteristics of cosmetics with skin care and cosmetics. The biggest advantage of online sales is that it is convenient and fast. There is no need to spend time selecting products, which meets the consumption needs of young people.

3   Audience Feature Extraction Method for Cross-Border Cosmetics Online Marketing in Japan

3.1   Exploring Japan's Cross-Border Cosmetics Market Positioning

Market positioning is a prerequisite for any enterprise to enter the market smoothly. This also exists in Japanese cosmetics enterprises, and there are multiple types of cosmetics in Japan. Among these brands with the same use effect and different types, consumer layered dumping is also worth considering. China's developed cities are concentrated in coastal areas and major provincial capitals. Korean enterprises in cosmetics often start from these areas. The main reason is that they have the characteristics of "three highs", that is, the average consumption level, economic level and population are high. The market for women's demand is divided into three levels, which are divided by coverage, That is, women aged 18–40 are subdivided, which is a coverage division of age dimension covering economic income and other factors, with clear priorities. For women at this stage, the focus is on consumers aged 25–30 who have a certain economic foundation. Such groups have the protection of economic income, and the speed of human metabolism is accelerated after the age of 25, Skin aging, water shortage and other problems are obvious, which maximizes the number of potential consumers. It also has a sense of innovation and attempt, has low brand attachment, is deeply penetrated by Japanese makeup style, and is willing to try new products. The concept of consumption focuses on "innovation" and "difference", pursues product performance, pays attention to personalized selection, and has a certain purchasing power for high-end products, but the purchasing power of top cosmetics brands is not as good as that of women in 30–40. Now, the most popular Japanese cosmetics for the Post-00 group still belong to the middle and low-grade cosmetics with relatively popular prices. The typical characteristic of this group is that most of them are studying in Colleges and universities, with low economic ability, but also have a greater pursuit of cosmetics [12, 13]. Therefore, it is reasonable that brands such as canmake are favored by this group. Moreover, the skin problems that perplex young women due to environmental and dietary reasons, such as closed mouth, acne and large pores, have also attracted the attention of many consumers to the field of pharmaceutical makeup. Japanese products for this group, such as FANCL, are also popular and suitable for younger people. Japanese cosmetics enterprises take age income as the basis for market positioning investigation in Japanese cosmetics marketing strategy in China, which is reasonable and scientific, and market-oriented marketing production is also in line with the market law [14, 15]. However, many enterprises have not noticed the rapid change of China's cosmetics market environment, blindly following the trend of production, resulting in market saturation and serious economic losses caused by unsalable products. In Japan's cosmetics marketing strategy, there are certain diversified requirements for product R & D and creation, which is to fully meet the needs of consumer groups of different genders, different regions and different age groups. Besides, the product's type not only covers the skin products of the face, but also produces products for hair care and perfume, and also for men's production of special cleansing cream and lotion. Because men also have the right to pursue beauty and pay more and more attention to exterior decoration and skin care. In terms of product efficacy, for example, several series of Kanebo can slow down the skin aging and collagen loss of middle-aged women. SHISEIDO series of eye cream and hyaluronic acid are also favored by consumers because of the effect of water desalination and fine lines. The essence of SKII has great effect on water supplement and shrinkage pores of young women. CUREL sets are natural and non irritating to pregnant women and children. This is the right remedy for the needs of different consumers according to the product function. Based on the above description, complete the steps to explore the positioning of Japan's cross-border cosmetics market.

3.2   Optimizing the Online Marketing Mode of E-commerce Platform

Online marketing needs to take the e-commerce platform as the media and combine the corresponding marketing strategies to optimize the traditional marketing model. Such enterprises focus their development direction on cosmetics and cosmetics surrounding fields, and provide platform enterprises with in-depth information and related services about cosmetics. Their business is aimed at similar products [16, 17]. For example, xiaohongshu, Jumei premium products, honey bud, meimeishuo and mushroom Street are vertical enterprises for cosmetics products. This paper will take xiaohongshu as a case for analysis. The cross-border e-commerce platform for comprehensive cosmetics refers to an enterprise that only takes the cosmetics field and the fields around cosmetics as one of the development directions. In addition to providing information and services for products in cosmetics and its surrounding fields, it also engages in other product fields unrelated to cosmetics. Such platforms in China include JD beauty, tmall global, Dangdang, etc. This paper chooses xiaohongshu as a vertical cross-border e-commerce platform in the cosmetics industry not because of its large scale. Xiaohongshu's market share is not the highest, but xiaohongshu is developing rapidly. The online community e-commerce model it creates is unique among the cross-border e-commerce platforms in the cosmetics industry, and has strong research value and reference significance. The operation mode of xiaohongshu is shown in Fig. 1:

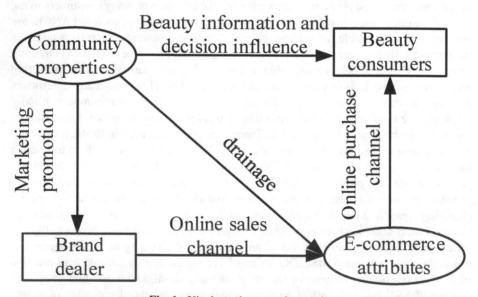

Fig. 1. Xiaohongshu operation mode

As shown in Fig. 1, brands carry out marketing and promotion activities in the online community. Consumers get corresponding information in this community. Those who are willing to buy can directly place an order in the e-commerce section of the community. The community plays a role in attracting e-commerce by providing consumers with beauty information. A complete cross-border e-commerce platform includes six links:

commodity procurement and management, payment, logistics, customs clearance and commodity inspection, marketing and after-sales service. Among them, old e-commerce platforms such as tmall global and jd.com have formed strong barriers in the fields of procurement, payment and logistics with their own advantages. As an emerging cross-border e-commerce enterprise, the key to breaking the competition barrier lies in how to obtain high-quality supplier resources in the procurement link. It adopts the mode of direct cooperation with brands such as Japan and South Korea, implements the bonded self-supporting mode, and controls the quality risk of products. In addition, the traffic conversion rate of xiaohongshu is high. The specific forms of cosmetics cross-border e-commerce trade include direct mail, bonded and goods collection. Among them, the direct mail mode and bonded mode are the two most basic modes in cross-border e-commerce trade, and the goods collection mode is equivalent to an upgraded version of the direct mail mode. This mode uses centralized transportation instead of scattered transportation to reduce costs. Cosmetics import direct mail mode refers to the trade behavior that domestic consumers purchase beauty products and skin care products through cosmetics cross-border e-commerce platform, and these products are directly sent to consumers from abroad by mail, sea parcels, etc. Cosmetics import and preparation mode refers to the trade behavior that platform enterprises purchase cosmetics and peripheral products mainly sold through centralized procurement, cross-border e-commerce enterprises directly pick up goods from the special supervision area and then send them to consumers through logistics. The bonded mode is to enter the country first and start customs clearance after the user places an order, while the direct mail mode is to start distribution after the user places an order and need to go through customs clearance procedures when entering the country. The main difference between the two lies in the order of order placement and customs clearance. Based on this, complete the steps of optimizing the online marketing mode of e-commerce platform.

3.3 Hybrid Recommendation Algorithm to Identify Audience Preferences

The main audience of cross-border cosmetics online marketing in Japan is female consumers, and female consumers are a special consumer group. They are born to pay more attention to emotional communication than men. This congenital psychological feature makes it easy for women to consult others when making consumption decisions. In the trend of online shopping, online word-of-mouth will affect the purchase intention of female consumers [18–19]. The theory of consumer behavior analysis holds that the generation and change of consumer behavior is a long process, which includes four stages: formation, prototype, performance and change. The information received in each stage will have a specific psychological orientation for consumers and affect consumer behavior. Generally speaking, consumer behavior includes motivation generation, purchase decision and purchase behavior process. Motivation generation includes internal demand and external factors. The more comprehensive consumers understand the product information, the easier it is to produce purchase behavior, and the higher the perceived evaluation of the product. Therefore, the purpose of consumer behavior analysis is to adopt different information strategies for consumers through feature and demand analysis, so as to improve consumers' understanding of the product as much as possible. As the audience group of cross-border cosmetics online marketing in Japan, the preference of female consumers is not completely independent, and there will be inter-action between friends and relatives. Therefore, the average preference of user groups for beauty products is defined as:

$$\hat{D} = \sum\nolimits_{l \in t} g \cdot \frac{1}{|t|} \tag{1}$$

In formula (1), t represents the randomly selected users, g represents the user's positive feedback on the item, and l represents the total number of users. On this basis, the loss function expression formula of the specified beauty products is obtained as follows:

$$L = -\sum\nolimits_{j=1}^{i} \sum\nolimits_{e \in k} + \ln j \left(G - \hat{h} \right) \tag{2}$$

In formula (2), i, j represents two adjacent users in the data set, e represents similar users, k represents the integer set, G represents the regularization coefficient, and h represents the implicit feedback data. In the e-commerce scenario, there are many types of implicit feedback data of user behavior, which is called heterogeneous implicit feedback data. BPR and a series of improved algorithms of BPR can not be directly used for recommendation. The conventional channels for female consumers to buy cosmetics mainly analyze the general purchase methods of female consumers' cosmetics from the aspects of network, comprehensive shopping malls, counter stores, purchasing overseas shopping and other channels. The survey found that the cosmetics purchased by the interviewed samples are mainly online channels, followed by counters, stores, purchasing agents and overseas shopping. Based on this, complete the steps of identifying audience preferences.

3.4 Establishing Feature Extraction Mechanism

Under the e-commerce platform, the user's behavior data represents different user pref-erences, that is, the user's heterogeneous implicit feedback data reflects the uncertainty of user preferences [20]. Heterogeneous implicit feedback contains a variety of user behavior data. The user's behavior type and behavior frequency of a product represent the user's different preference for the product. Therefore, the user's relative preference for two commodities is sometimes obvious. For example, it is generally believed that the user's preference for a commodity with multiple clicks is stronger than that with only one click, the user's preference for the final purchased commodity is stronger than that with only one click, and the user's preference for the final purchased commodity is stronger than that without behavior. However, there are still some relative preferences that cannot be directly judged by experience. Therefore, in the e-commerce scenario, due to the par-ticularity of heterogeneous implicit feedback data, the recommendation algorithm needs to solve two key problems in the definition of user preference: first, how to measure the user's preference between two goods. Second, how to measure the confidence of this relative preference. Consumers' purchase of cosmetics includes the purpose of use and brand value. They mainly obtain information through the Internet, take the price as the main factor affecting their choice, and prefer to choose plain cosmetics. Subsequently, further analysis was conducted on consumers who had purchased products on a certain platform, and it was found that consumers obtained cosmetics information more through online channels. Therefore, it is necessary to analyze the commodity attributes, classify the commodities, calculate the total score of users on each commodity attribute, and get the user preference similarity. The two kinds of similarity are linearly combined to obtain a more accurate user comprehensive similarity, find the user nearest neighbor set, predict the user score, and get the recommendation list. The results of clustering based user similarity and preference based user similarity are selected for linear combination. Firstly, the user similarity obtained by the two algorithms is calculated separately, and the appropriate value is taken through the balance factor to make the best user comprehensive similarity result. Spectral clustering is to transform the clustering problem into a graph partition problem. This algorithm needs to cluster the users, regard the users in the set as the vertices in the graph, and determine whether there are edges between users according to the proximity discrimination method. If there are edges, the edge weight is the similarity between users. After determining that there are edges between users, calculate the edge weight between users:

$$f = \exp\left(\frac{-\|p, q\|^2}{2\beta^2}\right) \tag{3}$$

In formula (3), p, q represents two adjacent users respectively, and β represents similarity parameters. In the investigation of marketing media preference of female consumers, firstly, according to the division of traditional media and new media, investigate the use preference and information recognition of different media of female consumers, and then divide the traditional media into TV broadcasting platform, newspaper and magazine, square marketing, outdoor advertising and other categories according to the division of different media categories in traditional media and new media, And further divide the specific categories of detailed platforms, and investigate the platform use and information recognition of female consumers. In the new media, search engines, social networking platforms, shopping websites and post bar forums, mail messages and so on are taken as the basis of division, and further specific platforms are divided. Then, the platform application and information recognition of female consumers are investigated. Consumers said that online cosmetics are cheap and convenient. For example, JD's self operated cosmetics have guaranteed quality, open and transparent price, door-to-door delivery and very high cost performance. Other consumers trust the product quality of counters and specialty stores, and some consumers believe that buying cosmetics from overseas shopping, purchasing on behalf of others and other places of origin, on the one hand, makes the price cheaper and the quality better than that produced by OEM factories, so they choose this way to buy cosmetics. Based on the above description, the steps of establishing a feature extraction mechanism are completed.

4   Conclusion

This study attempts to use the post feminist perspective to focus on the female audience of cosmetics advertising on the basis of the body framework, focus on their consumption habits in daily life, try to find the multiple meanings of "beauty" and confirm its internal tension, so as to further explore the subjectivity and hidden power mechanism in Discourse. Finally, it is found that according to the development trend of e-commerce and the current marketing strategy of cross-border cosmetics in Japan, it can be predicted that online marketing is an inevitable way to expand its influence, break regional restrictions and improve the awareness of female consumers. In the specific marketing methods, we will pay attention to the innovation of marketing to meet the needs of consumers and obtain consumers' unique value recognition. Due to the limited research conditions, the research on other types of cross-border commodities is not thorough enough. In the future, we will continue to conduct in-depth research and achieve results.

References

1. Hoang, T., Nguyen, H.K., Nguyen, H.T.: Towards an economic recovery after the COVID-19 pandemic: empirical study on electronic commerce adoption of small and medium enterprises in Vietnam Manage. Market. **16**(1), 47–68 (2021)
2. Yu, S., Huang, X., Li, J., et al.: Research on the development strategy of cross-border electronic commerce under the strategic background of belt and road initiative. In: 2019 International Conference on Management Science and Industrial Economy (MSIE 2019) (2020)
3. Azmi, I., Phuoc, J.C.: International norms in regulating ecommerce: the electronic commerce chapter of the comprehensive trans-pacific partnership agreement. Int. J. Bus. Soc. 21 (2020)
4. Kirichenko, L., Radivilova, T., Zinkevich, I.: Forecasting weakly correlated time series in tasks of electronic commerce (2019)
5. Marianus, S., Ali, S.: Factors determining the perceived security dimensions in B2C electronic commerce website usage: an Indonesian study. J. Account. Investment **22**(1), 104–132 (2021)
6. Madi, F.A., Al-Sarayreh, R.: The impact of electronic-commerce on gaining competitiveness in the jordanian telecommunication sector a field study. Eur. J. Econ. Finance Adm. Sci. **57**, 6–18 (2021)
7. Haile, T.T., Kang, M.: Mobile augmented reality in electronic commerce: investigating user perception and purchase intent amongst educated young adults. Sustainability **12**(21) (2020)
8. Hamid, O., Allaymoun, M.H.: Murabaha application for electronic commerce internet of things utilisation in Islamic fin-tech Int. J. Electron. Bank. **2**(3), 212 (2020)
9. Yao, Y.: Changes of Chinese cosmetics consumers markets by scale China. Deterg. Cosmet. **4**(04) 22–23 (2019)
10. Huang, S.: Identity construction of female consumers in Chinese and American cosmetics advertisements: a critical pragmatic study. Int. Linguistics Res. **3**(4), 131 (2020)
11. Yano, Y., Kato, E., Ohe, Y., et al.: Examining the opinions of potential consumers about plant-derived cosmetics: an approach combining word association, co-occurrence network, and multivariate probit analysis. J. Sensory Stud. **34**(2), e12484 (2019)
12. Kim, H.W., Seok, Y.S., Cho, T.J.: Risk factors influencing contamination of customized cosmetics made on-the-spot: evidence from the national pilot project for public health. Sci. Rep. **10**(1), 1561 (2020)
13. Chen, S., Xia, J.: How can cosmetics brands deal with new generation becoming the mainstream?. China Deterg. Cosm. (1) (2019)
14. Long, V.T.: Research on the influence of transportation services quality on purchasing intention of customer in e-commerce - evidence from purchasing intention of vietnamese consumer in cosmetic industry. Int. J. Soc. Sci. Educ. Res. **3**(5), 45–53 (2020)
15. Zhang, Z.T., Ying, Z., et al.: Cosmetic safety and risk assessment under the "new" regulations. China Deterg. Cosmet. **5**(4), 24–32 (2020)

16. Zbib, I., Ghaddar, R., Samarji, A.: Examining country of origin effect among lebanese consumers: a study in the cosmetics industry. J. Int. Consum. Mark. **33**(2), 1–15 (2020)
17. Sohn, H.J., You, S.H., Park, C.H.: Relationship between consumers' exploring cosmetics information behavior and satisfaction and recommendation intention. Asian J. Beauty Cosmetol. **17**(4) 499–509 (2019)
18. Sama, R., Trivedi, J.: Factors affecting consumers loyalty towards Halal cosmetics: an emerging market perspective. Int. J. Bus. Emerg. Mark. **11**(1), 1 (2019)

Author Index

Printed in the United States
by Baker & Taylor Publisher Services